1967

.e kept

Teaching the Language Arts in the Elementary School

BROWN

EDUCATION SERIES

Edited by

Lowry W. Harding, Ph.D.
The Ohio State University
Columbus, Ohio

Teaching the Language Arts in the Elementary School

Martha Dallmann

Professor of Education
Ohio Wesleyan University

WM. C. BROWN COMPANY PUBLISHERS
135 SOUTH LOCUST STREET • DUBUQUE, IOWA 52001

Library of Congress Catalog Card Number: 66-28710

Manufactured by WM. C. BROWN CO. INC., Dubuque, Iowa
Printed in U. S. A.

Acknowledgments

It is impossible to write a book on teaching the language arts in the elementary school without accumulating a great indebtedness. In a sense a book in this area is the result of the combined efforts of many persons, known and unknown to an author. Publishers of materials in the language arts, teachers in the public schools and in the colleges in which the writer of this book has worked in some capacity, student teachers she has supervised, students in her classes through the years, and boys and girls in the elementary schools have helped the author gain the insight into the problems of teaching the language arts that is reflected, it is hoped, in this book. To all these she is, indeed, grateful.

The author wishes to acknowledge her gratitude to the school administrators who provided photographs that make clearer the verbal content of the book. She is grateful to the publishing companies who gave permission to reproduce copyrighted materials, namely: the Bobbs-Merrill Company; Field Enterprises; the Garrard Publishing Company; Holt, Rinehart and Winston; the Honor Products Company; the Mast Development Company; the A. N. Palmer Company; and the Zaner-Bloser Company. She also acknowledges the fact that some of the photographs of illustrative materials appeared earlier in the magazine GRADE TEACHER.

The writer is indebted to the many students who kindly permitted inclusion in the book of photographs illustrating projects they had done in connection with work in the author's classes. It is with regret that credit cannot be given in the case of a few students of earlier years where records no longer indicate who made the illustrative material. Thanks are due to the former students who wrote teaching plans of which adaptations are included in Chapter 14. The helpfulness and skill of six students at Ohio Wesleyan University who drew most of the sketches in the book, namely, Jean Campana, Anne Castle, Carol Graham, Sue Meck, Joan Monoski, and Katherine Ratliff, are acknowledged with gratitude. Some of these sketches are adaptations of drawings by other students in past years.

Special mention is due various other persons. The writer is greatly indebted to the editor of the series of books on education of which this book is one – to Dr. Lowry W. Harding, Professor of Education, The Ohio State University, for his interest in the project and for his many helpful suggestions. Thanks need to be expressed to Dr. John J. DeBoer, Professor of Education, University of Illinois, senior author of the book *The Teaching of Reading,* published by Holt, Rinehart and Winston, which he wrote with the author of this book. The writing of *The Teaching of Reading* had a marked influence on the content of the chapters on reading in this book.

Thanks also go to various members of the library staff of Ohio Wesleyan University, especially to Mrs. Hilda Wick and Mrs. Katherine Schlichting, for their help in the search for bibliographical data. The writer owes a debt of gratitude to Dr. C. Francis Alter, Chairman of the Education Department, Ohio Wesleyan University, for his valuable responses to the many questions with which the writer went to him for advice. The suggestions by Mrs. Alma Forbes, formerly teacher of remedial reading and of religious education at Ohio Wesleyan University, are also acknowledged.

A list of persons named in these ACKNOWLEDGMENTS would be incomplete without mention of two individuals, Maria Dallmann, sister of the author, for her painstaking reading of the manuscript, and Mrs. Christine Bizer Dallmann, the writer's mother, who was living when the work on the book was begun, for her inspiration and for her interest in the writing activities of the author.

Martha Dallmann

Delaware, Ohio

Preface

The workable relationship between theory and practice that is made clear in *Teaching the Language Arts in the Elementary School* constitutes one of its major strengths. While a considerable part of the book offers practical suggestions for teaching various phases of the language arts, these are not given as isolated devices or procedures. Rather they are shown as they fit in with the guiding principles and other theoretical considerations that are presented in a clear-cut manner in connection with each facet of the language arts.

Although the interrelationship between theory and practice is stressed, the placement in the book of the theoretical and the practical is such that the reader should have no problem in locating either. Typically when a topic is presented, guidelines for teaching it are first given and other matters of general import are discussed. Thereupon suggestions are presented as to how the theory can be implemented. The ease with which the reader can find suggestions on theory when theory is wanted and on practical application when that is desired adds to the value of the book.

A variety of types of specific methods and procedures is recommended. Some are given in terms of possible practice exercises, some in the form of teaching plans or other descriptions of illustrative classroom situations, and still others as purposeful procedures that can be incorporated as part of the ongoing classroom activities. They are made more meaningful and easier to comprehend by means of the large number of pictorial illustrations that are scattered throughout much of the book. It is recommended that at all times only those procedures that seem best to fit the needs of the pupils should be selected by a teacher. It is hoped that the ideas that are presented will suggest to him many that are especially well adapted to the various individuals in his charge.

The main organization of the book also throws light on the philosophy underlying the writing of it. Part One "Basic Considerations" sets forth simply and directly the principles of child growth and development. It is they that serve as a foundation on which the rest of the book is built. Part Two, by far the longest part of the book, entitled "Developmental Procedures in Guiding Growth in Communication Skills," emphasizes, with attention to both theory and practice, means by which the teacher can guide the child in both oral and written communication. In addition to the topics usually given in a book on the teaching of the language arts, an entire chapter is devoted to a subject frequently not taken up in much detail in such books, namely "Guiding Growth through Dramatic Expression." Part Three, "Specialized Procedures and Resources," begins with a chapter on appraisal of the work in the language arts. The succeeding chapter, entitled "Illustrative Teaching Situations," should be particularly helpful to the reader who is looking for many practical suggestions. In it are given illustrations of classroom techniques to complement and supplement those to which reference is made in Part Two. The final chapter gives a somewhat detailed index of many of the resources in the area of the language arts that can prove very helpful to the classroom teacher.

A word of explanation about a matter of repetition is necessary. Many of the specific procedures relate to more than one of the topics discussed in the book. The question that arose in the writing was whether these should be repeated from time to time as they apply to various topics or whether many cross-references should be made to them. For the sake of practicality of use and at the sacrifice of brevity it was decided, as a rule, to list them in the context whenever they are appropriate without much use of cross-references.

This book has been designed particularly with the prospective teacher and the classroom teacher in mind. It is hoped, however, elementary school principals, supervisors, and curriculum workers will also find the book an effective combination of theory and practice, through application of which the language experiences of boys and girls can be enriched and extended.

Martha Dallmann

Contents

PART ONE

Basic Considerations

PART TWO

Developmental Procedures in Guiding Growth in Communication Skills

PART THREE

Specialized Procedures and Resources

To

My mother Christine Bizer Dallmann

and

My sister Maria Dallmann

PART ONE

Basic Considerations

OUTLINE FOR CHAPTER 1

Child Development and the Language Arts

CHAPTER 1

Child Development and the Language Arts

To accomplish effectively the aims of a desirable program in the language arts, the methods and procedures should be in harmony with what is known in the field of child growth and development. Without knowledge of the tenets emphasized by specialists in that field, the teacher may have objectives in mind that are too limited. Without such guidance he may be content to settle for aims that deal only with skills, ignoring the contribution that the language arts can make to the personality of the growing individual. It is for these reasons that throughout this book the relationship that should exist between what is known in the field of child development and the teaching of language arts is recognized.

Since incidental references to the contributions of the field of child development that are made in subsequent chapters are not sufficient to emphasize and demonstrate the known points, this first chapter is devoted exclusively to pointing out the relationship between child development and the language arts and the impact that knowledge of the former should have on teaching the latter. For the same reason the second chapter deals with a consideration of the developmental patterns of growth as they affect the program of the language arts.

The relationship between child development and the language arts is not one-way. It is reciprocal. An application of knowledge from the field of child growth and development affects the pupil's learning in major aspects of the language arts favorably — in listening, speaking, reading, and writing. At the same time, acquisition of abilities and skills in the language arts can — indeed, should — have a beneficial influence on the growth and development of the child. Let us now turn our attention to the first of these two points.

BEARING OF KNOWLEDGE OF CHILD DEVELOPMENT ON TEACHING THE LANGUAGE ARTS

What then are the "big ideas" from the field of child growth and development that the teacher should keep in mind in relation to teaching the language arts?

Behavior Is Caused

One of the most important emphases of students of child growth and development is embodied in the statement that has become almost the motto of that branch of study, namely "Behavior is caused." Manifold application can be made of this principle to the teaching of the language arts. It is pertinent to all phases of evaluation, ranging from the most casual to the specially planned highly technical. It is significant whether the appraisal deals with data like the child's ability to use *went* and *gone* correctly or whether it is concerned with more intangible and more complex factors such as the attitude of the learner toward reading or the degree of assurance and poise with which a pupil gives a report.

The teacher of the language arts who shapes his instructional program in harmony with the principle that all behavior is caused will not, for example, be satisfied with noting errors made in written or oral communication of an informal type nor will he stop short of careful analysis of results when a standardized test has been administered in any aspect of the language arts. He will try to determine what caused the child to perform as he did. He will endeavor to be understanding when dealing with persons, including those with very serious shortcomings, as he realizes that somehow, somewhere the reactions have been brought about by factors for which, in many instances, the individual may not be responsible, at least not at the time. Praise will then not be reserved for the child who habitually has a high rating but will be given primarily to the person who has overcome deficiencies, especially if he has done so against heavy odds. Blame will all but disappear as far as the teacher's attitude toward the learner is concerned. This statement, however, is not to be interpreted to mean that the teacher will not point out to the child his shortcomings; nor does it mean that he may not reprove the pupil for some of his actions. Rather, it means that his attitude toward the learner will be one of sympathy as he attempts to assist him in overcoming difficulties and tries to help him attain ever higher goals.

Multiple Causes of Behavior

The tenet that the causes of behavior are multiple is parallel in significance to the generalization that behavior is caused. Even so-called simple reactions are the result of many factors. As the teacher tries to ascertain what brought about obtained results, he should not be satisfied when one cause has been found, even though some of the influencing factors may be so hidden that at first glance they seemingly defy discovery.

The Concept of "the Whole Child"

Unfortunately the expression "the whole child" has become almost a cliché. Statements made concerning "the whole child" are at times so vague that they may obscure rather than clarify known facts about learning.

Let us not, however, ignore the importance of the concept of "the whole child" because the term is at times used in a setting in which little help is given toward understanding the child's potentialities and shortcomings. It is far too significant a concept to be slighted because of misuse.

Studies of child growth and development demonstrate the fact that the living organism has a unity — a wholeness — that constitutes its pattern of development. How then can awareness of this essential oneness of the developing organism, this "wholeness" of the learner, affect the work of the teacher? Let us note a few of the ways.

1. Whenever the teacher is guiding the child in language development, the teacher should proceed so as not to interfere, in any phase of the child's growth, with his optimum development.

2. When the teacher is guiding the child in language development, he should strive to teach so that he will help the learner grow in other respects also. For example, at the same time the pupil is learning to write a friendly letter, he can be encouraged, in many instances, to have a greater awareness of his responsibility to others, manifested through courtesy and consideration shown in the letter.

3. The teacher should not try to force learning in the language arts at the expense of other phases of the development of the child.

The Design for the Individual

Each individual, even before birth, is influenced greatly in his development through an inner design in accordance with which, to a considerable extent, he unfolds. It is because of the likenesses in this design for growth among human beings that characteristic growth trends can be established. It must not be overlooked, however, that there are many differences in design among individuals also.

The concept of the unfolding design is of great importance to the teacher of the language arts since, through knowledge about it, he can expect certain similarities as well as many dissimilarities among the boys and girls whom he teaches. He can anticipate, for example, that listening will precede speaking, that speaking will precede reading, that reading will precede writing. By means of the characteristics — emotional, social, intellectual, and physical — that have been identified as growth norms, the teacher can obtain a clearer picture of the level of a child at any one time than he could without such information. For example, when dealing with six-year-olds, through information from growth studies he can note that it is normal for boys and girls of that age to be lacking in disposition to do much planning in a large group of their peers. At the same time, however, because of the factors of individual differences, he can not expect any one child to follow details of norms established by Arnold Gesell and others even though they are based on study of large representative samplings.

Variations in Growth Patterns

The sequence of the appearance in the developing child of many phases of growth shows relatively little variation from individual to individual. It is fairly constant in various language activities as well as in over-all physical development. However, there is great variation among boys and girls in the timing of the appearance of these characteristics. These deviations also are due in part to the differences in depth possible for given individuals.

Maturation and Environmental Stimulation

The unfolding of the individual according to his design for living (nature) and the stimulation from the environment (nurture) are important determinants of his growth and development. The inborn design can be affected adversely or favorably by environment. Provision of an environment that affords above average opportunities for developing the hereditary equipment of the individual can, within limits, stimulate development beyond that possible under average conditions.

A few significant implications for the teacher who is guiding the language development of boys and girls are as follows:

Courtesy of the Cincinnati, Ohio, Public Schools

Figure 1.1

1. In an environment unfavorable to language development, an individual is not likely to develop in communication skills to the extent that he might if he were growing up under more promising conditions.

2. In an environment highly favorable to language development for a child of given potentialities, he will probably develop in communication skills beyond the point likely to be achieved by another child with equal potentialities but with only the usual degree of favorableness of environment.

3. There is a point beyond which an especially favorable environment for a child cannot stimulate further development that can be maintained even if temporary gains are made.

4. Immediate gains made because of an unusually favorable environment often are lost when excessive stimulation is removed unless the stimulation followed a period of deprivation of proper environmental circumstances.

Readiness for Learning

Readiness for a given task may be thought of as the "teachable moment," which Robert Havighurst defines thus:

> When the body is ripe, and society requires, and the self is ready to achieve a certain task, the teachable moment has come.[1]

These points further clarify the concept of readiness:

1. Readiness for an activity implies that the child is sufficiently mature so that under favorable environmental conditions he can learn the activity with success and without undesirable effects upon him in other respects that would counterbalance or outweigh the gain made through acquisition of the skill.

2. Into activities like "learning to walk" a child cannot be forced. Readiness for walking, like that for many other activities, is primarily a matter of the "unfolding of the design" of the individual. Barring highly unfavorable environmental influences, the child will acquire such a skill in its rudimentary form almost by himself. For the initial acquisition of such skills there is not much that the adult can do to facilitate learning other than provide a background that is not inimical to acquiring them. What is usually referred to as "teaching" is, in such cases, of little or no avail.

3. In the acquisition of many types of skills there is not merely one stage of readiness, namely that for the initial learning of the skill. There also is need for readiness for later stages in learning the skill. For example, there is not only a necessity for readiness at the beginning stage of reading instruction but also at later stages that include the development of skills like learning to use the dictionary.

4. Because frequently the best evidence of "readiness" for one of the non-initial stages of acquiring a skill is excellent performance in the preceding stage, it is important that the teacher should recognize the desired sequence of stages in the development of the skill.

5. All pupils in one classroom are not, as a rule, ready for acquiring a new skill at the same time. Consequently careful diagnosis of the needs and abilities of boys and girls is of paramount importance, and provisions for adapting instruction to individual differences are necessary.

Goals for Learning

Specialists in child development will attest what even casual observation confirms, that many of the goals for the young child, if they are to be genuinely his, must be of value to him at the present or in the near future. To be sure, by the time a child is six he should be able to work for worthy goals more than a few minutes removed from the present. A still older pupil should find as stimulus to action incentives that are realized considerably farther in the future. In fact, one of the tasks to be accomplished during the elementary school is to become able to accept, as reason for effort, various goals farther and farther removed from the present.

What then are some of the aims that may be real for the elementary school child as he is guided in development of the skills of communication? Statements like these may incorporate reasons for action for some children: (1) Read this story to find out how a dog saved the children of Nome. (2) Let us plan now how we can give good book reports for our assembly program. (3) Some of you have trouble using the words *ran* and *run* correctly. I will help you find out how you can decide which word you need. Goals like these are more likely to evoke the best efforts of the learner than substitutes such as: (1) Read the story beginning on page 25. (2) Read page 12 in your textbook to find out the rules for giving a good book report. (3) Today we will find out the difference in the use of *ran* and *run*.

Pupil-Participation in Planning

Since boys and girls often learn more effectively when they have a part in planning their activities, a

[1] Robert Havighurst, *Developmental Tasks and Education*. Longmans, Green and Company, 1952, page 5.

few pointers on pupil-participation in planning are listed here.

1. The teacher should frequently share in the responsibility of planning. The amount of responsibility that the pupils should assume is to be determined in part by the maturity, age, and experience of the children.

2. Boys and girls should be held to a choice of procedure once it has been approved by the teacher unless there is adequate reason for altering plans. Half-finished work or easy discontinuance of one procedure to follow another should be discouraged.

3. When children are given a part in choosing a procedure, the choice of a few should not be mistaken for that of all. In some classrooms the most vociferous pupils determine the goals to be sought and the procedures to be followed.

Courtesy of the Wichita, Kansas, Public Schools

Figure 1.2 Creativity as an Aid to Learning

Creativity as an Aid to Learning

The use in this book of the term *creativity* is not confined to the work of the artist who produces a masterpiece. It is not even limited to activities like writing original stories or poetry. Whatever an individual does that in some way expresses his own feelings or preferences for action is considered in this book a creative act. It may be merely a word chosen happily by the pupil as he states his own reaction, a letter that in one or more sentences shows his own convictions, or a message that illustrates his personal way of communicating an idea, for in method of work as well as in results creativity may be shown.

Some teachers seem to have the mistaken idea that all they need to do to help pupils be creative is to abstain from giving detailed instructions. The quality of the learning thus often is impaired more than if such instructions were given. In order to thrive, creativity needs more than a vacuum. In various ways, some of which will be pointed out in later pages of this book, the teacher can encourage boys and girls to be creative. When a child has expressed himself through the felicitous choice of a word, the teacher may comment on the selection. When the teacher at times uses methods that are original and reflects the satisfaction that comes from such abandon of routine procedures, the pupils may be able to sense the joy resulting from doing work to express one's own ideas. Sometimes the teacher can encourage creativity as he explains to the children that although he has shown them one way in which they can attack a given assignment, they are free to try others. Occasionally some of the boys and girls may be asked to explain their procedures after introductions like these: "Dick has figured out an excellent way to.... I think you would like to have him tell you about it."

Self-Confidence as an Aid to Learning

Probably in no other area is the effect of self-confidence on learning shown more than in that of the language arts. Anxiety about success has blocked the way to learning to read for many a child. Lack of self-confidence can unnerve even scholars as they give talks.

There is no intention here of encouraging a "know-it-all" attitude. Self-confidence must be based on fact. To make a child feel self-confident when he is doomed to fail is very likely to have a detrimental effect on future learning.

Here are a few ways in which the teacher can, in teaching the language arts, encourage reasonable self-confidence in the learner.

1. If a pupil's contribution has been good, the teacher can tell him so.

2. If a pupil has shown improvement in giving a talk, the teacher can praise him.

3. If a pupil is fearful of his ability to give a talk, the teacher can help him analyze the difficulties involved and possibly overcome them, at least in part, before he gives his talk.

Effects of Attitude toward Others on Learning

In all situations what an individual thinks of his fellowmen can affect his learning. The person suspicious of others or hateful toward them is likely to be poisoned by his own thought. Energy that could be used constructively for learning purposes is then consumed in devastating emotions. This generalization is strikingly true in the area of communication. Incentive for development of skills of communication may be lacking in persons to whom their fellowmen seem unworthy. There are, of course, exceptions to this rule, for fear or hate impels some to read, to write, to speak, and to listen.

What then is the teacher's role here?

1. The teacher can help the child attain self-respect. Self-respect can breed respect for others.
2. The teacher can work toward creating a climate of good will in the classroom.
3. The teacher can help the boys and girls learn to give criticism constructively and to take suggestions from others — their peers, the teacher, and other individuals.

EFFECT OF LEARNING THE LANGUAGE ARTS ON PERSONALITY

So far we have directed our attention primarily to guidelines from the field of human growth and development, application of which can help the child learn the language arts better. Now let us take note of how adequate guidance in the language arts can affect the developing personality.

Courtesy of the Akron, Ohio, Public Schools

Figure 1.3 Beneficial Effect on Personality

Probability of Beneficial Effect on Personality

Normally as the child begins successively to listen, speak, read, and write, a new world is opened for him. As he improves in these skills that world often gradually, though sometimes suddenly, expands for him. This broadening of horizons can be the means of helping him achieve development in personality.

Let us note, for example, what may happen as Susie learns a new word, a word new to her understanding vocabulary, the word *independence.* As she acquires the word under the guidance of an alert teacher, she may add to her understanding of the word from time to time in such a manner that eventually she will take increased pride in doing things independently. But such growth in personality is often not accidental or even incidental; nor is it to be expected that Susie will feel the full import of the experience immediately. It may take years after the introduction of the word to Susie until she appreciates the fact that independence must not be confused with license; that independence may not be desirable at all times; that independence for self is not enough, but that the goal should be to help others to become independent also; that with independence comes responsibility; that the spirit can be free and independent even if the body is in shackles. But when, in the course of years and perhaps of decades, Susie has learned to comprehend points like these through reflection and/or actual experience, something beneficial, something broadening will have happened to Susie. Susie may be a different person because of learning the meaning of the word *independence.*

A caution must be expressed here. If conditions under which the pupil learns language skills or develops in them are inimical to the best in personality development, then the process of learning to communicate may have a decidedly detrimental effect upon him. For example, if when a child is introduced to reading, he develops an anxiety complex because of parents who are overanxious to have him succeed, that state of mind on the part of the learner may not only interfere seriously with his learning to read but may also do temporary or even permanent damage to him as an individual.

Comparative Importance of Effect on Personality and on Acquisition of Skills

If the choice needs to be made, it is more important that the child develop into a well-integrated personality than that he gain great facility in the use of communication skills. Happily, however, the two types of development are not mutually exclusive. One

Courtesy of the Delaware, Ohio, Public Schools.

Figure 1.4 Satisfaction through Learning

frequently supplements or complements the other. The boy or girl who is guided effectively in learning the language arts is likely to be helped thereby in the development not only of language skills but also of his personality. The child who is assisted in such a manner that he develops into a wholesome personality by that very act of guidance will probably become more receptive to learning the language arts. For example, as he becomes poised, speaking will be less of an effort than if he were "knotted up" inside.

Here are a few ways in which the teacher can assist the child in the development of his personality as he is learning the language arts.

1. The teacher encourages the child who through real effort has made improvement even if the end result is not up to standard for the grade.

2. The teacher finds reading material for the child that not only makes it possible for him to improve in reading skill but also helps him build up new worthwhile interests or develop old ones resulting in enrichment of his life.

3. The teacher adapts the spelling load to the capacity of the individual.

It must not be concluded that insistence on standards in the language arts is inimical to personality development. In fact, lack of standards may be instrumental in developing an irresponsible individual, unwilling to comply with the many restrictions encountered throughout life, violation of which may have disastrous results. There must be standards. What standards there are and how they are enforced make the difference.

Bearing on Self-Expression

Each child should be encouraged to express his own thoughts when communicating with others. To force him to give the ideas of other people as if they were his own makes him commit a lie; to tell and — probably worse yet — to act a lie is a step toward disintegration. To help the child express his own ideas is an emancipatory step.

Figure 1.5 Self-Expression through Art

Provisions for Interpersonal Relationships

As the child is guided in the acquisition of communication skills, there is much chance for developing the personality through provisions for rich interpersonal relationships. Much opportunity, with wise guidance, should be given for informal conversation among boys and girls. Committee work, discussion, speaking to an audience — all are important.

Courtesy of the St. Louis, Missouri, Public Schools

Figure 1.6 Provisions for Interpersonal Relationships

Following are a few points, in accordance with which the teacher should plan for improvement of interpersonal relationships among his pupils, as he guides them in development of skill in communication.

1. Unless consistent guidance is provided, boys and girls may develop unsatisfactory rather than satisfactory interpersonal relationships.

2. Boys and girls should not be allowed more freedom in their interpersonal relationships than that for which they can assume responsibility.

3. In committee work the line between license and liberty should be drawn, and the pupils should be helped to make the differentiation.

4. While committee work and other group activities are highly desirable, there should also be much opportunity for the individual to work alone.

5. The child should be guided so that he does not assume that group standards are necessarily correct. He should be helped to realize that he is responsible for his action even when he follows the group. Furthermore, he should receive guidance so that he will not use the group as his standard of conduct when the group is wrong.

FOR STUDY AND DISCUSSION

1. Cite instances in which a teacher's method of dealing with a problem situation would have been different had he made wise application of the principle "Behavior is caused."

2. Of what import to the teacher of remedial work should knowledge of the following statement be: "Immediate gains made because of an unusually favorable environment often are lost when the excessive stimulation is removed unless the stimulation followed a period of deprivation of proper environmental circumstances"?

3. Name ways in which creativity in the language arts can be evident on the part of a primary-grade pupil; an intermediate-grade pupil.

4. In this chapter are named several ways in which the teacher can, in teaching the language arts, encourage self-confidence in the learner. Name additional ways in which he can affect the personality of the child favorably, with likelihood of resulting improvement in language arts skills and abilities.

5. Read a chapter in a book dealing at least in part with child growth and development. What ways are mentioned, in addition to those given in this chapter, in which knowledge of child development may affect personality development that in turn may have a favorable effect on a child's language development?

6. It has been said that readiness for an activity, such as learning to read, is not determined exclusively by the ability or the intelligence of the learner but also in part by the materials of instruction to be used and the methods to be employed in teaching. What, then, should the first-grade teacher consider, on the basis of a reading readiness test, before he decides that a child is not ready at that time to learn to read?

7. Name some language arts goals that are likely to be not too far in the future for serving as real motivation for a first-grade child. In addition name some that would be likely to be too far removed from the present to serve as true motivating forces for him.

REFERENCES

Almy, Millie, *Child Development.* Second edition. D. C. Heath and Company, 1959. 490 pp.

Baller, Warren R., and Don C. Charles, *The Psychology of Human Growth and Development.* Holt, Rinehart and Winston, 1961. 432 pp.

Blair, Glenn Myers; R. Stewart Jones; and Ray H. Simpson, *Educational Psychology.* Second edition. The Macmillan Company, 1962. 678 pp.

Eson, Morris E., *Psychological Foundations of Education.* Holt, Rinehart and Winston, 1964. 563 pp.

Jersild, Arthur T., *Child Psychology.* Fifth edition. Prentice-Hall, 1960. 506 pp.

Olson, Willard C., *Child Development.* Second edition. D. C. Heath and Company, 1959. 497 pp.

Strang, Ruth, *An Introduction to Child Study.* Fourth edition. The Macmillan Company, 1959. 543 pp.

OUTLINE FOR CHAPTER 2

Developmental Patterns

CHAPTER 2

Developmental Patterns

One of the most productive activities of specialists in child development has been study to determine characteristics of children — physical, emotional, social, and intellectual — at various stages of development. Since knowledge of these characteristics, coupled with information on the patterns of language development, is fundamental to the construction of effective programs of language instruction, this chapter is devoted to a summary of those findings.

LIMITATIONS OF AVAILABLE DATA

Although much valuable information has been gleaned through studies of the growth patterns of children, available data have certain shortcomings. Of these the teacher should be cognizant in planning a curriculum based in part on the findings of the characteristics of boys and girls at various stages of development. The following are important points in this relationship.

1. Much additional careful, painstaking study is needed either to reinforce or to contradict, if necessary, present-day generalizations on characteristics of children at various stages of development.

2. There are so many gaps in the information that has been gathered to date that many points in the planning of any course of study cannot be settled solely in the light of findings in the field of child growth and development. Common sense, informal observation of children, and knowledge of the psychology of learning should help where child specialists cannot supply the answer and should supplement, in general, their findings.

3. It is frequently difficult, even often impossible, to ascertain or to predict which children are exceptions to the rules or generalizations that have been formulated.

4. Although the sequence of appearance of a characteristic or trait is in many cases the same from one person to another, the timing of its appearance shows much variation from individual to individual.

GENERAL CHARACTERISTICS OF THE PRIMARY-GRADE CHILD

Keeping in mind the cautions that have been stated about interpretation of data, let us note the characteristics typical of children, six, seven, and eight years of age. Awareness of the physical, emotional, social, and intellectual natures of boys and girls at primary-grade levels will help us guide pupils in the first three years of school in their development of skills of communication.

Physical Development

The physical development of the child from six through eight is characteristically as follows:

1. Boys and girls increase considerably in size during this period, as a rule two or three inches a year in height and three to six pounds in weight, and the growth is at a steadier rate than in the preschool years.

2. The average girl at six is more advanced than the average boy of that age in general development, including skeletal structure, and she maintains this superiority throughout the usual span of ages of the primary grades. In both height and weight, as well as in other aspects of size, the average boy surpasses the average girl.

3. There is considerable increase in length of legs during this period. The chest becomes broader and

the heart increases a good deal in size. However, there is a decrease in the rate of the pulse and of breathing, negative manifestations that are nevertheless signs of development of the organism.

4. The size and general physical well-being of the primary-grade child greatly influence the personality of the growing individual.

5. Boys and girls in the primary grades are by nature so active that it is difficult for them to sit still for a long period of time.

6. The child entering the elementary school is still much more adept in his use of the large muscles than of smaller ones, but during the years in the primary grades he shows considerable growth in coordination of the latter.

7. In spite of relatively slow development of sex organs during the years of six through eight there is an increase in their size, and both boys and girls manifest development in sex feelings although these are much less intense and less obvious than those during later periods of development.

8. Typically the primary-grade child is subject to many colds as well as to childhood diseases and consequently is absent from school rather frequently.

9. Poor posture, as measured by adult standards, is characteristic of the primary-grade child, who is likely to have drooping shoulders and to show lack of strength of the abdominal muscles.

10. Uneven growth of various parts of the skeletal structure is likely, in part, to cause the awkwardness characteristic of the older primary-grade child.

11. The loss of deciduous teeth is one of the striking characteristics of the primary-grade child.

12. As in preschool years, the child in the primary grades continues to be somewhat farsighted. Consequently the length of time for close work and the nature of that work need to be under careful scrutiny by adults. Fusion, as a rule, is better than in earlier years.

Emotional Development

This statement by Willard C. Olson[1] well serves as introduction to a listing of the emotional characteristics of boys and girls.

> As might be expected, studies of emotional development and social adjustment, from the point of view of growth, have lagged because of the absence of easily applied techniques rather than through a lack of recognition of their importance. The available methods for study in these fields have been more successful in revealing individual differences among children than in plotting the course of the changes accompanying age and experience. An extensive miscellany of data based upon rating scales, projective tests, questionnaires, interviews, and anecdotes has been used to describe attitudes and feelings and social and emotional adjustment. The methods yield concrete data of unique significance which are difficult to generalize and to lay out on a scale which is meaningful for all children. The incidental and individual materials gained by observation and interview have often been incorporated by verbal description into accounts which also contain statistical and graphic portrayals of growth.

The following are some of the emotional characteristics of the primary-grade child that are of particular significance to the adult guiding the language development of boys and girls of ages six, seven, and eight.

1. One of the outstanding characteristics of the six-year-old is changeableness in level of expression of his emotional responses. He alternates between impulsive reactions characteristic of preceding, less mature stages in his emotional development (like temper tantrums, fighting, lack of intellectual responses) and the more reasoned, deliberate responses characteristic of later stages.

2. By the time some children reach the second grade they have developed an undesirable self-consciousness which at times results in withdrawal from both adults and peers. Insecurity, often precipitated by lack of felt love and lack of success, is frequently the cause of withdrawal tendencies at this age.

3. The six-year-old is likely to be self-centered to the extent that characteristics which in adults would be considered extremely selfish are much in evidence. He likes to be first and wants things done his own way. He is often overly aggressive. If he is frustrated he may resort to explosive behavior or to withdrawal. With increasing maturity the primary-grade child becomes less ego-centered and his reaction to not getting what he wants is more likely to be one of withdrawal than of explosiveness. He remains intent on preserving his own personality against all opposition.

4. The primary-grade child is greatly in need of feelings of success – success in work at home and at school and success in play.

5. To love and to be loved is one of the great needs of the human being. Lack of it during childhood is likely to result in a seriously warped personality.

6. Frequently even the well-adjusted primary-grade child shows mannerisms like biting nails, sucking the thumb, twirling a small piece of material of his wearing apparel, playing with the ears. Pronounced, numerous, or continuing behavior of this type is frequently the result of dangerous tensions

[1] Willard C. Olson, *Child Development*. D. C. Heath and Company, 1959, page 195.

that should be relieved in ways other than direct attack upon the offending act.

7. Boys and girls of the primary-grade age levels express their emotional reactions both through words and actions. When the two are at variance, it is probably the action rather than the verbal claim that is the truer index to the feelings of the child.

Social Development

The social development of an individual is inextricably knit with his emotional development. The relationship is evident between many of the following points indicating the social development of the primary-grade child and the emotional characteristics typical of a child of that age level.

1. Probably one of the most outstanding of the social characteristics of primary-grade children is that there is great variation among them in many respects. In spite of the differences, however, there are certain characteristic trends in their social development.

2. Without supervision the play of the first-grade child often degenerates into fighting.

3. Although the typical primary-grade child generally accepts the standards of right and wrong of his parents and teachers, it does not follow that he acts accordingly at all times.

4. The ego-centeredness, characteristic of the child in the early part of the primary-grade levels, while decreasing in strength, is evident in the contacts he has with peers and with adults.

5. The typical child entering first grade without kindergarten experiences is likely to be happier when he is with only one or two or three individuals than when he is a member of a larger group. The child who has attended kindergarten, profiting from the socializing activities of the preceding year or two, is usually more accustomed to the larger groups.

6. At the beginning of the first grade the child is still greatly interested in associations with adults. Gradually, however, as he associates more with his peers, they begin to count more and he seemingly becomes less dependent upon adults for the satisfaction of his social needs. However, adults continue to be of great importance to him even though they do not pre-empt the center of the expanding stage of the child's life. He needs the security of their affection as he sallies forth into explorations of social living with his age-mates.

7. The emotional instability of many boys and girls during part of the period of the primary grades is reflected in their social behavior and at times they tend to be rude and impetuous and stubborn and then again cheerful, cooperative, and generous.

8. As boys and girls progress through the primary grades, they increasingly like to tell others, children and adults, in small and later in large groups, of their experiences.

9. As the child grows from being a six-year-old through being an eight-year-old, he becomes more aware of the need of skill in associations with others. Under appropriate guidance he makes strides in group planning and in executing and evaluating plans. He also becomes more interested in serving occasionally in the capacity of leader. He can learn the difference in leadership and followership roles. He can also comprehend the fact that he should not expect to be leader at all times.

10. During the latter part of the primary grades the child becomes more interested than formerly in the faraway in place and the remote in time. However, these periods and places must be made quite concrete to him if they they are to get his prolonged interest and he is to profit from them. Abstractions still are frequently beyond his comprehension.

11. The primary-grade child continues to learn the customs and the prejudices of the culture of which he is a part. Nevertheless, social rank usually means little to him.

Intellectual Development

There are no sudden cataclysmic changes in intellectual development of the child between the time when he is of preschool age and the time when he enters first grade. Yet the intellectual development of the child as he leaves the third grade of the elementary school is strikingly different from that of the same child three years before.

These are some of the usual characteristics of the intellectual growth of the primary-grade child that should have considerable bearing on methods of guiding him in his development of communication skills.

1. One of the outstanding characteristics of the intellectual development of the primary-grade child is the existence of striking individual differences. The range of intelligence is so great that no uniform curriculum can satisfy the varying needs of all the children.

2. The intellectual activity of the first-grade child is to a considerable extent determined by factors that have direct influence upon him. He is too ego-centered to care much about many matters not pertaining to him. His intellectual curiosity is greater, as a rule, in regard to the near in time and space than in the distant.

3. The difference between reality and fantasy is not always clear to the beginner in the primary

grades, but usually by the end of the third grade differentiation is no problem. Even when the child knows the difference, however, he likes to engage in highly imaginative incidents, especially in the first grade. These are enjoyed vicariously and in dramatic play.

4. Interest in immediate goals rather than remote, which is highly characteristic of the child when he begins his years in the elementary school, gives way in part, under wise guidance, to interest in less immediate goals.

5. During the three years of the primary grades the child develops more objectivity in his intellectual considerations.

6. Interest in the concrete rather than the abstract, in fact, frequent failure to comprehend the abstract, is an outstanding quality of the six-year-old. Even at nine, though abstractions can be understood better than earlier, interest in and comprehension of the concrete are still predominant.

7. The primary-grade child develops markedly in ability to reason as his innate powers unfold in an environment rich in stimulating experiences.

8. Because of paucity of experience and ability to profit from many types of experiences, the six-year-old has a relatively small number of concepts. However, during the first three years of his elementary-school education, under desirable environmental conditions, growth in this respect is phenomenal.

9. The attention span of the six-year-old is brief but under appropriate guidance it can be greatly increased by the time he completes the primary grades.

10. Purpose becomes increasingly a significant factor in the persistence with which the learner performs. That purpose needs, however, to be the learner's purpose, not merely that of an adult.

11. The primary-grade child likes to put thought into action. The need for doing and making is characteristic of the intellectual development of the child of that age range.

12. At the beginning of the first grade the child has difficulty in following directions other than very simple ones. Marked development, however, takes place during the course of the next few years.

GENERAL CHARACTERISTICS OF THE INTERMEDIATE-GRADE CHILD

Upon entrance to the fourth grade the typical child has changed considerably in physical, emotional, social, and intellectual development from the time three years before when he started in the first grade. These changes have not been cataclysmic, but in their steady development, have been none the less certain and significant. They continue in the next three years, during the period of time usually spent in the intermediate grades (grades four, five, and six).

Physical Development

The following points explain characteristics of boys and girls in the period of middle childhood. They all have bearing on guidance in the development of communication skills that should be given the child of that age.

1. Throughout middle childhood the typical girl continues to be at least one year more advanced in physiological development than the typical boy of the same chronological age.

2. For both boys and girls in the period immediately preceding the spurt of preadolescence, there is for a short time almost a seeming cessation of physical growth.

3. Girls make their greatest gain in height during the last year of the intermediate grades and during the first of the junior high school. The rapid increase in height of boys usually takes place two years later. Much of the gain is in length of legs.

4. Middle childhood marks a period with fewer illnesses than there were during early childhood, resulting in more regular attendance at school.

5. Development in coordination continues during the period of middle childhood. However, a relatively small number of pupils in the sixth grade are awkward in movements. They tend to be girls who are approaching early adolescence. Their awkwardness is due, in part, to uneven skeletal development and to emotional changes of that period.

6. Posture continues to be relatively poor for many during this period.

7. Middle childhood is a time of much physical endurance and great energy.

8. During the period of middle childhood organs of circulation, respiration, and digestion approach those of adulthood in size.

Emotional Development

To probe into the inner world of human beings is, at best, a difficult task. During the years of middle childhood it is more baffling than during some other stages of development.

What the individual reports about his feelings gives one index of his emotional life. But often the child is not accurate in his responses, made either casually or in more formal set-ups as in questionnaires or interviews. At times this lack of accuracy is undoubtedly the result of wilful evasion of facts. In many other instances the response is unreliable because the child is unaware of his true feeling. Since he often has more difficulty in understanding himself during the intermediate-grade years than he has during some other periods of life, his own confusion about himself leads to reports about his feelings that are likely, in many instances, to be incorrect.

A second method of gathering data on the emotions is by studying actions. But middle childhood is a period when there is much contradictory behavior – one minute reversion to earlier immature stages and another progression to more adult standards. Furthermore, the intermediate-grade child has "learned" more successfully than when he was in the primary grades to camouflage his true feelings at times by not revealing them through behavior. Consequently, gaining insight into the inner world of the intermediate-grade child through his actions as well as through his reports is a process subject to many errors.

In spite of the problems involved in ascertaining characteristic feelings of the intermediate-grade child, however, we do have access to valuable though incomplete information. When coupled with common sense, a love for children, and a desire to observe them, the available information can make a great difference in the skill and artistry with which teachers guide boys and girls in their language development. A few comments on the trends of emotional development of the intermediate-grade child are here listed.

1. One of the characteristic patterns of the typical intermediate-grade child is lack of consistency in his actions, which frequently vary between rather adult responses and immature behavior. Often this outward state indicates an inner emotional condition that fluctuates between the impulsive expression of emotions of early childhood and the more intellectual responses of the adult. It would seem that the variation frequently is in the emotion itself not in only its expression.

2. Both boys and girls continue to care more and more about what their peers think and correspondingly less about what adults want. In fact, there is a growing rejection of adult standards of conduct. Nevertheless, the children of this stage typically still accept the correctness of many of the moral standards that their parents taught them, even though, unfortunately, they do not necessarily live up to the rules they consider right.

3. Boys and girls in the intermediate grades continue to need love and affection from both adults and peers. Behind the seeming indifference to adults there is a deep craving for their affection which if not satisfied is likely to have damaging effects upon the child. To be thought of highly by the peer group is, however, also necessary to the emotional well-being of the child in fourth, fifth and sixth grades; in fact, the peer group counts much more during this period than it did in preceding stages. Middle childhood is a time when the child feels real need of a chum with whom he can share intimately his joys and his sorrows, his shortcomings and his assets.

4. The intermediate-grade child becomes more and more aware of himself as an individual. Together with this growth in self-awareness come self-analysis and self-criticism. When kept within the bounds of normalcy, such analysis and criticism of self are healthy. That it is a time of self-awareness and self-criticism is not strange in the case of boys and girls approaching adolescence, for there often are many inner confusions resulting in part from lack of understanding of the new role to be played.

5. To please the parent or the teacher in most cases is no longer sufficient incentive for perseverance in work. More lasting objectives need to supplement or substitute for this goal that, rightly or wrongly, was often the driving purpose in the early primary grades.

6. As boys and girls approach adolescence, they become increasingly conscious of the opposite sex and in time increasingly interested in it; the girls, as a rule, clearly manifest such interest earlier than the boys.

7. Boys and girls are responsive to the idealism of heroes in life and in story.

8. Boys and girls are often greatly concerned in this period of growth about what their conscience dictates to them. When kept within proper limits, this concern is highly desirable. However, at times they become too involved in decisions of conscience and develop so-called "guilt complexes." They are too immature during middle childhood to carry the burden of making many decisions, the solution to which might bother them a great deal. Adults do the child a favor when they decide many matters for him and thus save him the need of making certain emotional involvements, even if the child does not like the decision. However, unless the boy and girl increasingly are given freedom to make their own decisions and to assume responsibility for them, they are likely to be stunted in at least one phase of their development.

9. It is very important to the intermediate-grade child that he be successful in some activities significant to him and that other people consider him capable. Without the satisfaction of success the child's emotional responses may not develop normally. Sometimes under such circumstances he becomes introverted, developing an "I don't care" attitude. At other times he may try so hard to succeed that his disappointment at failure can be highly detrimental to

him or undue concentration on certain activities, for which success is greatly coveted, may make him one-sided.

10. As the intermediate-grade child approaches adolescence, he frequently feels more keenly than before the joy and the pain that typically accompany all development.

Social Development

For a discussion of the close relationship between the emotional and social development of the intermediate-grade child, the reader is referred to the statement by Willard Olson on page 14. They are as appropriate for consideration in connection with the following points as in the setting in which they were earlier quoted.

1. In the emotions of the intermediate-grade pupil as well as his actions, unpredictability is one of the most outstanding characteristics during the period of middle childhood. One minute the reaction in a social situation involving one or more people may be that expected during earlier stages of development. The next time, shortly thereafter, it may be on a much more adult level.

2. The typical middle-grade child no longer cares to do as many things alone as he did in earlier years. He seeks the company of others.

3. The company that the intermediate-grade pupil desires increasingly becomes that of his peers rather than that of adults, with whom he had contentedly spent much time earlier. There is such a pronounced change in this respect that the "poor parent" who formerly had been enthroned by his child now thinks he is "deserted" for members of the child's peer group. But the parent should not be disconsolate. First of all, he is not really "deserted" for the child still depends on him for warmth and security and love although his actions at times seem to belie this fact. Second, this emergence from the close parent-child relationship of earlier days is part of the development from the dependency of infancy to the independency of adulthood which every thinking parent desires for his child, painful for the parent though this process often may be.

4. The intermediate-grade child likes to have a close pal, but he is also interested in groups, small groups as well as groups larger than those he chose to join in early childhood.

5. The groups to which intermediate-grade boys and girls belong are more highly structured than the informal groups of former years.

6. Increasingly boys and girls prefer to be with members of their own sex, a preference that reverses during adolescence.

7. Children of this stage of development often adopt as their own the mannerisms or other actions of those persons who to them are heroes; some are flesh-and-blood persons whom they have met while others are characters from fiction or biography.

8. Problems of juvenile delinquency frequently show up for the first time during middle childhood.

9. The intermediate-grade child is likely to be greatly concerned that his wearing apparel and other possessions should be similar to those of his best friends.

Intellectual Development

In planning the program in the language arts, the intermediate-grade teacher should be conscious of the relationship between the following intellectual characteristics of the pupil and the procedures to be employed in guiding the child to optimum language development.

1. The range in intellectual capacity among intermediate-grade pupils within a class is usually greater than that in any one of the preceding grades. This increase in variation is due, in part, to the fact that the child with above-normal intelligence continues to grow intellectually each year more than does the average child of the same chronological age, while the child with below-normal intelligence continues to develop less each year than does the average child.

2. Variations in the use made of the potentialities with which an individual was endowed are greater by the time a pupil has reached the intermediate grades than formerly, and consequently there is even greater difference in ability.

3. These are some of the ways in which the intellectual development of the typical intermediate-grade child are manifested:

> He is more interested than formerly in the remote in time and space.
>
> He is keenly interested in the world in which he lives so that questions of *how* and *why* are asked frequently.
>
> He is greatly interested in making classifications so that his ever-expanding world can be arranged in his mind into some kind of order.
>
> He is more understanding than formerly of cause-effect and other logical relationships. Under wise guidance he is able to make generalizations on a fairly difficult level.
>
> He has increased in ability to comprehend numerous abstractions but he continues to be in need of many concrete experiences.
>
> He can concentrate for a longer period of time than formerly.

He can follow directions better for he can put into action more complex directions than earlier.

In general, by the time he leaves the intermediate grades he has developed a great deal in understanding truth and various abstractions of goodness.

The intermediate-grade boy is considerably less interested than formerly in fantasy, but some girls very much enjoy reading poetry and prose that give free sway to the imagination.

LANGUAGE DEVELOPMENT OF THE ELEMENTARY-SCHOOL CHILD

We have now observed those phases of the general development of the child as he passes through the primary and intermediate grades that have particular implications for the guidance of growth in language abilities. Let us next note the chief characteristics of the elementary-school child as far as growth in language is concerned.

1. Basic to the understanding of growth in the language arts — in listening, speaking, reading, and writing — is the fact that they are inextricably interrelated. Even in the early stages of speaking it is plainly evident that this facet of the language arts is greatly influenced by the listening that the child does — by what he hears of the many sounds in his environment. His background for learning to read is conditioned to a considerable extent by what he has heard and how he has conversed previously. Further development in reading is affected similarly. The child's writing is also influenced by what he has heard spoken and by what he has read.

2. At the time the child enters the first grade most of the physical organs needed for performing functions in communications are mature enough not to furnish reason for delay in development of the skills. In fact, from early infancy the child's hearing apparatus is mature enough to enable him to pick up sounds in the world around him. Similarly, the speech organs are well developed even at the time of birth. In spite of the fact that the organs are physiologically mature enough to serve functions of speaking and listening well, the elementary-school child often needs assistance in developing clearer speech and greater auditory acuity.

There is a difference of opinion as to whether the eye is mature enough by the time the child enters first grade for that to be the desirable time for beginning to learn to read. At that time the child is still inclined toward farsightedness. However, long postponement of learning to read is not urged on these grounds by most specialists in the field. Rather than waiting a few years after the child enters school, until he is no longer likely to be farsighted, they recommend that care be taken that reading materials appropriate in size and clarity of type be used, and that the amount and time spent on close eye work be regulated in the interest of the hygiene of the eye.

By the time the child has come to the first grade his physiological set-up for muscular coordinations has been greatly developed although it still is easier for him at that time to make large-muscle rather than small-muscle coordinations — a fact of great importance for consideration in planning a program in handwriting.

3. By the time the child enters school he has had almost six years of very fruitful practice in listening and about five in speaking.

4. The broad outline of the sequence of the pattern of the development of the communication skills is essentially the same for all normal human beings. However, the details of language development as they affect the time for taking up various topics in the program of oral communication, for example, have not been established.

5. Although the sequence in the development of communication skills in broad terms is approximately the same for all normal human beings, the timing of the appearance of various phases in this sequence varies greatly from one individual to another.

6. Typically even in the first grade the child has learned to use all types of sentences — declarative, exclamatory, interrogative, and imperative and simple, complex, and compound. In vocabulary development he has made tremendous strides, much greater than he is likely to make after entering school or any time thereafter. The problem in his vocabulary development lies not so much in the small number of words that he uses as in the limited and erroneous meanings that he associates with some of them.

7. Although there is a close relationship between language ability and intelligence, intelligence is only one factor that helps determine language development. As set by the innate pattern of the individual, intelligence marks the limit of the development that is possible — determines the potentialities for growth. However, environment has a significant part in determining to what extent those potentialities will be realized and in what manner they will be developed.

8. As the child progresses through the elementary school, there is rather steady continuity of growth in language abilities and skills rather than development characterized by sudden spurts.

9. As the child advances from six years to thirteen years of age, he shows marked gain in ability to use

language skills effectively in group situations involving planning, executing, and evaluating.

10. The following statements indicate some environmental influences that affect language development.

> A favorable socioeconomic background seems to be beneficial to the child in the development of language skills.
>
> The extent of a child's experience, first-hand and vicarious, and the richness of it determine in part the development of his skill in communication.
>
> The "only child" is likely to be more advanced in language development than the child who has brothers and sisters, probably due to the closer, more exclusive contact with adults with greater language facility than sisters and brothers.
>
> Twins are inclined to be less advanced in language development than other children during their early years partly because much of their association usually is with one another, not with adults.
>
> The quality of the language of the adults with whom the child comes into contact, both at school and at home, greatly affects his power of communication.
>
> In homes where a language other than English is spoken, the child upon entrance to school is likely to be handicapped in his ability to communicate in English, regardless of advantages in other respects that may accrue for him because of his knowledge of two languages.
>
> In general, girls excel boys in various language abilities. However, boys have been found, too, in many instances to excel girls. The superiority of some boys in this respect may be due in part to the fact that fewer boys than girls seem to be shy in asking questions and in other aspects of communication affected adversely by shyness.
>
> The opportunity the child has to use communication skills helps determine the extent of his language development.
>
> A critical attitude toward the child's language development frequently affects communication skills unfavorably. This statement is not to be interpreted, however, as an argument against wisely given constructive criticism.

FOR STUDY AND DISCUSSION

1. In what ways is information about the physical development of an elementary-school child of particular significance to the teacher in the program of the language arts?

2. How can the teacher relate the program in the language arts to the fact that boys and girls in the intermediate grades are greatly influenced by the sanctions of the peer group?

3. How can the teacher through the language arts help boys and girls learn to distinguish more clearly between reality and fantasy?

4. On page 17 these two statements occur: "The intermediate-grade child becomes more and more aware of himself as an individual. Together with this growth in self-awareness come self-analysis and self-criticism." Cite ways in which the teacher can gear the language arts program so that the boys and girls develop mentally healthy practices in self-analysis and self-criticism.

5. On page 19 it is stated that when the child enters first grade "most of the physical organs needed for performing functions in communication are mature enough not to furnish reason for delay in development of the skills." What then are some reasons that in your estimation may serve as cause for delay in teaching boys and girls to read shortly after they start first grade?

6. How can the teacher help the elementary-school child to attain optimum physical maturity as he develops from early childhood to adolescence?

7. Describe an elementary-school child whom you know as to his physical, emotional, social, and intellectual characteristics. Include in your description comparisons with the characteristics listed in this chapter.

REFERENCES

Anderson, John E., *The Psychology of Development and Personal Adjustment*. Holt, Rinehart and Winston, 1949. 720 pp.

Harding, Lowry W., *Arithmetic for Child Development*. Second edition. William C. Brown Company, 1964. 428 pp.

Havighurst, Robert J., *Developmental Tasks and Education*. Second edition. David McKay Company, 1952. 100 pp.

Jersild, Arthur T., *Child Psychology*, Fifth edition. Prentice-Hall, 1960. 506 pp.

Lindgren, Henry Clay, *Educational Psychology in the Classroom*. Second edition. John Wiley and Sons, 1964. 574 pp.

Pressey, Sidney L.; Francis P. Robinson; and John E. Horrocks, *Psychology in Education*. Harper and Row, 1959. 658 pp.

Smith, Louis M., and Bryce B. Hudgins, *Educational Psychology: An Application of Social and Behavioral Theory*. Alfred A. Knopf, 1964. 533 pp.

PART TWO

Developmental Procedures in Guiding Growth in Communication Skills

OUTLINE FOR CHAPTER 3

Common Problems in Teaching the Language Arts

CHAPTER 3

Common Problems in Teaching the Language Arts

In spite of the close interrelatedness of the various aspects of the language arts that must be respected in teaching if maximum results are to be attained, a consideration of the methods of teaching each of these phases is important. It is impossible to give concise suggestions for teaching, which this book presents, without somewhere dealing specifically with each of the major components. It is for this reason that in Part Two of this book, which deals primarily with methods of teaching, that the suggestions are classified as indicated in the following chapter headings:

Guiding Growth in Oral Communication
Guiding Growth in Written Expression
Guiding Growth in Skills Common to Oral and Written Communication
Guiding Growth in Handwriting
Guiding Growth in Spelling
Guiding Growth Toward Readiness for Reading
Guiding Growth in Reading Skills
Guiding Growth in Independent Reading
Guiding Growth Through Dramatic Expression.

Although in succeeding chapters attention is paid separately to each of the foregoing phases of the language arts, nevertheless in this chapter there are discussed some of the problems common to two or more aspects of the language arts. This plan of organization is followed in order to prevent repetition.

PURPOSE OF THE LANGUAGE ARTS PROGRAM

What are we aiming to accomplish through the teaching of the language arts? That is indeed an important question for teachers to attempt to answer as they plan their work.

General Objectives

There are various degrees of specificity with which the objectives can be expressed. They can, for example, be given in such general terms as in the statement that the teaching of the language arts should help the learner to lead a more personally satisfying and socially useful life than he would be likely to have without the guidance he gets in the area.

General objectives in the language arts can also be stated in terms of the often-cited facets of the language arts in this manner:

1. To help the learner express himself better orally
2. To help the learner to be a more attentive listener and increase in ability to comprehend better what he hears
3. To help the learner comprehend better the meaning of the written word
4. To help the learner express himself better in writing.

Specific Objectives

For the day-in, day-out work in the classroom specific goals are a requirement for maximum effectiveness. They should spell out in more usable terms the general objectives. In this book specific objectives are considered in connection with various phases of the language arts that are taken up in the chapters to follow.

Enumeration of objectives in the different aspects of the language arts program should not be interpreted as a recommendation to teach them independently of one another. In all teaching the interrelatedness of the various phases should be recognized even though at times it is important to place primary emphasis on one phase, or even on a small segment of it, before it is integrated into the total program.

IMPORTANCE OF THE LANGUAGE ARTS PROGRAM

The significance of the role that development in the language arts can play in the growth of the individual and in turn in the improvement of society has already been pointed out in part in the statement of general objectives. The following list of statements highlights some of the points made and adds others.

1. Through development in the language arts the learner can increase his ability to think.
2. Through language development the individual can increase his power to affect the behavior of others.
3. Through language development the learner can increase his skill in the various fields of human learning.
4. Through guidance in the language arts the learner can not only increase his skills and abilities, but also improve his attitudes and develop his understandings.
5. Through an individual's effectiveness in the language arts the choice and success of his vocation or profession can be greatly influenced.

INCIDENTAL VERSUS SYSTEMATIC INSTRUCTION

One of the most debated questions in the teaching of the language arts in the elementary school centers around the place of incidental versus systematic instruction. Lack of agreement on the meaning of the terms causes some of the argument. Usually *systematic instruction* in the language arts refers to a program in which the skills are taught according to a systematically thought-out plan. On the contrary *incidental instruction* indicates a program of instruction by means of which the pupils acquire the communication skills incidentally as need for their use arises within lifelike situations that confront the learner.

Many persons favoring systematic instruction do not ignore the opportunities for the development of language skills through lifelike situations. Rather, their argument is that total dependence on such situations as the only means of developing desirable skills does not guarantee that all needed skills will be taught adequately. They do insist upon systematic instruction to supplement or parallel the incidental.

Adherents to the claim that the rule should be incidental instruction seldom go as far as to exclude all systematic work. In many cases they insist only that most of the learning be done in bona fide situations in which the child recognizes the need of the skills. There are some teachers who favor incidental instruction only in speaking, writing, and listening phases of the language arts while they want systematic instruction in reading. Others also may agree to systematic instruction in spelling though they object to it in handwriting. Thus the difference between those favoring incidental and those arguing for systematic instruction is frequently one of the extent to which each of these two means should be used.

Arguments Advanced for Incidental Instruction

Some of the commonly advanced arguments for incidental rather than systematic instruction in the language arts are as follows:

1. Learning in the language arts takes place in a program in which the pupils use the skills in communication in a challenging environment.
2. Learning language skills in lifelike situations assists the learner in recognizing the value of the skills he is acquiring and consequently motivates him to try to become proficient in them.
3. Learning communication skills in lifelike situations is likely to provide the learner with the opportunity to practice various language arts skills in the same situation.
4. Learning communication skills in lifelike situations places emphasis on application of what is learned to other situations, while frequently practice in more formal set-ups does not carry over into later use to the extent desired.

Arguments Favoring Systematic Instruction

The following are some of the arguments given in favor of systematic instruction:

1. The reaction against systematic instruction set in at a time when much meaningless drill served as the chief means of teaching the language arts. The criticism should be against almost exclusive use of ineffective drill, not against well-planned systematic instruction.
2. Incidental instruction is often accidental instruction, with learning left to chance.
3. In incidental instruction more time than necessary is spent on some skills.
4. Unless there is systematic instruction, some important skills will not be learned at all, while others

will not receive the attention needed for the desired degree of mastery.

5. Economy of learning some skills requires that special emphasis be placed on teaching them and that a planned program of practice on them be followed.

6. In nonsystematic programs of language instruction the chief emphasis is usually placed on something other than the skills of language. For example, when the language work is correlated with the social studies to the exclusion of separate work on the development of communication skills, the major attention is usually on the subject matter of the social studies rather than on the development of communication skills.

7. Use of a systematic program of instruction in the language arts does not preclude incidental instruction. Consequently the advantages of incidental instruction, without its disadvantages, can be achieved in a program in which systematic instruction takes care of those learnings that are not adequately and economically acquired through incidental instruction.

Point of View Emphasized in This Book

While the writer realizes the importance of the use of lifelike situations for learning in the language arts, she nevertheless believes that there should be a planned program, richly supplemented by one in which such situations are used. She believes that many pupils need adequate practice in the perfection of many of the skills required for efficiency – more than can frequently be relied upon to be provided by incidental means only. However, the writer emphasizes the fact that pupils should be helped to find purpose for learning such skills by recognizing their significance in true-to-life situations and that they should be assisted in making application of what they are learning through systematic practice in such situations.

SELECTION OF CONTENT

What is taught in the language arts is important. There is so much information that could be acquired and so many skills that could be developed that selectivity is essential. How then can the content of the program in the language arts in the elementary school be determined wisely? Here are some guiding principles.

1. The language arts are tools of communication rather than subject matter to be learned. In the selection of the content the emphasis, therefore, should be on the language arts as tools.

2. When planning the curriculum in the language arts, application should be made of what has been established by research in the field of child growth and development.

3. The content of the language-arts program should be selected in terms of the objectives that have been accepted.

4. The content of the language-arts curriculum should be determined in part by the ongoing activities of the classroom in other areas and, at the same time, the ongoing classroom activities in other areas should be chosen in part in terms of the needs and interests of the child in his language development.

5. The content of the language-arts curriculum should not be limited to the needs of the pupil at the time; attention should be given to future needs also. Fortunately, present and future needs of boys and girls are often the same.

6. In the selection of content, provision needs to be made for individual differences.

7. When selecting content, the teacher needs to begin where the child is, not where he thinks the learner ought to be.

8. The selection of the content for the elementary-school curriculum should be a cooperative enterprise in which teachers on all levels have an opportunity to contribute their knowledge.

9. Each teacher, sometimes with assistance of pupils, should have freedom in determining details of content within the framework of the program planned for the school.

SEQUENCE AND GRADE PLACEMENT

After the content of the curriculum in the language arts has been determined, it is necessary to decide on sequence and grade placement. Unfortunately there is a great deficit in available information as to desirable sequence and grade placement of content and activities. The curriculum maker cannot state with confidence that any particular order is the most advantageous. However, even now there need not be groping in total darkness when deciding upon sequence and grade placement. Guidelines such as the following can be of service.

1. From the field of human growth and development help should be utilized from data, such as those presented in Chapter 2, which indicate in general terms the sequence in the development of communication skills in the normal individual.

2. From the field of human growth and development data should be utilized that show the most likely times of appearance of particular abilities and skills. As these data are considered it should, however, be borne in mind that there is more variation in time

of occurrence than in sequence in appearance of many language abilities.

3. Psychological rather than logical factors should be the determinants of sequence and grade placement whenever there is a conflict between the two types of factors.

4. The abilities, needs, and interests of boys and girls should play important parts in determining sequence and placement.

5. Emphasis should be placed on what Robert Havighurst calls the "teachable moment" when the learner is ready to learn what will be taught.

6. There should be flexibility within the framework of the curriculum so that within it each teacher has leeway in terms of sequence to be followed.

7. The curriculum for any one grade should make provision for the wide range of abilities within the grade.

8. The difficulty of learning an activity or acquiring information should determine in part the sequence and placement.

9. The grade placement of a topic or an activity should be determined in part by the number of other activities or topics already allocated to a grade.

10. There should be a balance of types of subject matter or activities allocated to any one grade.

11. The content of the language-arts curriculum for any one grade should be chosen in relation to that of other grades.

12. The textbook should not be the sole determinant of sequence and grade placement.

13. Provision should be made for review and application of learnings acquired in preceding grades.

PROBLEM SOLVING

Contrary to popular opinion even very young children engage in problem-solving activities. Teacher guidance can be valuable in assisting boys and girls in solving problems more effectively than they would unaided. The teacher can surround the boys and girls with an environment conducive to the solution of problems and can help them in the various steps.

Steps in Problem Solving

The steps in problem solving have been identified in various ways. Here is one simple listing:

1. Sensing the problem
2. Defining the problem
3. Making hypotheses as to how the problem may be solved
4. Deciding on a likely hypothesis (to try first)
5. Testing the hypothesis
6. If the hypothesis does not stand the test, deciding on another hypothesis and testing it and then proceeding in this manner until a hypothesis that works is found.

Arriving at Generalizations

One type of problem solving takes place through arriving at generalizations inductively and then, through deductive reasoning, applying the generalizations. A value in helping boys and girls learn and apply rules in this manner is that they seem to remember longer and to make better use of generalizations when they arrive at them inductively than when they are merely told to study the rule and apply it. Another value lies in the practice that this procedure affords in problem solving — practice that, with guidance, can be helpful to the pupils in other situations. For illustration of this method the reader is referred to pages 305 to 307.

MEANINGFUL REPETITION

Provisions need to be made for meaningful practice since as a rule skills are not perfected through one exposure. To be sure, much needed practice can be provided by the ongoing classroom activities. Furthermore, some class projects, like writing a class paper or putting on a puppet show, can be designed primarily to give pupils needed practice in writing or in appearing in front of an audience. However, use of all these kinds of activities frequently does not give opportunity for the desirable amount and type of repetition for perfecting skills.

Guidelines for Providing Meaningful Repetition

These are some of the guidelines that the teacher should keep in mind when it is necessary to isolate somewhat for practice certain elements of a learning situation.

1. Practice should not be "busy work."

2. The purpose of practice work as a rule should be clear not only to the teacher but also to the learner and the boys and girls should be helped, if necessary, to recognize the purpose as significant.

3. Frequently the purpose of practice work can be made clear to boys and girls if they see its relationship to what they are doing in major classroom activities or in important out-of-school activities. For example, if boys and girls are planning to write a class paper, special practice in writing paragraphs in order to have a good paper is likely to be more meaningful than work on topic sentences taken up merely because paragraphing is the next topic in the textbook.

4. Practice is likely to be more effective if boys and girls have a standard they wish to attain through practice.

5. The pupils should have the opportunity to participate in the evaluation of the success of their practice.

6. As a rule a pupil should be provided with practice only on those points with which he is likely to have difficulty if such practice were not given.

7. There should be variety in types of practice work. This guideline is important for several reasons, among them these: (a) The work is likely to become monotonous if the same procedure is followed uninterruptedly. (b) Variety in type of exercise is likely to be of value in emphasizing more than one angle of strength desirable in perfecting a skill.

8. Pupils' difficulties in relation to a given skill for which practice is provided should be carefully analyzed and the children, if possible, should help in the analysis. Provisions should then be made as specifically as possible to overcome the shortcomings.

9. As a pupil is perfecting his skill in a given language arts activity, he should be provided with opportunity to apply the ability in a life-like situation.

10. Practice should be spaced in harmony with the findings of educational psychologists, with short intervals between early practice periods and longer intervals between later ones.

11. The practice provided should have considerable likeness to the situations in which the skill will later be exercised.

Games in the Language Arts

Occasional games, when well chosen and well conducted, can provide meaningful practice. Following are given a few shortcomings of many games as language arts exercises, as well as criteria for their selection. For further information on the topic the reader is referred to page 198. In chapter 15 (see page 337) are given a list of publications about games and a list of distributors and publishers of games.

Shortcomings of Many Games. Many games planned as activities to increase language skills can be criticized because of the following reasons.

1. Frequently the child who makes an error is eliminated from the game even though he might be the one who most needs the practice.

2. Often the length of time spent on a game is not commensurate with the amount of helpful practice provided.

3. At times the pupils become so interested in a game that instead of its serving as a motivation for other language arts activities, the other activities seem less rather than more desirable after they have taken part in the game.

4. In many games little if any opportunity is given to help the person who made an error know the cause of the error and to assist him in correcting it.

Criteria for the Selection of Games. Some of the points the teacher should bear in mind when selecting games for the language arts are implied in the list of "Shortcomings of Many Games." Here are additional criteria.

1. As a rule, the pupils should be able to recognize the purpose of the game in terms of language arts learnings.

2. The game should be on the interest level of the players.

3. If there is competition, it should be primarily with self, not with others.

TEACHER-PUPIL PLANNING

Teacher-pupil planning can be done on various levels. Over-all planning for the year is one important kind, as the pupils help in determining some of the goals for the year and give suggestions for attaining these objectives. Planning for a single unit of work can also be done with pupil participation. Furthermore, there is frequently much opportunity for desirable planning by boys and girls when an activity like putting on a dramatization or giving a program of choral readings is contemplated. Even in the day-by-day work, such as writing a letter to thank the principal for his help in providing the room with a portable bulletin board, the pupils can assist in planning what is to be included in the letter, on what type of paper it should be written, who should write it, and how it should be sent. For guidelines to effective pupil participation in planning the reader is referred to pages 6 and 7.

When pupils are participating in planning for an activity or a series of activities in which they will be engaging for a rather long period of time, these are some of the steps that it may be profitable for the teacher and pupils to follow.

1. Decide on the major goal or goals for the activity, regardless of whether it was originally teacher- or pupil-selected.

2. Define the scope of the problem in rather general terms so that redefinement later will not seem out of order.

3. Determine some of the means by which the goals may be reached.

4. List materials that will be helpful in the attainment of the goals and, if necessary, suggest means of making these available.

5. Try to determine what are some of the difficulties that are likely to be encountered in the course of the work on the problem and study means of overcoming these hurdles to success.

6. Make assignments for work to each person in the group in harmony with his needs for optimum development.

7. Plan a time schedule which can be altered, if advisable, as the work progresses.

8. Plan for continuous evaluation while the work is in progress as well as for a final evaluation.

9. Help the pupils set standards for their conduct while working on a problem.

ADAPTING INSTRUCTION TO INDIVIDUAL DIFFERENCES

For effective teaching-learning situations, it is essential in the language arts, as in other areas, that the procedures be adapted to individual differences. In Part One of this book, in the chapters "Child Development and the Language Arts" and "Developmental Patterns," statements are made as to the extent of individual differences among boys and girls in language development and causes of these differences are discussed. Let us now consider additional points related to individual differences of import to the teacher when planning and executing an effective program in the language arts.

Guidelines for Adapting Instruction to Individual Differences

The following points, important in planning instruction adapted to individual differences in all areas, should serve as guidelines to the teacher.

1. One of the assets of the human race lies in the lack of uniformity of all of its members.

2. Careful diagnosis should be made of individual differences and their causes should be studied.

3. Individual differences are likely to increase among individuals as they develop.

4. Good teaching is likely to result in greater increase in individual differences than poor teaching.

5. Each child has a right to be helped, if necessary, to feel that he can make a significant contribution and to be aided in making one.

6. Because of the great variations among boys and girls, it is probably unwise to construct a list of minimum essentials for any heterogeneously grouped grade of pupils. It seems sounder to plan a continuum of steps in development along the various phases of skills, attitudes, and knowledge to be acquired.

7. Pupils seem to learn better when they have a part in setting their goals (seeking), in deciding upon means of accomplishing them (self-selection), and in determining how fast they should proceed in the learning activities (pacing).

Organization for Grouping

Various plans of organization for grouping are followed in order to adapt instruction to individual differences. Here is one classification, with overlapping even among the three types listed.

Homogeneous Grouping Within a School. In some cases the grouping is made by dividing the total grade population into several almost equal groups, the number depending upon how many room teachers will be available to teach the pupils of a given grade. In other instances, the gifted pupils have been put into a room by themselves, often with some who are not in the same grade. Similarly provisions are frequently made for pupils who are slow learners or who are retarded for other reasons.

Homogeneous Grouping Within a Classroom. In many cases this type of grouping is done in only some of the subject areas. An example of homogeneous grouping within a classroom is the division into reading groups. At times the organization into groups is only temporary, as for instance with special interest groups. An interest group might, while work is in progress on a unit on Modern Americans, be primarily responsible for making a "movie" to show the outstanding work of the persons studied. The homogeneity in interest groups consists of similarity of interest. Boys and girls of varying abilities often are included in the same group. In fact, one argument for interest groups is that they give the pupils the opportunity to work in some groups with others of different ability. Often while a child is a member of an interest group he also belongs to another group classified according to achievement, like a reading group.

The Nongraded Plan. Gaining increasing popularity is the nongraded plan, which is frequently restricted to the primary grades. There are many variations of this type of organization. One frequently used plan is that of not designating a child's grade while he is in the first three years of the elementary school. In such a set-up the child progresses as rapidly as he can during the three years ordinarily spent in the primary grades. In some schools pupils may be advanced into the intermediate grades after fewer

Courtesy of The University School, The Ohio State University.

Figure 3.1 Adapting Learning Activities to Individual Differences

than three years in the primary division or they may be detained more than the customary three. Where the nongraded plan is followed throughout the elementary school, frequently there is a division into nongraded primary and nongraded intermediate.

Points to Consider when Grouping

Any teacher who expects grouping to be a panacea for all problems in adapting instruction to individual differences is unduly optimistic. No matter what system of grouping is employed, even where there are only two persons in a group, there are bound to be individual differences which need to be considered for best teaching.

Here are some of the points to note when grouping, in addition to the one stressed in the preceding paragraph.

1. Even if the members of a group show relatively little variation in the criterion used for grouping (and often there is considerable range even in that respect), there are usually many other ways, significant to learning situations, in which there are marked differences. For example, if pupils are classified according to intelligence, the differences in achievement, in age, in social maturity, in interest in work will make the group far from homogeneous.
2. Pupils need opportunity to associate with people who are unlike them in achievement or intelligence in order to be well equipped to take their places in a democracy.
3. Snobbery or feelings of inferiority may result from homogeneous grouping — snobbery for those in the best group and feelings of inferiority for those not in it.
4. The attitude toward the school of parents of children not in the highest groups is at times such that the parent-school relationship is impaired.
5. Parents of children not in the highest groups frequently put undue pressure on them for greater achievement, and parents of children in the highest groups sometimes similarly put too much pressure on their children to maintain their membership in such groups.
6. Flexibility in grouping is desirable. This point should be noted for various reasons, among them these: (a) Sometimes pupils are misplaced at the time the groups are organized, even according to the criterion used for classification. (b) Some pupils who seemed to belong in a given group at the beginning of the school year would later in the year, because of differences in learning rate and other factors, be placed to better advantage in a different group.
7. As a rule it is probably better not to try to hide the basis of grouping from boys and girls. Even first-grade children are likely to discover it before long. It is wiser for the teacher to explain the classification on a rational basis than for pupils to come to an irrational conclusion by themselves.
8. Each child has a right to be in a group in which he feels accepted.
9. Sociometric testing and the construction and use of sociograms may help the teacher discover how pupils in a group react toward one another.

COMMITTEE WORK

When committee work is wisely organized and executed, it can greatly add to the effectiveness of the program of instruction in the language arts.

Values of Committee Work

Some of the ways in which committee work can make contributions to the language arts curriculum are here suggested.

1. Through committee work instruction can be adapted to individual differences even though frequently the adaptation may not be the major reason for organizing a committee.
2. Opportunity for interest grouping can be provided through committees. However, uniformity of interest should not at all times be considered a requirement for membership in a committee. Sometimes membership can well be determined primarily by a divergence of interests and abilities that are needed in order to accomplish best the purpose for which the committee is organized and in order to help most in the all-around development of the participants.
3. Committee work gives boys and girls the opportunity to engage in small-group activities. The give-and-take in well-planned committee work is a significant experience for boys and girls, especially for the older children in an elementary school. Small-group participation gives opportunities for socialization not provided by membership in large groups, such as an entire class.
4. Organization into committees makes possible a more flexible method of grouping than some other types of grouping. If a person is not well suited for work on the committee of his choice or of his assignment, the error in placement is likely not to be as serious as it might be in a group selection or assignment of longer duration.

Guidelines for Committee Work

Following are guidelines for organizing committees and for providing for effective functioning.

1. Committees should be organized to serve significant purposes — purposes accepted by boys and girls as important.

2. Considerable planning of committee work by the teacher is important.

3. With pupils unaccustomed to working in committees the organization of the work should be very simple. As the boys and girls gain more familiarity with committee work, more complicated types of organization should be used. The first times pupils meet in committees the purpose may be as simple as to read orally to each other materials agreed upon beforehand. The chairman of each group may be appointed by the teacher in order to assure adequate leadership. The plan of procedure may be outlined and recorded on the chalkboard beforehand and directions given for (a) position of reader, (b) order of performance, (c) length of selection to be read by each individual, and (d) methods of helping pupils who need assistance.

4. Pupils should plan with the teacher for an orderliness conducive to work.

5. While rotating chairmanships are desirable in many instances, care should be taken that those who serve are competent. To assure good leadership, the teacher can plan with a chairman before a committee meeting some of the points in procedure and if necessary "coach" him in the performance of his responsibilities.

6. Frequently even when pupils are organized for committee work, much of the work can be done best individually. For example, in a committee responsible for making a notebook on writing friendly letters, the assignment for actual writing of a given letter can probably best be given to one individual even though that person may have received help from others in the group while planning the letter and later will receive aid from them in the evaluation of his efforts.

WORKING WITH THE RETARDED PUPIL

The problem of the retarded learner in the area of the language arts cannot be neglected in any effective curriculum.

Points to Keep in Mind when Searching for Reasons for Retardation

The teacher should be cognizant of the following points.

1. Attention should be paid not merely to the immediate but also to the long-time factors that contribute to retardation.

2. Symptoms must not be confused with causes. While the former are often of great value in diagnosis, unless the underlying causes are discovered, any resulting remedial work is likely to lack in effectiveness.

3. Usually no one single factor constitutes the total reason for a deficiency. As a rule a constellation of factors, sometimes closely interwoven, is at the root of the trouble.

4. Frequently a primary cause of retardation in a language art, especialy if the difficulty is of long duration, results in one or more secondary causes which may in turn greatly influence the productivity of the individual. For example illness, with resulting irregularity of school attendance, may be the original cause. It may result in lack of interest in learning, which even by itself is significant enough to bring about grave learning problems.

Common Causes of Retardation

Common among the causes of retardation are:

1. Low intelligence
2. An undesirable environment at school and/or at home
3. Poor physical or mental health
4. An inadequate experience background
5. Lack of interest in developing skill in the language arts
6. Poor methods of teaching.

The possibility of a brain lesion should not be excluded before examination when there is a serious difficulty unexplainable by other possible causes.

Guidelines for Working with the Retarded

Methods used with the retarded learner should be in harmony with the following recommendations to the teacher.

1. Be encouraging, but not beyond the point of truthfulness.

2. Stimulate the pupil so that he will want to improve.

3. Find an appropriate time of the day for remedial work. Do not use periods when the pupil is robbed of participation in activities he particularly enjoys, like physical education, art, or music. Furthermore, do not schedule remedial work for a time of day when he is likely to be tired.

4. Use suitable materials of instruction. They should if possible, be on both the interest and ability level of the learner.

GUIDING THE GIFTED

On any grade level the child above average in intelligence or singularly endowed in some other respects should be helped to improve beyond the norm for his class. He can be provided with reading material of difficulty commensurate with his ability to read. He can be guided in developing the reading skills required for his expanding field of interest. In handwriting provisions can be made for improving the quality and increasing the rate beyond that of the average. Greater efficiency and increased artistry in both so-called functional and creative writing can be encouraged. The pupil can be assisted in developing beyond the class norms in various forms of oral communication. Furthermore, most of these provisions can be made without interfering with the work that the child is likely to do in suceeding grades in a well-planned and intelligently executed program of the language arts.

The following are additional points that should be observed when guiding the gifted child.

1. Care should be taken that the gifted child does not consider himself more important than his peers who are not blessed with as much ability as he possesses.
2. Care should be taken that the classmates of the gifted child do not become alienated from him.
3. In making provisions for work for the gifted, the assignment of additional work along the same level of difficulty on which his peers are working often is not best procedure.
4. In planning the work for the gifted, the curriculum to which he will be exposed in later years should be taken into consideration. If a gifted pupil is in a school where a lockstep system of curriculum organization exists in which in subsequent years he will be required to do, let us say, the regular fourth-grade work regardless of whether or not he has already mastered it, the third-grade teacher, in order to avoid boredom in the following school year, is advised not to have the pupil do work that he is likely to have to repeat the following year.
5. Double promotions should not be given to the gifted child unless careful attention has been paid not only to his intellectual level but also to his social, emotional, and physical maturity. Enrichment, rather than acceleration, should be the rule.
6. The gifted child should be aided in accepting the responsibility incumbent upon the person possessing "many talents." The challenge of the responsibility, however, not its burden, should be emphasized with many children of superior ability.
7. The gifted child should not be exploited. Sometimes the pupil who is particularly capable in a certain activity, like dramatics, art, or music, is given a part in a disproportionate number of dramatic productions or is chosen to make most of the posters in the room or is asked to sing solo parts again and again. Participation in such activities should be distributed in the best interests of both the gifted pupil and the other boys and girls, who should not be deprived of their share in such activities.

FOR STUDY AND DISCUSSION

1. On page 25 this statement is made: "The content of the language arts curriculum should be determined in part by the ongoing activities of the classroom in other areas and, at the same time, the ongoing classroom activities in other areas should be chosen in part in terms of the needs and interests of the child in his language development." Give illustrations as to how the ongoing classroom activities in areas other than the language arts can be chosen in terms of the needs and interests of the child in his language development.
2. What advantages and what disadvantages do you see in the nongraded primary plan of organization? in the nongraded intermediate plan?
3. It is agreed that meaningless drill is poor. Describe a possible "drill situation" in connection with the development of one or more language arts skills that would be meaningful and in other ways desirable.
4. In what respects does work in the language arts lend itself particularly well to adapting instruction to individual differences? What special difficulties do you see in making such adaptation?
5. Read in one or more professional magazines or books articles or sections that deal with the topic of sociometric measurement. What procedures might you follow in making a sociogram? What cautions would you observe in applying to grouping data about pupils whose ratings are indicated on a sociogram? What benefits would you expect to derive from construction of a sociogram?
6. Write a description of a gifted child (hypothetical) in a third grade whom you might consider for possible double promotion. Indicate which points in the description give reason for double promotion and which constitute arguments against it. State what your verdict about double promotion would be in the case you described.

REFERENCES

Blair, Glenn Myers; R. Stewart Jones; and Ray H. Simpson, *Educational Psychology*. Second edition. The Macmillan Company, 1962. 678 pp.

Eson, Morris E., *Psychological Foundations of Education*. Holt, Rinehart and Winston, 1962. 563 pp.

Klausmeier, Herbert J., and Katharine Dresden, *Teaching in the Elementary School*. Second edition. Harper and Row, 1962. 622 pp.

National Council of Teachers of English, *Language Arts for Today's Children*. Appleton-Century-Crofts, 1954. 431 pp.

Smith, Louis M.; and Bryce B. Hudgins, *Educational Psychology: An Application of Social and Behavioral Theory*. Alfred A. Knopf, 1964. 533 pp.

OUTLINE FOR CHAPTER 4

Guiding Growth in Oral Communication

CHAPTER 4

Guiding Growth in Oral Communication

Although the child upon entering the elementary school has already acquired, in the course of normal growth, considerable skill in oral communication, much additional development is needed to meet the demands that the school and society in general make of him and those that society makes of the adult.

THE SCOPE OF THE PROGRAM

What then is the scope of the program in oral communication? In answering this question, let us consider the following topics: (1) general objectives, (2) types of skills and activities needed, and (3) grade placement.

General Objectives

The elementary-school teacher will want to help the boys and girls to:

1. Develop skills and abilities essential to effective speaking and listening
2. Become more closely-knit members of social groups, such as the classroom group and the family, of which they are a part
3. Express their thoughts and emotions better and thereby achieve the self-expression important to mental health and maximum contribution to others
4. Become increasingly thoughtful of the persons with whom or to whom they are talking or to whom they are listening, and give evidence of the improved attitude.

Needed Skills and Abilities

Listed below are skills and abilities important in various types of speaking situations.

TYPES OF SKILLS. A listing of skills needed should include:

1. Speaking in a clear, pleasant voice
2. Pronouncing words correctly
3. Enunciating distinctly
4. Having good posture
5. Having a pleasant manner
6. Using words that express the intended meaning accurately
7. Using sentences effectively (when it is desirable to express thoughts in sentences)
8. Organizing thoughts well
9. Knowing when to speak and when to listen and acting accordingly
10. Speaking tactfully and listening politely.

TYPES OF ACTIVITIES. On various levels of the elementary school, boys and girls should be given help in the following types of activities involving oral expression:

1. Taking part in conversation
2. Discussing
3. Giving reports
4. Telling stories
5. Making explanations and giving directions
6. Making announcements
7. Giving riddles
8. Telling jokes
9. Showing courtesies demanded in social situations of various types.

TYPES OF SITUATIONS. Somewhere in the elementary school the pupils should receive help in observing the accepted civilities in social situations such as the following:

1. Telephoning
2. Making and acknowledging introductions
3. Greeting callers and guests.

Because of the contributions that effectiveness in the following types of situations can make to the learner while in the elementary school and later on, help in oral communication should be given in connection with situations (1) in which the child participates in a program and (2) in which he is a member or leader of a club or a committee.

Grade Placement

In matters pertaining to grade placement of skills and abilities to be acquired and attitudes to be developed in oral communication, the teacher should follow the general principles considered under "Sequence and Grade Placement" on page 25. Furthermore, he should be cognizant of the objectives for oral communication to be achieved and the skills and abilities and attitudes to be developed to which reference is made earlier in this chapter. Growth in the achievement of these goals should be taking place without interruption throughout the years the pupil spends in the elementary school.

GUIDELINES

In Chapter 3 reference is made to some points that the teacher should bear in mind when teaching any of the language arts. Let us now consider some of those that have special bearing on teaching various phases of oral communication.

Even when the emphasis is on oral communication, the teacher should be aware of the close interrelatedness of the language arts. For example, when he helps the boys and girls give better talks, he should recognize the fact that skill in reporting on events in the order of their occurrence often is needed in both oral and written communication. Furthermore, knowledge of this fact should be reflected in the teaching.

For many boys and girls the teacher should provide direct help in improvement of skills in oral communication. For instance, after the teacher has developed with the pupils the importance of having an interesting beginning for a talk, he may find it desirable to have definite periods of practice on giving talks with interesting beginnings when the pupils might perform activities such as these:

1. Examine records of oral reports to determine which have good beginning sentences
2. Decide which of a list of sentences would make good beginning sentences
3. Give sentences of their own that would serve as beginning sentences.

The teacher should encourage the pupils to develop an ever-wider background of experience, through either firsthand or vicarious participation. Paucity of experience is one reason for lack of effectiveness of expression. The child with a wide background of experience has something to talk about. He is also more likely to be interested in what others are saying than is the pupil with a more restricted background.

The teacher should help the boys and girls understand the importance of telling interesting and significant points in acceptable form. There should not be a question as to whether content *or* form is important. Emphasis should be on both for the two are not mutually exclusive but can add value to each other. Content in poor form is undersirable; form without content is intolerable.

The teacher can help the boys and girls recognize the importance of good form in oral expression by:

1. Discussing with the pupils the importance of good form
2. Having the children listen to two talks identical in content but with extremes of form – desirable and undersirable – and then having them tell which is more interesting to hear
3. Having an employer tell the class the importance of good form in speech when applying for work and having other adults tell the class of the significance they attach to good form in expression.

The teacher should help the boys and girls to be considerate of others in oral communication. Courtesy should be an aim both in speaking and in listening. These are points that should be considered and emphasized:

1. When to speak and when to be silent
2. What types of topics are acceptable in oral expression under various circumstances
3. How, through demeanor, to show courtesy to listeners
4. What voice qualities to develop.

The teacher should provide for many opportunities for oral expression. Improvement in oral communication is brought about primarily through participation in speaking and listening. There should be an abundance of situations in which language can be used functionally. Definite provisions should be made in the ongoing program of the room for many activities that involve speaking and listening. Provisions should also be made, however, for somewhat structured situations involving oral communication when pupils give reports, tell stories, participate in dramatization, and take part in choral speaking.

The teacher should strive to help create a classroom atmosphere that is conducive to self-expression through oral communication. In a regimented classroom optimum development of this type is not encouraged. A free and informal spirit should prevail in the room. On the other hand the maximum benefit from participation in activities involving oral communication is not likely to be obtained in a room where license is confused with liberty and where confusion reigns rather than the considerate give-and-take of an orderly classroom.

The teacher should serve as a model in oral communication. The importance of this point cannot easily be overemphasized. Whether he is taking part in conversation or discussion, giving a report, making an explanation, or participating in oral communication in any other way, he should observe the specifications for excellence that he expects the pupils to observe (and many more!).

TAKING PART IN CONVERSATION AND DISCUSSION

Of the situations calling for oral communication, none, other than listening, occurs more frequently than that involving participation in conversation and informal discussion. It is probably also the type of speaking situation that is most neglected in terms of the amount of specific help given to boys and girls for taking part in it.

Let us now define terms. *Conversation,* as used here, refers to the free, easy-flowing exchange of ideas in an informal setting where, usually without previous planning, individuals express their ideas or make other comments or ask questions without holding themselves long to any one topic. In *discussion,* on the other hand, attention is typically concentrated on one or a series of topics. To be sure conversation often involves discussion. Discussion is part of conversation whenever in the exchange of ideas one topic is considered for a longer time than is characteristic of conversation without discussion. Discussion, like conversation, is usually informal. It can be structured, however, as it is, for example, in the panel discussion or in the even more complex situation involving debate.

Because there are many similarities between conversation and informal discussion, suggestions as to how to develop abilities in each of these are combined in this part of the chapter. Separate consideration is given in succeeding pages of the chapter to a more formal type of discussion, the panel discussion.

Appropriate Topics for Conversation

As boys and girls progress through the elementary school and later, they should be learning increasingly to make finer lines of distinction between topics that are and those that are not desirable for conversation.

CRITERIA FOR JUDGING SUITABILITY. The pupils should learn to check the appropriateness of conversation by noting whether the topic is:

1. Of interest to the group
2. Not embarrassing to anyone in the group
3. Not gossip
4. Entertaining or informative or inspirational.

LIST OF APPROPRIATE TOPICS. From time to time through discussion or explanation or suggestion, boys and girls can be helped in considering topics suitable for conversation in harmony with the criteria listed.

Some such topics are:

Hobbies
Summer trips
School events
Sunday school
Clubs
Content of any school subject
Current events
Books
Motion pictures
TV programs
Exhibits
Something unusual that happened
Pets.

Inappropriate Times and Places for Conversation

In many instances, it is important to help boys and girls become aware of when it is improper or impolite to carry on conversation.

LIST OF INAPPROPRIATE SITUATIONS. The pupils should learn to recognize the fact that, as a rule, conversation in situations such as the following is either entirely inappropriate or improper, or is inappropriate or improper when carried on for any length of time or other than in a very subdued voice:

1. While in church
2. While at a funeral
3. While at a program
4. While seeing a motion picture
5. When someone is talking
6. When someone is studying
7. When someone is sleeping who would be disturbed by conversation
8. When someone listening to a program would be disturbed by conversation
9. When someone is saying his prayers.

Methods of Helping Pupils Decide Upon Appriate Times for Conversation. The following means can be used to help boys and girls decide when it is inappropriate to talk or when only a few remarks should be made in a subdued voice:

1. Making a list of places or situations in which, as a rule, it is inappropriate to talk
2. Discussing situations in which members of the class have noticed someone talking when quiet should have been observed (without mentioning names)
3. Checking a series of written descriptions of situations to indicate in which of them it would be improper to carry on conversation
4. Making a bulletin board that draws attention to the appropriateness or inappropriateness of conversing under indicated circumstances
5. Recording and illustrating, in a section of a class or individual language-arts notebook, learnings in regard to situations in which it is inappropriate to talk.

Introducing or Changing a Topic of Conversation

Some pupils may need help in developing skill in introducing a topic and in changing a topic of conversation. Procedures such as the following may be used:

1. Listing types of situations in which it is important for someone to change a topic of conversation
2. Making a list of polite expressions that may be used when changing a topic of conversation
3. Checking a series of written descriptions of desirable and undesirable means of changing a topic of conversation
4. Giving a dramatization to illustrate polite and impolite methods of changing a topic of conversation
5. Making a bulletin board that draws attention to something learned about introducing or changing a topic of conversation
6. Recording and illustrating, in a section of a class or individual language-arts notebook, learnings in regard to introducing or changing a topic of conversation.

Expressing an Opinion

Some important points that elementary-school children should keep in mind about expressing an opinion have been discussed on preceding pages. They should also remember that: (1) All opinions that people express as their own should honestly be theirs. (2) At times it is kinder not to express than to express an opinion. (3) As people express their own opinions they should also be willing to listen to those of others on the same subject. (4) At times it is important to substantiate opinion with facts. (5) When older people have expressed their opinions, boys and girls should take special care before they express a contradictory opinion. (6) If people have been wrong in an opinion they have expressed, they should admit their error. (7) People should recognize times when it is essential to express an opinion.

Listed here are some procedures by means of which pupils can improve in skill in expressing their ideas in conversation or informal discussion:

1. Discussing the importance of expressing an opinion politely and otherwise properly
2. Listening to explanation by the teacher as to important points concerning how and when to express an opinion
3. Reading information in a textbook or on duplicated sheets as to how to express an opinion
4. Listing criteria to observe when expressing an opinion
5. Discussing times when it is essential for a person to express his opinion even though he would prefer to be silent
6. Discussing the importance of expressing opinions that are "honestly theirs"
7. Making a list of polite expressions to use when about to state a contradictory opinion
8. Checking a series of written reports of desirable and undesirable means of expressing an opinion
9. Demonstrating ways in which an opinion can be substantiated
10. Dramatizing situations in which opinions are expressed politely and otherwise properly and situations in which they are expressed impolitely and otherwise improperly
11. Making a bulletin board that draws attention to something learned about how to express an opinion
12. Recording and illustrating, in a section of a class or individual language-arts notebook, what has been learned about expressing an opinion.

Developing and Maintaining a Voice Suitable for Conversation

The pupils should be helped to act in accordance with points such as these when engaging in conversation or informal discussion: (1) The participant in a conversation should speak so that everyone in the group can hear him without strain. (2) The participant in conversation should guard against talking unnecessarily loud. (3) A pleasant voice should be maintained at all times. (4) No person in a small group should whisper to another.

Some of the ways in which boys and girls may be helped in developing or maintaining a voice effective in conversation are:

1. By discussing and listing the characteristics of a voice desirable for conversation
2. By taking part or observing a dramatization of a conversation situation in which undesirable and one in which desirable characteristics of a voice are illustrated
3. By making recordings of conversations and then evaluating the voices in terms of criteria that have been accepted
4. By making a bulletin board that draws attention to something learned concerning a desirable voice in conversation
5. By making a "movie" pointing out in word and picture some important learnings about the use of the voice in conversation or discussion
6. By recording and illustrating, in a section of a class or individual language-arts notebook, learnings about a desirable voice in conversation and discussion.

General Procedures

Guidance in achieving greater ability in participating in conversation and informal discussion can be given through use of informal conversation situations and through planned lessons.

USE OF INFORMAL SITUATIONS. Development in conversation skills can be encouraged through many informal situations in which conversation and discussion occur. The period on the playground or in the gymnasium, the free periods before school in the classroom, and the time devoted to the various planned school activities afford excellent opportunity.

It is not enough that pupils have adequate opportunity to engage in conversation. While practice is essential, it does not provide a guarantee that it will not be practice in error. Consequently the teacher should help the pupils develop ever higher standards even on those occasions where learning to converse better with others is not the reason for the activity, or at least not as far as the boys and girls know.

1. Informal conversation during "free periods." These are some ways in which guidance can be provided during "free periods":

> The teacher can draw into the conversation or discussion those pupils who have not been participating by asking them questions and by suggesting that everyone be given an opportunity to express himself.
>
> The teacher can comment from time to time on the observance of any of the points about conversation that have been emphasized in developmental lessons for improving conversation and discussion and he can give the pupils opportunty to do likewise.
>
> The teacher can provide many "conversation pieces," and encourage the pupils to do likewise, for display on bulletin boards, on shelves, and on tables.

2. Informal conversation during ongoing activities. The suggestions for guidance given in the preceding paragraph hold, for the most part, not only for "free periods" but also for times of planned work in the ongoing activities of the classroom. Such guidance can also be given in situations such as the following in which:

> The boys and girls plan the work for activities, of short or long duration, discussing questions like "How can we do our finger painting so that everyone has a chance?" or "In what different types of activities might we engage in order to find an answer to our problem?"
>
> The pupils discuss questions that have been raised dealing with the subject matter they are studying, like "Why had Mexico been called a beggar sitting on a bag of gold?" or "How should we show our visitors what safety rules we try to observe?"
>
> The pupils evaluate their work in response to questions such as "Which of these points do you think we observed particularly well?" or "On which of these points do we need much improvement?"

USE OF PLANNED LESSONS. For some boys and girls the incidental work on development of skills in conversation and discussion afforded by situations that can be utilized during "free periods" or during the course of ongoing activities is not enough to insure efficiency in these ways of oral expression. Consequently planned lessons, designed particularly to help the pupils in the development and maintenance of skills, are advisable. These lessons are of two types, developmental and maintenance. (The reader is referred to page 303 for a discussion of how a developmental lesson can be structured and to pages 305 and 307 for illustrations of such lessons.)

Developmental lessons often need to be supplemented by maintenance lessons. Presentation of a point at one sitting and making application of it at that time usually does not suffice in learning a generalization of considerable complexity or in establishing a habit. For many boys and girls it often is important to provide at intervals considerable opportunity for further application of what has been developed. At times it is sufficient to provide such practice incidentally; however, in many cases, such practice is not enough. Incidental practice then needs to be supplemented by planned lessons in which the pupils have the opportunity to make secure their earlier learnings.

In both developmental and maintenance lesson procedures such as these can be utilized: teacher explanation, pupil explanation, silent reading, oral reading, discussion, summarization, written work, question-and-answer procedure, demonstration, dramatization, and evaluation.

Suggestions for utilization of the methods listed are given at various places in this and other chapters. Description of procedure, therefore, of only one – namely dramatization – is given here.

Dramatization is of special value in the work on oral expression because dramatization itself is a means of oral communication. To help boys and girls see the need of learning when and when not to interrupt, as well as how to interrupt when necessary, for example, the teacher could ask several pupils to plan with him beforehand a skit in which they include several rude and untimely interruptions and one in which interruptions are made politely. The teacher can then during class time announce that two or more pupils have prepared two skits, one in which they are going to demonstrate how interruptions should not be made and another in which they illustrate how they can be made politely. The pupils in the audience can then be asked to watch the demonstration in order to find out what rules they can make to guide them on that point. After the skits have been presented, the discussion can follow on what was done properly and what improperly and through listing on the chalkboard rules to observe concerning interruptions during conversation.

Similarly dramatizations of rules can be given during phases of lessons in which the pupils are provided with opportunity to apply what they have been taught in the presentation part of a lesson. For example, the class could be divided into several groups, with each group given a slip of paper indicating what the members of the group are to dramatize later while the rest of the class are spectators. Each group should probably have a different set of directions. Examples of statements follow that can be listed on slips of paper describing situations to be dramatized by various groups.

1. While the boys and girls are having an interesting conversation, one pupil interrupts to remind the group that it is time to do a task that their teacher had asked them to begin at that time. The interruption is made politely.
2. Someone in a group brings into the conversation a pupil who has not been taking part.

A few general suggestions to bear in mind in planning dramatizations of the types described are:

1. The directions for a skit should be simple enough that the pupils can follow them with success.
2. The directions should allow for some ingenuity.
3. The skit should be brief.
4. While some of the skits might advisedly demonstrate what not to do, the emphasis, in general, should be on portrayal of correct procedures.
5. Provisions should be made for opportunity for all pupils to take part in skits, even though the participation may be spread over a period considerably longer than one day.
6. Care should be taken that the skits are on a refined plane of expression, without vulgarity, even those in which incorrect procedures are demonstrated.

Development of Skills in Special Types of Situations

Many of the suggestions in the preceding pages have been limited to those that apply to almost all types of situations involving conversation or discussion. In the next pages are given suggestions for somewhat specialized types of conversation or discussion, namely "sharing time," panel discussions, and conversation at mealtime.

SHARING TIME. *Sharing Time,* as the term is here used, refers to the time of the school day set aside for boys and girls to report to their peers events or other points of interest to them. Because frequently the participants illustrate what they tell by showing objects, at times this period is called the "show-and-tell" time. Although it is used more frequently in the primary than in later grades, it is by no means confined to the former. However, when it is used effectively in the intermediate grades, the structure is more complex than it should be in lower grades.

Sharing Time is considered by some educators one of the most useful periods of the school day, one in which pupils have the opportunity to express themthemselves informally. For others, however, this period is the butt of many uncomplimentary remarks. Evaluation of the Sharing Time results in the conclusion that both praise and criticism of it are well deserved. Which should be given depends upon how the period is conducted.

1. Guidelines. To achieve the values that can be attained through Sharing Time, the teacher needs to observe the following guidelines.

> *Sharing Time should be a happy time.* It should be a period toward which the pupils look with anticipation. The "contribution" should be given in a relaxed atmosphere in which the participant is assured of a sympathetic audience.
>
> *Sharing Time should afford the pupils the chance to learn to speak well in an audience-type situation.* If this objective is to be accomplished, pupils must be encouraged to speak in good English; otherwise the period may have a negative effect on the pupils' oral expression. Standards for use of good English, varying in complexity from grade level to grade level, could be set.
>
> *Standards should be drawn up as to types of "contributions" that are acceptable.* Even in the first grade criteria may be established. For example, pupils may be discouraged from reporting on anything that may hurt the feelings of someone in the room. Another standard that the pupils should be helped to apply is that there is no place for the cheap and the tawdry.
>
> *Help should be given beforehand to those boys and girls who have difficulty in deciding upon what to present to the group.* For example, to a child in the first grade who does not voluntarily participate, the teacher may lend an interesting object, like a novel kite, to show to the class. Or better yet, he may be able to encourage the pupil to show or tell something that the child has spontaneously shown or told the teacher.
>
> *Provisions should be made for pupils to exhibit articles, pictures, or clippings that they have brought.* Unless such materials are made available for later examination by the audience, frequently all the learnings that could be achieved are not possible. Bulletin board space or an exhibit table can be provided. Standards for making attractive displays should be formulated.

2. Procedures. Some of the means by which a presentation can be made are: telling, demonstration, puppetry, skits, other methods of dramatization, book reports, reports on current events, reading poetry or prose, make-believe radio or television programs, showing objects, pictures, diagrams, or maps.

Additional suggestions for procedure are as follows.

> The Sharing Time might consist of two parts. During one part of the period anyone could contribute who has something of special importance to tell which he just must tell that day (like the arrival of baby kittens!). During the other part of the period a planned program for the day could be presented, possibly one in which various children selected beforehand make their contributions individually on whatever topic they have chosen. For the non-planned part of the period those pupils could be called upon who before class had told the teacher or a pupil chairman of something they want very much to tell the class that day. During the more structured phase of Sharing Time the pupils who are on the program for the day could plan ahead of time how they could make an effective presentation. Care should be taken that no child is on the program for this part of the period a second time before each one has been on it once. A chart can be posted on which each pupil signs up for the day he will appear on the program.
>
> Sometimes during Sharing Time there can be informal discussion of some important topic of the day such as an eclipse or an adventure in orbiting or Lincoln's birthday.
>
> In the intermediate grades planned variety could characterize the contributions over a period of time. There may be a schedule of the type of contribution to be made on a given day of the week. For instance, Monday may be designated as a day for reports on science, Tuesday as a day devoted to books, Wednesday as a day for reports in the area of the social studies.
>
> Evaluation of contributions should be made. Questions like these may be asked: "What was particularly fine about our contributions today?" or "How could our audience make it easier for a person to talk to the group?"

PANEL DISCUSSIONS. Although the term *panel discussion* suggests to many teachers a type of procedure so complex that it is reserved for pupils beyond the elementary school, some types of discussion that can be designated as such are so simple in structure that they can be used even in lower grades. The expression *panel discussion* as used in this book applies to any discussion by a group of persons with an audience who listens. Descriptions of how such panel discussions may be conducted are given under the topic "Panel Discussions" on page 298.

Following are listed some topics, in the areas indicated, that are suitable for panel discussions; others are indicated in Chapter 14.

1. Social studies: (a) How is the life of children in Switzerland like and unlike that of boys and girls in our country? (b) How can we help our community helpers?

2. Science: (a) wild flowers in our neighborhood, (b) the migration of birds, (c) orbiting

3. Physical education or health: (a) how to take care of our teeth, (b) games around the world, (c) how to keep our bodies clean

4. Language arts: (a) what to do during Sharing Time, (b) what to remember about conversation at the dinner table, (c) books you may wish to read.

Conversation at Mealtime. If we judge by the reports of remarks made at mealtime at school and at home, it seems important that boys and girls in the elementary school should get help in learning significant points about conversation at the table and that they should be stimulated so they will want to observe them.

1. Points to be stressed. Although many of the points that pertain to all types of conversation may need to be stressed in connection with conversation at mealtime, the following probably need special emphasis: (a) Conversation at mealtime should be pleasant. (b) Matters of sickness or accident should not be discussed. (c) Nothing should be said that will be embarrassing or upsetting to anyone at the table. (d) There should be no criticism of food. (e) A person should feel responsible for entering into conversation at the table.

2. List of procedures. Many of the learnings that are needed concerning conversation at mealtime can be acquired through incidental means such as participation in school parties and eating lunch at school. However, for some pupils special emphasis is needed in situations specifically planned to help them with table conversation. Some possible procedures are here indicated:

Discussing the importance of appropriate conversation at mealtime

Participating in skits that demonstrate desirable and undesirable conversation at mealtime

Reading descriptions of reports of desirable and undesirable table conversation and noting each type

Drawing up rules for conversation at the table

Discussing the importance of being polite to any individual who disobeys the rules about conversation at mealtime

Making a booklet on what has been learned about conversation at mealtime

Drawing cartoons illustrating desirable and undesirable comments at mealtime.

For more specific suggestions for procedure the reader is referred to a teaching plan given on page 298.

DEVELOPMENT IN ABILITY TO GIVE TALKS AND REPORTS

This outline is followed in this section as consideration is given to talks by children about their own experiences and to reports: (1) guidelines for teaching, (2) topics and titles, (3) methods, (4) book reports.

Guidelines

The following are helpful guidelines for a program for the improvement of ability to give talks.

1. There should be a reason for giving a talk, one recognized as worthwhile by the pupils.

2. The total program should be well planned.

3. The program should include talks the pupils give in connection with work in the content areas as well as on personal experiences.

4. Included in the program should be developmental lessons in which there is presentation of skills to be attained or knowledge to be acquired in relation to giving talks.

5. For some pupils the program should include practice-type lessons in which major emphasis is placed on the practice of a skill rather than on the subject matter of the talk.

6. The pupils and the teacher should frequently make evaluations of talks given and of the total program for the development in ability to give talks.

7. Means of expression like demonstrating, illustrating, or dramatizing should at times be used to supplement the statements by the speaker.

Topics and Titles

Many of the topics and titles on which pupils will talk can be determined by the activities significant in the ongoing school program involving the social studies, science, health, literature, and even modern mathematics. However, since the more or less incidental selection of topics does not supply all the guidance that some pupils need in learning to select topics or titles for talks, it may be of value to name a few suitable ones.

List of Topics and Titles. What then are some of the topics and titles which boys and girls can use for talks? The following topics, with suggested titles, are merely illustrative of many others:

1. Pets: (a) Tricks I have taught my dog, (b) My pet crow hides things.
2. Hobbies: (a) My vegetable garden, (b) Trees are my hobby.
3. Trips: (a) An exciting moment on our trip, (b) We rediscovered the source of the Mississippi.
4. People: (a) A real friend, (b) My unforgettable character.
5. Personal experiences: (a) Something funny, (b) It happened to me.

Selections of Topics and Titles. The boys and girls may be helped in choosing appropriate topics and titles for talks as they:

1. Discuss topics from other curricular areas on which they can give talks that would help others get worthwhile information.
2. Look at pictures on a topic, such as pets or funny experiences or vacation experiences, to see if they would like to report on an event suggested by one of the pictures.
3. Bring things for a "show-and-tell" table and then decide whether an explanation of an object they brought would constitute a good topic for a talk.
4. Suggest topics on personal experiences on which they would like to hear reports.
5. Place in a box, possibly called "Our Idea Box," suggestions for topics or titles.
6. Suggest attention-getting titles that may be used for a talk on a given topic.

Methods

Listed here are activities in which the pupils can engage to improve in ability to give talks:

1. Deciding on questions they would like answered if someone else talked on the subject and then answering these questions in their talks
2. Studying the beginning sentences of recorded reports and deciding which are interest-arousing
3. Choosing from a list of beginning sentences for reports those that would make them want to hear reports beginning with those sentences
4. Giving reports with good beginning sentences
5. Listening to evaluation by their peers or by the teacher of the beginning sentences of their reports
6. Studying the ending sentences of recorded reports and deciding which are good endings
7. Giving reports with good ending sentences
8. Listening to evaluation by their peers or by the teacher of the ending sentences of their reports
9. Indicating which sentences in a series of recorded talks do not keep to the topic
10. Listening to evaluation as to whether any of their sentences did not keep to the topic by their peers or by the teacher
11. Indicating which of a series of pictures on a topic are not arranged in the order in which the events they represent are given in a written paragraph illustrated by the pictures, and then arranging the pictures in the right sequence
12. Indicating which sentences in a series of recorded talks are not given in the right order and then rearranging them
13. Listening to evaluation by their peers or by the teacher as to whether any of their sentences were out of order

Figure 4.1 Pictorial Illustration as a Means of Appraisal

14. Making a list of requirements for a good talk such as an interesting topic, a good beginning, keeping to the topic, arranging points in the correct order, good posture, good audience contact, freedom from mannerisms, good sentences, correct pronunciation, clear enunciation, a good ending (The reader is referred to the list of standards on page 285 and 286.)
15. Rehearsing their talks to someone at home or to one or more of their classmates or to the teacher
16. Evaluating their own reports in terms of chief difficulties, deciding on means of overcoming major

problems, and then giving talks in which each pupil tries hard to eliminate a problem with which he requests the help of his classmates and the teacher

17. Evaluating their own talks by means of tape recordings

Figure 4.2 A Checklist of Self-Evaluation

18. Keeping a card on which, with the help of the teacher, each pupil checks his strengths and weaknesses on each talk as he uses the criteria that have been worked out by the class

19. Participating in programs in which talks are given, some perhaps as mock radio or television programs

20. Participating in radio programs

21. Showing ways in which talks can be vitalized through illustrations, demonstrations, and the like.

Book Reports

A special type of report that pupils in the elementary school, even in the primary grades, can give is the book report. In general the suggestions that are given in the preceding pages for reports of various types apply to book reports also. Following are given additional points, which are supplemented by others in Chapter 5 and Chapter 12.

Guidelines. The following are some guidelines which the teacher may find helpful.

1. Reports should be given on only worthwhile books. While the banal should be avoided, the teacher must remember that the books should be on the pupils' level of appreciation.

2. Through oral book reports the pupils should be stimulated to want to read worthwhile books.

3. In oral book reports the pupils should apply what they have learned about giving reports of other types.

4. The pupils should learn to give book reports in their own words.

5. The pupils should be encouraged to give book reports without notes. (They may, however, wish to include in the reports the reading of a selection from the books.)

6. The boys and girls should be encouraged to report only on books that they enjoy.

7. All pupils should give one or more book reports during the year.

8. Giving book reports should be adapted to individual differences. Some ways in which this guideline can be observed are: (a) The teacher helps pupils who are likely to have difficulty in giving book reports to select books that will be relatively simple for them to review. (b) The teacher gives extra assistance to the pupils who without it could not give a successful report – successful from the point of view of the reported and of the audience. (c) Extra book reports are given by brighter children as one means of providing worthwhile additional activities.

9. The boys and girls should be given guidance in learning how to prepare a book report. Help can be given in these ways: (a) The teacher or a librarian gives reports of the complexity that the pupils can be expected to give. (b) The pupils, with the help of the teacher, draw up standards for reports after having heard several good reports or after having read some that are poor and some that are good. (c) The class discuss what should be included in a report. (d) The class work out a list of ways in which illustrative materials can be used with book reports. (e) The teacher and pupils evaluate reports given by the pupils.

10. Provisions should be made for an effective setting in which book reports will be given. The class may like to form a book club, an important feature of which can be giving book reports. Or the pupils in a grade may give weekly or bimonthly or monthly so-called "broadcasts" of book reviews for which one

or more classes serve as audience. Another procedure that may be followed is to have book reports given as a "book-of-the-week" activity. Each pupil could then be held responsible for an excellent book report for one week or two of the school year. Another possibility is to have pupils go to different classrooms, one or two at a time, especially to pupils in classes less advanced than they, to tell the children about interesting books that they might enjoy.

CONTENT OF A BOOK REPORT. In the lower primary grades the reviewer may merely show his book as he gives the title, tells what the book is about, and shows and explains a few interesting pictures. In later grades the class might draw up a list of points to include in a book report such as:

The name of the author
What the book is about
The main characters
A few interesting incidents
The reviewer's opinion of the book
Where the book can be obtained.

MEANS OF ILLUSTRATING A BOOK REPORT. The class may make a list of ways in which a book report can be made interesting and clear. Such a list may suggest:

1. Showing the book and/or pictures in the book
2. Drawing a picture of a scene or character in the book
3. Putting on a short skit, with the help of one or more classmates, illustrating a scene from the book
4. Making a poster about the book
5. Making a "movie" illustrating the book
6. Making an accordion-like folder of pictures illustrating the book
7. Pantomiming part of the book
8. Putting on a puppet show dealing with a part of the book
9. Constructing a pictured time-line showing the events in a book
10. Dressing in simple costume while giving a report in first person. (For example, a paper hat resembling that worn by Doctor Dolittle is enough if the book to be reviewed is *The Story of Doctor Dolittle.*)

DEVELOPMENT IN ABILITY TO TELL STORIES

Since telling of personal experiences is discussed on preceding pages of this chapter, in this part such accounts are not included. Here are given suggestions for reproducing stories that have been heard or read and for telling original stories. The differentiation observed between the stories and accounts of experiences is that the latter are factual without necessarily involving a plot. In the story, plot is essential. To be sure, the line of demarcation between the two types is not a clear one, and for practical classroom purposes does not need to be.

Values of Storytelling

Storytelling, which no longer is done as much in the home as it was before the time of mass communi-

Poster was prepared by Marilyn Kershaw Williams.

Figure 4.3 An Illustrated Outline of a Book Report

cation and mechanization, is an art that our civilization can ill afford to lose. Let us note some of the values that the child can derive from listening to stories and/or telling them. He can:

1. Become more familiar with the culture of the race.
2. Learn some of the values that are permanent in society.
3. Develop appreciation of literature.
4. Improve his vocabulary.
5. Get functional, meaningful practice in many skills of oral expression like talking in a pleasing voice, being considerate of the audience, speaking in correct sentences, organizing the thoughts to be expressed, and using good English.
6. Become emotionally involved in such a way that the involvement adds to his mental health.
7. Get a closer grip on things of the spirit. (Bible stories are very valuable in this respect.)
8. Add to his fund of information and gain vicarious experiences.
9. Develop his imagination.
10. Derive pleasure and give it to his audience.
11. Increase his interest in reading.

Guidelines

Guidelines are listed here on which to base a program in storytelling.

1. No pupil should be required to tell a story that he does not like.
2. No pupil should tell a story to a group unless he has made preparation for telling it.
3. Storytelling should take place in a relaxed atmosphere. (If feasible, the audience should be arranged in a compact but informal group around the storyteller, who, as a rule, should be seated.)
4. Standards for storytelling should be worked out by the class with the help of the teacher.
5. Evaluation of storytelling should take place in such a manner as to encourage future interest in telling stories.
6. The teacher should encourage individuality of expression and manner in the storyteller.

Choosing Stories to Tell

Among the guidelines in the preceding paragraph one important principle in the selection of stories to be retold has been stated, namely "No pupil should be required to tell a story that he does not like." Following are additional suggestions.

1. Only worthwhile stories should be retold.
2. With the help of the teacher the pupils should draw up standards for the selection of stories to be retold.
3. The pupils should have an important part in the selection of stories for retelling.
4. The pupils should have readily available many sources of fine stories of the type that they would be able to retell.
5. The storyteller should select a story that he thinks his audience will enjoy hearing.
6. During the course of the school year a variety of stories should be told to the class. (Some may be folk tales of long ago, some modern folk tales, and still others, stories about present-day adventures and other happenings.)
7. Each child, when of an age and maturity to retell stories, should be encouraged to learn to tell more than one type.

Choosing Topics and Titles for Original Stories

It may be that many boys and girls who could get great satisfaction out of telling or writing original stories do not do so because they do not know what to tell or write.

Aids in Choosing Topics and Titles. One of the most important points for the teacher to remember as he guides boys and girls in the selection of topics or titles for original stories is that the same topic, especially if it is a quite restricted one, is not likely to appeal to all children in a room even if it is one that seems just right for some in the class. Following are enumerated a few ways in which the pupils can be assisted in deciding upon topics or titles for original stories.

1. The teacher can tell or read to the pupils or suggest that the pupils read myths, fables, and other fanciful tales, and then the teacher can ask for suggestions for topics or titles of myths and other fanciful tales that the pupils can tell after the characteristics of such stories have been discussed.
2. The pupils can be encouraged to post on the bulletin board pictures that they think may suggest titles for stories to others in the room. (As caption on the bulletin board might be the question "What Titles for Stories Do These Pictures Suggest?")
3. The teacher may discuss with the boys and girls the importance of having "catching" titles for their stories.
4. The pupils may check a list of possible titles for stories to indicate which sound particularly interesting. (In the list might be titles like these: (a) An

Adventure, (b) Thanksgiving Day, (c) A turkey's Thanksgiving, (d) Alone in the dark forest.)

5. The pupils may make a composite list of interest-catching titles that they made up or that they have heard or read.

LIST OF TOPICS AND TITLES. The list that is given here contains both topics and titles. No attempt has been made to separate the two, for sometimes what constitutes a topic for one person's story might be a title for that of another. For example, "My Pet" might be either topic or title; or the title on the topic "My Pet" might be "Peter, the Crow."

The topics or titles in the following list are not some on which necessarily each pupil in a room can develop an original story. It may even be that for some children not one of them is suitable. However, it is hoped that the list may suggest to the teacher others which he may in turn propose, directly or indirectly, to a pupil.

Peter Groundhog's Shadow
Doctor Dolittle Goes into Orbit.
"Do Not Cry over Spilled Milk."
"Cast Your Bread upon the Waters."
The Life History of a Frog
We Entertained a Pilgrim Girl at Thanksgiving.
Hungry on Christmas Eve
If Houses Could Talk
With Christopher Robin
Make Way for Puppies
The Discontented Princess
Thanksgiving in Animal Land
Christmas in Animal Land
Brooms for Witches.

METHODS. Some of the methods that may be used in helping pupils tell stories are suggested under "Guidelines" on page 46. Others follow.

1. The teacher gives the beginning of an original story and then asks the pupils to plan a continuation of it.

2. The teacher (a) displays a series of pictures on a bulletin board, three for example, to illustrate a story, (b) has the pupils discuss what they think is happening in the pictures, and (c) suggests that some may like to plan a story of their own about the pictures.

3. After the teacher has read or told stories to the class, the pupils discuss characteristics that made the story a good one.

4. The pupils analyze some of the stories they have read in terms of characteristics that made those stories good stories.

5. The class draws up a list of characteristics of a good story. In the first grade the pupils may name criteria such as these: (a) Is it interesting? (b) Does it have a surprise? In the intermediate grades the analysis might be more detailed, on points like these: (a) Does it have a good beginning? (b) Does it have action? (c) Do interesting things happen? (d) Is it given in descriptive language? (e) Does it have a suitable ending?

6. The teacher gives a make-believe story or retells one of the complexity that the pupils will be able to give, and then the class may name characteristics of his method of telling the story that showed skill as storyteller. The list may include points like these, in addition to those already mentioned in the preceding paragraph: (a) good sentences, (b) pleasant voice, (c) telling events in order, (d) use of conversation, (e) correct pronunciation and clear enunciation, (f) freedom from interfering mannerisms, (g) correct use of words, (h) use of interesting and descriptive words, (i) telling the story without notes, (j) desirable length, (k) evidence of enthusiasm.

7. In the lower grades the pupils give their stories to small groups.

8. In the first grade storytelling may be confined primarily to telling original stories although pupils should not be discouraged from retelling stories if there is a point in doing so or if both the teller and the audience will enjoy the activity.

9. At times there will probably be need for practice lessons in which the chief objective is not enjoyment but improvement in the art of storytelling. At such times the pupils may discuss the points on which they need help. Each storyteller may announce to the audience what his chief problem is and ask the class to see whether he has shown growth and to give him suggestions for further improvement.

10. Children in one room invite others to hear stories. For example, Christmas stories can be practiced and then shortly before the holidays another class be invited to sing Christmas carols and to listen to stories as they gather around the Christmas tree.

11. The class has a period during the day or week set aside for storytelling. However, storytelling should not be confined to such times only. For example, the time when the boys and girls are studying about Indians in the social studies may be appropriate for telling an Indian "why" story.

12. The pupils determine which one of a group of recorded sentences given orally constitutes a good beginning for a story. The criteria applied may be these: (a) Does it tell something significant? (b) Does it make you think the story will be interesting?

(c) Does it answer the question *who, when,* or *where* about the story? (d) Does it make you wonder what will happen in the story?

13. The class make a list of good beginning sentences for stories and indicate what makes them desirable.

14. The class listen to some records of stories well told or to stories told on the radio or television and evaluate them in terms of the criteria that they have set up for storytelling.

15. The pupils rewrite a brief story in which the events have been listed in scrambled order.

16. The pupils study stories to note interesting endings.

17. The pupils tell stories as tape recordings are made. These recordings can be used for programs and for purposes of evaluation.

Figure 4.4 Illustrations as Aids to Storytelling

Storytelling by the Teacher

As is suggested in preceding pages of this chapter, one way the teacher can interest pupils in storytelling is by telling stories to them. Through his selection he can help develop in his listeners an appreciation of "the good, the beautiful, the true." He can also aim to serve as a model for the boys and girls in storytelling. In fact, whether or not he wishes to be a model, he is. Whether the teacher will be a good or poor one, however, lies in part within his power to determine.

By following the suggestions given in this chapter for storytelling by boys and girls, the teacher can set goals for himself. For further help he is referred to discussions of the art of storytelling in books listed at the end of this chapter.

DEVELOPMENT IN ABILITY TO MAKE EXPLANATIONS AND GIVE DIRECTIONS

What adult among us has not at times been puzzled when others have given explanations or directions in such a manner that they were incomprehensible?

Figure 4.5 A Suitable Environment for Storytelling

And who among us has not at times himself given them so poorly that his listeners have been in a similar predicament!

Guidelines

Some basic points to observe in helping boys and girls develop in ability to make explanations and give directions are listed following.

1. *Boys and girls should be helped to see the need for giving clear explanations and directions.* The resulting understanding can give them purpose for attention to correct ways of proceeding when, in informal situations, the need arises for giving explanations and directions. Similarly it can give the children incentive for engaging in learning situations in which special emphasis is placed on how to perform these activities.

2. *The work in each grade should be introduced in a bona fide situation.* In the modern elementary school there are many opportunities for giving explanations and directions. They should be utilized by introducing the work for a grade in a functional setting. For example, in a first grade as a pupil explains how he made his model airplane, help can be given to him and the rest of the class in learning how to

give clear-cut explanations. As a sixth-grade pupil explains to the class how to get to a place showing the undesirable effects of erosion, for example, the situation can be utilized for learning how to give directions well.

3. *The boys and girls should be given a part in developing standards.* Points like these, with wording to suit the grade level, could be listed:

Include all essentials.
Omit all nonessentials.
Decide on good sequence.
Choose words well.
Suit the explanation or the directions to the audience.
Give clear-cut examples and illustrations when helpful.

4. *Some boys and girls should be given more help in learning how to make explanations and give directions clearly than is afforded by the situations arising in the ongoing program of the school.* As in the case of the development of many other language-arts skills, special practice lessons may need at times to be set up to provide the desirable amount of explanation and practice. However, there must be in the mind of the pupil a clear relationship between such lessons and the value of application of what is learned to life situations requiring the use of the skill.

Situations Requiring Explanations or Directions

Boys and girls may find themselves in situations in which needs for explanations or directions like the following occur.

1. How policemen help us, how bread is made, why the colonists objected to taxation by England, why the Indians fought the white men
2. How heat travels, what is meant by the water cycle, how we can tell time by the Big Dipper, why we have time belts, why we always see the same face of the moon
3. How to get from one place to another
4. How to make things like candles, butter, puppets, puppet stages, costumes, paper-sculptured articles, dioramas, panoramas
5. How to play a game, make a gift, make a model airplane, paint an Easter egg, make a Christmas decoration, arrange a bulletin board
6. How to administer various types of first aid
7. How to feed a rabbit and take care of a pet.

Methods

Here are some suggestions as to how pupils can be aided in the acquisition of skills important for giving explanations and directions.

1. Make a chart or have some pupils make one listing the points that have been decided upon as standards.
2. Give the boys and girls copies of different explanations or directions written on various levels of understanding and ask them to decide for which grade level each is suitable.
3. Provide the pupils with copies of explanations or directions in which one or more points are included that are not important to the topic and have them indicate which points are superfluous.
4. Give the pupils copies of explanations or directions in which one or more points are out of the right order and ask them to arrange the sentences correctly.
5. Through skits, help the pupils show the difference in effectiveness if an explanation or directions are given at a proper tempo rather than too fast or too slowly.
6. Through skits, help the boys and girls show effective and ineffective ways in which visual aids can be used when giving explanations or directions.
7. Assist the class in listing types of visual aids that can be utilized in some instances to make clearer an explanation or a set of directions and have the pupils demonstrate how some of these (such as maps, diagrams, materials needed in construction) can be used effectively.
8. Discuss with the class *do's* and *don'ts* about responding to questions on explanations or directions asked by the audience when stressing points such as the following: (a) Be courteous. (b) If you do not know the answer, say so. If possible, suggest ways in which the questioner can find the answer or tell him that you will try to find it for him. (c) Answer to the point.
9. Through skits, help some pupils show how the question-and-answer period following the giving of an explanation or of directions can be conducted according to accepted standards and how it sometimes is conducted in violation of them.
10. Interest one or more pupils in making a poster to emphasize how to give explanations or directions.
11. Provide practice in giving directions and then check the effectiveness by having one or more persons in the audience follow them.
12. Have pupils give directions necessary to proceed from one place to another in the neighborhood or some other known territory.
13. Emphasize the importance of including in directions for going to another place the location of easily recognized buildings or other things in the environment that will help the person follow the directions.

14. Have pupils give orally a set of directions that indicates how to go from one place to another as outlined on a map of the city or of the neighborhood.

DEVELOPMENT IN ABILITY TO MAKE ANNOUNCEMENTS

Closely akin to the ability to make explanations is the ability to make announcements. This is important to the elementary-school pupil. It is an ability amenable to teaching.

Guidelines

The guidelines for development of skill in making announcements are similar to those for development of skill in giving explanations and directions. Essential suggestions are given here.

1. Boys and girls should be helped to see the need for learning to make announcements.
2. As a rule the help that boys and girls receive in making announcements should be provided at times when bona fide announcements are necessary.
3. Some boys and girls should be given more help in learning how to make announcements than is afforded by the situations arising in the ongoing program of the school.

Methods

Some of the ways in which the boys and girls can develop skill in making announcements are listed following. The pupils can:

1. Help draw up a list of standards for making announcements similar to those given on page 287.
2. Read in their language-arts books or on duplicated copies of materials that the teacher has written what some of the important points are that should be watched when making announcements.
3. Make posters emphasizing one or more points of importance when making announcements.
4. Discuss when it is of value to use visual aids while making announcements.
5. Criticize written reports of announcements, some of which include all essential points while others are lacking some.
6. Put on skits to illustrate desirable and undesirable ways of making announcements, for discussion by the class.
7. Summarize, verbally and pictorially, in a language-arts notebook the essential points learned about making announcements.
8. Restate some announcements made to lower-grade children so that they would be suitable to make to intermediate-grade pupils, and vice-versa.

DEVELOPMENT IN ABILITY TO ASK RIDDLES AND TELL JOKES

It is worthwhile to guide boys and girls in development of ability to ask riddles and tell jokes for several reasons, these among them: (1) Riddles and jokes are frequently told by children and adults and at times so inadequately that special attention should be directed toward improvement. (2) Through attention to asking riddles and telling jokes a functional setting can be provided for practice on various language-arts skills of value in other types of situations. For example, practice can be given in choice of words, in speaking with poise, and in use of good sentences.

Cautions

Some cautions to observe when helping boys and girls learn to give riddles and jokes are as follows.

1. Guard against having the pupils give riddles or jokes that are in any way "shady." (It may be necessary for the teacher to be informed beforehand about the joke a pupil plans to tell. Care should be taken, however, if such a procedure is followed, that no attitude of undesirable censorship is built up.)
2. Help the pupils to avoid the common errors of telling so much when asking a riddle that the point is given away in the mere statement of the riddle or of telling so little that the riddle is incomplete.
3. Try to prevent the pupils from telling jokes that may hurt someone's feelings.

Methods

Listed following are some suggestions for guiding boys and girls in development of ability in asking riddles and telling jokes. The pupils may:

1. Discuss criteria for desirable riddles and jokes.
2. Read riddles and jokes and evaluate them in terms of established criteria.
3. Tell riddles and jokes that they have heard or read, at times primarily for the enjoyment of the audience and at other times partly for evaluation by their peers of the method of telling the riddles or jokes.
4. Make up riddles and ask them of the class. (The *Who Am I* riddle is one on the level of children even in the primary grades when it is on a topic such as (a) objects with which the pupils play, (b) means of transportation, (c) animals. An example of a very simple *Who Am I* riddle is: I have long ears. I am a big animal. I have a trunk.)
5. Make a collection of riddles and jokes, including some original ones, and exhibit them on a bulletin board or in a booklet with a title like "Smile a While."

6. Examine a list of jokes in some of which the point is brought out well and in others of which it is given poorly, to determine which jokes are well stated.

DEVELOPMENT OF SOCIAL COURTESIES

Increased emphasis is being given to helping children gain poise in observance of social courtesies in activities such as telephoning, making and acknowledging introductions, and making and accepting or refusing invitations.

Telephoning

Since even the preschool child uses the telephone, the first grade is not too early to begin giving guidance in its use. Furthermore, even by the time the pupil is in the sixth grade he still has need, in many instances, of help in the proper use of this means of communication.

What Should Be Learned. Here are some of the learnings that should be acquired by the elementary-school child:

How to hold the telephone
What kind of voice to use when telephoning
What to say when answering the telephone
How to dial a number
What to say first when one telephones to someone
When to telephone
What topics are appropriate and what inappropriate for telephone conversation
Why courtesy is important
How long to phone
Who should terminate a telephone conversation
How to take a message over the telephone.

Methods. Following are listed a few suggestions for procedure:

1. Explanation by the teacher. The teacher can explain to the pupils some of thc important points to observe and give reason for observing them.
2. Reading on the topic. The pupils can read parts in a textbook or material on duplicated sheets that give suggestions on telephoning and show the importance of good telephone manners.
3. Discussion by the class. The boys and girls can discuss what they have learned about good manners in telephoning and help make a composite list of points to observe. The list can serve for purposes of appraisal. Items listed in the preceding section on "What Should Be Learned" can be changed to statements of rules.
4. Putting on skits. The pupils can participate in putting on skits or in observing them and in evaluating them. Skits can be used to introduce the work on telephoning in a grade by having two persons demonstrate poor and then good telephone manners so that the class can later discuss rules governing telephone courtesy. Skits can be used in later stages of work on telephoning when the boys and girls apply in a functional setting what they have learned. Slips of paper can be handed to pairs of children with directions like this one indicating what they should do for later evaluation by the group:

> Dramatize a telephone conversation in which someone responds correctly when a person asks to speak to an individual who is not at home. Then present another skit to show an incorrect way of answering the telephone when someone asks for a person who is not at home.

Figure 4.6 An Illustrated Checklist

5. Making displays for a bulletin board. On a poster entitled "What's Wrong Here?" can be depicted a scene in which two children are talking over the telephone, with evidence such as the following of violations of rules for courtesy as revealed either through the illustrations or through the remarks on the poster: (a) having the mouth too far from the transmitter, (b) calling at mealtime, (c) asking the other person to guess who is speaking.
6. Drawing pictures illustrating a series of rules for telephoning.
7. Making an illustrated booklet on how to use the telephone.

8. Studying written records of telephone conversations to determine which rules for telephoning are followed and which violated.

9. Practicing various points about telephoning, such as distance of the mouth from the transmitter and suitable voice, with a toy telephone.

10. Giving a demonstration as to how to dial a number.

11. Making a telephone directory of names and telephone numbers that each child may want.

12. Checking a list of times when it is appropriate or inappropriate to call, such as: mealtime; after school; at six o'clock in the morning; at eleven o'clock at night; at half past seven in the evening.

13. Checking a list of remarks to indicate which are appropriate and which inappropriate, such as: (a) Get your mouth closer to the telephone. (b) I can't hear a word you are trying to say. (c) Do you like Susy? (d) I hope you can come to my party. (e) My mother bought me a new dress. (f) Why doesn't your mother get you a new dress?

Introductions

Making and acknowledging introductions are activities that fall within the realm of the elementary-school child. Besides learning how to acknowledge introductions, elementary-school children may learn how to make introductions under circumstances such as the following: (1) introducing a speaker, (2) introducing a younger person to an older person of the same sex, (3) introducing a boy to a girl or to a woman, (4) introducing a man to a woman, (5) introducing a girl to a man, (6) introducing two persons of about the same age and the same sex, (7) introducing a new child or a visitor to the class.

Knowledges and Skills to Be Acquired. These are some points that children should learn and be able to put into practice when introducing a person, like a new pupil or visitor or speaker, to a group:

1. The name of the person being introduced should be given distinctly.

2. Something should be told about the person being introduced that will make the group especially interested in him.

3. No uncomplimentary remarks should be made.

4. The introduction should be brief.

When introducing one person to another it is important to observe which person is to be introduced to the other. Furthermore, points such as these are worthy of special note: (1) The names of both persons should be spoken distinctly. (2) Something should be told about each person that will make each interested in the other or that will facilitate conversation. (3) No uncomplimentary remarks should be made. (4) The persons being introduced should acknowledge each other by giving an appropriate greeting and by repeating the name of the other person. (5) The persons introduced should engage in conversation with one another if there is opportunity to do so.

Methods. The following methods can be used to help boys and girls acquire needed learnings.

1. The teacher can serve as model as he makes and acknowledges introductions within the hearing of the children.

2. The boys and girls can read about how to make and acknowledge introductions through the use of textbooks or duplicated sheets.

Figure 4.7 An Accordion-like Folder Emphasizing Sequence in Introduction

3. With the guidance of the teacher, the class can discuss points essential in making and acknowledging introductions.

4. The pupils can make a check list of points for evaluating the making and acknowledging of introductions.

5. The pupils can participate in or observe skits in which, for the pupils' evaluation, correct and incorrect procedures are used. Slips of paper can be distributed to groups of pupils with specifications for skits such as: (a) Introduce a classmate to your mother correctly and then tell the class what rules you observed. (b) Introduce a boy to a girl incorrectly and ask a classmate to explain what was wrong.

6. The pupils can check a list of written words of introductions and indicate which are done properly and which improperly. In the case of those not done correctly, they could state which rules were not observed.

7. The boys and girls can indicate which of a list of remarks for use in an introduction are undesirable, like: (a) I heard your team was really defeated. (b) So you are from California. That is one state I do not care to see. (c) Hello, Mrs. Johnson (said by a sixth-grade pupil). (d) I hope you will enjoy our schoolroom. We do many interesting things.

8. The pupils can make a poster showing a correct way of introducing two persons through picture and words.

9. The pupils can check *true* or *false* a list of statements about introductions such as these: (a) A girl should be introduced to a boy. (b) A man should be introduced to a woman. (c) It is all right to say something uncomplimentary about the town from which the person to whom you are being introduced comes if the statement you make is true.

10. A tape recording can be made of an introduction for later evaluation.

Greeting Callers

Following are a few suggestions for receiving callers, the need for which frequently occurs in the life of an elementary-school child. Boys and girls should learn:

1. To greet a person who comes to the door politely

2. Not to let a person they do not know enter the home

3. To invite a person they know into the home if he has come to call on a person who is at home

4. To go to the person who has a caller in order to tell him of his caller if he is in another room, not to shout for him

5. To take careful note of the name of a person who called on someone not at home and later to report the name to the person for whom the call had been intended.

How to receive callers can be learned through these and other methods: reading, discussing, listing criteria, making or studying posters, presenting skits, indicating which statements about the proper way to receive callers are true and which false, having a host or hostess in the classroom to receive callers.

DEVELOPMENT OF EFFECTIVE LISTENING

Development of skill in listening has probably been more neglected than any of the other three main facets of the language arts – more than speaking, reading, or writing.

Facts about Listening

Although there is a scarcity of conclusive research on methods of improving skill in listening, attention to facts such as the following, it is generally agreed, brings about development in that skill.

1. *Physical factors affect listening.* Relative quiet seems to be one of the factors that is conducive to listening and to development in ability to listen. However, while it is desirable that when boys and girls are being helped to become better listeners there should be a fairly quiet environment, it would be undesirable to depend on almost total quiet for the development of skill in listening. Children, especially in this age of mass communication, need to develop in ability to listen even if complete silence does not characterize the background for a listening situation. At first when concentration is placed on improvement in listening, it is particularly important to provide a background of many distracting sounds.

A fairly comfortable position for the listener also seems to be a valuable factor in improvement. A person who is in physical discomfort, like one who stands through a lecture, probably misses some of the points that he would get if he were seated fairly comfortably. For some levels of listening, however, where active rather than passive attention is demanded, it is possible for the listener to sit on a chair so comfortable that he fails to be as alert as he would be if he were on one less conducive to lounging.

Temperature also seems to affect the ability to do prolonged listening on a high level of concentration. Either too cold or too warm temperature seems to have an adverse effect.

2. *Health affects listening.* While many persons in poor health undoubtedly are excellent listeners, it seems that, other things being equal, the person in good health has the better chance of effective listening, especially on the levels of listening requiring considerable concentration and the exercise of the higher thought processes. Some interfering factors in the physical health of children in attendance at school are colds, headaches, and fatigue.

3. *A stable emotional state of mind is conducive to listening.* Perhaps the relationship between the emotions and listening can be stated more accurately if it is given in negative terms in a statement like "An unstable emotional state of mind is detrimental to listening." Fear, anger, jealousy, resentment, insecurity, and other destructive emotional states can cause a person to be unable to comprehend well what he hears. Even extremes of joy and happy excitement seem to interfere with the best concentration. A state of emotional equilibrium or one approaching it in which a peaceful, contented state of mind prevails is likely to be accompanied by better powers of listening than an imbalance.

4. *An atmosphere of good will in a classroom, in which the pupils feel they are liked by the teacher and by their peers, is background in which skill in listening is more likely to develop than in one that lacks this feeling of warmth of personal relationships.* Unless a person feels kindly toward those who are speaking, he is not under many circumstances as likely to pay undivided attention as when he knows he is listening to a friend. Furthermore, in an atmosphere in which the child does not feel accepted, he is less likely to participate constructively in the give-and-take of speaking and listening.

5. *A classroom in which there are many opportunities for communication through oral and written means is a factor in the development of skill in listening.* It is not enough to emphasize the importance of opportunities solely for listening. Instead the emphasis should be placed on all the facets of the language arts — reading, writing, speaking, and listening. Without emphasis on the various communication skills, the program in the language arts can easily become unbalanced. There is decided danger in spending so much time on listening that the school program is deplete of other activities, activities that by themselves are needed for the well-rounded development of the individual.

6. *There are various levels of listening to be recognized by the teacher.* These range in the elementary school from the fleeting, almost momentary attention that may be given to sounds to the type of listening characterized by concentration and critical analysis, as well as other kinds of personal reactions requiring higher thought processes. Intermediate levels, between which there is overlapping, when compared with the lower range of attention identified above, are characterized by growth in attention that:

Is of longer duration
Is more active than passive
Is less wavering
Recognizes the speaker's plan of organization
Produces associations in the mind of the listener.

7. *Recognition of the desirable purposes for listening can be of help in growth of skill in listening.* The pupil who recognizes a purpose for listening is more likely to profit from the experience than the one who does not. Boys and girls, therefore, should often be given reason for listening. It is not enough, as a rule, to tell the pupils to listen to a report on a given topic. They are likely to gain more in power to listen and in the acquisition of information if they are asked, for example, to listen to find out how the schools of the children of Switzerland differ from those in the United States or why irrigation is not carried on more extensively in a territory under consideration.

8. *Interest is a significant factor in listening.* Interest can be aroused through the selection of a topic of appeal to the boys and girls. It can be stimulated through questions that the teacher may point out would be answered in a report, providing the questions asked seem worthwhile to the children. It can be aroused by giving the pupils a background for the topic to be presented. For example, after the teacher has told the boys and girls an interesting incident in the life of Benjamin Franklin, he may announce that a child will give a report telling about other occurrences in Franklin's life he thinks they will enjoy hearing.

9. *Participation in drawing up standards for listening is conducive to better listening, especially when these same standards are used for evaluative purposes.* Standards can be drawn up by the class after participating in activities such as reading selections on how to listen; listening to the teacher talk about important points to observe when listening; observing some people as they listen attentively; discussing the characteristics of a good listener; watching a skit in which attention and inattention are demonstrated. For a list of standards the reader is referred to page 287.

10. *Children vary greatly in ability to listen even within a grade.* Because of this fact the teacher should try to ascertain the listening levels under various

Courtesy of the Public Schools of New York City

Figure 4.8 Interest as a Significant Factor in Listening

types of situations and provide needed individual attention.

11. *Special help in listening under selected types of situations can be of value.* For example, since listening to a speaker involves some skills that listening to a person with whom one is conversing does not, improvement in these two types of listening situations may require different methods of procedure. Some of the types of situations under which listening may need to be improved are shown by the listing given below:

Listening to a record
Listening to television
Listening to the teacher
Listening to a person who is talking with one
Listening when in a small group
Listening to directions and explanations
Listening to a play or a story
Listening to a speaker
Listening to poetry
Listening to sounds around one
Listening to the conversation of others
Listening to announcements

Courtesy of the Gary, Indiana, Public Schools

Figure 4.9 Listening Is Fun

Listening to choral speaking
Listening to panel discussions
Listening when being introduced.

12. *The length of time during which pupils can listen effectively varies.* No exact number of minutes can be cited for the attention span of listening of any type. Variation is caused by factors such as previous listening habits, interests in what is being heard, difficulty of comprehension of what is being heard, purpose for listening. While care should be taken that no attempt is made to try to force the child to extend his span of attention beyond that which he can attain without undue strain, efforts should be made steadily to increase it by exposing him to longer and longer periods of listening and by aiding him in holding his attention throughout that time.

13. *Taste in listening can be developed.* Boys and girls can be guided to higher levels of appreciation in music and in other types of listening. No effort, however, should be made to try to force a child whose highest level of appreciation is the wildest of Wild West jazz to appreciate, without intermediate steps, a Bach recording.

14. *Skill in listening is frequently affected by vocabulary, and vocabulary can be affected by listening.* In the vocabulary used by a speaker or by a storyteller there may be so many unfamiliar words that the listener's comprehension is affected adversely and that consequently he may lose interest in listening. On the other hand, if a limited number of words above the child's level of understanding are used, his vocabulary can be increased. This improvement in vocabulary is possible especially when meanings of "new words" are built into that which is being said. For instance, if the pupil does not know the word *burrow*, the use of the word in a comment like the following may help him figure out the meaning and make it easier for him the next time he meets the word to understand it even if its use is not made clear through the context:

The mother rabbit had dug a hole for the new home in the bushes near the big house. The little rabbit had watched her make the burrow.

15. *Skill in listening is affected by experience, and listening extends experience.* The child lacking in experience background is not likely to be greatly interested in a large variety of listening experiences. The pupil who has been to Quebec will probably be more alert when hearing about that city than the one who has not been there. Happily, too, experience can be extended through listening in many instances that are so self-evident that no enumeration is needed.

Methods

Since there are many different types of listening situations as well as varying purposes and levels, it is important that teaching procedures should be varied. To improve in power to listen, boys and girls can:

1. Listen to sounds of farm animals or to sounds around them of which recordings have been made on records available commercially.
2. Play games in which they identify sounds they hear when they are blindfolded such as beating a drum, playing notes on the piano, rapping a pencil on a table.
3. Give rhyming words.
4. Make a list of happy sounds such as a mother singing a lullaby or children laughing, and of weird sounds such as the hooting of an owl or the blowing of a fog horn on a dark windy night.
5. Say the rhyming words in couplets or short selections from poems that the teacher reads or tell which of a series of three or more words written on the chalkboard finish the rhyme scheme of an incomplete rhyme that the teacher reads such as:

   Tell me not in mournful numbers
   Life is but an empty dream,
   For the soul is dead that (sleeps, slumbers, rests).[1]

6. Listen to someone read a poem or play a recording of one in order to comprehend the story, to "see" the pictures that it brings to mind, to tell how they like it, to note how it is being read without undesirable singsong, to decide whether it is suitable for inclusion in a program, to answer a question that has been asked by the teacher.
7. Listen to a story to see if they will like it, to decide whether it is suitable for reading for a program or for dramatization, to compare it with another version of the same story.
8. Draw up criteria for telling stories and then listen to recordings of stories or to stories told over television or radio in order to note how the criteria are met.
9. Listen to the recording of an individual's reading of a poem or story or of a talk by him in order to apply criteria worked out by the class, with the view to possible improvement.
10. Discuss when it is important to give entire attention to something being heard and when it is enough to give only secondary or no attention to it. (For example, when one group is reading with the teacher in one part of the room, the boys and girls working elsewhere should learn not to pay attention to the teacher unless he addresses a remark to them.)
11. Compile a list of action words that describe sounds, like *tapping, thumping, rattling, barking, shouting, squeaking,* and then identify each sound.
12. Discuss which radio and television programs are suitable for children and then give exact information about when these can be heard or viewed.
13. Make a list of statements made in a record of a talk which are controversial or which state opinions and make a similar list of points made in a talk given orally.
14. Discuss the importance of looking at a speaker while he is talking and observing other niceties such as not playing with something, not talking, and not interrupting unnecessarily.
15. Discuss the responsibility of the speaker to make his remarks worthy of being heard.
16. Listen to a talk of which the pupils have been given an outline so that they learn to follow the plan of organization of a speaker and then to listen to other talks to decide upon the outline followed.
17. View a sound "movie" after the teacher has prepared the pupils for it through activities such as: (a) presenting background data; (b) giving them an outline of the main parts of the "movie"; or (c) listing on the chalkboard questions that will be answered in the "movie" and asking them to read them before they see the "movie."
18. Give summary of something the pupils have heard such as story or a television program.
19. Participate in putting on a skit or observe it as different types of listening (secondary, fairly attentive, and very attentive) are demonstrated and then discuss the points brought out in the skit in regard to learning to become better listeners.
20. Listen to directions for games and then play them.
21. Make a poster showing through words and picture some *do's* and *don'ts* about listening.

---

[1]Henry Wadsworth Longfellow, "The Psalm of Life."

22. Arrange in order of occurrence the events of a story that has been told by unscrambling a list of sentences in which those events are given in mixed-up order.

23. Make a check list individually of points each pupil thinks he needs to observe in particular as he tries to become a better listener.

24. Mark *True* or *False* a list of statements about listening such as: (a) It is important to listen carefully to everything. (b) If a speaker makes a statement during his talk to a small group, anyone who disagrees with him has a right to interrupt him immediately even if the speaker has not asked for interruptions. (c) Even if a talk is uninteresting, the audience should be polite to the speaker.

OPPORTUNITIES FOR GROWTH THROUGH SPECIAL ACTIVITIES

The program of the modern elementary school provides many rich opportunities for development of oral communication. To many of these reference has been made in preceding pages of this chapter. Two are discussed here, namely (1) planning and participating in programs and (2) being a member or leader of a club.

Planning and Participating in Programs

Programs can be planned for presentation to other pupils in other groups in the same classroom, to pupils in other rooms, to parents, or to the general public. They can deal with a large variety of subjects as indicated by the following types: Christmas programs, Thanksgiving programs, Mother's Day programs, Lincoln's and Washington's birthday programs, and programs consisting of the culmination of a unit the children have been studying such as on safety, China, or adventures in space.

Programs suitable for the elementary school can also be classified as to method of presentation. A program may consist of any one of the following types or of a combination of them: a dramatization, a puppet show, a pageant, folk dances, a pupil-made "movie," a make-believe radio or television performance, a panel discussion, an exhibit with explanations.

Guidelines. A few helpful guidelines follow.

1. *The program should be of educational value to the participants.* While there is nothing wrong in having as one of the purposes in putting on a program that of maintaining or developing school-home cooperation (which, in fact, is a desirable goal when it is not the only one), the children should not be used merely as agents for public relations. The work should be planned with objectives to benefit the pupils such as, for example, development in oral and written communication. It can also serve legitimately as incentive for some of the work of the regular school curriculum, for instance, for summarizing the work on a unit on our community.

The fifth grade has studied a unit on "Our European Background." Our program will include:

1. An introductory talk
2. The life of Verdi (report)
3. Playing "The Nutcracker Suite"
4. "The Child Handel" (report)
5. Galileo and the Telescope (report)
6. Slides of European buildings
7. Costumes of Europe (report)
8. European customs (report)
9. Telling stories
10. Motion picture on Sweden
11. Explanation of our exhibit.

Figure 4.10 Variety in a Program

2. *The program should be of value to the audience.* It is of particular importance that the time be well spent when the audience consists of boys and girls excused from other school activities. To be sure, to have fun when watching a program can be a desirable objective. However, there usually should be more than entertainment. When inviting pupils to a program care should be taken that the subject matter or method of presentation is neither below nor beyond the level of the audience. The range in grades for which most programs are suitable is not as inclusive as from grade one through grade six. As a rule, a program of real value to a first-grade audience is too juvenile for sixth-grade boys and girls.

3. *Throughout the time of preparation for a program, methods should be used that will make the*

work of educational value. The goal should not be merely a good end performance. For example, the boys and girls should be given an opportunity to help plan a program partly because such thinking through of what is to be included and of what the procedure should be will, if the planning is well done, help the pupils plan better in the future.

4. *There should be wide participation by pupils in programs.* It is not to be expected in short programs which one group gives for another in the same room, or even always in short ones given for another grade, that at all times all pupils will take part. Over a period of time when several programs are given by a group or grade, however, each pupil should have the chance to participate. When programs are presented to parents or to the general public or when they are given to another grade as culmination of a unit of work, every child should have a part. Unless there are children of such exceedingly low mentality as are seldom found in other than special rooms in the public elementary schools or children with physical defects that would prohibit their taking a regular part in the program, each child should be given a responsibility that is of educational value to him and one that is recognized by his peers and the audience as having such merit. To let a pupil do nothing repeatedly in programs other than work like passing out the songbooks, straightening the chairs, or distributing the programs is likely not to help him as much as he could be benefited through such programs. Furthermore, it is likely to be embarrassing to his family and him if his part is always limited to that type of participation.

5. *There should be a high standard of performance.* How high it should be will vary with the situation. A program for another group in the room probably will not need to be as finished as one to which the public is invited. The purpose for the program will determine in part the quality of the end-product desired. There is no situation, however, when a slipshod performance is excusable. Adherence to this general principle does not mean that so much time should be spent on a program that it is cameo perfect. Such procedure would usually involve a gross waste of time. The teacher needs to decide where on the scale of excellence of a program the law of diminishing returns would set in, the point where the time could more justifiably be spent on activities other than perfecting the program.

6. *Care should be taken not to invite another room very often.* Each room has certain educational objectives and each teacher should try to make optimum use of the time of his pupils toward the achievement of these goals. Frequent attendance at programs put on by other rooms may well interfere with making the best use of the time of the children in accomplishing the aims set for their own class.

7. *There should be evaluation of the program.* Self-evaluation is very important. At times, however, help in appraisal can be obtained from the pupils in the audience also. If children in lower grades constituted the audience, a pupil or a committee from the group who gave the program may go to the other rooms to ask the children what they liked particularly about the program and even, at times, what suggestions they may have for its improvement. If intermediate-grade pupils served as audience, the same procedure may be followed or a questionnaire or a check list, similar to the following, may be given for their appraisal.

Evaluating Our Program

We tried to observe these points in our program:

........1. Talking so all could hear us
........2. Having an interesting program
........3. Helping our audience learn something
........4. Being well prepared.

Put a check to the left of each point that you think we accomplished.

IDEAS FOR ASSEMBLY PROGRAMS. Most of the suggestions about programs given in the preceding pages apply to all kinds of programs. Let us now turn our special attention to one kind of program on which teachers are earnestly seeking assistance, namely the assembly program.

1. *Planning for an assembly program should be done well ahead of time.* If the practice in a school is that the teacher is assigned responsibility for an assembly program only a short time before the event is to take place, he will, of course, need to make the best of an undesirable situation. In that case, however, at teachers' meetings he may wish to suggest the importance of long-time planning. He may point out the value in each teacher's knowing near the beginning of the school year for how many assembly programs his room will be responsible and at least the approximate dates for them.

2. *Effective use can be made of bulletin boards to announce assembly programs and to create interest in them.* For a program on Columbus Day a poster can be displayed with illustrated questions on Columbus under the statement "We Will Help You Answer These Questions." Below the questions may be recorded the time and place of the program.

3. *Participation of the audience is often a good device to use.* Singing a song known to all, such as "The Star-Spangled Banner" or "America," makes the audience tend to feel a unity. Singing is of particular value in this respect when it comes at the beginning of a program.

4. *The persons putting on a program may encourage the audience to use good manners.* This device should be used sparingly and with considerable caution. In a skit serving as prologue to a program, good and poor manners of an imaginary audience may be demonstrated. Points that may be stressed are: (a) being orderly when entering and leaving the room, (b) keeping quiet during the performance, (c) looking at the performers, (d) not laughing at mistakes, (e) applauding with restraint.

5. *Provisions can be made for the distribution of copies of the program to the audience.* While it is not necessary at all times to give to each member of the audience a copy of the program, it often adds to the interest in and the clarity of the program to do so. As practice in handwriting in a functional setting, the boys and girls in the room giving the program can make enough copies of it for each person in the audience. Art may at times be correlated with this activity by having the pupils make simple appropriate illustrations on each copy. At other times, instead of providing every member of the audience with a copy, the sequence of events may be listed on a portable chalkboard or on a bulletin board.

Illustrative Programs. For description of programs that might be presented by primary-grade pupils and others by intermediate-grade pupils the reader is referred to page 301.

Being a Member or Leader of a Club

"Why have a club?" is a logical question to ask, for unless sound educational objectives can be fulfilled in part by means of it, it is questionable procedure to organize one. Fortunately, however, many worthwhile purposes can be served through club activities.

The following list of objectives may suggest others:

1. To give the boys and girls practice in parliamentary procedure
2. To help the pupils realize some of the rights and privileges as well as duties and responsibilities that are concomitants of democratic procedures
3. To give the boys and girls insight into election procedures
4. To help the boys and girls take more effectively the roles of leaders and of followers
5. To provide the boys and girls with the opportunity to acquire worthwhile information or skills such as those needed in either oral or written communication, for example, dramatization or writing a paper to be read
6. To give the pupils pleasurable experiences.

While the objectives stated are given in terms of teachers' objectives, the pupils, too, should have in mind rather specifically some of the goals they hope to obtain through a club. The wise teacher will not only help the pupils decide on ends to be obtained but also will guide them from time to time in their evaluation of how well they are accomplishing them. A few objectives that pupils may seek to attain are: (a) to learn how to conduct a meeting, (b) to get practical experience in voting wisely, and (c) to improve their room through this organization.

The initiative for organizing a club may well be taken by the teacher if the pupils do not suggest one. If the pupils do not know of rooms that have clubs, they are not likely to suggest that they have one. If the project is not proposed by the boys and girls, the teacher can interest them in a club by telling them of some grades that have clubs. Or he may begin more directly by asking the pupils how they would like to have a club to take care of some situations that may have arisen, such as the need for keeping the room more attractive. If the class is genuinely interested in forming a club, it matters little, if at all, whether the initial step is taken by the pupils or by the teacher.

Kinds of Clubs. Frequently a room club is formed, of which every pupil in the room is a member. Often such clubs serve a large number of purposes, depending upon the changing needs of the group. To these clubs are delegated many responsibilities such as: (1) improving the room, (2) putting on a party, and (3) giving good programs.

Some boys and girls prefer special-interest clubs, with the possibility of choosing the group to which to belong. A few possible types are science clubs, hobby clubs, nature-study clubs, bird-study clubs, and dramatic clubs. It is practical for interest clubs to meet during school time if each pupil in a room or group of rooms belongs to a club. Then, if several rooms join in organizing the clubs, all the clubs, preferably not more than about three, can meet at the same hour. If there were three clubs for the intermediate grades of a small school, the fourth-grade teacher may, for example, be the adviser of the hobby club, the fifth-grade teacher of the science club, and the sixth-grade teacher of the nature-study club.

Parliamentary Procedure. Some of the important points for boys and girls to learn about parliamentary procedures are: (1) how to organize a club, (2) how to select officers, (3) what the duties of the officers are, (4) how to make and vote upon motions, (5) how to write the minutes of a meeting, (6) how to appoint committees, and (7) what the steps in conducting a meeting are. Information that pupils should know on each of these topics is given on page 302.

TYPES OF CLUB PROGRAMS. In the special-interest clubs the type of club defines quite well the kind of program that is likely to be given. If it is a nature-study club, the program will deal with nature; if it is a book club, most likely book reports will be given. If the club is not organized to serve as well-defined needs as the special-interest clubs, the programs can show great variations as to subject.

Club programs can also be different in method of performance. Some may be talks; others may be planned around plays, readings, games, motion pictures, slides, or exhibits. Many may well be given by the members or part of the membership, while occasionally others may be presented by adults or boys and girls not belonging to the club.

OTHER SUGGESTIONS. The following points may also be of importance to keep in mind when guiding club work.

1. Many teachers find it profitable to have a regular time, weekly or every two weeks, set aside for club meetings.

2. In most cases it will be best to have the meetings of the club during school hours.

3. It is usually wise to have a change of officers several times during the school year so that more than one pupil has a chance to perform the duties of a president, vice-president, secretary, or treasurer.

4. It may be best not to charge any membership fees in a school situation. If there are dues, at times their payment is a serious problem for some of the boys and girls. Before dues are designated, the teacher should consult with his principal concerning the policy of the school.

FOR STUDY AND DISCUSSION

1. Name ways in which a teacher of any grade (designating the grade level) can help create a classroom atmosphere which serves as useful background for the development of skills of oral communication.

2. What precautions can a teacher take, after the class has studied matters of social courtesy in telephoning, in conversation at mealtime, and in making or acknowledging introductions, that pupils whose parents do not observe the dictates of social custom will not look down upon their parents?

3. Design a bulletin board to be used in connection with work on development in ability (a) to participate in conversation, (b) to give interesting talks, or (c) to give clear directions or explanations. Designate the grade level for which the bulletin board is intended.

4. Write the words for a skit of the type that pupils can present (designating the grade level for which it is intended) highlighting a language arts learning. It may be on a topic such as (a) telephoning, (b) engaging in conversation, or (c) greeting callers.

5. Plan somewhat in detail an assembly program that can be presented by any one grade (designating the grade level). Your description should be of a program that is of decided value from the language arts point of view.

6. For a period of time take special note of any jokes that you hear a person give in a speech. If you note any, report which were relevant and which irrelevant to the talk.

7. Prepare a story suitable for telling to an age level of children with whom you are particularly interested in working. If possible, tell the story to your classmates and ask for their suggestions.

REFERENCES

Anderson, Paul S., *Language Skills in Elementary Education.* The Macmillan Company, 1964. 447 pp.

Eisenson, Jon, and Mardel Ogilvie, *Speech Correction in the Schools.* Second edition. The Macmillan Company, 1963. 399 pp.

MacCampbell, James E., (ed.) *Readings in the Language Arts in the Elementary School.* D. C. Heath and Company, 1964. 470 pp.

Pronovost, Wilbert, and Louise Kingman, *The Teaching and Listening in the Elementary School.* David McKay Company, 1959. 388 pp.

Shane, Harold G.; June G. Mulry; Mary E. Reddin; and Margaret C. Gillespie, *Improving Language Arts Instruction with Children.* Charles E. Merrill Books, 1962. 526 pp.

Trauger, Wilmer K., *Language Arts in Elementary Schools.* McGraw-Hill Book Company, 1963. 392 pp.

OUTLINE FOR CHAPTER 5

Guiding Growth in Written Expression

CHAPTER 5

Guiding Growth in Written Expression

Before entering elementary school, the child has made much progress in ability to communicate orally. In contrast, in many cases he has done no writing other than possibly his name. It does not follow, however, that he has not had significant preparation for development in this means of communication even though crude drawings and unintelligible scribblings may be the extent of objective evidence.

In preparation for more or less formal experiences in writing, the children assembling in September in a first-grade room show many differences. Some have backgrounds of rich experiences so full of interest that it will not be difficult to guide them in wanting to share them with others, both orally and later more permanently in writing; others come with very limited backgrounds. Some come from homes where parents have taken time to let the children dictate to them brief messages, maybe a sentence or two to include in a letter to a grandmother or grandfather; others come from an environment devoid of such experiences. Some have been drawing pictures as gifts for their parents, with or without dictation of what the picture means; others have not been given the satisfaction of realizing that the pictures they produce or even the scribbling that they do, with proper interpretation by an older person, forms a way of expressing their thoughts and a means of giving pleasure to others. Some have received letters which were read to them by grownups; others have had no correspondence addressed to them. Some have observed the satisfaction that older persons in the family receive from expressing their thoughts in writing; others have witnessed writing by others only as drudgery. Some have come to school with anticipation because older brothers and sisters have told them that they will learn to write; others have been discouraged by their peers concerning all school activities, including writing. Some have attended excellent kindergartens where writing readiness has been developed, often seemingly incidentally; others have not.

With such variation in preparation, highlighted by differences in native ability, the children come to the first grade ready or not ready to begin work in written expression. As the teacher in the first grade and those in subsequent grades ask themselves the question, "How can I best assist this child in acquiring or developing ability in the various types of writing that will help him express himself?" they should have in mind points such as the following:

1. The child has need to express himself adequately in writing in order to meet various requirements of the typical school.
2. Writing is important to the individual for utilitarian purposes in his adult life.
3. Writing is a means of self-expression which may be of therapeutic value to an individual, both as child and as adult.
4. Although the limits as to how far a person can progress in writing are set by his capacity as determined by his heredity, there is wide latitude in achievement for most individuals. In fact, most persons do not nearly approach their maximum possibilities that under proper guidance they could achieve in this and other areas.
5. Each child should find satisfaction in writing effectively so that he will develop the desire to continue to write and to improve in writing throughout his school years and later.

THE SCOPE OF THE PROGRAM

Written communication consists of the expression by the individual of his thoughts in written form and of comprehension of the words recorded by others. This chapter is devoted to the phase commonly referred to as writing. It deals with reading only insofar as the interrelationship between the two needs to be made clear when considering methods of teaching written expression. The development of some skills common to both oral and written communication, like correct usage, are studied in Chapter 6. Chapter 7 is devoted to the teaching of handwriting and Chapter 8 to spelling. In this chapter are given suggestions for helping children do the following: (1) write letters and reports, (2) do other types of practical writing (such as writing lists, filling in blanks, and keeping records), (3) do creative writing, (4) develop skill in using capital letters and punctuation marks, and (5) grow in writing through special activities (like publication of a paper).

General Objectives

The teacher should help the boys and girls to do the following:

1. Develop greater efficiency in all types of written expression that are on the level of the elementary-school child.
2. Attain proficiency in use of capital letters and punctuation marks.
3. Become effective in taking part in activities such as helping write a class or school paper or magazine or writing an original "book," either as a group or individual project.
4. Maintain or develop interest in writing and in writing well.
5. Develop those skills in written expression that are needed for effective participation in other areas of the curriculum.
6. Become increasingly considerate of the persons to or for whom they are writing.

Grade Placement

Since many boys and girls attend the first day of school with the idea that this day they will learn not only to read but also to write, it probably is wise not to disappoint the children by failing to provide opportunity to learn to write. To give the pupils a satisfying though very elementary start in learning to communicate through written symbols is doubly important because in many instances a child will at the end of the school day be asked, jokingly as far as the parents are concerned but seriously as far as the child knows, "Have you learned to write?" If first-grade teachers have children who have not previously learned to write their names, they may want to have copies ready of each pupil's name, written in manuscript on small cards, for distribution to every boy and girl in the room. Then, for example, when the children have drawn a picture, each pupil can write his name on his picture as he reproduces the copy given him. In many instances the teacher may need to have other means of identification, for the writing done by the child may not be legible enough to serve that purpose.

From the first grade to the end of the elementary school, the child should be helped to achieve the goals established for the program in written expression. He should be guided to attain them as rapidly as he can but without any haste or hurry and without neglecting other phases of the total curriculum. He will start work on some of the skills in the first grade and on others in subsequent grades.

After work on any skill has once begun, the skill should be further emphasized as the child progresses through the elementary school. This additional attention to it may be in terms of review as is the case, for example, if the child has learned to use a capital letter at the beginning of a sentence. To help the pupils make consistent use of what they have learned about capitalizing the first letter of the first word of a sentence, spaced practice is needed in many instances. In the case of many writing skills or abilities it is necessary, after a beginning that paid attention to only the rudimentary elements of a skill, to help the boys and girls acquire proficiency in the use of its other elements. For example, letter writing in its simplest form can be started in the first grade as the boys and girls dictate the message for a letter to the teacher, who writes the letter in three parts. Later additional features of letter writing can be added to the agenda of work to be learned in each of the succeeding grades.

GUIDELINES

The following are helpful guidelines for developing skill in written expression.

1. The teacher should recognize the close interrelatedness of written expression with other facets of the language arts.
2. Both content and form should be emphasized in written expression.
3. The boys and girls should have a purpose for any writing they do.
4. The work in written expression should be closely correlated and frequently integrated with other school activities.
5. There is a place for lessons that help pupils concentrate on how to improve upon their written expression.
6. The pupils should be helped to learn the qualities of effective writing.

7. The boys and girls should be provided with considerable opportunity for writing of various types like creative writing, letter writing, writing reviews or reports, writing announcements, outlining.

8. Forms for certain aspects of written work should be uniform throughout the elementary school, beginning possibly with the second or third grade. (Some matters in which there may well be uniformity are heading of papers, width of margins, method of folding papers, symbols used for indicating need of corrections.)

9. The pupils should be helped to recognize the style of writing, including vocabulary, which is suitable under various writing situations.

10. Boys and girls should understand policies followed in the evaluation and correction of written work.

11. The pupils should not be expected to write on topics about which they know little.

GRADATIONS IN DEVELOPMENT OF GROWTH IN WRITTEN EXPRESSION

From the time a child enters until he finishes the elementary school, he typically progresses from a stage where he is unable to write to one where he can record his thoughts fairly well and often independently. The stages through which he passes may be identified thus: (1) readiness for writing, (2) dictation, (3) copying, and (4) writing by the pupil, developing from decided dependence to considerable independence.

Readiness for Writing

The teacher can be of aid to the child as he becomes ready for the initial experiences in expressing himself through writing by: (1) making him feel secure in his classroom, (2) helping him achieve an attention span favorable for writing, (3) helping him realize some of the values to be obtained through writing, (4) broadening his experience background, and (5) providing him with many opportunities for oral communication.

DEVELOPING A SENSE OF SECURITY. The child who is not assured of the good will and confidence of his peers and his teacher is not as likely to want to write as the one who feels secure. He will frequently be so tense that he cannot free himself of his feelings of insecurity long enough to concentrate on writing.

ACHIEVING A LENGTHENED ATTENTION SPAN. Since writing usually requires concentrated work, especially for the beginner, some boys and girls seem to be unable to write well in part because of the brevity of their attention span. As their minds flit from one thought to another, often wholly unrelated to the writing that they presumably are doing, the writing either stops entirely or ceases to be effective. Furthermore, because of lack of desirable results from such attempts, the pupil is likely to develop an aversion to writing that will increase his difficulties in concentrating on it at future times.

What can the first-grade teacher do to help the child increase his attention span? Here are a few suggestions:

1. Compliment a child when he has shown perseverance in a task.

2. Discuss with a child from time to time the importance of attending to one thing at a time.

3. Provide an environment for writing that is free from a large number of overstimulating and distracting factors.

4. Have work requiring concentration come when the child is not fatigued.

5. Do not expect the child to engage in an activity longer than he is likely to be able to pay the needed attention.

6. In harmony with the child's maturity, continue to increase the length of time when he is engaged in various activities requiring considerable concentration.

REALIZATION OF VALUES ATTAINABLE. Since one of the best ways to prepare boys and girls for writing experiences is to interest them in writing, anything done to help them realize the values they can acquire through writing can serve as means for developing readiness for it. Some of the ways in which beginning first-grade children can learn to see reasons for expressing themselves through written symbols are:

1. Telling what they think may be the writing under a picture in a book that the teacher is reading to them and then being told what it is

2. Taking home to their parents duplicated lists of things needed or some other message that the boys and girls recognize as important for their parents

3. Noting the many types of written materials in the room and their use on bulletin boards and on tables in the form of labels, pictures with brief explanations, posters with captions, magazines, and books

4. Discussing why it would be convenient to know how to record one's thoughts.

BROADENING THE EXPERIENCE BACKGROUND. The first-grade teacher can help his pupils extend their experiences so that they will be more ready for writing by:

1. Providing many interesting and informative pictures and discussing them with the children
2. Having a sharing table on which the boys and girls display objects of interest
3. Having exhibits for which the teacher himself provides the materials
4. Taking the children on field trips of various types
5. Having speakers come to the room to talk
6. Showing films and filmstrips
7. Making available good television programs
8. Telling or reading stories to the children.

Providing Opportunities for Oral Communication. Because of the close interrelationship between oral communication and written expression, much can be done by the teacher of pupils in the first grade, through providing opportunities for oral communication, in fostering readiness for giving expression to their thoughts. Some means are as follows:

1. Maintaining a classroom atmosphere in which talking at appropriate times is encouraged
2. Providing children with much opportunity for listening to worthwhile and interesting oral means of communication
3. Letting boys and girls meet in small groups for discussion purposes
4. Providing time for unstructured dramatic experiences
5. Encouraging boys and girls to dramatize stories
6. Having a telling time.

Dictation by the Teacher

After the pupils have attained reasonable readiness to start expressing themselves through the written symbols, they are prepared to dictate their thoughts, individually or in a group, to their teacher.

Occasions for Dictating. The school day affords many occasions for pupils to dictate their thoughts. Here are only a few:

1. Telling a "make-up story"
2. Making plans for the day's activities
3. Listing articles needed for a project
4. Listing plans for a project
5. Listing questions to ask a person who will speak to the group or who will show them something (like the farmer whose farm is to be visited)
6. Giving information about the work of one's father for a class booklet
7. Reporting on an experience
8. Dictating a letter (possibly to a sick child or to someone who assisted the class in a project).

Sequence in Method of Dictating. When the child first starts dictating to the teacher, it is desirable to have only brief records made. He may help compose a list of articles that he needs to bring from home or a one-sentence note to take home, or he may give a name to a picture he has drawn, which the teacher writes below it.

When the child starts giving dictation of more than a list of items or of more than one sentence, the teacher may want to record verbatim what the child is saying without stopping him to improve upon points such as sentence structure, sequence, or vocabulary. Through interruptions for errors in form during the early stages of dictation, the teacher may make the child lose desired spontaneity of expression as he might then be concentrating on how he says something rather than on what he is saying. After the teacher has recorded all the pupil wishes to say, the teacher can do the necessary editorial work as he rewrites the material. He should not make so many changes that the thoughts are chiefly the teacher's rather than the child's.

A more advanced step in dictation is reached when the pupil is able to take responsibility for improvement of parts of what he is dictating or to note corrections by the teacher before the latter makes a record of some points the child has named. For example, when the child gives a statement out of order, the teacher may ask, "But what is the next thing that happened?" or when the child uses *ran* instead of *run*, he may say, "Let's say, 'Toy had *run* home.'" Prompting the child by asking, "What do we want to say next in our report?" also may help the learner to do more organized thinking. When the first draft has been written, it is suggested that the teacher read it to the child to see if he has any suggestions for improvement. It is at this time that the teacher may wish to recommend further changes, possibly through questioning the child.

When a group of boys and girls rather than only one child dictate to the teacher, a similar sequence of procedure from less to more complex planning is recommended.

The Language Experience Chart. The experience chart is a record of happenings dictated by the boys and girls to the teacher. Two somewhat distinct types are recognizable – the reading chart and the chart which for lack of a more descriptive name is at times referred to as the language or language arts chart. The difference is primarily one of purpose. Important in the planning of a reading chart is the fact that the boys and girls will get practice in "reading" the material they have dictated. This type of chart constitutes an important element of the reading-readiness program in many first-grade rooms. The language-arts chart is not designed chiefly for use in progress in reading but is made primarily for a record of the content and for experience in language activities other than reading.

For a rather detailed description of the reading experience chart the reader is referred to page 184 and to page 310. In addition to the difference in purpose, the language-arts experience chart differs from the reading chart primarily in the following respects:

1. Less attention needs to be paid in the language-arts chart to keeping the vocabulary restricted.

2. Less practice is usually needed in reading the language-arts chart than in reading the reading chart since mastery of vocabulary is not as likely to be a major purpose for which the former was constructed.

Copying

Copying, in one sense, is not a stage distinct from dictating. In fact, it can be thought of as an act that accompanies much of the dictating to the teacher by the boys and girls.

At first when children dictate material to the teacher, they may have no part in the actual writing. At such times the final draft may be in the form of a teacher-written chart, a chalkboard record, or a copy typewritten or written in manuscript on a piece of paper or it may be a duplicated copy of what the teacher has written. A beginning step toward pupil participation in writing may be the actual copying of the entire message by them from the copy that the teacher made. It is difficult for beginners to copy from a large piece of paper posted on the wall or from the chalkboard because of the distance between them and the copy and because of the difference in size between the original and the copy they are making. It, therefore, is advisable that in the early stages of copying the child have a copy of the writing on a sheet of paper on his table. This could be in the teacher's own manuscript writing. Incentive for copying may result from mention of the fact that the child's parents would enjoy receiving a note in his own writing or would like to read, in the child's handwriting, the story that he has dictated.

Greater independence in copying may be achieved as the child copies a report or story or letter written only in part by the teacher and then adds a sentence or two of his own, with help from the teacher. At times all but the ending of a story or letter could be duplicated and then each child make up his own ending.

Writing by the Pupils

The final stage in learning to write is the semi-independent or independent writing by the child. The pupil is not ready for this stage until he can write the letters that he knows he needs for the words he will record and until he has acquired some skill in spelling some of the words that he will want to use in written expression.

Sufficient experience background and opportunity for discussion preceding the writing are of particular importance for the child who is a novice at writing. Frequently such a child may be given the chance to talk on the topic on which he will later write. In this way at a time when the act of writing is still accompanied by need of much attention to the mechanics of writing, the child is not also burdened while writing by trying at the same time to decide what he wants to write.

When the pupil first begins writing without a copy, the teacher should be readily available for help. Some teachers may want only a relatively small proportion of the class to write at one time so that they can give much individual help to these pupils while the others are engaged in activities that do not require supervision.

Assistance in Spelling. Teachers can handle the problem of words that the writers can not spell in various ways. Here are some suggestions.

1. Before the boys and girls begin writing, the pupils can think through what they wish to write and then ask for the spelling of words with which they think they may have trouble. The teacher can write these words on the chalkboard.

Figure 5.1 The Chalkboard as an Aid to Spelling

2. If all the boys and girls are writing on the same topic, such as "A Christmas Dream," the teacher may write on the chalkboard words that are later likely to be used by many – words that might, without help available, cause difficulties in spelling, such as *dream, Christmas, Santa Claus, gift, present.*

3. When the pupils come to a word in their writing that they can not spell, they may leave a blank space on their paper and continue writing until the teacher has time to help them as he progresses around the group. The teacher can then write on a slip of paper the word or words that the pupil requests.

4. Each child can develop a small file of spelling words, arranged according to the first letter of a word, which he can use when writing.

5. As soon as a pupil has developed skill in looking up the spelling of a word in a dictionary, he should be encouraged to make use of that tool.

DEVELOPMENT IN ABILITY TO WRITE LETTERS

With the possible exception of note-taking, none of the types of written expression is employed more frequently than letter writing. Because teachers recognize the importance of providing help in letter writing, the subject has been included in the curriculum throughout the elementary school, in many instances starting even in the kindergarten and continuing in high school. In spite of all the attention that has been afforded the topic, the letters written by many adults are woefully lacking in both form and content. Furthermore, for a variety of reasons many letters that should be written never materialize.

With facts like these in mind, teachers are asking in effect, "What can we do to make the work on letter writing more effective?" This section of this chapter gives a partial answer to the elementary-school teacher by means of consideration of these questions: (1) What do boys and girls need to learn about letter writing? (2) In what sequence and on what grade levels should guidance in meeting these needs be provided? (3) What guidelines should the teacher observe when teaching letter writing? (4) What additional suggestions are valuable in teaching the writing of personal letters? (5) What additional suggestions are valuable in teaching the writing of business letters?

Learnings to Be Acquired

The learnings to be acquired in relation to letter writing can be divided as to knowledge, abilities, and attitudes. It is according to this classification that they are here discussed.

Knowledge to be Acquired. Instruction in the elementary school should be geared so that the child acquires the following knowledge about letter writing:

1. The type of paper that is acceptable for writing letters for various purposes
2. The medium – pen, pencil, or typewriter – appropriate for writing various types of letters under differing circumstances
3. The color of ink to be used when a letter is written in ink
4. The parts of a letter, personal and business, and the reason for each part
5. The points to be included in the heading, inside address (in case of a business letter) salutation, complimentary close, and signature
6. The placement of the items in the various parts of a letter in relation to the page and to one another
7. The capitalization and punctuation of the parts of a letter
8. The points of importance to note in relation to the body or message of various types of letters
9. Acceptable methods of folding a letter
10. The points to be included in the send and return addresses on an envelope
11. The placement of the various items of the send and return addresses on an envelope in relation to the envelope and to one another
12. The placement of the postage stamp
13. Methods of determining how much postage is required.

Abilities to Be Developed. Acquisition of the knowledge needed concerning letter writing is not enough. Knowledge does not insure ability. The teacher thus will want to make certain that the boys and girls will make use of the various items of knowledge listed in the preceding paragraph.

Attitudes to Be Developed. How a child feels about letter writing is going to determine to a considerable extent his effectiveness in it while he is in school and when he is on his own. Indicated below are some of the attitudes the teacher will want to try to help boys and girls develop.

1. The pupils should want to be careful that their letters will seem courteous to the recipient.
2. The boys and girls should understand that when they receive letters that seemingly are lacking in courtesy the writer may not have intended to be discourteous.
3. The pupils should desire to be as prompt in writing letters as the situations demand.

Figure 5.2 A Chart to Emphasize How Addresses Should be Written on Envelopes

Dear Jim,

We miss you.

This is a picture of

my new fire-engine.

It has a ladder.

Dan

Figure 5.3 A Three-Part Letter

Dear Mr. Warner,

We had a good time at your farm. We learned about your animals. Thank you for showing us your farm.

The First Grade

Figure 5.4 Letter Writing, A Cooperative Venture in the First Grade

4. The boys and girls should want to be prompt in mailing letters that they have written.
5. The pupils should be tolerant of the errors of others but critical of their own.
6. The pupils should be interested in putting into effect everything they know about letter writing.

Sequence and Grade Placement

In what order should the various learnings be acquired and on what grade levels? Courses of study and expert opinion expressed in other ways show lack of uniformity. Furthermore, research does not provide us with the answer. However, the following points indicate areas of general agreement.

1. In the kindergarten or first grade the letters which then ordinarily consist of but three parts – the greeting, the body, and the signature – are usually composed by the group and written by the teacher on the chalkboard or on large sheets of paper such as newsprint. Then the letter is frequently duplicated and copies distributed to the children. At times one or more pupils in the later months of the first grade copy the letter.
2. The five-part personal letter is often introduced in the upper primary or lower intermediate grades.
3. Beginning in the second grade, the boys and girls often write letters individually, frequently with help from the teacher.
4. Writing of composite letters by the group is often continued even after pupils have begun independent writing of letters.
5. When boys and girls can use a pen effectively, the pencil is often discarded for letter-writing purposes.
6. Emphasis is usually not placed on business letters before considerable skill in writing personal letters has been acquired.

Guidelines

Guidelines for the teacher to follow in teaching letter writing, such as those given following, will help him in deciding upon more specific points of pro-

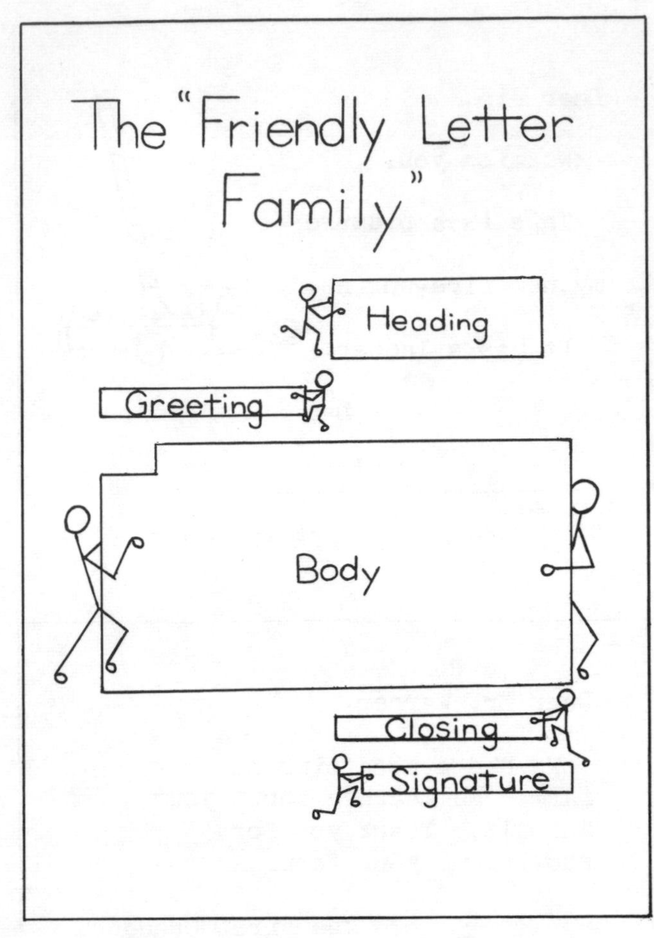

Figure 5.5 The Five-Part Letter

cedure than those enumerated in the preceding paragraph.

1. Writing of the usual type of personal letter (not a letter of complaint, for example) should be taught in such a manner that it becomes an activity that the writer enjoys, not a chore that he tries to avoid.

2. Much of the work in letter writing should consist of writing bona fide letters.

3. In addition to writing of meaningful letters that are to be sent, provisions should be made for lessons devoted primarily to helping boys and girls master the skills of letter writing.

4. The pupils should be allowed to write some of their own letters at school, aside from any school assignment.

Methods

Suggested following are procedures applicable to both personal and business letters. Those that pertain only to letters of one of these two categories are given in the next two sections of this chapter, where special consideration is given to each of these two types. In connection with either personal or business letters the pupils may do the following:

1. Examine letters that have been posted on a bulletin board.

2. Examine a bulletin board on which is posted a chart showing a neat letter written in ink and on proper writing materials as well as a letter in sharp contrast with it. A question like "Which Kind of Letter Do You Write?" can be posted near the illustrations on the bulletin board.

3. Make or help make a chart on which lines are drawn showing where various parts of a letter should be written. While the following lines indicate how the placement of the parts of a business letter can be shown, a similar diagram can be made for a personal letter.

Figure 5.6 Form of a Business Letter

4. Participate in discussion on various phases of letter writing.

5. Assist in making a check list for evaluating letters.

6. Make a list of different types of situations for which boys and girls on their grade level might need to write letters.

7. Participate in a skit or observe one which shows the reactions of recipients of well written and poorly written letters.

8. Make or contribute to making a booklet on letter writing. Such a booklet may contain samples of well-written letters of all types studied; poorly writ-

ten letters with comments as to how the letters can be improved; explanations of the purpose of various parts of letters; rules for writing various types of letters; an explanation as to how courtesy can be shown in letter writing; examples of envelopes written in block and in slant style (if both are taught); an article on "The Story of a Letter"; information about the Post Office Department; and a report on the history of written communication.

9. Do exercises similar to those to which reference is made on page 303.

Additional Suggestions Concerning Personal Letters

As indicated earlier, the comments about letter writing in the preceding pages are applicable to both personal and business letters. Let us now consider some additional points about personal letters.

Types of Personal Letters. The following types of personal letters may advisedly be studied somewhere in the elementary school: the usual so-called friendly letter, the letter of congratulation or praise, the letter expressing sympathy, the letter of invitation, the letter of acceptance of an invitation, the letter of regrets in answer to an invitation, the letter of apology, the letter of complaint, the thank-you letter.

1. The usual friendly letter. The following are some of the learnings about the usual friendly letter that boys and girls should acquire.

> The content should be of interest to the person to whom the letter is written.
>
> Questions should be asked or comments made about the welfare or other concerns of the person to whom the letter is written.
>
> The writer should, as a rule, avoid brief reference to many topics, for more detailed treatment of fewer is more interesting.
>
> The style should be appropriate to communication with the person to whom the letter is written. (The tone of a letter addressed to Grandmother should be more dignified than one written to a classmate.)
>
> The letter should be friendly. (There is no place in it for anger, discourtesy, irritation.)
>
> The letter should express opinions of the writer.
>
> The letter should be free of trite statements like "I have wanted to write to you for a long time but . . . ." or "I better quit or you will be too tired to finish reading this."

2. The letter of congratulation. Boys and girls have opportunity to write letters of congratulation when friends have achieved an honor or have done something praiseworthy without recognition for it. These are a few specific situations that may call for a letter of congratulation or praise from a pupil in the elementary school: (a) A classmate has received a medal at a pet show. (b) A friend has been chosen to represent the Brownies at a district camp. (c) A friend has shown bravery in a situation.

A few points to be noted about writing letters of congratulation or praise are as follows:

> The letter should make clear for what event or achievement the person to whom the letter is written is being complimented or congratulated.
>
> The expression of congratulation or praise must be sincere.
>
> The wording should be such as to convey real appreciation without showing exaggeration.
>
> The letter should not include any statements that may detract from the expression of congratulation or praise. For example, the following would violate this requirement: (a) I want to congratulate you on having won second place in the pet show. Isn't it too bad that you did not get first place? (b) I want to congratulate you on having won second place in the pet show. I know it is the first time that you have won a place in the pet show. My sister won second place two years and first place one year.

3. The letter of sympathy. Even boys and girls in the elementary school have occasion to write letters of sympathy. Sympathy can be expressed by them to a sick friend, to a person who has been in an accident, or to someone whose relative has died.

Expression of sympathy can be included in the usual friendly letter or in a letter in which nothing else is discussed. If sympathy is expressed in the usual friendly letter, the tone of the rest of the letter must be in harmony with the expression of sympathy. Nothing should be included in it that would be likely to make the recipient more unhappy than he probably is. For example, in a letter to a boy who has broken his leg, inclusion of a part like this would show poor judgment: "I know you hate to miss the baseball game this Friday afternoon. Why did you have to break your leg just at this time? I surely am thankful that I don't have a broken leg and have to miss that game."

4. The letter of invitation, the letter of acceptance, and the letter of regret. Boys and girls may write letters inviting (a) their parents to school, (b) the principal to see an exhibit in their room, (c) the pupils of another room to come to a program they are giving,

or (d) a person who helped them with a study of a unit of work in science or the social studies to come to their culminating activity for that unit.

Elementary-school pupils at times have need for writing invitations outside of school when, for example, they invite someone to a party or to be a week-end guest.

For both school and out-of-school use pupils will need to know how to answer invitations and how to accept them or send their regrets. They should learn what points should be included in a letter of invitation, namely: (a) a clear statement as to the event to which the person is being invited, (b) the exact time of the event, and (c) the place where the event is to take place. Sometimes additional information is necessary. For example, if the party is a birthday party, it may be advisable to make clear whether or not presents are intended. At times it is desirable to let the person to whom the invitation is extended know the length of time of the event. If there is to be an admission charge to an event, the amount of admission should be stated in the invitation.

Boys and girls should be taught the following:

That every letter of invitation should say something that makes the person invited feel he is really wanted

That courtesy, as a rule, demands an answer to invitations either in the form of acceptance or regrets. The pupils could also be helped to understand when responses are not mandatory, as, for example, when all the boys and girls in a school are invited to an ice-cream social for which there is a charge

That when an invitation is extended in writing, it usually should be answered in writing

That regardless of whether or not an invitation is accepted, in replying the person invited should thank the sender of the invitation

That in a letter of acceptance it is important to restate the time and place of the event for which an invitation has been extended, since such a statement can help clear up any misunderstanding as to time or place

That preferably in a letter of regret the writer should as a rule, possibly in general terms, indicate why he cannot accept the invitation.

5. The letter of apology. One of the ways boys and girls can express their regret about their wrongdoings or unintentional inconveniencing, harming, or saddening of others is through the letter of apology. The following situations are typical of some of the times when letters of apology by elementary-school children may be in order: (a) when a boy or girl has unintentionally run over and broken a plant that his neighbor, who is out of town, has in his yard; (b) when a person is sorry for an unkind remark he has made; (c) when children playing ball have broken a window in the home of a neighbor who is out of town; (d) when a discourtesy has been shown to a speaker or visitor in a classroom.

These are some of the points that boys and girls should be taught about writing letters of apology:

That it is usually better to apologize in person than by letter if the individual is within reasonable distance from the one to whom an apology is due

That at times, even after one has apologized in person, it is courteous and thoughtful to write a letter of apology also

That if a person has unintentionally acted in such a manner as to make necessary an apology, it is often advisable to explain how he happened to act as he did

That if an individual has done something to require an apology, he should make it clear that he is genuinely sorry for his action. (An apology that is not genuine should not be written.)

That if a person can make amends for what he has done, it is important to state what he will do or to ask what he can do to try to make up, at least in part, for his actions

That if a letter of apology is desirable, it should be sent promptly

That if a person receives an apology, he should be forgiving and let the person who apologized know that he holds no grudge.

6. The letter of complaint. Boys and girls may send a letter of complaint, other than in business situations, on occasions such as the following: (a) if an exhibit that a class has put in the hall is being molested by pupils from another room; (b) if a speaker who has been engaged by a class to speak at a program to which pupils from another room have been invited is not treated with politeness by the visitors.

These are some of the points about personal letters of complaint that boys and girls should learn:

That it is often better to state a complaint orally rather than in writing

That the writer should be careful not to attach wrong motives to the person to whom he is complaining. It is well to assume that the possible offender may be innocent in this respect unless he has been proved guilty

That a letter of complaint should be written with great courtesy.

7. The thank-you letter. Pupils can write letters thanking: (a) boys and girls from another room who have invited them to a program or an exhibit; (b) pupils in an upper grade who have done something for the room, such as making a pen for a pet rabbit belonging to first-grade pupils; (c) a person who has served as speaker or who has allowed them to visit a farm, bakery, fire station, or other place on a field trip; (d) parents when pupils are away from home.

Some points about writing thank-you letters that children should learn are:

The importance of writing thank-you letters promptly

The fact that frequently even if one has thanked a person orally it is also desirable to send him a thank-you letter

The desirability of saying something about a gift for which one is thanking the giver

The importance of trying to write a letter of thank-you in such a manner that the recipient will be convinced of one's gratitude.

Methods. Below are several suggestions for methods of procedure that apply in particular to writing of personal letters.

1. The boys and girls can evaluate a group of statements by writing *Yes* on the line to the left of a statement if it is a desirable statement to include in a thank-you letter and by writing *No* if it is undesirable. Statements such as these may be listed:

........Thank you for the gift that you sent me even though I wish you had sent me money instead.

........It was kind of you to send me a pencil with my name on it. I wish you could see some of the presents that I received. Some are very expensive. My aunt sent me a transistor radio.

2. The boys and girls can indicate by writing *Yes* or *No* which statements of a list are suitable for inclusion in the usual friendly letter and in some of the various special types of personal letters such as those of complaint, of invitation (as well as acceptance or regret), of apology, of sympathy, or of congratulations or praise.

3. Some of the pupils can put on a skit in which they show the right and wrong way in which to write a letter of complaint. One part of the skit can show what effect a letter written by a person who was angry may have upon the recipient. In the other part there can be shown how a letter of complaint was written in such a way that it had no undesirable effect upon the receiver.

4. The group can draw up a check list of points by means of which to appraise each of the various types of personal letters.

Additional Suggestions Concerning Business Letters

Here are a few additional points that should be emphasized in writing all types of business letters.

1. A business letter should have an inside address.

2. Some salutations and complimentary closings that are appropriate for personal letters are inappropriate for business letters and vice versa.

3. A colon should be the final punctuation mark of the salutation of a business letter.

4. A business letter should be as brief as possible while still including all needed information, expressed in good English and with politeness.

5. The signature of a business letter is often different from that of a personal letter.

6. Some types of stationery that are suitable for personal letters are inappropriate for business letters.

Types of Business Letters. Boys and girls in the elementary school have occasion to write business letters of the following types, either as class projects or as individual writing: (1) letters ordering things, (2) requests for free materials, (3) requests for services, (4) letters of complaint, and even (5) letters of application.

1. Letters ordering things. Pupils at times order books by mail. They also order other articles such as model airplane kits, small rock exhibits, pets (like hamsters), shell exhibits. Some learnings that boys and girls should acquire about writing letters ordering things are:

The need of checking on the reliability of a firm

An evaluation of the true worth of an article they wish to order

A careful decision as to whether the article will most likely meet their needs

Knowledge of items to include in a letter ordering things and of the method in which they should be included in a business letter, such as the title and author of a book; the catalog number of an article other than a book, with exact specifications as to size, color, etc.; a statement as to how the article will be paid for;

inclusion of a check or money order unless the thing ordered is to be sent COD; the correct way of writing dollars and cents in a business letter.

2. Requests for free materials. Both in and out of school boys and girls write letters requesting free materials from travel agencies, chambers of commerce, publishing companies (copies of catalogs, for example), manufacturing companies, consuls, state departments, and many other sources. (Since companies have been bombarded with letters asking for free materials, it is important that boys and girls learn to judge when it is right and when it is not right for them to request materials.)

Here are a few additional learnings that boys and girls should acquire concerning the writing of letters asking for free materials.

> The writer should state clearly why he wants the materials he requests.
>
> As many specifications as are valuable to insure getting only what is useful should be stated. (For example, if a fourth-grade child is requesting material on England, he should indicate his grade level.)
>
> When a letter asking for free material is composed as a class project, only one copy of the letter should be mailed so that unnecessary time is not spent by the recipient of the request in reading many letters.
>
> An expression of thanks should be made in every letter requesting free materials.

3. Requests for services. The following are examples of situations in which pupils find reasons for writing business letters requesting the services of others.

> The class wants permission to make a field trip to a bakery, post office, fire station, telephone office, telegraph office.
>
> The class would like to have someone talk to them on a specified subject.
>
> One or more pupils would like to have the opportunity to interview someone about a matter of significance to the class.

The following are points for boys and girls to note when writing letters requesting services.

> The letter should include information such as (a) what services are wanted; (b) by whom the services are wanted; (c) for what purpose they are wanted; (d) when they are wanted; (e) who the writer of the letter is.
>
> The letter should be businesslike in wording.
>
> The letter should show appreciation for consideration of the request. A self-addressed stamped envelope should, under many circumstances, be enclosed.

4. Letters of complaint. Business letters of complaint are still another type of letter that boys and girls may need to write in situations such as these: (a) when an article that has been ordered is not satisfactory; (b) when material that has been ordered has not been delivered.

Points listed in connection with the personal letter of complaint (nonbusiness letter) in a preceding part of this chapter apply also to business letters of the same type. In the case of an article that has been ordered which proves unsatisfactory, the letter should indicate when the article was ordered and explain what is wrong with it. Inquiry may also be made as to which of several possible procedures should be followed in making up for the deficiency.

5. Letters of application. Although most applications for work made by boys and girls (for example, work as lawn boy, errand boy, newspaper carrier, or baby sitter) should be made in person, there are times when a written application seems preferable. When writing a letter of application the writer should remember that:

> It is important to make the letter as nearly perfect as possible since the applicant will probably be judged in part by the letter.
>
> The letter should ask that the writer be considered for the work, give his age and grade level, describe his business experience (if any), supply the employer with names and addresses of persons (other than relatives) who will serve as references, and express appreciation for the consideration that may be given the application.

6. Other business letters. Occasionally boys and girls will find need for writing thank-you letters that are also business letters. They may, for instance, thank a travel bureau for a generous supply of free materials of use in a unit in the social studies or they may write a letter of thanks to the city council for having taken measures to insure greater safety around the school.

There may be occasion when business letters of apology need to be written by elementary-school pupils. One such situation might arise when a class had previously sent a letter of complaint stating that an article ordered had not been received, only to find out that it had reached the school promptly but, through no fault of the sender had not been delivered to the right persons.

METHODS. On page 70 reference is made to methods that apply to both personal and business letters. The statements that follow indicate additional points of procedure for helping boys and girls write effective business letters.

1. On the bulletin board may be exhibited various types of business letters, some well and others poorly written, for evaluation by the boys and girls.

2. The pupils may check a series of statements, some well and some poorly expressed, in a business letter of complaint.

3. A business man may talk to the class about desirable and undesirable features in business letters that he and others in his company receive.

DEVELOPMENT IN ABILITY TO WRITE REPORTS

It should be noted that many of the suggestions given in Chapter 4 in relation to oral reports (beginning on page 42) also apply to written reports.

Guidelines

Helpful guidelines for the teacher when assisting pupils in development of ability to write reports are as follows.

1. There should be a purpose for written reports that the boys and girls recognize as worthwhile.

2. At times the purpose the pupils have for writing reports may be, at least in part, that of perfecting language-arts skills important in writing reports.

3. The person making a written report should know well the topic on which he writes.

Courtesy of the Gary, Indiana, Public Schools

Figure 5.7 Research as an Aid to Report Writing

4. Oral work frequently should precede the writing of reports.

5. When writing reports boys and girls should try to apply everything they have learned about writing regardless of whether the reports are for a language-arts class or for one in the social studies or other content areas.

6. Boys and girls should be encouraged to show originality of expression.

Methods

Suggested procedures for guiding growth in writing reports are as follows:

1. In the lower primary grades the pupils may as a group make an experience chart as described in Chapter 14.

2. Even in the intermediate grades the pupils may at times work as a group on a brief report. The procedure can be that of the class first discussing what may be included in the report and then giving sentence after sentence as the teacher writes them on the chalkboard. The pupils then can read the report and decide upon improvements to be made.

3. For longer reports suggestions can be given by the group as to the type of information that should be included. For example, if a committee had decided to write a report on Christopher Columbus for reading to others in the room on October 12, they may first of all make an outline similar to the following, which can be recorded on the chalkboard:

Early life
Plans
Search for aid
First voyage
Later voyages and death.

Next, the pupils can suggest different points that should be included under the various parts of the outline. A note written under "Early life" might be "place and date of birth"; under "Plans" a note might state "different from what others believed." After the note-writing has been completed, individual pupils may be assigned various parts to write, with the understanding that they can later get help from others in revising their reports.

4. In the lower grades the pupils can report on happenings by drawing a series of illustrations with or without captions or sentences to explain each. If they made a mask out of a paper bag, they may report by using illustrations of the steps like these:

Get a bag. Cut. Color. Paste.

5. The boys and girls can make a notebook on the topics of various units in the social studies or science in which reports are included. For example, in a unit on famous persons a notebook can be made by each pupil in which he writes on various phases of the life of the person he studied. A class notebook may be made to which each pupil contributes a report. In the lower grades in a notebook on "Our Homes" single sentences or simple paragraphs of possibly not more than two or three sentences can explain illustrations drawn by the pupils.

6. Accordion-like illustrated folders can be made by individuals or groups of pupils. To these folders, made of heavy paper such as mounting board, can be attached illustrations of steps in a process with a brief explanation of each step written on the part of the folder immediately preceding or following the illustration. On such a folder, for example, the steps in mailing a letter or in making applesauce can be indicated.

7. While working on a unit in science on "The Sky above Us" the boys and girls can put on an imitation broadcast in which they read reports some of them have written. In some communities opportunity may be given for actual broadcasts on a radio station of reports written by pupils on topics of general interest to the public. In schools with a public address system the boys and girls can broadcast on a topic of interest to the school audience.

8. The pupils may make an illustrated report on something they have studied by drawing a mural, supplemented by a booklet in which are given reports explaining the illustrations. For example, they may illustrate life in Colonial times and write reports to accompany the mural on topics such as "The First Permanent English Settlement in America," "The Year 1619 in the Virginia Colony," "Life in Old Plymouth." The booklet can be made available for reading by visitors to the room.

9. The boys and girls may make a "movie" showing the chief events in the life of a person like Thomas Edison or Abraham Lincoln or Marian Anderson, and write a booklet containing reports on various events of importance in the life of the person depicted. In lower grades a "movie" may be made on "Our Community Helpers" with possibly only a sentence or two explaining the work of each helper pictured.

10. Logs or diaries form another type of report writing. The diaries or logs may be kept on the pupil's own activities or on those of the class. In some cases, in connection with work in the social studies, the boys and girls may like to write imaginary diaries of persons, real or fictitious, of long ago. To make such

diaries worthwhile it is important that the writers be well acquainted with the life of the times about which they are writing.

11. Class books and class papers furnish excellent incentive for report writing. (For discussion of this topic the reader is referred to page 94.)

12. Reading of material on report writing and then discussing it can be a worthwhile activity for pupils.

13. Comparing the qualities of well and of poorly written reports can serve useful purposes.

Book Reports

Many of the suggestions given for oral book reports, (page 44) as well as those in the pages immediately preceding this one in relation to written reports in general, also apply to written book reports. Consequently only a few additional points are made here.

1. *Frequently oral reports should precede written.* However, it is not necessary that all reports given orally should be written, or that all that are written should be given orally.

2. *The boys and girls should recognize a real purpose for the reports they write.* They may write to keep a record of their reading for their own future reference or for the benefit of others.

3. *Book reports can be preserved in various ways.* They may be kept on cards for individual files of the reader or for a common file to which all pupils in the room have access. They may be kept in loose-leaf notebooks, one for each child, or in a notebook on book reports for the whole grade. Some may be selected for inclusion in a class paper. Posting book reports, with pictures or objects to illustrate them, serves as incentive for writing and for reading. Book reports in connection with a unit in the content subjects can form part of an exhibit of materials of interest on the unit.

4. *Written reports should be brief.* If boys and girls in the elementary school are required to write long book reports on all books they read, they may be discouraged from doing much reading.

5. *The form of written reports can be worked out by the group.* This suggestion is of special value if the reports are to be used in a common file or in a class notebook of book reports. Points such as the following may be included in the lower grades:

Author
Title
What the book is about
More about the book
Name of the writer of the report
Date of writing the report.

For intermediate grades items such as these may be suggested or required:

Bibliographical data (author, title, publisher, address of publisher, date of publication)
Summary of the book (in one or a few sentences)
Interesting incidents or significant information
Writer's opinion of the book
Signature of the person making the report
Date of writing the report.

6. *Even if a form is worked out by the class for use for most written reports, originality on the part of boys and girls in writing book reports should be encouraged.* The pupils can be helped to understand how even when following a form that has been agreed upon, they can show originality in their comments summarizing a book, describing one or more incidents, stating significant information, or expressing their opinion of the book. At times they may want to write some of their reports without following a given form.

7. *The pupils can help in making a score sheet for evaluating written book reports.* If a score sheet is constructed, the pupils should have opportunity to evaluate book reports by using it.

DEVELOPMENT IN ABILITY IN OTHER TYPES OF PRACTICAL WRITTEN EXPRESSION

In addition to writing letters and reports elementary-school pupils have need for learning how to do the following types of practical writing: (1) writing lists, (2) filling in blanks, (3) writing announcements, explanations, and directions, (4) keeping records, (5) writing bibliographical data, (6) taking notes, and (7) outlining.

Writing Lists

Even before the beginner in the elementary school can make his own lists, there often are many opportunities for him to participate in helping with lists which the teacher records on the chalkboard or on large sheets of paper. Often beginning some time in the first grade the pupils copy some of these cooperatively constructed lists and later boys and girls in the modern elementary school have frequent occasion to make lists of their own.

TYPES OF LISTS. Some of the types of lists that the elementary-school child can make or participate in making are:

1. Names of pupils who are absent
2. Names of boys and girls who want milk or juice or lunch
3. Names of pupils who have been assigned special duties like watering flowers, arranging books on the library shelf, passing the wastepaper basket
4. Names of persons who have made a contribution to a given cause
5. Names of persons who have not returned permission slips
6. Names of important people studied in a unit of work
7. Materials needed for a proposed project or experiment
8. Questions to be studied in a proposed unit of work

OUR QUESTIONS ABOUT THE DUTCH IN AMERICA

1. Why did the Dutch come to America?
2. When did they come to America?
3. Where did they settle?
4. What work did they do?
5. Who were the leaders?
6. What were their schools like?
7. What were their churches like?
8. Did they have any interesting customs?
9. Why did the English take the land away from the Dutch?
10. What did the Dutch do after the English took their land away from them?

Figure 5.8 Questions as a Means of Giving Direction in the Study of a Unit

9. "New words"
10. Minimum essentials to be learned
11. Flowers or birds or trees.

Points to Learn. Boys and girls should, if necessary, be helped so that they will know points such as the following and so that they will put into use their knowledge of them:

WHAT WE WANT TO STUDY ABOUT THE NEW ENGLAND STATES

1. Location and size
2. Surface and climate
3. History
4. Occupations
5. Schools
6. Cities
7. Other places of interest

Figure 5.9 A List of Topics as a Means of Giving Direction in the Study of a Unit

1. When it is of value to keep lists
2. In what form to write lists (sometimes horizontally across the page and other times vertically)
3. How to classify points in a list
4. How to punctuate items
5. What media to use when making lists for various purposes (pen, pencil, crayon)
6. How to use various types of lists effectively (by checking off items, for example).

Methods. The pupils can acquire information, skills, and attitudes about keeping lists by:

1. Watching the teacher make lists
2. Assisting in compiling lists as they dictate points for the teacher to record

WHAT WE WILL DO WHEN WE WORK ON OUR UNIT

1. Read
2. Draw pictures
3. Give talks
4. Write reports
5. Study pictures
6. See a "movie"
7. Make things
8. Draw maps
9. Give a play

Figure 5.10 A List as Record of Plans for Work on a Unit

3. Listening to the teacher's explanation as to capitalization and punctuation of points in a list and answering questions as to how the teacher should capitalize or punctuate items to be recorded
4. Helping to arrange points in order
5. Examining and evaluating tidy and untidy lists that have been posted on a bulletin board for appraisal.

Filling in Blanks

It may be that one reason why filling in blanks, especially in long questionnaires, is distasteful to many adults is that they have not had adequate training in so doing.

TYPES OF BLANKS. A few of the many types of blanks that the elementary-school pupils can profitably learn to fill in are as follows:

1. Blanks for enrollment in school
2. Applications for library cards
3. Cards for withdrawing books from a library
4. Applications for membership in groups
5. Blanks as a means of obtaining free materials
6. Blanks on standardized tests
7. Deposit and withdrawal slips for school banking.

LEARNINGS TO BE ACQUIRED. The following are points to be learned about filling in blanks:

1. When to use pen and when pencil
2. How to spell words often needed in filling in blanks (such as the father's name or his occupation)
3. Why it is important to try to write within the space provided
4. How to proceed in trying to write in the space provided
5. Why it is important to fill in all applicable parts of a blank that asks information suitable for recording
6. Why accuracy is important in filling in blanks
7. What to do when an item of a blank does not apply
8. What types of information to be willing to supply
9. Why it is important to write the name and address very distinctly
10. Why it is important not to sign a paper unless one is certain what one is signing.

METHODS. The following types of activities can be used in helping pupils develop ability to fill in blanks:

1. Discussion of many of the points listed in the preceding paragraph
2. Practice in filling in blanks
3. Skits indicating circumstances under which it is wise and others under which it is unwise to sign one's name
4. Examination of types of blanks posted on a bulletin board.

Writing Announcements and Directions

Although much of the work in the elementary school in making announcements and giving directions is likely to be oral, there is also a place for writing announcements and directions.

TYPES OF SITUATIONS. The following suggest some of the meaningful ways in which boys and girls in the elementary school can write announcements and directions:

1. A poster or a written statement on the bulletin board or chalkboard announcing an event such as a program or the coming of a dental clinic
2. A notice of a coming event in the school paper or the community newspaper
3. A list of directions as to how to do things, such as making a bird feeder, a Christmas ornament, or a May basket
4. A record for a card file for use by the teacher and others as to how to get to the home of a pupil
5. A card for a file giving directions as to how to get to various places of interest in the community
6. A chart giving directions for writing a good paragraph
7. A chart giving a list of directions for operating a filmstrip projector or other equipment that the pupils can operate.

POINTS TO LEARN. Following are listed some of the topics on which information concerning writing announcements or directions may be helpful to boys and girls:

1. Brevity and conciseness needed in making announcements and giving directions
2. Circumstances under which it is proper and improper to post announcements
3. Physical appearance of writtten announcements
4. Rules for making attractive posters, including attention to balance, proportion, color harmony, emphasis, mounting
5. Items to include when making announcements of various types
6. Importance of stating points in correct order when giving directions
7. Value in checking written announcements or directions before making them available to others
8. Value of diagrams with some written directions
9. Value, at times, in itemizing the parts of a direction.

METHODS. Boys and girls can be helped in writing announcements and directions by:

1. Being provided with practice in giving announcements and directions orally.

2. Making a list of suggestions to keep in mind when giving directions such as: (a) Have clearly in mind what the directions are. (b) Determine the best order for giving the various points in the directions. (c) Check against the inclusion of unnecessary details. (d) Check the directions to make certain that all necessary points have been given correctly. (e) Draw a diagram if you think it will be of value in making the directions clear.

3. Judging which of a series of directions presented in written form are clear and which are not clear and then indicating what is wrong with those that are inadequate.

4. Checking a written list of descriptions of situations in which it would be proper or improper to post announcements such as: (a) posting an announcement about an event in the classroom in the principal's office without having obtained permission from him; (b) posting an announcement about an event in the classroom on newspaper print that has become torn through poor or extended storing.

5. Making a list of situations in which it would be improper to post announcements.

6. Arranging in sequence a set of directions in which the steps of the directions have been written in scrambled order.

7. Writing directions for getting from one place to another as indicated on diagrams on the chalkboard or on duplicated sheets of paper.

Keeping Records

In the modern elementary school the ongoing program of the school affords many opportunities for keeping records.

OPPORTUNITIES FOR KEEPING RECORDS. Some of the opportunities for keeping records are indicated in the following list:

1. Keeping a record of the temperature or other phases of the weather such as sunshine, precipitation, wind velocity, humidity
2. Making a chart showing the return of birds to the vicinity
3. Keeping an attendance record
4. Making a class notebook in which are recorded important events of the year
5. Making a time line showing important events that took place in the classroom
6. Keeping a record of books read.

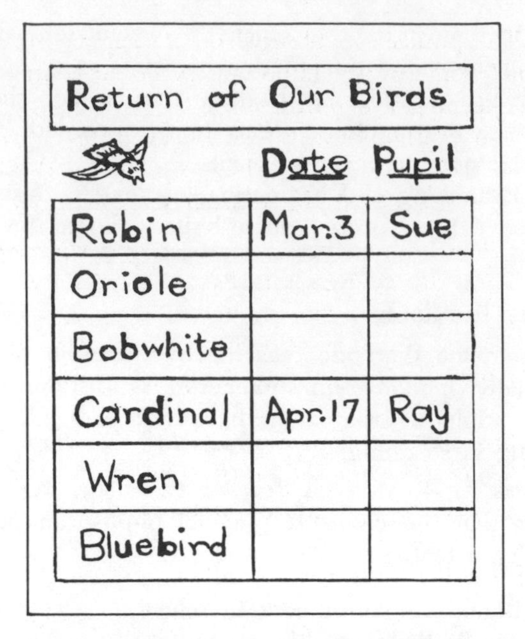

Return of Our Birds

	Date	Pupil
Robin	Mar.3	Sue
Oriole		
Bobwhite		
Cardinal	Apr.17	Ray
Wren		
Bluebird		

Figure 5.11 A Chart for Record Keeping

POINTS TO LEARN. Some of the points boys and girls should know about keeping records are:

1. The importance of accuracy
2. The need of promptness
3. The value of neatness
4. Types of records it is important to keep
5. Uses to be made of records
6. Means of storing records
7. Private nature of some records.

METHODS. Suggested methods for helping pupils grow in ability to keep records are given following.

1. The pupils can observe the teacher as he keeps a record, possibly of class attendance, while they note the care with which he checks the data, the promptness with which he records them, the neatness of his record, and the safety of the place in which he stores the record.

Figure 5.12 A Time Line to Show Important Events in a Classroom

2. The pupils can observe or participate in a skit in which some of the important points to learn about record keeping are portrayed.

3. The boys and girls can check a list of items such as the following to show which are desirable places for storage of the indicated records:

........The bulletin board for posting a chart showing the return of birds to the vicinity

........The library table in the classroom, for placement of an individual's record of the money he has deposited in the school bank.

4. The class can make a notebook in which they record and, in some instances, illustrate the points they have learned about keeping records.

Recording Bibliographical Data

Bibliographical data written by boys and girls in the lower grades usually consist of only the author and title. In the intermediate grades author, title, name of publisher, address of publisher, and date of publication can advisedly be included. In these grades some boys and girls might also learn how to record needed data on stories or articles in magazines, pamphlets, or children's encyclopedias.

Situations for Recording Bibliographical Data. Some of the reasons why pupils in the elementary school record bibliographical data are to:

1. Introduce others to a book by means of a poster giving an illustration and the title and author of the book
2. Keep a list of books or stories or articles helpful for work on a given unit of study
3. Keep a record of books recommended
4. Make an inventory of books in the room library
5. Make a list of books wanted from the public library.

Points to Learn. So that pupils will not be confused it is recommended there be agreement among the teachers of a school on the form to be used for recording bibliographical data. With such a uniform method of recording in mind, the teacher should help them learn:

1. The reason for inclusion of all the items listed as bibliographical data
2. The order in which bibliographical data should be written in an entry
3. The capitalization, punctuation, and underlining of parts of bibliographical entries
4. The placement of bibliographical data on a sheet or card.

Methods. Some methods that may be used to help pupils acquire needed information and skills and desired attitudes concerning the recording of bibliographical data can be utilized as the boys and girls:

1. Engage in discussion led by the teacher and listen to his explanation as to the reason for inclusion of each point in a record of bibliographical data
2. Engage in discussion led by the teacher and listen to his explanation as to capitalization, punctuation, and underlining used with bibliographical entries
3. Make corrections on sheets containing bibliographical data in which errors have been made
4. Arrange in desirable order a list of references to books and articles in magazines, children's encyclopedias, or pamphlets pertaining to a given topic.

DEVELOPMENT IN ABILITY TO DO CREATIVE WRITING

What is creative writing? If we define creative writing as any writing that shows originality of thought or expression or organization much so-called practical writing, including many letters and reports and even at times announcements, can be considered creative. In a certain sense, one word well chosen that truly reveals the sincere thought of the writer is evidence of creativity. Although in this chapter for purposes of clarity a division has been made into practical and creative writing – designating as creative the writing that is not primarily for practical purposes – no clear line of demarcation can be drawn to establish a discrete dichotomy.

Guidelines

Let us consider some guidelines the teacher should follow as he tries to help boys and girls develop in ability to do creative writing in prose and poetry form.

1. *Creative writing can serve significant purposes.* Important among these are: (a) It can be a means of self-expression, with the accompanying release to the writer. (b) It can prove to be a happy leisure-time activity. (c) It can give a start to boys and girls who have literary talent that should be developed. (d) It can interest boys and girls in reading additional worthwhile materials. (e) It can furnish practice in applying language-arts skills (even though that should not be a major purpose for creative writing).

2. *Creativity is encouraged through a classroom atmosphere that is relaxed and permissive yet orderly*

and conducive to success in learning activities. No regimented school program in which decisions are authoritatively made by the teacher furnishes an atmosphere in which creativity of any type is likely to flourish. If respect for the individual's thoughts is not shown throughout the school day, the child is likely to be hampered in expressing his own ideas in any line of art.

3. *The physical environment can have an encouraging effect upon creativity.* A barren, untidy, austere classroom is likely to discourage creativity. Through ways like the following the teacher can help furnish a stimulating physical environment:

Figure 5.13 Pictures as Motivation

Displaying pictures that are interesting and stimulating to the child

Having a pet in the classroom

Having a "sharing table," used by pupils and teacher

Encouraging pupils to use a room bulletin board for things they wish to exhibit

Having in the room articles of beauty such as a lovely vase or figurine

Having flowers or plants in the room

Arranging things artistically in the room

Arranging for adequate places for storage purposes

Keeping the room from being cluttered by displaying too many things at any one time

Having an interesting-looking reading corner, with books pleasingly arranged and with an object of interest as centerpiece on a reading table or as ornament on a shelf of a bookcase

Dressing attractively and being well groomed.

The teacher whose classroom is in an old building need not despair of providing a physical environment conducive to creative expression. While he cannot change the walls or ceiling or floor, he can make the room interesting in spite of problems. While surely a new classroom can be an asset to a learning situation, there is also danger in having one. Sometimes teachers who are privileged to teach in a new building may become less ingenious than those who are almost forced into resourcefulness through the very fact that they are in a seemingly discouraging environment. An unimaginative teacher can make a classroom in a new building look sterile and empty, while a teacher with imagination can make an old one into a veritable treasure chest of sources of stimulation.

Equipment can also serve as means of encouraging creativity. Examples of such equipment are slides, filmstrips, motion pictures, projectors, tapes, tape recorders, records, phonographs, radios, television sets. The room can be equipped with work benches, reading tables, bookcases, easily operated duplicators (which some children can learn to use), typewriters. However none of these is essential. Substitutes can be supplied by the wide-awake teacher. Instead of films, filmstrips, and motion pictures, for example, well-selected and attractively mounted still pictures can be used. Field trips can be a substitute for either visual or auditory learning aids. A reading table can be made by pushing together four pupils' desks, and a bookcase can be constructed from bricks for the sides and three or four boards as shelves.

4. *Exposure to good literature can serve as a means of stimulating interest in and development of ability in doing creative writing.* Telling and reading to children stories of literary merit but yet on the level of their comprehension and appreciation can arouse an interest in the pupils to write their own stories and poems or even their own "books." Ways of stimulating a child in this manner are discussed under "Writing Prose" beginning on page 85, and suggestions for interesting him in writing poetry are recorded under "Writing Poetry" starting on page 87.

5. *Boys and girls can be stimulated to creative writing through exposure to writing done by their*

peers. Such exposure can be made by: (a) reading by the teacher to the class poetry or prose written by some of the pupils; (b) reading by boys and girls to their peers some of their creative work; (c) reading to the class by the teacher poetry or prose written by pupils in other schools; and (d) posting on the bulletin board or placing in a notebook stories or poems written by members of the class or by boys and girls in other schools.

6. *A pupil's creative work should not be made available to others without his full consent.* Before a teacher reads to the rest of the class or makes available the copy of a pupil's creative writing, he should make certain that the writer has no objection. Furthermore, he should not make the child feel that he ought to read his own work to his classmates unless he wants to do so. His writing should not be published in a school or community publication or in a magazine without the writer's consent. However, at times the teacher can influence a reticent pupil whose original reaction was against sharing his writing so that he is willing to have it shown if the teacher explains to him that he believes others will enjoy it. But the final decision must come from the child. Before using a story or poem for a children's magazine published commercially, the consent of one of the parents should also be secured.

7. *There are advantages and disadvantages in displaying a pupil's creative writing even when the child is willing, in fact, even if he is pleased, to make his writing available to others.* Advantages are rather evident. Such practice may encourage the child who lacks confidence, may give others needed exposure to writing by peers, may encourage the writer to write more stories or poems, and may stimulate others to write. However, the advantages need to be carefully weighed with possible disadvantages such as the following: (a) The writer may develop a tendency to become set at his present level of writing if considerable attention is given to something that he has written. (b) When the writer is not given similar publicity at other times, he may become discouraged. (c) The writer may get more joy from the publicity than from the expression of creativity he has experienced. (d) The writer may become more interested in writing for the honor than for the sake of expressing his thoughts. (e) It may be discouraging to others in the room if their writing does not receive publicity, especially when there may develop a tendency to put emphasis on "publication" rather than on expression of what one thinks.

8. *Boys and girls should not be forced to do creative writing.* The arts do not flourish at command. However, the child can often be guided gently so that he will want to participate in creative writing. No assignment should be made requiring every boy and girl to write a story or poem. After careful motivation for creative writing, the children who want to write a story or poem may be invited to go to one part of the room while others are allowed to perform other activities that will not interfere with the writers. Frequently boys and girls who at first were not in the writers' group may, of their own free will, ask if they may join it.

9. *The main emphasis in the first draft of creative writing should be on content rather than form.* Observance of this guideline is particularly important in the early stages of learning to write when much emphasis on form can easily interfere with needed attention to ideas. The child should feel free to record his thoughts as they come to him without stopping when he is making the first draft, to look up a word in a dictionary or ask for the spelling of it. If he plans to read a story or poem to others, however, he should check his first draft in order to note whether he has expressed himself as best he can. Furthermore, if he intends to have others read his story, he should also do editing for capitalization, punctuation, handwriting, spelling, and desired neatness of paper. In most cases such editing will probably require rewriting the paper before it is shown to others.

While needed emphasis on perfecting a pupil's form in writing should be placed on that skill when the child does practical writing and when he makes a second draft of creative writing, there is probably also a relationship that should be noted between form and content even in the first draft of creative writing. While a pupil should not be restricted in his first draft through over-attention to form, he can nevertheless be encouraged even then to write as best he can without undue concentration on form. There is no virtue but there is possible harm in jotting down points in the first draft, for example, without spelling words to the best of the pupil's ability.

10. *Evaluation of creative writing should be done with care.* Here are a few points to observe in terms of evaluation of creative writing:

> The teacher should not insist on reading all creative writing done by the boys and girls. If a child does not want to show his writing to the teacher, his wishes should be respected.
>
> Frequently if a story or poem is to be shown to others at the discretion of the writer, the teacher may help the pupil correct his writing after he has made all corrections that he can without assistance.

Making many revisions of creative writing usually is not as profitable as spending time that might be used for such rewriting, on further writing in which the child tries to improve upon former writing.

The teacher should be tactful in criticisms that he makes on any creative writing.

There are dangers involved in criticisms by peers — sometimes more serious than when given by the teacher. Consequently criticism by classmates should be used with caution.

Figure 5.14 Illustrated Checklist Serving as Impersonal Means of Evaluation of Stories

The teacher should guard against high praise for any piece of creative writing. If too much praise is given, the child may feel, by contrast, discouraged at times when he does not receive it. Furthermore, there is always danger that he may then begin writing for recognition rather than for self-expression.

11. *There is probably a close relationship between creative writing and creativity in other areas.* While many people can not express themselves with satisfaction in various forms of art, it would seem that participation, either vicariously or firsthand, in some creative activities other than writing may serve as means of stimulating growth in writing. This relationship may be due, in part, to the release of tension afforded by any form of self-expression, which in turn may affect happily further self-expression.

12. *Through guidance in becoming more observant boys and girls can develop in ability to do creative writing.* Their attention may be drawn to things of beauty such as a sunrise or sunset, a snowflake, the patter of rain, the designs of Jack Frost, the murmur of a stream, the strength of massive machinery, the majesty of the mountains. In fact, the pupils may to advantage be helped to become more aware of all types of environmental factors, including the concrete and the abstract, the feelings of people, the cause and effect of various circumstances.

13. *Boys and girls who are helped to express themselves more clearly are likely to make progress in creative writing.* One reason for lack of a high level of creativity undoubtedly is the paucity of thoughts to be expressed. Another is scarcity of words at the command of the pupils with which to express adequately the thoughts that they have.

14. *Frequently boys and girls reveal their inner lives through writing.* This revelation can be made, of course, in part through direct statement of their feelings as they write on topics such as "The Subject I Like Best" or "An Embarrassing Moment." In many instances the affective nature of an individual is shown more clearly through writing that is not on the surface as self-revealing as it gives the impression of being. As boys and girls write about others, often in fanciful tales, the problems and difficulties they themselves experience are, at times, indicated. Frequently conditions the opposite of those bothering a child are pictured in his writing. The child who is being wounded by lack of love from his parents may reveal his soul by means of a heroine who is showered profusely with love not only from her parents but also from others. The writer may express his hunger for love in his own thwarted life, with its almost inevitable accompaniment of animosity, by picturing a child-dominated situation. In cases in which the creative writing taps the often hidden consistent desires of a child it may give him some release and help him solve his problem in part. Furthermore, through wise guidance the child can at times be helped to overcome some feelings of "hurt" that he harbors. While therapy in circumstances such as this when poorly done can do more harm than good, nevertheless, as in

Courtesy of the Hamilton, Ohio, Public Schools

Figure 5.15 A Close Relationship between Creativity along Various Lines

the case of bibliotherapy and other types of therapy for healing personalities, when approached cautiously and with understanding, it can be truly therapeutic.

15. *The optimum method of motivation for creative writing varies greatly from one individual to another.* One person may be stimulated to write a poem because the teacher read one to the class. Another may get the idea for his writing from a casually made remark. Still another may be inspired to write following a class discussion of the plight of wild geese that on their southward migration were deterred for hours when confused by the bright lights of a city over which their flight had been "scheduled."

16. *Patience is a requisite for guiding boys and girls in the development of abilities in creative writing.* Often the beginning of true creativity in writing seems slow. The results at first may seem, to the casual eye, less desirable than the concise statements written by boys and girls who are doing not much more than following directions as they write on topics like "How I Spent My Vacation." Growth that is inner often does not show up outwardly for a long time. Impatience on the part of the teacher may block a child's flow of free expression, possibly forever.

17. *Thinking is an integral part of creative writing.* If the teacher wishes to help children grow in ability to do creative writing, he should stimulate their thinking. However, no time should be set aside for stimulation of thought; no "thinking period" should add further to the clutter of periods found in the daily schedule of some classrooms. Boys and girls, instead, should be helped to think through real problems arising during the school day.

18. *The teacher who wishes to help boys and girls in creative work should expose himself to conditions that make him more creative.* In order to guide boys and girls in creative work, it is not enough for the teacher to have knowledge of and apply methods for guiding them in doing creative writing. If he will write some poetry or do some creative writing in prose form (maybe for inspection by no one else), he may be better able to understand the trials, tribulations, and joys that boys and girls experience when they write. Should the teacher, however, decide not to try creative writing, at least he should read good literature so that he can develop a deeper appreciation of it, which in turn should make him better able to guide boys and girls in creative writing.

Writing Prose

The guidelines stated on the preceding pages apply equally to writing poetry and prose. Let us now pay special attention to means of guiding growth, first in writing prose and then in writing poetry.

1. The pupils may note interesting legends for bulletin boards or captions for pictures, discuss them,

and then make up and evaluate some for other bulletin boards on which pictures are posted.

2. The class may listen to the teacher discuss differences and likenesses between creative and practical writing.

3. The children can select from various types of practical writing some sentences or groups of sentences that make that part of the writing creative because it expresses the writer's own feelings or thoughts.

4. The pupils may copy words or groups of words in selections of practical writing that show various signs of creativity for inclusion in a notebook or for posting on a bulletin board.

5. The class may listen to and read myths and then draw up, with the help of the teacher, characteristics of the myth. Next they may suggest topics for original myths such as "What Happened to the Rabbit's Tail." Thereupon some boys and girls may write myths and then be willing to read their production to the class. The original myths can be placed in a class notebook on fanciful tales, or can be included in each writer's own collection of original writings.

6. The class may listen to and read fables and then decide on differentiating characteristics of the fable.

7. Some of the boys and girls may write fables and then read them to the class or use them for inclusion in a class notebook on fables or in an individual notebook on creative writing.

8. The members of the class may compile a list of proverbs and then read them to each other, with possible discussion of some.

9. The boys and girls may make up stories about pictures that suggest topics for good stories. Near a picture posted on a bulletin board may be stimulating questions such as: (a) Why do you think Jack looks worried? (b) What do you think his sister will suggest that he do? Or the caption above a group of pictures may be "What Stories Do You See in These Pictures?"

10. After the boys and girls have read a series of tall tales and have discussed outstanding characteristics of the tall tale, they may like to make a list of topics about which such stories can be written such as "Paul Bunyan's Dressmaker" or "Porky the Porcupine Tells a Tall Tale."

11. After reading and hearing some puzzles or riddles, the boys and girls can be helped to draw up a list of criteria for judging them. Among these might be cleverness, appropriateness (excluding the cheap), brevity, and plausibility of the answer. Then the pupils may make up puzzles and riddles of their own. An interesting bulletin board can be made with a legend like "Who Knows the Answer?" An illustration of a boy or girl scratching her head could be given near the list of riddles or puzzles. Provision should be made for supplying the readers with the answers, probably on a separate sheet of paper. A collection properly edited could be sent to a member of the class absent because of illness.

12. Boys and girls can show originality in writing various types of greeting cards – for Thanksgiving, Christmas, Easter, Mother's Day, Father's Day.

13. At times group endings of stories may be recorded. After the teacher has read or told all but the ending of a story, the pupils may be asked for various suggestions as to the ending that could be written.

14. Occasionally the teacher may announce to the class that he is going to tell a story he made up. Sometimes he may stop at a crucial point and let the boys and girls suggest different endings. He may write the part of the story he told and then, with possible endings recorded by boys and girls, place it on the reading table in a folder on which are written the words, "Which Ending Do You Prefer?"

15. The boys and girls may draw up a list of points to observe when writing stories such as: (a) Decide what you want to write about, about whom your story will be, where it will take place, how you will start it, what interesting or exciting things will happen, how you will end it. (b) Put your thoughts into writing. (c) Read the story silently (or if possible, orally to yourself) to see whether you have told it in the best way you can. (d) If you plan to let others read your story or if you intend to keep it, correct it for any errors in writing and in many cases rewrite it. (e) If you wish ask your readers or listeners for suggestions for improvement.

16. Boys and girls may write original stories in connection with a unit of work. For example, after they have studied about community helpers and have read stories about the policeman, they may make up a story about something funny that might happen to a policeman or about how a policeman might help a child.

17. In the lower grades the teacher may record the "make-up stories" suggested by boys and girls. A child should feel free to ask his teacher to serve as his scribe. With the young child or the one who has no more skill in storytelling than the young child, the teacher may wish to take down verbatim what he says without asking him to make any improvements before the teacher makes a record of his thoughts. Then the teacher may himself edit the work or he may have the child help in improving it as the teacher reads it. The pupil may also be asked to help with capitaliza-

tion and punctuation as the teacher asks questions such as this: "Why did I put a question mark after the sentence 'Would you like to go with me?' "

18. At times the teacher may find it wise to record the endings for stories at the dictation of boys and girls. For example, when a pupil who is still finding it difficult to manipulate the mechanics of writing has written the first part of his story and then is too tired to finish it or finds it too exacting to complete it alone, the teacher may offer to serve as scribe for the rest of his story. By so doing, the teacher may keep the child from writing an ending that is so abrupt that it displeases the child and may cause him to lose interest in future creative writing.

19. Diaries can serve as expression of creativity. To be sure, diaries can also be thought of as practical writing. However, when they show originality, they can well be classified as creative writing. The boys and girls may read selections from diaries and with the teacher discuss the important characteristics of well-kept diaries. They should be helped to see the importance of dating the entries. They should recognize the fact that unless a diary is about interesting or significant points or serves as an interpretation of the writer's feelings or thoughts, it is often not worth keeping. Boys and girls may wish to write diaries of their own or, as a class project, want to keep a diary of important happenings in the room, or decide to write diaries of people like: (a) a girl who came with the Pilgrims to Plymouth in 1620, (b) a child who is taking an imaginary trip through a country about which the boys and girls are studying. If the diary deals with a period of history or a far-off land, the boys and girls should have enough background for writing so that the diary does not help make permanent erroneous conceptions the writer may have.

It is also fun for boys and girls to write imaginary diaries of mythical characters. After studying about wild animals, some child may, for example, like to write a diary of Chip, the chipmunk.

20. Children may write stories for gifts for Mother's Day or Father's Day or Christmas or Mother's or Father's birthday.

21. Sometimes after boys and girls have shown great enjoyment of a story character such as Doctor Dolittle, Winnie the Pooh, Mole (in *The Wind in the Willows*), or Miss Hickory, they might suggest additional experiences that such characters might have and write stories reporting on these adventures.

22. The teacher may encourage the pupils to report when they have written a story they would like to share with the class. Such stories might be submitted for consideration for reading by being placed in a box entitled "Our Very Own Stories."

23. Sometimes boys and girls who do not do creative writing alone are encouraged if for a while they can have a partner in their writing. Some types of writing lend themselves better to such cooperation than others. An imaginary diary of a young page during the feudal ages is one example. Before the partners start writing, they should have acquired considerable information about that period of history; they should have discussed important points they wish to include in the diary and the moods that they wish to portray; they should have an outline; and they should have decided who will write the various entries. After each child has done his individual writing, the two should read the entire diary carefully to determine needed changes.

24. The pupils may collect a list of beginnings of stories that they think are unusually interesting or may check a duplicated list of beginnings to indicate which make them want to read the stories. At times they may as a class suggest opening sentences that would make the reader want to find out what happens in the story.

Writing Poetry

The reader is referred to page 81 for guidelines for helping children write both prose and poetry, since the suggestions that follow are supplementary to those given there.

METHODS. In connection with the following suggestions for the teacher, of methods for guiding children's growth in writing poetry, it must be remembered that the teacher should not try to force his pupils to write poetry.

1. Introduce the boys and girls to writing poetry by reading it to them frequently.

2. Provide the boys and girls with opportunity to read poetry orally to themselves and their classmates.

3. Before reading a poem to the class, as a rule, prepare the audience for appreciation of it.

4. After a poem has been read to the class, frequently give the audience opportunity to read it themselves, possibly to find lines that they may like particularly well or to note how the poet states a certain point or to find out to what he compares something. Sometimes the teacher may wish to have the boys and girls read the poem to see if there are any lines that appeal to them in particular.

5. Encourage the boys and girls to look for words or groups of words in poems they read by themselves that are particularly expressive, picturesque, beautiful, or imaginative. The teacher may give them the

Courtesy of the Portland, Oregon, Public Schools

Figure 5.16 Sharing One's Writing with Others

opportunity at times to show or read these selections to the class. The pupils may want to keep the quotations as a class or individual collection.

6. After reading limericks to the class and showing them copies of some, help the pupils work out the pattern and rhyme scheme of the limerick. The pupils may either as a class or individually make endings for a limerick of which they are given the first two lines. Some might be encouraged to try to write limericks of their own.

7. After the pupils have been on a walk to see different signs of fall, encourage them to speak of what they see. Then when they return to the classroom, they may be given a chance to continue their conversation and the teacher may record some of the words used in describing signs of fall. As the teacher is writing on the chalkboard or on a piece of newsprint, the pupils could be encouraged to give not only expressions that they had already used in their conversation but also additional interesting ones that tell how they feel. Thereupon the teacher might tell the class that she plans to use some of their expressions in a poem that he will write. Possibly the following day the teacher will want to read the poem to the class and give each child a copy on which are underlined all the expressions received from the class. The next time when boys and girls have an experience to which they wish to react poetically, such as a walk through newly-fallen snow, they can again dictate to the teacher expressions that are symbolic of a suggested mood or idea. The children who wish to write a poem on the experience may be invited to use any of these expressions in their poems.

8. Give the boys and girls suggestions such as these as to steps in writing a poem by themselves: (a) Think of some idea or act or feeling about which you would like to write a poem. (b) Think of what you would like to say about the topic. (c) Jot down

your thoughts in note form without paying any attention to rhyme. (d) Revamp what you have recorded so that it is poetry form, either rhyming or not rhyming.

9. Discuss with the class characteristics of a fine poem. The pupils then can note how these characteristics are exemplified in various poems.

10. When in free play or other spontaneous activities you find that a child starts singing, making up words to accompany his actions, jot down at times the words he is saying. Then the teacher may show the song to the composer and at times, if he readily assents, to the rest of the class.

11. Provide various rhythmic experiences for boys and girls such as being in a band or listening to one, so as to develop their natural sense of rhythm. However, the teacher should guard against beginning experiences in poetry writing by beating out the rhythm of poems for fear that the result would be a set of stilted jingles in which the emotional quality is lacking. When boys and girls have had considerable experience in writing poetry without special attention to rhythmic pattern, they can at times profit from explanation and demonstration of various rhythmic designs. They can then discuss the importance of suiting the pattern of rhythm to the mood to be portrayed.

12. Introduce the boys and girls to simple rhyme schemes – the couplet, the triplet, and the quatrain – and help them discover which lines rhyme. In some instances the teacher may wish to introduce older boys and girls to some types of poetry forms that do not rhyme such as the Japanese haiku, tanku, and senryu described by Nina Willis Walter in her delightful and informative book *Let Them Write Poetry.*[1]

13. Help boys and girls realize the economical manner in which words are used in poetry by asking them to express in prose some thoughts given in poetry and in poetry some recorded as prose.

14. Help boys and girls determine which of a group of poems written by persons whom they do not know, either children or adults, merely give an image and which go farther in that they also tell how the writer feels concerning that about which he is writing.

15. Encourage the pupils to look for beauty. They can discuss things of beauty in the room, using as appropriate words to describe them as they can. They can also report on beauty they have experienced outside of school. The boys and girls can be encouraged to go beyond the concrete in their appreciation as they note circumstances such as these: (a) an older sister tenderly helped a young child after his tumble, (b) a mother sang a lullaby to her baby.

16. Encourage the pupils to collect pictures or objects of beauty that may inspire someone to write a poem. A brief discussion of a few possibilities for stimulating poetic expression, such as a shell or a picture of the starry heavens, may at times be appropriate.

17. Encourage the children who would like to illustrate a poem that they have heard or read to do so. Those who wish may first draw a picture of how they feel about something and then "draw" that picture in the words of poetry.

18. Have older boys and girls classify the emotions in some poems in which they are expressed simply.

19. Discuss points such as these with older boys and girls: (a) the importance of selecting words that state the thought concisely; (b) the fact that a poet needs to show originality either in the topic selected or in handling an old topic in a new way; (c) the undesirability of awkwardness in sentence structure; (d) the desirability of avoiding the use of overworked expressions or slang (unless the slang is used in a direct quotation); (e) the fact that all poetry does not rhyme.

20. Through explanation, class discussion, study of models, and copying of poems by the pupils, help them acquire knowledge of these points concerning the appearance of poetry on paper: (a) Free verse is often not indented. (b) Indentation in poems that rhyme is not required. (c) Lines that rhyme should have the same margin.

21. Help the pupils acquire inductively generalizations such as these about rhyming, listed in *Let Them Write Poetry by Nina Willis Walter*:[2]

> Avoid trite rhymes, such as *love* and *above*, *trees* and *breeze, sing* and *spring*.
>
> Except in a tercet, do not have more than two successive lines rhyming.
>
> Avoid near rhymes, such as *home* and *alone*, and rhymes identical in sound, such as *see* and *sea*.
>
> Do not use the same rhyme more than once in a short poem, unless the poem has a refrain.
>
> Do not use forced rhymes, twisting words out of their meaning for the sake of rhyme or saying things awkwardly in order to make the rhymes come out right.

EXHIBIT OF POETRY. One way in which boys and girls can be encouraged to write poetry is by suitable

[1]Nina Willis Walter, *Let Them Write Poetry*. Holt, Rinehart and Winston, 1962, pages 122-129.

[2]Nina Willis Walter, *Let Them Write Poetry*. Holt, Rinehart and Winston, 1962, pages 138-139.

display of poems written by the pupils or by others. Care should be taken that pupils are not strongly urged and never forced to share their original writing with others. Care needs also be taken to avoid dangers in exhibiting children's poetry even when the writers are willing to share their poems with others.

Here are some suggestions for display of poems.

1. Have in the room interesting-looking books of poetry with, at times, one or more on special display.

2. Post poems, sometimes groups of poems, on a bulletin board. There may be a picture to illustrate the poetry, drawn by the pupil or otherwise obtained, together with a challenging legend written on the bulletin board.

3. Copy a poem, if it is short, on the chalkboard, possibly in a section entitled "Our Poems" or "Do You Like This Poem?" The latter caption should not be used when the poem was written by someone in the class.

4. On the first "page" of an accordion-like folder post a poem and on the succeeding "pages" let the pupils illustrate parts of the poem. The words illustrating a picture could be written near it.

5. Encourage pupils to make individual collections of their poetry and possibly to illustrate it. The collection could be kept in a notebook or in a card file.

6. If you have a class or school paper, submit some of the poems for inclusion in it.

7. Help the class compile a notebook for display on the reading table containing a favorite poem by each pupil in the room. Children are interested in having the name of the person who chose each poem indicated in writing.

8. Help the class keep a notebook in which they record interesting expressions of poetic quality said or written by boys and girls in the room.

9. Make or help one or more pupils construct a poster on which a poem is written, with illustrations to accompany some of the lines of the poem. The lines illustrated could be rewritten near each picture.

10. Encourage the pupils to write poems for their father or mother for Christmas, Easter, Mother's Day, Father's Day, their mother's birthday, their father's birthday.

11. Help the boys and girls participate in making a book, even possibly for publication, similar to some extent, yet definitely original in others, to *Children's Voices* by Bertha E. Roberts and Arreta Beckman.[3]

DEVELOPMENT OF SKILL IN CAPITALIZATION AND PUNCTUATION

Even though considerable time and energy are spent in the elementary school and in high school in helping boys and girls learn to capitalize and punctuate correctly, the written work of high school and college students and of adults shows many errors in capitalization and punctuation. Furthermore, many of the mistakes occur on points to which much attention has been directed in the elementary school and in later schooling.

Guidelines

What are reasons for the ineffectiveness of the program of instruction in capitalization and punctuation? One of them probably lies in the teacher's lack of knowledge or understanding or application of guidelines such as these:

1. Work on capitalization and punctuation should be carried on in such a way that the pupils sense the worthwhileness of capitalizing and punctuating correctly.

2. The teacher should be careful not to assume that pupils already have information they lack.

3. The boys and girls should be given many opportunities to apply in writing situations what they are learning about capitalization and punctuation.

4. Incidental learning situations do not provide all practice that many boys and girls need on points to be learned and skills to be acquired in capitalization and punctuation.

5. The teacher should try to ascertain the needs and capacities of each learner.

6. The work on capitalization and punctuation should be adapted to individual differences.

7. The teacher should not assume that more transfer of training takes place than actually does.

The Program in Capitalization

The results of studies as to what should be learned in the elementary school are inconclusive. Consequently any suggested lists lack authenticity.

Points to be taken up in the elementary school undoubtedly should be determined to a considerable extent by the needs of the pupils. Those that are used most should be given priority provided they are simple enough for the child to learn.

By the time boys and girls have completed the elementary school, those of average ability should probably have learned the following uses of capital letters:

1. The first word in a sentence

2. The word *I*

3. Names of persons, initials, polite titles, races, nationalities

[3]Bertha E. Roberts and Arreta Beckman, *Children's Voices*. Silver Burdett Company, 1939.

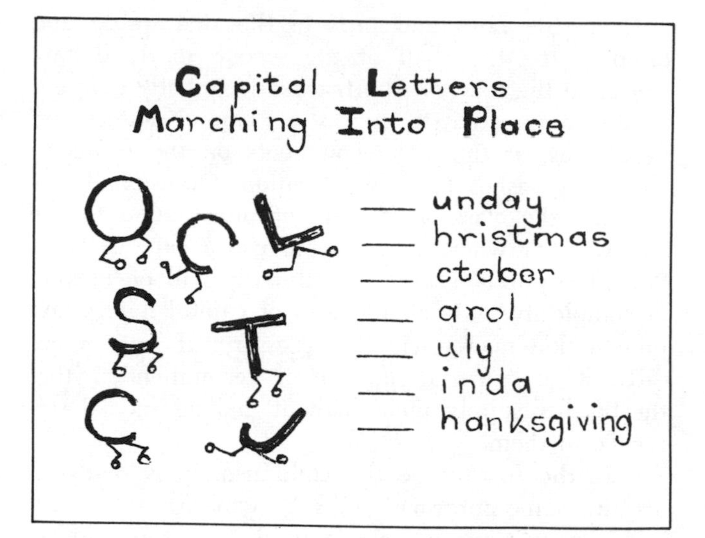

Figure 5.17 Interesting Children in Use of Capital Letters through an Illustrated Chart

4. The first word, the last word, and every so-called "important word" in a title and in the name of a company, firm, special product, television program, radio program. (Children should learn that words like *a, an, and, at, from, in, into, on, or, the, to, with* are not considered "important words" in titles.)

5. The first word and each "important word" in the name of a city, state, school, club, building, geographical feature such as valleys, mountains, oceans, rivers, continents

6. Proper adjectives such as *Bostonian, American*

7. The first word of a direct quotation

8. The first word and every "important word" in a salutation of a letter and the first word of the closing of a letter

9. Many abbreviations. (Although pupils should learn that many abbreviations are capitalized, they should be expected to learn the abbreviations of only a few frequently used ones like *Mr., Mrs., Dr., C.O.D., R.R.,* and *P.O.*)

10. The word *God* and other words for the Deity

11. The word *Bible* and other names of writings sacred to a religion

12. Words such as *Father, Mother, Aunt, Uncle, Sister, Brother* when they are used as a name

13. Words such as *North, Southwest, Far East* when they refer to a part of the country or of the world.

The Program in Punctuation

By the time pupils leave the elementary school, those of average ability should probably have learned the following uses of these punctuation marks,

THE PERIOD

1. At the end of a declarative and an imperative sentence (although the terms *declarative* and *imperative* may not necessarily be taught)
2. After abbreviations
3. After initials
4. With numbers or letters preceding a list in outlines
5. With numbers or letters to help indicate items in a list of words or sentences or longer thought units even if the items are not included in an outline

THE COMMA

1. After the greeting in a personal letter and after the closing in a personal or business letter
2. Between the date of a month and the year
3. After the name of a city when it is written directly to the left of the name of the state
4. With words or groups of words in a series
5. After *yes* or *no* when used as a part of an answer
6. In a sentence containing a direct quotation (to separate the quotation from the rest of the sentence unless a question mark or an exclamation point sets the quotation off from the rest of the sentence)
7. After a word or group of words, other than a sentence, which shows some, but not much, surprise or expresses moderately strong feeling
8. After the name of a person addressed
9. With appositives
10. After the last name of a person if it is written before the first name, as in an alphabetical list

Can You Abbreviate Me?

Doctor Dr.
Mistress Mrs
Mister
Street
Avenue

Figure 5.18 A Device for Practice in the Writing of Abbreviations

THE QUESTION MARK

1. After an interrogative sentence (although the term *interrogative* may not necessarily be taught)
2. After a direct quotation in question form given as part of a sentence

QUOTATION MARKS

1. In a direct quotation to set off the exact words of the speaker
2. Around the title of a story (but not of a book) or of an article

THE EXCLAMATION POINT

1. At the end of an exclamatory sentence (although the term *exclamatory* may not be taught)
2. After a single word that shows surprise or expresses strong feeling
3. After a word or group of words expressing strong feeling given as a direct quotation

THE APOSTROPHE

1. In a contraction
2. In a possessive noun

THE HYPHEN

1. Between syllables if a word is divided at the end of the line so that one or more syllables occur at the end of one line and the remaining syllable(s) at the beginning of the next line
2. In a compound word, including compound nouns, compound adjectives, and compound numbers

THE COLON

1. After the salutation in a business letter
2. Between the hour and minutes when expressing the time of day as in *9:30* A.M.

UNDERLINES

With a title of a book or magazine when used as part of a sentence, in handwritten or typewritten form.

Grade Placement

The needs of the pupils as they participate in a rich, comprehensive program in the language arts should probably be the chief determinant of grade placement. However, only those skills should be taught that are on a difficulty level within the ability of the boys and girls to acquire without undue stress. The following points may be of value in allocating topics to various grade levels.

1. As the boys and girls in the first grade and often in the first half of the second grade dictate stories to the teacher, the teacher frequently supplies whatever punctuation marks or capital letters are needed as, at times, he comments on the forms to which he wishes to draw attention. Occasionally he may ask the class what mark of punctuation to use and why, or where and why to use a capital letter. Since the pupils' sentences ordinarily will be lacking in complexity, only simple uses of capital letters and punctuation marks will be necessary. If some more difficult uses are needed, it is recommended that the teacher supply them without making special reference to them.

In the first grade the child usually is ready to acquire some information as to why capital letters and punctuation marks are used (as *stop* and *go* signs) and as to what are the name and form of the comma, the period, and the question mark. First grade pupils may be ready to learn these uses of the capital letter:

At the beginning of the sentence
In names of persons, their town or city, the days of the week, and the months
With the word *I*.

Some first-grade pupils can advisedly be helped to learn to use capital letters in writing the name of the avenue or street on which they live as they write their own addresses. Capitalization of names of holidays or other special days can also be noted by first-grade children.

The first-grade pupil usually is ready to learn that a sentence that tells something needs a period at the end while one that asks a question calls for a question mark. At times in this grade boys and girls can well be taught to put periods after figures given in lists when they write lists of words.

2. In the second and third grades it is important to review points taken up in first grade that have not been mastered. Additional points of capitalization that many boys and girls are ready to learn in those grades are the capitalization of:

The names of towns and cities
The first word in the salutation of a letter
Titles like *Mr., Mrs., Dr.*
Initials
Names of countries and states as well as of rivers, lakes, and other geographical terms that they will use in their writing
The first and last words and all "important words" in a title

Words such as *Father, Mother, Sister, Brother, Aunt, Uncle* when they are used as names.

The following uses of punctuation marks may be stressed with boys and girls in the second and third grades:

The period with abbreviations and initials and after letters or figures given in outlines

The comma after the greeting in a personal letter; after the closing in a letter; between the date of a month and the year; after the name of a city or town when it is written directly to the left of the name of the state.

The exclamation point at the end of an exclamatory sentence and after a single word or group of words not constituting a sentence if it expresses surprise or strong feeling

The apostrophe in a contraction.

As some boys and girls write book reports, they might learn that titles of books when written in longhand or typed should have underlines if they are included in sentences.

3. In grades four, five, and six there should be review of all points that have been studied and not mastered in earlier grades. Sometimes review requires reteaching as well as further practice in making application of what is in the process of being learned. Additional points under "The Program in Capitalization" (page 90) and "The Program in Punctuation" (page 91), not already introduced in the primary grades, can constitute the new work of these grades.

Methods

The following list of ideas as to methods of teaching needed skills in capitalization and punctuation may suggest others to the reader.

1. The teacher can discuss with the boys and girls the fact that capital letters and punctuation marks are used in order to make it easier for the reader to comprehend what the writer wants to communicate.

2. The teacher or the boys and girls can make a chart showing the chief functions of punctuation marks.

3. In the intermediate grades the teacher can help pupils note how at times punctuation makes a decided difference in the meaning of sentences. He can give illustrations such as the following for discussion as to meaning and he can encourage the boys and girls to make up other sentences for presentation to the class.

My brother who is away at college will not be able to come home for Mother's Day.

My brother, who is away at college, will not be able to come home for Mother's Day.

4. The class can make a handbook of rules for capitalization and punctuation that they have learned.

5. As the pupils in the lower primary grades dictate stories or reports to the teacher while he supplies the needed capitalization and punctuation, the teacher can at times comment on his use of capital letters or ask questions concerning the need for capitalization. As he uses punctuation marks he can similarly ask questions and make comments.

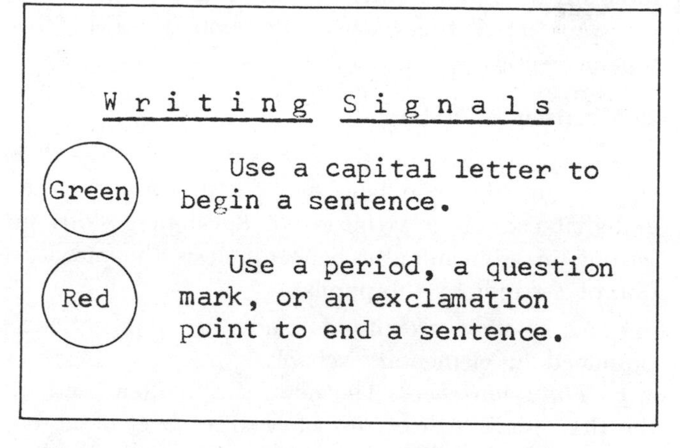

Figure 5.19 Writing Signals for the Lower Grades

6. Under the guidance of the teacher the pupils can examine books to note certain uses of capital letters and punctuation marks.

7. As boys and girls begin doing their own recording of their thoughts (rather than dictating them to the teacher), the teacher can make himself available to answer questions about capitalization and punctuation as well as about other points about which boys and girls may wish to ask him. He can also help the children individually as they examine their stories or reports for possible errors, those in capitalization and punctuation included.

8. For correction by the class the teacher can copy on the chalkboard sentences containing errors in capitalization and punctuation taken from a set of papers written by the boys and girls in the class.

9. The pupils can give reasons for use of capital letters and punctuation marks in sentences, stories, reports, or letters in textbooks. Only those uses of capital letters and punctuation marks that the boys and girls have studied should be discussed.

10. Pupils who need practice on some uses of capital letters or punctuation marks beyond that furnished by their own writing can use exercises in textbooks or in workbooks or on duplicated sheets. (For further suggestions the reader is referred to page 304.)

OPPORTUNITIES FOR GROWTH THROUGH SPECIAL ACTIVITIES

The program in written expression should be closely interrelated with the ongoing activities of the classroom in the various curricular areas and in activities and projects that cut across the boundaries of the separate subjects.

Publication of a Paper

One special activity that can be stimulating, that can be fun, that can help in work in various areas, and that can serve as means of developing skills in writing in a meaningful background is the publication of a paper by the pupils.

KINDS. Below are listed kinds of "publications" produced in elementary schools.

1. *The news sheet.* The news sheet, often used in the first grade, can consist of a large sheet of newsprint on which the teacher writes the news items that the boys and girls planned. In place of this on a large sheet of paper can be attached small pieces of paper on which are written the news stories the boys and girls have helped compose. Some rooms have daily news sheets. These can be saved in a portfolio to become a record of some of the year's activities. Duplicate copies can be made of some or all of the editions, one for each child.

Figure 5.20 A News Sheet

2. *The class "newspaper."* Commonly a class "newspaper," written by a class in the intermediate grades, consists of several sheets of paper stapled together, with enough copies so that each child can have his own. Sometimes this paper deals with a variety of happenings in the room that publishes the paper but it may also contain notes, written by pupils in the grade producing the paper, on what is happening in other rooms. Sometimes each issue is devoted chiefly to one topic such as a unit in the social studies or a science project.

3. *The school paper.* In some schools the entire school cooperates in "publishing" a school paper. In such cases the main responsibility for the paper often rests with the fifth or sixth grade. An editor-in-chief is selected from the room that has major responsibility for the paper. A room editor might represent each grade cooperating with the room issuing the paper. He could be charged with the responsibility of acting as liaison person between the room for which he was chosen and the room that is putting out the paper.

4. *The department paper.* Sometimes the pupils of the grades four, five and six together write a school paper. Such a paper follows the general plan described for the school paper excepting that the paper tells primarily or exclusively about the work of the three intermediate grades.

5. *The room magazine, the department magazine, or the school magazine.* Instead of writing a "newspaper," the class or department or school might "publish" a magazine, possibly two or three times a year.

6. *The column in the community paper.* Although columns in community papers are more likely to contain articles by or about the high school than the elementary school, there is no reason why steps may not be taken in small communities by the principal to encourage the inclusion of a column in the town

paper that would be devoted, at least in part, to happenings in the elementary school.

GUIDELINES FOR THE CLASS "NEWSPAPER." Although the following guidelines are written for class "newspapers," many of the suggestions, with slight adaptation, can be used for other types of "publications" listed.

1. *The paper should convey the well-rounded program of the class.* Emphasis should not be put only on fun. The value of "digging" at times to learn should be made clear. The inclusion of a letter by the principal or the room teacher can help interpret the program not only to boys and girls but also to their parents.

2. *All boys and girls in the room should contribute to the class paper.* This point should apply whether or not the names of the writers are included with the articles. Each pupil should have a part in gathering information, planning its organization, actual writing, or in proofreading, not merely in tasks like stapling the sheets.

3. *The writing should be in correct English.* The argument that the paper should reflect the unedited writing of the children is not convincing. These are a few of the reasons why every article should be written in good English: (a) The pupils should be given practice in editing their work so that they will get into the habit of careful checking. (b) The boys and girls who read an article written by their classmates are entitled to one written correctly. (c) Errors in English in the paper make an undesirable impression upon adult readers and, therefore, because of the class paper the school may get unfavorable publicity.

4. *The first page should give, in attractive form, the name of the paper and other identifying data.* The name of the paper should be written in letters larger than those of the typewriter used for the rest of the writing. It should be centered across the page even if the paper is in two-column form. Below the name of the paper the following information might be presented, as here indicated.

School	City, State
Date	Edition

5. *Every page should look interesting.* On every page there should be something other than the regular type to keep the page from forming too solid a block. For the first page the variety may be furnished by the heading. On subsequent pages diagrams, blocked-in parts, changes in type for names of sections of the paper (which could be written in all-capital form or in cursive writing), poems, or statistical tables can help make a page look interesting.

6. *The diagrams and pictures should almost always be the children's work.* If an illustration is copied, due credit must be given to the source and care must be taken that no copyright laws are violated. It usually is wise to reproduce authentic maps so that the pupils do not get erroneous impressions from their own or their classmates' inaccurate sketches.

7. *Poems in the paper should be original.* The class paper furnishes too good an opportunity to use poetry by the pupils to take the space for that written by other people.

8. *Any joke to be considered for inclusion should be carefully scrutinized.* Since the publication represents the children's work, space should not be used for jokes that are not original. When jokes involving boys and girls are used, great care must be taken that they do not embarrass anyone. (Most of us do not wish to be the butt of a joke, especially not one that is published.)

STEPS IN WRITING A CLASS "NEWSPAPER." Many of the steps listed can be followed, with slight alteration, when producing one of the other types of "publications" to which reference has been made earlier.

1. *Interest the boys and girls in writing a paper.* If the incentive comes spontaneously from the class, this step will be omitted. However, if boys and girls have not previously participated in writing a class paper, interest in the idea will most likely have to be aroused.

2. *If possible, give the pupils adequate opportunity to study papers written by other classes.* These can be obtained, in many instances, from other rooms in the school or from other school districts.

3. *Discuss with the class the general nature of the paper desired.* Decisions need to be made on questions such as: (a) On what size sheet should the class paper be written? (b) How many pages should it be? (c) What should be the format of the paper?

4. *Help the class decide upon the content.* The teacher may list on the chalkboard the suggestions given by the class and add some of his own. The list made on the first day of discussion should be considered temporary.

5. *Choose or have the class choose an editor and one or more assistant editors.* In some instances the teacher may wish to appoint the editor and his assistant(s) while in others he may want the selection to be made by vote.

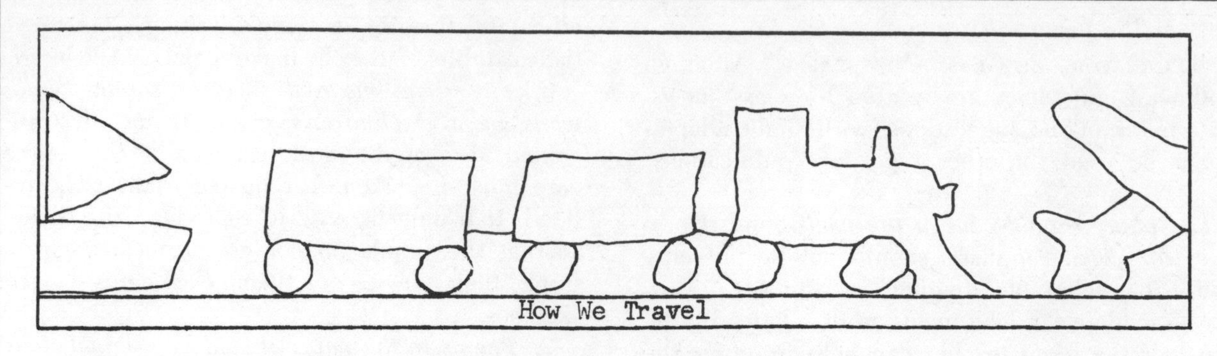

Primary Grades Study Transportation

The children in the first, second, and third grades have been studying transportation. They have read many stories about land, water, and air travel.

An Airplane

I saw an airplane
In the sky.
It did tricks
So high! So high!
--Kenneth Peterson

***

My Boat

My little boat went sailing,
Sailing on the sea.
The waves took it out so far
It couldn't come back to me.
--Jerry Kramer

***

Choo-Choo!

Choo-choo-choo!
Goes the train on the track.
Choo-choo-choo!
Clickety-clickety-clack!
--Alan Rivers

Children Ride on School Bus

We went to the airport in our school bus. We saw many different kinds of travel on the way. We saw a dredge, a rowboat, another bus, a tractor, a horse, a hayrack, a baby carriage, a motor cycle, bicycles, a freight train, and many people walking.

Boys and Girls Visit Airport

We saw many airplanes in the hangar. Some were ready to use, and others were being made. One plane taxied to the end of the field, rode into the wind, and took off.

The Mississippi River Works

The Mississippi carries barges with heavy cargo. It carries many pleasure boats, too. The "Golden Eagle" stopped at Winona this summer.

Children Make Many Things

We made a big boat. We used builder blocks, brown paper, and boxes.

Our train has a locomotive and two cars. This train will really go.

Our airplane will carry two people. We like to ride in it. We keep it in our hangar.

Figure 5.21 Example of a Page of a School Paper Featuring Lower-Grade Activities

Early Methods of Communication

Room Studies Communication

Since the fourth, fifth, and sixth grades have been studying about communication this summer, we decided to use our section of this paper for showing and telling about the development of communication. This part will be followed by articles on "Guides Explain Telephone" and "Children Plan Visit to Western Union."

Cavemen Use Signals

Signals were one of the earliest means of communication. The cavemen used their hands to signal. Messages were often sent by smoke. People of today still occasionally use smoke signals. Boy Scouts learn many signals.

Early People Invent Alphabets

The people of long ago wrote on clay tablets, on the sand, and on the walls of caves. The Babylonians wrote on clay tablets. The earliest Egyptian writing was made up of very simple pictures, each of which stood for a word. By and by a picture came to have a meaning different from that which it actually showed. A vase upside down meant a priest, for example. Finally alphabets, on the order of those we now use, were developed.

Egyptians Develop Alphabet

The drawings below show the Egyptian signs for some of our letters.

-- I   -- B

-- G   -- K

-- KH   -- P

Printing Press Aids Communication

John Gutenberg invented the printing press in 1439. He invented the type, the ink, and the press. He modeled the press after the wine press. The printing press of today is a great improvement over Gutenberg's press. The invention of the printing press was the turning point in the history of communication.

Newspapers Come into Use

All of the newspapers in the early days were written by hand. In the fifteenth century monks wrote the newspapers. The papers of long ago were small. Some of the newspapers were only headlines while others were more like those we have today. Many of these told about battles and fires. Two countries, Germany and Italy, published the first papers. Nowadays we get much of our news from newspapers.

Figure 5.22 Example of a Page of a School Paper Featuring Intermediate-Grade Activities

6. *Help the group determine the responsibilities of each individual.* While the editorial board should give guidance and make some decisions, all the boys and girls in the room should have a part in making others.

Toot, toot, I hear a train.
The Hiawatha is coming.
Orange, white, and silver
Smoothly it rolls along.

Airplanes go flying.
Birds go flying, too.
They go where the clouds are white
And where the sky is blue.

Figure 5.23 Original Poems in a School Paper, as Encouragement for Creativity

7. *Provide time for writing the first draft.* The first writing can be done before or after discussion of possible content and form of each article.

8. *Make provisions for revisions.* Most of the changes should be made by the pupils. However, often they will need the guidance of the teacher.

9. *Type a rough draft of the paper.* In many instances if the teacher can type, he will probably do this step. If he cannot type, he may be able to secure secretarial help.

10. *Provide for the revision of the rough draft of the paper.* Even if the articles for the first draft were in good form, changes might need to be made because of space limitations. If major changes are necessary, the person making a given contribution should be the one to assume at least part of the responsibility of making them. Minor editorial changes can be made by the editorial staff or in some cases by the teacher.

11. *Cut the stencil.* The typing of the stencil will, as a rule, be the responsibility of a secretary on the staff of the school. In the intermediate grades the boys and girls may be able to transfer their pictures, diagrams or maps, if the illustrations are simple, to the stencils.

12. *Assemble the paper.* The assembling of the paper, including the stapling, can be done by the boys and girls.

13. *Guide the evaluation of the paper.* Final evaluation may come after the boys and girls have had opportunity to hear comments on the paper by persons outside the classroom. Questions such as these may be considered: (a) How could we have made our paper better? (b) How could we have worked more effectively on the paper?

Other Special Activities

Following are listed a few of many interesting and significant school activities that involve much writing:

1. Writing the script for a puppet show, play, or pageant
2. Making class books on special activities in which the group has participated during the course of the school year
3. Making a booklet on a unit of work such as "The Clothes We Wear" or "News from Outer Space."

FOR STUDY AND DISCUSSION

1. Explain why the vocabulary for the language experience chart does not need to be as carefully controlled as that for the reading experience chart.
2. Outline a procedure that can be followed in a presentation lesson on writing a thank-you letter in a third-grade classroom.
3. Draw up a list of guidelines for helping boys and girls in a primary grade write a class news sheet. (Designate the grade level that you have in mind.)
4. Draw a diagram of a hypothetical classroom, choosing any one of the first six grades, in which the physical equipment is such that it would encourage creativity in written communication. Label the equipment and designate the grade level, and write a brief paper explaining the diagram.
5. Plan a balanced program of written communication for any one of the first six grades. Include in your outline of the program: objectives, subject matter to be studied, activities to be included, materials of instruction to be used, and means of evaluation.
6. After reading on the topic of creative writing in one or more professional books or magazines, add to the suggestions given in this chapter for helping boys and girls write creatively.
7. Examine papers written by the elementary-school pupils, noting the excellences of the writing and the problems that are revealed. What suggestions do you have for helping the writer of each paper?
8. If you have access to the book *Let Them Write Poetry* by Nina Willis Walter, read Chapter 7 entitled "Rhythms and Patterns." Then you may wish to ex-

periment with writing poetry in the form of the Japanese haiku, tanku, or senryu.

REFERENCES

Anderson, Verna D., et al. (editors), *Readings in the Language Arts.* The Macmillan Company, 1964. 503 pp.

Burrows, Alvina Treut; Doris C. Jackson; and Dorothy O. Saunders, *They All Want to Write.* Third edition. Holt, Rinehart and Winston, 1964. 281 pp.

Greene, Harry A., and Walter T. Petty, *Developing Language Skills in the Elementary Schools.* Second edition. Allyn and Bacon, 1963. 572 pp.

Herrick, Vergil E.; and Leland B. Jacobs, *Children and the Language Arts.* Prentice-Hall, 1955. 524 pp.

Roberts, Bertha, and A. T. Beckman, *Children's Voices.* Silver Burdett Company, 1939. 184 pp.

Walter, Nina Willis, *Let Them Write Poetry.* Holt, Rinehart and Winston, 1962. 179 pp.

OUTLINE FOR CHAPTER 6

Guiding Growth in Skills Common to Oral and Written Communication

CHAPTER 6

Guiding Growth in Skills Common to Oral and Written Communication

Because of the close interrelationship among the various facets of the language arts, they have many skills of value in common. The skills needed for both oral and written communication discussed in this chapter are those pertaining to (1) vocabulary, (2) sentence structure, (3) paragraph structure, (4) note-taking, (5) outlining, and (6) correct usage.

VOCABULARY

Words are the basis of much of listening, of speaking, of reading, and of writing. Without suitable command of words, the individual is likely to be unable to speak or write interestingly and concisely, to listen intelligently, and to comprehend written material that with a larger vocabulary he might understand.

Kinds of Vocabulary

An individual has several kinds of vocabularies. Commonly they are classified as (1) the listening or hearing vocabulary, (2) the speaking vocabulary, (3) the reading vocabulary, and (4) the writing vocabulary. Although these terms are essentially self-explanatory, a few comments about the nature of each may be helpful.

1. *Listening or hearing vocabulary.* An individual's listening vocabulary consists of the words he can comprehend when he hears them in oral expression. The listener may understand one meaning of a word but be ignorant of others. Furthermore, there are differences in comprehension of even the same meaning of a word. For example, a person hearing the word *love* may understand that it refers to the state of being liked very much, but he may have no idea of the depth of feeling that is associated with the word if the speaker is talking about love that expresses itself in sacrifice.

The child's listening vocabulary surpasses in number of words his other types of vocabulary. He can, as a rule, understand as he listens more words than he uses in his own speech and more than he can comprehend in his reading or uses in his writing.

2. *Speaking vocabulary.* The child has a sizeable speaking vocabulary before he starts to learn to read. Ordinarily, the speaking vocabulary continues larger than the reading vocabulary well through the primary and often fairly long into the intermediate grades. By the time the pupil leaves elementary school, however, he typically does not use nearly as many words in his speech as he can comprehend with some degree of interpretation when he meets them in print.

3. *Reading vocabulary.* In the early stages of learning to read, the child's reading vocabulary remains small chiefly because he cannot recognize many words in print, not because he does not know the meaning of many. In fact, reading material for beginners is usually planned so that the words the children encounter are those whose meaning they know. It is only as the pupil progresses into later stages of learning to read that he is likely to find many words he does not understand. (Very little is said in this chapter about the development of the reading vocabulary since the topic is taken up in Chapter 10.)

4. *Writing vocabulary.* The last of the four types of vocabulary that the child acquires is the writing vocabulary. Even after a child has been writing for several years, his writing vocabulary lags behind his speaking vocabulary. Some adults, however, have a larger writing than speaking vocabulary. Research has not established where the reversal in size of the

two typically occurs in individuals in which it does take place.

Guidelines

Following are listed helpful guidelines.

1. *Even though intelligence greatly affects an individual's vocabulary, environment also is a powerful determinant of it.* Heredity sets the limits of possible development but rarely if ever does an individual make use of all leeway in growth possible for him. In fact, the person with an intelligence quotient slightly below normal who has grown up in an environment favorable to language development is likely to have a better vocabulary than the person with an intelligence quotient slightly above normal who has been reared in surroundings inimical to vocabulary development.

2. *One of the best ways of helping boys and girls in vocabulary development is to furnish them with a variety of rich, meaningful experiences and opportunities to discuss them.* Types of situations that encourage such incidental development of the child's vocabulary are listed in the next section of this chapter.

3. *At times direct methods of teaching vocabulary development should be supplemented by indirect methods.* While vocabulary development is stimulated through an environment rich in meaningful experiences in which vocabulary seemingly receives but incidental attention, such an environment for many boys and girls needs to be supplemented by situations set up primarily in order to help him grow in word power.

4. *When direct methods of increasing word power are used, the pupils should be convinced of the worthwhileness of the activities.* "Busy work" is inexcusable because it is wasteful. For good results not only the teacher but also the pupils should realize the worth of what they are doing.

5. *Recognition should be given to the fact that the words an individual uses differ somewhat in formal and in informal speaking and writing situations.* In informal conversation, such as that in which the pupil engages when he converses with members of his family or friends, he is likely to use words that he would not use in more formal situations. Furthermore, in the informal writing of personal letters or personal memoranda, he will probably use some words that he would not use in more formal business letters or in report writing. The child should be helped to recognize these facts and to learn some types of words appropriate for one kind of situation but not for the other. This differentiation in type of vocabulary should not be made, however, in such a manner that the child thinks words that are cheap or vulgar or incorrect are permissible in informal speech or written expression.

6. *The vocabulary of the home and the playground greatly affects the program in vocabulary development of the school.* Even before the pupil enters first grade, he has had several years during which he has been speaking and listening. After he has enrolled in school, he continues to spend most of his waking hours outside of school in such activities. Consequently, if the type of vocabulary the child uses outside of school is meager or otherwise unsatisfactory, it may offset in part efforts by the teacher to help him improve his vocabulary. Care needs to be taken that in no way will the child develop a feeling of shame about his home because it is lacking in high standards in choice of vocabulary.

7. *Pupils who fall behind their peers in vocabulary development often are in need of many rich, meaningful experiences.* Erroneously, some teachers believe that the best remedy for this deficiency is to provide the child with more and more practice exercises or to use other direct means of improving his vocabulary. Usually it is wiser to spend part of the effort in vocabulary improvement in giving the child many experiences that will give him real reason for using an improved vocabulary.

8. *Boys and girls frequently experience difficulty because of the fact that many words have a variety of meanings.* The teacher should realize that the meaning an individual associates with a word is often determined by his experiences with that word. To the child of a miner living in the area of the Mesabi Iron Range in northern Minnesota the word *range* is likely to have an entirely different meaning than to the boy who has been saturated with stories of cowboys on the ranges of the West.

9. *Many children need to be helped to appreciate the value of an effective vocabulary.* This point needs particular note when the pupil comes from an environment in which the value of attention to the words used is not emphasized.

10. *In the lower primary grades increases in the pupil's meaning vocabulary is obtained primarily through oral means of expression.* The words that the pupil reads in suitably graded reading material in the lower grades are selected, in part, in terms of words that have meaning for him. It is in these grades that much emphasis, therefore, needs to be placed on vocabulary improvement through oral communication. As the pupil progresses through the upper primary and the intermediate grades, he will have increasing

opportunity to improve his vocabulary through words that he reads. Throughout the elementary school, however, oral communication should be utilized in furnishing the child with greater word power.

11. *As boys and girls read materials in the content areas, including the social studies, science, mathematics, and health, they need special help meeting various vocabulary problems.* One problem lies in the fact that many words of which they already know one meaning have a different meaning as part of the more specialized vocabulary of a given field of knowledge. The child who has long used the word *mouth,* for example, may be confused when he hears or reads about the mouth of a river. A further problem lies in the fact that a large number of new words is introduced per given number of running words. In the reading material in the content subjects the vocabulary burden usually is not as carefully determined as in the reading textbooks to which the child has been accustomed. The problem of meaning is increased by the fact that the pupil frequently does not have the concepts, for example, of words such as *liberty,* that the writer of the material assumes he has.

12. *Boys and girls need to learn that some words are used primarily to give information and others chiefly to produce a certain emotional effect.* The concept of "loaded words" may need explanation as the child learns to recognize such words as *native land* (rather than the name of the country) and *loved ones* (rather than *relatives*) as emotive words. The pupils should be helped to understand that even though it is proper to use words that reveal one's emotions or that are likely to produce a certain emotional effect on the listener or reader, emotive words are often dangerously used by persons who wish to influence others unduly.

13. *The teacher's attitude toward vocabulary improvement, his own vocabulary included, is likely to affect that of boys and girls.* Through precept and example the teacher can help pupils realize that acquiring more power over words can be fun as well as useful.

Situations that Encourage Vocabulary Development

Probably the chief means of encouraging growth in the vocabularies of boys and girls is to provide them with many meaningful experiences such as:

1. Talking with one another, with the teacher, and with visitors
2. Listening to stories told by the teacher, the librarian, and other boys and girls
3. Listening to directions and explanations and giving them
4. Listening to poems read or given by the teacher, librarian, and other boys and girls
5. Reading, telling, or listening to stories
6. Reading poems silently and orally
7. Listening to a radio or television program
8. Seeing a "movie"
9. Reporting on events that have taken place
10. Taking care of a pet
11. Listening to recordings, including tape recordings of the pupils' own speech
12. Giving, writing, and listening to book reports
13. Doing creative dramatics
14. Planning and giving a puppet show, a play, or pageant
15. Making a mural or a movie
16. Writing a news sheet or a class or school newspaper or magazine
17. Singing or composing songs
18. Participating in choral reading
19. Writing letters, reports, and announcements
20. Doing creative writing
21. Planning and putting on a book fair or a school exhibit.

Methods

The following are some of the procedures that may be used to help boys and girls grow in power to understand and use words. Some of the suggestions are usable in connection with situations in the ongoing program of the school, such as those listed in the preceding paragraph. Others are adaptable when a more direct approach to the problem of development in vocabulary seems indicated. (Suggestions for helping boys and girls use the dictionary to gain in knowledge of the meaning of words are given together with ideas for developing other dictionary skills, on page 210.)

1. Draw attention to words that are used in oral communication. Some ways in which the attention of the pupils can be drawn to words are as follows:

As the teacher uses a new word in a sentence when he is talking to the class, he writes the word on the chalkboard and explains what it means in the context in which it is used.

Comments are made on the appropriateness or descriptiveness of words that pupils use in their speech.

Before the teacher reads a selection to a class, he writes on the chalkboard one or more difficult words that they will hear and questions them about the words or makes comments on them.

2. Have the boys and girls make lists of synonyms and antonyms of specified words; homonyms, with sentences containing them; descriptive action words (verbs), name words (nouns), and other parts of speech; special vocabulary encountered in a unit of study; substitutes for overworked words such as *nice, lovely, terrible;* prefixes and suffixes; compound words.

3. Encourage the pupils to make charts, possibly illustrated, giving the new words met in connection with an area of study or with a unit in that area such as a chart with new words used in a unit on Switzerland, as, for example, *glacier, chalet, alp, altitude.*

4. Have the pupils make a picture dictionary of words of which they will want to remember the meaning.

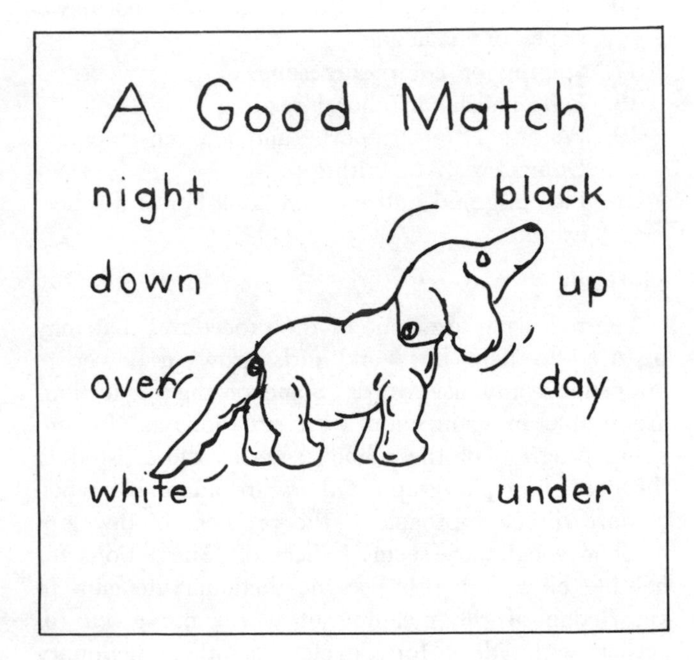

Figure 6.1 Means of Motivating Work on Antonyms

5. Have the pupils keep individual notebooks or a file system of words the meanings of which they are learning. The pupils might be encouraged to write each word, tell what it means, use it in a sentence and, if possible and helpful, draw an illustration of it.

6. Develop with the pupils the meaning of commonly used prefixes and suffixes. Thereupon they can identify the prefixes and suffixes in words presented to them and show how the meaning of the root is affected by the affix.

7. Have the pupils form derivatives from root words such as *happy – unhappy; wrap – wrapped, unwrap, wrapping.*

8. Give the pupils crossword puzzles based on knowledge of words and encourage them to make or help make some. For example, in the lower grades a simple puzzle using questions like these can be constructed:

(1) What word means the opposite of *short*?
(2) From what smaller word is *running* made?
(3) What word means more than one boy?
(4) What is a baby cat called?

9. Discuss with the boys and girls the importance of expressing themselves well, bringing out points such as these: (a) the relationship to clarity and interestingness; (b) the value at school in various subject areas; (c) the value when looking for work or working; (d) the importance in terms of showing refinement.

10. Encourage the pupils to make cartoons or other illustrations showing the importance of careful choice of words.

11. Help the boys and girls figure out the meaning of a word in context by: (a) asking them what meaning(s) would fit into a sentence containing a blank space for a word; (b) having them tell what an underlined word in a sentence might mean judging from the rest of the sentence and then check the word in the dictionary; (c) asking which possible meaning of a word fits into the context of a given sentence.

12. Guide pupils in putting on a skit showing the value of choosing words well.

13. Ask the pupils to restate in a more interesting manner underlined words or expressions used in sentences.

14. Have the pupils dramatize the meaning of specified words that are used in sentences such as "The children *sauntered* home from school."

15. Give the pupils practice exercises of the types described on page 210.

SENTENCE STRUCTURE

To be unable to talk in good sentences presents a problem in the clarity and interestingness of oral expression. Furthermore, lack of sentence sense can interfere with comprehension of what is read, especially when the sentences are long and involved. Similarly, written expression and ability to comprehend what is communicated orally seem to be affected adversely by lack of sentence sense.

Results, as revealed in the speaking and writing of boys and girls leaving the elementary school and their written and oral expression during later years,

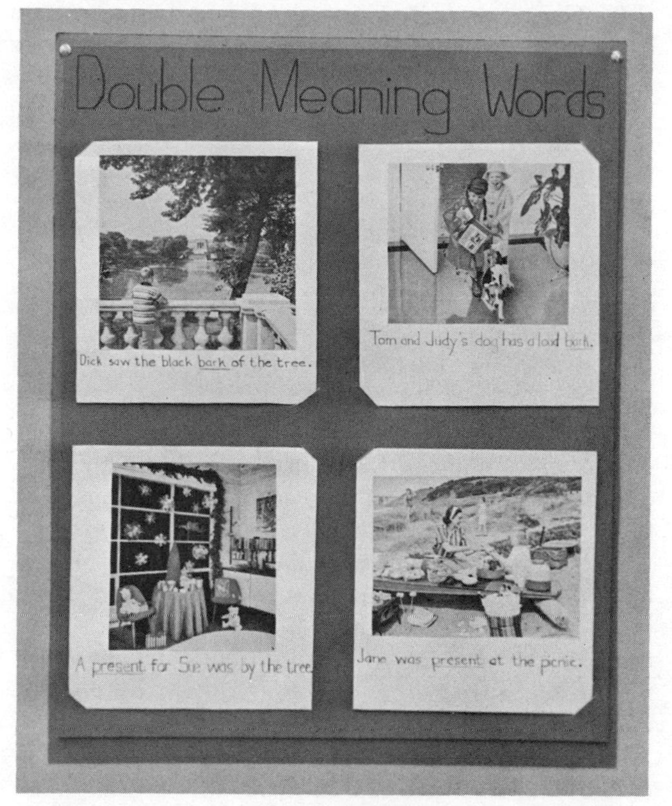

Bulletin Board was prepared by Marcia Palmer Pyle.

Figure 6.2 A Bulletin Board Illustrating the Dependence of Meaning of Words on Context

seem to indicate that either not enough emphasis has been placed on improvement of sentence structure or the teaching has not proceeded in accordance with well-known principles. Noting the emphasis placed on sentence structure by many elementary-school teachers and the space devoted to that topic in textbooks, one is inclined to conclude that much of the inadequacy in the recognition and use of good sentences may be due to inferior teaching.

In the discussion of sentence structure that follows, these points are taken up: (1) objectives, (2) guidelines, and (3) methods.

Objectives

The teacher will want to have the pupils become able during the course of the elementary school to understand or do the following:

1. Know the value of good sentence structure.
2. Recognize sentences.
3. Know the kinds of sentences (declarative, interrogative, exclamatory, imperative).
4. Begin a sentence with a capital letter and end it with the proper punctuation mark.
5. Write and speak in clear-cut sentences.
6. Know under what circumstances it is important to use complete sentences and to use them at such times.
7. Avoid run-on sentences.
8. Avoid many short, choppy sentences.
9. Have variety in sentence structure.
10. Comprehend rather long and involved sentences in oral and written communication.

Guidelines

Important guidelines are as follows:

1. *The emphasis in teaching sentence sense or sentence structure should be placed on helping boys and girls express themselves clearly, concisely and interestingly, not primarily on teaching them the mechanics of saying or writing or recognizing sentences.* The pupils should be helped in becoming conscious of the fact that the important goal is to speak and write in such a way that others can comprehend the material fairly readily. Questions like these are relevant when checking sentences the pupils have given: (a) Do these words express a whole thought? (b) Is it clear what you are trying to say?

2. *Growth in ability to use sentences is to a considerable extent a matter of maturation.* As in other areas of human achievement, the limits for development are set for the individual by his inheritance. Furthermore, unless interrupted there is a sequence in sentence development that seems to be part of the pattern of inner unfolding of the individual. First the child talks in words or in substitutes for words. Next he talks in words that form the skeleton of a sentence. Then follow complete sentences, simple in form. Sentences more involved and longer come next. Consequently environmental factors need to be selected to "go with the current" of the pattern of growth not against it.

3. *There is a close relationship between thinking and sentence sense.* When the pupil is helped to clearer thinking, he is directly or indirectly given assistance in expressing himself in sentences.

4. *Criticism of the child's sentences at times when he speaks in somewhat formal situations other than those specifically designated for purposes of improving in sentence structure may have a detrimental effect upon his spontaneity of expression.* If he is interrupted other than in training situations or corrected after he has finished speaking, he may become shy about expressing himself in the future or he may pay so much attention to the mechanics of speaking that he neglects suitable concentration on what he is saying. On the other hand, if the child is never helped

to improve his speech through appraisal of the sentences that he uses when his purpose is to tell a story, give a report, or engage in conversation, there is danger that he will use one set of standards for sentences when he is given specific help in talking in sentences and a set of lower standards at other times. Probably the best rule to follow is to spend most of the time on criticism and complimentary evaluation of the pupil's ability to talk in good sentences when lessons for specific help are set up but also not to neglect to draw the child's attention, at times, to sentence structure after he has spoken in nonpractice-type situations.

5. *There is a place for lessons definitely planned with the objective of helping boys and girls develop a better sentence sense and of helping them talk and write in effective sentences and comprehend such sentences in both oral and written communication.* Some such lessons should be devoted to introducing boys and girls to various phases of the problem of developing effectiveness in relation to sentence structure. Others should be used for practice purposes at well-spaced intervals.

6. *The fact that as pupils are enrolled in the intermediate grades they sometimes make more errors in sentence structure and have additional difficulty in comprehending what they hear or read, due to problems related to sentence structure, than they did in the years immediately preceding, is not necessarily reason for discouragement or alarm.* The increase may be accounted for in some instances by the fact that boys and girls typically speak and write in more involved and longer sentences and listen to and read sentences of that nature when they are in the intermediate grades than when they were younger. Furthermore, the ideas to be expressed are more advanced and consequently harder to put into words than those of earlier days. The lag may thus be only apparent, not real.

7. *There is a close relationship between use of sentences in oral and in written expression.* Attention to sentence structure in oral situations can often be given in such a manner that its value will also be accruing in written communication and vice versa. However, because of the greater difficulty pupils often have in written expression, it is frequently desirable to have the work on various phases of development of sentence skill begin with emphasis on oral communication.

Methods

In harmony with the guidelines given, methods such as the following may be used.

1. The teacher discusses with the pupils why it is usually desirable to talk and write in sentences.

2. The pupils are guided to note why it is usually desirable to talk and write in sentences as they compare two paragraphs written on the chalkboard, the first in sentence fragments so that it is difficult to comprehend the meaning and the second in sentences in which the first paragraph was rewritten.

3. Provisions are made for first-grade children to express themselves orally. The teacher at times records what the pupils say as he comments on the capital letter at the beginning of a sentence and on the terminal punctuation mark. For example, he may say, "I will use a capital letter here because it begins our second sentence." Or he may ask, "Since this is a question, what punctuation mark should we place at the end?"

4. The teacher makes incidental reference to sentences in connection with what the pupils read when, for example, he gives directions such as: (a) Read the next sentence in order to find out. . . . (b) Read the sentence that tells us why Susan wanted an apple.

5. The pupils note which words given in writing or orally express a complete thought.

6. The boys and girls read in a textbook an explanation of the fact that a sentence is a group of words expressing a complete thought.

7. The teacher explains to the pupils what constitutes a declarative, an interrogative, an exclamatory, and an imperative sentence as the pupils note sentences on the chalkboard or as the teacher records on the chalkboard sentences of the various types that the boys and girls give orally.

8. The teacher explains to the boys and girls that some groups of words look like sentences but are not. He asks the boys and girls to select those in a list of groups of words (some of which are sentences and others sentence fragments) which are not sentences and then to change them to sentences.

9. The pupils match a group of sentence fragments like the following as they comply with the direction given.

Direction. On the line to the left of each group of words in the first column, write the number of the group of words in the second column that finishes the sentence.

........Stephen had found	1. a broken leg.
........The crow had	2. Stephen's pet.
........Stephen took	3. a crow.
........The crow became	4. the crow home with him.

10. The boys and girls state what kind of sentence each of a series is, though written without final marks of punctuation, and then supply the needed punctuation in sentences like the following:

Where are you going with that crow
I am taking the crow home with me

11. The pupils finish a sentence by selecting the ending word from a list and then supply the final mark of punctuation.

I will show my crow to .... (school, Mother, garage).

12. The pupils write in sentences series of words that are listed in scrambled order.

Mother crow me food gave the for

crow a has pet Jim

Jim has a pet crow.

Figure 6.3 Arrangement of Words into Correct Sequence

13. The boys and girls finish sentences of which only the first few words are given.

I like .... My crow never ....

14. The children rewrite sentences in which no capital letter nor final mark of punctuation is given.

15. The teacher asks the pupils to observe how the voice is raised at the end of a question. He then tells them that while in oral expression raising the voice helps a person to know that a question is asked, in writing a question mark helps identify it.

16. The teacher puts on the chalkboard some poorly expressed sentences written by boys and girls, possibly in paragraph form, and asks the class to plan ways of improving them.

17. The teacher writes on the chalkboard sentences that are confusing because they contain irrelevant material and then asks the pupils to decide what should be deleted. Sentenecs like the following might be recorded:

When I ran to school today with my little rat terrier that Father gave me for my last birthday, when I was nine years old, I lost my tablet.

18. The teacher helps the boys and girls express themselves in better sentences by suggesting that when they want to say something that is rather difficult to explain, they first ask themselves the question that they want the explanation to answer.

19. The teacher helps the pupils recognize the fact that it is not always important, not even desirable, to talk in complete sentences as, for example, he draws attention to complete and incomplete sentences like the following that he has recorded on the chalkboard:

How much is the bus fare? Fifteen cents.
Who is with you? My sister.

20. The teacher puts on the chalkboard a record he made of what a pupil said who had run his sentences together with *and, and-uh, then, and then,* or *and so.* He then asks the pupils to read the paragraph, omitting unnecessary words and indicating needed capital letters and punctuation marks.

21. The teacher emphasizes the fact that at times *and's* are desirable as they combine groups of words, closely related in thought, that could form independent sentences, like the following:

I put my books in the house and then I quickly hurried out to see the fire.

The pupils can be given practice in deciding in which instances, in relation to sentences on the chalkboard, it is desirable and in which it is undesirable to use *and's* to connect groups of words that could, with the omission of the *and,* be written as separate sentences.

22. The teacher writes on the chalkboard a series of sentences in which words such as *when, while, since* are used instead of *and* to connect two parts of a sentence, each of which can form a separate sentence, as in the following:

It was very cold *and* I wore my winter coat.
Since it was very cold, I wore my winter coat.

The pupils can then be asked to rewrite other sentences containing unnecessary *and's* by using connectives such as *when, while, since, because, after.*

23. The class discusses reasons why many people run sentences together when speaking. Some reasons that may be mentioned are: (a) Since the speaker is not certain of what he wants to say next, he tries to give himself time to think by including an unnecessary connective. (b) The speaker has formed a habit of using unnecessary connectives. (c) The speaker

does not know that use of words such as *since, because, while* can keep sentences without unnecessary *and's* from being short and choppy.

24. The pupils indicate what connectives can be used in cases like the following to combine two thoughts into one sentence:

My coat is blue ___ Mary's is red.

25. The pupils note the contrast between a written report in which all the sentences begin in the same way and one in which some of the sentences have been changed so they have different beginnings. They then decide which makes the more interesting report.

26. The boys and girls note different ways in which a sentence can be structured as they read sentences like these that the teacher has written on the chalkboard:

> When I came home late last evening, I was very tired.
> I was very tired when I came home late last evening.
> Last evening, when I came home late, I was very tired.

Then the boys and girls can rewrite other sentences to show possible variety in sentence structure.

PARAGRAPH STRUCTURE

Although at the beginning of the first grade the paragraphs dictated to the teacher by boys and girls as well as those they read are usually limited to one sentence, later the children become ready to learn that when we have more to say on a topic than we can express in one sentence, we often use two or more sentences to form a paragraph. While throughout the elementary school the one-paragraph written report or story is typical of the child's writing, it is not unusual to find boys and girls in the upper elementary grades ready to express themselves effectively in more than one paragraph. How the pupils can be guided in the development of skill in constructing paragraphs is discussed in the following paragraphs as these points about paragraphing are stressed: (1) objectives, (2) guidelines, and (3) methods.

Objectives

As the teacher helps boys and girls in the development of ability to structure paragraphs, these are points of information or skill that he should aim to have them acquire somewhere in the elementary school:

1. Knowledge of what a paragraph is
2. Knowledge of characteristics of a good paragraph
3. Knowledge of the importance of the use of good paragraphs
4. Skill in the use of topic sentences
5. Skill in making all sentences in a paragraph contribute to its central thought
6. Skill in relating points in the correct order
7. Skill in using good beginning sentences
8. Skill in using good ending sentences
9. Skill in making transitions from one paragraph to another. (This objective might be emphasized with only the more able boys and girls.)

Guidelines

Points such as the following serve as guidelines in helping boys and girls acquire the information and the skills listed in the preceding paragraph.

1. *Work on paragraph development should continue throughout the elementary school.* It can begin when in the first grade the teacher writes, first, one-sentence paragraphs and later longer ones, at the pupils' dictation. In every grade thereafter there should be emphasis on paragraph structure until by the end of the sixth grade the boys and girls have attained considerable knowledge about the types of information listed under "Objectives" and until they have developed to a considerable extent the skills named under the same topic.

2. *Much of the work on paragraphing can be done through incidental means.* As the boys and girls are writing paragraphs or as they are giving short talks as part of the ongoing school program, real purpose for good paragraph structure can be demonstrated.

3. *As a rule, incidental means of teaching paragraph structure need to be supplemented by lessons the chief aim of which is to help boys and girls develop in skill in paragraph structuring.* These lessons can be both presentation lessons, where points new to the children about paragraphing are developed, and practice lessons, through which at well-spaced intervals the pupils can consolidate their learnings.

4. *It should be recognized that the paragraphs in books for children often do not serve as models in paragraphing.* In due time boys and girls should be familiarized with the fact that this shortcoming exists. If the teacher helps them they will probably not be as inclined as they might be if they made the discovery by themselves to think that it is not important to have good organization of paragraphs.

Methods

Here are some means by which boys and girls may be able to attain the needed knowledge and skills.

1. Knowledge of what a paragraph is through:

   Hearing the teacher use the term *paragraph* during the beginning stages of somewhat incidental learning about paragraphs even though the boys and girls will not be expected at that time to use the term. Reference can be made to it as the teacher mentions to the class when he writes a paragraph of more than one sentence that he is writing the sentences in one paragraph because they are all on the same topic.

   Hearing an explanation by the teacher, with samples of paragraphs, as to what is meant by a paragraph.

   Following directions given by the teacher like "Read the first two paragraphs on page 31 to find out what Bobby wanted to get for his mother" or "Read the paragraph orally that tells us what Bobby's mother said she would like for her birthday."

2. Knowledge of characteristics of a good paragraph through:

   Participating in a series of developmental lessons in which each of the following characteristics of a good paragraph is studied: (a) keeping to the topic, (b) giving points in correct sequence, (c) having a good beginning sentence, (d) having a good ending sentence and in the case of written paragraphs also (e) beginning a paragraph on a new line and (f) indenting the first word of a paragraph (unless the block form of paragraphing is used)

   Making a chart in which the characteristics of a good paragraph are listed

   Finding paragraphs that do and some that do not possess the characteristics of a good paragraph and giving reason for the classification made

   Participating in a developmental lesson in which the use of paragraphs in direct quotations is made clear

   Giving reasons for division into paragraphs of direct quotations in a series in which different people are quoted

   Dividing into paragraphs a written record of conversation involving direct quotations in which the division into paragraphs had not been made

   Constructing good paragraphs.

3. Knowledge of the importance of using good paragraphs through:

   Participating in class discussion of the importance of good paragraphs

   Listening to explanation by the teacher

   Noting the difference in desirability between a series of poorly written and a series of well-constructed paragraphs

   Rewriting a poorly constructed paragraph into a well-constructed paragraph.

4. Skill in the use of topic sentences through:

   Finding in a series of paragraphs the sentence around which the rest of a paragraph is built and then being told by the teacher that such sentences are called topic sentences

   Selecting the topic sentence in a series of paragraphs

   Changing paragraphs that do not contain topic sentences into some that do

   Building a paragraph around a sentence like "Our room contains many interesting things" to be used as topic sentence

   Determining (a) which paragraphs in a series contain topic sentences, (b) which do not contain topic sentences.

5. Skill in making all sentences in a paragraph contribute to the central thought of the paragraph through:

   Telling what each sentence in a given well-organized paragraph, relating to an incident, tells about the incident

   Stating which sentences do not contribute to the central thought of the paragraph in which they are used

   Writing paragraphs in which all sentences contribute to the central thought

   Taking part in a discussion, while examining paragraphs, that brings out the fact that in well-organized paragraphs some sentences contain main points bearing on the topic, others give details, and still others give illustrative or background material

   Checking paragraphs to find out which type of contribution, if any, each sentence in each of the paragraphs makes to the central thought, namely: (a) contains main point bearing on the topic, (b) gives details, (c) illustrates a point, (d) gives background data, (e) serves another useful purpose.

6. Skill in relating points in a correct order through:

   Arranging in order a series of pictures illustrating a paragraph or a series of paragraphs.

The pupils may arrange in sequence a series of cut-out pictures illustrating the steps listed in a paragraph explaining a simple process

Finding the sentences that are out of order in paragraphs not in acceptable sequence

Putting in order scrambled sentences that when arranged correctly constitute a good paragraph

Rewriting paragraphs in which thoughts are expressed out of order when more than a rearrangement of the sequence of the sentences is needed to produce a good paragraph.

7. Skill in using good beginning sentences through:

   Examining a series of paragraphs to note which have beginning sentences that indicate what the paragraph is about and that interest one in the rest of the paragraph

   Planning improved beginning sentences for paragraphs that do not have a good beginning and stating why the revision is an improvement

   Writing paragraphs that have a good beginning sentence.

8. Skill in using good ending sentences through:

   Examining a series of paragraphs to note whether or not the ending sentence of each contributes to the rest of the paragraph

   Examining a series of sentences each of which would make a good ending sentence and another series which would not

   Making a list of sentences that would not make a good ending sentence like: (a) That's all that I know about this topic. (b) I hope I have not bored you.

   Planning improved ending sentences for paragraphs that have poor endings.

9. Skill in making a transition from one paragraph to another through:

   Noting paragraphs in which a satisfactory transition is made and explaining how it is made

   Discussing the need of having sentences that show transitions between paragraphs

   Listing sentences that show how a transition can be made from one paragraph to another

   Writing sets of two or more paragraphs in which a good transition is made.

NOTE-TAKING

Notes can be useful for talks boys and girls give as well as for papers they write either about their own experiences or on data that they have acquired through reading, talking with others, or other experiences.

There is real need for helping elementary-school pupils learn how to record notes effectively and how to use them. Efficiency in writing and using notes can help them in self-expression. It can be of value to them in that it provides them with a form for recording information basic to improved thinking and greater enjoyment.

Guidelines

Important points to note in helping boys and girls develop skill in taking notes and using them are as follows:

1. *Emphasis should be placed on skill in note-taking throughout the elementary school.* In the first grade drawings may serve as notes. By the time a pupil leaves the elementary school he will, it is hoped, have learned to take notes on a topic by consulting various sources.

2. *The boys and girls should be helped to see the value of taking notes.* Probably the best ways in which they can learn to recognize the value of taking notes are by taking them for purposes that to them serve a real need and by being helped to take them and use them effectively.

3. *Help should be given in the development of various types of note-taking skills.* It should not be assumed, for example, if a pupil has learned to take effective notes for organizing a talk based on personal experiences or on what he has heard one or more persons say, that he will be able to write useful notes for organizing a paper on information he has gathered through reading books on a given topic.

4. *The boys and girls should be helped in locating information in books and other written materials.* Discussion of how such help can be provided is given in Chapter 10.

Methods

The teacher can guide boys and girls by doing the following in order to help them in recording and using notes.

1. In recording notes through:

   Using, as the teacher tells a story, illustrations he has drawn or secured which follow the sequence of the story and letting the boys and girls see the picture as he tells the story

   Guiding the pupils in drawing pictures to illustrate a story that the teacher has told or read to them so they can tell it

   Guiding the children in drawing illustrations of a personal experience that later they can tell the class or dictate to the teacher or they themselves record in writing

Using and showing to the class sketches the teacher has drawn or has otherwise obtained of steps in a process he is explaining

Guiding the boys and girls in making sketches of the steps in a process the teacher or the pupils are explaining or about which they are reading

Showing the pupils two sets of notes taken on a given selection from an encyclopedia in order to find the answer to a specified question and then asking the pupils to decide which is the better set and to tell why. One of the sets of notes might: (a) contain irrelevant material, (b) be so sketchy that they are almost meaningless, (c) omit some important points. The contrasting set of notes should be without these shortcomings.

Showing the pupils a set of notes that the teacher took on a question on which they may want information as he draws attention to points such as these: (a) the inclusion of the title of the book and author from which the notes were obtained; (b) the pages in the book on which the information was found; (c) the use of quotation marks when the exact words of the writer were recorded; (d) the fullness of the notes; (e) the brevity of expression used without sacrifice of clarity; (g) the relevancy of the notes. The group can then give reasons for the desirability of observing in note-writing each of the points noted.

Making a chart headed with a question like "What Are *YOUR* Notes Like?" on which are posted an excellent set of notes as to form and content and one poor in both respects

Helping the class decide on sub-topics on which they would like information on a topic like hamsters (in case the boys and girls are planning to get a hamster as pet) and then having the group divide into committees to find information on each of the sub-topics such as: (a) what a hamster looks like, (b) food, (c) shelter, (d) value, (e) habits.

Having the pupils decide on a topic on which they want information and after they have gathered the information and recorded it, giving them an opportunity to have their notes evaluated

Guiding the boys and girls in looking up information on a topic when they do not know on what sub-topics they will need or find information

Giving the class an opportunity to discuss the importance of taking accurate notes

Providing the pupils with an opportunity to think of an interesting experience they have had as the teacher jots down notes while they organize the material for a talk or a written report

Discussing with the boys and girls points to observe when taking notes on a talk, possibly heard over the radio or on television, such as: (a) Do not concentrate so much on your note-taking that you fail to comprehend much of what the speaker is saying. (b) While you listen to the opening sentences, try to get your clue as to the outline the speaker will follow. (c) In many instances, to get the full value of your notes, rewrite them more fully shortly after the talk has been given.

Helping the pupils take notes as they carry on experiments or take field trips.

2. In using notes through:

Discussing with the class the importance of not, as a rule, following the organization given in their source(s) when using the notes for a paper or talk and explaining to the class if the same organization is followed in many instances credit should be given to the source

Discussing the importance of using quotation marks and indicating the source whenever in a paper the exact words of the speaker or writer are given

Discussing with the class why it is usually undesirable when giving a short talk to use notes while one is talking

Discussing with the class how to use notes in a talk if it seems desirable to use them

Having some of the pupils put on skits as they demonstrate correct and incorrect methods of using notes when giving a talk

Providing the pupils with practice in writing a paper or giving a talk after taking notes on a topic.

OUTLINING

Outlining can help boys and girls in listening, in speaking, in reading, and in writing. More specifically, these are some of the chief ways in which outlining can serve the elementary-school child:

1. As an aid to recall of what he reads or hears or otherwise experiences
2. As a study aid, if he is furnished an outline of what he is studying

3. As a guide for talks that he will give or of papers he will write
4. As an aid in planning dramatizations.

Skill in outlining can be acquired by the average pupil during the course of his years in the elementary school if he is given adequate guidance. Some teachers, unfortunately, have assumed that pupils need only spasmodic help in learning to write outlines and in using them. Putting this theory into practice in many schoolrooms has resulted in a large number of boys and girls leaving the elementary school and even high school who have not learned how to make effective outlines and how to make effective use of them.

Guidelines

Following are points on which a sound program of guiding boys and girls in acquiring skills related to outlining should be based.

1. *Outlining is one means of organizing material.* Consequently, experiences of value to the child in growth in skill in organizing are likely to assist him in becoming more adept at outlining.

2. *Outlining, like other means of organizing materials, is closely interwoven with thinking.* Even after the pupil has comprehended what he has read or heard or otherwise experienced, he needs to think as he tries to decide upon the main points. He needs to think as he tries to select less major points (sub-topics) that support the main points. He needs to think as he figures out the interrelationship between sub-topics and supporting details.

3. *Outlining should be taught in such a way that boys and girls see the usefulness of the learning.* Outlining or any activity preliminary to learning how to outline, such as learning to organize materials not in outline form, should frequently be taught in situations in which the pupils readily recognize the value. Such situations include many that can easily be identified by the teacher within the scope of the ongoing activities of a modern elementary school. For example, one is classifying a rock collection for display on an exhibit table.

4. *So-called incidental training in outlining is not enough for many boys and girls.* In addition to the opportunities afforded by incidental learning, for a large number of pupils lessons need to be provided in which new learnings are developed about organizing material the pupils need to acquire, like the identification of the details to serve as sub-points for sub-topics in an outline or the form to be followed in outlining. Furthermore, from time to time lessons need to be set up to supplement the incidental work and the development lessons so that well-spaced practice will be provided.

5. *The teacher should, in part, plan the program in outlining in harmony with the sequence of steps arranged as to difficulty.* In the primary grades much of the work is usually preliminary to actual outlining. There the chief emphasis in this respect can be on organizing material without putting it into outline form. For example, boys and girls may help decide what event should come first in a play, what books should be placed in a space marked "Books on Nature," or what should be the order of events in a program that they are planning. In the fourth grade, frequently considerable attention is paid to the organization of the paragraph in terms of (a) selection of the topic of the paragraph, (b) identification of the topic sentence if there is one, (c) decision as to whether only relevant points are made, (d) consideration of the desirability of the sequence in which points are given, and (e) study of the appropriateness of the beginning and ending sentences. In the fifth grade, if not before, boys and girls are ready to learn to outline single paragraphs and in the sixth grade, again if not before, to outline two or more consecutive related paragraphs. Work on the form of outlining is often begun in the later primary grades and continued in the intermediate grades with attention to increasing complexity of form, often through sub-points supporting sub-topics.

Methods

In the listing of methods that follows, suggestions for organizing material are given that are considered of either preliminary or supplementary help in the actual teaching of outlining.

1. Methods for organizing material for help in outlining

CHIEF PRODUCTS

Farm Products	Manufactured Products	Minerals
wheat	watches	coal
corn	silverware	iron
oats	gloves	copper
beans	machinery	

Figure 6.4 Classification That Can Be Worked Out by Class

The teacher can list on the chalkboard items that the pupils dictate to him, like articles needed for a field trip or what was seen on a field trip, and then have the pupils work out a classification of the points.

The pupils can make a classified list of products found in a country that they are studying.

The teacher can point out to the pupils the fact that words such as *first, second,* and *third* when used in context frequently give a clue to part of the structure of the paragraph or a group of paragraphs in which they are used.

The pupils can draw a series of pictures illustrating in sequence events in a story.

The boys and girls can make a list of questions or topics on which they want to obtain information when studying a unit and then they can list the questions or topics under different headings.

The pupils can arrange in correct order a series of paragraphs on a topic in which the sentences are presented to them in scrambled order.

The boys and girls can study the table of contents of a book to note its organization. The teacher can ask questions such as: (a) Which story do you think is about a pet? (b) How many stories are given in the section about "Animal Friends"?

The boys and girls can read a story to plan the scenes they want to include in a dramatization. After the scenes have been listed on the chalkboard, the pupils can check to see whether they are arranged in the right order and, if they are not, arrange them correctly.

2. Methods for outlining (beyond those dealing with organization in general)

Before the teacher gives a short report, he can place on the chalkboard an outline, with the main topics only, of the talk and tell the class that he will follow that outline as he gives a talk. Later on when the boys and girls are ready for learning the use of sub-topics and sub-points of sub-topics, the teacher can place on the chalkboard before he gives a talk, a more complete outline of it.

As the boys and girls make plans for an exhibit the room is presenting, the teacher may ask them to name articles they wish to include in the exhibit and then to classify them. After the pupils have made the classification, the teacher may write it in outline form as the pupils state points to be recorded. The class can then use the outline as they plan how they will secure each article and where they will display it.

In outlines that the teacher places on the chalkboard, attention may be drawn to the lettering and numbering of the main points, the sub-topics and the sub-points, as well as to the use of capital letters, punctuation marks, and indentation.

As the teacher is working out the points of an outline with the boys and girls, he can have them take responsibility for telling where the various points should be placed in the outline, what numerals and letters should be used, and where capital letters and punctuation marks are needed.

The pupils can be given a paragraph and told that it deals, for example, with four points, one of which is already recorded on the chalkboard. Then the pupils can be asked to find the other three points and name them for the teacher to write on the chalkboard. A paragraph on "Clothes of the Indians" may be duplicated and part of an outline on it, in a form such as the following, written on the chalkboard for the pupils to complete:

Clothes of the Indians

I. What the men wore
II. ....
III. ....
IV. ....

The teacher can give the pupils a written report and an outline of it in which some of the sub-topics are in incorrect order, with the direction that they rearrange them correctly.

The boys and girls are helped in learning the terminology of outlining, such as *main points* and *sub-topics,* first by seemingly incidental reference to them by the teacher. Later the teacher may write the words on the chalkboard and after explaining what parts each designates, the pupils may be asked to use those terms in their discussion and explanation.

To give the pupils practice in writing the form of an outline correctly, the teacher may give them an outline correct in content but incorrect in form in that periods, capital letters, and numerals and letters for lists are omitted.

The teacher can give the boys and girls an outline of a reading assignment and suggest ways in which they can use it as they are studying.

The teacher can give the pupils an outline form with the name of the subject as in the following case:

Old and New Ways of Communication

I. ....
  A. ....
    1. ....
    2. ....
  B. ....
II. ....
  A. ....
  B. ....
  C. ....

With an outline form like the foregoing the boys and girls may be given a list of topics to serve as main topics, sub-topics, and sub-points to sub-topics, with the direction that they should fit them into the outline form.

The pupils can be helped in learning that the divisions of the same order in an outline must be "mutually exclusive and collectively exhaustive" by: (a) showing them some outlines in which the principle is observed; (b) showing them some outlines in which it is not observed; and (c) having them write an outline in which it is observed, which they can discuss with the class in terms of the principle.

The pupils can be given help in keeping points under a given division or subdivision in an outline parallel in structure so that if *I* is given in sentence form, *II* and *III* are also so listed or that if *A* under *I* is in phrase form, *B* and *C* are also listed as phrases. They can be helped to understand this point by the teacher doing the following: (a) emphasizing the point as models are studied; (b) helping them observe the point as an outline is being worked out by the class as a whole; (c) providing them with opportunity to check outlines that they write to note whether or not they observed the point.

CORRECT USAGE

There has long been controversy as to whether the work on correct usage in the elementary school should include grammar and, if it should, what grammar should be taught and how. Part of the controversy is due to fundamental differences of opinion. At one extreme are those who believe in formal grammar; at the other are those who contend that all work on correct usage in the elementary school should be incidental study, without any attempt at helping the pupil arrive at rules or generalizations or names of the parts of speech, of the parts of sentences, and other so-called grammatical terms. Between these two extremes are various shades of opinion.

Part of the controversy is due to lack of definition of the term *grammar*. If grammar is thought of as the formal study of rules governing the structure of the words and groups of words within a sentence, to be applied in practice situations without close relationship to meaningful experiences involving true communication, then many teachers are definitely opposed to teaching grammar in the elementary school. However, if grammar is thought of as the study of words or groups of words within a sentence in such a way that the sentences an individual uses will therefore tend to be structurally correct (whether or not such study involves arriving at some generalizations that are meaningful to the learner) then many teachers favor teaching grammar in the elementary school. Unless terms have been clarified in any argument on the subject the possibility of misunderstandings due to lack of clarity must be recognized.

Guidelines

In the writer's opinion the following points can be used as guidelines.

1. *In the elementary school there is no place for formal grammar which deals primarily with the study of rules.* Memorizing many rules of grammar seems to have little effect on the English an individual uses. Persons who know many rules may fail to apply them. Individuals who use good English do not necessarily have knowledge of the rules of grammar.

2. *In the elementary school much emphasis should be placed on learning correct English through teaching-learning situations that to the learner seem incidental.* Since an individual is greatly influenced in his speech and in his written expression by the type of English he hears, the importance of the example the teacher sets in his speech is of vital concern. Furthermore, with due consideration of habit formation, the teacher needs to give the child many opportunities for speech in informal as well as in more or less formal speaking situations.

3. *Incidental teaching of correct usage, through the ongoing classroom activities, does not for many pupils constitute an adequate program.* Direct attention to matters of correct usage, beyond that which

is given through more or less incidental attention to them, needs to be given as a rule.

4. *There are different levels of English.* The level of what is considered acceptable English varies with socioeconomic conditions. Then, too, in varying situations an individual may advisedly use a different level of English. The informality of speech that is perfectly acceptable for communication on the playground often is not satisfactory in somewhat more formal classroom and out-of-school situations.

5. *In trying to help the child advance from the level of English, if it is a low level, to which he is accustomed in his home, the teacher needs to proceed with tact.* Children may resent insistence by the school on a level of expression markedly different from that to which they have been accustomed. In fact, the child whose family background of oral expression is directly or indirectly criticized by the school may develop a feeling of insecurity. The intimate language of his own family is tied up in the child with awareness of belongingness that, if destroyed, may leave the child at loss in a world where he needs all the security he can get in order to develop to the maximum during the critical years of his childhood. On the other hand, unless the English being taught at school is going to function outside of school, there is not much chance for marked improvement. Any policy, therefore, on the part of the teacher to encourage the child to think that it is quite all right to speak in whatever way he has been speaking outside of school is also detrimental to progress in English.

6. *Pupils need to be convinced of reasons for improving their English.* Unless boys and girls are truly motivated to change their patterns of expression, attempts by the teacher to alter them may result in resentment.

7. *Much of the work on the improvement of English in terms of correct usage should be oral rather than written.* One reason for this preference for the oral over the written when concerned with matters of correct usage common to both methods of expression is that many more such errors are made in oral expression. Many a pupil who is not likely to write *it don't* may, in speaking, when he has less time to think as he is expressing himself, make that error. Since many of the incorrect expressions have been heard rather than read, it seems reasonable to attack the difficulty in the type of situation in which the errors have become somewhat ingrained in the individual.

8. *As a rule, it is undesirable to interrupt a child while he is speaking, in order to correct his English.* If a child is corrected while speaking, especially when he is giving a talk, he will probably be embarrassed. He can easily then lose the train of the easy flow of his thought and in the future may be paying more attention to the form of his speech than to the content. There are times, however, when the agreement might be — when the class has been working on the overcoming of a specific type of error (let us say, the use of the unnecessary *and*) — that a child should be stopped when he makes the error. In such cases the value of the interruption should be clearly recognized by the boys and girls.

9. *There are times when the pupils should have responsibility for correcting the English of their peers.* Some teachers shy away from this practice for fear that an individual may be hurt if he is criticized by his classmates. They know that it is often harder to take even just criticism from one's equals than from one's superiors. They also realize that at times boys and girls may be criticized by their peers in an unfriendly manner. However, the values that can be attained through evaluation by classmates are so great that use of this important source of help should not be neglected in a classroom in which the teacher has been able to help the pupils establish an atmosphere usually characterized by mutual trust, good will, and helpfulness. Nor should pupil appraisal of each other be limited to noting points of strength. Such evaluation would be weak and often insincere.

10. *There is no sound objection to teaching some of the terms of grammar such as declarative sentence, subject, predicate, the names of the parts of speech, common noun, proper noun.* To steer away from all use of such terms and, for example, throughout the elementary school call nouns *name words,* seems to the writer to be somewhat insulting to a child's ability to learn new words. Teachers should realize how much children can enjoy extending their vocabulary and how quickly they acquire terms such as *countdown, capsule,* and *orbit.* No teacher will think that he should say *circle around* instead of *orbit* as he talks with sixth-grade boys and girls, to whom the meaning of the term *orbit* can readily be made clear. Why then think that pupils who enjoy adding new words to their vocabulary when they are presented, must always, in the elementary school, talk about *words that tell how, when, or where* instead of referring to them as *adverbs*?

11. *As a rule, emphasis should be put in any one grade on only those points the knowledge of which when put into practice will improve the pupil's skill in expression.* For example, if no pupil in a room uses double negatives, prolonged drill on them may be worse than useless.

12. *The teacher can determine the needs of pupils through a variety of ways, both those of individuals and those of the class as a whole.* Some teachers like to keep a record of errors that they hear in the classroom or playground during the first weeks of school. A tally as to the frequency of each error, insofar as practical, and a record as to who made each mistake are valuable. Or the teacher may wish to make a count of errors occurring in the pupils' written work. If the check is on written work, the teacher should remember when interpreting his data that errors in correct usage of word forms occur much more commonly in oral than in written communication. The use of standardized tests or of teacher-made tests if they are carefully checked for validity is a further device for determining points that should be emphasized.

13. *Emphasis should be placed on application rather than on memorization of rules.* This statement is not to be interpreted as meaning that no generalizations or rules are to be learned. The writer of this book believes that there are generalizations that children should know, even though he recognizes that in many instances they should not be developed with the boys and girls since many learnings in the area of correct usage can be acquired through repeated exposure to correct speech or written expression without conscious formulation of generalizations. We do not hesitate to help boys and girls develop generalizations in the natural world of science for we know that they can be of real value to them in various situations. Similarly we should not keep from helping boys and girls develop generalizations about matters of correct usage. Fear of teaching formal grammar should not keep the teacher from tying points being learned, together in the form of generalizations. However, the value of generalizations lies in their application. Boys and girls seem to be more likely to understand and to make use of rules if they have been learned inductively and then applied rather than if the rule has first been stated by the teacher. A teaching plan showing how to help boys and girls develop and apply generalizations is given in Chapter 14. (See page 305.)

14. *Since many errors in the use of English may have become a habit for a pupil, they usually cannot be eradicated at once.* The teacher should make provision for repeated emphasis on points that have been studied. Patience is required by the teacher when he wishes to help a child break a habit and acquire a new one in its stead.

What Should Be Taught

Criteria to be applied in determining in part what should be taught are discussed on preceding pages of this chapter. Need, level of difficulty, and importance are mentioned. In the application of these criteria there are real difficulties. No one study has yet ascertained even on a national level (to say nothing of what should be done in any particular room) what topics should be taken up in the elementary school. Although these are shortcomings in any list that has been compiled, two that the teacher may wish to check are those by Robert C. Pooley[1] and Paul McKee.[2]

Methods

Suggestions for teaching pupils to recognize sentences and helping them identify kinds of sentences are given on preceding pages of this chapter. The suggestions following are grouped as to ideas for teaching (1) subject and predicate, (2) verbs, and (3) other phases of correct usage.

SUBJECT AND PREDICATE. The teacher can be of help to the pupils by:

1. Writing on the chalkboard a list of simply constructed declarative sentences and then asking the class about what each of the sentences tells as he underlines the complete subject of each sentence
2. Telling the boys and girls that the part of the sentence that tells what the sentence is about is the subject of the sentence
3. Asking the pupils to name the subject of declarative sentences written on the chalkboard or on paper and to give the reason for their selection
4. Asking the pupils to form sentences in each of which one of a specified group of words is used as the subject, like: (a) the boys, (b) some men
5. Having the boys and girls select the subject and predicate in each of a list of declarative sentences
6. Asking the pupils to find the subject of an interrogative sentence. The teacher may help the pupils find the subject after he has changed the question to declarative order as in:

Interrogative form: What are you doing?
Declarative form: You are doing what?

Then the teacher may point out to the pupils that when they try to find the subject of an interrogative sentence, they may find it of help to change the question to declarative order.

7. Pointing out to the class that when they try to find the subject of an exclamatory sentence not in the same order as the usual declarative sentence, it

[1] Robert C. Pooley, *Teaching English Usage.* English Monograph No. 16. D. Appleton Century Company, 1946, pages 180-181.

[2] Paul McKee, *Language Arts in the Elementary School.* Houghton Mifflin Company, 1939, pages 292-294.

may help them to change the exclamation to declarative form

8. After writing on the chalkboard a group of imperative sentences, the teacher may, for example, ask questions like this one about the sentence "Come here right away": "When I say, 'Come here right away,' whom do I want to come right away?" Then the teacher may point out that the sentence really means "You come here right away." Next he may ask the pupils for the subject in that changed sentence and tell them, if necessary, that *you*, which is understood, is the subject. Then he may have the pupils examine a list of imperative sentences in order to be able to arrive at the generalization that *you* (understood) is always the subject of an imperative sentence.

9. Having the boys and girls act out a sentence to help them in determining the subject and predicate

10. Asking the pupils to find the subject and predicate of each of two short sentences that can be combined into one sentence with a compound subject like:

> The boys went on a picnic.
> The girls went on a picnic.

Then the teacher may have the pupils find the subject of the sentence "The boys and girls went on a picnic," as well as of other sentences with a compound subject. He can next tell them that subjects connected by *and*, *or*, or *nor* are called compound subjects. Work on compound predicates can be done similarly.

11. After the boys and girls have selected the complete subject of a sentence in which the subject consists of more than one word, asking them to name the most important word in the subject – the one word that names what the sentence tells about. After they have selected the most important word in the subject of each of several sentences, the teacher may tell the class that such a word is called the *simple subject*. Thereupon the pupils may be asked to select the simple and the complete subjects of several sentences. Work on the simple and complete predicates can be done similarly.

12. Encouraging the pupils to make a poster that will remind them how to find the subject and the predicate of a sentence

13. Asking the pupils to find in a paragraph a sentence with a compound subject, a sentence with a compound predicate, and a sentence with both a compound subject and a compound predicate

14. Providing the boys and girls with practice in forming sentences with compound subjects and sentences with compound predicates out of short groups of sentences that can be combined in that manner

15. Helping the pupils find the subject and predicate of declarative sentences in which the subject is not at the beginning of the sentence, like "Early in the morning they left for home."

16. Asking the boys and girls to match the subjects in one column with the predicates in another like the following:

The rain	went to the bakery.
The book	will make the grass green.
We	are blooming.
The flowers	contains many interesting stories.

VERBS. The teacher can help the boys and girls in learning about verbs by:

1. Correcting a pupil who uses the past participle instead of the past tense, or vice versa, as the teacher tells the pupil the correct form and asks him to repeat it. For example, when a child says, "I done it," the teacher says, "We say, 'I *did* it.'"

2. Teaching which verb form to use, when developing generalizations such as the following:

> *Done* is usually used with a helping word.
> It is never correct to use *did* with a helping word.

A teaching plan illustrating a developmental lesson of this type is given in Chapter 14. (See page 305.)

Figure 6.5 Use of Illustrations to Emphasize Correct Usage

Courtesy of The University School, The Ohio State University.

Figure 6.6 Reading, an Aid to Oral and Written Expression

3. Correcting the pupil who uses a singular verb when a plural form should be used, or vice versa, as the teacher tells him the correct form and asks him to repeat it

4. Following some of the suggestions given below under "Other Phases of Correct Usage."

OTHER PHASES OF CORRECT USAGE. Here are additional suggestions that the teacher can follow in helping the boys and girls learn to speak and write correctly.

1. Have the pupils make application of their learnings by filling blanks in sentences, by choosing the correct form in sentences of the multiple-choice type, and by using sentences of their own to illustrate the correct form.

2. Encourage the pupils to make a handbook on correct usage or on some phase of it.

3. Encourage some pupils to put on a skit showing the value of speaking according to what they have learned about the correct usage or about a phase of it.

4. Suggest that some pupils make cartoons or posters illustrating points in correct usage.

5. Encourage the pupils to make crossword puzzles that are based on knowledge of correct usage.

FOR STUDY AND DISCUSSION

1. Name meaningful situations, in addition to those listed in the chapter (see page 103), through which vocabulary development can be encouraged in the elementary school.

2. Devise a practice exercise to help boys and girls in any one of the intermediate grades improve in some phase of sentence structure.

3. Plan a developmental lesson in which boys and girls in an intermediate grade receive help in paragraph structure.

4. To apply some points on outlining stressed in this chapter, write the outline for this chapter using letters and numerals to indicate the various parts.

5. Name ways in which growth in the correct use of words (correct usage) can be stimulated in the elementary school.

6. Devise diagrams of bulletin boards that can be used to encourage and to help boys and girls with correct word usage.

7. Examine a recent language-arts series for use of elementary-school pupils and note what items of grammar are taught and the grade level at which each is presented.

8. Devise a crossword puzzle based on knowledge of words as a device for helping boys and girls increase their word power.

Figure 6.7 Cartoon to Emphasize Comparison of Adjectives

REFERENCES

For references for this chapter the reader is referred to those given at the end of Chapter 5 and of Chapter 6 and to those given in Chapter 15.

OUTLINE FOR CHAPTER 7

Guiding Growth in Handwriting

CHAPTER 7

Guiding Growth in Handwriting

Regardless of whether or not there is justification for the complaint that handwriting has deteriorated, it must be acceded that the quality of the handwriting of the American people is on a much lower level than it could be expected to be in a nation that has been and is giving unparalleled attention in terms of time, money, and man power to providing educational opportunities for its citizenry.

What are the evidences of the inadequacy of writing ability in school and out of school? Research has given partial answers; however, no scientific study is necessary to establish convincing proof. Commonly known facts such as the following provide it.

1. Addresses on so many letters are illegible or almost unreadable that some of the large post offices have on their staff individuals whose responsibility it is to try to decipher such addresses.

2. Many of the letters received at the Dead Letter Office are referred to it because the handwriting could not be figured out by the personnel in the post office. Many of the letters relegated to that office never reach their destination because even experts in the Dead Letter Office are not able to determine to what addresses they are to be sent.

3. Business yearly loses large amounts of money because of errors and wasted time caused by illegibility of writing on sales slips, on checks, and in letters ordering things.

4. Students receive lower marks than they otherwise might on examinations and on other handwritten papers because their handwriting is such that the teacher cannot readily comprehend the meaning that the writer is attempting to convey.

5. Recipients of friendly letters have difficulty in figuring out the meaning that their correspondents are attempting to express and at times are unable to ascertain it even after considerable attention has been given to trying to decipher it.

6. The character of much writing, even when legible, is so inartistic that the reader is deprived of a certain aesthetic satisfaction that can result from viewing something well done.

7. Many persons, it seems, refrain from writing because they know they are inefficient in that skill in terms of effort required and of the results they achieve.

BASIC CONSIDERATIONS IN TEACHING HANDWRITING

Before turning to a study of specific procedures for guiding growth in handwriting, let us give attention to certain important considerations.

Causes of Neglect of Handwriting

Light may be thrown on how to guide growth in handwriting by inquiring as to the reasons for the partial neglect in the past by many teachers of the development of skill in handwriting. The following are among contributing causes.

1. There has been a lack of knowledge on the part of many teachers of the psychology of handwriting in that (a) they do not recognize the skill aspects of written communication and (b) they do not understand the principles underlying the teaching of skills.

2. There has been a tendency to emphasize incidental learning rather than an efficient combination of systematic instruction with the incidental.

3. The disappearance of the penmanship supervisor was not followed by steps to give the classroom teacher adequate preparation for the teaching of

handwriting, which was delegated almost solely to him.

4. The alleged claim, prevalent in and out of school, that excellence in handwriting is no longer very important in the modern world of the typewriter and other machines used for communication purposes, took away motive for effective teaching and learning of how to write.

5. Recognition of the shortcomings of writing practices that had been popularly followed caused many persons to revolt against systematic practice of any kind.

Shortcomings of Earlier Practices

Following are listed undesirable features of some earlier practices in teaching handwriting.

1. An overemphasis was often placed on handwriting as a skill.

2. Undue attention was frequently paid to the mechanics of handwriting.

3. There was at times excessive emphasis on formal, isolated drill.

4. Much drill was of a mechanistic type.

5. There was little correlation made, on the part of some teachers, between drill on handwriting and the work in the content subjects.

6. Skills acquired during the writing period often did not carry over into writing done at other times of the school day or outside of school.

7. There was in some schools a great preponderance of group instruction over individualized instruction.

8. Uniformity of style was stressed by some teachers to the neglect of individuality.

Goals of Instruction

A sound program of instruction cannot be planned merely through an avoidance of past teaching errors. A constructive program must (a) be determined by worthy goals of instruction and (b) be in harmony with sound principles of teaching.

General Objectives. Simply stated, the aim of handwriting instruction is to help boys and girls learn to write legibly and neatly without undue strain and at a commendable rate. The quality that is often considered desirable for the upper-grade pupil and for the adult is that represented by a score of 60 on the Ayres' Handwriting Scale, with 50 as the absolute minimum of acceptable handwriting. For teachers a score of 70 on the same scale is frequently considered the lowest satisfactory quality. An acceptable rate depends to such a great extent upon the purpose of the writing that no one over-all minimum desirable rate can be quoted.

There is another objective in teaching handwriting that is important to achieve if improvement is not to be an unduly difficult attainment and if results are to be permanent. That objective has to do with the desire of the learner. Unless he really wants to write well, acquiring skill in handwriting is likely to be a more laborious process than it would be were the learner truly interested in becoming a good writer.

The general objectives of handwriting instruction can be summarized thus:

1. The pupil should learn to write legibly, probably with the quality of handwriting represented by a score of 60 to 70 on the Ayres' Handwriting Scale.

2. The pupil should become able to produce a neat paper, written without smudges, signs of erasures, or crossing out what had been recorded. He should use a format suitable to the material and the purposes for which the writing is being done.

3. The pupil should acquire the ability to write for a rather long time without undue strain.

4. The pupil should learn to be able to write at a fairly rapid rate.

5. The pupil should acquire or maintain the desire to write well.

Specific Goals. Whether or not a teacher uses a commercially-produced handwriting series, the programs suggested by the better series may be of help to him in determining the specific aims he wishes to accomplish. Following are indicated the goals as recorded for grades one and six in *I Learn to Write* by E. C. Seale and Company.[1] For statements of the goals in that program for grades 2, 3, 4, and 5, the reader is referred to the teachers' manuals of that company.

1. Grade One

"By the end of grade one, most children should have achieved these objectives: [page 17, Book One]

They enjoy writing.

They are interested in improving their writing.

They have developed the ability to criticize their writing and to improve it.

Their writing is easy to read.

They make each letter so that it is not confused with any other letter.

They write words so that each is easily recognized as it stands alone.

They have made obvious progress in different technical phases of writing."

[1] E. C. Seale and Company, *I Learn to Write* (teacher's edition), Book One and Book Two. E. C. Seale and Company, 1963. Material used with permission of the Bobbs-Merrill Company, Indianapolis, Ind., publishers of the E. C. Seale and Company *I Learn to Write* Series.

2. Grade Six
"Children should have attained these goals by the time they begin their sixth-grade work: [page 23, Book Two]
Realize the functional value of writing
Recognize the necessity for legible writing
Can make, without hesitation, good, legible letters in context
Can evaluate their own writing and detect causes of illegibility
Have established habits of posture and movement necessary for easy and uniform writing."

"Goals to be achieved by the end of Grade Six are:
To improve upon the skills developed during previous years
To increase ability to express thought in clear, correct language
To organize material in such a way that it makes a neat, attractive page
To be aware of the personal responsibility for easily-read writing in all social and business situations."

Guidelines

The relationship between the selection of goals such as the following, and the formulation of guidelines should be two-way. The goals should in part determine the guidelines, and the guidelines should to some extent be useful in arriving at the goals.

1. Readiness for writing and for the various stages in learning to write should be determined and, if necessary, developed.
2. Handwriting should be correlated with work in other areas, including not only the other language-arts activities but also other phases of the school curriculum and out-of-school activities.
3. Since handwriting is in part a muscular-neural skill, the laws governing economic development of skills should be observed in the teaching.
4. Practice conditions should approximate as much as possible those under which a skill will be required in nonpractice situations.
5. Since handwriting is more than a skill – also a means of self-expression – more than the drill aspects should be emphasized.
6. Since example is important in learning, the teacher's handwriting should serve as a model of what he wants to teach.
7. Although legibility of handwriting calls for considerable uniformity, nevertheless individuality of writing, within limits, should not be discouraged.
8. A pupil in the elementary school should learn to write so well that in his written communication he can, in time, give his almost complete attention to the ideas he wishes to express rather than to the phases of the writing act.
9. Systematic instruction should be paralleled with much opportunity for incidental learning.
10. Attention should be paid not only to legibility but also to the ease and speed with which writing is done and the attitude of the writer toward it.
11. Emphasis should not be placed primarily on letter strokes or letter forms but on thought units of expression – on words, sentences, paragraphs, and longer forms of written communication.
12. There should be emphasis on the attainment of good posture, rhythmic movement, and other mechanical features of good handwriting; but the learner should be helped to realize that these aspects of the handwriting program receive their significance primarily through their relationship to the final outcomes as shown in improved handwriting.
13. Individual differences should be recognized and the program planned to meet them adequately.
14. Standards of good handwriting against which he can compare his own writing should be made available to the learner, and he should be given needed help in making self-evaluations.
15. Pupils should not only be cognizant of sound goals for the handwriting program as a whole but should also have specific goals in mind for each day's work on improvement in ability to write.
16. The value of rewards should be recognized, with major emphasis on the intrinsic which knowledge of progress offers, but also if it seems desirable on extrinsic rewards in the form of praise. Only limited use, if any, should be made of such signs of accomplishment as awards, buttons, or badges.
17. There should be a working atmosphere in the classroom that can greatly contribute to the probable effectiveness of learning – characterized by pupils happily busy with an activity they consider worthwhile and an orderliness which prevents undue interference with anyone's success by others in the room.

ORGANIZATION

No final answer, convincing to all educators, has been found to the question, "How can the classroom best be organized for providing an effective program of instruction in handwriting?" Two of the points of controversy related to this question will now be discussed.

Incidental versus Systematic Instruction

The chief point of argument in the debate seems to deal with whether or not the most effective organization is to have class periods set aside for teaching handwriting or whether the instruction should be given incidentally in other than handwriting periods. Let us examine arguments for and against the use of class periods set aside for that purpose.

ARGUMENTS ADVANCED AGAINST PERIODS FOR TEACHING HANDWRITING. Arguments such as the following are commonly given against separate periods for handwriting instruction.

1. There is danger of lack of carry-over from separate periods for writing practice to ordinary writing situations.

2. Boys and girls find more purpose in writing that is done as part of the ongoing activities of the school program than in that done during periods set aside specifically for learning to write.

3. There are so many individual differences among boys and girls, as reflected in the type of help they should be given in handwriting, that large-group instruction is impractical.

4. It is a waste of time for many pupils to have regular class work for the improvement of handwriting.

ARGUMENTS FAVORING PERIODS FOR TEACHING HANDWRITING. Following are listed not only arguments advanced in refutation of those enumerated but also additional ones in favor of setting aside periods in the school program for teaching handwriting.

1. Handwriting is too complex a skill to be trusted for proper development to only incidental methods of procedure.

2. Without systematic instruction boys and girls are likely to develop poor habits of writing which need to be broken because the learner is left "on his own" at crucial stages in the development of handwriting habits.

3. When separate periods are used for instruction in handwriting, it is possible to develop a program in which the pupil is helped to progress from easier to more difficult phases in learning to write more effectively than in incidental programs.

4. Primary focus on a skill to be developed, at a time when other considerations are secondary, is frequently characteristic of a more effective teaching procedure than a less direct attack on a problem.

5. Systematic instruction can provide the learner with the practice needed at well distributed intervals.

6. Even in handwriting classes much attention can and should be paid not only to the skills needed for effective handwriting but also to the use of writing in meaningful situations.

7. Even in a program in which a separate period is used for handwriting, much attention can and should be paid to it in all writing activities in which the pupil engages.

8. Often fundamental skills and basic habits can be developed most economically through group rather than individual instruction.

9. The handwriting class can and should be taught in such a way that not all instruction is given as a group process but that work is individualized as needed.

10:20 - 10:25	Presentation of new work to class
10:25 - 10:32	Work on practice exercise on new work by class as group
10:32 - 10:45	Application of new learning to activities requiring writing by various individuals, with teacher guidance

Figure 7.1 Plan for Group and Individual Help during Handwriting Class

10. Pupils who require less time for the development of writing skills and habits — less than others in the class — can and should be excused from class whenever attendance seems not to be indicated for them.

Nature of the Handwriting Period

Surveys indicate that the predominant practice in the schools of the country seems to be to set aside a period in the school program for the teaching of handwriting.

FREQUENCY AND LENGTH OF WRITING PERIODS. There is, as might well be expected, considerable variation in the frequency and length of periods for handwriting. In some school systems systematic instruction in handwriting ceases at the end of the sixth grade while other schools continue the program through grade eight. In many schools provision is made for a handwriting class daily, while in others handwriting is taught fewer than five days a week. From 15 to 20 minutes is often the length of a handwriting period, but in the lower grades periods of only 10 minutes are also found in some schedules.

THE WRITING PERIOD AS PART OF A LANGUAGE-ARTS BLOCK. A practice followed with success in an increasing number of schools is that of providing for systematic instruction in handwriting by means of a block of time set aside for all the language arts other than reading. In such a block, for example, 20 minutes may be used daily for spelling class, 20 minutes on some days for handwriting class, and 20 minutes or more for other language-arts activities. In place of this, separate classes in handwriting may be held within that hour only two or three times a week, varying from week to week. During these periods special emphasis can be placed on the development of basic habits and skills of handwriting and on individual diagnosis followed by appropriate remediation. On the other days of the week the only writing done during the language-arts period is in connection with the writing in spelling class and in other language-arts activities, such as writing a report or writing a poem.

MATERIALS OF INSTRUCTION

One way in which the teacher can obtain a good idea of the materials available for teaching handwriting is to examine the catalogs of leading publishers.

Materials Distributed by One Company

The following are among the handwriting materials listed in a recent catalog of the Zaner-Bloser Company for the *Guiding Growth in Handwriting* series by Frank N. Freeman.

1. Recorders, in which the pupils write, with special provision for variation in grade level from school to school, at which the transition is made from manuscript to cursive writing
2. Reference manuals for teachers
3. Other books for teachers or pupils, namely:

   Writing on the Board (96 pages)
   Solving Handwriting Needs as We Look Ahead to the Pace-Setting Sixties (by Frank N. Freeman, 34 pages)
   The Whys and Hows of Teaching Handwriting (by Emma Myers, 160 pages)
   Penmanship Step by Step (by Max Rosenbaum, 80 pages)
   Greatest Book on Modern Engrossing (136 pages)
   Readable Handwriting (by Max Rosenbaum, 80 pages)
   Manual 96 (96 pages)
   Lessons in Ornamental Penmanship (96 pages)
   Pocket Alphabet (by Max Rosenbaum, for pupil use, 24 pages)
   Our Print Letters and How to Make Them (for pupil use, 64 pages)
   Our ABC's and How to Improve Them (cursive, 64 pages)

4. Scales, for both manuscript and cursive writing
5. Wall strips, in both manuscript and cursive writing
6. Aids to correct writing position, including: (a) "writing frame," as illustrated, into which any pen can be inserted and which can be used by right-handed or left-handed writers; (b) "Body position charts," illustrating correct position for manuscript and for cursive writing for the right-handed writer; (c) "Left-handed body position charts," illustrating correct position for manuscript and for cursive writing for the left-handed writer; and (d) "Hand charts," showing a correct arm position
7. Transparent rulers, including the "Diagnostic ruler" and the "C-thru-Ruler"
8. Other aids to correct letter formation including: (a) three alphabet worksheets, entitled "Manuscript Alphabet Worksheets," "Transition Alphabet Worksheets," and "Cursive Alphabet Worksheets"; (b) two "Alphabet Sheets," one for manuscript and one for cursive writing; (c) a chart entitled "Handwriting Faults and How to Correct Them"; (d) two booklets entitled "Alphabet Antics," one for manuscript and

<u>Plan for Oct. 1.</u>

1:00 - 1:20	Spelling: presentation of words for week
1:20 - 2:00	Language: writing stories

<u>Plan for Oct. 2.</u>

1:00 - 1:20	Spelling: oral and written work
1:20 - 1:40	Handwriting: developmental lesson
1:40 - 2:00	Language: oral work on correct usage

<u>Plan for Oct. 3.</u>

1:00 - 1:20	Spelling: trial test
1:20 - 2:00	Language: planning a puppet play

Figure 7.2 Illustration of a Language-Arts Block

one for cursive writing; (e) "Peek-Thru" alphabets, for manuscript and cursive writing; (f) "Your Alphabet Guide Chart"; and (g) two units, one called "Word-Building Unit," for use in making the transition from manuscript to cursive writing, and the other the "Size Reduction Unit," of help in reducing the size from one-half inch to one-quarter inch

9. Writing paper, with a large variety available, both lined and unlined, with rulings ranging from two inches to one-quarter inch apart, some with alternate light and heavy lines, of various sizes and colors, in tablet and in separate-sheet form. Various sizes of large chart paper, ruled, is also available.

10. Crayons, pencils, penholders, and pen points, including among others:

Readiness to Write Crayon
Finger-fitting Guest Pen Ballpoint
Primary Ballpoint
Finger-fitting Penholders
Double-end Ballpoint Pen
Double-end Primary Ballpoint Pen
Primary Pencil (manuscript)
Z. B. Finger-fitting Pencil (standard size lead)
Double-end Pencil (standard size lead)
The Zanerian Fine Writer Point
Lucky Color Quartette Guest Pen Set
Flo-Master
Felt-Tip Cado-marker.

11. Film strips, on manuscript and cursive writing
12. Awards, "for writing legibly," another "for improving my writing," and a third "for writing effort."

Selection of Materials

In choosing suitable materials for the various age or grade levels, the teacher may be guided by suggestions such as those given in the teacher's edition of *I Learn to Write,* Book One, published by E. C. Seale and Company (1963), pages 8 and 9.

CHOOSING PENCILS. Concerning pencils the following recommendations are given in the teacher's edition of *I Learn to Write,* Book One, to which reference is made in the preceding paragraph.

> Children in the first or second grade require special tools which will aid in developing those finer muscles used for writing. Most of them can write more easily with a larger diameter pencil — somewhat reduced for second grade — than with one of regular size. The pencil should have a smooth, round surface and be of average length. An extra-soft, large-diameter lead which produces, without pressure, the firm, broad strokes necessary for large writing is recommended. Third-grade pupils usually write with a standard-size pencil; however, a round, smooth design is still advisable. Extra-soft lead is preferable to medium-hard lead because it allows a child to make a darker mark without applying undue pressure.
>
> Rubber-tipped pencils are not recommended for primary youngsters. Stopping where a mistake occurs, marking a line through the error, moving the pencil a space, and rewriting the word improves page appearance and is a valuable time-saver.

CHOOSING PAPER. In the teacher's edition of *I Learn to Write,*[2] these points are emphasized about the paper on which the pupils write.

> Paper for primary grades should be a good quality newsprint, which is the type best suited for soft lead pencils. Rulings must be clearly marked and should conform to the generally approved and accepted specifications for each grade level.
>
> Grade One: one-inch spacing between top and baseline with center guide line, and additional half-inch space for letters that extend below the baseline.
> Grade Two (manuscript and transition); three-fourths inch spacing between top and baseline with center guide line, and additional three-eighths inch space for letters that extend below the baseline.
> Grade Two (reduced manuscript) and Grade Three (transition): one-half inch spacing between top and baseline with center guide line.
> Grade Three (cursive): one-half inch spacing between top and baseline with no center guide line.
> Grades Four through Eight: three-eighths inch space between top and baseline.

MANUSCRIPT VERSUS CURSIVE WRITING

A very radical change in style of handwriting was introduced into the American schools in the 1930's when manuscript writing began to be taught in quite a number of primary grades. The method quickly spread from school system to school system. Because of differences in samplings and in sampling techniques, investigations vary in their findings as to the extent to which manuscript writing is now being taught in the elementary schools of our country. A conservative estimate is that it is used in at least 85 per cent of the schoolrooms of the nation as a beginning method of instruction. Research has established the fact that in by far the greater number of the schools in which manuscript writing is used as the beginning method of handwriting a change is made to cursive writing after one or more years of manuscript writing.

---

[2]Material used with permission of the Bobbs-Merrill Company, Indianapolis, Ind., publishers of the E. C. Seale and Company *I Learn to Write* Series.

Arguments Advanced for Manuscript Writing in Lower Grades

Reasons such as the following seem to have convinced the vast majority of educators that as an introductory system of handwriting manuscript is superior to cursive writing.

1. Because of the muscular immaturity of the beginner it is easier for him to write manuscript than cursive. In manuscript writing, which consists of straight lines, circles, and parts of circles, he has chance for more periods of rest since he lifts his crayon or pencil more frequently – typically at the end of every stroke of a letter – than in cursive writing. In the case of many words in cursive writing, the writer lifts his tool only after he has completed the entire word.

2. For a beginner, because of his muscular immaturity and his comparatively low mental age, it is easier to master the three separate strokes of manuscript writing – the straight line, the circle, and the part of a circle – than it is to gain facility in making the larger number of strokes in cursive writing.

3. Since manuscript writing more closely than cursive resembles the print which the pupil finds in the books he reads, use of manuscript reinforces his learning to read rather than confuses him.

4. In the early stages of manuscript writing the child can write meaningful messages sooner than if he were learning cursive writing.

5. Manuscript writing is more legible than cursive.

6. Manuscript writing takes less time than cursive.

Arguments Advanced Against Manuscript Writing in Lower Grades

Even though manuscript writing is used almost universally in our schools as a beginning method, there are some persons who question its use. Arguments advanced against the use of manuscript writing, such as those given following, should be considered because there has been no absolute scientific proof to establish the superiority of one system over the other. Popularity of a method must not be confused with excellence.

1. It is poor policy to have boys and girls learn two systems of handwriting.

2. There is considerable difference even between manuscript writing and print – a difference that many teachers of beginning reading do not seem to take into account and consequently do not give the pupils the needed guidance in either reading or writing.

3. With manuscript writing it is not possible to use the rhythm and the arm movement attained in cursive writing that are seemingly essentials for minimum fatigue in writing situations of considerable duration.

Consideration of Arguments

In connection with some of the arguments given for or against the use of manuscript writing these points should be kept in mind.

1. There is no conclusive evidence that either manuscript or cursive writing is the more legible if conditions of practice and other factors are kept constant.

2. There is no proof that either manuscript or cursive writing can be executed with greater speed if conditions of practice and other factors are kept equal.

3. When the boys and girls make the transition from manuscript to cursive writing they are spending time and energy trying to learn two systems of handwriting rather than using them to learn one well.

4. Many teachers seem to assume, incorrectly, that the child who knows manuscript writing can automatically read print. It is true, however, that manuscript writing more closely resembles print than does cursive.

5. The argument that it is necessarily easier to achieve suitable rhythm and arm movement in cursive than in manuscript writing has not been established by scientific investigation.

A Dual System of Handwriting

Probably the most convincing of the arguments advanced against the use of manuscript writing lies in the fact that in most of the schools of today there is a subsequent change-over to cursive writing. Responses like the following, which are not accepted by those who oppose a dual system, are made to the objections to manuscript writing on the basis that a dual system is uneconomical of time and energy.

1. Boys and girls under good guidance can accomplish the change-over from manuscript to cursive writing without much difficulty providing the transition is made at the most felicitous time and in the best manner.

2. Learnings from the manuscript writing period can be utilized when learning to do cursive writing.

3. The advantages of using manuscript writing as the initial means of written expression outweigh the disadvantages of the need of a change-over.

4. Since or if the disadvantages of a dual system of handwriting are many and serious, it does not necessarily follow that the one style of writing that should be taught is manuscript. It might be more desirable to teach only cursive writing.

Objections to Manuscript Writing as the One Style of Handwriting

Whenever the desirability of teaching only manuscript writing is suggested, a storm of protest can be expected, not only from the relatively small number of persons opposed to teaching it as a beginning method but also from many who are ardent defenders of the present plan, in operation in most schools, of teaching manuscript writing to beginners and then later making the transition to cursive writing. The chief of these objections, with responses given to each, may be summarized thus:

1. Manuscript writing of signatures is not accepted by banks. (Yet in *Readings in the Language Arts* this information is given:[3]

> Vergil Herrick observed that most banks will accept a manuscript written signature if it is the writer's regular signature. Part of the confusion over this issue lies in the fact that officials may not distinguish between "printing" one's name, that is, the use of all capitals by a person unaccustomed to writing this way and the long-practiced hand of the manuscript writer.)

2. Manuscript writing for many persons is synonymous with the immature writing of young children. (If a large number of adults had been taught only manuscript writing, this objection would soon lose weight.)

3. Children like to learn to write like adults. (Again, as in the case of the preceding argument, this statement would hold little weight after the change to a single system of handwriting – the manuscript style – had been in effect for a decade or so.)

4. Cursive writing is more legible and can be executed with greater speed and with less accompanying fatigue than manuscript. (These claims have not been established scientifically.)

5. Teachers in the upper grades are not adequately prepared to teach manuscript writing. (Were it determined that it is desirable to have a single style of handwriting taught and that the style should be manuscript, provisions could be made for pre-service and in-service education of teachers to overcome this handicap in a relatively short time.)

Time for Transition

Surveys differ in the details of the findings reported as to when the transition is made. This variation undoubtedly is due to a large extent to the variety of the samplings used. However, a study of the reports indicates that while in a few schools the change-over is made as late as in the fourth grade, it usually occurs in the last part of the second or in the third grade. Authorities in the field of handwriting differ considerably as to when it should be made but most of them seem to favor transition not earlier than in third grade.

Here are guidelines that can be followed when trying to determine the optimum time for the transition.

1. The best time differs from class to class and even from pupil to pupil.

2. The methods used during the period of transition should help determine when the change-over should be made.

3. Care should be taken that pupils are not asked to learn a second system of handwriting until they have learned to express themselves with some efficiency and satisfaction in the first.

READINESS FOR WRITING

The importance of readiness for learning to perform an academic activity is not limited to reading and arithmetic, two subject areas in which there has been quite universal recognition of its significance. It needs to be given due attention in relation to beginning writing instruction. Trying to teach a child to write before he is ready for the activity may have detrimental effects on the development of the child in general. More specifically, it may affect adversely his handwriting and his attitude toward it.

Appraisal of Readiness for Writing

To the question "Is this child ready to learn to write?" no one quick answer can be given. The inability to provide a definite answer is due in part to the fact that a child may be ready for the program of beginning writing instruction of one teacher but not another. Even for the same program of writing instruction there are varying degrees of readiness, all of which may be sufficient for the beginner if due attention is paid to individual differences.

POINTS TO NOTE WHEN APPRAISING READINESS. Following are some of the factors that are closely related to success in handwriting and that, consequently, should be noted in an attempt to answer the question, "Is this child ready to learn to write?"

1. *Muscular coordination.* Since writing is in part a muscular activity, the extent of a child's muscular coordination is of great importance. If he lacks ability to do with his muscles what is necessary to produce legibility of handwriting, he is at a disadvantage. If

[3]Verna D. Anderson, Paul S. Anderson, Francis Ballantine, and Virgil M. Howes. *Readings in the Language Arts*. The Macmillan Company, 1964, page 163.

he needs to exert himself exceedingly in order to achieve the muscular coordination needed in writing, he may overstrain himself and he may develop an antagonistic attitude or something akin to fear toward handwriting.

2. *Visual acuity.* For writing the child needs sufficient visual acuity to recognize what is to be written and to be able to see what he has written. Fortunately even children with quite poor eyesight can be ready for writing with proper visual corrections when supplied with suitable writing and reading conditions and appropriate materials.

3. *Visual discrimination.* The child must have not only the necessary eyesight but also ability to make visual discriminations, an ability amenable to training. He needs to be able to recognize differentiating features of letters and words and of other points of importance in handwriting. He must be able to get a clear image of the *b* or the *d,* for example, and to take mental note of the difference in the visual image on his retina.

Which Are Alike?		
b d	m m	u n
d d	n m	n n
d b	n n	u u
b b	m n	n u

Figure 7.3 Exercise to Develop Visual Discrimination

4. *Reading ability.* To be sure, boys and girls can engage in some writing activities before they have learned to read in the sense in which we ordinarily use the word *read* when referring to the reading activities of first-grade pupils. They may, for example, copy a note they have dictated to the teacher who has written it on the chalkboard inviting their parents to visit the classroom. Though the very first stages of learning to write may not include recognition of any of the letters of a word, very early in the program of writing instruction it seems highly desirable that a pupil be able to identify the letters he writes if he is to get the maximum help from the instruction. In general the procedure, maybe almost universally followed, of having systematic instruction in reading begin before systematic instruction in handwriting is started seems justifiable.

5. *Ability to spell.* There is a relationship between writing and spelling that is close, indeed. The child who knows the spelling of a word he is about to copy, for example, is freed from the necessity of concentrating on the sequence of the letters. It is impractical to insist that a child learn to spell a word before he writes it, however, since through writing it he can also acquire the ability to spell it.

6. *Ability to differentiate between right and left.* When group instruction is given in handwriting, as is commonly the practice in the primary grades, it is especially important that the child should be able to differentiate between his right and left hand.

7. *Attention span.* To be ready to receive systematic instruction in handwriting, the pupil needs an attention span that will enable him to pay attention to one activity long enough to participate successfully in the various learning activities required in the program.

8. *Ability to follow directions.* Since a program in systematic instruction in handwriting involves following directions, the child who has difficulty in following simple directions is at a disadvantage. Furthermore, since most handwriting instruction in our schools depends heavily on group methods of teaching, the child who is ready to learn to write should be able to profit from instructions given not only individually but also in a group situation.

9. *Interest in writing.* Interest in an activity is one of the valuable aids to learning. Handwriting is no exception to this rule.

Methods of Appraisal. Of the factors related to writing readiness mentioned in the preceding paragraphs, two can be ascertained by means of standardized tests: (1) visual acuity, by the tests of vision (by a specialist if there is reason for suspecting poor vision) and (2) visual discrimination, by means of sections of some reading readiness tests. The other factors can be noted through observation or teacher-planned testing situations. For example, a child's muscular coordination can be checked by noting how well he handles objects, whether he seems to be free of undue tension when engaged in motor activities, and how well he can draw. Ability to follow directions can be observed as the pupil takes part in the ongoing activities of the classroom or as the teacher administers a test that he has constructed, with directions similar to this one: "On the first line draw a circle and on the second line draw a straight line." Interest in writing can be indicated by questions that the child asks the teacher about writing when he sees the teacher write or about his own "scribbling" attempts at writing.

Development of Readiness

The adult who wishes to see the child become ready to write does not need merely to wait for him to acquire so-called "writing readiness." There are ways in which readiness for writing can be encouraged and developed.

GUIDELINES. First of all, let us note some of the principles that can serve as guidelines in attempts to help the child develop readiness for writing.

1. Boys and girls should be encouraged to participate in the ongoing activities of the home and the school that help in the development of readiness for handwriting.
2. For some children activities should be provided with the intention on the part of the teacher of developing writing readiness. Some of these activities may advisedly be in the form of practice exercises.
3. Care should be taken that the pupils enjoy participating in writing-readiness activities, so that the similarity of the activities to those later used in writing will in some cases interest the child in writing and never prejudice him against it.
4. Tools for written expression should be made readily available to the child.

ONGOING ACTIVITIES IN THE HOME. Encouragement of participation in many of the activities that take place in the home can help the child become ready for handwriting. A few of these are:

1. Listening to interesting material that someone has written or read to the child such as a letter from an absent member of the family
2. Attempting to "write" a letter to an absent member of the family or other friend
3. Dictating to an older person a message to be sent to a friend
4. Drawing or painting
5. Cutting or pasting, which can develop muscular coordination
6. Playing with blocks or toys, which can help develop muscular coordination
7. Observing others in the family receive satisfaction out of writing
8. Modeling with clay
9. Participating in games that require the identification of the right and left hands.

ONGOING ACTIVITIES IN THE SCHOOL. Many activities in the regular school program can be utilized for the development of writing readiness, the following among them:

1. Dictating to the teacher "stories" for an experience chart, lists of materials needed, thank-you notes, and rules to observe
2. Participating in activities that develop hand-eye coordination such as painting, drawing, clay modeling, cutting, and pasting
3. Engaging in activities that develop coordination of the larger muscles, including skipping games, playing with toys and blocks, taking responsibility for a pet, caring for plants, and keeping books and classroom equipment properly arranged
4. Making use of the chalkboard through "writing" or drawing on it
5. Listening to directions and then following them
6. Taking part in some one activity such as listening to a story for an increasing length of time, thereby lengthening the attention span
7. Telling where on a large chart the teacher should start writing as the boys and girls dictate to him.

OTHER ACTIVITIES. Activities such as the following can be specifically designed to guide some or all of the pupils in the development of readiness for writing.

1. Arranging pictures in a left-to-right and a top-to-bottom sequence
2. Discriminating between pictures, words, and letters, that are arranged on the chalkboard or on paper, or discriminating between objects that are quite similar
3. Practicing how to hold chalk, crayons, or pencils for effective drawing or "writing"
4. Drawing circles in the air, on the chalkboard, or on paper to the rhythm of some action games such as "Farmer in the Dell" or "Here We Go"
5. Drawing circles and straight lines on large sheets of paper or on the chalkboard, at times according to directions as to size and placement.

DEVELOPING SKILL IN MANUSCRIPT WRITING

After some or all the boys and girls in a first-grade room have acquired a desirable degree of writing readiness, questions such as the following need to be answered by the teacher: (1) What constitutes acceptable form in manuscript writing? (2) What basic writing habits should be developed? (3) What are "first steps" in teaching handwriting? (4) How can the teacher proceed by means of systematic instruction to give boys and girls the needed guidance? (5) How can manuscript writing be used functionally?

Form of Manuscript Writing

For effective teaching of any skill the teacher should have clearly in mind what constitutes the desired outcome. In handwriting that goal can be defined in part in terms of the form of the writing.

THE ALPHABET OF MANUSCRIPT WRITING. Figure 7.4 gives the alphabet in manuscript form and the figures used by The Zaner-Bloser Company, with letters in the proportion that that company advocates for beginners.

To encourage uniformity of letters, it is helpful for the manuscript alphabet of one company, both capital letters and lower-case, to be displayed, probably in the form of the wall charts available from publishing companies.

THE STROKES OF MANUSCRIPT WRITING. One of the reasons why manuscript writing is relatively easy for beginners is that essentially the letter forms are three in number: (1) the straight line (vertical, horizontal, and slant); (2) the circle, and (3) the part of a circle.

Adding further to the simplicity of the writing is the fact that in order to secure the best form, the writer lifts his writing instrument at the end of every straight line and of every circle, and at times after a part of a circle. For example, in writing the word *runs* in manuscript, the writing instrument is lifted seven times at the places indicated below.

Practice differs as to whether or not the writing instrument is lifted before the end of the letter *o*. Some teachers teach the pupils to write the letter *o*

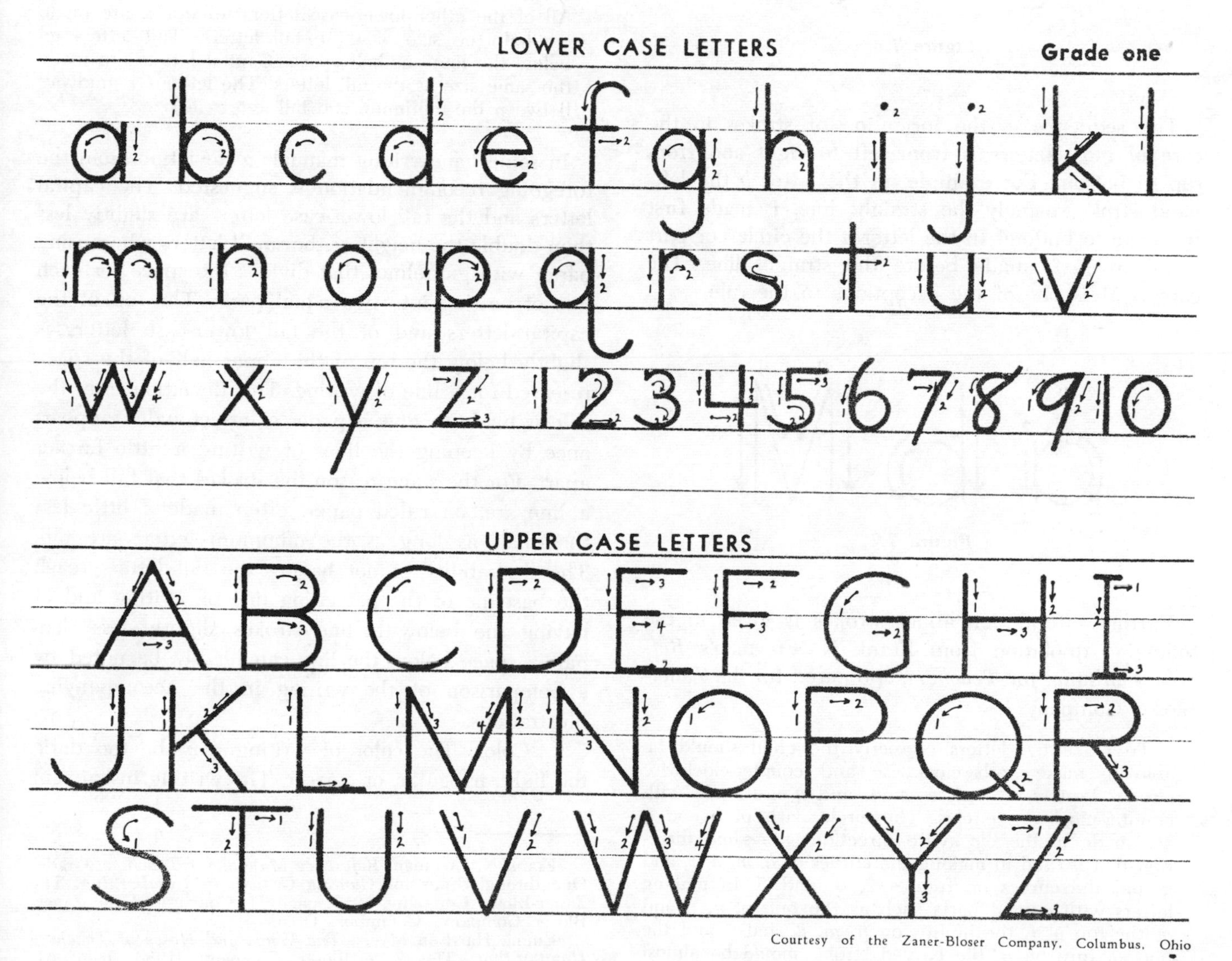

Figure 7.4 Manuscript Alphabet Sheet

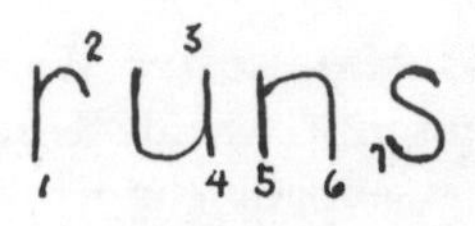

Figure 7.5

in two strokes, first the left half of the letter, beginning at the top and curving to the left and down and then curving to the right and up until a semicircle is formed, and then starting the second stroke at the point where the first began, to form the right half of the circle.

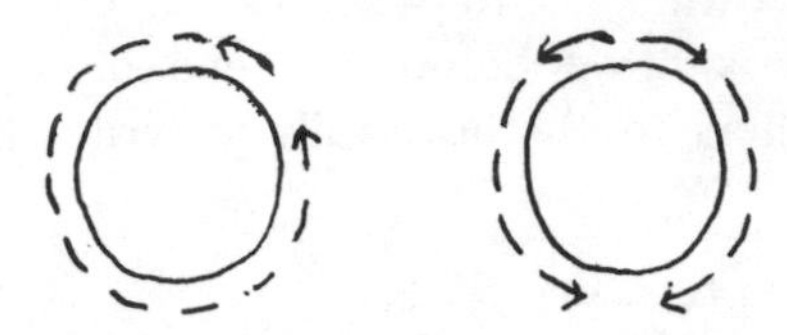

Figure 7.6

The sequence in the formation of strokes in the case of most letters is from left to right and from top to bottom. For example, in the letter *b* the left-hand stroke, namely the straight line, is made first from top to bottom. In the letter *a* the circle (or part of a circle) is made before the straight line. The capital *M* is one of the exceptions to the rule.

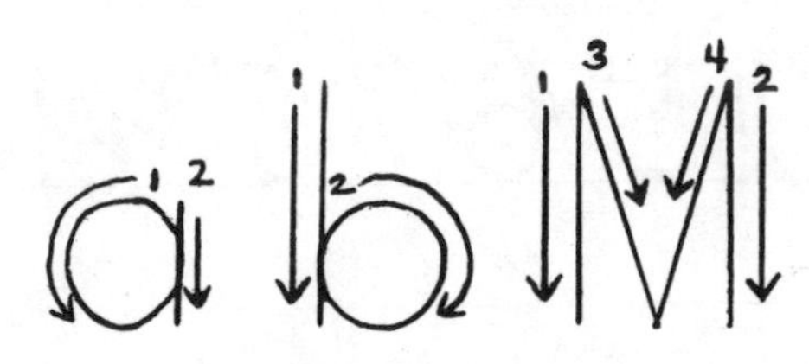

Figure 7.7

Further information about strokes is given in the following quotation from Frank N. Freeman's *Reference Manual for Teachers*,[4] prepared for the Zaner-Bloser Company.

> To make the letters correctly the child should be able to make both clockwise and counter-clockwise circles. Letters *a, c, d, e, g, o,* and *q* are made with counter-clockwise circles. The circle parts of *b* and *q* are made in the clockwise direction, the same direction that is used in making the curves of *h, m, n, r,* and *j;* and the curves on figures 2, 3, and 5. In making letters with curved parts such as the tails of *g, j,* and *q,* the top of *f,* the humps on *h, m, n,* and *r,* and the bottom turn on *u,* the curved stroke should be almost a half circle and equal in degree to the curve of the *o.*

Other Matters of Form. Also important in the consideration of the form of manuscript writing are matters of size and proportion, color or shading, slant, alignment, and space between letters and words.

1. Size and proportion. The following quotation from Emma Harrison Myers[5] indicates guidelines for both size and proportion of letters.

> . . . . There should be a gradual reduction in the size of the writing as the child's coordinations develop. Freeman recommends that paper with lines one inch apart be used in grade one. In grade two he reduces to three-quarter inch ruling. In each case he recommends a guide line at the half-way mark to develop the proper relationship in size between minimum letters and tall letters, i.e., the minimum letters are one-half the size of the tall letters and capitals for manuscript writing. By grade three he reduces the ruling another quarter-inch to one-half inch ruling, still keeping the same proportion of minimum letters to tall letters. In manuscript writing the tall letters are *l, b, h, k, f,* and *d.* All of the other lower-case letters, except *t,* are made one-half the size of these tall letters. Tail letters go below the line one-half space. Capital letters are made the same size as the tall letters. The letter *t* is midway between the minimum and tall letters in size.

In some handwriting manuals a deviation from the foregoing recommendation is suggested. The capital letters and the tall lower-case letters are slightly less than double the height of the small letters when using paper with guidelines that divides the space for each line of writing into two equal parts. The top of the capital letters and of the tall lower-case letters is slightly below the top of the upper half of the space reserved for a line of writing. This deviation from the rule is made to give a paper a less crowded appearance by keeping the lines of writing a little farther apart. For the same reason the strokes that fall below a line are, on ruled paper, often made a little less than half as long as the minimum letters are tall. The desirability of not having the tall letters reach the baseline of the preceding line of writing and of having the below-the-line strokes slightly less than half a space below the line can readily be noted by a comparison of the writing in the accompanying illustrations.

2. Color. The color of writing may be too dark, too light, irregular, or correct. The writing instrument

[4]Frank N. Freeman, *Reference Manual for Teachers.* Grades One through Four for *Guiding Growth in Handwriting.* The Zaner-Bloser Company, 1959, page 31. Courtesy of the Zaner-Bloser Company, Columbus, Ohio.

[5]Emma Harrison Myers, *The Whys and Hows of Teaching Handwriting.* The Zaner-Bloser Company, 1963, page 51. Courtesy of the Zaner-Bloser Company, Columbus, Ohio.

in part determines the color. However, pressure on the writing tool also plays an important part in determining color.

3. Slant. The basic slant in manuscript writing is "straight up and down." It is achieved rather readily

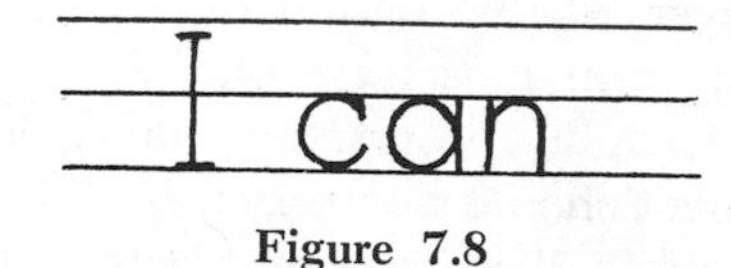

Figure 7.8

if the paper is parallel to the desk or table. Even though the basic slant is "straight up and down," many letters have other lines of slant. Some slant to the right and others to the left, as, for example, the second and third strokes of both the upper- and the lower-case letter in Figure 7.9.

K k

Figure 7.9

4. Alignment. Some writers do not stay on the line. They may begin a word on the baseline, but then swing upward or downward in their writing. Still others have irregular alignment with part of the writing above the line, part of it on the line, and part of it below the line.

5. Spacing. The space that should be left between the letters of a word and between words cannot be stipulated in terms of fractional parts of an inch, for it should be proportionate to the size of the writing. The suggestion is sometimes made to first-grade children that they leave enough space between letters for the forefinger to be placed there and that they double that space between words. If this suggestion is made, the boys and girls should be discouraged from frequent use of their fingers to measure spacing. Probably a better practice is to provide boys and girls guides in the form of copies of manuscript written the size that they are writing in which the spacing is correct. Attention of even fairly young writers should be drawn to the fact that the spacing between letters in manuscript writing differs with the width and form of the letters. For example, after wide letters such as the capital *M* and the capital *W* less space should be left than between two narrow letters such as the *l* and the *t*.

Basic Writing Habits

Some of the pointers given here concerning basic writing habits apply to both manuscript and cursive writing; others apply to manuscript writing only. In the section in this chapter that deals with developing skill in cursive writing, attention is paid to variations from those given in this part for manuscript writing.

POSTURE OF THE WRITER. In the book *Handwriting Aid for Elementary Teachers*[6] this list of points describing the posture of the writer is given.

> Sits tall.
> Sits well back in his seat and allows the back of his hips to touch the back of the seat and inclines his body slightly forward bending from the hips.
> Rests his feet on the floor.
> Faces the desk squarely.
> Keeps both shoulders at the same level.
> Rests both forearms easily on the desk and at an equal distance from the body.
> Keeps the head comfortably erect.

Figure 7.10

In order to insure desirable body posture, it is important that the seat and desk at which the pupil writes fit him. Here are some points to observe in this connection.

1. The chair and the desk should be of a height that is comfortable for the writer.
2. The seat should be high enough so that the writer's feet can rest on the floor when he sits back.
3. The seat should be low enough so that the writer's knees are not held high by the seat.
4. The desk should be of a height so that the writer's arms are in a comfortable position while he maintains correct body posture.

---

[6]Frank N. Freeman and The Zaner-Bloser Company, *Handwriting Aid for Elementary Teachers.* The Zaner-Bloser Company, 1948, page 15. Courtesy of the Zaner-Bloser Company, Columbus, Ohio.

5. The seat should be at such a distance from the desk that the pupil can easily maintain correct posture while writing.

POSITION OF PAPER, HAND, AND WRITING TOOL. In the *Reference Manual for Teachers*[7] for grades one through four to accompany the *Guiding Growth in Handwriting* series, Freeman gives this list of specifications for the position of paper, hand, and pencil that should be observed when doing manuscript writing.

> Paper is held straight on the desk, the lower edge parallel to the lower edge of the desk.
>
> Paper is held so that the writing being done is directly in front of the eyes. This means that the paper should be moved towards the left as the writing progresses across the line.
>
> Hand is roundlooking with the palm partially open – not a fist.
>
> Hand rests on the tips of the last two fingers.
>
> The end of the thumb is placed *against* the pencil; the first finger rests against the second finger. All three fingers are placed about one inch above the pencil point.
>
> The top of the pencil points in the direction of the upper arm and shoulder.

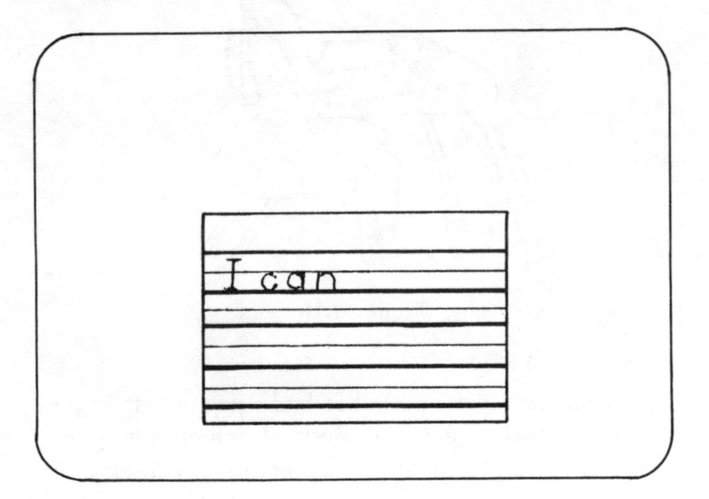

Figure 7.11

PLACEMENT OF AUXILIARY MATERIALS. Attention must be paid not only to the placement of the paper on which the pupil writes but also to any other materials, such as books or paper, which he needs to use while writing either for copy purposes or other references. However, teachers should encourage boys and girls to remove from their desks all materials not needed for writing so that ample space can be provided for freedom of movement. The pupils should be helped to form the habit of placing needed auxiliary materials to the left of the writing paper if they write with the right and to the right of the writing paper if they are left-handed. They should be asked to place the reference material at the angle that is most convenient for reading purposes.

MOVEMENT AND RHYTHM. Arm movement is important for excellence in writing. Finger movement should, however, not be barred but, if necessary, encouraged. The arm muscles should be used for the general left-to-right progression in writing while finger movement should be utilized for the production of smaller strokes that require greater care in performance. Even wrist movement has a legitimate place.

It is important that the movement should be rhythmic to avoid undue strain when writing for a rather extended time and to produce better-looking copy. Especially with the beginner it is valuable to stress rhythmic movement so that a habit of writing with jerky movement can be prevented.

"First Steps" in Manuscript Writing

An exact line of demarcation between readiness for manuscript writing, suggestions for which are given on preceding pages of this chapter, and the "first steps" in manuscript writing would be difficult to draw. With clear recognition of that fact, some suggestions for "first steps" are here given.

GUIDELINES. The following general suggestions are for application in the early stages of teaching manuscript writing.

1. The chalkboard should be used freely by both teacher and pupils, with the pupils' first writing experiences on the chalkboard on a space without lines but with later writing on a ruled chalkboard with lines probably not closer than four inches apart.

2. Large sheets of unlined paper, possibly newsprint – maybe folded to make the sheet of manageable size – can be used at first while later ruled paper with lines about four inches apart and still later with less space between lines is appropriate. (In time, even as little as one-inch lined paper, with two spaces used for capital letters and other tall letters, should be used.)

3. Crayons should be used at first with many children, and in many cases later the so-called "primary pencil," with thick lead and a larger circumference than the pencil for the adult, is usually recommended.

4. From the very beginning, instruction in writing should be based on meaningful units – on words and larger thought units.

[7]Frank N. Freeman. *Reference Manual for Teachers.* Grades One through Four. *Guiding Growth in Handwriting* series. The Zaner-Bloser Company, 1959, page 32. Courtesy of The Zaner-Bloser Company, Columbus, Ohio.

5. The words or groups of words written by the pupils should frequently serve a purpose such as writing one's name to identify possessions, writing words for a picture dictionary, or writing a letter to take home.

6. Copying, rather than tracing, should be encouraged and later reliance should be placed at least in part on visual memory of letters and word forms.

7. Attention should be paid even in the early stages of handwriting instruction to the formation of proper habits of position, sequence, and direction in letter formation.

SUGGESTED ACTIVITIES. Application can be made of the guidelines given in the preceding paragraphs and of others by means of activities described on page 307. Two suggested activities for use during the beginning period of work on manuscript writing are also mentioned following.

1. On the first day of school or thereafter the teacher may give to each pupil a small piece of tagboard with ruled lines, on which he has written the child's name in the size that is suitable for a beginning writer. From this card each pupil can copy his name to identify his drawings and other possessions.

2. If pupils have difficulty in knowing where to begin tall letters and where minimum-sized letters, the teacher, using paper with baselines and guidelines, for each child, may write before class a vertical line double space in height and one single space. He may then explain that on the first line he has a stroke for a tall letter and then he may ask the pupils to make a stroke of similar height to the right of it (after they have pointed out the place where they will begin the stroke). Next the pupils can proceed similarly with the line representing the beginning stroke of a small letter. After they have finished both lines by writing strokes of required height they can write a line of vertical strokes, at the direction of the teacher, some the height of small letters and the others of tall letters. (Emphasis throughout this exercise should be placed on the fact that the vertical lines are made from the top down.) A similar exercise can be done with large and small circles. With the circles, too, care should be taken that they are the right height and that the direction of the stroke is the desired one.

Systematic Instruction in Development of Skill in Manuscript Writing

It is hoped that some of the suggestions given here will be helpful not only to the teacher who endorses systematic instruction in handwriting but also to the teacher who is not in favor of such instruction.

DEVELOPMENTAL PROCEDURES. Systematic instruction in handwriting may be divided into (1) those class periods or parts of periods in which new points are presented and (2) those in which the pupils practice skills earlier presented. Procedures of the former type are here referred to as developmental. Examples of such procedures are given in Chapter 14. (See page 307.)

PRACTICE PROCEDURES. Some practice on a skill being presented is important in the class period when a new point is being given. Furthermore, in many writing lessons no new point should be presented but the entire class period should be devoted to strengthening a point developed earlier. To keep practice from being boring and fruitless, these guidelines may be followed.

1. The boys and girls should know clearly the purpose of the practice work and the purpose should be specific.

2. The pupils should be guided so they will accept a worthy purpose for the practice.

3. The pupils should have means of comparing their product at the beginning of a practice period with that later on during the period.

4. The boys and girls should be helped to understand that they need not be discouraged if every attempt at improvement does not result in advancement.

5. A practice period should not be so long that it exceeds the attention span of the boys and girls for the type of activity.

Functional Uses of Writing in Lower Grades

Functional use of writing can be made in the lower grades both in programs of systematic instruction supplemented by effective use of ongoing activities and in programs of handwriting that emphasize only incidental instruction. A few of the many ways in which boys and girls can engage in writing activities meaningful to the primary-grade child are as follows:

1. Writing their names for identification of their possessions and for other utilitarian purposes, such as listing who wants milk, who will be on a committee, or who is on a given team

2. Writing the day and date on a daily newsletter posted in the room

3. Writing the date on a large calendar

4. Making a picture dictionary or a picture-word file

5. Writing letters. In the lower primary grades the class letter dictated to the teacher may be the preferable procedure. All pupils may copy the letter, but only one usually should be sent to any one individual.

The other boys and girls may keep copies of their letters in folders of their own in which they save samples of their work.

6. Making a bird book. Below pictures of birds can be written the name of each bird and with older children one or more interesting statements about each.

7. Using workbooks for reading, spelling, or handwriting. Boys and girls may be motivated to do their best writing in their workbooks if they know that these will be on exhibit at parents' night or if they know that they will have an opportunity to take them home at regular intervals to show their parents.

8. Making books for Mother's Day

9. Making booklets for units of study

10. Making an accordion-like folder on which are drawn pictures and on which are written comments by the pupils about the pictures.

THE TRANSITION FROM MANUSCRIPT TO CURSIVE WRITING

The following factors should be given serious attention in deciding when to begin encouraging a child to make the transition from manuscript to cursive writing:

1. Muscular coordination sufficient to do a good quality of manuscript writing
2. Ability to do manuscript writing with correct body, paper, and pencil position
3. Ability to do manuscript writing with rhythmic movement and with well-formed letters
4. Interest in making the transition
5. Ability to read cursive writing.

Developing Readiness

Although the factors contributing to readiness for writing or for readiness for phases of writing are influenced in part by maturation, they are also amenable to training and education. Consequently the teacher should not merely wait for the appearance of signs of readiness but should strive to help the child reach the stage of development in which he can advisedly learn to do cursive writing (if a transition to cursive writing is made in a school system).

Here are guidelines that the teacher may wish to follow in helping boys and girls make the transition.

1. It is unwise to hurry the pupil into making the transition.

2. The best preparation for readiness to make the transition is doing manuscript writing well — with good movement, with correct position of body, paper, pencil, and in well-formed letters and correctly spaced letters and words.

3. The teacher can help develop interest in making the change-over in a variety of ways. He can emphasize the fact that after making the transition the pupils will be able to write in two different ways, not in only one. Although the point may be made that when the boys and girls are able to do cursive writing they will be able to write like grown-ups, care needs to be taken not to overemphasize it. Otherwise it may lead to a disdain of manuscript writing and cause the pupil to lose desire to continue to do any manuscript writing after he has acquired skill in cursive writing.

4. Unless a pupil is fairly efficient in reading cursive writing, he will be likely to have considerable difficulty in learning to write it.

5. Cursive writing is decidedly different from manuscript. It should not be assumed that the latter is merely an adaptation of the former, the transition to which a pupil can easily make without guidance from the teacher.

Position of Writing Materials

Although the correct body position of the writer is the same for manuscript as for cursive writing, the position of the paper is different. The lower line of the paper in cursive writing should be tilted to the edge of the writing desk at an angle of approximately 30 degrees. If the person writes with his right hand, the paper should be tilted toward the left, but if he writes with his left hand it should be tilted toward the right. The slanted position of the paper permits the line of writing to be about perpendicular to the forearm.

The Alphabet of Cursive Writing

There are variations, though relatively few and slight, in the forms of accepted alphabets of cursive writing. Two alphabets by leading publishers of handwriting programs are reproduced on the next page.

New Points to Be Taught

The following is a list of new points to be taught in cursive writing, according to Frank N. Freeman.[8]

1. Slanting position of paper.
2. Slant in writing.
3. Connecting strokes between letters.
4. Loops on letters to form upper and lower case letters.
5. Completely new form of letter — *b e f k r s z*.

---

[8]Frank N. Freeman and The Zaner-Bloser Company, *Handwriting Aid for Primary Teachers.* The Zaner-Bloser Company, 1948, page 95. Courtesy of The Zaner-Bloser Company, Columbus, Ohio.

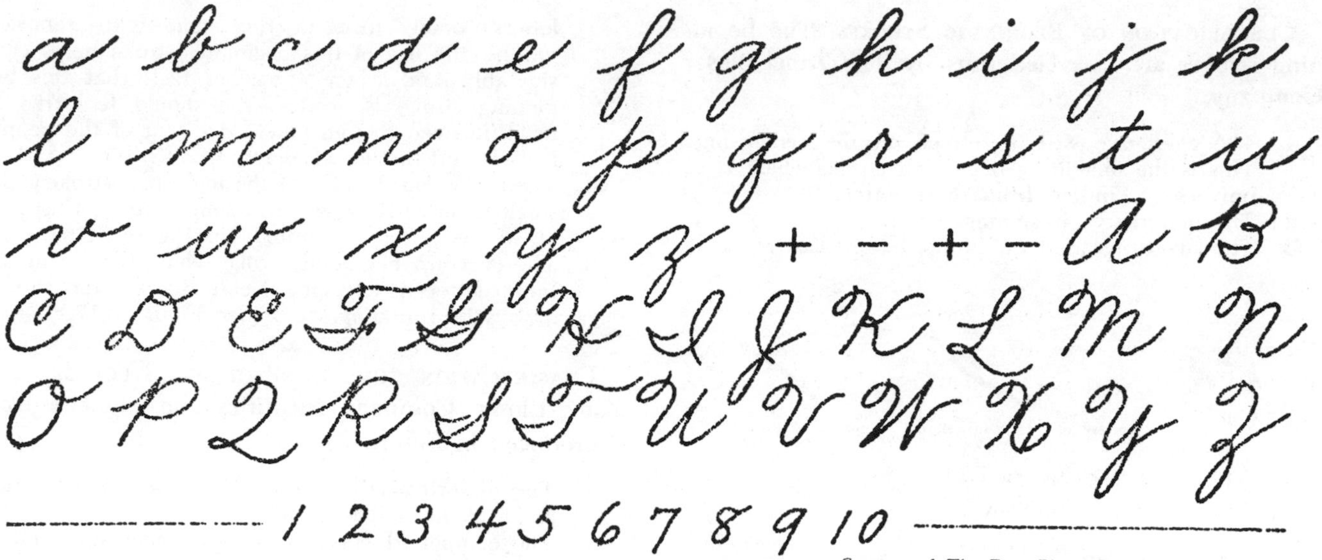

Courtesy of The Zaner-Bloser Company, Columbus, Ohio

Figure 7.12 Reproduced from cover of **HANDWRITING AID FOR PRIMARY TEACHERS** by Frank N. Freeman, Ph.D., and The Zaner-Bloser Company, 1948

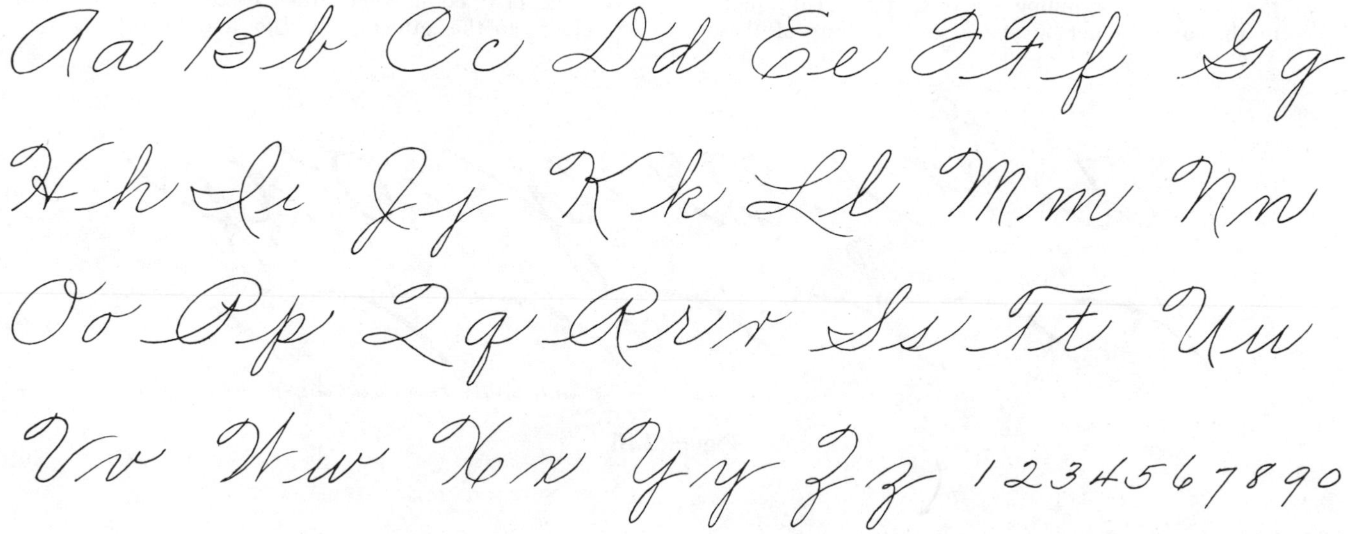

Courtesy of The A. N. Palmer Company

Figure 7.13 Reproduced from cover of **MY PROGRESS BOOK, CURSIVE WRITING THE EASY WAY,** published by The A. N. Palmer Company

6. Finish stroke on letters.
7. The initial strokes – undercurve and overcurve.
8. Close spacing between words.
9. Increase in speed.
10. New Capital Letter forms.
11. Correct number of letters per line.
12. Dotting of *i* and crossing of *t* after word is finished.
13. Retraced letters *b v r s w*.
14. Relative heights of letters *p d t*.
15. Lighter quality of line.

Groupings of Letters and Parts of Letters

Various companies that publish handwriting materials have made different groupings of letters and of parts of letters for teaching purposes. Helpful groupings with suggestions made by the Zaner-Bloser Company are here reproduced.[9]

[9]Frank N. Freeman and The Zaner-Bloser Company, *Handwriting Aid for Primary Teachers.* The Zaner-Bloser Company, 1948, pages 81-88. Courtesy of The Zaner-Bloser Company, Columbus, Ohio.

Classification of Beginning Strokes. The beginning strokes are classified thus by The Zaner-Bloser Company:

1. The overcurve with a retrace on the center line. This is the imaginary beginning stroke which is so universally omitted from these letters.
2. The undercurve beginning stroke.
3. The overturn, used on hump letters like *m* or *n*.

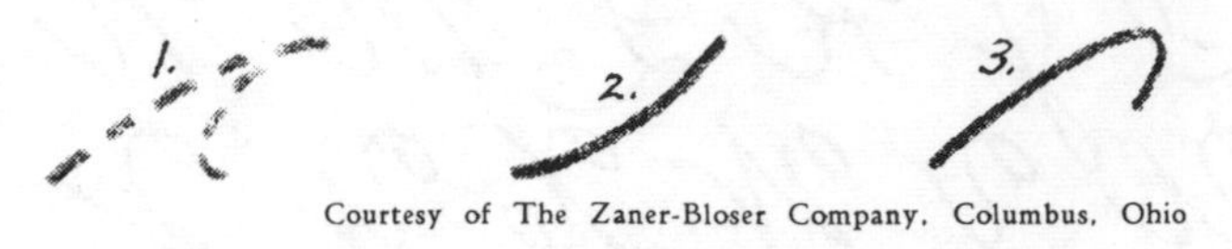

Courtesy of The Zaner-Bloser Company, Columbus, Ohio

Figure 7.14

The following illustrative examples and explanation of these strokes are given in *Handwriting Aid for Primary Teachers*, pages 81 ff.

1. In the illustration [below], the dotted line shows the imaginary beginning stroke that is usually made in the air as a person starts to make any of these letters. Some teachers find that with retarded groups, the use of this beginning stroke helps considerably, and where a teacher feels that this beginning stroke is needed, she should feel free to teach it, even though ninety per cent of the people leave it off in actual practice. . . .
2. The easiest application of the underturn stroke is the small letter *i*. However, this same stroke is used in all of the letters illustrated [in Figure 7.16]. . . .
3. The overturn beginning stroke which is used in the hump letters needs special care, for the top should always be rounding. . . . (See Figure 7.17.)

Classification of Connecting Strokes. The Zaner-Bloser Company identifies the eight strokes reproduced in Figure 7.18.

1. The underturn stroke used to connect letters such as *ai*, *ci*, *hi*, and so forth.
2. The compound curve used to connect such letters as *an*, *dv*, *to*, and so forth.
3. The check swing on this stroke is used to connect *b* to *i*.
4. The check overturn used to connect such letters as *ov*.
5. The next connection stroke used to connect lower loops to the letters, *a*, *b*, *d*, *o*, and so forth.

Courtesy of The Zaner-Bloser Company, Columbus, Ohio

Figure 7.15

Courtesy of The Zaner-Bloser Company, Columbus, Ohio

Figure 7.16

Courtesy of The Zaner-Bloser Company, Columbus, Ohio

Figure 7.17

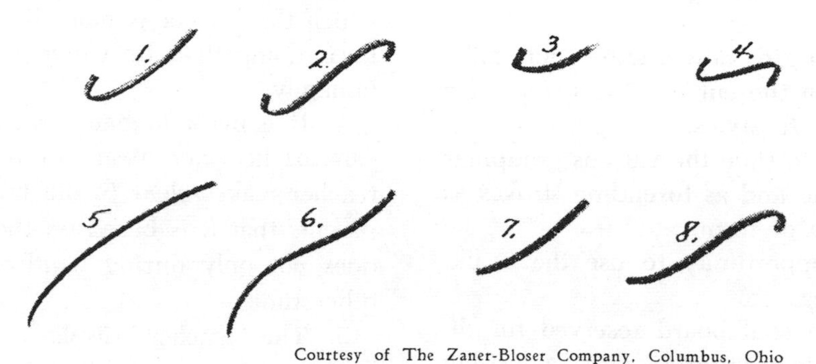

Courtesy of The Zaner-Bloser Company, Columbus, Ohio

Figure 7.18

6. The compound stroke used to connect the lower loops, to *i, u, s,* and so forth.
7. The underturn stroke used to connect *q* to *u, s* to *i,* and other similar letters. This stroke is very similar to number one but it is distinctly different in that it starts on the base line and curves up, while number one starts with a downstroke and then turns into the same curve.
8. Starts on the baseline and is a compound curve used with such letters as *fa, pd, so,* and so forth.

Classification of Ending Strokes. The Zaner-Bloser Company classifies the ending strokes of lower-case letters thus:

1. The under turn which is the same as number two beginning stroke.
2. The small check ending stroke. Some teachers refer to this as the retrace ending stroke.
3. The tail letters ending stroke such as *y* or *z.*

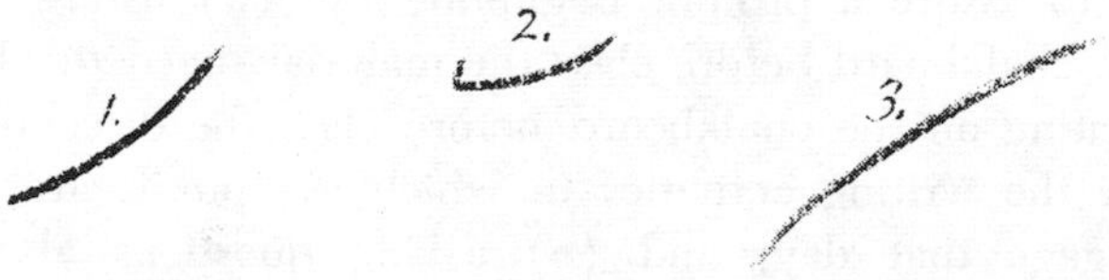

Courtesy of The Zaner-Bloser Company, Columbus, Ohio

Figure 7.19

Classification of Letters as to Form. In *Learning a New Way Recorder*[10] the classification of capital letters, reproduced on page 140, is given.

"First Steps" in Making the Transition

There is no one best way for making the transition from manuscript to cursive writing. However, here are some points that the teacher may find of value for the change-over.

1. Discuss with the class the fact that there are two commonly used kinds of writing and show the same word or words written in both types.

2. Familiarize the boys and girls with the terms *manuscript* and *cursive.*

3. Have pupils tell where or when they have seen examples of cursive writing.

4. Encourage them to want to learn another way of writing.

5. Help the boys and girls note some of the differences between manuscript and cursive writing, stressing points such as those named on page 136 under "New Points to Be Taught."

[10]Frank N. Freeman, *Learning a New Way Recorder.* Grade 3, of the Guiding Growth in Handwriting series. The Zaner-Bloser Company, 1959, page 1. Courtesy of The Zaner-Bloser Company, Columbus, Ohio.

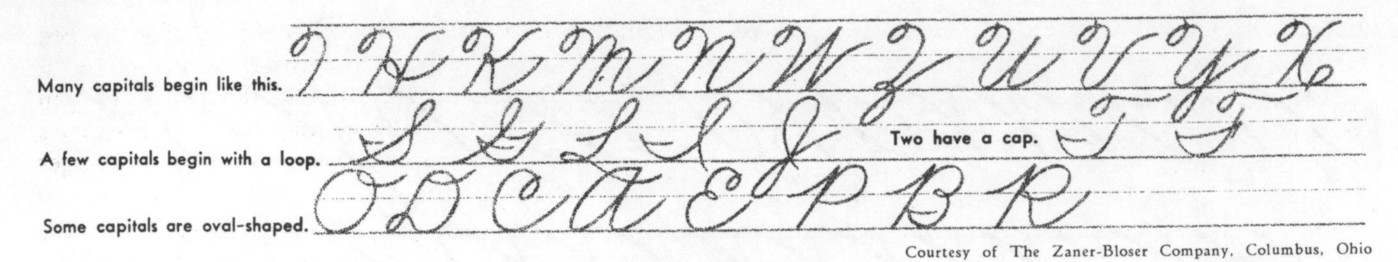

Figure 7.20

6. Check the pupils' ability to read letters and words in cursive and provide practice in reading cursive writing.

7. Show the boys and girls how a letter quite alike in the manuscript and in the cursive, the letter *i*, for example, is written in both styles.

8. Present from time to time the various groupings of letters as to beginning and as to ending strokes as well as to other aspects of form.

9. Give the pupils opportunity to use the chalkboard for cursive writing.

10. Have part of the chalkboard reserved for directions and assignments written in cursive writing and give needed help in reading these directions and assignments.

TEACHING CURSIVE WRITING

Many of the suggestions given in the preceding part of this chapter, entitled "The Transition from Manuscript to Cursive Writing," also apply to the program of cursive writing beyond the transitional stage. Additional suggestions for the handwriting program in its later stages are here given.

Motivation

To offset the drudgery that might otherwise be associated with phases of practice in the development of any skill and the lack of purpose for doing one's best that might characterize the attitude of the writer, the teacher should try to encourage the child to learn to write and to make application of what he has learned. Following are some ways in which the pupils may be stimulated to want to do their best.

1. The teacher shows samples of writing that are difficult to decipher and has the pupils discuss the problem of the reader.

2. The teacher encourages the pupils to set individual goals for themselves by the use of handwriting scales and then from time to time study their progress toward their objectives.

3. During handwriting class the teacher tries to secure a relaxed, happy classroom atmosphere, in which the learner is more likely to enjoy the activity he is doing than he would in one that is tense and unhappy.

4. If a mark in handwriting is given on a report card or in other means of reporting to parents, the teacher makes clear to the boys and girls and to the parents that it is based on the writing that the pupil does not only during handwriting class but also at other times.

5. The teacher displays better papers written during classes other than handwriting class.

6. The pupil keeps a folder in which he saves dated samples of his handwriting. These samples may be selected for the folder without previous announcement that the paper will be put into the folder at a given time.

7. The pupils engage in many activities in which they see the importance of good handwriting such as bona fide letter writing, making booklets, and making charts.

8. The pupils participate in the evaluation of their handwriting.

9. The teacher helps the pupils realize that illegible handwriting may be interpreted as errors in spelling.

10. The teacher displays posters in the room, often pupil-made, encouraging the boys and girls to write well.

11. The teacher encourages an atmosphere of work during handwriting period by using the time at the beginning of the period when paper is distributed so as to assure a prompt beginning by: (a) listing on the chalkboard before class the materials needed; (b) writing on the chalkboard before class the directions for the writing activities in which the pupils are to engage that day; and (c) asking questions about handwriting, such as "How far below the line should the below-the-line loops extend?"

Achieving Characteristics of Legible Cursive Writing[11]

Legibility in cursive handwriting is determined by characteristics that can be classified as to: (1) size and proportion, (2) color shading, (3) slant, (4) letter spacing, (5) beginning strokes, (6) ending strokes, (7) word spacing, (8) alignment, and (9) letter forms.

SIZE AND PROPORTION. The desired size and proportion of letters vary according to the maturity and skill of the writer. Published handwriting programs give suggestions for the reduction in size from the time the pupil starts cursive writing, when lines, one-half inch apart are recommended, with the small letters about one-half the size of the capital letters (often in the second half of the second grade or in the third grade) until the time (frequently in the fifth or sixth grade) when the pupil is ready to write the size and proportion recommended for the adult.

In general, these recommendations as to size are made for adults when writing on paper on which the lines are 3/8 of an inch apart:

Capital letters and the loop letters *l, b, h, k,* and *f*: 3/4 space
The letters *t, d,* and *p*: 1/2 space
The small lower-case letters: 1/4 space
The below-line loops: 1/2 space below the line.

Boys and girls should be helped in diagnosing errors in the size of their letters by noting whether they are too large, too small, or irregular. They can be helped in recognizing the following frequent causes of each of these shortcomings and in correcting their errors.

1. Too large writing. Too large writing is often caused by using primarily arm movement rather than a desirable combination of hand and finger movement and by holding the pen too far from the point.
2. Too small writing. Too small writing is often caused by using a disproportionate amount of finger and hand movement rather than sufficient arm movement, and by holding the pen too close to the point.
3. Irregular size. The cause of irregular size frequently is unsteadiness in writing, resulting from not curving the thumb enough when holding the writing instrument.

COLOR OR SHADING. The boys and girls can be given help in understanding that too light or too dark shading may be caused by a too fine or a too heavy pen point. They may need help in recognizing the fact that too heavy writing is frequently also caused by holding the pen too close to the point; in learning that too light writing is frequently caused by holding the pen too far from the point or by turning the pen point (if it is not a ball-point pen) so that the eye of the pen is not up; and in realizing that heavy downstrokes often result from too much pressure of the forefinger onto the writing tool.

SLANT. The relationship of slant to position of the paper and to the pull of the pen or pencil toward the middle of the body needs to be made clear to some boys and girls. A tilt of the paper at an angle of about 30 degrees to the edge of the desk helps secure correct slant. Moving the paper from right to left in case of the right-handed writer, with the left hand several times, maybe three, as the writer progresses across a line of writing can be demonstrated to the child as a means of securing correct slant while failure to do so may cause a problem of slant. (It should be noted, however, that very few adults, even among good writers, make this adjustment of the paper as they write. Usually those who maintain good slant make up for this lack of motion by a change in the position of the fingers, hand, or arm as they progress from left to right.)

The cause of irregular slant often is failure to shift the paper or failure to make the downstrokes of letters toward the center of the body of the writer. Too slanting writing is frequently the result of tilting the paper more than 30 degrees to the edge of the desk, while lack of slant often results from tilting it less than 30 degrees.

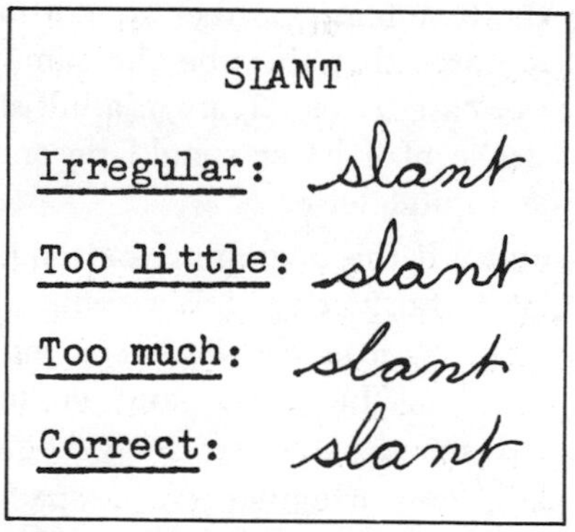

SLANT

Irregular: slant
Too little: slant
Too much: slant
Correct: slant

Figure 7.21

LETTER SPACING. Defects of letter spacing consist of: (a) too crowded writing, (b) too scattered writ-

[11]The classification of characteristics of handwriting is, with but slight alteration, the one followed in the SELF-CORRECTIVE HANDWRITING CHARTS by Ellen C. Nystrom, no longer in print. Acknowledgment is also here made of the fact that suggestions from these charts are incorporated in comments as to how to achieve these characteristics.

ing, and (c) irregular spacing between letters. As a rule, difficulties in letter spacing are closely related to defects of slant. Scattered letter spacing is often caused by too much slant, crowded letter spacing by too little slant, and irregular letter spacing by irregular slant.

BEGINNING STROKES. Boys and girls should know that ordinarily the first stroke of the letters *a, c, d, g, o,* and *q* does not begin on the line but starts at or near the top of the letter. They can check whether they use beginning strokes starting on the line for letters that need them and do not use them for those that are usually written without them. They can also be helped to note whether the strokes they write for letters beginning on the line are too long, too short, or irregular. They can get suggestions for overcoming shortcomings from knowledge of facts such as these:

1. Irregular beginning strokes are often caused by writing letters that show irregularity of size.
2. Too short strokes of letters beginning on the line are often associated with letters that are too small or with letters of too little slant.
3. Too long strokes that begin on the line are often associated with letters that are too large or that have too much slant.

ENDING STROKES. Errors in ending strokes include in addition to those of form of the ending strokes: (a) irregular strokes, (b) too short strokes, and (c) too long strokes. The causes of irregularity of ending strokes, of too short strokes, and of too long strokes are the same as those for beginning strokes (i.e., for those letters beginning on the line) with the corresponding shortcomings. Correct proportion of ending strokes requires that they be the same height as the small lower-case letters. Thus in adult-size writing the ending stroke of a letter should be one-third the height of the capital letter.

WORD SPACING. If the beginning and ending strokes are correct, it is fairly easy for a writer to achieve correct spacing. Scattered word spacing is often caused by too long beginning and ending strokes, crowded word spacing by too short beginning and ending strokes, and irregular word spacing by irregular beginning and ending strokes.

Boys and girls should be helped to note that the space left between the last word of a sentence and the first word of the following sentence should be wider than that between two words within a sentence.

ALIGNMENT. By correct alignment is meant writing that rests on the baseline. Irregular alignment is often caused by not placing the paper in the correct position and by not moving it to the right two or three times, at regular intervals, as the writer progresses along a line of writing.

Writing above the line is often the result of lack of slant of the paper, with the paper placed at an angle of less than 30 degrees to the edge of the desk. Writing below the line is frequently the result of too much slant of the paper.

LETTER FORMS. Two alphabets, that by The Zaner-Bloser Company and that by The A. N. Palmer Company, are given on preceding pages of this chapter. A helpful publication in pocket-size form is one entitled *Points to Remember about Each of the Letters of the Alphabet.*[12] The nature of the booklet is summarized on the first page in these words:

> In writing the alphabet, there are many important points for each letter that help both teacher and pupil with letter structure. We are listing here, under each letter, some of the important points to keep in mind: the numerical count for the letters and a descriptive word count.

A page is devoted to each lower-case and each upper-case letter of the alphabet and to each of the figures from 1 through 10.

There are some letters on which many pupils need special practice. Probably more illegibilities in cursive writing result from incorrect writing of the letters *a, e,* and *r* than from poor writing of any other letters. Additional letters frequently written so poorly that they cause spelling problems are *t, s, c, n, d, b, h, c, v,* and the capital *I*. Other frequent causes of illegibilities are:

1. Not crossing the *t* nor dotting the *i*
2. Leaving letters "open" that should be closed, like the *o*, the *d* (which is then confused with *cl*), and the *a*
3. Not using loops in loop letters
4. Making loops in some letters that should be written without loops
5. Making straight lines where there should be curved lines
6. Writing an *n* like a *u*, an *r* like an *i*, and a *c* like an *a*.

Development of Appropriate Speed

The two major objectives in teaching handwriting are (1) to write legibly and (2) to write at an appropriate speed. Means of developing legibility are

[12]The Zaner-Bloser Company, *Points to Remember about Each of the Letters of the Cursive Alphabet*. For Upper Grades. The Zaner-Bloser Company, 1963. Courtesy of The Zaner-Bloser Company, Columbus, Ohio.

discussed in preceding paragraphs. Let us now note points of value to consider in relation to the development of speed of writing.

1. In the lower grades practically no emphasis should be placed on speed. However, dawdling habits should be discouraged even in those grades.
2. Speed varies, and rightly so, from individual to individual.
3. As a child grows toward maturity, there tends to be a positive relationship between speed of writing and quality of cursive writing.
4. Even in the intermediate grades, speed develops chiefly as greater skill is acquired.
5. Care should be taken that slowness in writing is not due to the learner's drawing rather than writing the words by means of which he plans to communicate.
6. With improved rhythm in writing increased speed seems to come.
7. In the intermediate grades from time to time the pupils may be given tests in which both rate and legibility are checked.

TEACHING THE LEFT-HANDED CHILD

Since studies seem to indicate that on the average two or three pupils in an elementary-school classroom can be expected to have a preference for the left hand over the right, the question as to how to teach the left-handed child to write is a problem that almost every elementary-school teacher needs to face.

Determining Hand Dominance

There is disagreement among psychologists and specialists in handwriting as to the cause of left-handedness, right-handedness, and ambidexterity. Some claim that preference of one hand over the other or of no preference is determined by the hereditary pattern of the individual. Others claim that which hand is the dominant one is primarily or solely a matter of early practice or training. The great difficulties often encountered when attempts are made to change a left-handed writer to a right-handed one are frequently used as argument for the former position. However, it can be argued that the tenacity of a once-established habit could account for the difficulty of change-over. Regardless of whether or not hand preference is chiefly an inherited trait or primarily the product of practice, it does seem as if often by the time a child reaches school age, his hand preference is quite firmly established.

In order to deal with the question as to which hand the child should be encouraged to use, it is important to try to determine his hand dominance. Casual observation of the child as he goes about activities in which he uses his hands is one means of giving an answer to the question, "Is this child left-handed?" But such informal observation is hardly enough to try to answer as important and far-reaching a question as that of hand preference. Simple tests, if a variety of them are used, can be given by the classroom teacher as he sets up testing situations in which he takes note in writing of the preferred hand of the child in activities such as these:

1. Picking toys off the floor
2. Handing an article to the observer
3. Taking an article that the observer hands to the pupil
4. Throwing a ball
5. Bouncing a ball
6. Drawing with crayon or pencil or painting
7. Cutting
8. Using a fork or spoon when eating
9. Holding a cup when drinking
10. Pointing at things
11. Washing the face with a washcloth
12. Combing the hair
13. Driving nails.

One test that has been used to try to determine hand dominance is given by placing a pencil directly in front of the child on a table or desk so that the lead points toward the middle of his body and then asking him to pick up the pencil or asking him to draw or write with it.

If a test is made comprising probably five or six of the items suggested and if that test is given to an individual at two or three different times, the per cent of times that he uses the right hand rather than the left is a rough index of handedness. If 100 per cent of the attempts in all the times that the test is given show preference for the right hand, it can be assumed, for practical purposes, that the pupil has a decided right-hand preference. If in no case the child shows a preference for the right hand over the left, it can probably be assumed that his left hand is the dominant one. If the number of times a pupil uses the right hand is the same as the number of times that he uses the left hand, then there is indication of ambidexterity. If in 75 per cent or more of the attempts a pupil shows preference of one hand over the other he might be considered to have a definite, though not perfect, preference of the hand used the more frequently.

To Change or Not to Change

"That is the question" that has long puzzled teachers and parents. In spite of much research, agreement has not been reached. There seems, however, to be considerable evidence for the recommendation by the late Frank N. Freeman, psychologist and specialist in the field of the teaching of handwriting, who believed that if a child has a definite preference for the left hand especially when at the same time he does not follow rather readily the suggestion that he write with his right hand – he should be allowed to write with the left hand. This point is readily accepted by many teachers particularly in the case of the child who has already begun to write with his left hand. It is this recommendation that the writer accepts.

Reasons given for not insisting that the child with decided left-hand dominance or the child, regardless of dominance, who has long written with the left hand should write with his right hand include:

1. The child with left-hand dominance or the one accustomed to writing with the left hand, regardless of dominance in terms of his hereditary pattern, is often able to write more legibly if he is allowed to write with his left hand.
2. Writing with the right hand by a child with left-hand dominance at times seems to cause nervousness. Even though the incidence has not been established as a frequent result, the seriousness of such a possible development makes many teachers and parents unwilling to risk much encouragement for a change-over.
3. Change from left-handedness to right-handedness in writing seems in some instances to bring about speech difficulties.
4. Change in handedness may cause reversals in reading and writing.

There are some authorities in the field of the teaching of handwriting who insist rather persistent effort should be made, if necessary, to influence the child to write with his right hand. They argue that the likelihood of resulting nervousness, speech difficulties, or problems of reversal in reading and in writing is so small that the change-over should be made in order to avoid the disadvantages of left-handedness. The claim could be made that the undesirable results from a change-over could possibly be prevented if the transition were made in the best manner feasible.

In general, authorities seem to agree that the child who may, as far as heredity is concerned, be equally able to use both hands but who prefers his left hand, should be encouraged to make the change if he has not at the time rather firmly established the habit of writing with the left hand.

If a change to right-hand writing is attempted, the teacher and parents should explain to the child the advantages and try to obtain his cooperation. They should assure him at the outset that if he finds it very difficult to make the change, it will be all right if, after making an honest attempt, he continues to write with his left hand. Such assurance is of value in keeping the child from being unduly concerned with the matter of success or failure.

Disadvantages of the Left-Handed Writer

The disadvantages of the left-handed writer result to a considerable extent from lack of instruction in correct body and paper position. Without guidance the child may develop a backward writing slant. Furthermore, he may develop an awkward body position as he writes in a so-called "hook position" in an attempt to see what he is writing while he tilts his paper to the left. He may have his paper in that position in accordance with instructions given to the right-handed child because it has not been explained to the left-handed child that his paper should not be turned in the same way.

Position of Paper and of Body

If the child who writes with his left hand is given early guidance in acquiring and/or maintaining the position of paper and body described below, the disadvantages of left-handedness can be reduced considerably.

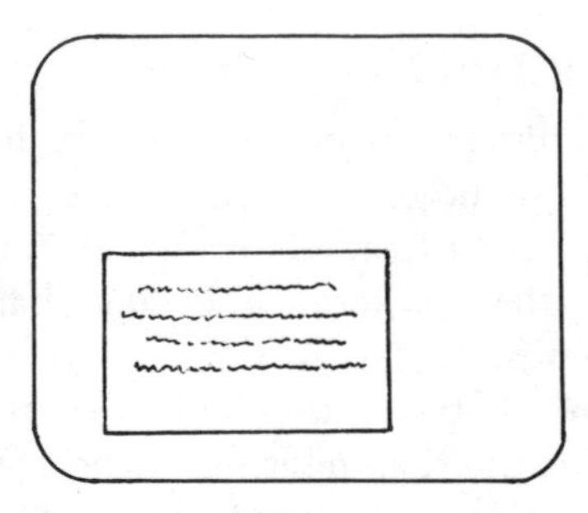

Figure 7.22 Position of Paper in Manuscript Writing for Left-Handed Writer

1. In manuscript writing the paper should be held as it is for the right-handed child, parallel to the edge of the desk.
2. In cursive writing the paper should be slanted to the right at an angle somewhere between 30 and 45 degrees from the line formed by the edge of the desk.
3. The paper should be placed in front of the writer or a little to the left. The second alternative

given here is preferable when the child is copying something from a book or paper on his desk and if the desk provides rather limited space. The forearm should be at approximately a right angle to the line of writing.

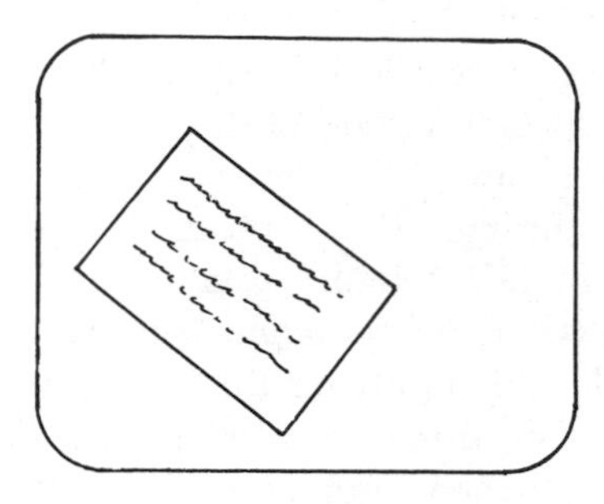

Figure 7.23 Position of Paper in Cursive Writing for Left-Handed Writer

4. The writing instrument should be held in much the same way as is recommended for the right-handed child except that it should be held farther from the tip so that the writer can quite readily see what he is writing. An inch or even an inch and one-half is recommended. The pencil or pen should slant toward the child's left shoulder.

5. The left arm should be quite close to the body so that the tendency toward curving the wrist is offset, at least in part.

6. To achieve a writing slant to the right in the position here recommended, the pupil should be encouraged to push his downstrokes toward the left elbow and his curved upstrokes toward the right. It should be noted, however, that there are people who believe that the left-handed child should be allowed to write with a backward slant or with no slant. In fact, some teachers furnish left-handed writers with models of handwriting in backward slant.

Other Teaching Suggestions

The following recommendations should be observed when helping the child who writes with his left hand once it has been decided not to try or not to continue to try to have him acquire the habit of writing with his right hand.

1. Help the left-handed child feel that there is nothing wrong or odd in being left-handed.

2. Provide the left-handed child with much practice in doing manuscript writing on the chalkboard during the early stages of learning to write as he stands directly in front of his writing.

3. Let the left-handed writer postpone the changeover from manuscript to cursive writing longer than most of the right-handed children. In fact, arguments against a change-over from manuscript to cursive handwriting are more convincing in case of the left-handed child than in case of the right-handed.

4. Furnish the left-handed pupil with a pencil with hard lead to avoid smudging, and if he uses a ball-point pen, give him one that does not smear.

5. Supervise carefully a left-handed pupil's experiences in the early stages of learning to write so that he places his paper correctly, holds his writing instrument properly, sits in good position, and uses correct arm and hand movements.

OTHER CONSIDERATIONS

In this last section of this chapter consideration is given to the following points: (1) adapting instruction to individual differences, (2) the instructional program, (3) writing numerals, and (4) use of the chalkboard.

Adapting Instruction to Individual Differences

In Chapter 3 general suggestions are given for adapting instruction in the language arts to individual differences. Consequently, in this chapter only a few points are mentioned.,

1. Boys and girls should be helped to understand why individuality in handwriting can be a decided detriment to ease in communication and that courtesy to the reader demands an easily read style of writing.

2. Careful diagnosis should be made of each pupil's needs and then individual or group attention given to his problems.

3. Pupils may at times be grouped into sections like the following: (a) those who are slow writers, (b) those who have particular problems with posture, (c) those who are left-handed, (d) those who have particular problems with size, slant, beginning and ending strokes, spacing, or alignment, (e) those who have particular troubles with letter formations, and (f) those who have difficulty in achieving good format.

4. The program in handwriting should be so flexible that variation is possible in the time when individuals within a classroom make the transition from manuscript to cursive writing.

5. Each child should be competing with his own best record. Use of handwriting scales and diagnostic charts can be of great value in this respect.

The Instructional Program

In some school systems the instructional program in handwriting is based almost entirely upon that advocated by one of the companies publishing handwriting materials such as The A. N. Palmer Company, the E. C. Seale Company, or The Zaner-Bloser Company. Pupils' recorders for the various grades are purchased for or by the children. With the help of the teacher's manual and other aids the main structure of the educational program is laid. In other schools the program is determined either without the use of a published program or with relatively little dependence on one.

PLANNING THE SCHOOLWIDE PROGRAM. Even when much dependence is placed upon a published program in handwriting, the need of schoolwide planning should not be overlooked. If plans for initiating a schoolwide program or for drastically revising one are considered, attention should be paid to: (1) formulation of objectives, including knowledge to be gained, abilities to be acquired, and attitudes to be developed; (2) deciding upon the sequence of the parts of the program; (3) determining, in general terms, the grade placement of various abilities or attitudes to be acquired; (4) listing resources available, including professional books and materials for use by the boys and girls; (5) studying methods of teaching; (6) planning means of evaluation; and (7) considering ways of correlating and integrating handwriting with other parts of the school program.

Frequently as the result of rather intensive study there may be produced a resource unit on handwriting which is written chiefly by members of a committee but to which contributions from the entire staff of the elementary school are solicited. In such a unit may also be included suggestions as to work that can be done in the secondary school to supplement that begun in the first six grades.

PLANNING THE PROGRAM FOR A GRADE. Even if a schoolwide program has been accepted and a commercial program in handwriting is followed to a considerable extent, there is need of planning by each teacher the details of a handwriting program for his grade. However, a good schoolwide program will simplify the work of the teacher as he plans for his room. Similarly many suggestions can be utilized by the teacher from programs worked out by companies that publish the better handwriting materials. After the teacher has studied available guides, he should do the following:

1. Set goals.
2. Determine the scope and sequence of the program.
3. Decide on means of testing the pupils to determine their general level of achievement as well as their strengths and weaknesses, and later on their progress.
4. Decide on general teaching procedures.
5. Make a list of methods and specific techniques to utilize.
6. Keep record of available materials and resources.

Writing Numerals

Boys and girls should be helped to realize the need of paying special attention to accuracy in writing numerals. At times a letter poorly formed can be deciphered through the context of the sentence in which it is found. A figure usually needs to stand on its own, however, for the context in which it is found is of no value in supplying the reader with a clue as to what the figure may be. (This difficulty, however, does not exist when figures are given in serial order. For example, a poorly written *2* can be recognized as such when written in a *1, 2, 3,* sequence.)

Here are a few suggestions for teaching numerals in addition to those given.

1. Draw attention to the fact that the numerals are written the size of the "small small letters."
2. Discuss with the boys and girls which figures are often confused with others when written carelessly such as the *6* and the *0*, the *1* and the *7*, and the *9* and the *7*.
3. Make certain that the boys and girls in the primary grades associate each figure with its correct value or order. Pupils may, for example, be asked to draw a line from one figure to an illustration showing the corresponding number of objects. Or opposite a given number of objects they may write the correct figure or may draw the required number of objects opposite a figure.

The Chalkboard as an Aid to Handwriting

It is to be regretted that in many modern elementary-school classrooms relatively little chalkboard space is provided. It is hoped that the elementary-school teacher will use his influence as new buildings are being constructed, to help those in authority realize the importance of considerable chalkboard space.

USE OF THE CHALKBOARD. With the limited chalkboard space in many classrooms it can easily be assumed, though erroneously, that the chalkboard is almost solely for the teacher's writing. However, if its use is reserved almost entirely for that purpose, some of the most significant possible values of the chalkboard, such as those indicated here, are overlooked.

1. There is less danger of developing cramped writing if the pupils use the chalkboard frequently,

for the movement in chalkboard writing is almost entirely arm and shoulder movement.

2. The larger handwriting on the chalkboard shows up — more readily than writing on paper — the problems and deficiencies in handwriting of a pupil.

3. The teacher can watch many pupils, perhaps 10 or even 12, almost simultaneously as they are writing on the chalkboard.

4. The teacher can guide the child's hand while he is writing at the chalkboard more effectively than when he is writing on paper.

5. The boys and girls enjoy writing on the chalkboard.

Position at the Chalkboard. Here are a few suggestions concerning the position at the chalkboard recommended by Frank N. Freeman[13] for the teacher, who should serve as model for the boys and girls.

> "Stand at nearly an arm's length from the board." [Another way of indicating the distance that the writer should stand from the chalkboard is to say that he should stand at least eight inches from the baseboard. In fact, it has been recommended that a line eight inches from the baseboard below the chalkboard be drawn parallel to it, as an indication to the pupil that he should not get his feet beyond the eight-inch line.]
>
> "Balance the body by standing with the feet apart, distributing the weight of the body equally on both feet.
>
> "Face the board squarely and write the first line of copy at eye level in order to keep a straight line." [It is recommended that the left-handed writer turn a little to the right. It should be noted that while the best writing position for a right-handed person is to face the chalkboard; for purposes of demonstration the teacher should stand a little to the right so that the pupils can observe him as he writes or he should write above his head.]
>
> "Hold the writing arm so the elbow is down and away from the body. As the writing progresses along the line, allow the hand to lead the elbow.
>
> "Lean leftward with the weight on the left foot in starting to write, gradually shifting the weight to the right foot as the writing progresses. This permits writing for a distance of about twenty to thirty inches before shifting the feet again."

Holding the Chalk. For holding the chalk Frank N. Freeman, in the book *Reference Manual for Teachers*, makes these suggestions (page 17):

> Hold the chalk between the thumb and first two fingers, pointing the chalk toward the center of the palm. A half piece of chalk is better to use, especially for people with small hands.

On page 5 of *Cursive Writing The Easy Way*, written and published by the A. N. Palmer Company in 1963, these statements are made:

> Two methods of instruction for placement of chalk in the hand are common, (a) as illustrated in the picture [accompanying this text] have the student place the chalk between the thumb and finger-tips so the base of the chalk points on a line to the elbow; (b) a variation of this method is to hold the chalk between the thumb and the finger-tips so the chalk is at an angle, parallel to the floor.
>
> Keep the end of the chalk blunt and rounded by turning it frequently.

Another suggestion of importance concerns the angle at which the chalk is to be held in relation to the chalkboard. It should be held at an angle somewhere between 20 and 40 degrees according to the suggestion of The Zaner-Bloser Company in *Writing on the Board*.[14]

Characteristics of Chalkboard Writing. The following points give information that characterizes good writing on the chalkboard.

1. Size. The size of the writing on the chalkboard for primary-grade children should be larger than that for intermediate-grade boys and girls. It is recommended that the size of the board writing be about five times as large as the writing that boys and girls do on paper. For first-grade it should be about five inches in height (for capital letters), for grade 2 four inches, for grade 3 three and one-half inches, and for grades 4 and above three inches. However, the desirable size depends not only on the grade level of the child but also on the distance from which the material is to be viewed, the quality of the stroke, and the type of writing surface.

2. Color or shading. The quality of the stroke should be such that the writing can be clearly and readily recognized from the distance from which it is to be read. The writer should press the chalk enough that he obtains a clear, sharp stroke. To maintain such a stroke as the writing proceeds, it is important to turn the chalk in the hand frequently enough to avoid writing with a rounded piece of chalk that would result in an uninteresting stroke, lacking in sharpness. The desirable stroke for manuscript writing is broader than that for cursive writing.

3. Slant. It is often less difficult to obtain the slant (or lack of slant) for manuscript writing on the chalkboard than to obtain the proper slant for cursive writing. The latter should be at an angle that deviates somewhere within the range of 20 to 30 degrees from

[13]Frank N. Freeman, *Reference Manual for Teachers.* Grades 5 through 8. Building Growth in Handwriting series. The Zaner-Bloser Company, 1959, page 17. Courtesy The Zaner-Bloser Company, Columbus, Ohio.

[14]The Zaner-Bloser Company, *Writing on the Board.* The Zaner-Bloser Company, 1958, page 17. Courtesy The Zaner-Bloser Company, Columbus, Ohio.

a perpendicular. To achieve correct slant at the chalkboard it is suggested on page 44 of *Writing on the Board*[15] that boys and girls be shown a figure like the accompanying one, which indicates the slant zone. Since the term *degrees* is likely to have meaning for only the older boys and girls, the explanation of the desired angle of slant should be simplified for beginners in cursive writing.

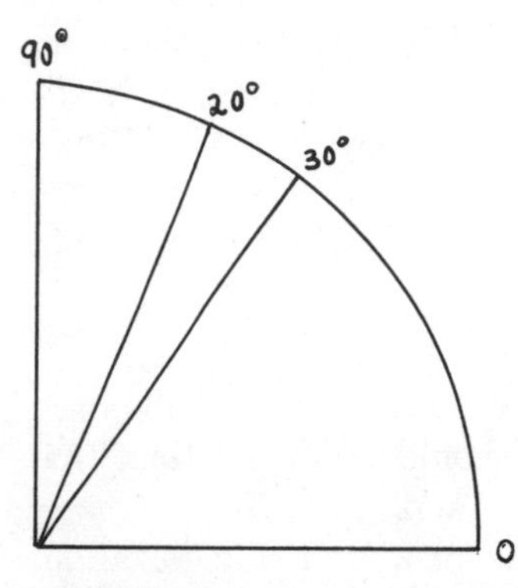

Adaptation of a diagram by The Zaner-Bloser Company: Courtesy of The Zaner-Bloser Company, Columbus, Ohio.

Figure 7.24 Illustration of the Slant Zone, Which Is between 20 Degrees and 30 Degrees to the Right of the Perpendicular

4. Beginning and ending strokes. The suggestions for achieving correct beginning and ending strokes for cursive writing on paper that are given earlier in this chapter are also of value in obtaining correct beginning and ending strokes in writing on the chalkboard.

5. Spacing. For correct letter and word spacing in cursive writing on the chalkboard the same proportionate distance should be maintained as in cursive writing on paper.

6. Alignment. Alignment on the chalkboard presents a problem beyond that which the writer meets when he works for correct alignment on paper. While a teacher should try to learn to write straight across an unlined chalkboard, often for demonstration purposes he will want a lined board. If the board is lined the boys and girls can better visualize the alignment as well as the size and proportion of letters as they will want to write them either on the chalkboard or on paper. For the pupil in some of the beginning stages of writing (though not the very first, when he should not be impeded by lines) it is important that a lined surface be provided.

Suggested Procedures. Following are a few suggestions as to methods of procedure in board writing.

1. It is good practice to have pupils who are beginning to learn to write to do much of it on the chalkboard. Sometimes one or more pupils may write on the board while the others are watching. At other times those at the seats may be writing on paper for a short time, maybe five to ten minutes, while others are at the chalkboard. A system of rotation to give all pupils a chance, though not necessarily daily opportunity, for writing on the chalkboard before any one pupil has had a second chance can be worked out.

2. Even after pupils in the primary grades have learned to write fairly well with the pencil, they should not be deprived of gaining the advantages that board writing offers. Practice on the chalkboard beyond the primary grades is often reserved for those boys and girls who are in need of special help. However, it could also be of much help to others, especially when a skill is being presented in a developmental lesson.

3. The boys and girls should be encouraged to use arm and shoulder movement almost exclusively when writing on the chalkboard.

4. It is good practice to have the pupils whose seats are near the back of the room come forward at times while the teacher is demonstrating at the chalkboard. Similarly those sitting near the sides of the classroom, if the teacher uses a chalkboard area near the middle of the front wall for demonstration purposes, may be invited to come toward a place of better visibility.

5. In a lesson in which the chalkboard is used, after the pupils have seen purpose for the lesson, these steps may be followed: (a) demonstration by the teacher; (b) explanation by the teacher; (c) demonstration by one or more pupils; (d) evaluation of the pupils' demonstration; (e) practice by the class; (f) comments by the teacher on points of difficulty, with suggestions for correction as the teacher again demonstrates the point; (g) further practice by the boys and girls, and (h) further evaluation.

Materials of Instruction and Their Care. This part of this chapter deals with two major "materials of instruction" for chalkboard writing, namely the chalkboard and the chalk.

1. The chalkboard. There are still in existence in quite a number of classrooms, especially in the older schools, chalkboards made of slate. Composition chalkboards have, however, to a large extent replaced

---

[15]The Zaner-Bloser Company, *Writing on the Board.* The Zaner-Bloser Company, 1958, page 44. Courtesy The Zaner-Bloser Company, Columbus, Ohio.

the slate boards. In turn, the composition boards are giving way in some schools to glass chalkboards.

Listed here are a few suggestions for care of chalkboards made of slate or composition board: (a) Do not use water, for it is likely to wear off the surface of composition boards and to take color out of the slate, graying it so that illegibility may result. (b) Do not use oiled cloths on slate or composition boards. (c) Use clean erasers, supplementing their use with a chamois skin, when washing slate boards or composition boards. (d) When erasing the board, start at the top and proceed to the bottom so that the dust falls into the chalk tray. (e) Have clean erasers, clean chamois skin, clean chalk trays, and clean chalkboards.

2. The chalk. Parker, Zaner, and Bloser on page 19 of *Writing on the Board* make these comments about the quality of chalk.

> Quality and kind of chalk varies in different communities from very cheap, soft and dusty chalk to the very hard, expensive and dustless kinds. As a general rule, it is best to avoid the extremes for while one may be a little hard on the health of the children, the other may be equally damaging on the eyes, by being too fine and faint. In some school rooms are found the traditional chalkboards where a medium, dustless chalk is advisable. In other rooms imitation slate chalkboards are used and give better results with a very hard chalk. In still other cases will be found some of the newer glass chalkboards. When teachers meet these varying conditions, it is well to try to find the chalk most suitable for the schoolroom conditions.
>
> The efficient teacher makes the most of the materials and does the best that he can with the tools which can be secured.
>
> The softer grades of chalk should be used in large or dark rooms and the harder grades in the small or light rooms. Care and judgment are needed in this as well as in the other conditions mentioned previously.

FOR STUDY AND DISCUSSION

1. Suggest methods that you could use for motivating boys and girls in a primary-grade room to improve their handwriting; in an intermediate-grade room.

2. How would you answer the question that a pupil in the intermediate grades might ask as to why many successful adults do not write legibly?

3. Write the alphabet in both manuscript and cursive writing, including upper-case and lower-case letters. Then compare your letter formation with that recommended by a good publishing company of handwriting materials. What suggestions for improvement of your own writing can you give?

4. Draw a diagram of a classroom for one of the elementary-school grades in which you show adequate space for chalkboards. Indicate recommended space for pupils' wraps and for bulletin boards. Also show desirable placement of windows, doors, teacher's desk, pupils' desks or tables, and other furniture.

5. If you are a right-handed writer, how would you try to demonstrate writing to the left-handed writer? If you are a left-handed writer, how would you try to demonstrate it to the right-handed writer?

6. Make a list of ways in which handwriting can be correlated with other school subjects in any one grade of the elementary school.

7. Make a study of several handwriting scales available commercially and evaluate them.

8. Study the handwriting materials, materials for boys and girls, teachers' manuals among them – produced by one or more publishing companies. Note the extent to which suggestions given in this chapter are implemented in those materials. Also note and evaluate any suggestions to the contrary that you may find, as well as additional ideas that you consider useful.

REFERENCES

Burns, Paul C., *Improving Handwriting Instruction in Elementary Schools.* Burgess Publishing Company, 1962. 66 pp.

MacCampbell, James C., (editor), *Readings in the Language Arts in the Elementary School.* D. C. Heath and Company, 1964. 470 pp.

Myers, Emma Harrison, *The Whys and Hows of Teaching Handwriting.* The Zaner-Bloser Company, 1963. 160 pp.

Shane, Harold G., and June Grant Mulry, *Improving Language Arts Instruction through Research.* Association for Supervision and Curriculum Development, 1963. 153 pp.

The Zaner-Bloser Company, *Writing on the Board.* The Zaner-Bloser Company, 1958, 97 pp.

OUTLINE FOR CHAPTER 8

Guiding Growth in Spelling

CHAPTER 8

Guiding Growth in Spelling

One of the most frequently heard complaints against the American school is that boys and girls "can't spell." Such statements are made not only by consistent critics of American education but also by parents and teachers. Although research data seem to indicate that the boys and girls today spell better than their forefathers who attended school in America, there should be little comfort in that. The ability to assert the superiority of spelling results of the present day over those of the past, should, indeed, be expected. With the greater advantages that pupils in attendance at school now have over those of forty years ago, for example, in terms of better-schooled teachers, improvements in materials of instruction, and benefits of research, there surely ought to be an advance over norms of the past. Such a comparison, therefore, should not keep us from striving for better and better results in spelling.

BASIC CONSIDERATIONS IN TEACHING SPELLING

As background for a subsequent emphasis on methods and materials of instruction, the following points are considered in the introductory pages of this chapter: (1) shortcomings of earlier programs, (2) goals of spelling instruction, (3) motivation for spelling, and (4) time allotments.

Shortcomings of Earlier Programs

In order to avoid some of the deficiencies of earlier programs of spelling instruction, let us note what they were.

1. Emphasis was put on a very long list of words.
2. The words in spelling lists were far more difficult than those included in modern lists.
3. The words in spelling lists were not scientifically selected in terms of use in writing.
4. The lists were poorly allocated to grade levels since neither usefulness of the words nor difficulty of learning them were established by research.
5. Too great faith seemingly was placed on transfer of learning.
6. Little help was given boys and girls in the method of studying words.
7. Inadequate provision was made for systematic review.
8. There was an overemphasis on the value of writing a word — one that had been misspelled — a specified number of times for practice purposes.
9. There was an overemphasis on oral spelling.
10. There was an overemphasis on spell-downs.
11. Inadequate attention was paid to individual differences.
12. Relatively little time was spent on improving the spelling of words not included in spelling lists, words which the boys and girls used in their functional writing.
13. An unnecessarily large amount of time in the school day was often allotted to spelling.

Goals of Spelling Instruction

In the modern elementary school, teachers try to:

1. Help the boys and girls see the importance of correct spelling
2. Help the pupils write correctly the words they use in written communication
3. Guide the pupils so they will want to spell correctly the words they use in their writing
4. Develop in the boys and girls independence in spelling so that in time they need not rely on the teacher or a textbook for the spelling of a word

5. Guide the pupils so they will habitually use methods of learning to spell a word that for them are effective.

Motivation for Spelling

The following two aims listed in the preceding paragraph deal with motivation in spelling: (1) to help the boys and girls see the importance of correct spelling and (2) to guide the pupils so that they will want to spell correctly the words that they use in their writing.

THE IMPORTANCE OF SPELLING. The need for uniform spelling can be pointed out to elementary-school children by explanation, discussion, and demonstration of the effect on written communication if each person were spelling in whatever way he wished. Furthermore, the teacher can discuss with the boys and girls the fact that when people seeking work make a written application, the employers often judge them in part by any errors of spelling that may appear on their letters of application.

The fact that many people other than employers judge an individual in part by spelling ability could also be pointed out. Since it is considered good form to spell correctly, the boys and girls could be helped to realize that failure to do so in many cases constitutes reason to believe that a person is slow of learning, unschooled, or careless.

THE DESIRE TO SPELL. In a sense the realization of the importance of spelling is merely preliminary to the next step – that of wanting to spell. The child should realize that the goal of being a good speller can be accomplished, at least in part, if he really wants to become a good speller – enough to be willing to follow suggestions for improvement.

OTHER POINTS. As emphasis is being placed on knowledge of the importance of correct spelling and on developing a desire to become a good speller, the following points should be noted.

1. If boys and girls realize that the words that they are asked to spell are important to them in their writing, they are likely to want to learn them.

2. Competition with self, rather than with others, should be stressed.

3. It is not necessary, not even desirable, that every day when the boys and girls study spelling the teacher try to motivate them to better spelling. If daily the teacher urges them to become better spellers, his comments may have an effect the opposite of what was intended.

4. Knowledge of results serves as motivation, especially, if the results are desirable. In fact, one of the best ways for interesting a person to strive for further improvement is to show him that he is improving.

5. Purpose for spelling can be highly meaningful to boys and girls when they engage in bona fide writing situations in which they are truly interested. Consequently the teacher who provides many occasions such as the following is likely to aid growth in spelling: writing and proofreading articles for a class paper or magazine; writing a letter to a pupil who is absent from school; writing a thank-you letter to an adult who has spoken to the group.

6. The attitude of the teacher toward spelling can serve as a motivating influence. The teacher who shows enthusiasm for teaching spelling is more likely to inspire it in his pupils than the one who gives the impression, though unwittingly, that he thinks of it merely as a task to be performed. His own care in spelling correctly can also motivate the class to pay more attention to spelling, especially if they like him.

Time Allotments

What is the optimum length of time to be spent on spelling in the daily or weekly schedule? One reason it is impossible to give an authoritative answer to this question is that the extent to which spelling is given incidental attention during the school day undoubtedly affects the length of time that might advisedly be set aside for learning-to-spell periods. Another reason is that research has not thus far, with surety, pointed to any one length of time as the best. In fact, since so many factors, such as means of using the class period and the number of spelling words studied, have bearing on the desirable length of time, it is doubtful whether research can ever say with conclusiveness that a given number of minutes a week is *the* optimum length of time for spelling classes.

Research, together with expert opinion, has, however, thrown some light on the problem of time allotments. It is now rather commonly believed by persons specializing in the field of the teaching of elementary-school spelling that 75 minutes a week spent in spelling classes is somewhere near a desirable length of time. In applying this recommendation the teacher must bear in mind the fact that the length of time he will want to use for spelling classes should be determined in part by factors to which reference is made in the preceding paragraph.

How the total number of minutes a week for spelling can best be allocated to the daily schedule has not been determined. Some teachers favor spending 15 minutes five times a week on spelling. Others favor an unequal division of the time, with limits to be determined in the light of the type of work to be done each day. For example, some teachers who follow the plan of working on a given set of new words for five class periods during the week like to have a longer period of time on the day when they present the words than on other days. The following, or a variation of it, might be their schedule.

First day: 25 minutes
Second day: 15 minutes
Third day: 10 minutes
Fourth day: 10 minutes
Fifth day: 15 minutes.

Still other teachers set aside daily a block of time, possibly an hour in length, commonly referred to as the language-arts period, during which all the language arts except reading are taught. Thus they do not specify how much of the block should be used daily for spelling, how much for handwriting, and how much for so-called "English." The length of time they use for spelling may vary from day to day. Some teachers may decide not to spend time on spelling every day of the week.

READINESS FOR SPELLING

Before regular instruction in spelling begins, the child should be ready for the task. Let us then consider these points about spelling readiness: (1) the need for spelling readiness, (2) prerequisites for spelling, (3) appraisal of spelling readiness, and (4) methods of developing spelling readiness.

The Need for Spelling Readiness

It is now generally conceded by specialists that formal instruction in spelling should not take place in the first grade. In fact, some educators question starting such teaching even at the beginning of the second grade. Reason for this delay in teaching the child to spell is that he may suffer in the following ways if he is confronted with formal teaching of spelling before he is ready for it.

1. He may develop an aversion for school activities because of inability to do what he is expected to do in spelling.
2. It may become difficult in the future to interest in spelling the child who had been defeated in his early efforts to learn to spell.
3. If the child received formal spelling instruction at the time he was beginning to learn to read, learning to spell may interfere with learning to read.

Prerequisites for Spelling

Some of the factors that will determine whether a child is ready to learn to spell are his (1) mental age, (2) ability in visual and auditory discrimination, (3) reading ability, (4) knowledge of the alphabet, (5) knowledge of phonics, (6) ability to write, (7) ability to spell a few words, and (8) interest in learning to spell.

1. Mental age. If any one desirable mental age for beginning formal instruction in spelling had to be named, it might be about 7 or 7 1/2 years. However, as in the case of readiness for reading, no one mental age can be set as the optimum or even the minimum age at which formal spelling instruction should begin. If a child ranks high on the other prerequisites of spelling listed in the preceding paragraph, he may be able to learn to spell before he has attained a given mental age that might ordinarily be considered desirable.

2. Visual and auditory discrimination. The ability to discriminate between symbols for letters and words is essential to success in spelling. In addition to needing visual acuity the child must be able to differentiate quite readily, for example, between letter forms such as *m* and *n*. He needs to be able to note quickly that the vowel, for example, in *sat* and *sit* is not the same. Auditory discrimination also is an important aspect for readines for spelling. Many errors in spelling seem to be caused by "hearing" words incorrectly.

3. Reading ability. The child who has completed successfully the reading of material equivalent in difficulty to that of most first-grade readers seems to be well enough equipped as far as reading ability is concerned for work in a desirable program of beginning spelling instruction.

4. Knowledge of the alphabet. The pupil who does not readily recognize the names of the letters of the alphabet as capital letters and as lower-case letters is likely to be handicapped even in a beginning program of spelling. The recommendation is that in the beginning program in both reading and spelling instruction the words should be written in manuscript.

5. Knowledge of phonics. To be successful in learning to spell, the child should have knowledge of the rudiments of phonics. Knowledge of common sounds of the consonants and vowels, in various positions in words, as well as of much-used consonant blends, seems to be a prerequisite. (The relationship of phonics to spelling is explained somewhat in detail later in this chapter.)

6. Ability to write. Since spelling is useful almost exclusively in writing situations, the ability to do some writing is essential to spelling. A child who cannot write the letters of the alphabet legibly without undue effort is hardly ready to learn to spell the words as he writes them.

7. Ability to spell a few words. Before formal instruction in spelling is begun, it is helpful if the pupil can spell a few words in addition to his own name – words that he has used rather frequently in writing and to the spelling of which the teacher has drawn special attention.

8. Interest in learning to spell. The teacher should, during the spelling readiness period, try to motivate the child so that he will be eager to learn to spell. This objective can be accomplished, at least in part, through helping him realize that in order to write effectively one must be able to spell.

Appraisal of Spelling Readiness

A few suggestions are given here as to how the teacher can ascertain whether or not a child is ready to learn to spell. They are organized around the prerequisites for spelling readiness listed in this chapter.

1. Mental age. The best index of mental age that is obtainable for a child is secured through intelligence tests. (The reader is referred to listings of intelligence tests given in Chapter 13.)

2. Visual and auditory discrimination. It is important that the teacher have clearly in mind the difference between visual acuity and visual discrimination, as well as between auditory acuity and auditory discrimination. A child who has visual acuity – one who can see plainly, for example, the letters *u* and *n* – may not be able to differentiate between the two. To test a child's ability to make visual discriminations an exercise with items like the following can be used as he is asked to cross out the word in a row that is different from the others:

dime dime dine dime dime.

Or he may be asked to draw a line under the word in a row that is the same as the first word in the row, as in this illustration:

dine dime dime dine dime.

Since skill in visual discrimination is checked in many reading readiness tests, some teachers may find the child's level of performance by means of such a test.

A child who has considerable auditory acuity – that is one who can hear well – may not be able to differentiate, for example, between the sound of the words *bear* and *hair,* a skill important to spelling. (For a discussion on appraising auditory discrimination the reader is referred to Chapter 10.)

3. Reading ability. One very simple test for reading ability, if the child was not given a standardized reading test, is to have him read orally to the teacher in the last part of a first-grade reader or the first part of a second-grade reader of the series used in the school. If he can read the material with no more than a few errors per page, he would seem to be ready for spelling instruction as far as level of attainment in reading is concerned.

4. Knowledge of the alphabet. The teacher can ask the child to read the letters of the alphabet, written in manuscript. The letters should not be given in alphabetical order, for the pupil might be able to identify the letters by their order rather than by their form if they are given in *ABC* order.

5. Knowledge of phonics. Following are some ways in which a child's knowledge of phonics, important for beginning spelling, can be tested:

> The teacher can ask the child to write the letter with which each of a series of words begins as the teacher names them.
>
> The teacher can ask the child to point at the letter *d,* for example, which the teacher has written on the chalkboard, when he names a word beginning with *d.* The child can further be instructed to point at the letter *p,* also written on the board by the teacher, when the teacher names a word beginning with *p.* Other consonants whose sounds are frequently confused can be identified in a similar manner.
>
> The pupil can be asked to name words that begin with the same sound as one that the teacher names.

6. Ability to write. The teacher writes on the chalkboard one or a few short sentences that the pupil is able to read, which he is to copy. If the pupil has done the copying so that it is legible and so that there are no more than a few errors in writing the letters (omissions, substitutions, or repetitions), it would seem that the writing ability of the child would be advanced enough that he ought not to be handicapped in beginning spelling because of his handwriting.

7. Ability to spell a few words. A child's ability to write his own name without a copy is one index of readiness for spelling. If from time to time the teacher has drawn the attention of his class to the spelling of a few words frequently written by pupils, such as *Mother* or *today,* the teacher may ask them to write those words without copy. Failure to write such words correctly should not be interpreted as a serious shortcoming.

8. Interest in learning to spell. One way in which the teacher can appraise the child's interest in learning to spell is by noting his reactions when the teacher

informally refers to the spelling of words. For example, he can note whether the child is interested in responding when the teacher asks questions like this one as he writes on the chalkboard: "With what letter should I start the next word you dictated, the word *man?*"

Methods

The methods used to help boys and girls grow toward readiness for spelling should not be pigeonholed into a period of the day designated for spelling readiness. Rather, means for getting the children ready to learn to spell should be employed throughout the school day, many of them, as far as the children know, incidental in the ongoing program of the room. The following are some of the ways in which the teacher can guide the boys and girls so that they will become ready for systematic instruction in spelling.

1. Providing the boys and girls with a large number of interesting and worthwhile experiences so that they will have the background for dictating to the teacher reports or stories which they would like to see in writing
2. Writing at a child's dictation a caption for a picture that he has drawn
3. While writing a story at the dictation of one or more pupils, occasionally making comments or asking questions like these that draw attention to spelling: (a) What is the first letter of the word *mother?* (b) Who can write the letter with which our next word *farmer* begins? (c) The next word for our story is given on this word card. Write it here in our story. (d) Let's spell this word *run* together, for it is a word we often use in writing.
4. Helping the children who are lacking in auditory discrimination by any of the means suggested for development of that ability in Chapter 9
5. Orientating pupils to the left-to-right and top-to-bottom sequence in writing by: (a) drawing attention to that sequence in reading; (b) showing the child where the teacher starts and how he continues when writing something on the chalkboard, a chart, or a piece of paper; (c) asking a child occasionally where he (the teacher) should start as he writes at the pupil's dictation and asking him in what direction the writing should progress; (d) having a pupil name the first letter in a word and the next and the next
6. Helping boys and girls who have difficulty with enunciation
7. Having the pupils copy a story or letter the teacher has written on the chalkboard at the dictation of the class
8. Helping the pupils copy lists they may need such as lists of supplies; names of room duties to be performed and names of those who are to do them; the sequence of activities for the day
9. Having the pupils do semi-independent writing with the teacher available to help in spelling of the words in the simple sentences that the children write
10. Having a pupil who asks for the spelling of a word write the first letter of the word before he is given help by the teacher
11. Providing a series of picture cards which the children are to match with letters of the alphabet
12. Having the pupils give words that start with the letter of the alphabet to which the teacher points
13. Having a "pupil-teacher" point at the letters of the alphabet given on the chalkboard in mixed-up order as others name them
14. Providing the pupils with sheets of paper on each of which are two columns, with capital letters in the first column to be matched with lower-case letters in the second

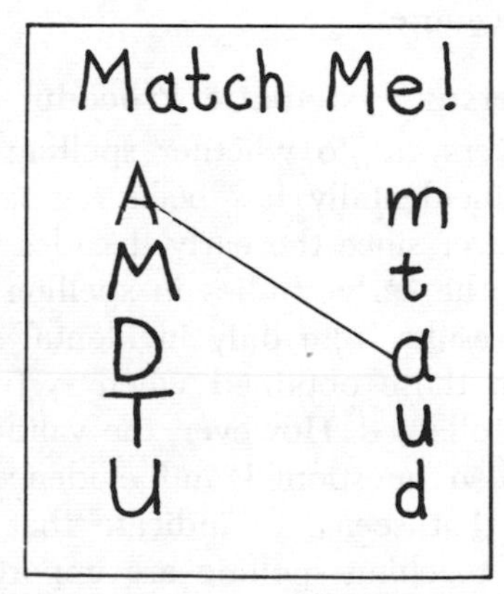

Figure 8.1 An Exercise for Matching Upper- and Lower-Case Letters

15. Playing a game on the order of Bingo in which are used letters of the alphabet in mixed-up order. The caller can either name the letters to be covered on the cards provided or name words beginning with the letters to be covered.
16. Providing the boys and girls with picture dictionaries and helping them use these books
17. Helping the pupils make picture dictionaries either as a class or individual project
18. Helping boys and girls learn to write according to suggestions given in Chapter 7
19. Helping boys and girls acquire the rudiments of knowledge of phonics and various other skills in reading as suggested in Chapter 10.

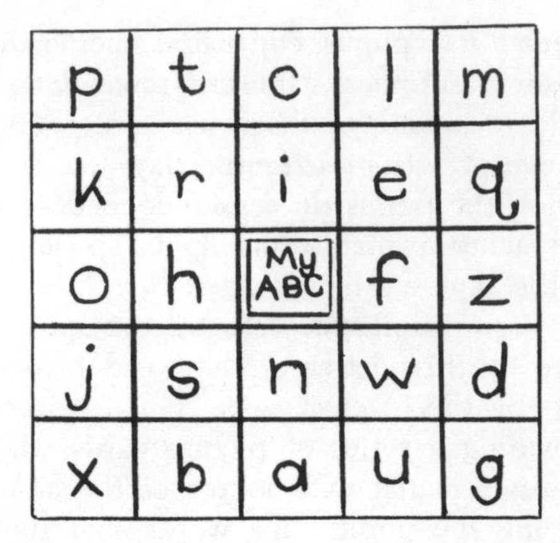

Figure 8.2 A Game for Letter Recognition or for Practice on Sounds

ORGANIZATION FOR SPELLING

Three questions of organization of the spelling program that have far-reaching effects are here considered. They deal with (1) incidental versus systematic procedures, (2) the multiple-day versus the daily plan of procedure, and (3) study-test versus test-study procedures.

Incidental versus Systematic Procedures

The controversy as to whether spelling should be studied only incidentally has been raging in educational circles ever since the early decades of the century. Some of the early studies in spelling seemed to indicate that results from only incidental study were not inferior to those obtained when systematic procedures were followed. However, the validity of those studies has been questioned and evidence has been accumulating that seems to indicate that systematic procedures in teaching spelling are important. While there still is no unanimity of belief on the question, many specialists in the field have the point of view, to which the author subscribes, namely that the best results are obtainable when incidental means of teaching spelling are utilized in the various activities of the school program providing these are supplemented by systematic teaching of spelling in a separate period of the school day or during a part of a block set aside for the language arts.

The Multiple-Day versus the Daily Plan of Procedure

If a teacher or a school has decided to use a systematic procedure for teaching spelling, supplemented, it is hoped, by many incidental means of learning to spell, the question arises as to its plan of organization. A very popular plan, according to which most of the recent spelling textbooks in the elementary school are organized, is the five-day plan. It calls for the repeated study for five consecutive school days of a list of words, usually ranging in number from about seven or eight to twenty, with the number varying according to grade level and the spelling series. This plan is sometimes referred to as the weekly plan, with Monday thought of as the first day of the five to be spent on a given list of words, Tuesday as the second, and so on. However, authors of some spelling books and probably some teachers think of it as a five-day plan — not a weekly plan — on which the first work on a list does not necessarily fall on Monday. Some find that designation more convenient because of the fact that vacations of part of a week or other events that may interefere with having spelling every day can throw off the schedule for the weekly plan.

In contrast to the five-day plan is the one that was used extensively in earlier times and still has not been abandoned. According to it a smaller number of words is presented than in the five-day plan and new words are studied each day. However, reviews are also provided or can be provided for on later days at spaced intervals in the one-day plan.

Not all plans for systematic teaching of spelling are the so-called one-day or five-day plans. Four days or three days for study on a list of spelling words are used by some teachers. However, the most common of the multiple-day plans undoubtedly is the five-day plan.

Research on the comparative value of the two types of plans, the multiple-day and the daily plan as those terms are here used, is inconclusive. There is a difference in opinion of writers and of teachers on the question of relative worth, even in regard to the following statements, but it can be said, at least, that no conclusive evidence has been presented that contradicts them.

1. When systematic spelling instruction is first begun in primary grades, it is probably advisable to present a few words several times a week with continued study on succeeding days.
2. Pupils with low intelligence seem to profit more from having only a few words presented daily, with provisions for adequate review, rather than more words presented to them once a week.
3. Pupils with many difficulties in spelling, regardless of their grade placement or their intelligence, would probably profit more from a one-day plan of procedure with adequate review than from a multiple-day plan.
4. After pupils of near-average, average, or above-average intelligence who are near-average, average,

or above-average spellers are beyond the stage of beginning work in systematic instruction in spelling, the multiple-day plan is probably superior to the one-day plan for them.

Study-Test versus Test-Study Procedures

One question often raised by persons who wish to recommend or use a multiple-day plan of procedure is that of the comparative desirability of study-test and test-study procedures. More specifically, the question is: "Is it better to test the boys and girls on a list of words before they study them or is it more advantageous to have the first testing follow some study of the words?"

To make clearer the two procedures, let us note how they can be used in the five-day plan. If less than five days are spent on a given list of words, the methods used in the five-day period as here outlined can be telescoped into fewer days.

TEST-STUDY PROCEDURES. Although there are many variations of test-study procedures, these steps are somewhat typical of them: (1) Either before the pupils have seen a list of new words or after they have had only a brief approach to the new words, they are given a pretest on the list. (2) Thereafter each pupil studies the words that he missed on the test. (3) Next he is retested. (4) Thereupon every pupil again studies the words that he missed. (5) A so-called final test is then given.

To summarize, the five steps enumerated in the preceding paragraph can be identified as (1) pretesting, (2) studying, (3) testing, (4) studying, and (5) testing. The procedure is sometimes called the test-study-test-study-test procedure. In the five-day plan, in many instances roughly each of these steps constitutes the work for one day. Provisions are made for further study of any words a pupil misses on the final test given on the fifth day, and provisions for systematic spaced review of all words in the weeks and months to follow are made.

STUDY-TEST PROCEDURES. These four steps are typical of those followed in study-test procedures, in which study of words precedes testing: (1) The pupils study the new words rather carefully. (2) The pupils are tested. (3) The pupils study the words missed. (4) The pupils are again tested. When these four steps are followed, the procedure is sometimes called the study-test-study-test procedure. If five days of consecutive study are devoted to a list of words, the first and second days can be spent on study, the third on the trial test, the fourth on more study, and the fifth on the final test. In lieu of this, the first day can be devoted to study, the second to the trial test, the third and fourth to further study, and the fifth to the final test. Provisions are made for further study of words that a pupil misses on the final test and for systematic spaced review of words in the weeks and months that follow.

RELATIVE VALUE OF TEST-STUDY AND STUDY-TEST PROCEDURES. Although research has not established which of the two methods is superior, at the present time there is some reason for believing that considerations such as the following should help determine which of the two should be used.

1. An argument against the test-study procedure is that pupils might be discouraged in studying a list of words if they found out in a pretest that they have missed a large per cent of the words.

2. Another argument against the test-study procedure is that a pupil might spell a word correctly on a pretest and then miss it in a test given later. For example, when he writes the word *receive* in a pretest, he may be in doubt whether the vowel sound in the second syllable is spelled *ei* or *ie*, but, without any surety, he may happen to spell it *ei*. If he gives no further attention to the word before the time of the next test, he may again wonder whether the long *e* sound should be spelled *ei* or *ie* and then by chance happen to write it *ie*. The child studying the word before his first testing will at least have the benefit before the final test of some study of a word that he really does not know.

3. An argument for the test-study procedure is that a pupil who has spelled almost all words correctly is encouraged by knowing he has only a few words to learn.

4. Another argument for the test-study procedure is that a pupil does not waste time studying the spelling of words he already knows. For pupils who do not know how to spell a large proportion of the words on a list, the study-test procedure is probably superior to the test-study plan. For others, the test-study procedure probably is better. To obtain an estimate of whether a given pupil is likely to miss many words on pretests, his achievement on tests given on earlier lists may be considered or he can be given a semester pretest on a sampling of the words for the term.

STEPS IN LEARNING TO SPELL A WORD

Merely to tell a child to study a word or to study it by writing it a specified number of times is no longer considered adequate procedure.

Learning to Spell a Word with Teacher Guidance

Although many teachers as well as writers on the subject of spelling have developed plans for studying the spelling of a word, there is no one system that has been established as superior to all others. Many, however, would agree in general on the following as significant steps in learning to spell a word when a teacher is present to guide the work: (1) pronunciation of the word; (2) clarification, if necessary, of the meaning of the word; (3) getting a clear image of the word; (4) recalling the word; (5) writing the word; (6) checking the writing; and (7) repeating steps 3, 4, 5, and 6 in case of error until the word is learned.

Figure 8.3 Illustrated Steps in Learning to Spell a Word

Pronunciation of the Word. Acceptable practice for this step of the procedure varies. Some teachers like to write the list of new words on the chalkboard before class, numbering the words for easy reference. Then at the beginning of the period they pronounce each word as they point at it, and have the pupils pronounce it after them in unison. Others prefer to have pupils who do not recognize a word get help in word recognition through other than the sight method, according to which every word is pronounced for them. Consequently some teachers, referring to the numbered list of words on the chalkboard, ask the pupils to give the number of any word that they cannot pronounce. Then the teacher tries to help the child who has difficulty with the word to decipher it by means of context clues (as the teacher writes a helpful sentence on the chalkboard in which the word is used), structural analysis (including syllabication), or phonetic analysis. Thereupon the teacher pronounces the words as he points at each and the pupils say each word in unison after him.

Clarification of Meaning. After the pupils know the pronunciation of the words on a list, attention should be paid, if necessary, to the meaning. If the words are well-graded, there should not be many words about which there is question of meaning. Since the pupil's meaning vocabulary exceeds his spelling vocabulary, the emphasis in spelling lists is put on words of which the pupils know the meaning not on those of which they do not know it. Still, since published grade lists are planned for the entire country, there may be on any list some words the meaning of which an individual or even an entire class does not know.

The question of multiple meanings of words might be raised in connection with this step of the process of learning to spell it. Usually at this point – when the new list of words is being presented – the teacher can be satisfied if the pupil knows one common meaning of a word. Emphasis on multiple meanings can be placed later on during the multiple-day sequence when through extended activities the child is helped to learn more about word meanings and other matters related to spelling.

For a list of steps in a procedure for helping boys and girls learn the meaning of a word, the reader is referred to page 309. Additional points are here listed.

1. If a homonym is included in a list and there is reason to think that the meaning of the other spelling of the homonym may be known by a pupil, it is wise to have a child explain the meaning of the word and use it in a sentence. In some instances it may also be desirable to write the homonyms on the chalkboard and then use them in sentences.

2. It is often a waste of time to have the pupils use all the words on a spelling list in oral sentences, because it is likely that everybody knows the meaning of many of the words without such practice.

3. Helpful practice on the meaning of words can be given through the context which many spelling books provide for use when a list of words is presented. The context is often in the form of a story

that contains all the words on the spelling list. Some teachers have pupils read the whole story silently in the hope that the use of the words will be made clearer. (The teacher should be cautioned not to have someone read the story orally while the rest read it silently because such practice discourages effective oral reading and encourages slower habits of silent reading for the pupils who can read more rapidly silently than orally.)

GETTING A CLEAR IMAGE OF THE WORD. Even while the child pronounces and/or hears each word pronounced and while he learns the meaning of a word, he should be encouraged to note the spelling of the word. Furthermore, after he has concentrated on the pronunciation and if necessary on the meaning of the word, he should try to form a clear mental image of the word as he looks at it with the intent of learning the spelling. With some longer words children sometimes seem to profit if the word is written on the chalkboard twice, once without division into syllables and once with it. It is at this stage of learning to spell a word that saying distinctly each syllable may be advisable.

It is at this step that distinguishing or irregular features of the spelling of a word can be pointed out. Questions like these can be asked as the pupils look at a word: (1) What double letter is found in this word? (2) How is the long-*a* sound spelled in this word? In the case of a word that is spelled as it sounds, the teacher may wish to make a comment similar to this: "I believe that you will not have trouble with this word because it is spelled the way you would expect it to be spelled."

RECALLING THE WORD. In this fourth step the learner, without looking at the word, thinks of its spelling. Some teachers ask the pupils to close their eyes to try to "see" the word. Others merely tell them to "say" the letters silently to themselves without looking at the word and without vocalization. The pupils are encouraged to check their recall by again looking at the word.

WRITING THE WORD. The pupils are then ready to write the word. This writing is frequently done on scratch paper or in the case of a few pupils on the chalkboard.

CHECKING THE WRITING. After the pupil has written the word, he checks it. He can do so by looking at the word, hearing the teacher spell it by syllables, or using both of these methods. As he checks it, if he has made an error he takes special note of his mistake. It may be helpful in the case of an error to draw a circle around the part misspelled or to rewrite the word correctly, drawing a line under the part in which an error was made.

REPEATING STEPS IF NECESSARY. The last four steps, as here listed, should be repeated until the child has written the word correctly.

Learning Independently to Spell a Word

Any spelling program in which the teacher does not help the boys and girls to form good habits when studying a word without teacher guidance is falling short of accomplishing an important objective that should be attained in guiding growth in spelling. The steps to be recommended for individual study should be similar to those used for group work, though not necessarily identical, with possible variations. The following should prove useful.

1. Look at the word.
2. Say the word softly to yourself.
3. Think of the spelling of the word as you look at the word.
4. Without looking at the word "see" it in your mind.
5. Compare your "picture" of the word with the copy.
6. Write the word.
7. Check your writing of the word.
8. Repeat the steps if necessary.

To facilitate memory of the steps they could be abbreviated on a chart in a manner like this:

1. Look.
2. Say.
3. Think.
4. "See."
5. Compare.
6. Write.
7. Check.
8. Repeat, if necessary.

The children should understand that the steps in learning to spell a word are given to help them. They may be told that many pupils who have followed these or similar steps have improved their spelling. They should also be told that if after a while they can learn to spell well without going through each of these steps, they should omit those that they do not need.

METHODS

The suggestions for methods of procedure given in the preceding pages of this chapter are for the most part rather general in nature. In this part specific suggestions are listed. They are discussed under this grouping: (1) studying the meaning of words, (2) formulating generalizations, (3) using phonics as an aid to spelling, (4) studying word forms, (5) other activities, and (6) questionable procedures.

Studying the Meaning of Words

Suggestions are given on page 158 for helping boys and girls acquire one meaning for any word in a spelling list with which they are familiar. Additional methods are here suggested for helping them acquire more than one meaning and for learning meanings of homonyms. The pupils can do the following.

1. Write the correct homonym as the teacher reads sentences such as this one:

 Did you *hear* him?

2. Select the correct homonym in a set or sets of homonyms given in parentheses in a sentence and then write the correct one(s) in space provided for that purpose.

 (Their, There) is no reason to think that they will be (hear, here) soon. ...., ...

3. Make a list of homonyms and use each in a sentence, orally or in writing, to illustrate the meaning of each word.

4. Proofread some material, possibly written by the children, in which there are errors in spelling homonyms or other words they have studied.

<u>What's</u> <u>Wrong</u> <u>Here</u>?

Have you scene hour knew aquarium? I hope you will come too our room this afternoon two sea it. Sum of the boys and girls helped plan it. Miss Hill said that they have put the write plants into it. Did you no that won has to be very careful in choosing the food for an aquarium?

Figure 8.4 An Exercise in Detecting Wrong Homonyms

5. Match homonyms given in one column with words or groups of words explaining them in a second column, like:

sea also
two at this place
too more than one
here water
hear look
see understand through listening.

6. Match the words given in one column with the meaning given in a second column. (This suggestion is similar to that given for homonyms in the preceding item.)

7. Find in a dictionary the meaning that best fits the use of an underlined word in a given sentence.

8. Study the different uses of a word with multiple meanings as listed in a dictionary, and then use sentences illustrating the meanings within the pupils' comprehension.

9. Read a series of sentences containing various meanings of words of which the boys and girls are studying the spelling and then explain the meaning of the spelling word in each of them.

10. Solve a crossword puzzle in which all the words to be filled in are spelling words.

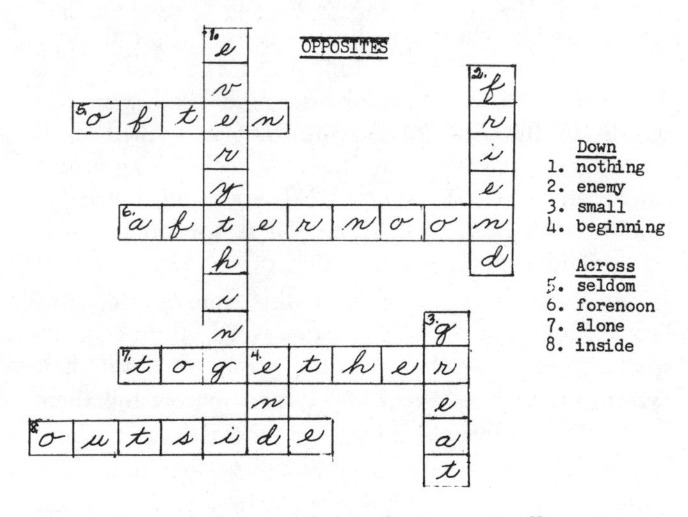

Figure 8.5 A Crossword Puzzle as a Spelling Device

11. Make a crossword puzzle for others in the class to solve in which all the words to be filled in are spelling words.

12. Give synonyms for words in a list.

13. Substitute synonyms in context for overused words.

Formulating Generalizations

There seems to be general agreement that learning generalizations, when certain guidelines are observed in the process, can be of real benefit to boys and girls. Through knowledge of a few generalizations they do not have to think of every word they learn to spell without relationship to what they have already learned about spelling some other words.

GUIDELINES FOR TEACHING GENERALIZATIONS. The following are some of the points that the teacher should bear in mind as he helps boys and girls form and apply generalizations.

1. Only those generalizations should be taught of which the pupils can make fairly wide application to words they need to spell.
2. Only those generalizations should be taught to which there are not many exceptions, especially not among words that the pupils need to spell.
3. Only those generalizations should be taught that are simple enough for the learner to comprehend and remember without undue difficulty.
4. Boys and girls should be helped to develop generalizations rather than to be asked to memorize a set of rules.
5. After formulating a generalization, boys and girls should be given adequate opportunity to apply it.

GENERALIZATIONS TO BE LEARNED. Even among persons who favor learning generalizations according to guidelines like those listed, there is disagreement as to which ones should be taught. Here are some that are frequently considered important for boys and girls to learn in the elementary school, though not necessarily in the language in which they are here stated.

1. When adding a suffix beginning with a vowel to a word ending in a silent *e*, the *e* is usually dropped.
2. When adding a suffix other than one beginning with *i* to a word ending in *y* preceded by a consonant, the *y* is usually changed to *i*.
3. *I* comes before *e*, as a rule, excepting after *c* when the *ie* has the sound of the long *e*.
4. The final consonant usually should be doubled when adding a suffix to a monosyllabic word or to a word of more than one syllable accented on the last syllable, if the word ends in a single consonant preceded by a single vowel.
5. The letter *q* in a word is followed by the letter *u*.
6. Plurals of nouns are often formed by adding *s* to the singular.
7. Nouns ending in the *s, sh, ch, x,* or *z* sound in the singular usually form the plural by adding *es* to the singular.

Courtesy of the Hamilton, Ohio, Public Schools

Figure 8.6 Reinforcing Generalization about Adding the Suffix **Ing**

Directions: Add a suffix not beginning with an i to each of the following words. Remember that if the y is preceded by a consonant, the y must be changed to an i.

occupy occupied
try tried
enjoy
destroy
stay
supply
pry
deny

Figure 8.7 Making Application of a Generalization about Adding Suffixes

8. Many nouns that end in *f* or *fe* in the singular form the plural by changing the *f* or *fe* to *v* and adding *es*.

9. The *k* sound is usually spelled *c* when it comes before *a*, *o*, or *u*. When it comes before *e* or *i*, it is usually spelled *k*. After a long vowel sound the *k* sound is usually spelled *k*.

10. The long or short *i* sound at the end of a word is usually spelled *y*.

Developing Generalizations. Undoubtedly many boys and girls develop some spelling generalizations by themselves. The teacher's role is to help them form more accurate generalizations than many would be likely to form without assistance. The following description illustrates how, through induction; the teacher can help the pupils make the generalization that *i* should usually be written before *e* excepting after *c* when the long sound of *e* is being produced.

The teacher can proceed by having on the chalkboard a few words in which *ei* and *ie* have the sound of the long *e*, such as *believe, piece, conceit, receive, mien.* The pupils may be asked to note that in every one of those words the *ie* and the *ei* have the long sound of *e*. Then they may be helped to observe each of the words as they note what letter precedes the *ie* or *ei*. A listing such as the following may be developed and put on the chalkboard:

Before *ei*	Before *ie*
c (conceit)	l (believe)
c (receive)	p (piece)
	m (mien)

Next the pupils may summarize their finding that *ei* was used when preceded by *c* and that *ie* was used when preceded by a letter other than *c*. The teacher may then state that this finding holds true in other cases when the *ei* or *ie* has the sound of the long *e*. Thereupon the pupils can note the spelling of other words in which *ie* or *ei* has the long sound of *e* and explain how the generalization applies in each case. When additional words are studied that are governed by this generalization, the teacher may frequently wish to help the pupils note the application.

Using Phonics as an Aid to Spelling

For several decades there had been many teachers who were highly critical of phonics as an aid to reading and spelling. Their criticism, elicited partly by the sterile, ineffective manner in which phonics had formerly often been taught, was in many instances against all systematic instruction in phonics. Consequently in many schools, especially in those in which many "progressive" methods were used, phonics was not taught. In these schools the main method by which boys and girls were taught to read was the look-say or sight-word method.

Figure 8.8 Illustrating a Rule of Phonics

Recently teachers have realized that teaching no phonics is not the proper substitute for the former inadequate teaching. When no phonics was taught, in spite of many advances in the professional education of teachers, many boys and girls failed to become good readers and good spellers. It also became evident that when pupils were not taught phonics, many of the brighter ones taught it to themselves. We now recognize the fact that it is the poor teaching of phonics, not all teaching of phonics, that should be deplored.

To illustrate the importance of a knowledge of phonics in learning to spell, let us imagine a situation in which a person has absolutely no understanding of phonics. To be sure, he might be able to learn to spell a limited number of words without the ability to distinguish one sound from another. He could, for example, learn to spell, – that is write without copying – his name even if he were unable to identify a single letter or sound in it. To set out to learn to spell even a moderate number of words without knowing the sounds of letters would be a stupendous undertaking. It is therefore little wonder that a pupil without knowledge of the elements of phonics is a poor speller; the wonder often is that he can spell as well as he does.

One argument advanced by people opposed to emphasizing phonics needs special consideration. Occasionally we hear the statement that because of the great inconsistency in spelling in the English language, it is not important to stress phonics. To be sure there is no rule to explain why *might* is not spelled *mite* or why *burglar* is not spelled *bergler.* There is no rule to explain why all letters but the first are alike in two words pronounced as differently as *bough* and *rough.* Nevertheless, in spite of the many exceptions to the rules of the English language, there are no words in it that are not, at least in part, spelled the way they sound.

Teachers need also to face the fact that knowledge of phonics may in some instances be detrimental to spelling, if the teaching of phonics is not supplemented by other desirable methods of teaching spelling. For example, while the child who begins the word *mother* with an *s* most likely lacks knowledge of phonics important to spelling, on the other hand the child who begins the word *knee* with an *n* has probably allowed his partial knowledge of phonics to interfere with the correct spelling of the word.

GUIDELINES. The following points have bearing upon how phonics should be used as an aid to spelling.

1. *Phonics has a different function in spelling than in reading.* In reading, phonics is used to determine what sound a certain letter or combination of letters has in a word. In spelling, phonics is used to determine what letter or combination of letters is used to produce a given sound.

2. *Because of the different function of phonics in spelling and in reading, it is not advisable to begin systematic study of phonics in the two areas at the same time.* After pupils have had some acquaintance with phonics as used in reading, the knowledge gained thereby can be used advantageously in spelling. However, if phonics is introduced simultaneously in reading and spelling situations, confusion can easily result.

3. *The teaching of phonics should be functional.* In neither reading nor spelling should elementary-school boys and girls be engaged in the systematic study of the science of sounds.

4. *Pupils should be taught those elements of phonics that are of value in gaining proficiency in reading and spelling.* There is no one program that has been scientifically established as the best. There are certain minimum essentials to be included, however, on which there is considerable agreement. In order to become an effective speller a pupil needs to learn the common sounds of the vowels and consonants. Furthermore, he needs to learn the sounds of: (a) the common consonant blends, such as *bl* and *st;* (b) the two-consonant letters used as one, or digraphs, such as *th* and *ng;* and (c) the two-vowel letters used as one, such as *ai* or *ie.* He must not only know the sound of these but he must also be able to associate them with the correct forms of the letters or groups of letters.

SUGGESTED PROCEDURES. The following are some of the ways in which phonics can be taught for spelling purposes.

1. *Training in auditory perception.* When a pupil is unable to distinguish some of the sounds of the language, he may need specific drill. The teacher may give plainly a word beginning with the sound of *m* such as *man,* for example. Then the pupil may be asked to tell which of a series of words the teacher pronounces begins with the same sound. He may also be asked to name words that begin with a given sound.

2. *Associating the form of a letter with its sound.* The problem of associating a letter with its sound is complicated by the fact that in the English language there are more sounds than letters. Consequently many letters have more than one sound. Furthermore, the same sound is spelled in different ways in a number of instances. It is not enough that the pupil be able to recognize or produce the initial sound in *cat* or *kitchen.* He also needs to know which letter represents that sound. A simple device for developing this power with primary-grade children is to have on the chalkboard a list of words such as these, all of which begin with *b* or *d*: *bird, boat, dig, dark, bark, big, deep.* A pupil then draws a circle around a word that begins with whatever sound – *b* or *d,* in this case – the teacher gives.

3. *Pronunciation of spelling words.* In many cases it is helpful to assist pupils in deciphering phonet-

ically a word in the spelling list that they cannot recognize without help.

4. *Studying the nonphonetic elements of a new spelling word.* If the pupils take special notice of the words in a spelling list that are not spelled as they would expect them to be, the primary emphasis can be put on probable difficulties. For example, in the word *wreck* the teacher or pupil may draw attention to the *w* and to the *ck* combination. The practice of noting double letters is also recommended.

5. *Using other procedures.* Other devices frequently used with success are: (a) supplying the missing letters in blanks left in words that contain "hard spots," (b) marking the sounds of vowels, (c) marking the accent, (d) selecting words in a list in which a letter or a group of letters has a given sound, and (e) matching a rule with words whose spelling is governed in part by it.

Studying Word Forms

Following are given, in addition to those mentioned in connection with other topics in this chapter, suggestions for helping boys and girls study word forms.

1. Have the pupils tell how many pronunciation parts there are in each of a list of words that the teacher pronounces.

2. Tell the pupils that each pronunciation part is called a syllable and have them use the term *syllable* as they refer to such a part.

3. Spell the words in syllables as the pupils check their spelling.

4. Have the pupils look up the syllabication of words in a glossary or dictionary.

5. Discuss with the class why division into syllables sometimes helps in spelling a word.

6. Tell the class that words can be divided at the end of a line only between syllables and have them show on the chalkboard how given words would need to be divided.

7. Have the pupils give a list of words, as the teacher writes them on the chalkboard, beginning with the prefix *un*, for example. Then ask them to tell what the prefix does to the meaning of the rest of the word. Next, similarly, the pupils can study other common prefixes.

8. Help the boys and girls arrive at the generalizations involving word forms listed on preceding pages of this chapter.

9. Have the pupils name compound words as the teacher writes them on the chalkboard and have them tell whether they are written (a) as two or more words, (b) as one hyphenated word, or (c) as one unhyphenated word. The teacher can then tell the pupils how to find out from a glossary or dictionary how a compound word is written and provide them with practice in finding out how a series of words, some of which are compound words, is to be written.

10. Introduce the boys and girls to the word *contraction* by showing them, for example, how the words *does* and *not* are combined to form *doesn't.* Then the pupils can state from what words other contractions are formed and match two columns of words, in one of which are given contractions and in the other words from which the contractions are formed. The class also can discuss when it is proper and when improper to use contractions.

11. Provide the boys and girls with practice in building words from root forms by adding prefixes and suffixes as, for example *interest, interests, interested, interesting, uninteresting, interestingly.*

12. Have the boys and girls underline the root words in derived forms.

13. Demonstrate to the pupils the fact that when one recognizes a root word he knows how to spell, often it is not difficult to learn the spelling of forms derived from it.

14. Help the pupils develop the following generalization for forming possessive nouns: (a) Write the name of the owner. (b) Add an apostrophe. (c) Add an *s* if that *s* is pronounced in the possessive form.

15. Have the pupils tell which of a list of words are possessive singular and which are possessive plural.

16. Ask the pupils to use possessive nouns in writing groups of words like these: (a) the coats belonging to the boy, (b) the coats belonging to the boys, (c) the coats belonging to the lady, (d) the coats belonging to the ladies, (e) the coats belonging to the man, (f) the coats belonging to the men.

Other Activities

The following additional suggestions for activities may prove useful in teaching spelling.

1. The pupils write words that rhyme with given words.

2. The pupils tell which of sets of two words the teacher names in pairs rhyme.

3. The boys and girls check which pairs of words given in written form rhyme, such as:

bat, rat; seat, feet; by, lie; made, bad; feel, fed

4. The boys and girls draw a line under each of a given series of words that have the same vowel sound found in a word for which an illustration is given. For example, a picture of a ball can be drawn and the

words *bat, cat, baby, barn, play* be written near it. A variation of this is to have a word given in which the letter or letters spelling that sound are underlined and a list of words given in which the pupils are to underline the letters spelling the same sound. For example, one item in such an exercise may be:

cake: made, neighbor, receive, make, sat.

5. As the teacher names words, the pupils supply the vowel of those words listed on paper in which a vowel has been omitted. Examples are:

b .... t, n .... ce, r .... n.

6. The teacher dictates sentences to the boys and girls. At times he may wish to give the pupils a chance to study the sentences before they write them. When dictating a series of sentences, this procedure may be used:

a. Give the number of the sentence.
b. Read the sentence as a whole.
c. Read the sentence in parts as the pupils write the parts.
d. Reread the sentence.

It is probably desirable to mark the entire sentence wrong if any error in spelling, capitalization, or punctuation occurs.

7. The pupils proofread their written work. At times it is advisable for the teacher to work with each child as he does so.

8. The pupils make a picture dictionary, as an individual or class project, in which words of which the spelling may be needed are written and illustrated.

9. The pupils make files of cards with words that may be needed for spelling. These cards, possibly illustrated, could also contain meaningful sentences in which the words are used.

10. The pupils make a list of words that belong to various "word families" such as *eat*: *meat, seat, beat, heat, neat* (and, with older children, *wheat, feat, treat* can be included).

Figure 8.9 A File for Spelling Words

11. The pupils make a list of words which illustrate the generalizations about spelling they have helped formulate.

12. The boys and girls list words containing different spellings of the same sounds such as *meet, meat, receive, believe.*

13. The pupils underline in groups of words the phonograms common to some of the words in the list.

Draw a line under the k sound.

1.	wreck	5.	cent
2.	knit	6.	come
3.	cat	7.	kit
4.	look	8.	book

Figure 8.10 An Exercise for Recognizing Phonograms

14. The pupils match words in two columns so that they form a compound word, as in this example:

grand	ball
base	father
tea	spoon

15. The pupils use the dictionary to find the spelling of words: (a) when one of two spellings of a word (one correct, the other incorrect) is suggested; (b) when a blank is left for a letter or letters in a word, such as *bel* .... *f;* (c) when a word is pronounced by the teacher.

Questionable Procedures

Three questions that puzzle some teachers are here briefly discussed. They are: (1) Is "sky-writing" desirable? (2) Is tracing words good practice? (3) Should homework be assigned in spelling?

SKY-WRITING. *Sky-writing,* as the term applies to spelling, is the practice of having pupils "write" in the air with their fingers the words they are learning to spell. It is used by some teachers as part of the presentation of a word. After the pupils have pronounced a word or heard it pronounced, after it has been ascertained that they know the meaning of the word, and after they have looked carefully at the word, the teacher using this method may ask the pupils to close their eyes as they "write" in the air the word that they are studying. Then the pupils are asked to look again at the word in order to compare with it the word that they have "written" in the air.

In the opinion of the writer of this book, the practice has only questionable merit. As a pupil who has "written" a word in the air compares it with his copy, he has no assurance that he remembers exactly how he "wrote" it in the air. Consequently errors may remain undetected. If instead of "writing" the word in the air he writes it on the chalkboard or on paper, this criticism cannot be made.

TRACING WORDS. The tracing method as commonly used by teachers for spelling purposes is an adaptation of the Fernald kinesthetic method, which is frequently employed with retarded readers.[1] When used as a spelling method, the pupil is encouraged to trace with a finger or pencil (or with chalk if the chalkboard is used) the word he is trying to learn to spell.

Figure 8.11 Using Three-Dimensional Letters for Tactile Reinforcement of Learning to Spell

After the teacher has pronounced a word, the child pronounces it in parts while he traces the copy of the word supplied to him. When he has traced it, he pronounces the entire word. The pupil repeats this process as long as he thinks he needs the practice before he can write the word from memory. After he has tested himself, if he has not spelled the word correctly he repeats the procedure until he masters it.

It is highly questionable whether this time-consuming method of learning to spell is to be recommended for most children. It might, however, be tried with boys and girls who are retarded in spelling. It might occasionally also be used with the average or above-average spellers with words that are particularly difficult for them.

HOMEWORK IN SPELLING. If the school provides about 75 minutes a week for spelling instruction in addition to time spent on incidental teaching of spelling, and if the school makes good use of that time it would seem that it should be unnecessary, as a rule, for children to take home a spelling assignment. Dawdling habits of work may be developed through such practice. However, the child who has been absent from school for a while may occasionally profit from homework.

TESTING AND REVIEW

One of the features of well-planned test-study and study-test procedures is the emphasis put on tests and on reviews.

Provisions for Testing

The following provisions are frequently made for testing.

1. The pretest, given before the boys and girls have studied words in a spelling list.
2. The trial test, sometimes given after the pupils have studied the words that they have missed on a pretest and, in many cases, after they have engaged in other activities involving the use of spelling words. This test is frequently given on the third day of a five-day procedure. (It should be noted that sometimes the pretest is also referred to as the trial test.)
3. The final test, given on the last day of the five-day period (or the fourth day if the fifth day is used for review or restudy). Often this test contains not only the words for the week but also review words from earlier weeks.
4. The test on words missed the preceding week. This test is often given individually to each child.
5. A test on words of a few weeks before, possibly three, four, five, or six weeks before. Sometimes one such test on words of a given list is followed by another weeks later.
6. The semester test or the year test on new words or review words studied during the course of the semester or year. In some classes a pre-semester test is also given in order to find out what procedure for teaching may be the better with a given group or individuals, the test-study or the study-test plan. The pre-semester test also serves as a means of measuring progress during the semester. For similar reasons a test at the beginning of the year on words to be studied during the course of the year also may be given.

Suggestions for Testing

Following are listed a few additional suggestions for testing in spelling.

1. *In planning a pre-semester, a semester, a beginning-of-the-year, or an end-of-the-year test, there should be a representative sampling of the words for the semester or school year.* If a test is to serve as an

[1]Grace M. Fernald, *Remedial Techniques in Basic School Subjects.* McGraw-Hill Book Company, 1943.

adequate end-test or as an index of the level of the child's ability in spelling, the more difficult words or easier words must not be weighted in number. One way in which to avoid such a shortcoming is to select, in terms of placement on lists, the words to be included in the test. For example, after the teacher has decided how many words he wants in a test and knows how many words will be studied during the semester or year, he can divide the number of words to be studied by the number of words he plans for the test. If the answer were about six, he could then decide that he would include every sixth word in the list until he has the desired number for the test.

2. *Pupils should not be given opportunity to study the spelling words immediately before a final test or a review test.* If the boys and girls study the words shortly before they are tested, the test will indicate immediate, not long-term, recall.

3. *In dictating a list of words a procedure such as the following can be used.*

   a. Give the number of the word (so that the pupil will not be likely to omit a word or otherwise become confused in his own numbering).
   b. Pronounce the word distinctly (without "overpronouncing" it).
   c. Use the word in a sentence (so that the pupil can be certain that he heard the word correctly, not with the thought that he writes the entire sentence).
   d. Repeat the word.

If this procedure is followed, it is probably advisable to tell the pupils that if the teacher is giving the test too fast for them, they should raise their hands as soon as they have difficulty keeping up. In that case it would be unnecessary after the list has been dictated to repeat all words or to answer questions asked by the pupils as to what various words on the list are.

4. *While most of the words in a test could be written by the pupils in column form, it is at times advisable to have one or more sentences dictated so that the children will write the entire sentence(s).* Each sentence should contain one or more words from the list being studied or from review words. It should contain no words the pupils are not expected to know how to spell unless the teacher has written the unknown words on the chalkboard, from which the boys and girls can copy them.

5. *Words that are not written legibly should be counted wrong.* There should be no question as to each letter of a word if it is to be counted right. However, lack of excellence of the form of a letter should not be reason for counting the word wrong if it is plain what letter is intended.

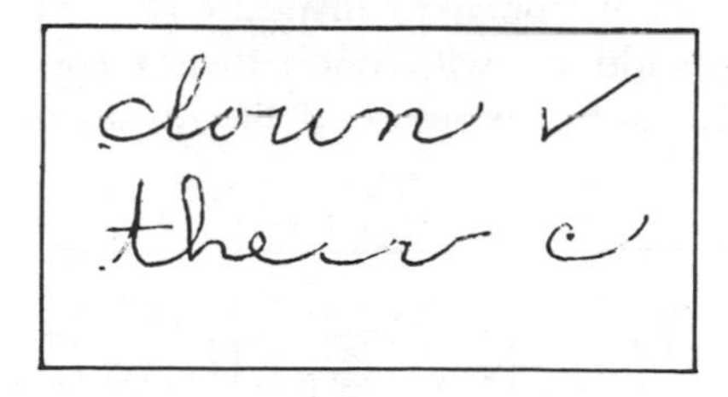

Figure 8.12

6. *While no authoritative answer can be given to the question as to whether a word should be counted wrong if it has been crossed out or erased in case the final spelling is correct, there is good argument for counting wrong all words in a spelling test that were not written correctly the first time.* A supporting claim is that if a pupil does not know the spelling of a word well enough so that he can immediately write it correctly, he perhaps has not mastered the word.

7. *There are convincing arguments that can be advanced for or against having the pupil correct his own test papers.* An argument for that practice is that the child is given additional opportunity to scrutinize carefully his own spelling of a word. Argument against it is that the child may cheat or may have the wrong image so firmly established in his mind that it is difficult for him to recognize his error. As far as cheating is concerned, the teacher should try to educate the boys and girls so that they see the futility of that practice as well as its wrongness. Furthermore, the teacher should be alert enough as he gives the spelling test to know when there is cheating. To avoid in part the temptation to cheat, the teacher may ask the pupils to correct the papers with a different medium than the one in which they wrote them. If a pencil was used in writing, a crayon or a pen may be used in correcting. Furthermore it is advisable that usually the teacher himself recheck at least the final test. If a pupil has difficulty in checking his own paper or that of a classmate, the teacher may wish to give him individual practice in checking the spelling of words. Probably at times one method of checking should be used and at other times another.

8. *Opportunity for adequate checking should be provided when boys and girls do the correcting.* It is recommended that the teacher spell the words by syllables and that after all the words have been spelled by him, the pupils refer to a list to note any words that they may wish to recheck.

9. *Graphing the results of a final test is helpful practice.* Every pupil can keep a simple graph showing his attainment on each final test. It is best not to have the graphs open to inspection by others. Competition should be with one's own record, not with that of others. Furthermore, if the results on a test are posted, the pupils with lower marks who had worked hard may become discouraged and those who easily get a perfect score may be kept from being humble about their achievement.

Figure 8.13 An Individual Spelling Graph

10. *If marks for spelling are recorded on a report card, more than spelling achievement on the words in spelling lists should be taken into consideration.* A pupil who has a perfect score on every final and review test during a marking period should not be given an excellent mark on his report card if he spells poorly on papers written during the school day other than the spelling period. The proposed marking policy, however, needs to be carefully explained to the boys and girls (and in some cases to the parents) if it is contrary to earlier practice with a given class.

Provisions for Review

Ample opportunity should be provided for review. Follow-up on the trial test by study of words missed is not enough. Other opportunities for systematic well-spaced review are here indicated.

1. *Review in the form of restudy of "new words" missed on a final test.* Boys and girls should be asked to keep a list of words that they miss on final tests and then restudy those of the preceding list one or more days after work on a new list has begun. They can then be individually tested on the words they missed.

2. *Review after the final test of some words previously included in spelling tests.* Some publishers of spelling textbooks have a built-in plan for review in which the words of a given number of weeks before are automatically included among the words in a final test of a week's work. The teacher must try to make certain the words in the review list that are missed by a pupil are restudied to the point of mastery.

3. *Review of words included in end-of-the-semester or end-of-the-year tests.* Because of the time element review of words missed on a test given at the end of the year is at times not possible. However, it is probably desirable to try to schedule end-tests in the elementary school so that they are not given after all regular classes are over in order that the pupils will have an opportunity to do necessary review indicated by the testing.

4. *Review of some words studied the preceding year.* Some spelling series make provision for restudy of many review words during the first few weeks of a school year.

5. *Review of lists of word "demons" or very commonly used words.* Some teachers provide pupils with copies of words on a "demon" list or on a list of very frequently used words and make provisions for study as well as for review and testing of these words.

6. *Review of words on individual lists.* If the pupils are keeping lists of words they want to learn to spell other than those given in spelling or class lists, opportunity for systematic review and testing of these words should be provided.

WORD LISTS

One of the questions of great importance in connection with the teaching of spelling is "What words should the child learn to spell?" Those who do not believe in systematic study of spelling may answer the question simply by stating that each pupil should learn to spell the words that he needs in his writing. However, a child in the upper primary grades and intermediate grades who expresses himself adequately in writing will often use many more words in his written communication than it seems practical for him to learn to spell. Consequently this question also may need to be answered: "What should be the criteria

Courtesy of the Cincinnati Public Schools.

Figure 8.14 Aids to Correct Spelling

for determining which of the words a pupil uses in his writing he should learn to spell?"

Regardless of whether or not systematic procedures for spelling instruction are followed, these criteria for word selection are considered important: (1) frequency of use of a word in children's writing and (2) likelihood of use of word in adult writing. Difficulty of learning a word may also be given consideration.

The criterion of "likelihood of use of a word in adult writing" presents a problem. While many words used frequently by children in writing are also much used in adult writing, others are not. Which of the words frequently used by children in writing but not by adults should be included in spelling lists cannot be answered with finality. The problem is further complicated by the fact that by the time boys and girls are adults many of the words they will then use often in their writing may not be the ones now frequently written by adults. In general, perhaps the best procedure is to teach boys and girls the spelling of those words they use much in their writing and help them acquire a method of learning to spell new words – a method they can also use in later years when learning to spell additional words they need as adults.

Published Lists

Research studies culminating in lists of words for spelling purposes have taken into consideration (1) the words that pupils use frequently in writing, (2) the words that adults use frequently in writing, and (3) the words that are often misspelled. Some of the lists are: Ernest Horn's "A Basic Writing Vocabulary," appearing in the University of Iowa Monographs in Education, First Series, No. 4, Iowa City, Iowa; "The 222 Spelling Demons," listed in a four-page publication by that name by James A. Fitzgerald, published by the Bruce Publishing Company, Milwaukee; and Leslie W. Johnson's, "One Hundred Words Most Often Misspelled by Children in the Elementary Grades," which appeared in the *Journal of Educational Research,* October, 1950.

Class Lists and Individual Lists

Lists of spelling words based on the needs of a given class or individuals in it are often used in schoolrooms in which no standard list of words nor lists in spelling textbooks are employed. However, such lists are also used in many rooms in which pupils study the words of a published list. In fact, a desirable use of a class or individual list is made when it complements a list based on research.

Some teachers suggest that every pupil should keep a notebook or file of the words that he wishes to use in his writing but cannot spell. Other teachers compile a class list of words that the group is likely to need in writing, including many words in the content areas. There are objections to this procedure. One is that the list is likely to become too long,

Figure 8.15 A Spelling Notebook

especially for the poor speller who will probably find that he has difficulty in spelling a considerable proportion of the words that he uses in writing – too many for him to try to include in his spelling vocabulary. Another is that many of the words a pupil uses in writing may not be used by him often in the near future. Merely because boys and girls in their writing in connection, for example, with a unit on Alaska may be writing about kayaks is no reason why they need to add the word *kayak* to their spelling vocabulary, especially when they may not know how to spell commonly used words like *their.* Maybe all that is needed is to have *kayak,* together with other words used in connection with the study of Alaska, written on a chart headed "New Words" from which boys and girls can copy the word *kayak* when they use it in writing.

Other Points

The following points about word lists may throw further light on their use.

1. The number of words included in lists of spelling words for the elementary school is considerably smaller than formerly. While there is no agreement on the desired number, many include no more than 4,000 words in their basic lists.

2. In spite of the research in the field, there is far from unanimity of opinion by authors of spelling textbooks as to which words should be included. A comparison of the words on lists in spelling books shows surprisingly great differences.

3. There is marked lack of agreement on the grade placement of words given in the basic lists of various spellers.

ADAPTING INSTRUCTION TO INDIVIDUAL DIFFERENCES

Since boys and girls within the same class differ greatly in ability and interests, it is important that spelling instruction be adapted to individual differences.

Factors in Diagnosis

If spelling is to be adapted to individuals, diagnosis is vital not only for pupils with pronounced difficulties but also for the average or above-average speller. How much time the teacher should spend on diagnosis cannot be stated with certitude. However, it is certain that careful diagnosis of individual needs of the boys and girls within a classroom, although the process of making it may seem quite time-consuming, can save much time in subsequent teaching-learning situations. For the puzzling cases perhaps a detailed study should be made while for the others less intensive study may suffice. Under all circumstances the initial diagnosis should not end the appraisal, but evaluation should be continuous throughout the year. Factors such as the following should be considered in diagnosis.

1. *Intellectual ability*. Even though the correlation between intelligence and spelling ability is lower than it is between intelligence and many other school subjects, there is a positive relationship. It is seldom that the child with low intelligence is an excellent speller. It is uncommon that the very intelligent child is unusually poor in spelling.

2. *Spelling ability*. Spelling ability can be checked by giving the pupils a pre-semester test in which a sampling of the words of the semester are included, or standardized tests or scales can be used effectively if they are valid for the purpose.

3. *Nature of spelling difficulties*. Study can be made through careful attention to the words a given individual misspells during spelling class and at other times. The pupil's errors in spelling can be recorded and the teacher, with the pupil, can look for any recurrent types of mistakes such as omitting so-called "silent letters" or not following the letter *q* within a word by a *u*.

4. *Pupil's method of study*. The following and similar points about a pupil's method of study may be investigated.

> Does he pay good attention during periods when the teacher is helping thc class?
> Does he begin to study spelling promptly when time is provided for such study?
> Does he make good use of his study period?
> Does he observe recommended steps for learning to spell a word?

5. *Attitude toward spelling*. Insight into the child's attitude can sometimes be gained through noting his verbal response when time for spelling is announced or by observing his bodily response during spelling class. Whether or not the pupil has pride in being a good speller can sometimes be gathered by the meticulousness (or lack of it) with which he does his work in spelling.

6. *Skill in reading*. Reading ability can be checked by means suggested in Chapter 10.

7. *Ability in phonics*. A child's ability in phonics can be tested by means such as these:

> The teacher asks the pupil to name words beginning with a sound that starts a word he gives.
> The teacher asks the pupil to write the letter with which each word in a series he names begins or ends.
> The pupils name various spellings of the same phonogram.

8. *Physical well-being*. Vision, hearing, and general health are health factors important to reading. Suggestions for checking the physical condition of a child are given in Chapter 9.

9. *Pronunciation*. The child who mispronounces a word is more likely to misspell it than the one who pronounces it correctly. To check the ability to pronounce words correctly the teacher can ask the child to read a list of words or a selection orally or he can ask the child to repeat words after him.

10. *Handwriting*. Errors in spelling are at times traceable to illegible handwriting. Slowness in writing may also cause a pupil to receive a poor mark on a spelling list. Consequently analysis of a pupil's handwriting in terms of legibility and observation of the time it takes him to write are effective means of checking this factor.

11. *Errors in correcting*. A child's deficiency in spelling may be due to the fact that he makes errors in checking his work. Rechecking of papers by the

teacher is needed in diagnosis as well as for other purposes.

12. *Materials.* Careful study of materials of instruction is important in terms of validity of the word lists, provisions for individual differences, suggestions for method of study, and provisions for review and testing.

13. *Methods of teaching.* The teacher should examine his methods of teaching spelling critically.

Spelling Tests and Scales

Some teachers use standardized tests or scales to ascertain a pupil's level in spelling. Others prefer those provided in manuals accompanying spelling books and some that they themselves made from words in the spelling lists. If spelling scales or standardized tests are used, it is advisable to check the words for frequency of use as established by research unless evidence on the validity of a test or scale for a desired purpose is given, making unnecessary further checking by the teacher. (Some commercial tests and scales are listed in Chapter 15.)

Instructional Procedures

The following are a few ways of adapting instruction in spelling to individual differences.

1. Some spelling books have a differentiated list of words, with a small number of words of high frequency of use and relatively low difficulty, for all or almost all of the pupils to study. They have additional words for the pupils of average ability, and still more for those of above-average ability. In some spellers the extended activities show similar differentiation.

2. When individual lists of words are used, the pupils can be encouraged by the teacher to study as many words as they should be expected to learn without undue stress or strain.

3. In the use of standardized and nonstandardized lists, the teacher can help each pupil diagnose his types of errors or difficulties. Some common types are: substitutions of certain letters, repetitions, reversals, lack of knowledge of phonics, application of limited knowledge of phonics to nonphonetic elements of words, illegible handwriting, and lack of speed in writing (if words are dictated).

4. The teacher can encourage the pupils to keep a record of their spelling achievement and discuss it from time to time with them.

5. The teacher can help the pupils individually in studying spelling according to steps recommended. He may ask each child, while in individual conference, to explain how he proceeds as he studies several words.

6. The teacher can check with an individual the length of time that he spends on studying spelling and then make needed recommendations.

7. The teacher can try to help a child determine whether his spelling difficulty lies primarily in lack of immediate or delayed recall of the spelling of words.

8. Some pupils may be excused during part or all of a spelling period to engage in other worthwhile activities.

9. The pupils can be grouped for help when common problems exist.

10. Thc teacher can teach some pupils by the study-test plan and others by the test-study plan if such differentiation seems advantageous.

FOR STUDY AND DISCUSSION

1. Outline a spelling-readiness program for a first grade.

2. Examine carefully several recent spelling series for the elementary school, studying both the pupils' books and the accompanying teachers' manuals. What likenesses and what differences do you note among the series? What points of excellence characterize them? What if any questionable procedures do you note?

3. Select a five-day spelling list as found in a recent spelling textbook for an elementary-school grade. Write a teaching plan based on it, in which you show clearly what class procedures you might follow each of the five days to be devoted to the study of the list. (You may wish to refer to the plan given on page 308 for some suggestions.)

4. Explain how you would develop with boys and girls in a fifth grade the generalization "when adding a suffix beginning with a vowel to a word ending in a silent *e*, the *e* is usually dropped." Also show how you might help pupils apply this generalization.

5. Note what elements of phonics are taught in some of the recent spelling series and pay particular attention to the methods of teaching these elements that are suggested either in the pupils' book or the teachers' manuals.

6. What games could be used in teaching spelling? (Suggestions are given in professional books and magazines and in teachers' manuals accompanying spelling series.)

7. Several spelling lists are named in this chapter. Study professional literature on the teaching of spelling to find information on additional ones.

8. Give suggestions for dealing with a request by a parent that a child be given homework in spelling.

REFERENCES

Anderson, Paul S., *Resource Materials for Teachers of Spelling*. Burgess Publishing Company, 1959. 118 pp.

Fitzgerald, James E., *The Teaching of Spelling*. The Bruce Publishing Company, 1951. 233 pp.

Hildreth, Gertrude, *Teaching Spelling*. Holt, Rinehart and Winston, 1955. 346 pp.

Shane, Harold G., and June Grant Mulry, *Improving Language Arts Instruction through Research*. Association for Supervision and Curriculum Development, 1963. 153 pp.

Tidyman, Willard F., and Marguerite Butterfield, *Teaching the Language Arts*. McGraw-Hill Book Company, 1959. 403 pp.

OUTLINE FOR CHAPTER 9

Guiding Growth Toward Readiness for Reading

CHAPTER 9

Guiding Growth Toward Readiness for Reading

It is not strange that one of the major problems with which many a first-grade teacher at the beginning of the school year concerns himself, as he thinks of each of the pupils in his charge, is whether the child is ready to learn to read. In fact, that the teacher has this concern is encouraging for it is one of the most far-reaching problems that confronts him at that time. If he tries to force a child to learn to read before he is ready, he may cause him to dislike reading as well as school, to get a poor start in reading, or to have other unfavorable reactions in the form of feelings of inferiority, even of frustration. On the other hand, if the teacher postpones reading instruction too long, there also is danger. Such postponement is probably harmful in the case of the child who even before he starts school has looked forward with anticipation to the time when he can learn to read. Undue delay may also cause frustration and boredom as well as general loss of interest in school.

BASIC CONSIDERATIONS RELATED TO READINESS FOR READING

Basic to a consideration of the problem of readiness for beginning reading are points such as these:

As far as practical, whether or not children in a room are ready to learn to read should be decided on an individual basis. Even if only one or two pupils are ready near the beginning of the school year, reading instruction should not be postponed for them merely because they constitute a small minority. Similarly, if all but a few are ready, those few should not be confronted with the task of learning to read before they seem equal to it.

Whether a child should be considered ready to learn to read depends in part on the methods and materials of instruction to be used. If the teacher shows skill in adapting reading instruction to the level of various individuals and if he uses material adapted to individual needs, some children, who under more rigid conditions should be excluded from reading for a time, can be started in learning to read.

FACTORS RELATED TO READINESS FOR READING

The factors that the teacher needs to consider in trying to determine whether or not a child is ready to learn to read can be classified roughly, as they are by various writers, into the following four groups: (1) mental, (2) physical, (3) social and emotional, and (4) educational.

Mental Factors

No one mental age can be quoted as the optimum age for beginning reading. It has often erroneously been assumed that the desirable mental age for beginning reading is six years and six months. It has, however, been shown that it is not necessary to postpone reading for all children until they are six years and six months mentally. With simpler materials and suitable methods of instruction adapted to children with lower mental ages, some boys and girls with mental ages of less than that can be taught to read successfully. Furthermore, all children are not necessarily ready when they attain that mental age. Nevertheless, mental age is an important factor to consider in relation to others for judging readiness and for determining, in part, the approach to reading in terms of methods and materials to be used.

Physical Factors

Physical factors also are closely related to readiness for reading. Especially significant are vision and hearing. That vision is important has long been recognized. Not so clearly understood has been the relationship between difficulties in hearing and learning to read. It has been reported that in the classrooms of our country there are many children with hearing problems unidentified by teachers, yet so serious that lack of acuity of hearing interferes with learning to read. Often such boys and girls are considered dull, lazy, or even insubordinate.

Social and Emotional Factors

A child unaccustomed to participation in large groups before entrance to school frequently is so ill at ease that he is not able to concentrate on something as abstract as learning to read, especially not in group situations. Environmental preschool situations as well as the hereditary pattern of a child may also have kept him from normal social and emotional development and thus have constituted a negative factor as far as readiness for reading upon entrance to first grade is concerned.

Educational Factors

The group of factors affecting readiness for beginning reading that is often referred to as educational factors includes a variety of points. Important among these are interest in reading; richness of experience background; auditory discrimination; visual discrimination; language ability; skill in interpreting pictures; skill in using ideas; and knowledge of how to handle books.

DETERMINING READINESS FOR READING

How then can we determine whether a child is ready to learn to read? While directing our attention to each of the groups of factors described in the preceding paragraphs, let us bear in mind the fact that it is not essential to successful beginning reading that a pupil have a high rating in respect to each one.

Determining the Mental Age

An index of the mental age of an individual can be secured by means of a group or individual intelligence test. However, intelligence has been an elusive characteristic to measure for no test has been devised that is not partly invalid because of the lack of isolation of those test elements that measure the results of environmental factors from others that truly measure native ability.

MENTAL TESTS. In choosing a standardized intelligence test the teacher or administrator should note not only data on the validity of a test but also other characteristics of good standardized tests such as reliability, availability in more than one form, ease of administration, cost. (The reader is referred to a listing of intelligence tests given in Chapter 15.)

OTHER MEANS OF DETERMINING MENTAL AGE. Even if the teacher has data on the mental age of a child according to a standardized intelligence test, because of lack of perfection in all intelligence tests he is advised also to take into account information that can be attained through means other than mental testing. Observation of the child's intellectual reactions to a variety of situations can give some indication as to whether he seems as bright as others of his chronological age. Furthermore, through study of books on child growth and development the teacher can compare the reactions of the child being observed with those noted for various age groups and can thereby get some insight as to the approximate mental age of the child.

Evaluating Physical Health

Checking with school records if the child has been in kindergarten, consulting with the school health staff, and conferring with parents are often means of securing valuable information on health to supplement that gained through observation.

These are some of the questions to which it will be profitable for the teacher to try to find answers as he attempts to determine a child's readiness for beginning reading as far as health factors are concerned.

1. Does he frequently complain of being tired?
2. Does his posture indicate tiredness?
3. Does he enjoy active games?
4. Is his muscular coordination as good as that of the average beginning first-grade child?
5. Does he have a healthy color?
6. Does he have frequent colds?
7. Is he often absent from school because of reported poor health?
8. Does he have a history of poor health?
9. What are his eating habits?

CHECKING VISION. No teacher should consider himself in a position to determine whether a pupil's vision, with or without correction, is sufficient for effective reading without eyestrain or other danger to the eyes. However, through screening tests and through observation of the pupil in nontesting situations the teacher alone or with the help of the school health service can get some clues as to possible vision difficulties of some of the children.

1. *Use of screening tests.* If a test seems to indicate that a pupil's vision is impaired, the school should not make a pronouncement, unless it employs an eye specialist, that the child's vision is unsatisfactory. All the school should do is to recommend to the parents, usually through the school principal, that the child's eyes be examined by a competent doctor.

There is danger of false security if screening tests are used in a school. A pupil may have a defect in vision not discoverable by the test given so serious that it interferes with effective reading and that, uncorrected, it may cause increasingly greater problems of vision. Consequently the teacher should be careful not to rule out the possibility of a defect merely because none shows up in the screening test being used.

2. *Other means of checking vision.* In place of or in addition to giving one or more screening tests, the teacher can note, as he observes each child, whether or not he is often characterized by any of the following, all of which may be indicative of difficulty with his eyes:

Squints
Does not enjoy looking at picture books
Rubs his eyes
Has watery eyes
Can not see pictures at a distance
Has headaches, especially after doing close work
Has inflamed or crusted eyelids
Has sties
Frowns or scowls habitually
Blinks
Holds book too close or too far from eyes.

CHECKING HEARING. Many of the large school systems now have audiometers – machines for testing hearing. Audiometers are of two types, those by means of which one individual at a time is tested and those by which all the pupils in a small class can be tested at the same time. The latter type is not diagnostic as to the type of hearing difficulties that the person tested may have. It is of value in screening those pupils who should be tested later by means of an audiometer designed for individual testing, preferably by a specialist. Information about audiometers can be secured by writing to the distributors, among them the Otarion Listener Corporation, Ossining, New York 10562 and the C. H. Stoelting Company, 424 North Homan Avenue, Chicago, Illinois 60624.

Courtesy of the Cicero, Illinois. Public Schools

Figure 9.1 Using an Audiometer

Even without the benefit of an audiometer the teacher can try to determine whether his pupils have significant hearing loss, by means of informal tests such as these:

1. *The watch-tick test.* The teacher checks the child's acuity of hearing by means of a watch whose tick is plainly audible by a person with good hearing at a distance of a yard or so. It is recommended that the teacher stand behind the child as he tests first one ear and then the other. The child can hold his hand over the ear that is not being tested. The teacher can first stand about four or five feet behind the child, so far away that the examinee cannot hear the watch. The child is instructed to notify the examiner as soon as he can hear the tick as the examiner slowly approaches. This test is more valid when comparative data are obtained on a group of children (not information on only one child) who are tested by the same watch and in the same room. If a child's hearing by this test seems to place him among those in the group with the most acute hearing, there probably is not much need of suspicion concerning his general hearing ability. The fact must not be overlooked that a child may not report accurately.

2. *The whisper test.* When giving the whisper test, the examiner at first stands far enough from the examinee, perhaps about 30 inches, so that the latter

cannot hear him as he names words or figures in a whisper, which the examinee is asked to repeat while he has one ear stopped up. He should have the other ear toward the examiner. The pupil should not be able to see the face of the examiner, to preclude lip reading. The examiner comes closer and closer to the pupil until the latter is able to repeat correctly what the examiner is saying. The test is helpful as a rough screening device if a fairly large number of children, such as an entire class, is examined under the same testing conditions.

3. *The low-voice test.* The low-voice test is similar to the whisper test except that the examiner talks in a low voice, not in a whisper, and that he stands farther away from the examinee, perhaps about 20 feet at first. It is important that initially the examiner should be so far away from the pupil that the latter cannot hear accurately what is being said.

Betts[1] lists the following symptoms of which the teacher should be conscious as he observes each child in his room, for they may be indicative of problems of hearing:

1. Monotonous or unnatural pitch of voice
2. Faulty pronunciation and lack of clear or distinct speech
3. Turning one ear toward the speaker
4. Poor spelling
5. Inattention
6. Frequent requests for repeating questions or statements
7. Difficult breathing, including mouth breathing
8. Earache
9. Discharging ears
10. Catarrhal conditions
11. Sinus infection
12. Frequent colds
13. Excessive accumulation of earwax
14. Rubbing and picking at the ear
15. Head tilt
16. Reports of
    A. Dullness or blocked feeling in ear
    B. Head noises, such as ringing or buzzing.

Determining Social and Emotional Readiness for Reading

To try to determine to what extent the child possesses social and emotional characteristics that affect readiness for reading, the teacher can observe the child for points suggested by the following questions:

1. Does he prefer being alone to being in a group?
2. Does he seem to come to school reluctantly?
3. Does he show evidence that he likes school?
4. Does he talk with others when he can do as he pleases?
5. Does he cry without adequate cause?
6. Does he often try to insist on getting his own way?
7. Does he cooperate?
8. Is he overly aggressive?
9. Is he stubborn?
10. Does he seem happier in the company of adults than in that of his peers?
11. Is he interested in what he is doing?
12. Does he consider the rights of others?
13. Can he work independently for a while?
14. Has he many interests?
15. Is he a good listener?
16. Does he respect authority?
17. Is he self-confident?
18. Is he easily irritated?
19. Is he able to take criticism?
20. Does he share materials with others?
21. Is he willing to await his turn?
22. Does he show more than an average degree of day-dreaming or emotional upsets?
23. Is he afraid?
24. Is he very noisy?
25. Is he quarrelsome?

Appraising Educational Factors

Educational factors closely related to readiness for reading can be measured by so-called reading readiness tests as well as by other less formal means.

Reading Readiness Tests. Although reading readiness tests are not a perfect means for determining whether a child is ready to begin to learn to read as far as educational factors are concerned, they are helpful. By using a reading readiness test, the teacher can probably find out more within an hour or so than in any other ways during the same length of time about the extent to which a pupil possesses some of the characteristics of educational readiness for beginning reading. However, because of the shortcomings of even the best of readiness tests, other data that the teacher can collect on the child's readiness for reading as far as educational factors are concerned should also be considered with care.

There are now on the market many reading readiness tests which are of merit when used in the light of the caution stated in the preceding paragraph. Some of the much-used ones are listed in Chapter 15.

Other Means of Evaluating Educational Factors. The teacher can obtain much information about so-called educational factors affecting readiness for reading through: (1) less formal observation of the pupils than provided for by reading readiness tests; (2) examination of the school records if the child has

[1]Emmett A. Betts, *Foundations of Reading Instruction.* American Book Company, 1950, page 208.

attended kindergarten; and (3) conferences with the child and with his parents. A few ways in which the teacher can check on some educational factors related to reading readiness are described following.

1. *Testing for auditory discrimination.* When checking auditory discrimination the teacher needs to keep clearly in mind that he is not obtaining data on auditory acuity but on auditory discrimination. The two are not the same. Auditory acuity indicates how well the child is able to hear with the hearing apparatus that he has. Auditory discrimination refers to the child's ability to differentiate among sounds. A child may have auditory acuity above the average and yet be low in discriminating between sounds. He may, even with average hearing acuity, for example, have difficulty in differentiating between the *b* and the *d* sound, an ability important in learning to read. Fortunately, auditory discrimination is a trait subject to improvement through training.

To check on auditory discrimination the teacher may, for example, do the following:

> Have the pupils tell in which groups of words, named by the teacher, such as the following, the words begin with the same sound: *Mary, mother; nose, more.*
>
> Ask the pupils to indicate which of the groups of words such as these rhyme: *fun, run; comes, goes; big, beg.*
>
> Ask the boys and girls to name words beginning with the same sound as a word the teacher names.

Most boys and girls entering first grade, it would seem, have sufficient auditory discrimination, providing their hearing is acute, to begin to learn to read without much special training.

2. *Testing for visual discrimination.* The difference between the terms *visual acuity* or *vision* and *visual discrimination* must be kept in mind by the teacher. Visual acuity refers to keenness of vision; visual discrimination refers to the ability to make visual differentiations of that which is seen by a given individual.

To test visual discrimination the teacher may wish to devise test items such as the following.

> Test 1. One of the pictures below in each row is different from the first one in that row. Draw an *x* through the one that is different.
>
> Test 2. Draw an *x* through each word in a row that looks like the first one in the row. (The pupils are not expected to recognize the words.)

three green found buy three sleep
long round long yellow white read

Figure 9.2

> Test 3. If two words in a group look alike, draw a circle around the group. If two words in a group look different, draw an *x* through each word in the group.

sing sing run run man men he me

3. *Checking the ability to remember words.* The teacher can check a pupil's ability to remember words in ways such as the following.

> He can give oral sentences, beginning with short ones and progressing to longer ones, which the pupil is to repeat verbatim. Examples are: (a) We are going on a walk. (b) This afternoon we will play in our room. (c) Before we go home tonight Miss Smith will tell us a story.

4. *Noting interest in books and stories.* The teacher can obtain significant data on the pupil's attitude toward books and stories by:

> Noticing the child's reaction when the announcement is made that a story will be told
>
> Noting whether the pupil seems attentive when a story is being told
>
> Observing whether the child looks at picture books placed on the library table
>
> Taking note as to whether the pupil brings books that he likes to school.

5. *Checking method of handling books.* Readiness for beginning reading can be checked in part by how a pupil handles books in terms of questions like these:

> Are his hands clean when he picks up a book?
> Does he turn the pages of a book carefully?
> Does he treat books as if he liked them?

6. *Checking language background.* The teacher can check a pupil's language background by:

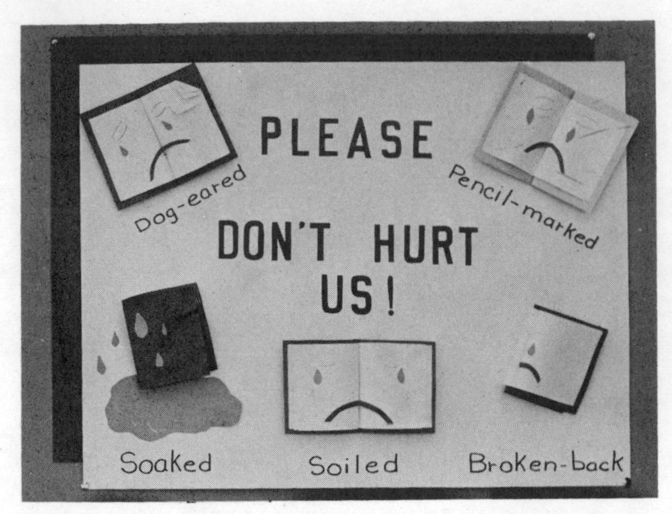

Bulletin board was made by Diane Hartman.

Figure 9.3 An Illustration of How Not to Treat a Book

Asking him to give the opposite of words like: *over* (*under*); *big* (*little*); *good* (*bad*); *awake* (*asleep*)

Noting the extent to which he takes part in class discussion

Noting whether he uses words correctly

Checking on how clearly he expresses his ideas

Checking on the length and structure of the sentences he uses.

7. *Checking other educational factors.* Some of the other factors related to reading readiness that the teacher can check through informal exercises, questionnaires, and observation are: (a) ability to follow directions; (b) right-to-left and top-to-bottom adaptation when "reading" picture books or following an experience chart; (c) ability to think critically; (d) experience background; (e) knowledge of the alphabet; (f) skill in interpreting pictures.

DEVELOPING READINESS FOR READING

Although in part readiness for beginning reading is a factor of maturation, there are many aspects that are subject to training. Suggestions for developing readiness for reading are given in the remaining pages of this chapter.

Developing Emotional and Social Readiness

The child who is overly aggressive, shy, or self-conscious will not be as ready to learn to read, other things being equal, as a child who does not have these or other emotional problems. To help boys and girls become ready to learn to read, as well as to become socially and emotionally well adjusted for other reasons, the teacher needs to provide a school atmosphere in which the following prevails:

1. Respect for each individual in the group
2. A feeling by each child that he is liked by the teacher at all times, even when he is not "good"
3. A feeling on the part of each child that he is accepted by the group as a whole and liked very well by some individuals in the group
4. A spirit of cooperation.

One way in which the teacher can help the child develop in social and emotional maturity is to provide him with many worthwhile experiences such as taking field trips, listening to stories, participating in sharing time, engaging in dramatic play, playing games, seeing pictures. Other ways are:

1. Providing the shy child with opportunities to become increasingly involved in activities well graded for him
2. Helping the overly-aggressive child take a rightful place in the social scene of the classroom
3. Using praise when deserved but resorting to criticism sparingly
4. Adapting the curriculum to the needs of each child so that he is likely to have a maximum of success experiences and a minimum of frustrations
5. Helping boys and girls appreciate the difference between license and liberty
6. Giving responsibilities to all pupils
7. Helping boys and girls in self-evaluation
8. Helping boys and girls become more self-reliant
9. Avoiding much competition with others
10. Placing a child in a group in which he is likely to be happy
11. Encouraging the child to do without assistance chores that he can do alone
12. Encouraging a child to express his own opinion
13. Encouraging every pupil to develop his special talents.

Helping the Child with Physical Shortcomings

Attention of the teacher to such matters as are suggested in the following paragraphs can be of real value in helping the child become ready to read as well as to develop in many other respects.

1. The teacher can help the pupil who has problems of vision by having him sit in the part of the room where he can best see the chalkboard; paying particular attention to the lighting facilities where he is; providing him with printed materials of suitable

type; writing large enough on the chalkboard and on materials that are duplicated so that the writing is suited, as well as feasible under the circumstances, to his poor vision; encouraging him to wear glasses if they have been prescribed for him; helping him get emotionally adjusted to glasses if he needs to wear them; developing among the other boys and girls in the room a mentally healthy attitude toward an individual who has problems of vision.

2. The teacher can help the child who has problems of hearing by giving him a seat in a part of the room where audibility is excellent; speaking distinctly and loud enough so that he can hear; encouraging all the boys and girls to speak distinctly and loud enough; using visual rather than auditory methods of teaching more frequently; helping him realize that a defect is not an excuse for not trying; helping him get emotionally adjusted to his handicap; developing among the other pupils a mentally healthy attitude toward an individual with hearing problems.

3. The teacher can assist the pupil who has problems of health other than those connected with vision or hearing by providing rest periods for the fatigued child; alternating periods of concentration with periods of freedom; trying to provide a room free of drafts; consulting with parents about the child's health habits and needs; encouraging the pupil to eat properly in so far as the food he eats is subject to his choice; emphasizing good posture through precept, example, and opportunity to practice; isolating the child with a cold if it does not seem necessary to send him home; assisting a pupil in accepting health handicaps that cannot be overcome; helping him remedy health handicaps that can be remedied; having a good program of physical education and health education; providing proper seating.

Developing Auditory Discrimination

Many of the boys and girls in a beginning first grade will probably need no help in auditory discrimination other than that afforded by the ongoing school activities. Others may require help in terms of supplementary practice exercises. The major emphasis should be on the type of discrimination the child will find of value when reading. However, included among the list of activities given below are also some that may be of value to a pupil in becoming ready for making the type of discrimination that he will need to make when reading. The pupils requiring help in making auditory discriminations could do some of the following activities:

1. Listen for sounds and report on those they heard during a few minutes of silence.

2. Guess the sources of sounds as one child, hidden from view, produces sounds by crumpling paper, using an egg beater, pouring water from one container to another.

3. Tell which note is the higher as the teacher plays two on the piano.

4. Tell which of two voices the teacher imitates is a happy voice and which a sad voice; or which is a kind voice and which is a cross one.

5. Distinguish, with closed eyes, whether the teacher taps on a table, the chalkboard, a glass, or something else.

6. Dramatize stories in which a variation of soft and loud voices is needed such as "Three Billy Goats" or "The Three Bears."

Further suggestions for exercises for developing auditory discrimination are given in Chapter 14. (See page 311.)

Developing Visual Discrimination

Following are listed means through which some pupils can improve in ability to make visual discriminations that will help them get ready for beginning reading. Some will be of value even after the pupils are in the early stages of learning to read. Additional methods are suggested in Chapter 14. (See page 311.)

1. Checking a series of pictures in each of a group of rows to show which is the largest (or smallest)

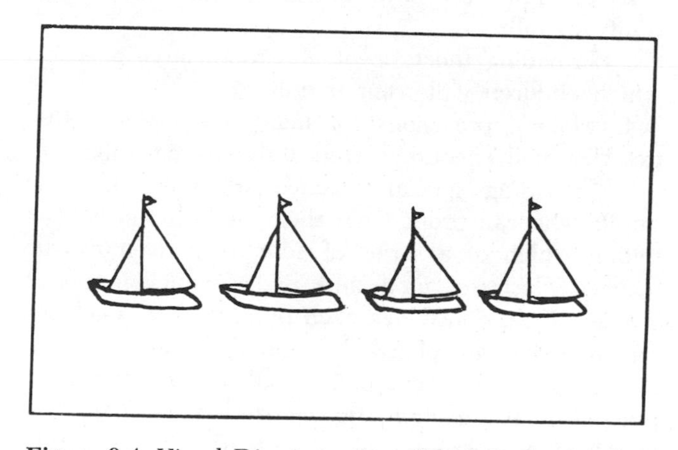

Figure 9.4 Visual Discrimination: Which Is the Smallest?

2. Telling what is wrong in a series of pictures that have been duplicated, some of which have an incongruity. For example, a picture of a door may be without a knob or both shoes that a child is wearing may be made for the right foot.

3. Solving picture puzzles

4. Completing one of each of a pair of pictures duplicated on paper so that it looks like the other.

For instance there may be a picture of two pumpkins, one without a stem.

5. Matching the cut-off part of each of a series of pictures with the part of the picture of which it originally formed a part

6. Indicating which of a series of letters or words in each row, such as the following, is different from the first one in that row

run run ran run run

7. Looking for words on a chart that begin in the same way as a given word

8. Doing an exercise for which the pupil is supplied with a duplicated sheet of paper on which are given rows of words, with each of the words in a row different from any other word in that row. As the teacher holds up a word card with a word like one in a specified row, the pupil puts a circle around the corresponding word on his paper.

Developing in Ability to Speak

The following are ways in which the teacher can help during the reading readiness period and later not only to keep speech problems from interfering with the pupil's reading but also to make the joy of oral self-expression affect the reading situation favorably.

1. Serving as model of good speech himself
2. Providing the boys and girls with much opportunity to talk
3. Providing the type of classroom atmosphere in which children will want to talk
4. Making provisions for many interesting activities that will encourage free and informal talk
5. Providing special practice activities for those pupils who can profit from them, such as these: (a) telling which of a series of sentences given by the teacher illustrate good and poor enunciation; (b) playing a game in which each pupil tries to reach the top of a diagram of a ladder on the chalkboard, on the rungs of which are pictures illustrating words for practice in enunciation such as *running, yellow, bus;* (c) having recordings on tape made of the pupil's talks; (d) participating in "sharing time."

Developing the Vocabulary

The understanding and the speaking vocabulary are factors that help determine a child's readiness for reading. Consideration is therefore given here not only to the development of a rudimentary reading vocabulary but also to an increase in the child's understanding and speaking vocabulary. The teacher can help the boys and girls in vocabulary development by:

1. Using words in sentences in which the meaning is indicated
2. Providing much opportunity for conversation
3. Reading poetry and prose
4. Making experience charts
5. Providing the pupils with new experiences
6. Asking the pupils to find their names in a list
7. Making "helper" charts

Figure 9.5 Learning to Recognize Names of Pupils

8. Having the pupils use labels for exhibits, for identification of supplies, etc.
9. Providing color and number charts.

Developing Listening Abilities

The relationship between listening abilities and learning to read is especially close when reading is taught primarily in a group situation. However, even when individualized reading programs characterize beginning instruction, there is interrelationship so that development in ability to listen is likely to affect beginning reading advantageously. Through listening the child acquires the vocabulary that will make reading meaningful later. Through listening he can develop sentence sense — an essential for intelligent reading. Through listening activities the foundation is laid on which phonetic analysis is built later in connection with reading. (In Chapter 4 there is a discussion of how the listening abilities of boys and girls can be developed.)

Learning the Rudiments of Handwriting

Although beginning reading instruction should precede writing instruction, some writing activities or activities related to writing such as the following can

Poster was prepared by Ann Patton Herron.

Figure 9.6 Learning to Recognize Names of Supplies

have a favorable effect on the development of readiness for reading and on success during the initial period of reading instruction.

1. The boys and girls can write their own names from name cards written by the teacher.
2. In a picture dictionary made by the class or individuals the pupils can write the word that is illustrated by each of the pictures below that written by the teacher.
3. The pupils can note where the teacher begins when writing on a chart or on the chalkboard as he asks questions such as: (a) Where should I start my first word? (b) Where should I start the second line?

For further suggestions on this topic the reader is referred to Chapter 7.

Developing in Ability to Think Critically

When reading is considered an activity through which thought can be acquired, as it should be, the relationship between ability to think critically and readiness for reading is self-evident. The teacher can help the boys and girls develop in ability to think critically by doing the following:

1. Asking questions that involve thinking before, during the time, or after he tells or reads stories to the class
2. Asking thought questions of the boys and girls as they plan school activities
3. During "sharing time" discussed in Chapter 4, asking questions such as these of children who are planning their contributions: (a) Where do you think you should stand when you show your shell (b) When would it be best to pass around your shell — before you begin talking, while you are talking, or after you have finished?"

Learning the Sequence in Reading

Although it is not difficult for most boys and girls to learn the left-to-right and the top-to-bottom sequence in reading, sometimes definite instruction is needed. Practice in interpreting pictures that are arranged on a page from left to right and from top to bottom may be valuable. Some pupils may profit by arranging pictures in that order on a chart. To help further, as the teacher writes on the chalkboard or reads from it, he may point out the sequence that he is observing.

Developing Other Abilities Important for Reading

Only a few of the abilities important for reading — more specifically for readiness for reading — have been discussed in the preceding pages. Others to which the teacher will want to pay attention in his efforts to help in the development of reading readiness are the ability (1) to remember, (2) to follow directions, (3) to handle books with skill and (4) to interpret pictures. The teacher will also want to help boys and girls extend their experience background. Since reading is a process involving thinking, the richer the experiences, regardless of whether they are definitely related to reading, the more likely the child will be able to approach reading with intelligent anticipation of the content. The teacher will also wish to do what is in his power to develop and help maintain an interest in reading. Many of the activities already suggested as means of guiding growth toward readiness for reading, if they appeal to boys and girls, can be used to stimulate their desire to learn to read.

THE USE OF EXPERIENCE CHARTS

The reading experience chart is one of the most widely used means of developing readiness for beginning reading. The two most common types of reading charts are those that give a record of an experience that a group has had or indicate plans that have been drawn up for a proposed activity.

Values

The popularity of the experience chart is undoubtedly due in part to the fact that it can contribute to the accomplishment of many of the objectives of the reading-readiness period.

1. It can be the means of extending the pupil's experience background as the class discuss experiences.
2. It can provide experience in democratic living with its contribution to the social and emotional development of the child as he learns to take turns, to respect the ideas of others, to feel the encouragement and satisfaction of a worthwhile contribution, and to work in an orderly manner.
3. It can help interest the child in reading.
4. It can provide orientation in the left-to-right and top-to-bottom directional sequence of reading, especially if the teacher draws attention to it.
5. It can stimulate the development of sentence sense as the teacher uses the term *sentence* when he makes comments or asks questions such as: (a) What shall we have for our next sentence? (b) Where shall I begin the next sentence? (c) Please read the next sentence.
6. It can serve as a means for the child to learn a limited number of words as sight words.

Purpose for a Chart

When making an experience chart, it is important that the boys and girls see purpose for engaging in the activity. It will be noticed that in the following listing the suggested purpose in some cases is not only for making a chart and reading it but also for follow-up activities.

1. The boys and girls can make a series of charts on a trip that they have taken. The purpose may be, as far as the pupils are concerned, to remember important and interesting things they learned on their trip.
2. The class can make a series of charts, one on each field trip that they take during the course of the year. Their purpose may be similar to the one stated in item 1.
3. The class can make a booklet after they are able to "read" an experience chart based on a walk on which they had observed signs of fall (or winter or spring). Every child may be given a duplicated copy of the chart for his notebook. Then he can draw an appropriate cover for his booklet. On one page in the booklet may be the "picture words" the pupils learned while reading the chart, with pictures drawn by them to illustrate each word learned that can be pictured. After a pupil is able to "read" his booklet, he may be allowed to take it home to give to his parents and to "read" it to them.
4. The experience chart can be written on paper that will serve as a page in a large class notebook, in which the pupils can keep an illustrated record of interesting activities of the year, possibly for turning over to the first grade who will the next year follow them in the room.
5. Before Thanksgiving the boys and girls can participate in making an experience chart so that they will be reminded throughout the year of some of the many reasons they have for gratitude.
6. The boys and girls may be stimulated to want to make an experience chart to serve as a written record of plans for an activity they intend to perform.
7. The class can take part in planning and using a series of individual charts, with each chart being about a pupil in the room or about his family or foster family. Each child could work out the wording for his chart with the help of the teacher, who would write it on large tagboard or on large sheets of paper to be used as pages of a class notebook. Each child could draw an appropriate illustration for his chart.

Planning, Constructing, and Using an Experience Chart

Steps in planning, constructing, and using an experience chart are given in Chapter 14. (See page 310.)

Points to Remember

Following are additional points for the teacher to bear in mind when he plans, constructs, or uses experience charts for reading-readiness purposes.

1. It is important to have wide participation in the planning, so that the chart is not primarily the work of a few pupils and the teacher. If this precaution is not observed, many of the pupils may in time lose interest in the activity. Furthermore, many of the possible benefits will not accrue to all.
2. If the experience chart is to be of maximum value as a reading experience, special attention needs to be paid by the teacher to the selection of some of the words for the chart. It is not recommended that the boys and girls be expected to learn all the new words included in an experience chart. If they learn

two, three, or four from each chart, perhaps no more should be expected. If the words to be learned are those that the boys and girls will be likely to use in the near future in their reading, the word study has increased value. The teacher needs to be careful, however, when planning for the inclusion of certain words in the chart not to violate the caution stated in the preceding paragraph.

3. The words from a chart that are to be added to the child's sight vocabulary should be used at frequent intervals even after the work on the chart has been discontinued. Without violating the principle to which reference is made in the two preceding paragraphs, a teacher can guide the structuring of the story on the chart in such a way that some "review words" are used in subsequent charts. For some pupils direct practice on those words may be needed. Word cards or picture word cards could be made for practice purposes.

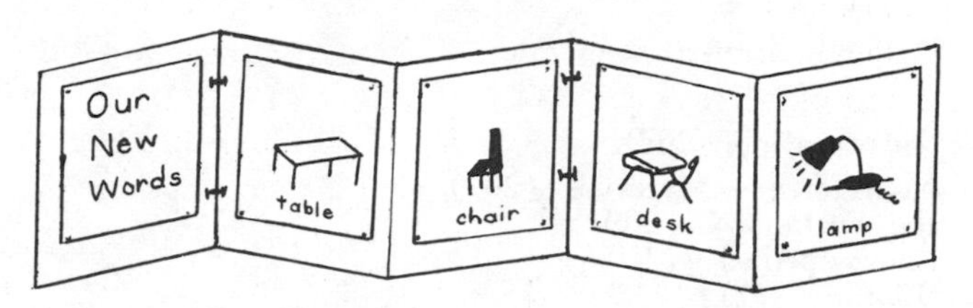

Figure 9.7 A Folder for Displaying Illustrated Words

4. Experience charts should not be considered substitutes for early reading in a book. It is not as important now to emphasize this point as it was several decades ago when a substantial number of teachers advocated using experience charts as practically the only reading for boys and girls during the early stage of learning to read. One argument given by some proponents of this point is that boys and girls enjoy reading more if they have dictated the material to be read. This point is refuted by those who point out that in time it can also become very boring to keep on reading only that material which the reader had helped plan. Other arguments against almost exclusive use of the experience chart as a beginning reading activity are: (a) The pupils are not really reading when they reproduce the sentences they have memorized, since reading is or should be primarily a thought-getting process. (b) The vocabulary is not as controlled as that in text books even if the teacher tries, within reason, to have some words used in the charts that will later appear in the child's reading books. (c) Boys and girls find, at times, that reading what someone else has written can be more intriguing than that which they have helped "write."

FOR STUDY AND DISCUSSION

1. Study reading-readiness materials published by commercial companies and evaluate them. What suggestions for teaching did you receive from them?

2. In what ways, in addition to those suggested in this chapter, can the teacher of beginning first-grade children set about to help them grow toward the emotional and social maturity as a prerequisite to beginning reading instruction?

3. Suggest procedures that can be used, in addition to those mentioned in this chapter, for development in the following elements of educational readiness for beginning reading: (a) auditory discrimination, (b) visual discrimination, (c) ability to speak, (d) vocabulary, (e) listening, (f) handwriting, (g) thinking critically, (h) ability to remember, (i) following directions, (j) handling books, (k) following the sequence in reading, (l) experience background, (m) interest in learning to read.

4. Write a teaching plan for developing and using an experience chart during the pre-reading period. (You may wish to refer for suggestions to page 310.)

5. A few audiometers are listed on page 177. Study the professional literature to find more information on audiometers as a means of checking the hearing of children during the period preceding that of the initial teaching of reading.

6. One question on a check list for evaluating a program in reading-readiness might be: "Are individual differences given adequate consideration?" What other questions do you consider important for inclusion in such a check list?

REFERENCES

Bond, Guy L., and Eva Bond Wagner, *Teaching the Child to Read.* Third edition. The Macmillan Company, 1960. 416 pp.

DeBoer, John J. and Martha Dallmann, *The Teaching of Reading.* Second edition. Holt, Rinehart and Winston, 1964. 422 pp.

Harris, Albert J. (ed.), *Readings on Reading Instruction.* David McKay Company, 1963. 466 pp.

McKim, Margaret, and Helen Caskey, *Guiding Growth in Reading in the Modern Elementary School.* Second edition. The Macmillan Company, 1963. 454 pp.

Russell, David H., *Children Learn to Read.* Second edition. Ginn and Company, 1961. 612 pp.

Tooze. Ruth, *Your Children Want to Read.* Prentice-Hall, 1957. 222 pp.

OUTLINE FOR CHAPTER 10

Guiding Growth in Reading Skills

CHAPTER 10

Guiding Growth in Reading Skills

When the child is ready to learn to read, how can he be guided in the development of skills important to reading? That question is considered in this chapter.[1]

DEVELOPING INDEPENDENCE IN WORD RECOGNITION

Specialists in the field of child growth and development emphasize the fact that it is the responsibility of adults to help the child grow from the dependence of infancy to the independence of adulthood — a point, which with modification, can well be applied to the venture of teaching boys and girls how to recognize words. It could be paraphrased thus: It is the responsibility of the teacher to help the child to grow from complete dependence on others in word recognition, which the beginning reader necessarily has, to total independence in word recognition (often, to be sure, with the help of the dictionary) that characterizes the skilled adult reader. In other words, it is the teacher's challenge to help the pupil develop from the stage where a word needs to be told to him to the stage where he can, without help from others, recognize any words in the English language which he meets in his reading. Furthermore, the pupil should be helped to proceed from complete dependence toward complete independence as rapidly as possible but without any haste or hurry.

When the term *word recognition* is used in this chapter, it refers to the ability to identify written words, not to the knowledge of one or more meanings of the word. Undoubtedly word recognition without recognition of the meaning of a word is rather futile. The two must go hand in hand in practice. However, for the sake of clarity, word recognition is here discussed first.

Guidelines

As the teacher plans the work in word recognition, he should keep in mind the following points.

1. *Although skill in word recognition does not guarantee skill in reading, it is absolutely essential to effective reading.* Although a person cannot read without being able to recognize words, excellence in that skill does not assure efficiency in reading.

2. *No one method of teaching word recognition should be used to the exclusion of all others.* One of the characteristics of the effective reader is that he knows how to use a variety of methods of attacking new words. He should be able to recognize words through the sight method (including observance of the general configuration or striking characteristics of a word), context clues (both visual and verbal), phonics, and structural analysis.

3. *All phases of the school program should contribute to development of skill in word recognition.* When pupils tell about their experiences, the teacher may write on the chalkboard a word that serves as topic of a talk. When working on a unit on community helpers, the class could refer to a chart listing the names of the helpers.

4. *Systematic instruction should be given in word recognition.* While effective use should be made of opportunities that arise during various parts of the

[1]For a more comprehensive treatment of many of the topics discussed in this chapter and in the preceding one, as well as for many other points bearing on the subject of these two chapters, the reader is referred to the book THE TEACHING OF READING, of which the writer is co-author with John J. DeBoer (second edition, published by Holt, Rinehart and Winston, 1964).

Courtesy of the Chicago, Illinois, Public Schools

Figure 10.1 Books That This Little Girl Will Use in Her Schoolwork from Kindergarten through Grade 12 in the Chicago Public Schools

school day for growth in skill in word recognition, there should also be a carefully planned developmental program, with emphasis not only on providing initial help in learning to use a method or a phase of a method but also on provisions for the maintenance of skills.

5. *Words should, as a rule, be taught in context, not in isolation.* The context can frequently be of help to a learner in identifying a word. Furthermore, if a child learns a word in context, he sees it in the type of setting in which he will usually encounter it in his reading. It is not always a poor policy, however, to present a word separately. At times the teacher may wish to introduce a word as he writes it on the chalkboard. He may not want it to appear initially in context because he may wish to have the learner decipher the word by means other than context clues. Later he may want the child to read the word in context.

Use of the Sight Method

As the term *sight method* is here used, it refers to the so-called look-say method, where a word is learned without any analysis of it and without any reference to context. The pupil is merely told the word by someone – by the teacher, another adult, or a child. The expression *sight word* is used in this book to designate words that were presented by the sight method. (It should be noted that some writers refer to words as sight words when the learner knows the words by sight, regardless of the method by which the word was first presented.)

If the teacher wishes, for example, to present the word *school* as a sight word, he may write it on the chalkboard or show it on a word card as he says to the child, "This word is *school.*" Thereupon the pupil may be asked to repeat *school* and to find the word in a sentence, preferably in one that contains no other word new to the child's reading vocabulary.

It should be noted that a heated controversy has been raging about the use of the sight method. While many persons have recommended that as many as 75 words should be taught by that method during initial reading instruction, others have contended that phonics should be taught from the very beginning so that from the start the reader achieves some independence in word recognition. These people have thought of the sight method as presenting the child with an impossible task as far as learning to read effectively is concerned.

The adversaries of the sight method are right in their claim that if all words were learned only by that method, no one could hope to become an efficient reader. Consequently the sight method should be supplemented by the phonetic method and other methods. An example of how the sight method can be, in an early stage of reading instruction, combined with phonics and with the context-clue and structural-analysis methods is given in the teaching plan presented on page 314.

Why then, if the sight method is a memory method whereby each word needs to be remembered as such, is it advocatd by anyone? It is recommended by many for use in beginning reading instruction because in a fairly short time a child can acquire a reading vocabulary sufficient to help him read meaningful material with a very limited vocabulary.

General Configuration and Striking Characteristics of a Word. Closely allied to the sight method, in fact often part of it, is that of pointing out the general configuration or striking characteristics of a word. The teacher may, for example, when he tells the child the word *book,* point out the fact that there are two circles in the word, or as he presents the word *morning* as a sight word, he may draw attention to the fact that it is a long word. The pattern of words with parts higher than the rest, such as the *f* in *farm,* or with parts below the line, such as the *g* in *go,* may also be emphasized. One fact that limits the value of this method is that there are many words with the same general outline. Consequently only a very small number of words should be presented with emphasis on configuration.

Practice on Words Presented by the Sight Method. To tell many children a word once does not, in the early stages of reading instruction, assure that they will remember it. It is for this reason that publishers of books for beginning instruction have provided considerable subsequent use of a word in context after the initial presentation. Even so, many teachers realize that unless the use of a word in the textbook is supplemented by other opportunities to strengthen the association with a word taught as a sight word, a large number of boys and girls will probably not remember it on a subsequent day, maybe not even as they find it in the reading of that day.

Some of the procedures here suggested can be employed either at the time of the presentation of a sight word or later, while others are applicable only for practice at the time when a word is presented as a sight word.

1. After the teacher has told the class the name of a word, one pupil or the entire class pronounces it after him.

2. A pupil matches the word on a word card with a word on the chalkboard.

3. A pupil names the words presented as they appear on the chalkboard or on word cards.

Figure 10.2 "Balloons" Used as Word Cards

4. The teacher names a word that a pupil is to find among the words listed on the chalkboard or on word cards.

5. One pupil points to a word while another names it.
6. A child finds the new words named by the teacher as they occur in a list of sentences that the teacher has written on the chalkboard.
7. The pupils point in their reading book to a word that the teacher names or for which he shows a word card or at which he points as it appears on the chalkboard.
8. After two words similar in general configuration which have been presented as sight words, such as *this* and *that*, have been written on the chalkboard, a pupil encircles the parts that are alike in the two words.
9. One or more pupils indicate which pairs of a series such as the following written on the chalkboard, are alike:

this, that that, this that, that this, this.

10. Special attention to the contour and length of a word can be drawn by means of an exercise like the one that follows. The children may be asked to draw a line from the word in Column A to the frame in Column B into which it would fit.

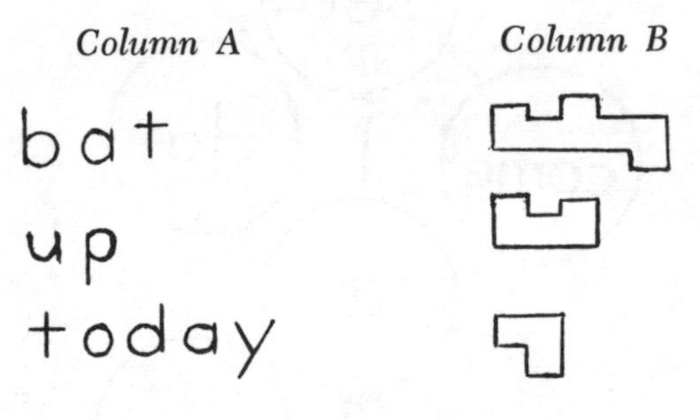

Figure 10.3

The reader will find further suggestions that can be applied for reinforcement of association between the written symbol and the name of the word presented by the sight method as he reads the ideas given in subsequent pages of this chapter dealing with means of providing practice on words suggested in connection with other means of word recognition.

Use of Context Clues

Somewhat less dependent than learning words by the sight method is learning them through pictorial or verbal context clues.

PICTURE CLUES. Obviously not nearly all words can be presented or remembered through picture clues. Nouns that are names of concrete objects or persons or places, not of ideas or other abstractions, can most readily be recalled in this way. Even with them there may be confusion. For example, if the word *mother* is presented with a picture of a young woman holding a baby, it may not be clear to the beginner whether the word is *mother* or *baby*. Action verbs can be illustrated, but frequently there is no certainty as to what the word is. For example, to illustrate the verb *run*, there may be a picture of a boy running. The reader may, however, be uncertain as to whether the word written below the picture is *boy, run, runs,* or *running*. The other parts of speech are even more difficult to illustrate pictorially.

To overcome the shortcoming of the picture-clue method, words are often presented in the first grade by a combination of the sight method and the picture-context method. For example, the teacher may show the picture of a boy with the word *boy* written below it and ask the pupils what they think the word is. If they do not suggest the word *boy*, the teacher tells them the word. Then the card can be posted for possible later reference by the pupils.

Following are additional suggestions for using the picture-clue method, either alone or in combination with another word-recognition method, as a means of learning for the first time the word pictured or of reinforcing the original learning.

1. The boys and girls may have their own sets of picture-word cards, made on a smaller scale than those for class use. It is recommended that in the first grade, in most cases, the teacher do the writing on the cards, for the pupils should have a good model of handwriting when learning to read. To study the word the pupil looks on the side on which both picture and word are given. To test his recall he tries to pronounce the word or recall without pronouncing it as he looks at the side without a picture. To check his response he can turn the card around to see what picture is given on the reverse side.
2. Before the pupils are about to read a selection, the teacher may discuss accompanying pictures with them. He may then direct comments and focus his own statements so that the names for the words pictured are the ones to which reference is made in the text. For example, if one of the new words of the story were *apple*, he might ask questions like these about a picture given on the page: (a) What does Johnnie have in his hand? (b) What do you think he will do with the apple? If the teacher wishes to use a combination of both the picture-context clue and the verbal-context clue methods later on during the lesson, he may tell the pupils, without presenting the word *apple* beforehand, to read a given page. To

check word recognition after the pupils have read the page, the teacher may ask or say: (a) What did Johnnie give his mother? (b) Point to the word on this page that tells us what Johnnie gave his mother.

3. Sometimes, especially in the intermediate grades, the pupils may find a word which they do not have in their hearing or speaking vocabulary illustrated in a picture. For example, they may be unfamiliar with the word *glacier*. The teacher can then give the necessary background for understanding both the picture and the general meaning of the word as the boys and girls look at the picture. He may even wish to tell children that he believes they will be able to spot the word *glacier* when they run across it in the context. This procedure, of course, is a combination of the picture and verbal context methods.

4. The boys and girls or the teacher can make a chart of words that can be illustrated – words learned as the class study a unit in the content subjects. For example, after studying about Switzerland, the class may use a chart with words like *alphorn* and *glacier* illustrated.

Figure 10.4 A Booklet of Picture-Word Pages Used with a Unit on the Circus

5. The teacher and/or the pupils may make a picture word-card file, to which the pupil can refer when necessary, of words for geographical features such as *equator, isthmus, peninsula.*

VERBAL CONTEXT CLUES. If a reader is helped to determine what a word is by means of the phrase or sentence or paragraph in which it occurs, he is learning it through a verbal context clue. This method should be used alone only if the context gives a clue as to what the word may be. For instance in the sentence "It is a warm day," the child cannot determine by context alone what the word *warm* is, for it could be *hot, cold, mild, rainy, sad,* or one of a large number of other words and still fit in with the rest of the sentence.

Even in beginning reading the method of verbal context clues can be combined with one or more other methods. For instance, if the pupils were given the sentence, "It is a warm day," providing they recognize every word other than *warm,* the teacher may ask what word fits into the sentence which he has written on the chalkboard twice, once with and once without the word *warm,* in this manner:

It is a .... day.
It is a warm day.

Then after the pupils have named a number of words which he may want to write in column form on the chalkboard, including the word *warm* (which if necessary he himself may name), he can say, while pointing at the second sentence illustrated, "The word which is used in this sentence is *warm.*" If this procedure is followed, a combination of the verbal-context clue method and the sight method is used.

When used correctly and at appropriate times, the method of learning to recognize words through context clues is one important aid to word recognition. For the beginning reader it can be a great boon because it is an additional method through which he can learn new words before he is ready for much work in phonics. Even the effective mature reader can use it advantageously when, in combination with other methods such as that involving attention to the beginning sound, he is able to tell what a word in context is without resorting to phonetic or structural analysis.

The danger in the use of context clues is that the method is undesirable when used as a guessing procedure. It is for this reason that it should be emphasized that when the pupil is expected to use the verbal context method alone there should be some indication in the phrase or sentence or paragraph as to what the word in question may be. It is also for this reason that it is imperative that not many cards are unknown to the reader within a given context – probably not more than one in any one sentence, especially in the case of beginning readers.

Following are other ways in which intelligent use of context clues, either with or without the use of other word-recognition methods, can be encouraged. Some are for pupils in the initial stage of reading instruction; others are for more advanced readers, while still others can be used advantageously on any level.

1. Having pupils tell which of a series of given words fits into a blank for a missing word in a sentence such as:

Winter is my .... season. (favor, favorite, favorable)

2. Asking the pupils to draw a line from the blank for a missing word in a sentence to one of a series of pictures indicating the word needed

3. Giving pupils practice in choosing the appropriate pronunciation of a word that has two pronunciations by having them read sentences like the following orally, after silent reading:

I like to *read* stories about the West.
I *read* this book last summer.

4. Asking pupils to fill the blank in a sentence with a word of which the meaning is built in, in the rest of the sentence, like:

He was not friendly but very ....

Use of Phonetic Analysis

One of the sharpest controversies in the teaching of reading has centered around teaching phonics. For several decades the question asked was "Should phonics be taught?" Now it is generally accepted that it should be taught. A question of current debate is "When should it be taught and how should it be taught?"

There are those who believe that phonics instruction should be given during the initial stage of reading instruction without being preceded by the sight-word method or emphasis on context clues. Some recommend (1) that pupils follow a planned program according to which many of the sounds of letters or of combinations of letters associated with the proper written symbols are taught before they begin to read consecutive reading material and (2) that the pupils begin reading consecutive material only after they have at their command the phonic elements necessary to an independent or almost independent unlocking of the words they will meet in their reading. According to some of these same advocates of phonics as the means of teaching beginning reading, a sizable number of generalizations pertaining to phonics also need to be taught before regular reading instruction is begun or at least before it is far advanced.

There is argument not only about when phonics should be taught but also how. The question centers in part on whether or not practice on phonics should be independent of the regular reading activities or in conjunction with them. In recent years there also has arisen the question, "Shall the Initial Teaching Alphabet method be used?" Question has also been raised as to whether beginning reading should be taught by a method designated as the "words-in-color" method. Both of these methods attempt to reduce or eliminate the difficulty inherent in many systems of beginning work in reading. They try to simplify the process by having the same sound (or the same color in the case of the "words-in-color" method) of a letter always represented by the same written symbol (or the same color). For further information concerning these two systems, the reader is referred to the last section of this chapter.

THE PROGRAM IN PHONICS. Before considering the subject matter to be taught and the generalizations to be learned, let us note the following explanation of commonly used terms.

1. A *digraph* is made up of two letters producing one sound. There are two kinds of digraphs, *consonant digraphs,* such as *th* and *ck,* and vowel digraphs, such as *ei* and *ay.*

2. A *diphthong* represents two vowels that are blended almost to the extent that they produce one sound, such as *oy* and *eu.*

3. A *consonant blend* is a combination of two or three consonants, such as *gr* or *str,* that are blended in such a way that each letter in the combination continues to be heard.

The following outline of subject matter is cited from *The Teaching of Reading,*[2] page 97, which is given there as indicative of points on which there is essential agreement as to the elements of phonics that should be taught.

Single consonants in monosyllabic and polysyllabic words
- a. In initial positions in words
- b. In final positions in words
- c. In medial positions in words

Consonant blends, like *st, gr, br, cr, tch, pl*
Consonant digraphs, like *ch, th, sh*
Single vowels
- a. "Short"
- b. "Long"

[2]John J. DeBoer and Martha Dallmann, *The Teaching of Reading.* Second edition, by permission of Holt, Rinehart and Winston, 1964.

c. Vowels modified when preceding *r*
d. The *a* when preceding *l* or *w*
e. Other vowel sounds

Vowel digraphs, like *ea, oa, ai, ay, ee, oo*
Diphthongs, like *oy, oi, ou, ow*
Silent letters

Also quoted from *The Teaching of Reading* (pages 97 to 98) is the following listing of generalizations rather commonly recommended for teaching in the elementary school.

A single vowel in a syllable is usually short unless it is the final letter in the syllable. (Examples: *baby; bat*)
If there are two vowels together in the same syllable, the first vowel is usually long and the second silent. (Example: *boat*)
If a final *e* in a syllable is preceded by a single consonant, a single vowel preceding the consonant is usually long and the *e* is silent. (Example: rat*e*)
The sound of a single vowel preceding an *r* is usually modified by the *r*. (Example: col*o*r)
The sound of a single *a* preceding an *l* or a *w* is affected by the *l* or *w*. (Example: f*a*ll, cl*a*w)
A final *y* in words of more than one syllable is usually short. (Example: bab*y*)
A *c* before *e, i,* or *y* has, as a rule, the soft sound. (Example: *c*ity)
A *g* before *e, i,* or *y* has, as a rule, the soft sound. (Example: *g*em)

It is hoped that the following descriptions of possible procedures in helping boys and girls learn to recognize words through phonetic analysis will suggest others.

1. The boys and girls name a list of words that begin with the same sound as the teacher writes the words on the chalkboard, recording only those in which the beginning sound is also spelled in the same way. It is suggested that at the beginning of work on phonics the teacher record only words that begin with consonants that always have the same sound or about the same sound, namely *b, h, J, l, m, p, t,* and *v*. Later the same type of practice can be used with consonant blends or consonant digraphs and with single consonants other than those that have the same sound or approximately the same sound at all times.

2. To provide practice in identifying words through substitution of a letter at the beginning of a word, the pupils may be asked to draw a line under the words in each row, like the following, that are like the first word in a row excepting for the beginning letter.

can	fame	tan	tar	car	fan
sang	swim	rang	rung	bang	jam

A similar exercise can be worked out for practice in identifying words through substitution of a letter at the end of a word.

3. For boys and girls who can write letters and numbers, this type of exercise can be provided for help on initial sounds of words. After the boys and girls have numbered, say to ten, the teacher tells them that the words he will pronounce begin either, for example, with an *m* or *n*. The pupils are then instructed to write an *m* opposite every number if the word that is named for that number begins with an *m*, and if a word begins with an *n* to write an *n* opposite the number. Then the teacher proceeds by giving a list of words like the following as he names the number of each:

(1)	mother	(6)	number
(2)	Nancy	(7)	make
(3)	made	(8)	Mary
(4)	not	(9)	more
(5)	nothing	(10)	nose.

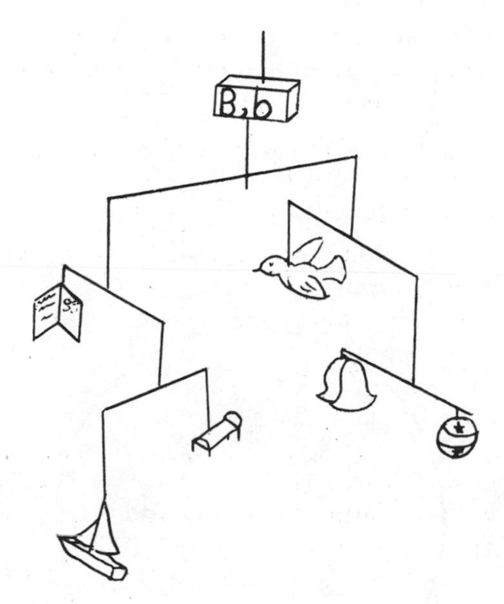

Figure 10.5 A Mobile Illustrating Words Beginning with the Same Sound

4. After the boys and girls have learned the hard and the soft sound of the letter *c*, the pupils may tell which of a list of words written on the chalkboard or on paper begin with the soft sound and which with the hard sound. Similarly emphasis can be placed on words beginning with the hard and soft sound of *g* or with the voiced and the voiceless sound of *th*. The exercise may further be adapted for use for identifi-

cation of various sounds of the same letters found in other than the initial positions of a word.

5. A commonly recommended type of exercise on phonetic sounds is the phonic wheel, by means of which the boys and girls can get practice in recognizing words through emphasis on the beginning consonants, consonant blends, or consonant digraphs.

The wheel can be made in the form of two concentric circles fastened by a brass fastener through a hole punched in the center of the circles. As the pupil rotates the outer circle, he names the words that are formed by a combination of the beginning sound on the smaller wheel and the endings of words on the larger wheel. In the second part of the accompanying illustration is an example of what the writing on the outer circle might be, most of which is hidden from view at any given time.

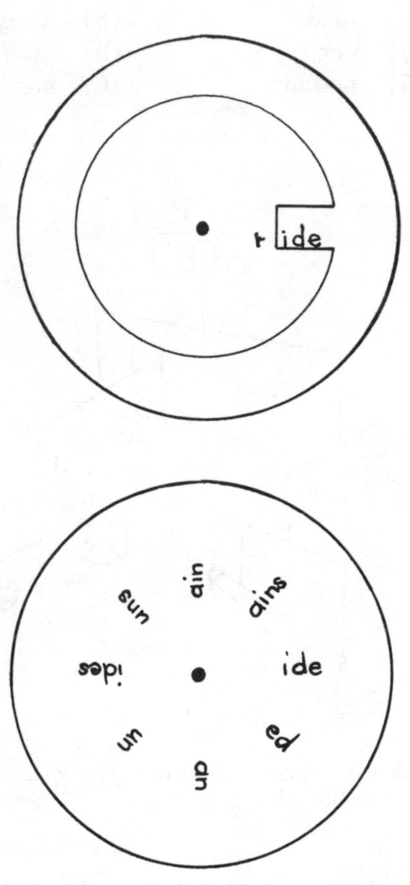

Figure 10.6 A Phonic Wheel

6. The boys and girls may draw pictures of objects the names of which rhyme, like *boy, toy.*

7. The pupils can be asked to sort, according to initial consonants or according to rhyme, small pictures pasted on uniform-sized pieces of cardboard.

Figure 10.7 2a Variation from the Phonic Wheel; *At* Ending Used with Different Consonants

8. The boys and girls may supply the initial letter of words in a sentence in which the first letter or combination of letters of some words has been omitted.

The ....oys and ....irls were ....aying ....all.

9. A chart can be made showing that the silent *e* at the end of a word is important in the pronunciation of the word. Words to illustrate this fact are *rat, rate; rid, ride; hop, hope.*

10. The pupils can find pictures of objects the names of which begin with stated consonant sounds. For example, for the sound of *p* they could find pictures of a pie, a pail, and a party. Each pupil could make his own picture dictionary with these pictures.

Use of Structural Analysis

So far we have considered three methods of learning to recognize words – the sight method, the use of context clues, and phonetic analysis. Now let us discuss a fourth method – and in some respects the last, for the use of the dictionary is really practical application of the phonic method and of structural analysis – namely that of structural analysis.

When a word is recognized through structural analysis, it is learned through identification of prefixes, suffixes, root words, parts of compound words, syllables, contractions, and form (if the word is possessive, like *father's*). It will be noted that in structural analysis the recognition is through the structure of the word, not in terms of the sound elements of a word as in phonetic analysis.

There is one important caution concerning the use of structural analysis. Pupils should not be encouraged to find "little words in big," as many teachers request, unless the "little words" form the root of the word or unless the word is a compound word. If pupils look, in general, for "little words in big," undesirable habits may result which may cause trouble in word recognition. For example, children encouraged in this practice may well find *moth* or *he* or *her* in *mother* and *so* or *on* in *soon* and thus be misled in attempts at recognition of words.

The work in structural analysis should include: (1) knowledge of syllables, (2) recognition of prefixes and suffixes, (3) recognition of compound words, contractions, and possessive forms of nouns, and (4) knowledge of common rules for forming the plural of nouns.

Teachers' manuals accompanying reading textbook series frequently indicate quite fully the important learnings to be acquired in relation to structural analysis.

The following listing indicates some procedures that can be followed to help boys and girls learn to recognize a word through its structure.

1. The teacher may explain to the class why structural analysis is frequently a quicker method than phonetic analysis and thus have the pupils see reason for recognition of common prefixes and suffixes.

2. A list of common prefixes, suitable for a given group of boys and girls, may be written on the chalkboard as the pupils suggest words that contain these affixes. Discussion may follow on the common meaning(s) of the prefixes. For permanence, information may be recorded on a chart summarizing the important points about prefixes.

3. Older boys and girls may be helped to realize that certain letters and groups of letters sometimes used as suffixes are not always such, as in the case of *ing* in *thing* or *ed* in *fed*. They can be asked to indicate in a list of words with endings that are often suffixes in which words they are used as suffixes.

4. The pupils may indicate in which instances in a list of words similar to the following the *es* or *ed* suffix forms a separate syllable and in which it does not. They can then pronounce the words.

drowned copied copies horses
sounded sounds washes

5. The boys and girls can be helped to learn the rules for forming singular and plural possessives of nouns and then make application of that knowledge to complete a form such as the following:

Noun	*Possessive Singular*	*Possessive Plural*
boy		
girl		
woman		
baby		

Or the pupils may tell which ones of a series of possessive forms of nouns, such as the following, are singular and which plural: *woman's, women's, babies', man's.*

6. The pupils can be given individual cards on each of which is written a contraction that is pronounced the same or almost the same as a possessive pronoun found on another card, such as: *its, it's; they're, their; there's, theirs.* As the teacher gives a sentence containing a word on a card orally, each pupil holds up the card he thinks is correct.

7. The pupils may be helped to draw up a list of words in which the last letter of a prefix is the same as the first letter of the word, as in *illegal, illegible, irresponsible, irreverent, immobile.*

8. To emphasize the point that care needs to be taken to know which words are hyphenated compound words, which are unhyphenated compound words, and which are not compound words, the pupils can be given guidance in the use of the dictionary to learn how to determine into which of these categories a word or group of words falls. Then, by inserting necessary hyphens or by separating two words in a group by a vertical line, they can complete an exercise with words written in the following manner: g r a n d m o t h e r, s i s t e r i n l a w, s c h o o l y e a r.

9. The pupils may find the compound words in a paragraph or story.

10. The boys and girls may be asked to choose the correct ending for words in sentences like:

She (visited, visits) us yesterday.

11. The boys and girls can indicate the number of syllables in a list of words like the following:

——unlikely ——situation ——geography.

Additional Considerations

Before leaving the topic of guiding growth in reading through word recognition, let us turn our attention to the following questions: (1) How is word recognition taught by means of the Initial Teaching Alphabet? (2) How is word recognition taught through the "words-in-color" program? (3) What is the role of the textbook in the program of word recognition? (4) How can workbooks contribute to the word-recognition program? (5) What use can be made of games in the program of word recognition? (6) How can picture dictionaries be used to develop skill in word recognition?

THE INITIAL TEACHING ALPHABET. In recent years a mode of writing, referred to as the "Initial Teaching Alphabet," often written as *i.t.a, I.T.A., or i/t/a,* has been used increasingly in schools, first in Great Britain and later in the United States. Because the English language lacks consistency in representation of sounds by letters or groups of letters, it is rightly claimed, that many a youngster — in fact, many an adult — has difficulty in reading. In an attempt to reduce the problems of the beginner in learning to read, the following alphabet for beginning reading is used in i/t/a materials.

æ	b	c	d	ɛɛ	
face	bed	cat	dog	key	
f	g	h	ie	j	k
feet	leg	hat	fly	jug	key
l	m	n	œ	p	ɹ
letter	man	nest	over	pen	girl
r	s	t	ue	v	w
red	spoon	tree	use	voice	window
y	z	ƨ	wh	ch	
yes	zebra	daisy	when	chair	
th	th	ʃh	ʒ	ng	
three	the	shop	television	ring	
ɑ	au	a	e	i	o
father	ball	cap	egg	milk	box
u	ω	ω	ou	oi	
up	book	spoon	out	oil	

Figure 10.8 The Initial Teaching Alphabet

In the i/t/a alphabet of 44 characters it will be noted that 24 are found in traditional orthography; some of the others are a combination of letters in the usual English alphabet; several are new characters. Each symbol in the i/t/a represents one sound and that one sound is represented by no other symbol or combination of symbols. In this respect the Initial Teaching Alphabet is in sharp contrast to that ordinarily used when writing English, in which many letters have more than one sound and in which many sounds are represented by different letters or letter combinations.

For information on the i/t/a and its use in schools the reader is referred, first of all, to the many articles appearing in professional magazines and in popular literature. He is also referred to the book *The Initial Teaching Alphabet,*[3] written by John Downing, the Englishman whose work in the United States has been greatly responsible for developing keen interest in the alphabet among many teachers in the United States. Suffice it here to note the following statements about i/t/a.

1. The proponents of i/t/a emphasize the fact that it is not a method of teaching but a mode of writing. They stress the point that the alphabet can be used with any method of teaching beginning reading (such as the sight method or the phonic method) the teacher uses, as based on his philosophy of education or upon the procedures by means of which he obtains the best results.
2. John Downing and others point out the fact that use of the Initial Teaching Alphabet should precede use of the traditional alphabet and that it should not be a substitute for it for lifetime reading. *When* the transition should be made from the initial teaching alphabet to the standard one has not been ascertained. Undoubtedly the optimum time for the change-over will depend upon many factors such as the interest, the intelligence, and the skill of the reader, not merely upon chronological age nor upon length of time in school. Some pupils make the transition at various periods during the first school year; others make it later.
3. Since i/t/a was not used in England before 1961 and not in America before 1963, convincing research on the use of the alphabet, it is claimed by many, is still lacking. This argument is advanced when consideration is given to some of the enthusiastic reports in schools where i/t/a has been used for a few years. Undoubtedly the real test will come when longitudinal studies of six or more years are made on the reading success of individuals who were initially taught by i/t/a.
4. While the United States is behind Great Britain in the number of available reading series and supplementary reading materials written in the Initial

[3]John Downing, *The Initial Teaching Alphabet.* The Macmillan Company, 1964.

Teaching Alphabet, the number is increasing. Initial Teaching Alphabet Publications, 20 East 46th Street, New York, New York 10017, will furnish on request a list of teaching materials to augment teaching by means of this 44-character alphabet.

"WORDS-IN-COLOR" PROGRAM. Another approach to minimization of the divergence between the sound and symbols in the English language is the "words-in-color" program, published by Learning Materials, Inc., Encyclopedia Britannica Press. To explain how color is used the publishers in one of their brochures state:

> Each of the 47 sounds of English is printed in a distinctive color on wall charts. Alphabet letters or groups of letters (280 signs of English) are colored according to how they sound in a given word. Thus color is used to make English phonetic without in any way changing traditional spellings.
>
> A sound is always represented by *one* color — regardless of its spelling. If it is the short sound of *a*, it is white whether it is in *pat* or *laugh*. Children use these color clues to help them fix the image in their minds.
>
> From the beginning, the pupil writes and reads in *black and white* each colored sign that he is introduced to so that there is immediate and constant transfer. Since he carries the images of these signs in color in his mind, the pupil can evoke and re-evoke the images if he needs them for reading or writing. Thus he is not dependent on printing in color.

As in the case of i/t/a the "words-in-color" program has not been used long enough for research to give evidence that many would accept as conclusive, for it was not until 1959 that Caleb Gattegno, the originator of the program, applied to the English language the results of earlier experimentation with the Spanish and Hindi languages.

THE TEXTBOOK IN THE PROGRAM OF WORD RECOGNITION. One of the advantages in the use of reading textbook series in the elementary school, especially in the first stages of learning to read, is that the reading vocabulary is controlled. Publishers and authors take pains to produce basal reading series in which new words are introduced gradually and in which there is enough repetition of the new words that the average child, with proper presentation and later attention to the words, will be able to develop and maintain a reading vocabulary that includes the words learned through use of the textbooks.

The matter of selection of vocabulary as to the words to be included is also an important consideration of authors and publishers of reading textbooks for the primary grades. Frequently some of the well-established word lists are consulted.

Attention also needs to be drawn to the excellent contribution that many publishers of textbook series in reading make through the development program in word recognition that is outlined in the teachers' guides accompanying textbooks.

WORKBOOKS AND WORD RECOGNITION. Many of the exercises in consumable books, either accompanying textbook series or published separate from any one single basal reading textbook program, are designed to help boys and girls not only learn the vocabulary presented but also develop skill in achieving greater independence in word recognition.

There was a time when there was justifiably much criticism of workbooks. In some instances they probably did not provide much more than "busy work." However, the quality of many consumable books is now so fine that the teacher using a basal textbook series is well advised to consider carefully the advantages of a good workbook before he decides against the use of one. Some boys and girls seem to need more practice on words than that afforded in the regular reading books of a series. This practice can be provided through workbooks.

READING GAMES AND THE DEVELOPMENT OF WORD-RECOGNITION SKILLS. Knowing the power of interest on learning and also recognizing the interest that

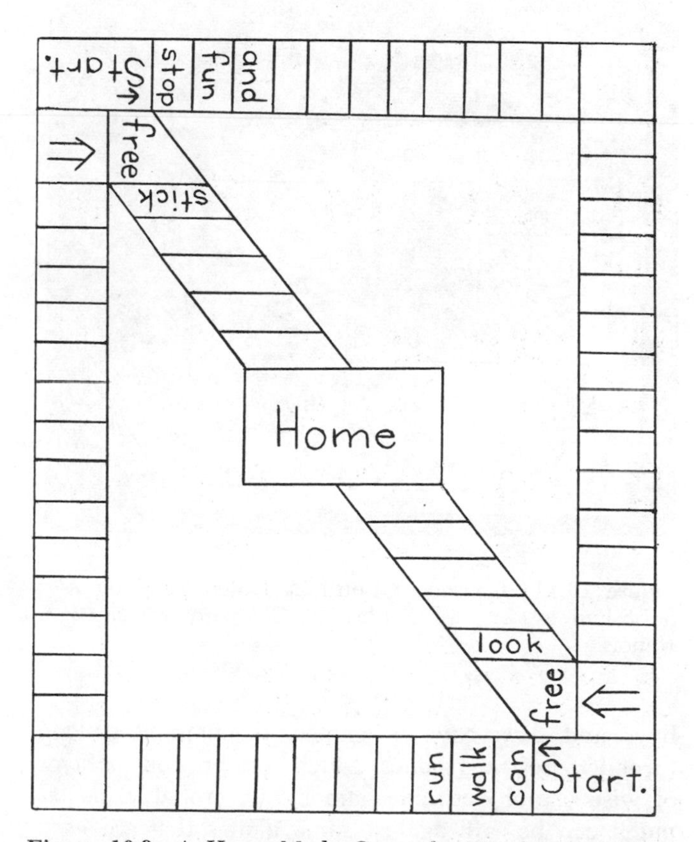

Figure 10.9 A Home-Made Game for Word Recognition

Figure 10.10 Vowel Lotto: A Dolch Teaching Aid, published by Garrard Publishing Company, Champaign, Illinois

Figure 10.11 Consonant Lotto: A Dolch Teaching Aid, published by Garrard Publishing Company, Champaign, Illinois

boys and girls have in games, teachers have long turned to reading games. Much can be said in favor of wise use of desirable games, but probably just as much can be said against some games that are used and against the manner in which some of the desirable ones are misused. On page 27 "Games in the Language Arts" is discussed. Suffice it to say that the purpose of a game will in part determine its appropriateness. The teacher should recognize that so-called reading games may serve one of two major purposes, that of helping boys and girls become better readers and that of giving them a recreational activity. When the main purpose is to use the game as a reading exercise it should not be used unless, to a considerable extent, it is in harmony with the rules of effective drill. If, however, a game is used primarily for the fun that it can provide and only secondarily for its reading value, it may be quite legitimate to use it even if it has doubtful value as a reading exercise. Probably a good deal of the time when recreation is the main objective, the teacher will want to use a game during a period for relaxation rather than during a time devoted primarily to learning to read. The reader is referred to page 337 for a list of publications about games and a list of publishers and distributors of games.

The Picture Dictionary and Word Recognition. Picture dictionaries are probably of primary value in the reading program because of the help they afford boys and girls in remembering words learned by the sight method. They can also serve as a means of learning new words and as an introduction to later work with non-picture dictionaries. A list of some commercially available picture dictionaires is given in Chapter 15. (See page 238.)

DEVELOPING SKILL IN COMPREHENDING WHAT IS READ

The term *reading with comprehension* is somewhat relative. One person reading a given selection may understand only part of the meaning that is revealed to another reader of the same material. Furthermore, one individual may receive a partially incorrect impression of what is stated by the author, while another may be able to interpret the meaning with great accuracy.

Guidelines

In helping boys and girls develop in ability to comprehend what they read, the teacher is advised to proceed according to these guidelines.

1. *Guidance in comprehension should not be postponed until the pupils have learned to recognize many words.* Skills in word recognition and in comprehension should be developed almost simultaneously. The teacher of beginning reading can encour-

age growth in comprehension by asking questions like: (a) What do you think will happen next in the story? (b) Why did Susan want to go to the park?

2. *Guidance in comprehension should not be limited to reading situations.* One way in which help can be given in nonreading situations is this: After a pupil has given a talk, the rest of the class can indicate what points mentioned by him brought out the thought the speaker wished to present. If irrelevant facts were mentioned, the classmates could designate them.

3. *The boys and girls should be helped to recognize various purposes for reading and to realize that different methods of procedure should be used for different purposes.* For example, they should recognize that at times they may be reading a selection only to get the main idea or ideas, at times to summarize what they have read, and at still other times to achieve any of the other abilities needed in order to comprehend effectively the various types of reading they will be doing. The preceding statements, however, should not be interpreted to mean that boys and girls at any level should necessarily be confronted with a list of types of comprehension skills similar to those following.

Finding the Main Idea

Reading for the main idea or ideas often suffices when a child reads a story or an article in a magazine for children or when an adult does leisure-time reading or reads the newspaper. Some ways in which the teacher can help boys and girls develop skill in finding the main idea(s) are as follows:

1. Letting the boys and girls know the purpose for which they are to read a given selection as the teacher gives directions or makes comments like "Read the next page to find out how Susie felt when her mother explained what had happened."
2. Having the boys and girls help determine how a certain passage should be read in order to accomplish a given purpose. For example, if the teacher asks the class to read a selection to find out whether Peter got his wish, the class may be asked whether they will need to read the story to get the general idea or to note details in order to be able to answer that question.
3. Asking the boys and girls to record on a card or in a booklet data on each book that they read outside of class. They may be asked to write a one-sentence summary of the book.
4. Helping the boys and girls learn what is meant by a topic sentence and providing them with practice in selecting the topic sentence of paragraphs containing them
5. Asking the pupils to write a question that a paragraph as a whole answers
6. Having some pupils draw a series of pictures, each of which summarizes the main action in a series of paragraphs and then having others match the pictures with the paragraphs
7. Helping the boys and girls plan the topic or themes of each of several scenes they may enact when dramatizing a story they have heard or read
8. Asking the pupils to tell what a longer selection is about after they have read only the author's introduction to it, providing the introduction gives the general idea(s) of the selection
9. Asking the pupils to change each sideheading of a chapter into the main question that they may expect to find answered under a given sideheading
10. Mounting a picture, with a short story written below it, on a firm piece of paper and writing on the back of the mounting titles of which the pupils are to select the most appropriate.

Reading for Details

A pupil reads for details when he looks for data to support a point he plans to make, when he wants to plan a costume for a play representative of a period of history, when he plans a report on current events, when he reads a problem in arithmetic. In helping boys and girls read intelligently for details, the teacher should emphasize the fact that the points to be noted should be pertinent to the objective of the reader. Consequently pupils can advisedly be given help in formulating questions on details that would be of value to them as they read for functional purposes. Emphasis should also be placed on the relationship of details to the central ideas.

Activities such as the following may help the boys and girls in learning to read for significant activities:

1. Finding the facts to support a generalization in one or more sources
2. Indicating which of a series of questions the readers should expect to have answered in a given selection and then checking their responses
3. Drawing pictures for a "movie" of a story showing the details brought out in the story
4. Reading to be able to describe how a character of a story should act in a dramatization to be given by the pupils
5. Matching illustrations with sentences that state important details
6. Quoting details in selections read that support the opinions of the readers

7. Drawing pictures to illustrate a character in a story showing many details, and then asking classmates to identify the character or to suggest other details that could have been shown.

Figure 10.12 Pupil-Made "Movie"

Organizing What Is Read

Several types of abilities in addition to that of finding the main ideas and selecting pertinent details are, at least in many instances, important to organizing. They include: (1) arranging events or ideas in a functional sequence, (2) relating details pertinent to the main idea, (3) outlining, (4) taking notes, and (5) summarizing. Suggestions for developing these abilities are given in the following listing of activities in which boys and girls may engage.

1. Making a "movie" illustrating a process such as "From Tree to Tire" or "From Ore to Steel"
2. Listening to a story told or read by the teacher as he shows pictures of the scenes and arranges them in view of the children in the sequence of events in the story
3. Making a mural that tells the main events of a story with the needed details to explain these events
4. Arranging in proper sequence the paragraphs of a story which are presented in mixed-up order
5. Classifying pictures on a flannel board and putting, for example, in one category pictures of fruits, in another those of vegetables, and in still another those of grains
6. Classifying words into various groups, like those naming clothing for a rainy day, for a sunshiny summer day, for a day when it snows
7. Making an outline for a report on a personal experience that will be given to the class
8. Noting the outline that the teacher has written on the chalkboard for a talk that he is giving
9. Completing an outline of which a skeleton like the following is given:

Caring for Our Teeth

I. Why it is important
 A.
 B.
 C.
II. Steps in brushing the teeth
 A.
 B.
 C.
 D.

10. Participating in making an outline of activities that the class may consider for work on a unit. Part of such an outline for a unit on Alaska may be similar to the following.

I. Reading
 A. Our textbook
 B. Library books
 C. Newspapers and magazines
 D. Travel folders
II. Art work
 A. Making a "movie"
 B. Making an accordion-like picture folder

Figure 10.13 A "Movie" on 'Little Mouse Dances' (pages 127-132 of THE NEW MORE FRIENDS AND NEIGHBORS by W. S. Gray and others, published by Scott, Foresman and Company, Chicago, 1953).

C. Making a diorama or panorama
D. Constructing an Eskimo village
III. Dramatization
A. Putting on a skit about the discovery of gold
B. Putting on a play showing life in Alaska

11. Learning the form of an outline by listening to explanation by the teacher

12. Having practice in rewriting an outline or part of an outline that violates the rules of good outlining, like:

WRONG: I. What we need
A. Scissors
B. Thread
II. Pins and needles

13. Before being able to outline, drawing sketches for use as notes when planning a talk or a report on a story. An example of actions of which pupils could draw pictures for such an outline is as follows:

Little Red Riding Hood's mother giving her a basket
Talking with the wolf in the forest
Talking with "grandmother" upon arrival at Grandmother's home
Being saved by the woodcutters.

14. Learning when to use the exact words of a writer for note-taking and how to indicate that they are the exact words

15. Dictating to the teacher notes to be used as memoranda for the class

16. Comparing the value of an organized and an unorganized set of notes

17. Writing summaries with attention to *who, what, where, why,* and *how* as key words for questions to be answered in a summary.

Critical Evaluation

The need of critical evaluation of what is read — that is, of examining what is read to ascertain its value — is, indeed, acute in this age of unprecedented use of means of mass communication for educational purposes, for entertainment, for dissemination of propaganda, for advertising. Following are suggestions as to how the teacher can help boys and girls evaluate what they read as they (1) distinguish between fact and opinion, (2) differentiate between the real and the fanciful, (3) note qualifications of the author, (4) check the accuracy of generalizations, (5) note the up-to-dateness of information, (6) decide whether propaganda is being disseminated, and (7) discern the attitude of the writer.

Fact or Opinion

1. Provide the pupils with statements like the following about which they are to state whether they are based on fact or opinion: (a) St. Paul is the capital of Minnesota. (b) Switzerland is the most interesting country of Europe.

2. Ask the pupils to find all statements of opinion made within a selection.

3. Have the pupils rewrite some statements expressing opinion in such a way that it is clear that they express an opinion.

Real or Fanciful

1. Give the boys and girls an opportunity to make up a fanciful story and have the class tell what their reasons are for considering it fanciful.

2. Ask the pupils to find examples of methods used in stories by which some authors let the reader know if a tale is fanciful.

3. Have the class compile a list of expressions like "Once upon a time" that often indicate that a tale is fanciful.

Qualifications of the Author

1. Discuss with the class the type of questions that a reader may like to have answered about an author of an article on current-day world affairs in order to know how much faith to have in the article.

2. Discuss with the class which of two hypothetical authors of an article has the qualifications (which are stated) that would indicate that the author's comments can be expected to be valuable.

3. Ask the pupils to write paragraphs giving the qualifications of an imaginary author of a selection dealing with a topic like, for example, "Behind the Iron Curtain." They may write one paragraph that includes insufficient background of the author to write with authority on the topic and another that would seem to show adequate background.

Accuracy of Generalizations

1. Discuss with the class dangers of overgeneralizations by showing them generalizations that are too broad or that are unwarranted because of lack of data.

2. Ask the pupils to write paragraphs in which facts to support a given generalization like the following are presented: (a) Air exerts pressure. (b) In the book *Rabbit Hill* the animals in some respects act like human beings. (It is important that the generali-

zations stated are some on which the pupils have, or can fairly easily acquire, information adequate for establishing them.)

UP-TO-DATENESS OF INFORMATION

1. Discuss with the class what types of information need to be kept up-to-date.

2. Have the class check a list of statements to indicate which are unreliable in present-day conditions if the information were received from data gathered a few decades ago, like: (a) The population of our city is . . . . (b) George Washington was born on February 22, 1783.

3. Ask the boys and girls to check for which of a series of facts (like the following) a book with the copyright date indicated would be a recent enough source of information: (a) the telephone number of an individual (directory of four years before); (b) the signers of the Declaration of Independence (1940).

4. Make available to the boys and girls a list of books, some with old and some with recent copyright dates. The pupils may be asked to answer questions or follow directions like the following: (a) Is your history book written recently enough so that it can report on events during the last five years? (b) What is the copyright date of Virgil Hilyer's *A Child's Geography of the World*? Find two items of information in that book that are now out of date. Find two items of information that still hold true.

PROPAGANDA TECHNIQUES

1. Discuss with the class the widespread use of propaganda techniques.

2. Have the pupils check selections, written for that purpose by the teacher found in current writing in newspapers, for various propaganda techniques employed.

3. Ask the boys and girls to write a paragraph in which they use one or more propaganda techniques.

ATTITUDE OF THE WRITER

1. Ask the class which of a pair of sentences shows a sympathetic attitude and which an unsympathetic attitude toward the persons or situations described, such as: (a) A group of busybodies met at Mrs. Smith's home last night to see what they could do to keep our boys and girls from having a good time. (b) A group of civic-minded women met at Mrs. Smith's home last night to see what they could do to help prevent vandalism by some of the boys and girls in our neighborhood.

2. Ask the pupils to rewrite sentences that show an unsympathetic attitude so that they show one of sympathy, and also to rewrite sentences that show a sympathetic attitude so that they show one lacking in sympathy.

Predicting Outcomes

Some ways in which boys and girls can be given help in predicting outcomes are given following.

1. After the boys and girls have read a selection, they find the parts that give a hint of the outcome.

2. The teacher asks questions like these during intervals while reading orally to the class: (a) What hints are we given as to the change that will take place in the main character? (b) Where did we get the first indication that he may change?

3. As the teacher reads the first part of a sentence, paragraph, or story, the pupils look at a picture that he displays and they give one or more expected endings.

4. The pupils predict what will happen next after reading an account on a current issue of a newspaper and then they check the following issue of the paper to see whether they were correct.

Growth in Word Meaning

Let us now turn our attention to ways in which boys and girls can be helped to improve their reading comprehension through the development of a more adequate meaning vocabulary. (For a discussion as to how the dictionary can be used for increasing the pupil's understanding vocabulary the reader is referred to page 209.)

1. Before the pupils read a given selection, the teacher can assist them with the meaning of some of the words by helping them study pictures given in the book, by providing them with other pictures that illustrate the meaning of one or more of the words, by having a pupil in some instances dramatize a word, or by asking a pupil to use a word in a sentence.

2. At times when there is a built-in definition of a word in the context of which a word is used, the teacher may list it on the chalkboard, within or without the sentence, and tell the class he thinks that as the pupils read the selection they will be able to tell what the word means. After the reading the check should be made.

3. The pupils may be provided with an exercise consisting of a series of sentences in each of which a word, with multiple meanings that may cause a problem in comprehension, is underlined. Below each sentence may be written three or more dictionary definitions of the underlined word, of which the

pupils are to choose the one that fits into the context of the sentence.

4. Experience can be extended and an emphasis put on vocabulary through field trips, motion pictures, filmstrips, slides, other pictures, talks by visitors, talks by pupils and teacher, book reviews, wide reading.

5. Flannel boards and bulletin boards can be used for posting new words. At times the word may be illustrated.

6. The pupils may try to see how many different meanings they can think of or find for a word with multiple meanings such as *run, bridge, tide.* Then they can use each in a written sentence. A booklet can be made in which some of the words with a large number of meanings are given in sentences illustrating each of the meanings the class has found. A page can be used for each word.

7. In connection with the study of a unit, the class or a committee can make an illustrated chart listing words learned in the study of that unit. For example, in a unit on the Western States terms like these may be included: *rodeo, plateau, ore, placer mining.*

8. The pupils may have individual files in which they keep a card for each "new" word they want to remember. They can include on the card the spelling, the phonetic respelling or diacritical markings, the part of speech (if the pupils know the parts of speech), the plural form of a noun, one or more common meanings of the word, and a sentence illustrating each of the recorded meanings.

9. The boys and girls can construct materials to illustrate the meaning of a word such as *lock* (of a canal), *volcano, pueblo, sombrero, drawbridge, portcullis.*

DEVELOPING SKILL IN REMEMBERING WHAT IS READ

Research corroborates what teachers and pupils and persons outside of school often attest, namely that a common problem is inability to remember what is read, to the extent desired. After one reading people retain, as a rule, for a short time, only a small per cent of the information in a selection. Furthermore, much of what is remembered for a short time is later forgotten.

Abilities Conducive to Retention

The following are some of the abilities related to power in retaining what is read that the average child leaving the sixth grade should have developed to a considerable extent:

1. Ability to formulate a purpose for reading a given selection
2. Ability to decide, even before reading a selection, what in general terms it will be important to remember
3. Ability to organize what is read
4. Ability to take notes
5. Ability to make summaries
6. Ability to decide what means should be employed to remember what is read
7. Ability to make application of points to be remembered.

Methods

Some procedures by means of which boys and girls can be helped to develop the abilities listed in the preceding paragraph are named in an earlier section of this chapter. Additional suggestions are here given for developing abilities to which reference has been made.

Ability to Formulate a Purpose. While in earlier stages of reading instruction the teacher frequently will state a purpose related to needed thoroughness of retention, even in the primary grades the boys and girls should at times be given help to formulate their own purposes for reading.

Some of the purposes related to remembering that the pupils may have in mind when reading are: to remember the general idea of a selection; to remember details bearing on a given problem; to remember verbatim, or almost so, what they read; to remember for only immediate recall what they want to remember; to remember points that are in contradiction to what they had known or heard; to remember descriptive words; to remember the conclusion to which the writer comes; and to remember the writer's method of presenting his information.

Ability to Decide What to Remember. It is of value for the reader to have in mind, in general, before he begins reading, not only to what extent it will be advisable for him to remember what he is about to read but also to know what type of information will be significant to remember. For instance, if he decides he is going to read a selection in order to note details, it will help him in reading if he decides what types of details he wants to retain.

Ability to Decide Upon Methods. The effective reader often knows when (in terms of the material, his purpose, and the time available) it is not enough for him to take mental note to remember what he wishes to retain. He must determine, for example, when written notes, outlines, or summaries are advisable. He will want to reach a decision on what distribution of practice in recall in a given situation is best for him. Another judgment that it is important to make is the length of each practice period.

Ability to Make Application of Points Remembered. If the reader sees the relationship between the points he wishes to remember and life situations of significance to him, he is more likely to remember what he reads than if he thinks of them merely as points to remember. Consequently when pupils are given opportunity to discuss their own experiences in relation to facts worth being remembered for a given purpose, help is provided in the development of ability to remember.

DEVELOPING DESIRABLE READING RATES

In this age of unsurpassed speed when man circumvents the globe in a matter of hours and sends missiles far out into space in an almost unbelievably short time, when astronauts orbit the earth with incredible speed, when reports of happenings in some of the far ends of the earth come to us almost instantly, when production is speeded up in an unprecedented manner, when inventions and discoveries in various fields of human endeavor are made at an unparalleled frequency, it is little wonder that much attention should be paid to the rate of reading.

Common Misconceptions

There are several misunderstandings about what is desirable in terms of the rate of reading.

1. *Many persons think that there is some one desirable rate of reading for an individual.* There is not. The ideal rate differs with the purpose of the reader and with the type and difficulty of material being read. Very fast reading may be desired when, for example, the reader wants to skim the material to find out what it is about or when he looks rapidly over the material to see if in it opinions are expressed or facts presented about a given point. Very slow reading is indicated when one is doing, for instance, study-type reading or when one wants to follow a set of somewhat complicated directions. At many others times when a person is reading only for pleasure or when, for other purposes, he wishes to get the main idea and not note many of the details, a rate between the fast and the slow would be the best rate.

2. *It is believed by many people that a fast rate is ordinarily accompanied by poor comprehension.* No such generalization can be drawn. While it is true that comprehension can suffer when a person reads too fast for his purpose, a slow plodding rate by no means assures superior comprehension.

3. *It is believed by a sizable number of teachers that there is a high positive correlation between rate of reading and comprehension.* Research does not substantiate such a claim. While it is true that there seems to be a positive correlation, it has by no means been proven high.

Basic Considerations about Reading Rates

The following are additional points that the teacher should keep in mind as he decides upon means of helping pupils to learn to read at appropriate rates.

1. In the lower grades the emphasis should not be on the increase of rate of reading.

2. In the upper primary and intermediate grades emphasis should be on reading at appropriate rates, but not to the extent that comprehension suffers.

3. Boys and girls should be helped to be able to determine when fast reading, average reading, and slow reading are desirable.

4. Overconcern by boys and girls about the rate at which they are reading should be discouraged.

5. One of the chief causes for reading slowly habitually is deficiency in other reading skills such as word recognition, comprehension, and locating information.

6. Much oral reading can have a disadvantageous effect upon rate of reading after the pupils have learned to read more rapidly silently than orally. Then they should only rarely, if at all, read silently the material that at the same time someone is reading to them orally.

7. Habits of word pointing, vocalization while reading silently, and moving the head instead of the eyes while reading should, in general, be discouraged. To discourage word pointing even in the first grade, the teacher may provide the reader with a marker, possibly a piece of stiff paper, four inches by one inch, which he can use to keep his place as he moves it from line to line. Markers should not be used after the pupils can get along without them. As far as vocalization while reading silently is concerned, there is no scientific evidence to tell us how soon the child should be discouraged in moving the lips while reading silently. It may be that the first-grade teacher who during the initial period of reading instruction emphasizes the importance of not moving the lips is trying to take from the child a crutch he still needs. There is no question, however, but that the practice is detrimental if the child continues it beyond the point where he can read more rapidly silently than orally.

8. There is a relationship between eye movements and reading rate. The following points have been established, partly through ordinary observation and partly through a machine known as the ophthalmograph, which photographs the movements of the eyes of the reader: (a) The eyes of an effective reader sweep from left to right along the line of writing. (b) There are usually three or more breaks per line in the sweeping movement of the eyes from left to right. Each of these breaks or stops is known as a *fixation.* (c) The actual reading seems to take place while the eye is in motion, not at the time of the fixation. (d) Much more time is normally occupied by a fixation than by the sweep itself. Consequently the number of fixations per line determines to a considerable extent the rate of reading. (e) At times the eye moves backwards in reading. Such a movement is known as a *regression.* (f) The sweep of the eye from the end of one line of reading material to the beginning of the next is called a *return sweep.* By an inaccurate return sweep is meant the failure of the eye of the reader to focus near the beginning of the next line as it moves from the end of the preceding line of reading.

There are characteristic differences between the eye movements of the effective reader and of the person who has not acquired efficiency in reading. Chief among these are: (a) The eyes of the efficient reader move in rhythmical sweeps across the line of writing, while those of the inefficient reader are likely to move jerkily. (b) Typically the effective reader has fewer points of fixation per line than the ineffective reader. (c) Aimless regressions in larger numbers are more characteristic of the ineffective than of the effective reader. Although even the good reader makes regressions when, for example, he wishes to consider more carefully something he has just read, his regressions are not, as a rule, characteristic of the reader whose eyes make fixations like those indicated in the accompanying diagram. (d) The effective reader is more likely than the ineffective reader to have accurate return sweeps from the end of one line of print to the beginning of the next.

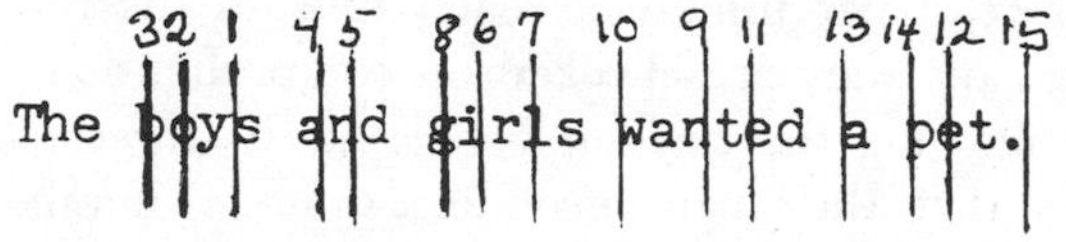

Figure 10.14 An Illustration of Numerous Aimless Regressions

There has been considerable argument as to whether or not the relationship that undoubtedly exists between the quality of reading and the eye movements of the reader is a causal one. Some persons have claimed that poor eye movements cause poor reading and that improvement of eye movements results in better reading. People endorsing this point of view are likely to encourage training in eye movements in the hope of improvement in reading. Others, however, contend that ineffective eye movements are the result, not the cause, of ineffective reading and that consequently there should not be training directly on eye movements. According to this point of view, improvement will result from better reading habits. The writer is of the opinion that the latter point of view is the correct one.

9. There is argument as to the value of so-called "controlled reading." By "controlled reading" is meant a method of spacing the exposure of parts of the reading, often, but not necessarily, by means of a mechanical device in which parts of a line progressing from left to right are successively exposed. Or the device may be one in which – as in the case of the SRA accelerator, – a shutter, at a rate that can be set, occludes line after line of reading material. The shutter prevents the reader from regressing to previous lines in case he does not read at a rate faster than the one at which the accelerator is set. (If the reader is a line or more ahead of the shutter, he can, of course, reread one or more lines that precede the one on which he is reading over which the shutter has not already moved.)

The claim for "controlled reading" is that the reader can be "forced" to read at a faster rate when his reading is controlled, that he can transfer reading at a faster rate from machine-controlled material to ordinary reading material, that the novelty of the device stimulates interest and purpose on the part of the reader, and that knowledge of measurable results (in terms of rate of reading) encourages increased effort. The effect of novelty of approach, especially for boys and girls who have failed to increase their speed through more commonly used methods of procedure, may serve as a strong incentive for concentration and increased speed. Knowledge of results, objectively measurable and almost immediately discernible, is another strong feature of various methods of "controlled reading." It should be noted, however, that even in "noncontrolled" reading frequent checks, with results made available to the reader, can be made.

Some people question the use of controlled reading, at least for elementary school pupils. They doubt whether the long-time effect on rate, of reading materials read under "controlled" situations, is greater than that which could be obtained if as much emphasis were put on rate in practice without reading controllers. Furthermore, they will argue that if we accept the principle that the effective reader often advisedly changes his rate of reading within a selection, use of a controller may under some circumstances even interfere with reading at desired rates. Another objection raised by some to extensive use of a controller is that a good reader at times justifiably makes regressions. It may well be, the argument runs, that an effective reader reads along at times at a relatively rapid rate and then wants to reread a point that he did not grasp at the rate appropriate for most of the selection. Or he may wish to reread a part in order to clinch in his mind a point that was stated before he continues with his reading.

Further criticism that is given of extensive use of a controller is that when a problem in rate is caused by inefficiency in word recognition – such as lack of ability to comprehend what is read or deficits in other reading skills – reading the material rapidly is unlikely to affect the total effectiveness of the reading favorably. Maybe a more rapid rate is the last thing a person lacking skill in word recognition needs to improve his reading. Although many people using "controllers" provide checks on comprehension, the main emphasis in "controlled" reading usually is on rate rather than on comprehension. Even in many studies that show considerable increase in rate, a corresponding improvement in comprehension is not evident. In fact, frequently after prolonged use of a "controller," comprehension scores show but little improvement.

In spite of arguments advanced against "controlled" reading, the reader is advised not to dismiss the whole question lightly but to be interested in results claimed through "controlled" reading with students beyond the elementary-school level. The reader is referred to Chapter 15 (see page 337) for a listing of devices and for names of distributors of mechanical aids for increasing the rate of reading.

Methods

Following are suggested procedures that may help some boys and girls learn to read at appropriate rates.

1. Discussion with the boys and girls of facts such as the following: (a) that there is no one best rate of reading; (b) that rate of reading should be thought of as rate of comprehension; (c) that points that help determine the optimum rate of reading at any one time are the ability of the reader, the difficulty of the material (for him), and the purpose for reading; (d) that other things being equal, the person who can accomplish a given purpose for reading a given selection the more rapidly is the better reader.

2. Discussion with the class of the rate of reading (i.e., very fast, average, slow) at which given types of selections, such as the following, should be read for stated purposes: (a) reading an article in a newspaper to get a rough idea of what is "going on" in the world; (b) studying a science lesson that is rather difficult for the reader for the purpose of giving a report on it; (c) reading a series of stories to determine which one(s), if any, are suitable for reading to a group during a program of Christmas stories; (d) reading a library book to get enjoyment from it, without planning to remember many details; (e) looking for a stated "new" word on a page in a primary-grade reading textbook.

3. Having pupils read a short selection such as the following, in which some words have been omitted (words without which the general thought of the selection can be comprehended) so that the pupils recognize the fact that one does not need to note with care every word in a selection in order to comprehend the general idea.

One .... most interesting experiences .... we .... our trip occurred .... day .... we............ fishing. .... father .... I .... started .... early .... morning, ... had had .... good breakfast of ham .... eggs.

4. Providing the boys and girls with practice in first skimming a section in a social studies book in order to get the general idea and organization of the material and then rereading it for detail.

5. Providing the boys and girls with exercises such as the following: (a) The pupils read for a given length of time (two or three minutes or longer) and then their rate per minute is figured and their comprehension of what they read is checked. (b) The pupils read a selection to answer rather general questions on it. Then they record the time or number of words read per minute as each finishes his reading. Thereupon, they are checked on comprehension.

6. Showing the boys and girls in the intermediate grades that they can recognize quite a number of words without looking at every letter of the word, especially when words such as the following are used in sentences:

Ch .... tm .... s S .... da .... s .... ho .... l.

7. Encouraging the pupil who habitually reads slowly to read much easy material.

8. Providing practice in skimming to find a story in a table of contents, to locate an entry in an index, to find a word in a dictionary, to find a telephone number, to find the date on which something happened.

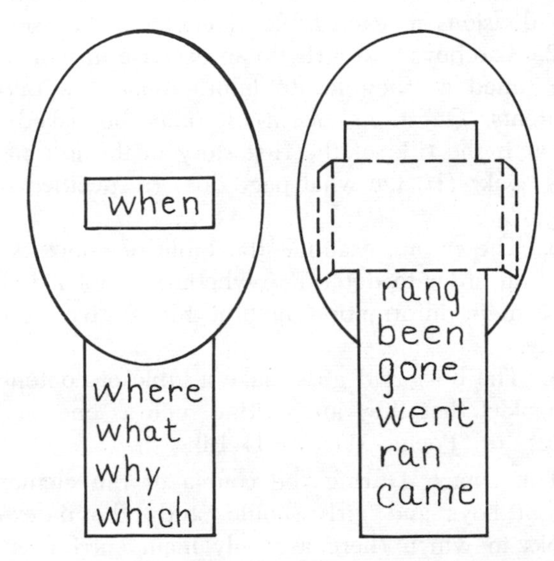

Figure 10.15 A Tachistoscopic Device for Word Recognition

Figure 10.16 A Tachistoscopic Device for Phrase and Sentence Recognition

DEVELOPING SKILL IN LOCATING INFORMATION

In order to achieve independence in reading a person needs to acquire skill in locating what he desires to read, both in terms of reference materials and nonreference materials.

Locating Information in Nonreference Materials

Boys and girls should acquire skill in locating materials in nonreference books by familiarity with the use of the title page, the copyright page, the introduction, the table of contents, and the index.

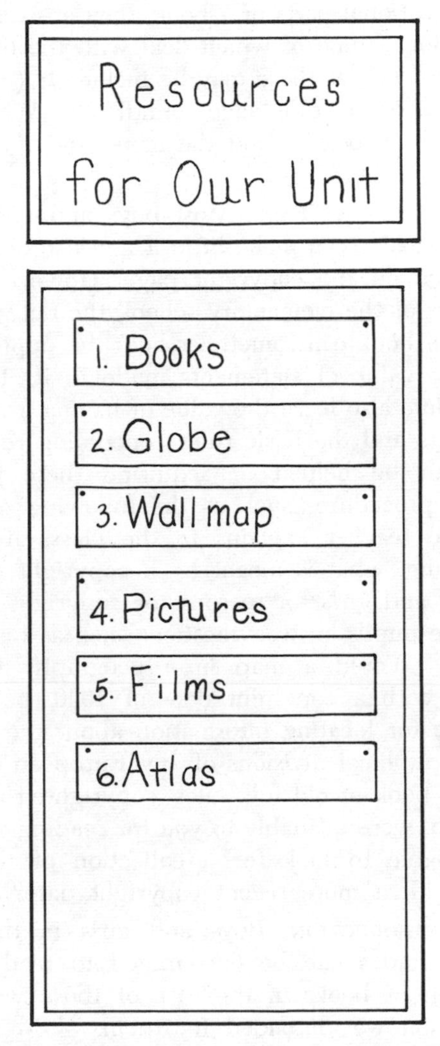

Figure 10.17 Chart of Usable Resources

The Title Page. Early in the elementary school the pupils can be referred to the title page in order to note where it is located and what is given on it. Their attention can be drawn to the title, the author, the publisher, and the address of the publisher. In the intermediate grades they may note the designation, if there is one, of the position(s) that the writer(s) hold(s). Information about the title page can often be acquired without much practice through procedures such as the following:

1. The pupils turn to the title page and through questions and comments by the teacher note where in the book the title page is found and what is given on it.

2. The teacher discusses with the class reasons for making accessible to the reader the information given on a title page.

3. After the boys and girls have studied several of the locational parts of a book, they answer a series of questions, some of which deal with the title page. Questions such as these may be included: (a) Where in a book is the title page found? (b) Where in a book do you look to find the name and the address of the publisher?

THE COPYRIGHT PAGE. Most boys and girls in the primary grades can make little if any use of information given on the copyright page. However, in the last years of the elementary school, the date of copyright of a book can sometimes help the pupils decide upon the value of statements made in it. They can at that time also learn the value of having a system of copyrights and the basic rules concerning copyrights. They can be helped in acquiring these learnings through procedures such as the following.

1. The teacher explains to the class, after brief questioning, what is meant by a copyright and asks the boys and girls for reasons for copyright laws.

2. The pupils answer questions such as the following: (a) Would a map in a geography book on Europe, with a copyright date of 1940, be a good reference for locating information about the present-day geographical divisions of any European country? (b) If a book of old folk tales, copyrighted about 20 years ago, were available to you for reading, would it be advisable to look for a collection of the same stories with a more recent copyright date?

THE INTRODUCTION. Boys and girls in the intermediate grades can be encouraged to read the introduction of books in the case of those where the introduction was intended for them.

THE TABLE OF CONTENTS. The pupils should be helped to realize that the table of contents can be very valuable in finding informatioin. They need to know that the table of contents (if there is one) is found near the front of a book; that it contains chapter headings (or other main divisions of the book, which at times are divided into chapters); that the chapters or other divisions are listed in the order of their appearance in the book; and that the page on which each chapter (or other division or subdivision) begins is given. They should acquire efficiency in using the table of contents in order to decide where to look for information on a given topic. To gain these learnings and abilities procedures such as the following can be used:

1. The boys and girls examine their textbooks to note which ones have a table of contents and how the divisions in each table of contents are arranged.

2. The boys and girls do an exercise in which they are timed as they locate information in a table of contents. Questions like these may be asked: (a) What is the title of the first story in the last part of this book? (b) On what page does [a specified story] begin?

3. The pupils examine the table of contents of a book in order to determine whether or not it is likely to contain information helpful for a given unit of study.

4. The boys and girls make a table of contents for a booklet that they are writing such as one on "Our Trips" or "Poems We [or I] Like."

THE INDEX. During the course of the elementary school boys and girls should study the indexes of books in which there are only main entries as well as some in which subdivisions of the main entries are found.

The following skills and abilities in using the index are some of the most significant ones for pupils to acquire: (1) ability to decide under what key word to look for information on a specified topic or question; (2) speed in finding an entry in an index; (3) skill in interpreting the various types of information given in an index, and (4) ability to make effective use of a reference in an index after it has been located.

1. Finding words arranged alphabetically. Basic to skill in using an index is facility in finding words that have been arranged alphabetically. Suggestions for doing so are included here under methods for acquiring skill in using an index, even though this ability is also needed for locating information in reference books.

Some ways in which boys and girls can be helped to acquire skill in finding words that are arranged alphabetically are as follows: (a) The teacher can display prominently in the room the letters of the alphabet in alphabetical order, so that the pupils can read them from their seats. (b) The boys and girls at times may say the alphabet in concert. (c) The pupils can indicate which of a series of words, either beginning with the same letter or with different letters, are in alphabetical order by writing *Yes* on a line if the series is in order and *No* if it is not, like:

walk, ring, sing ....
sun, sit, sat. ....

(d) Pupils may arrange series of words such as the following alphabetically by placing a *1* to the left of the first word in alphabetical order, a *2* to the left of word that comes second, etc.

.... baby
.... apple
.... chicken
.... fox.

2. Deciding upon key words. Skill in deciding upon key words is needed for finding information efficiently in an index as well as in reference books of many kinds. Here are a few suggestions for helping boys and girls develop skill in determining under what entry words they would be likely to find information they want. (a) If the boys and girls know the term *noun,* it should be explained to them that in indexes and reference books other than the dictionary, the entry words are nouns. (b) The boys and girls can draw a line under the word in parentheses (in an exercise) which would be the most likely one to be found as entry word of help in answering a given question. An example of an item of such an exercise is: "Were the French or the British victorious at the Battle of Quebec? (French, British, battle, Quebec).

3. Developing other skills. Other skills important for efficient use of the index can be developed through procedures such as these:

After the boys and girls have learned how to use other than main entry words in an index, they can be given a timed exercise, in which they are instructed to find the answer by consulting the index in one of their textbooks. Questions like these may be included: (a) On what page is a map given showing the land included in the Northwest Territory? (b) On how many consecutive pages is information given about the Gold Rush of 1849?

The boys and girls can make a chart giving significant information about the index of a book. One point that may be included is the fact that the index is found toward the back. Another is that entries are arranged alphabetically.

The pupils can be given help in understanding the employment of the various punctuation marks and abbreviations commonly used in an index.

The boys and girls can make an index for a class or individual booklet they have written.

Locating Information in the Dictionary

The following are chief among the skills that boys and girls should acquire in using a dictionary: (1) the ability to locate entry words in the dictionary (which involves knowledge of the alphabet, ability to open the dictionary fairly close to the page on which the desired entry word is found, skill in using guide words, and knowledge of how to find a derived form if it is not given as an entry word); (2) power in comprehending, through use of the dictionary, the appropriate meanings of words that the pupils are likely to meet in their reading or conversation (which involves understanding the various ways in which the dictionary gives information on the meaning of a word and skill in choosing the appropriate meaning of a word in relation to its context); (3) skill in determining the pronunciation of words (which involves information about syllables as well as information as to how the accent is marked and how to interpret diacritical markings and phonetic respellings); (4)

Courtesy of the Darien, Connecticut, Public Schools

Figure 10.18 The Dictionary, a Key to Discovery

ability to find out how words are spelled (which involves considerable background learnings); and (5) knowledge of various types of information given in the introductory and the last parts of the dictionary and skill in finding the information needed.

Following is a list of rather specific suggestions to implement the more general ones already presented for helping boys and girls locate information in a dictionary.

1. The boys and girls are helped to learn the value of guide words. The teacher may ask them to explain why they think guide words are called that.

2. The pupils indicate which of a series of words they can expect to find on a page in a dictionary in which specified guide words are given. For example, in an exercise like the following they can write *Yes* on the line to the left of a word if they expect to find it as an entry word between two words named as guide words for a given page and write *No* if it can not be found on that page:

Guide words: *droop, dry*

.... drink .... dull
.... drowsy .... drill.

3. To impress the boys and girls with the importance of finding the meaning of a word that best fits a sentence in which the word is used, the pupils can be given practice in supplying one of the meanings given in a dictionary as it is needed for each of a series of sentences in an exercise with items like the following:

"A stitch in time saves nine," is one of the *saws* that we memorized. (saw: a. a tool for cutting; b. a wise saying.)

4. The pupils can be directed to cross out the incorrect word, after consulting the dictionary if necessary, in sentences like the following:

The desks in the old schoolroom were (stationary, stationery).
What (advise, advice) did your father give you?

5. The boys and girls may write sentences using each of the different meanings of a word given in the dictionary.

6. The pupils may divide words into syllables and place the accent marks where they belong.

7. The pupils can pronounce a list of words like the following in which the placement of the accent determines the differentiation in pronunciation and then use the words in sentences given orally: *pro gress', prog'ress; con'tract, con tract'; rec'ord, re cord'.*

8. The pupils can be given an exercise the directions for which are: "If you know that a word begins with the sound given below, but do not know how to spell the word, under which letters or groups of letters should you look for it in the dictionary? Draw a circle around each letter or group of letters that shows your answer." Below these directions items like the following can be given:

the *f* sound: f, ph, gh, v, w
the *s* sound: s, z, c, t
the *un* sound: on, un, in, an.

Locating Information in Encyclopedias

There are several valuable sets of encyclopedias on the market designed, at least in part, for elementary-school boys and girls. Among the most commonly used of these are: *Childcraft* (especially helpful for use with primary-grade boys and girls); *Compton's Pictured Encyclopedia; Junior Book of Authors* (with biographical or autobiographical data on famous writers of books for children); *Junior Britannica; Our Wonderful World;* and *The World Book Encyclopedia.*

The boys and girls should learn how the information in reference books is arranged, what aids to the speedy finding of materials are given in each set of encyclopedias, and what method each uses for making reference to material in addition to that included with the main entry.

Following are listed some ways in which the teacher can help boys and girls learn to use encyclopedias effectively:

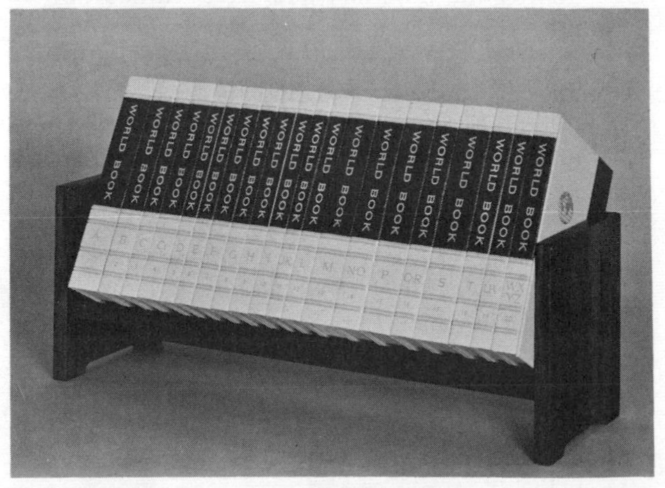

Courtesy of Field Enterprises

Figure 10.19 The Encyclopedia, an Aid to Learning

1. By asking the pupils to tell the number of the volume in which they would look for information on topics such as George Washington Carver; the Battle of New Orleans; the Declaration of Independence. (Beforehand the teacher can place on the chalkboard a diagram showing the volume guides of the set of encyclopedias that the class is using.)

2. By explaining to the boys and girls the system of cross references used in their set(s) of encyclopedias and providing them with practice in using cross-references.

3. By showing the class the filmstrip "How to Use an Encyclopedia," published by the Popular Science Publishing Company and distributed by the McGraw-Hill Book Company.

Locating Material in the Library

Boys and girls need to become familiar with the arrangement of books in their room, school, and public libraries. In the primary grades they can learn where to look for the picture file, where the picture dictionaries are kept, where *Childcraft* or other reference for their use are shelved, and where non-reference books of interest to them are placed. In the intermediate grades many skills related to locating books in the library should be taught. Among basic learnings that boys and girls should acquire before they leave the elementary school, providing they have library facilities for which such information is important, are: (1) the value and the arrangement of the card catalogue; (2) the three most common types of library cards — title card, author card, and subject card; (3) the arrangement of books on the shelves; and (4) the placement of magazines in the library.

To help the boys and girls learn more about the library and how to use it the teacher can:

1. Help the boys and girls make a card catalogue of books in their room library.

Courtesy of the Gary, Indiana, Public Schools

Figure 10.20 The School Library

2. Suggest that a committee make a large diagram showing the placement of books in the room, school, or children's section of the public library.

3. Have some pupils put on a skit showing how to behave in a library.

4. Give some of the pupils an opportunity to serve as librarian of the class library.

WHEN WE GET A BOOK FROM OUR LIBRARY

1. We find the book that we want.
2. We write our name on the card.
3. We hand the book and the card to the librarian in the correct way.
4. We say, "Thank you," when the librarian returns the book to us.

Figure 10.21 A Chart as an Aid in Getting a Book from the Library

DEVELOPING SKILL IN ORAL READING

When well done, oral reading can produce beneficial social and emotional results. The growth in literary appreciation that, under favorable conditions, children often make as they read orally or listen to others is probably one of the most significant values that can be gained from oral reading. Furthermore, as boys and girls read to each other, there often is created a stronger, more sympathetic relationship among the individuals of a group. These results are more likely to be attained in a true audience situation where no one reads silently while someone reads to him. The effect upon the reader of reading under such circumstances can also be beneficial as he realizes he is making a contribution, especially for the child who has not had much other opportunity to measure his achievement favorably.

Oral reading can also be of value in the following ways:

1. Through practice in oral reading some aspects of silent reading can be improved. Almost all the skills that are important to oral reading are needed in effective silent reading also. Consequently practice in one type of reading can have a salutary effect on the other. In fact, a word in print cannot be given orally unless the reader has recognized the word and by that very act has read it silently. Skill in word recognition, possession of a suitable reading vocabulary, and the ability to comprehend what is read are essentials of both oral and silent reading. Even rate of reading is a factor in both types, for the individual who cannot read as fast silently as he can say the words that he is reading is handicapped in oral reading.

2. Through oral reading, competencies and deficiencies of some types that occur in silent reading can be discovered. Difficulties such as the following, common to both oral and silent reading are often revealed: omission of letters, words, or phrases; insertion of letters, words, or phrases; substitution of letters, words, or phrases; skipping lines; repeating lines; phrasing so inadequately that it interferes with thought-getting.

Organization of the Program

One of the questions that is important when organizing the oral-reading program is the allotment of time. Factors in determining the proportionate time that should be spent on oral versus silent reading and the amount of time to be devoted to oral reading are: (1) the grade level, (2) the amount of time of the reading period actually spent in reading, (3) the amount of time spent in silent and oral reading during periods other than the reading period, (4) the amount of time spent in silent reading outside of school, (5) individual differences among boys and girls, including their past training and needs.

It is in the first and second grades that most children cannot read more rapidly silently than orally and therefore there is little danger at that time that much oral reading will have an unfavorable effect upon the rate of silent reading. However, the possibility should not be overlooked that even in beginning reading an undue amount of vocalization in silent reading may be caused by an overemphasis on oral reading.

The joy that boys and girls in the lower grades often receive from reading orally to their classmates and in listening to them read is another factor that ought not to be ignored when determining the emphasis to be placed on oral reading. A reason for mentioning the pupils' desire for considerable oral reading is that one argument for having less oral reading is the alleged boredom of the boys and girls during periods of oral reading. The observation of the writer in first grades has not been such as to substantiate this as a claim for less oral reading on that level.

Some teachers believe that after the boys and girls can read more rapidly silently than orally, there should be but little oral reading for fear that the rate of silent reading will be reduced. It is probably true that, in a situation requiring remedial attention because of a very slow rate of silent reading, it would be unwise to have the child do much oral reading until he has acquired a less plodding rate of silent reading.

Other considerations important in planning an oral-reading program are as follows.

1. There is a controversy as to whether or not non-oral reading should precede all oral reading during the stage of early instruction. Such procedure is advocated by John E. McDade. Some of the arguments that are given for a non-oral method of teaching beginning reading, by which the pupil's ability to read is tested by his power to get the thought without using oral reading, are: (a) Oral reading as a beginning method of instruction is likely to cause the reader to vocalize when he reads silently. (b) The child who learns to read by a non-oral method is less likely to develop poor eye movements and become a "word caller" than the one who learns, in part at least, by an oral method. (c) "Inner speech" or subvocalization, the practice of a reader mentally "saying" to himself the words he is reading silently, is encouraged by initial instruction in reading when the child reads orally. It is argued that thereby the rate of silent reading may be affected adversely. (d) The child who does not read orally during the period of beginning reading instruction is more likely to get the meaning of what he reads than is the one who does part of his reading at that time orally.

Arguments frequently advanced against any method of beginning reading instruction that excludes all oral reading are as follows: (a) Since the child has been communicating orally long before he begins to read, he should be allowed to make use of his ability in oral communication when he begins the intricate task of learning to read. (b) The teacher cannot readily tell whether a child recognizes all the words when he reads silently, even though the teacher is able to test the pupil's comprehension through means such as ascertaining the child's power to follow written directions and his ability to tell in his own words what he reads. (c) Vocalization seems to decrease without much difficulty in the case of most children by the time when they read more rapidly silently than orally. (d) Subvocalization possibly takes place in all silent reading, regardless of whether or not the reader has learned to read through an oral or a non-oral method of reading instruction. (e) If beginning reading is taught properly, comprehension is stressed in oral as well as in silent reading (f) There is the possibility that the seeming superiority of the non-oral over the oral method, claimed by Guy T. Buswell in his investigation, may have been due to reasons other than the differences in effectiveness between the oral and the non-oral approach. Facts such as enthusiasm and education of the teacher and the emphasis placed on reading under the experimental set-up may have kept that experiment like many others from being entirely scientific.

Although in the absence of conclusive scientific data opinion differs as to whether or not oral reading should be used with beginning readers before they acquire fluency in silent reading, it is the opinion of the writer that from the very beginning some time should be spent on both oral and silent reading.

2. *The effective oral reader must not only possess many of the silent reading skills but also additional competencies peculiar to oral reading.* One of these is correct pronunciation of words. While in silent reading the pupil must recognize the word and know its meaning, it is not essential that he know how to pronounce it. Many a reader does not know the pronunciation of a word he is reading. In fact, not infrequently a person who had repeatedly recognized a certain word when reading silently finds he did not even realize that he did not know its correct pronunciation until he was confronted with reading it orally to some one who could and would inform him of his error. Clear articulation, a pleasing and well-modulated voice, and contact with the audience are additional concerns of the oral reader. Furthermore, in oral reading thought-getting common to both oral and silent reading must be followed by thought-interpretation, for the responsibility of the oral reader is to reflect to his audience his own grasp of the meaning of a passage.

3. *There are likenesses and differences in the eye movements used in oral and in silent reading.* When an individual reaches the stage where he can perceive words more rapidly than he can say them, the silent reading rate exceeds the oral. The point at which the child can read material for many purposes more rapidly silently than orally is often reached some time between the middle of the second and the beginning of the third grade.

A term peculiar to oral reading is *eye-voice span.* By eye-voice span is meant the distance between the last word said and the last word recognized. It is the difference between where a person reads orally and where he reads silently. If a pupil reads aloud effectively the sentence "The little goats waited for their mother to come home," he will need to recognize words farther on in the sentence than the one he is pronouncing. Otherwise he is likely to be somewhat of a word-by-word reader. As he is saying, for example, the word *waited,* he may already have perceived all the words and comprehended their meaning through the word *mother.* While it is to the decided advantage of the oral reader to have an eye-voice span of several words, there is danger in having one that is too long. In the sentence given, if the eye-voice span is from the word *waited* through the word *home,* a reader may find that he needs to retrace part of that distance with his eyes because he may have forgotten some of the words he has seen before he is ready to say them. There is also danger that he will omit words or make substitutions if he allows his eyes to precede his voice by very far.

School Situations Involving Oral Reading

Oral reading can be done advantageously in a large variety of school situations involving purposes such as these.

1. Reading a poem or a story for the enjoyment of others
2. Reading the minutes of the meeting of a club
3. Reading to prove a point
4. Reading material to give information about a topic being studied
5. Reading part of a play preparatory to giving the part from memory
6. Reading lines for a puppet play
7. Participating in choral reading.

General Procedures

Here are some general procedures by means of which skill in oral reading can be developed:

1. *Through oral reading by the teacher.* Frequent oral reading to the class should continue throughout the elementary school. Through it boys and girls should get enjoyment, a greater appreciation of literature, and information. It can also serve as an example of good reading to the boys and girls. If it is to accomplish these purposes, the material read by the teacher must be interesting and on the pupils' level of comprehension. Furthermore, the teacher must read skillfully, exemplifying the various characteristics of an effective oral reader.

2. *Through audience reading lessons.* By the term *audience reading lessons* is meant the type of lesson in which boys and girls read for the enjoyment or information of the group, in a program set-up, materials that they have prepared carefully beforehand.

3. *Through silent reading.* While as a rule boys and girls should have the opportunity to read material silently or orally before they read it to the class, occasionally they should have the practice of reading orally without such preparation. One of the chief purposes of sight reading – oral reading without preparation – is the insight the teacher can get on the silent reading of the pupil. Sight reading for diagnostic purposes should as a rule be done when no one but the teacher serves as audience.

4. *Through choral reading.* For a discussion of choral reading the reader is referred to page 275.

Methods

Here are some specific suggestions for development of the following skills related to oral reading.

1. *Comprehending what is read orally and serving as interpreter to the audience.* Although some phases of the problem of comprehending what is read are alike in oral and silent reading, others are so different that special attention often needs to be given to their development in oral reading. Knowledge of the meaning of words, for example, is essential to both types. On the other hand skill in phrasing, also important to comprehension in both oral and silent reading, manifests itself differently in oral reading than in silent. Some pupils who seemingly have little or no difficulty in phrasing when reading silently show a marked deficiency in this respect in oral reading. In addition to comprehending the meaning of what the oral reader reads, he has the responsibility of serving as interpreter to his audience.

What has been said on preceding pages of this chapter about the improvement of comprehension in silent reading also applies, in general terms, to oral reading. Additional suggestions follow, in the form of pupil activities, for improving understanding as it is related to oral reading. Suggestions are also given for helping boys and girls develop in ability to serve as interpreters as they read orally.

Listening to the teacher read a sentence in correct phrasing and then repeating it

Noting the difference in clarity when a sentence is read with proper and with inadequate phrasing

Reading a selection orally in which the phrases have been marked by the teacher

Reading a selection orally or listening to someone else read it in order to answer questions the teacher has asked before the oral reading

Making a chart on which are listed points a reader should observe in order to interpret effectively what he is reading

Choosing material suitable for oral reading

Checking with the audience as to whether they were able to comprehend the meaning of what the pupil read and noting comments made by members of the audience.

2. *Pronouncing words correctly and enunciating clearly.* Help can be given to the pupils in pronunciation by making provisions for them to participate in activities such as the following:

Listing reasons why correct pronunciation is important

Getting help, if necessary, in pronouncing words before reading orally

Finding out from the teacher or others in the group whether they mispronounced words as they read orally or whether they were careless in enunciation

Learning to make use of diacritical markings and phonetic respellings so that by themselves the pupils can decipher "new" words

Learning how to find the number of syllables in a word by consulting the dictionary

Studying the relationship between failure to use various speech organs effectively and poor enunciation

Telling which one of various pairs of words ending in *ing, ed,* and *t* is enunciated correctly, as the teacher gives the words in pairs such as these: *running, runnin'; crep, crept*

Giving words that rhyme, in pairs, with words the endings of which are often slurred over in speech, such as *yellow* (*jello*), *again* (*Ben*).

3. *Using the voice effectively.* Some ways in which the pupils can set about to develop appropriateness and variation of tone, pitch, force, and rate in oral reading are as follows:

Listening to material intentionally read with monotony of tone, pitch, force, and rate in order to note how unsatisfactory such reading is

Reading material to show various moods through change in voice qualities

Deciding which words in a sentence are particularly significant within their context and then reading the sentence to emphasize those words

Answering questions asked by the teacher about sentences the pupils are reading so that emphasis on a certain word or group of words is desirable when giving the answer. For example, the question "Did John go home with his mother?" could be answered by saying, "He went with his *father*," or "He went *down town* with his mother," or "He went home with *my* mother," given in such a way as to place emphasis on the words in italics in those sentences.

Reading a sentence like the following several times, each time with the emphasis on a different word, as indicated by the word in italics:

(a) Did *you* walk home with your mother?
(b) Did you *walk* home with your mother?
(c) Did you walk *home* with your mother?
(d) Did you walk home with *your* mother?
(e) Did you walk home with your *mother?*

4. *Handling the material being read effectively.* To learn to handle a book or magazine or papers effectively when reading orally, the pupil may do the following:

Take part in a skit in which first a pupil handles the material awkwardly while reading and then handles it with grace.

Draw up a list of suggestions for holding a book or a magazine or papers while reading orally.

Make illustrations demonstrating how material should be handled while a person is reading.

5. *Being at ease when reading orally.* Sometimes it is desirable to have the pupils divided into small groups so that a child who might be bothered if he had a large audience will be more at ease if he has some practice in reading to a smaller number of listeners. The following are ways in which, with a sympathetic audience, readers can develop a feeling of ease when reading orally:

Reading orally often

Having real purpose for reading a selection orally

Knowing the selection to be read well

Making use of constructive criticism, with emphasis on the points that need improvement and on those that are well done.

6. *Being sensitive to the audience.* Development of sensitivity toward the audience is in part the product of having in mind a bona fide purpose for reading to them. Other suggestions for the teacher for stimulating development of sensitivity to the audience are:

Help the learner realize that since he takes someone's time when reading orally, he is under obligation to make it worthwhile for the listener.

Have the reader ask the audience, at times, what he can do to make his reading more enjoyable.

Suggest that the reader occasionally ask his audience what, if anything, he is doing as he reads that pleases the audience in particular. Points such as these may be mentioned: (a) looking at the audience occasionally, (b) reading so all can hear, (c) showing that he enjoys the oral reading.

FURTHER CONSIDERATIONS

In this last section of this chapter, a few problems are discussed that have bearing on helping the child acquire the skills in reading that have been considered in preceding sections.

Helping the Retarded Reader

Since in Chapter 3 the general principles for helping boys and girls retarded in the language arts are discussed, here only those points about retardation are brought out that have some special application to learning to read. They deal with: (1) causes of retardation in reading, (2) school organization for helping the retarded reader, and (3) methods for teaching the retarded reader.

Causes of Retardation in Reading. Among the causes of retardation, the following are important:

1. *Low intelligence.* It is to be noted that low intelligence is by no means the usual cause of retardation in reading as the term *retardation* is here used. (It applies, as here used, to those readers performing below the level of their grade who can be helped to become better readers.) Of the number of backward readers who come for clinical help a large percentage have an intelligence quotient above one hundred. Furthermore, according to the definition of *retardation* given, only those backward readers of low intelligence who would profit by additional help or special methods are considered in this chapter.

2. *Unsatisfactory conditions in the home.* What are often thought of as unsatisfactory conditions in the home may be the cause of retardation — conditions characterized by lack of interest in reading and poor facilities for reading. However, often the retarded reader comes from homes where reading is encouraged and where there are highly desirable physical facilities for reading, with an abundance of books, quiet needed, and time provided. In such homes, pressuring the child to become a good reader may have the opposite of the desired effect, especially when he feels resentment toward those who are possibly overanxious about his learning to read.

3. *A poor classroom atmosphere.* A classroom in which authoritarianism prevails, in which boys and girls do not feel happy with one another, in which there is no true interest in books, is not likely to encourage reading.

4. *A paucity of desirable reading materials.* Although no amount of appropriate reading material is sufficient reason for some boys and girls to learn to read on their possible level of achievement, a lack of it may be one of the contributing causes of retardation.

5. *Personality difficulties.* Personality problems may be either cause or effect of backwardness in reading. Perhaps too often the teacher has somewhat excused himself from blame for difficulties in reading on the assumption that problems of personality have been the cause of lack of a child's interest in reading. Undoubtedly at times they are. Even then, however, the teacher is not necessarily blameless since he may have contributed to the personality defects in that he has not dealt with them adequately. Furthermore, the correlation between personality problems and lack of reading ability may be due to the fact that the child who is not learning to read effectively develops a personality difficulty because he is having reading problems.

6. *Physical disabilities and health problems.* The child with uncorrected vision or hearing defects may find himself severely handicapped in reading. While sometimes boys and girls who have poor health are avid readers, low vitality, resulting from malnutrition, lack of sleep, or other factors may be the reason for inability to concentrate and for lack of interest in reading, with resultant retardation.

7. *Inadequate methods of teaching.* Poor teaching methods frequently seem to be the cause of retardation. Often they seem to be traceable to gaps in the developmental reading program under which the individual has been taught or to other program deviations from accepted sound principles of teaching.

School Organization for Helping the Retarded. Common organizational plans whereby the retarded reader is helped are: (1) referral to a reading clinic, (2) help from a special reading teacher not within a clinical set-up, (3) schoolwide special grouping according to reading needs, and (4) attention by the classroom teacher.

1. *Referral to a reading clinic.* As a rule, only the larger school systems believe they can afford a read-

ing clinic. Clinics vary greatly in organization. Frequently there is in charge of a reading clinic at least one specialist in working with children who are retarded in reading and one or more other teachers as well as one or more secretaries. The nonspecialist teachers in a clinic sometimes are on a rotating basis, each serving in the clinic for only one school year. The aim of such a plan often is that thereby an increasing number of classroom teachers within the school system will learn how to deal with the retarded readers in their own classrooms.

Equipment within a clinic varies greatly. Ideally a large number of devices for diagnosis (including a goodly supply of the better up-to-date standardized reading tests) are part of the equipment. Materials – mechanical and nonmechanical – for use with boys and girls as teaching devices are available in large numbers. Such equipment includes games and drill materials, basal textbooks in reading and in the content areas, supplementary reading materials from the content areas, and many books and magazines rich in interest for diversified and extensive voluntary independent reading. At times the clinic also serves as a professional center on reading for the classroom teacher. In those instances it may contain professional books on the teaching of reading, lists of suggestions for teaching the retarded reader, and copies of curricula emphasizing good developmental and remedial reading programs.

In some clinical set-ups a pupil referred to the clinic remains there throughout the school day for as many weeks or months as seems desirable. In such cases his daily program in the clinic ideally includes all types of activities that seem important for the all-around development of the child. In many school systems in which there is a reading clinic, however, the pupil comes to the clinic for only part of each day and spends the rest of his time in his regular classroom.

2. *Help from the special reading teacher.* Some school systems with a reading clinic employ one or more teachers to serve as reading specialists from whom the classroom teacher can get help in dealing with the problems of retardation in reading. In addition to responsibilities as consultant, such a teacher is often expected to do actual teaching of children in need of special help. Usually each referent is with the special teacher only part of each school day, per-

Courtesy of the Hamilton, Ohio, Public Schools

Figure 10.22 Help with Reading

haps for an hour or an hour and one-half, while the rest of the time he is in his own home room. The value of such an organizational plan depends to a large extent on the cooperation between the special teacher and the classroom teacher who share the responsibility of a smooth transition for the child from his work in the special-reading situation to his regular classroom activities.

3. *Schoolwide grouping according to reading needs.* Some schools are set up so that the pupils throughout the elementary school are grouped on a schoolwide basis according to their reading needs. In a few such schools all reading classes meet during a specified part of the day. Instead of each teacher having his home-room pupils in his reading class, he may be teaching only a few of his own with the majority coming from other rooms, all reading on the level which has been assigned to him. A shortcoming of this plan is the fact that some children may be embarrassed if they need to join a reading class made up primarily of pupils considerably younger. To offset this difficulty such a division into groups can be made in only part of the school such as the primary or the intermediate grades. Even if the plan is carried out on both of these levels, children from the intermediate grades may not be grouped with children of the primary grades. A second difficulty is inherent in any plan of departmentalization in reading, namely that of establishing unity between the work in reading and the rest of the school program. Through wise planning, however, this problem can be solved in part.

4. *Attention by the classroom teacher.* Many educators believe that the key to the problem of the retarded reader is the classroom teacher. They think that unless the child presents problems with which the regular teacher is unable to cope, it is best for him to be taught reading by his own teacher. Various plans for adapting instruction to the needs of the individual are advocated, among them individualized reading and the nongraded primary or the nongraded elementary school unit of organization. (For a discussion of individualized reading the teacher is referred to page 222, and for a discussion of nongraded plans of organization he is referred to page 28.)

METHODS. In general the methods for teaching the retarded reader do not differ in kind from those for teaching the nonretarded reader. However, special cautions should be observed by the teacher working with a retarded reader, some of which are discussed in Chapter 3. Additional general suggestions are given following.

1. Much of the work with the retarded reader should be done as he reads interesting material on his level.

2. With some pupils experience charts, which the teacher writes at the pupil's dictation, should be used as part of the reading material. (A discussion of experience charts is given on page 184.)

3. Some of the mechanical devices for improvement of reading seem to be helpful in guiding the reading of some retarded readers when used with other methods. (Mechanical devices are discussed on page 205.)

4. Some teachers have reported considerable success with retarded readers through use or through adaptations of a method advocated by Grace Fernald.[4] It has often been referred to as the tracing method, for when the pupil begins using this method he traces with his finger each word the teacher has written for him in large letters. As he traces it, he says the word to himself, part by part. As he thereupon writes it from memory, he also vocalizes the word. After comparison of his attempt with the teacher's copy, if he has made an error he takes note of the correction he should make and then again writes the word from memory. Again he compares his writing with that of the teacher. In later stages of the use of the method the child may omit the step of tracing. Often the words selected for use are those the pupil needs in reading experience charts he has helped plan, in labeling items, or in writing other messages. Many teachers using this method encourage the reader to keep a file in which each word is recorded on a separate card, maybe filed alphabetically according to the first letter, for use in independent or semi-independent writing.

The Fernald method should not be spurned, without trial, by the teacher working with the retarded reader who has been unable to gain results from other less laborious and time-consuming procedures.

Guiding Growth in Reading of the Gifted

The gifted child undoubtedly has not received the attention in the American school system that he deserves. For general suggestions for helping him achieve in accordance with his ability, the reader is referred to page 32. Following are additional suggestions.

1. The gifted child may not need all the systematic training in reading the average child requires, in terms of the development of skill in word recognition, comprehension of what he reads, and the like. However, care needs to be taken that it is not erroneously assumed that he is not in need of help with a given skill without evidence to substantiate the assumption. In many instances the best procedure is

[4]Grace M. Fernald, *Remedial Techniques in Basic School Subjects.* McGraw-Hill Book Company, 1943.

not to omit guidance in the development of a skill but to provide help in performing more difficult aspects of the skill than the average child can master. For example, if a gifted child already knows how to use the index of a book, he may, unlike the other children, be helped to use *The Reader's Guide to Periodical Literature.*

2. The gifted child should be supplied with reading materials on his level of reading comprehension. Some teachers make the mistake of encouraging the child to read widely on the same level as the average child instead of challenging him to read on higher levels. A gifted reader in the fifth grade probably should not spend all of his reading time on books like *The Singing Tree* by Kate Seredy, on the level of the average fifth-grade child, however good such books may be. Often he should be reading more advanced material such as *Oliver Twist* by Charles Dickens, *The Last of the Mohicans* by James Fennimore Cooper, or *Treasure Island* by Robert Louis Stevenson.

3. Much of the reading instruction of the gifted child may advisedly be in the form of individualized reading. (For a discussion of individualized reading the reader is referred to page 222.)

4. While the gifted child can at times be expected to perform activities primarily for the benefit of others in the class rather than chiefly for his own development, he should not be asked frequently to play the role of teacher by helping classmates who have difficulties with reading. It is wise to have each child – gifted or underprivileged or average – give a limited amount of time for the welfare of the group, for one of the objectives of the modern elementary school is to help develop boys and girls who will be willing to work for the good of others. However, it is unfair to the gifted pupil to expect him to do much tutoring. The superior child's time for reading should be spent chiefly in the development of his own skills. Furthermore, as a rule, the help that a retarded reader needs is expert guidance, not some that can be given satisfactorily by any one of his peers no matter how gifted the classmate may be.

Guiding Growth in Reading the Content Subjects

One of the persistent problems for the intermediate-grade teacher in teaching reading is that of helping boys and girls learn to read effectively in the content areas. Even in the primary grades the problem is recognizable. One reason for difficulty in reading content subjects is that some of the pupils in an upper-primary grade or an intermediate-grade class are below average in their general reading ability. Another is that some who have little or no difficulty when reading a textbook for their grade or when reading books of fiction on their level are nevertheless considerably handicapped when reading in the content areas such as science, mathematics, art, and the social studies.

GUIDELINES. As the teacher plans his program for helping boys and girls improve in reading in the content areas, these are guidelines that should be considered.

1. Every teacher of a content subject should be a teacher of reading in that subject.

2. The teacher of the content subjects should have goals in mind in relation to skills to be acquired in reading the material in that area.

3. The program in the improvement of skills for the reading of material in a content subject should, in many cases, include: (a) presentation lessons in which methods of acquiring skills in reading materials in that area are discussed and illustrated; (b) practice exercises, if necessary, in which specific practice is provided for perfecting a specified skill; and (c) periods in which incidental, but not accidental, application is made of the skills when reading materials in that subject area.

4. Means should be provided whereby every pupil can evaluate his growth in reading materials in the content subject.

5. The reading program involving reading in the content subjects should help stimulate the pupils so that "on their own" they will enjoy reading in the content areas.

PROVISIONS FOR GUIDANCE. Special problems in reading in the content subjects exist even though there is probably not one single problem in reading in those fields that is unique to them. The problems are special only insofar as they occur more commonly than in some other reading or as they differ in the best treatment required for their solution. Four of these difficulties relate to vocabulary, retention, cause-effect relationship, and critical reading.

1. *Vocabulary.* When reading in the social studies, boys and girls are likely to meet a fairly large number of new words. While new words or new meanings for familiar words are introduced in all reading material intended to aid in vocabulary development, the proportion of new words in a social studies or science textbooks is likely to be considerably greater than it is in the reading textbooks or in fiction that the boys and girls are reading. Words such as *products, treaty, industrial* are unfamiliar to many pupils when they leave the primary grades. When a large number of words like these are used in a reading selection, there is likely to be trouble unless the author explains the meaning or unless the teacher helps the pupils add these words to their vocabulary.

Probably a still more confusing vocabulary problem has to do with the number of words introduced for which the reader already knows one meaning, but not the one needed in the context. The meaning that the average fourth-grade child associates with the word *belt* is not one that will be of much value in comprehending a reference to a heat belt.

The following are suggestions to help boys and girls with vocabulary problems.

> Write on the chalkboard difficult words in the context of sentences with built-in meanings such as "The *source* of the Mississippi River is in Lake Itasca, where it begins as a very narrow stream." Then ask the pupils to read the sentence to see if they can tell what the underlined word means.
>
> Before the boys and girls read a selection, explain or ask a pupil to explain a word unknown to some or show a picture that illustrates the word.
>
> Have the children make a chart of words related to the unit currently being studied. In a unit on Mexico, for example, words or expressions such as *fiesta, market day, adobe, serape, gorge* can be included in the chart and frequent reference can be made to them until mastery is achieved.
>
> Encourage pupils to construct things that make clearer the meaning of a word like *drawbridge, moat, portage.*
>
> Plan a "quiz program" with the questions and directions limited to testing knowledge of the vocabulary of a given unit of work.

2. *Remembering what is read.* The need for retention when reading in the content areas often presents special problems. When a pupil is reading from a reading textbook, in which frequently a selection is designed for only one sitting, there is often little reason for him to try to remember what he has read for any length of time. This situation, however, does not, as a rule, prevail when a child reads from a social studies, science, or health textbook. Unless he can remember many facts that he read on a given day, he may be almost hopelessly confused when he continues reading in the same book on subsequent days.

Special attention needs to be given to names of persons and places as well as of events, such as the Missouri Compromise or the Bill of Rights, which frequently occur on pages of a textbook in the social studies. Many pupils need help in determining which names are important enough to remember in terms of their purpose for reading.

In science and mathematics there are also problems in retention somewhat unique to those areas. The generalizations presented in science often are a source of difficulty. The problem is due in part to the fact that many boys and girls have not learned to recognize generalizations as such when they are stated in written form. Sometimes, too, even when the pupils recognize a generalization as a statement of importance, they so little understand the meaning of it that retention is poor. Inability to see clearly in science material the relationship of points that together form the basis for the generalization itself may make both comprehension and retention a problem. At times lack of clarity of statement in a book is a cause of the difficulty.

In mathematics there also are special problems in recall that sometimes are the source of error. Immediate recall is necessary in all problem solving. The fact that exact recall is essential for the correct solution of problems is often a cause of difficulty for pupils who have not had practice in noting carefully what information is given. Permanent recall also plays an important role in many phases of mathematics. The pupil who, for instance, learns that three feet equal one yard must remember exactly how many feet are in a yard.

Here are a few suggestions for the teacher as he tries to help his pupils improve their retention when reading in content areas:

> Have the pupils make a list of points that are important to remember in a given selection for a stated purpose.
>
> Have the pupils indicate which of a series of details contribute to a stated reason for reading a selection.
>
> Emphasize the importance of frequent recall at well-spaced intervals.

3. *Cause-effect relationship.* The ability to comprehend the relationship between cause and effect when reading in the social studies is sometimes lacking in boys and girls who have no difficulty in understanding the often more easily grasped relationship to which reference is made in books of fiction or in reading textbooks. Even though an author indicates that a certain event figures as a cause of war, an immature reader unfamiliar with the intricacies of causes of war may fail to grasp the significance of the event or the complexity of contributing factors. Another difficulty is that pupils may assume that there is a cause-effect relationship between events simply because one occurred shortly before the other. Furthermore, they are at times prone to affix such

a relationship to two events that are the result of a common cause.

One way in which to help boys and girls understand causal relationships is to have them explain in what ways one event precipitated another. They can also at times be asked to surmise what might have been the turn of events if a given event had not occurred in the manner in which it took place. The boys and girls can also be encouraged to make a list of cause-effect relationships stated as such in materials that they are reading in the content subjects.

4. *Reading critically.* Another reason for confusion in the reading of the content subjects is that in many instances pupils have not developed sufficient skill in evaluating what they read. Much more than while reading material in reading textbooks, they are confronted with the need of asking questions such as: (a) Is the writer qualified to write on his subject? (b) Did an interested or disinterested person make this statement?

Adapting Instruction to Individual Differences. What can be done to meet the problem of individual differences in reading in the social studies and in science? For a partial answer to this question the reader is referred to page 28, where general suggestions for adapting instruction in all areas are given. Following are a few suggestions for the teacher as they apply rather specifically to the problem in the case of the social studies and science.

1. Find simpler reading on the same subject for the retarded reader and more difficult material for the more able.

2. Rewrite very simply some of the material written in too complicated form for the retarded reader.

3. Give the retarded reader an alternate assignment not involving reading or involving less or simpler reading while the other pupils do their reading assignment. The recommendation of making a non-reading assignment should not be followed often for the retarded reader is probably in more need of suitable practice in reading than the excellent one.

Have a pupil practice before class a short selection which he will read orally during class time.

5. While the rest of the class is reading a selection silently, give individual or small-group help to retarded readers.

Use of a Basal Textbook

Although it is not essential that a textbook series be used in a systematic program of reading instruction, it is usual. Suggestions for use of a basal reader are found in various parts of this chapter. Furthermore, in Chapter 14 is given an illustrative teaching plan showing how a basal reader can be used effectively. (See page 314.) Consequently here only a few additional comments for consideration in connection with a basal series are given.

Courtesy of the Wichita, Kansas, Public Schools

Figure 10.23 Auditory Aids to Learning to Read

1. *Choose a good basal textbook.* To make a wise choice is not such a difficult task these days when a growing number of publishing companies have very good series of textbooks on the market. (For a list of some the reader is referred to page 327.) Points such as these should be considered when making the selection:

Reputation of author and/or publisher
Format of book including pictures, type, general attractiveness
Interest value of the content
Educational value of the content
Supplementary aids for the pupil such as workbooks and books for independent or semi-independent reading
Teachers' guidebooks, with special attention in the lower grades in particular, on the point of view regarding the development of skills in word recognition
Continuity of the series
Price of the series
Date of publication.

2. *Make use of the teachers' guidebook.* It is not recommended that the guidebook be followed slavishly. Writers of teachers' manuals include more suggestions, as a rule, than they themselves advocate any one teacher follow. Furthermore, it is the well-founded hope that the suggestions given may stimu-

late the teacher to think of others adapted specifically to the needs and interests of the boys and girls in a particular class.

Unless textbooks in reading are in the form of supplementary books for the series, they are not intended for rapid storybook type of reading. With most pupils basal textbooks should be used as a basis for development of the various reading skills characteristic of the effective reader. To be sure, some advanced readers who possess the skills that can ordinarily be taught while studying the material of a reading textbook should be excused from detailed emphasis on these skills recommended for the average or below-average reader. In fact, they may be excused from reading the textbook in any fashion.

3. *Collect the textbooks in reading at the end of each reading class or upon the completion of each independent reading assignment.* This precaution should be taken so that boys and girls are not tempted to continue reading in the textbooks parts that will be studied later. Such earlier reading can later interfere with the optimum use of the class period in which pages that some pupils have already read silently are studied. To tell a pupil that he may keep his book in his desk but that he should not read ahead in it does not assure that each child will follow the instruction. It may be a recommendation for the book, though not for the extent of obedience to regulations by the teacher, that a selection is so enticing that in spite of an order to the contrary the pupil reads ahead during spare time.

4. *Do not, as a rule, ask boys and girls to read a selection in a reader during a study period preceding a reading class in which that selection will be discussed.* To get the maximum benefit out of the textbook, it is recommended that usually the introduction to the work be done during the reading class. Assignments for the study period can then be follow-up work. Such assignments may include: (a) finishing reading a selection started in class and answering questions on it, (b) illustrating some of the new words learned in the selection, (c) doing work in the consumable book accompanying the series. (In the case of *The Macmillan Readers* where the consumable books are preparatory to the reading in the textbook – after proper introduction to the work in these preparatory books – the pupils may do the work in the consumable books during independent work periods. These work periods would then need, of course, to precede the periods in which the work in the hardback books of the series will be done.)

5. *Break up the reading selection for a day into several parts as a rule, and give appropriate help before and after reading each part.* While there is admittedly a need at times for consecutive reading without interruptions for boys and girls in the elementary school, economical use of the teacher's time usually requires the pupils do the long uninterrupted reading during independent work periods. When the teacher is available to help the boys and girls, it is desirable that active help be given in terms of possible problems of reading each of the several parts into which the reading for the class period has been divided. These parts may range from a line or two in the primary grades to several pages in the intermediate grades.

Individualized Reading

Accepted beyond question by specialists in the field of elementary-school reading is the fact that reading should be individualized. Argument is only in relation to the extent of individualization and to the methods to be followed.

In a sense, there is nothing new about the practice of adapting the program in reading to individual differences and of including in this adaptation much opportunity for individual programs of reading. Effective teachers of reading have long tried to give pupils a share in the selection of materials that they would read on an individualized basis. However, usually they have thought of this program of individualized reading as but part of the total reading program, supplementary or complementary to the regular developmental program in reading, as a rule with a reading textbook basic to the program.

Individualized Reading, as the term is currently used by its advocates, refers to something other than a program supplementary or complementary to a basal reading program. It is recommended by them as *the* basal reading program in which each individual through a process of self-selection of reading materials determines his materials for reading. Help with the skills of reading is, in such a program, presumably given when the pupil needs it.

On the credit side of Individualized Reading – with scientific evidence inconclusive – is the fact that with capable teachers who have thoroughly studied plans for such a program, the results may often seem outstanding in terms of the atmosphere that pervades the classroom and the type of readers produced. However, such an enthusiasm can also exist when boys and girls are given ample opportunity to do worthwhile – in part self-selective – independent reading and still retain the benefits of systematic instruction in a program in which a basal textbook is used. The alleged superiority of results may not be over the better basal reading programs or excellent use of them.

The reader is cautioned to note that there is much variation in the systems of so-called *Individualized Reading,* even when the words are spelled with capital letters (to denote the recent interpretation of the term). Before one argues for or against Individualized Reading, one should state clearly for or against which form of it one is arguing.

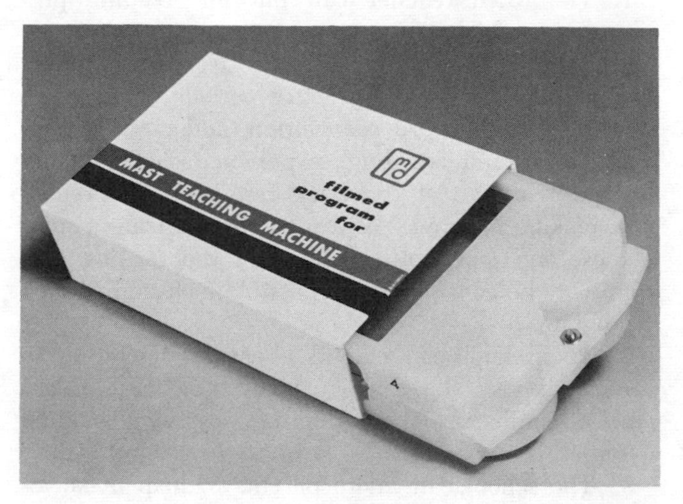

Courtesy of Mast Development Company

Figure 10.24 A Program on Film for Use with Mast Teaching Machine

Programed Learning

"Can the elementary-school teacher make effective use of programed learning when guiding boys and girls toward growth in reading?" is a question of current concern. Before venturing an answer to that question, let us note briefly what programed learning is.

Programed materials, if well constructed, usually possess these characteristics:

1. The material typically is produced in a series of small units called *frames.*
2. The content of the frames is arranged sequentially to insure a good order of learning.
3. The materials are tested and graded on levels of difficulty.
4. The materials are designed to be self-teaching.
5. The materials are self-evaluating. The pupil can check his own responses immediately upon completion.
6. The pupil can proceed at his own rate of learning.

Some companies have produced teaching machines to be used with programed materials. While engaged in programed learning by means of a teaching machine, a pupil sits near such a so-called machine and operates it according to instructions given to him orally or written into the program. However, teaching machines are by no means essential to programing. The programs can be written on cards, sheets of paper, or in consumable or nonconsumable books.

So far programs for reading have consisted chiefly of developmental or practice-type material. Objective-type questions based on the material are asked. True-false statements and multiple-choice responses have been used extensively. Furthermore, the programs have dealt primarily with the more mechanical skills of reading. Phonic exercises, work on structural analysis, skill in locating materials, work on factual comprehension seem to lend themselves better to programing than does work of the more interpretative types. Little has been done, it seems, with "reading between the lines" and with "reading beyond the lines" – aspects of comprehension that are highly significant but much more difficult than factual data to be tested

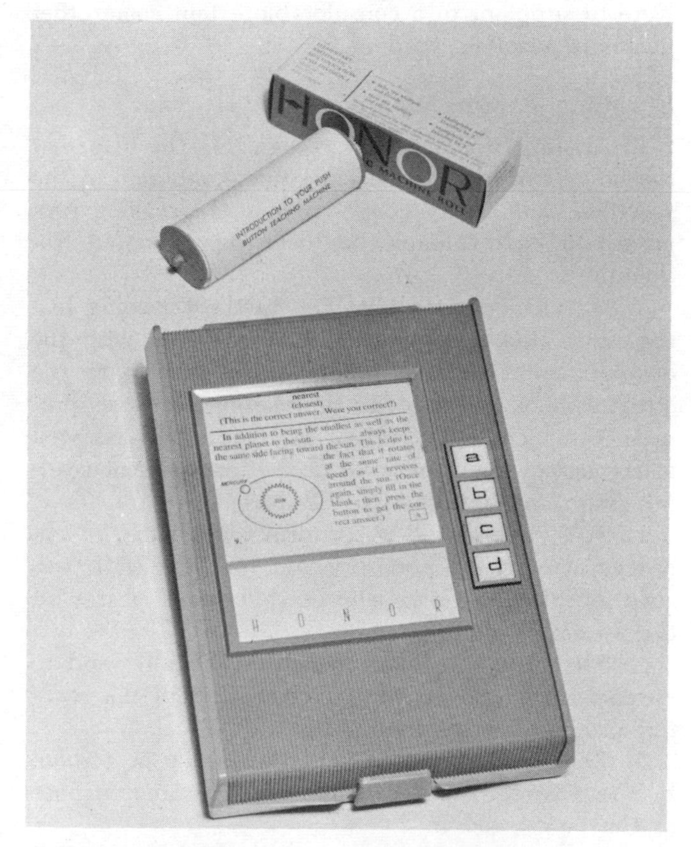

Courtesy of Honor Products Company

Figure 10.25 A Push Button Teaching Machine

by a device such as programed learning. To be sure, more can be done in programed learning than has been to develop skills such as the ability to predict outcomes or the ability to arrive at generalizations, for objective questions can be devised to test some aspects of these abilities. However, since to many matters of interpretation there is no one single acceptable answer and since discussion is often very desirable when determining the answers to thought questions, something beyond programed learning needs to be provided in the development of such competencies.

To answer the question "Can the elementary-school make effective use of programed learning when guiding boys and girls toward growth in reading?" the following responses can be made.

1. The elementary-school teacher will do well to look into the matter of programed learning, preferably if feasible, participating in the preparation of materials in addition to using some commercial programs.

2. Since the type of skills included rather extensively in programed learning in reading is limited chiefly to the more mechanical aspects of reading, it would seem that there is need of radical revision of the concept of programed learning, it is hoped, if it were to supplant to a considerable extent some other means of teaching reading.

Enrolling Parents as Helpers

Increasingly the school is recognizing the help that the home can give to the educational program of the school. That parents' cooperation in the reading program can be invaluable has been demonstrated frequently.

WHAT THE SCHOOLS CAN DO. In the following listing are included suggestions in connection with the developmental reading skills and in relation to the attainment of objectives of the reading readiness program – which is the subject of Chapter 9 – as well as the achievement of goals of the independent reading program considered in Chapter 11.

1. The superintendent or principal, with the cooperation of the supervisory and teaching staff, can send out letters or brochures describing phases of the reading program.

2. The classroom teacher can periodically send to parents a bulletin highlighting activities of the reading program of his room.

3. Letters to the parents of the pupils in a room by the classroom teacher can serve the same purpose as that suggested in 2.

4. Programs at parent-teacher meetings can deal with various phases of the teaching of reading such as: (a) the place of phonics, (b) aims and activities of the reading-readiness period, (c) recent trends in the teaching of reading, (d) the place of oral reading, (e) the program of recreational reading.

5. Parent conferences can emphasize a child's achievement in reading.

6. Teachers can recommend books or articles on the teaching of reading of particular value to parents. (A few references of this type are given in Chapter 15.)

7. The room teacher can put on "reading programs" in which, in a teaching-learning situation, various types of reading activities are demonstrated. Presentation lessons and practice periods for development of skills in word recognition, audience reading, constructing and "reading" experience charts, taking a silent-reading test to check rate and comprehension, making a "movie" of a story, dramatizing a story – these and many other phases of the reading program may be considered for possible inclusion in such a program.

8. The school can extend a cordial invitation to parents to visit the school at any time and, if desirable, emphasize the value of observing reading activities.

9. The school can invite parents to help make instructional materials, such as charts and word cards, and to help, under some circumstances, combine into a whole the children's work on murals, class notebooks, books of poems, and the like.

10. The teacher can explain and demonstrate to parents how they can help the child become a more effective reader.

WHAT PARENTS CAN DO. Parents are interested in knowing how they can help. Some ways are suggested under the topic "What the Schools Can Do." Other suggestions are here listed. The parent can:

1. Serve as an audience to the child for oral reading practice.

2. Emphasize, but not overemphasize, the importance of reading.

3. Avoid becoming upset when the child is not progressing as rapidly as might be wished.

4. Make provisions for the child to utilize the public library.

5. Find out what books make good gifts for a given child.

6. Praise the child when he makes progress even though the progress may be slow.

7. Encourage brothers and sisters in a home to serve as an audience for oral reading for one another and to discuss books and dramatize stories.

8. Provide the child with many experiences that will enrich his reading and stimulate him to do more.

9. Keep the child from engaging in too many activities.

FOR STUDY AND DISCUSSION

1. Make an outline for a thirty-minute talk that you could give at a parent-teacher meeting on the current controversy on teaching phonics. If you have available the book *Fact and Fiction about Phonics* by Roma Gans (which is listed under "References"), you may wish to read all or parts of that book when working on this assignment.

2. Evaluate the following newer practice in relation to the possible contribution to the program of teaching of reading: (a) the Initial Teaching Alphabet, (b) the "words-in-color" program, and (c) programed learning.

3. What difference may be implied by the terms *reading the lines, reading between the lines,* and *reading beyond the lines*?

4. For any one grade make an outline of what would constitute an effective program in the development of locational skills. Include in your outline: objectives, guiding principles, general methods of procedure, and some specific methods for accomplishing the objectives.

5. Outline for any one grade different ways in which you might try to implement an effective program in oral reading. Be as specific as seems feasible in your suggestions.

6. Devise samples of items for practice exercises to help boys and girls arrive at generalizations and apply them in the area of the social studies or science.

7. Examine several basal-reading series and compare them. What points of strength suggest themselves? If any weaknesses are evident, indicate ways of reducing or eliminating them.

8. If you have access to Jeannette Veatch's book *Individualizing Your Reading Program* (which is listed under "References"), read parts of it. Otherwise read other professional material on the topic of Individualized Reading (as proposed by advocates of no systematic instruction in reading). Then give your reactions to the recommendations made.

9. Make a visual aid that would be helpful in guiding pupils toward growth in reading skills.

REFERENCES

Austin, Mary C., and Coleman Morrison *The First R: The Harvard Report on Reading in the Elementary Schools.* The Macmillan Company, 1963. 263 pp.

Betts, Emmett Albert, *Foundations of Reading Instruction.* America Book Company, 1950. 757 pp.

DeBoer, John J., and Martha Dallmann, *The Teaching of Reading.* Second edition. Holt, Rinehart and Winston, 1964. 422 pp.

Dechant, Emerald V., *Improving the Teaching of Reading.* Prentice-Hall, 1964. 568 pp.

Gans, Roma, *Fact and Fiction about Phonics.* The Bobbs-Merrill Company, 1964. 107 pp.

Hester, Kathleen B., *Teaching Every Child to Read.* Second edition. Harper and Row, 1964. 384 pp.

McKim, Margaret G., and Helen Caskey, *Guiding Growth in Reading in the Modern Elementary School.* Second edition. The Macmillan Company, 1963. 454 pp.

Smith, Nila Blanton, *Reading Instruction for Today's Children.* Prentice-Hall, 1963. 594 pp.

Veatch, Jeannette, *Individualizing Your Reading Program.* G. P. Putnam's Sons, 1959. 242 pp.

OUTLINE FOR CHAPTER 11

Guiding Growth in Independent Reading

CHAPTER 11

Guiding Growth in Independent Reading

In the modern elementary school even when independent reading is just for the fun of reading, it is valued as a highly significant activity, worthy not only of stimulation and encouragement for hours outside of school but also legitimate and desirable during school time.

VALUES OF INDEPENDENT READING

Because of the large variety of materials – poetry, fiction, history, science, for example – that are read independently, many different values can be derived from a strong program of independent reading.

Independent Reading and the Needs of Children

May Hill Arbuthnot well classifies the needs of children in her book *Children and Books*[1] in this manner: (1) competence – the need to achieve; (2) material security – the need for physical well-being; (3) intellectual security – the need to know; (4) emotional security – the need to love and to be loved; (5) acceptance – the need to belong; (6) play – the need for change; and (7) aesthetic satisfaction – the need for beauty and order.

While, to be sure, books can rarely if ever make up satisfactorily for the neglect a child may have experienced in his environment at home or at school for satisfying his basic needs, books can, in ways suggested here, do much toward supplementing or counteracting undesirable features in the surroundings.

1. "*Competence – the need to achieve.*" As the child with unusual problems reads of persons who in story or in real life have achieved in spite of difficulties, the lives of such individuals can help him realize that achievement is not denied to those who are living under great disadvantages.

2. "*Material security – the need for well-being.*" If a child is lacking in a normal amount of material security, there are books that may show him that there are other types of security that are more significant than the physical. If he is fortunate in the extent to which he feels secure materially, he may be grateful as he reads of how many others need to strive for that which has been given to him without effort or special worth on his part.

3. "*Intellectual security – the need to know.*" Through the wealth of books on science, social studies, biography, the reader – handicapped or privileged – can learn many important facts. He can also gain insights deeper than those of the intellect only, as a consequence of improved understanding of problems.

4. "*Emotional security – the need to love and to be loved.*" Through the right books the child lacking a fair share of love can sometimes experience vicariously a taste of the security resulting from being loved. The child who is loved may develop appreciation of the love bestowed upon him through recognition of the power of love illustrated in books he reads. Both he and his less fortunate classmate who has seemingly been deprived – only temporarily, it is hoped – even of the right to be loving can gain from some books incentive for developing that trait. All, the favored and the neglected, can learn through folklore and other classics of the past as well as through books of the present era, the power of love to help make life worthwhile.

---

[1]May Hill Arbuthnot, *Children and Books*. Third edition. Scott, Foresman and Company, 1964. Pages 3-10.

5. *"Acceptance – the need to belong."* The many books for children that portray the need of belonging, of being accepted, can give boys and girls a greater appreciation of the security that they may possess, a more profound understanding of the fact that some great individuals have had to struggle to be accepted, and a deeper realization of the importance of their own willingness to accept others.

6. *"Play – the need for change."* Through reading for the pleasure of reading, without any objective akin to work, the child can satisfy in part the need for "play – the need for change."

7. *"Aesthetic satisfaction – the need for beauty and order."* Through reading about "the good, the beautiful, the right," (in the words of Goethe) and seeing illustrations of beauty, the child can be assisted in having his need for aesthetic satisfaction fulfilled. Better yet, he can derive from reading the ability to differentiate between the uplifting and the cheap, as well as the discrimination to recognize the beautiful around him even when ugliness and disorder sometimes almost hide the truth of beauty.

Other Values of Independent Reading

Other values, besides those named, that can be achieved through independent reading are here listed.

1. Independent reading can stimulate children to develop hobbies that can add zest to their lives and those of others.
2. Independent reading can lead to or strengthen interest in a vocation or profession to be taken up as a lifetime means of livelihood and service.
3. Independent reading can help boys and girls improve in reading skills.
4. Through independent reading pupils can grow in language skills other than reading (as, for example, in improvement of listening and speaking vocabulary.)
5. Through independent reading children can develop the power of critical thinking.
6. Independent reading can be instrumental in helping children establish moral and spiritual values that will endure.

"THE RIGHT BOOK FOR THE RIGHT CHILD"

To achieve the values of independent reading the program should not be left to chance. This chapter is devoted to a consideration of two major problems, namely (1) finding "the right book for the right child" and (2) interesting the child in independent reading of a worthwhile nature. Let us now pay attention to the first of these two problems.

Books on the Child's Reading Level

Perhaps the first point that should be made in connection with this problem is that the teacher must know the individual before he undertakes to help him work out a program of independent reading. Important among qualities that should be taken into account are the reading ability and the interests of the child.

Courtesy of the Portland, Oregon, Public Schools

Figure 11.1 The Right Book

Unless the teacher knows a child's reading skill, he is likely to recommend books that are too easy or too difficult. Whenever the reading material suggested by the teacher is not on the pupil's level of comprehension, the efforts to guide him will usually be futile, at least in part. If, for example, a boy has difficulty in comprehending the meaning of third-grade material, all attempts to interest him in reading Howard Pyle's *The Merry Adventures of Robin Hood* will likely end in failure, no matter how much the boy might enjoy reading more simply written stories about Robin Hood. Similarly, data on his reading ability are of value to the teacher in guiding the child to avoid material far below his level of comprehension. Although some easy books are good for any reader, continued exposure to them, to the neglect of more difficult books, does not foster best development.

Knowledge of the child's likes and dislikes plays an important role in determining what he is ready to read in his leisure time. Experiments have shown what casual observation has also made evident: namely that a pupil can read more difficult materials in areas in which he is greatly interested than in those in which he lacks a propelling motive.

An estimate of reading ability can be obtained through standardized and nonstandardized tests. If a teacher finds it impossible or not feasible to secure standardized reading tests, he can devise tests of his own whereby he can obtain fairly accurate data on a child's skill in reading. An index of achievement in reading can be secured by timing the boys and girls while they are reading a selection silently and then checking their comprehension or retention by means of true-false, multiple-choice, multiple-response, completion, or other types of questions. Reading ability can also be estimated by having a child read orally out of graded textbooks and then asking him questions on the material. No matter what kind of test the teacher uses, he must be careful to guard against attaching more significance to the interpretations than is warranted.

Determining Children's Interests

One way to gain insight into children's interests is to become familiar with published reports on this topic. Unfortunately the majority of these studies deal with groups of children. Although the information from these investigations is at times indicative of what to look for in a given child, the extent of individual differences makes them of limited value. They should be interpreted with this shortcoming in mind.

Unfortunately, too, some of the more extensive and formerly most reliable studies were made in the pre-television and pre-space days when the interests of children were less expansive. The individual who wishes to read accounts of studies on children's interests is referred to professional books on literature for children such as May Hill Arbuthnot's *Children and Books* and to *The Reader's Guide to Periodical Literature* and *The Education Index.*

The teacher himself can utilize various means to try to determine the interests of a given child. Three such means are mentioned and briefly discussed here.

1. *The questionnaire.* Some teachers with pupils advanced enough to fill out a questionnaire use questions on the order of the following:

> What books have you liked best?
> What *kinds* of books do you enjoy reading?
> What books do you remember having read this past year?
> What magazines do you read?
> What magazines do you like best?

2. *The interview.* Valuable information can also be gained through informal interviews. Questions such as these may prove helpful:

> What do you like to do when you can do as you please?
> What books do you like best?
> What do you look for in a book when you pick one out in the library?

Care must be taken to keep rapport with the child. A frank statement like this may be made by the teacher: "I am talking with some of the boys and girls about their reading so that I can help them find books they will enjoy. I would like to ask you some questions so I can help you, too." By no means should the child feel that the teacher is prying into his life or that the information is useless.

3. *Observation.* Throughout the school day the teacher has countless opportunities to discover what each member of the group enjoys doing. In order that the teacher will not forget a part of the observed happenings, he may find it helpful to keep records of significant occurrences.

BASIC CONSIDERATIONS IN GUIDING GROWTH IN INDEPENDENT READING

When the teacher has determined, as best he can, the plane of the child's independent reading, about all he can do to help the pupil receive the most pleasure and benefit from independent reading is to try to arouse or cultivate in him a deep and abiding interest in a variety of worthwhile books. In the teacher's attempts to stimulate this interest, he is advised to observe points such as thc following.

1. *Attention to individual differences is of paramount importance.* In the average classroom it is difficult and undesirable to have all teaching in the form of individual instruction. Even when group methods of stimulating recreational reading are employed, however, attention should be paid to adapting the procedures to the needs of every boy and girl.

2. *The child should be stimulated to develop new interests in reading.* In some schoolrooms we find children who in their free time read almost exclusively one type of book such as Indian stories or

stories about aviation. Frequently, too, the leisure-time reading is limited to fiction, while factual material related to the natural and social sciences and to the arts is neglected. Although it is desirable that an individual develop more along some lines than others, the narrowing effects of too much concentration on one type are evident.

3. *The child should be guided to develop more refined tastes in his reading interests.* Two children who are alike in that they have the same field of interest – adventure stories, for example – often differ greatly in their tastes. One may be satisfied with the crudest of Wild West stories while the other may enjoy Daniel Defoe's *Robinson Crusoe.* It is the responsibility of the teacher to help every child not only to broaden his interests but also to elevate his tastes.

4. *Children should not be forced onto higher planes.* Insight is needed to determine the extent to which the adult should try to interest a child in superior types of reading.

5. *A variety of approaches in stimulating recreational reading is usually more productive than any one procedure.* The point is particularly important when group methods are used to interest the children in reading. It will be found that one child will be reached more easily through one method while another responds more readily to another.

6. *Sincerity on the part of the teacher is a requisite.* If the teacher merely acts as if he enjoys books, the falsity of his action will probably soon become apparent to at least some of the boys and girls. The teacher who finds himself lacking in the appreciation of good books will do well to broaden his acquaintance with worthwhile reading material.

GENERAL PROCEDURES FOR INTERESTING CHILDREN IN READING

Perhaps the most important question to be faced in relation to independent reading is how the teacher can stimulate a child to want to read desirable books during part of his leisure time. A few procedures are indicated in the following paragraphs.

1. Oral reading by the teacher of parts of a book. The following experience had by one teacher with the book *The Flight of Pony Baker* by William Dean Howells can easily be duplicated in spirit. When she had read the first chapter or two to the class, she asked who would like to borrow the book. Since every child raised his hand eagerly, a schedule had to be worked out so that all would eventually have access to it. Later one boy, as he returned the book, said that he read it but that after it had made the rounds in the classroom, he would like to take it home again so that his father could finish reading it. The teacher who in an appropriate manner starts reading to his pupils books of the universal appeal of *Doctor Dolittle* by Hugh Lofting or *The Wind in the Willows* by Kenneth Grahame need not fear that many children able to read such books will not be eager to read them.

2. *Oral reports by the teacher and the boys and girls.* Because at times an insistence on a rigid form for a book report seems to kill interest in books, some teachers feel almost apologetic when recommending book reports. But they can be fun. The teacher may start by telling now and then of a book that he has enjoyed. In time it will probably be easy to get others in the group to share their reading experiences. Not infrequently there may be a happy response to a child's review when someone in the audience speaks up promptly with "When are you returning the book to the library?"

3. *Written reports by boys and girls.* A simple file of books read by the boys and girls with brief comments by the readers can be a source of great help. Children like to get the opinions of their peers on books. (The reader is referred to the discussion on book reports in Chapters 4 and 5.)

4. *Commercial motion pictures, filmstrips, and slides on books for children.* Motion pictures, slides, and filmstrips on books for children, which are available to schools in increasingly large numbers, can be used to create interest in reading. Much depends on the procedure used in presenting a picture. A statement by the teacher that certain scenes in which the children showed special interest are described more fully in the book can arouse a desire to read it. The boys and girls can be encouraged to read a book if after a discussion of details of certain occurrences shown in the pictures the teacher remarks that the book will throw further light upon their uncertainties. (In Chapter 15 are given aids to the selection of visual resources for interesting children in books.)

5. *First-hand contact with libraries.* One teacher found it practical to take her children, who had patronized chiefly the school library, to the public library shortly before school closed in spring. They thus became acquainted with the library through a talk by the librarian who explained various points of significance and pointed out especially interesting books. The children also were given time to browse. Opportunity was provided to obtain application blanks for library cards, while those who had library cards were permitted to check out books.

Exhibit was prepared by Myra Lou Smith.

Figure 11.2 Interesting Children in Books

Other procedures for interesting boys and girls in worthwhile reading are here listed. Many of these are described in subsequent pages of this chapter and in Chapter 12.

1. Dramatization of parts of favorite books
2. Contests
3. Exhibits
4. Book parties
5. Creative writing
6. Letters to an author of books for children
7. Reading clubs
8. Visits to bookstores
9. Pupil-made visual aids.

GAMES TO INTEREST CHILDREN IN READING

It sometimes is difficult to distinguish between games and exercises that are not games. Various procedures suggested in this book may be classified as games by some. Other exercises can be changed into games with slight alteration. For criteria to observe when using educational games the reader is referred to page 27 and for a list of sources of games to page 337.

Following are additional suggestions for games for interesting children in independent reading.

1. As a pupil describes a character from a story, the rest of the class guesses who is being described.

2. The pupils guess the title of stories suggested by headlines for newspapers such as: (a) Tom Boy Marooned on Rafters in Old Time Kitchen (Kate in Kate Seredy's *The Good Master*); (b) Pig Rescued by a Spider (Wilbur in E. B. White's *Charlotte's Web*).

3. The boys and girls guess titles of stories represented by articles on a display table such as a paper doll representing a girl next to a thimble (for *Thimble Summer* by Elizabeth Enright) or a troll and a billy-goat, both made of clay (for "The Three Billy-Goats Gruff").

4. The pupils guess the titles of books that are presented in picture form, as in Figure 11.3.

Figure 11.3 A Rebus

5. The children name the designated characters of a story of which the title is given in answer to questions such as: (a) Who in *Little Women* married Laurie? (b) Who in *Charlotte's Web* saved Wilbur?

6. A pupil pantomimes a scene from a story and the other pupils guess the title. For example, a pupil may stand "on all fours" and blow with all his might as he represents the wolf in "The Three Little Pigs."

7. The pupils make up and use in a contest rebuses representing titles of books. Examples are: (a) a picture of a jungle and an outline of a book (for *Jungle Book*); (b) the word *The*, a picture of a witch, the word *of*, a dab of black color, a picture of a bird, and the outline of a pond (for *The Witch of Blackbird Pond*).

8. The pupils match illustrations of book characters with phrases or sentences referring to the illustrations. For example, a picture of a toy rabbit made of cloth, preferably of velveteen, could be matched with the sentences from *The Velveteen Rabbit* by Margery Bianco, published by Doubleday and Com-

pany (page 18); "The nursery magic had happened to him, and he was a toy no longer. He was real."

BOOK WEEK

Book Week, which comes during the first part of November, is an especially good time for concerted effort to help boys and girls become more interested in independent reading of worthwhile materials.

Guidelines

The teacher who wishes to help his pupils obtain the maximum benefits from Book Week should observe guidelines such as the following:

1. *Book Week should be used primarily for teaching purposes.* In schools where the command from an administrative office is that each room must do something to observe Book Week there is danger that some teachers may be tempted to put on a "show" to demonstrate that they are following the injunction. The real purpose of Book Week can be entirely defeated by emphasis on "putting on a program."

2. *Book Week should in its emphasis be the beginning of a "Book Year."* The objective should be to interest the boys and girls in good reading the year round.

3. *Through educational Book Week activities parents can be made partners in the challenge of guiding the child in growth in independent reading.* Parents can be invited to programs that are planned in harmony with the true objective of Book Week. During Book Week special provisions, possibly through the Parent Teacher Association, can be made for discussion with parents of the problems involved in the challenge of Book Week. In one school during Book Week, at a meeting of the Parent Teacher Association, the librarian explained important factors in book selection and discussed the exhibit of children's books she had set up with the cooperation of a local bookstore. The list of good books for children which she distributed to the parents was timely, since many parents are eager to get aid in selecting books for their children for Christmas. Book Week may also be made a special time for individual conferences with parents about the independent reading of the children.

Procedures During Book Week

The points listed on preceding pages of this chapter as suggestions for interesting boys and girls in books can be used effectively during Book Week. The teacher can also obtain many suggestions from materials available from the Children's Book Council, 175 Fifth Avenue, New York, New York 10010. Yearly the October issue of the *Wilson Library Bulletin*, published at 950 University Avenue, Bronx, New York 10452, gives many excellent ideas. The teacher interested in books for children should not miss the Sunday *New York Times* book review section during Book Week. That section of the newspaper has for many years been exclusively devoted to children's reading during Book Week. Professional magazines such as *Grade Teacher* and *The Instructor* publish articles of help for Book Week in the November issues. From these and many other sources the teacher can get assistance in starting a year-round emphasis on books during Book Week.

The Book Fair

Special mention is made here of one of the activities often used during Book Week. It can also be used during other times of the year. The purpose of a fair should be to interest people – children as well as adults – in good books and to give information about them.

Book fairs differ widely in organization. The factor common to all is an exhibit of a fairly large number of books. Other displays to interest people in books and to give information about them are a feature of many fairs. In connection with some, programs are given in order to help accomplish the purposes for exhibiting the books. Sometimes the fair is put on by only the boys and girls in a school with the help of one or more teachers. At other times other adults, such as members of the Parent Teacher Association or of other clubs, may have a part in the work.

In planning a book fair, special attention should be paid to the development of lasting interest in reading. One way in which this objective can be achieved is to give children a part in planning the books to be purchased for the room, school, or public library. A poster entitled "What Books Would You Like for Our Room?" could be used. Another means of making permanent the work on a book fair is to encourage the pupils to keep a record of recommended books that they would like to read.

The following list shows some of the characteristics of a well-planned and well-executed book fair.

1. A goodly number of worthwhile books are displayed. The books can be from the children's personal libraries, from the room, school, or public library, from bookstores, from publishers, or from other interested people.

2. The books are suited to various levels of reading. They should cover a broad range of difficulty so that they serve as challenge to as many pupils as possible of those who either put on the fair or who are visitors.

3. The books are displayed attractively.

INDEPENDENT READING IN CONTENT AREAS

Some of the special problems of the reading of boys and girls in the content areas, with suggestions for meeting them, are discussed in Chapter 10. In that chapter the main emphasis put on reading in those fields is on guiding the child's growth in the development of needed skills. In this chapter consideration is given to interesting the child in independent reading in the content subjects. Obviously no strict line of demarcation between the two types can or should be drawn.

Guidelines

What are some of the basic guidelines in stimulating growth in independent reading in the content areas? Three are briefly described following.

1. *The teacher should try to make available to the boys and girls a large amount of reading material in the various subject areas on different reading levels.* Purchase of materials for the room library should be supplemented by reference to books in the different areas in the school and public libraries if possible. Many librarians in school and in public libraries welcome suggestions from teachers as to types of books that would fit with the subject matter in the content subjects taught in a given grade. Resources from county or state libraries are open to boys and girls in many communities.

2. *The teacher should help boys and girls recognize the importance of reading in various areas.* While the teacher should emphasize the importance of much reading along the line of an individual's specialty, he should also discuss the narrowness that can result if a person confines himself too much to only one or two areas. Discussion should be supplemented by challenging reports on books of various types. In some instances it also may be desirable, in drawing up specifications for outside reading, to indicate that each child should assume responsibility for reading one or two books of each of a number of types of books for children such as books about history, books of biography, books about geography.

3. *The reading that the teacher recommends in the various areas should not be confined to those topics about which boys and girls are studying while in a given grade.* While it is desirable that there be available to boys and girls a rich collection of books on the topics they are studying during a given school year and that the teacher encourage them to read along these lines, it is also important that the pupils read materials in the content areas other than those about which they are studying.

Books on History

Undoubtedly one reason why many boys and girls do not read many books dealing with history or having an historical background is that they have not been introduced to the good books in the field that would make interesting and significant outside reading for them.

Criteria for Selection. What criteria should the teacher keep in mind when recommending books dealing with history? Here are a few important questions that should be answered positively if a book is to be recommended.

1. *Is the book historically accurate?* A book is by no means to be excluded from consideration if it is historical fiction. However, even in historical fiction the background must be true to the facts of history. Marguerite de Angeli's *The Door in the Wall*, for example, while a story, has a background congruous with the history of the times.

2. *Are the theme and plot of a story constituting historical fiction adequate?* The fact that a story is based on history and can give the pupil an understanding of one or more periods of history does not constitute reason for accepting a poor theme or plot. The story should merit attention on its own — because it is a good story. The historical background should not overshadow the plot.

3. *Is the book informative without being didactic?* That book of historical fiction is the better of two, other things being equal, which does not seem to be written primarily "to teach something."

4. *Does the book give perspective resulting from a better understanding of the past?* A book for independent reading related to history should help the pupils appreciate the fact that we owe a debt to the past. The expert writer of historical fiction will try to avoid any tendency to didacticism in the undesirable sense of that term.

5. *Through reading this book will the reader be in a better position to live effectively in contemporary society?* To accomplish this implied objective the author does not need to resort to a clear explanation of the application of the problems of people of the past to those we face today. The content should frequently be presented so that the child himself, without being forced to a generalization involving the application of the problems discussed to present times, comes to an important understanding of how the knowledge of the past as given him in a book can throw light on present-day problems and their solution.

Suggested Procedures. How can the teacher interest boys and girls in reading material related to history as independent reading? How can he help them profit from such reading?

The first of these two questions is answered in part in discussions on preceding pages in which suggestions have been given for interesting boys and girls in books of any types. General procedures for interesting boys and girls in reading books with historical background are: having available to boys and girls interesting and worthwhile books on history on various reading levels; putting up attractive exhibits of books in the classroom; having charts to interest them in books; reading to the class a part of a book (often the introductory part) in order to stimulate them to want to read the book; and having pupils give exciting and significant reports on books with an historical background.

A few specific suggestions for interesting pupils in books on history and for helping them profit from reading them are listed following.

1. After a pupil has read a book dealing with the history of a period, he may make a poster or an accordion-like picture folder illustrating some of the learnings that he has acquired. For example, a book by Laura Ingalls Wilder may be illustrated by pictures authentically portraying the history of the times, by pictures of the interior of the home, of cooking utensils, of basic foods eaten, and pictures of schoolhouse furnishings. If the display is made by means of a picture folder on the space immediately preceding each picture, there may be written a quotation from the book explaining the point that coincides with the history of the times that is illustrated.

2. A date line can be made showing important historical happenings of the period on which a book is based. For example, for *Johnny Tremain* by Esther Forbes the events preceding and during the Revolutionary War can be shown on a time line. One suggestion for an interesting time line is actual use of a line (maybe a clothesline) strung across the room, to which placards are attached from above stating important events with dates and to which below the

Figure 11.4 A Three-Dimensional Bulletin Board

Figure 11.5 An Accordion-like Folder

line are attached illustrations of important happenings of the story.

Figure 11.6 Part of a Time Line

3. A frieze may be drawn showing significant events of the story with care taken that the details of the picture are in harmony with customs and habits of the people of the time.

4. After reading a book based at least in part on history, a pupil can study in reference books some of the topics suggested by the background of the story. For instance, after having read *Thanksgiving Story* by Alice Dalgliesh, the pupil can read authentic accounts of the voyage of the Mayflower and of the First Thanksgiving in Plymouth. The pupil can then write a booklet in which he reports on background events.

5. The pupil who plans to give a report on historical fiction can study about the lives of important men and women in history who lived at the time when the story took place. With the help of some of his classmates the reader may impersonate some of these people as he gives a report on the book and thereby makes history real to his audience.

6. One way in which readers can be helped to grasp historical sequence is by means of a series of shadow boxes that can be made out of shoe boxes. For example, Lois Lenski's *Boom Town Boy* can be illustrated by a group of shadow scenes in which one of the shoe boxes can depict the farm before the discovery of oil, another during the construction of the first oil well, and the third after it was covered with wells.

Books on Geography

As in the case of books with a historical setting, so with those of a geographical setting, even the details of background must be true, regardless of whether the material is fiction or nonfiction. Also as in the case of historical fiction the story element must not be sacrificed in order to teach facts. In a fascinating story, such as the great classic of childhood *Heidi* by Johanna Spyri, the background can make a lasting impression upon boys and girls, for the heroine moves in a real world, one made significant to the child because Heidi lived there.

Books that deal with other countries should not place emphasis on outmoded customs such as the wearing of wooden shoes in Holland. However, the pronouncement often made by writers in the field of the teaching of social studies in the elementary school – that the likenesses rather than the differences among people around the world should be stressed – needs to be interpreted with caution. To be sure, the common humanity of all should be emphasized. Nevertheless, what makes one individual lovable is based to a large extent on his unique characteristics. So, too, with peoples of other countries.

Here are a few suggestions for stimulating interest in reading books with emphasis on the geography of a region. These ideas may be considered by the teacher in addition to the many others given in this and the preceding chapter on how to interest children in books of all types.

1. In the case of a book with a regional setting, the reporter can beforehand exhibit on a bulletin board a map showing the places at which the chief events of the story occurred. For example, a child reporting on *Judy's Journey* by Lois Lenski can make his report not only more profitable but also more interesting if he sketches on a map the journey of the family of sharecroppers as they migrated from California to Florida and later to New Jersey.

2. Posting illustrations drawn by the pupil or otherwise obtained that provide background information can add to the interest of books such as Marguerite de Angeli's *Thee, Hannah!* the story of a Quaker girl whose critical attitude toward her garb was drastically changed during the development of the plot.

3. Dioramas showing the setting in which a major part of a book takes place can be especially effective as a motivating device in connection with books with a geographical setting. A scene showing the uncle's hut with the majestic Alps as background can be a stirring means of interesting the child in reading the book *Heidi*.

4. A display of travel folders, or even an imitation travel bureau in the room, can interest children in reading about peoples in distant regions.

Poster was prepared by Cynthia Fish Cormany

Figure 11.7 A Three-Dimensional Poster

Poster was drawn by Judith Cox

Figure 11.8 Poster Suggesting Background by Means of Lines

The teacher may wish to consult *Children's Books to Enrich the Social Studies* by Helen Huus (published by the National Council for the Social Studies) in which is given a brief review of 618 books. Since the titles are classified according to theme, it will be relatively easy to note books in areas needed in his room. He may suggest these as additions to the room or school or public library. Nancy Larrick's *A Teacher's Guide to Children's Books* published by Charles E. Merrill Books should also prove helpful.

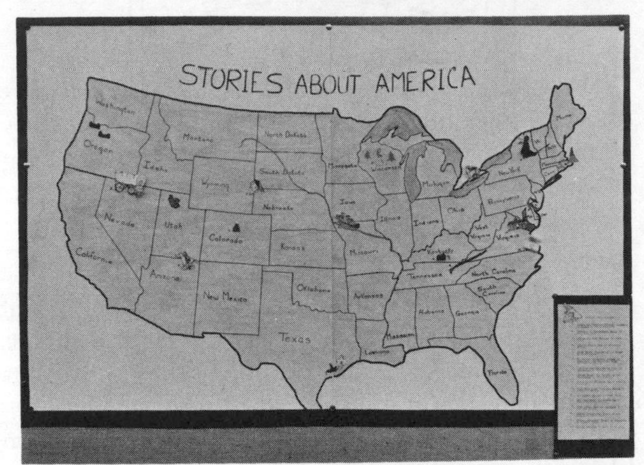

Poster was made by Gwen Stephens Meissner

Figure 11.9 Map of the United States Illustrating Books about Our Country

Books on Science

During the last few decades many books on science for boys and girls have appeared on the market. Some of them have been outstanding in their contribution; others have been mediocre.

Criteria for Evaluation. For listings of excellent science books for children the reader is referred to the book by Nancy Larrick to which reference has been made. Another excellent source for the adult interested in locating good books on science is the professional book *Elementary School Science and How to Teach It* by Glenn O. Blough and Julius Schwartz, published by Holt, Rinehart and Winston.

A few criteria to apply when judging books on science for boys and girls are these:

1. Is the book up-to-date in the facts presented?
2. Is the book accurate insofar as it teaches nothing that needs to be untaught later?
3. Is the book on the child's level of comprehension?
4. Is the book interesting?
5. Will reading the book interest the child in reading other books in the field of science?

SUGGESTIONS FOR STIMULATING INTEREST. There are many ways in which to interest boys and girls in books on science, whether they deal with animal life, plant life, or facts in the realm of physics, chemistry, astronomy, or geology. A few are here mentioned.

1. An exhibit can be set up to intrigue boys and girls in trying a simple experiment with the directions for conducting it explained in written form. On the same table with the materials for experimentation one or more books dealing at least in part with the subject of the experiment can be exhibited with a caption like this: "If you like to do experiments, here are some books you may enjoy."

2. An illustrated bulletin board entitled "Can You Answer These Questions?" may have challenging questions posted on it like "What makes an airplane move?" On a table in front of the bulletin board may be placed several books on science. Each question on the bulletin board may be connected by a narrow ribbon to the book that gives the answer.

3. To interest boys and girls in books dealing with animals, the homes or habits of one or more of the animals can be represented. For example, through use of papier-mâché or clay as the basic medium for molding, there can be portrayed on a board, possibly 18 by 24 inches, a model showing a cross section of the home of a beaver.

4. A chart entitled "Is It True?" can be used for listing various superstitions mingled with true facts. An illustrative chart may be used only for superstitions and facts about one topic such as the moon or travel in space. Near the chart can be placed a book with the sign "This book will tell."

5. A "migration map" can be made to interest boys and girls in books about birds.

6. Children can be interested in means of animal protection by a mobile. Examples of only a few of the many animals that can be represented on the mobile are the skunk, the rabbit, and a fish. The skunk can be made from black paper with a white stripe, also of paper. The rabbit can be made in part of cotton. The fish can be made from a paper plate with the rippled edges cut so they serve as fins and tail.

7. To interest boys and girls in reading about the activities of ants, a pegboard can serve as background for a poster entitled "Life in an Ant Hill." The ant hill itself can be made of brown construction paper with wood shavings sprinkled upon it. The tunnels and rooms can be made of white poster board outlined with a black magic paper. The ants may be represented by black construction paper. Drapery hooks can be used to attach the following three signs to the pegboard: (a) Queen laying eggs, (b) Guards at entrance, and (c) Food storage bins.

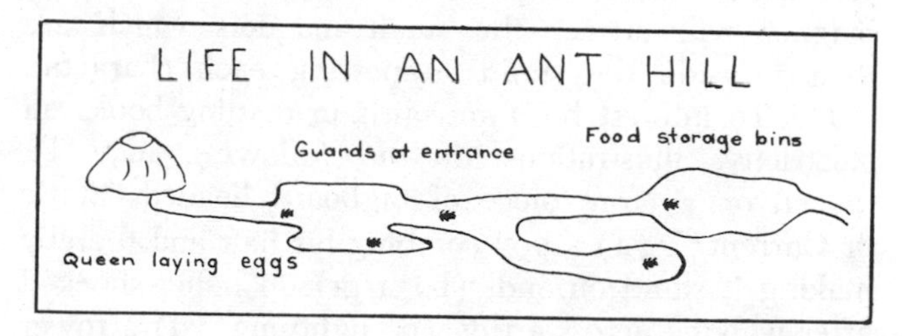

Figure 11.10 A Poster to Interest Pupils in Reading about Ants

8. Below a sign "All about Aviation" books on aviators and aviation may be displayed.

9. To interest boys and girls in reading about magnetism, on a large piece of tagboard or mounting board headed "What does a magnet attract?" may be fastened objects such as the following: (a) a piece of wood, (b) a thumbtack, (c) a nail, (d) a sponge, (e) a screw driver, and (f) a piece of wire. Below each of these articles can be written the substance from which it is made. For example, under the piece of wire the word *steel* may be written. A magnet, attached by a cord to the background, can be used by the boys and girls to test which objects are attracted to it.

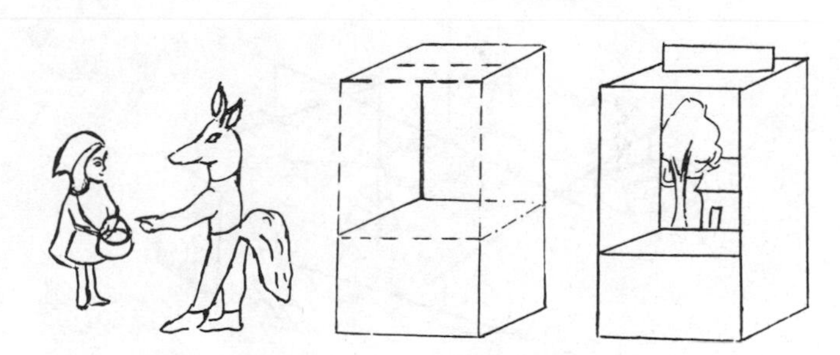

Figure 11.11 A Magnetic Theater

10. One exciting way in which to interest boys and girls in magnets is the construction of a "magnetic theater." The theater can be made from a cardboard box by cutting out one-half of the bottom and securing this piece of cardboard inside the box in the middle to serve as stage, as shown by the dotted lines in the accompanying figure. The backdrop can be illustrated with a scene to suit the story being dramatized. The piece of paper serving as backdrop can be slipped into a slit made across the top of the theater. The characters for the play can be made of

cardboard and construction paper and then taped to a low triangular stand containing a magnet. By moving a large magnet under the stage floor, the characters can be made to move across the stage. The large magnet will attract the small magnets which are placed inside the stand supporting each character.

11. To interest boys and girls in reading books on electricity, illustrations of the following may be placed on a large piece of tagboard headed "Static or Current?": (a) a boy combing his hair and thereby making it stand on end, (b) a person being shocked after walking across a rug, (c) lightning, (d) a tower transmitting electric impulses, and (e) a radio. To increase interest in the bulletin board the boy's clothes could be made of cloth and the rug of textured material.

12. A mobile may be used to interest the pupils in reading books dealing at least in part with electromagnets. The mobile may include pictures of the following objects mounted on poster board: (a) a doorbell, (b) a derrick, (c) a telephone, (d) a telegram, and (e) an automobile.

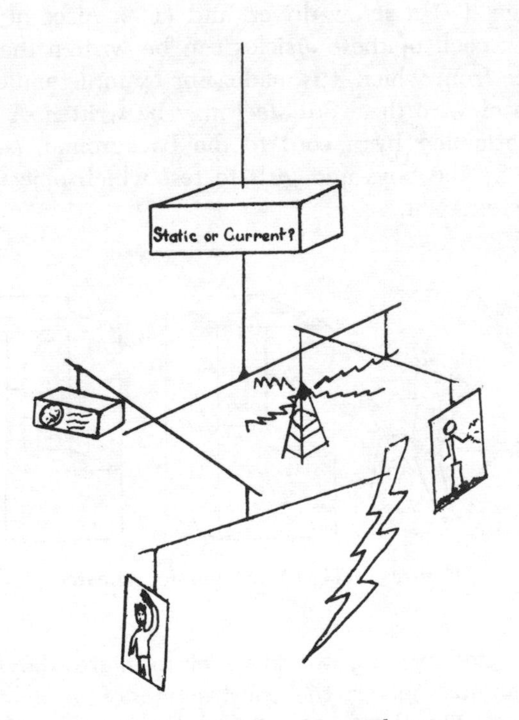

Figure 11.12 A Mobile about Electromagnets

13. To interest boys and girls in learning about famous botanists some of the children may make a "hall of fame" from a large box cut in the manner indicated in the accompanying illustration. The "stage" can be covered with white shelf paper. The curtain shown in the illustration can be made of blue taffeta and suspended from a thin wire serving as curtain rod. The four pedestals, also shown in the illustration, can be small tempera paint jars covered with white shelf paper. The pictures of botanists can be pasted onto a background of black construction paper and their names printed with white ink on black paper. These "name cards" can be pasted to the pedestals.

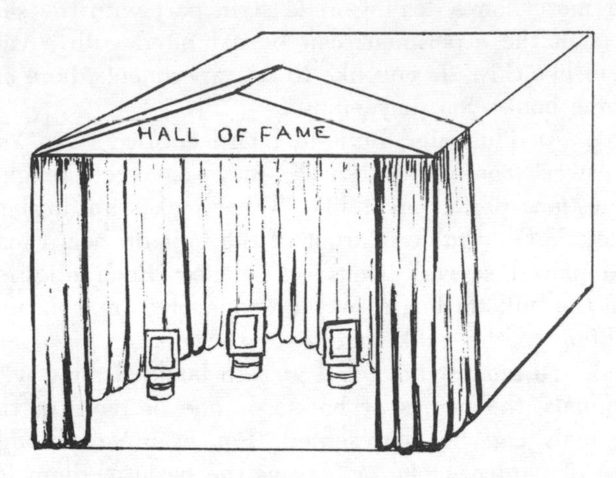

Figure 11.13 A Hall of Fame of Botanists

14. To interest boys and girls in reading about space travel, a bulletin board can be made indicating some of the characteristics of space that differ from characteristics of the earth. The bulletin board may be entitled "The Earth Has. . . . Space Does Not Have. . . ." Pictures cut from magazines can illustrate that the earth has (a) gravity, (b) particles to reflect light, (c) objects to absorb heat, (d) plants for oxygen, and (e) objects to reflect sound.

15. A bulletin board that can be constructed to interest boys and girls in reading about space travel can show how the different stages of a rocket work. The bulletin board can be made on blue poster board and can be entitled "Three-stage Rocket." The illustration of the rocket can be divided into four sections by using strips of gray construction paper to represent the rocket. The first section can show the rocket as a whole, the second section can show the first stage falling off, the third section can show the second part dropping, and the fourth section can show the third stage falling off with the capsule departing alone into space.

Books on Minority Groups

In general when we refer to the term *minority groups* we think not only of the opposite of *majority* but also of a group of people who by the majority are considered inferior, unique, or set apart in some important way.

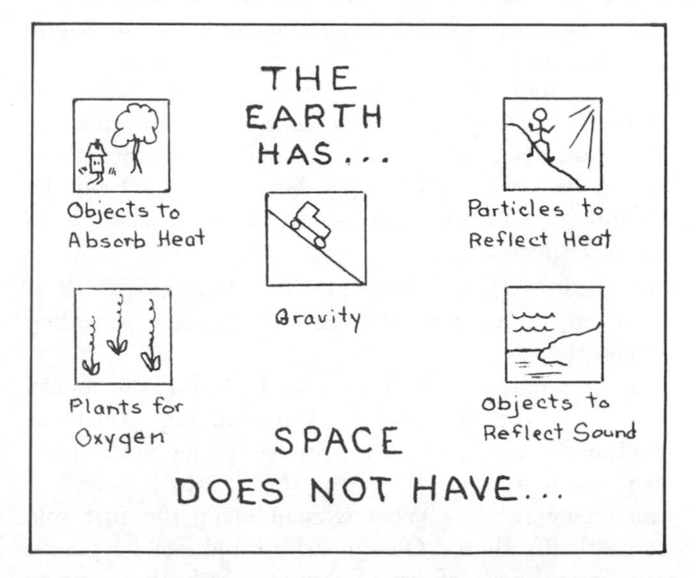

Figure 11.14 A Poster to Interest Pupils in Space Travel

Criteria for Evaluating Books. Some of the criteria on which we should evaluate books dealing with minority groups, in addition to those applying to all good books, are as follows:

Figure 11.15 Illustration of a Book about a Girl in a Minority Group

1. The books should treat of the differences between the minority group and others as variations rather than abnormalities. Merely to follow the dictum of omitting reference to differences does little, if anything, toward reaching the ideal of brotherhood.
2. The books should show that many problems of life are identical in minority and majority groups.
3. The books should emphasize the fact that pain in one person is as hard to bear as pain in another and that joy is joy regardless of who is experiencing it.
4. The books should refer to any problems existing between majority and minority groups as being common problems. Emphasis should be put on the point of view that hurting someone brings harm to the person who inflicts the pain because of what it does to him as a person.
5. The books should be such that they are of assistance to boys and girls of both minority and nonminority groups. It would, as a rule, be unwise to have different literature for the groups and thus possibly widen rather than decrease the chasm existing between them.

Teaching Procedures. How can the teacher interest the pupils in the variety of good books available that deal with minority groups, whether the differences are in race, social standing, religion, or nationality? How can he help boys and girls profit from the reading of such books? The ingenious teacher will know many ways in which to apply to reading of this type of book the suggestions for interesting children in books given in preceding pages. Here are only a few procedures with specific application for use with books on minority groups.

1. Without moralizing the teacher can ask questions about a book that will help the readers imagine themselves in the place of characters of the story who are members of a minority group.
2. Skits can be put on in which the pupils take the role of a minority group.
3. The boys and girls can be given background for understanding peoples represented in books on minority groups.
4. The background for reading books on minority groups as well as their reading can be correlated with work in art, music, drama, and dance.
5. The teacher, preferably with the help of one or more pupils, can prepare a bulletin board on famous people of minority races. Marian Anderson and George Washington Carver serve as two examples of persons to whom reference may be made on such a bulletin board.

Books of Biography

Boys and girls enjoy reading good books of biography. It is well that this is the case for through biographies of people with sterling qualities the child can be inspired to emulation of them. Furthermore, since many biographies written for children put considerable emphasis on the background of the times in which the persons lived, much historical information is acquired in this pleasant manner.

CHARACTERISTICS OF GOOD BIOGRAPHIES. Some of the criteria by which books on biography for boys and girls should be judged are the same that should be applied to any books on biography for adults or children. Others are somewhat unique to books for younger readers. The list that follows contains both types.

1. A biography should be an authentic, truthful presentation of the life of an individual. In books for adults heavy documentation, which is not found in books for children, is an index of authenticity of the facts related. In biographies for children the preface may give some indication of the source of the information.
2. A book on biography for children should not deal with problems beyond the realm of comprehension by the reader.
3. A biography for children should be written in a style that presents a suitable mood or background for recording the life of the person whose biography is being written.
4. A book of biography for young children usually should not include the sordid or the immoral. If no accurate biography can be written about an individual without such details, then the life of that person is not, as a rule, an acceptable subject as a biography for boys and girls.
5. A book of biography for children should be written about a person who is worthy of emulation. A person does not need to be flawless (for then there would be no biographies for boys and girls) but he should be a person who can serve as an example in many respects.

TEACHING PROCEDURES. The following points illustrate how boys and girls can be guided in reading biography.

1. Arranging a bulletin board. A bulletin board with the caption "Who's Who among American Women?" may have on it slips of paper with questions such as: (a) Who was the "Little Mother" of the prisoners? (b) What woman made the first solo transatlantic flight? On a nearby table can be placed attractive books of biography in which the answers to the questions can be found.
2. Dramatizing scenes from the lives of a few famous people such as (a) Jane Addams' ride with her father through slums, (b) Benjamin Franklin's arrival as a boy in Philadelphia, (c) Sacajawea's aid to Lewis and Clark.
3. Using a large map of the United States for indicating at appropriate places illustrations of some-

Poster was prepared by Marilyn Kershaw Williams.

Figure 11.16

thing important in the lives of famous people. For example, a paper airplane can be placed at Little Falls, Minnesota, in recognition of Charles Lindbergh or a picture of Hull House, perhaps given a three-dimensional effect by a mounting on an accordion-like piece of paper, can be attached to the site of Chicago for Jane Addams.

4. Making objects or collecting them to represent something of importance about the person whose biography had been read in order to interest others in it, like: (a) a collection of products, in connection with George Washington Carver that can be made from peanuts (cereal, flour, peanut butter) or (b) mottoes giving wise sayings of Benjamin Franklin.

Books on Religion

No listing of books for boys and girls in the elementary school would be complete without reference to books on religion. This fact remains true even though it has been ruled that religion as such is not to be taught in public schools.

Even without any court decision, many people had felt that the public school teacher has no right to teach boys and girls a religious belief, other than that which is in agreement with the wishes of the parents. Because of the differences in point of view, even among Christians — in fact, even among members of the same church — at best it is impossible or almost impossible to adhere to this principle and still deal with many matters of religion.

Various proposals have been made to help solve the problem posed in the preceding paragraph, among them the following.

1. Only those points about religion should be taken up in school on which there is agreement among the religions represented in a classroom. To this argument, the following comments are pertinent. If a teacher presents only the common elements of all religions, there are those who, with reason, object to such practice because it may detract from the significance of points emphasized in a given religion which the child is being taught at home and at Sunday school. Many parents do not want their children to be given the erroneous point of view that it matters little what is believed as long as we believe in one God and try to practice virtuous living.

2. Only the applications of religions should be emphasized in the public schools. Any such delimitation in practice results not in religious but in secular instruction. Morality is not synonymous with religion.

CRITERIA FOR BOOKS ON RELIGION. Although the use of books on religion or pertaining to it with all the boys and girls in a room may be greatly limited and in some instances not desirable, the teacher will want to know about books on the topic in order to be able to furnish parents with information on them. Furthermore, he may want to recommend to a child, within the boundaries of the religious beliefs of his home and church, suitable books on the subject. Consequently the teacher needs to know sound criteria pertaining to the choice of religious books.

First of all, books on religion should fulfill the general requirements of all good books as to illustrations, format, and content. Additional criteria pertinent to all books dealing with religion are here listed. Still others are mentioned later on in this chapter in relation to the types of books on religion that are discussed.

1. In books for boys and girls only those concepts of religion should be presented that are somewhat within the power of the child to comprehend. To be sure, many of the concepts of religion are beyond man's total comprehension. Nevertheless, some can be stated so simply that they have certain meaning for the child.

2. Religious concepts should not be oversimplified. If they are made to seem simpler than they are, the child later may find himself in the unhappy situation of unlearning what he once learned.

3. Books dealing with religion should show the respect for personality emphasized by the higher religions of the world.

TYPES OF BOOKS ON RELIGION. The books on religion or related to religion which may be of value to boys and girls can be classified in the following manner.

1. *Bible stories.* Many editions of the Bible, because of language problems, are difficult for boys and girls to read. Even modern versions have vocabulary beyond the comprehension of many boys and girls in the elementary school. Further difficulty in reading the Bible, or parts of it, for elementary-school children lies in the fact that concepts difficult to comprehend are scattered among those that are simpler to grasp. For these reasons, books on stories of the Bible written for boys and girls can serve a real need. The use of the latter should not, however, keep the child from having some of the passages of the Bible read to him or from reading parts himself. The beauty of much of the language of the Bible has not been equalled in any edition of Bible stories.

2. *Books about Jesus.* Attempts to give a consecutive account of important events in the life of Jesus that boys and girls can read with comprehension, pleasure, and inspiration have resulted in various books on His life. They include a wide range of difficulty, from the very simple picture-story books to

those read with profit by only the more advanced reader in the elementary school and by older people.

3. *Books about Bible characters other than Jesus.* The value of good books about Bible characters lies partly in the fact that strong characters, even though handicapped by human frailties, have been selected. As in other types of biography those points in the lives of persons selected as subjects for biography that are helpful and courageous should be emphasized, but only to the point of truthfulness. In a book about persons of the Bible the God-loving character of the individuals should be highlighted so that they are presented as persons who, in spite of evil in their lives, nevertheless show that God did matter a great deal to them.

4. *Books about various religions.* There is a difference in point of view among adults as to whether books about various religions should be given to children to read. Some will argue that exposing the child early in life to various religions may interfere with the child's highest spiritual development.

5. *Books about God.* Controversy also exists as to what books about God should be put into the hands of boys and girls. Some Christian people object to a child being given a book on religion that does not emphasize Jesus as the central figure. Similarly, objections to boys and girls reading books that tell about Jesus are raised by parents who are not Christians.

6. *Books of prayers.* One of the chief tests of any book of prayers for the adult or the child is whether it instills in the reader a worshipful attitude. In some books of prayers not only the words but also the accompanying illustrations help bring this about.

7. *Books of information about Bible lands.* Authenticity and clarity of presentation are two of the criteria that should be considered in books of this type. Importance of the facts selected constitutes another criterion.

8. *Other books of religious significance.* Books on persons other than Bible characters who were leaders in religious movements, such as Martin Luther and St. Francis of Assisi, are also written on a level of comprehension of older boys and girls in the elementary school. Books on religious holidays, although frequently emphasizing the secular rather than the religious elements (probably too much), also need to be mentioned in a well-rounded classification of books dealing with religion.

Books of Fiction

In the teacher's enthusiasm to introduce the boys and girls to excellent reading in the social studies, science, and other content areas, the teacher must not neglect his role in guiding the pupils in terms of the books of fiction not related to these areas that pupils can read. Books "just for fun," for the story involved, are important in the fulfillment of objectives related to the needs of children.

No special list of suggested methods of proceeding with the guidance toward growth in reading good stories is here given because those are enumerated in other parts of the chapter. For lists of books, many in fiction, the reader is referred to the Caldecott Medal books and the Newbery Medal books named in Chapter 15.

Books of Poetry

The teacher must be certain to make available books of poetry, with poems that will help the boys and girls achieve higher levels of appreciation of poetry. Suggestions for interesting boys and girls in poetry and for elevating their taste are given on page 87 under "Writing Poetry." Following are listed a few suggestions about the selection of poetry for children.

1. Start with poetry approximately on the pupil's level of appreciation.

2. Provide the boys and girls with poems about experiences, fanciful or actual, that they have had.

Figure 11.17

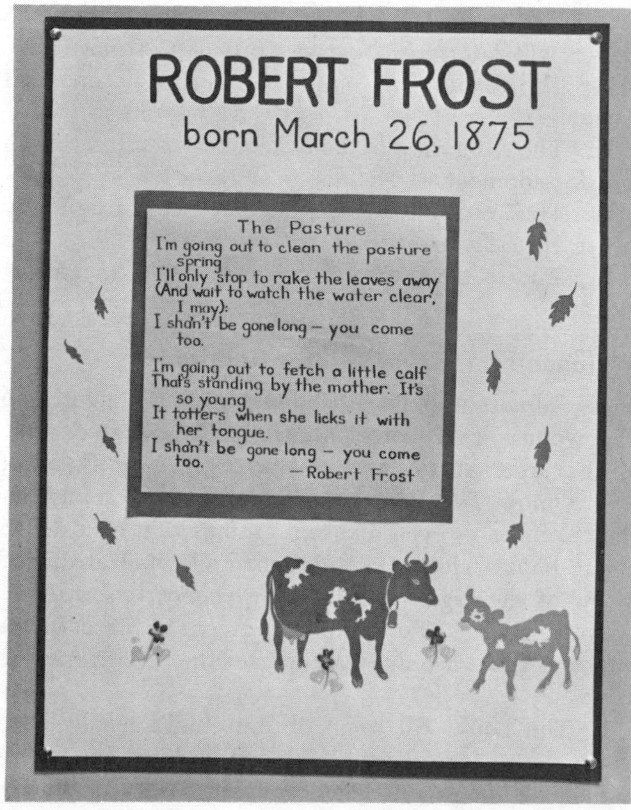

Poster was drawn by Susan Kuemmerling Van Orman and Judith Heis Rosene.

Figure 11.18

3. Do not make the mistake of thinking that a poem is suitable for a child because a child figures prominently in the poem. (For example, Eugene Field's "Little Boy Blue," though the main character is a boy, is unsuitable, for it is an expression of an adult's grief at the death of a child.)

4. Avoid selection of poems that "moralize."

5. Include in the selection some books with poems that are humorous and also some that tell a story.

6. While it is desirable to have an anthology of poetry available in the classroom for the teacher's use and in the intermediate grades for the use of the boys and girls, also provided for the pupil should be less ponderous-looking books than the typical anthology.

7. Make available to the boys and girls some books of poetry with wide margins, especially interesting-looking print, and illustrations that are reprints from masters of the art.

COMIC BOOKS

The importance of consideration of comic books is easily recognized as one realizes that a modest estimate of the per cent of boys and girls from ages 8 to 13 in this country reading comic books regularly is 90. Anna Wolf, in an article entitled "TV, Movie, Comics, Boon or Bane to Children?" published in *Parents Magazine*, volume 36, April, 1961, reports on page 47 that in 1961 comics had a monthly circulation of over 35 million. The estimate is that more money is spent on the purchase of comics than on textbooks for elementary and secondary schools.

Arguments Against Comic Books

Any unprejudiced evaluation of comic books, it seems to the writer, will need to take cognizance of the fact that, as in the case of other books, there is considerable variation between the best and the worst. Among the worst types are those that deal with crime and deeds of horror and those in which sex plays a predominant role. In a different class are the watered-down classics or Bible stories and stories such as those of Donald Duck with funny antics of

Poster was drawn by Gretchen Schmidt Grier.

Figure 11.19

animals. Some arguments against the comics apply equally to both extremes of comics; others are justifiable only when characterizing the poorer types. However, when the large per cent of comic books on the market that deal with deeds of crime and horror is kept in mind, the magnitude of the problem is self-evident.

Among the chief arguments given against the comics are the following.

1. The vocabulary of the comics at best is not such that the reader is likely to grow in a desirable command of the English language. In many instances it has a weakening effect.

2. The grammar used often is poor and the sentence structure frequently is not acceptable.

3. The spelling is at times not that accepted as standard.

4. The illustrations are frequently cheap and in many cases obscene and terrifying.

5. The illustrations do not follow accepted rules of techniques for illustrations for children.

6. The paper is poor and the print is hard on the eyes.

7. The reading lines, brief and irregular in length, counteract the establishment of effective eye movements in reading at a stage in reading progress (the intermediate grades, where the most avid readers of comics are found) when eye movements are being stabilized in many cases.

8. Many comic books deal with stories of horror and crime. In these typically the brawny man wins, methods used in committing crimes are demonstrated, techniques of torment are described and illustrated, and violent deaths are shown. These books can well give the child ideas for committing crimes. Furthermore, they can make boys and girls living in an overstimulated age tense with excitement of the undesirable kind. They are inimical to the development of sound and lasting standards of morality. They can lead to sadism and other types of delinquency. Books dealing with sex give children wrong ideas on that subject. The handsomeness of the men and the beauty of the women may give the reader a distorted idea of what is essential in love. The comics can be overstimulating in their effect on the sex life, especially for the age for which comics have the greatest appeal.

9. The illustrated classics are mediocre editions of the original. The same criticism can be made of those dealing with versions of Bible stories. The beauty of expression is lacking and the reader obtains an interpretation of some stories that the master writer did not mean to convey. There are those who claim that reading the classics in comic books may decrease rather than increase the chances that the reader will later turn to the work of the masters.

10. The reading of comics is a waste of time and money.

11. The vulgarity of many comics interferes with the development of standards of taste.

12. The characters are stereotyped, frequently either all good or all bad.

13. The comics are often used as a means of escape.

Arguments in Favor of the Comics

It is almost unbelievable that some intelligent men and women, even some educators, have stated some of the arguments that they have given in favor of the comics. Their points are nullified in many instances through even a casual examination of a dozen comic books selected at random. Following are listed a few of the arguments favoring comics that are frequently given. The sentences given in parentheses indicate the writer's reaction to the arguments as stated.

1. The books fill some of the child's needs, such as his desire for security, his need of using his imagination, his longing for achievement. The very stereotyped nature of the characters is used by some persons as an argument that they give a child security in that he knows what to expect. (In other literature we often condemn the use of stereotypes. Furthermore, the imagination of the child who reads many comics runs wild in areas where he might better not sojourn for the sake of his mental health.)

2. The comics are the fairy tales of today. (The comic books can easily fill the child with horror that many of the fairy tales of long ago do not do. One reason for the difference is probably the fact that the "long-agoness" of fairy tales prevents the child from suffering from feelings of gruesomeness that are experienced when reading horror tales of stories with the immediacy of a modern setting.)

3. The children will outgrow their liking for comic books. (But surely it is important in the formative period of childhood that everything within reason be done to keep the child's mental life healthy.)

4. The children learn to read by means of the comics. (Arguments against this statement is that reading does not need to be learned through resorting to undesirable material. It is no more appropriate to use low-grade reading material to learn to read than it is to use vulgar speech as means of self-expression.)

5. Reading of books on crime will not cause the well-adjusted child to commit wrong deeds or add to delinquency as commonly defined. It is admitted by

some people who use this argument that it may have that effect on a child who already has some emotional problems or a tendency to delinquency. (Surely this is poor argument for those of us who have seen the good and the bad intermingled in all children we know. Since when, too, are we going to cease feeling responsibility for the weaker brother whom we have not yet even learned, in many instances, to identify?)

What to Do About the Comics

Under the leadership of Charles F. Murphy, the Association of Comic Books produced the Comics Code Authority for the alleged purpose of having reform come from within the comic industry. How ineffective the resulting reform has been can be judged by the reader who examines a random sampling of comic books bearing the seal of approval by the organization. If the Comics Code Authority formulated in 1954 has not brought the needed results, what can be done about the polluting types of comics?

1. The good books on the reading and interest levels of the boys and girls should be made readily accessible to them in large numbers.
2. Various procedures, many of which are described elsewhere in this book, should be used to interest the boys and girls in good books.
3. More books should be written emulating features of the comics which are not undesirable and which attract the children to them such as ease of material, adventure, and quick action in the stories.
4. Teachers should forbid boys and girls to read comics at school. Many educators would object to this point of view on the grounds that prohibiting the reading of a comic book makes it more sought after. The writer of this book argues that we do not hesitate to forbid children to use vile language at school for fear that they may consequently use it more out of school than otherwise.
5. Parents should forbid boys and girls to buy or read harmful literature at home. (The writer recognizes the difficulty of enforcement of this rule.)
6. The school and the home should try to give the child a background of values that will help him like that which is fine.
7. The school and the home should provide the child with many experiences that will help satisfy the needs some persons think the comics satisfy.
8. Parents and teachers should examine the comic books on the newsstand and then take a firm stand for the abolition of all undesirable comics from the newsstands of the community.
9. Teachers should try to help boys and girls become discriminating readers. This suggestion should not, however, be observed by having the children waddle in trash for a period of time.
10. Parents and teachers should try to get laws passed that will forbid the sale of debasing literature. Why many persons with keen intelligence are specifically opposed to this suggestion is hard to comprehend. The argument seems to be that people do not become better through legal action. But we do have faith in laws that are passed against the use of marijuana even though through the passing of the law, per se, the individuals affected by it may not be reformed. We know that forbidding the sale of tobacco to minors does not eradicate the desire in the youngster who wants to buy tobacco, but we pass the law believing it wise not to leave up to children in their formative years the decision as to what is good for them in a matter of such moment.

KEEPING RECORDS OF BOOKS READ

Keeping records of books read, whether by the teacher or by the reader, can be valuable for two reasons, namely, (1) to know or remember what books have been read and (2) to stimulate further reading. The first reason mentioned is of significance because an individual often finds it helpful to remember the exact title and author of a book he has read. To the teacher a record is of value in that he will know better how to guide further growth in reading. Records in reading can stimulate the pupil to further reading especially if he has set for himself (alone or through the influence of the teacher) a goal of wanting to read many good books. The incentive that keeping records furnishes even for adults can readily be noted as one observes how commonly the device is used in an attempt to inspire greater effort in United Appeals drives and in other campaigns.

Cautions for Record Keeping

In keeping records that show books read by an individual, the following cautions should be noted.

1. Records that cause competition of the reader with others should be used sparingly, if at all. The child who has read only a few books (and sometimes for good reason) may feel discouraged if he is the one who lags behind as revealed in a posted chart showing the number or types of books read. Competition should be primarily with the reader's own past record.
2. When a pupil keeps record of the books or the number of books read, care must be taken, as a rule,

that the number of pages read is in some way considered. If this caution is not observed, a child may avoid reading some of the longer books.

3. Provisions should be made that the child does not feel obligated to read every word in a book and, on the other extreme, that he does not merely skim a book or parts of a book that he records as one he has read. One way in which pupils can be helped in this respect is through frank discussion of the degree of comprehension with which a book must be read in order to be recorded on a list.

4. Care should be taken that the child is not reading merely to have a good record of independent reading. If that is his objective, it is hardly one that will provide a good goal for adult reading.

Means of Keeping Records

Following are described types of records that can be kept of a child's reading.

1. A record of books read can be kept in a file box. After a child has read a book, he can make a card for it if someone else in the room has not already made one for the book.

2. On a bulletin board or chart can be attached small boats, made of colored construction paper, one for each child with a name on each. These can be arranged into a "classroom fleet." On the sail of each pupil's boat can be recorded the author and title of each book he reads while the record is being kept.

3. On an outer-space chart showing the planets of our solar system there can be attached a paper rocket for each pupil in the room, with the name of the child on it. The pupil's rocket ship can be moved from planet to planet as he reads an additional book.

4. The class can have a large class progress chart in the form of a bookworm, made of paper, with at first only the head of the worm displayed. When a child has completed a book, a new segment can be added onto the worm. The goal of the class would be to see the worm grow as long as possible.

5. Each pupil can record on a card the title and author of every book he has greatly enjoyed. These cards can be placed in a pocket chart so other pupils can note the recommendations of their peers.

VISUAL AIDS TO ENCOURAGE READING

Many visual aids that boys and girls can make to interest others in good books and provide for themselves values in connection with the reading they have done are described in preceding pages of this book. Additional ones are here given.

Courtesy of the Portland, Oregon, Public Schools

Figure 11.20 Record Keeping as Incidental to Absorption in Reading

Bulletin Boards

The descriptions of bulletin boards given in this section are divided into three groups, namely (1) bulletin boards dealing with one book, (2) bulletin boards dealing with a category of books, and (3) bulletin boards designed to interest children in reading any worthwhile books.

Bulletin Boards Dealing With One Book. Here are descriptions of a few of the many posters that can be used as bulletin boards to interest pupils in reading a given book.

1. On a poster entitled "Mike Mulligan and His Steam Shovel" depicting the book by that title by Virginia Burton, the steam shovel can be cut from red construction paper with facial features pasted on and a movable steam shovel arm, also of paper, used for a nose. For the background three shades of green construction paper can be used: light green for the ground, medium green for the foliage on the ground, and dark green for the leaves on a tree.

2. In a poster entitled "Twenty-One Balloons" on the book by that title by William Péne Dubois, a fairly large three-dimensional balloon made from thin papier-mâché covered with yellow cloth is the central object. Strings from the balloon extend down to a three-dimensional basket, shaped from light cardboard and covered with gray yarn in a basket weave pattern. These objects are mounted on light blue tagboard with a few white cotton clouds pasted onto the blue sky.

Poster was drawn by Kathy Kappel Rose

Figure 11.21

Figure 11.22

Poster was drawn by Alice Sharpe Barber

Figure 11.23

Poster was drawn by Mary Stewart Rutchow

Figure 11.24

Poster was drawn by Mary Helen Houck

Figure 11.25

Poster was drawn by Kathryn Newman Feld

Figure 11.26

Bulletin Boards Dealing with One Book

3. In a poster entitled "Paddle-to-the-Sea" illustrating the book by Holling C. Holling, white tagboard serves as a background. Across the poster an outline of the Great Lakes area is drawn in black ink. A heavy line of blue paint shows the border on the Canadian side of the lakes and a line of red paint that on the American side. A broken black line traces an Indian's voyage. The model of an Indian is in a three-dimensional canoe in the bottom left-hand corner of the poster.

4. In the accompaning illustration of the poster on the book *The Bears of Hemlock Mountain* by Alice Dalgliesch, the background is blue construction paper on a mounting of black paper. The lettering and the drops from the pail, which is made of tinfoil with black pipe cleaners for handle and feet, are also of black paper. The evergreens are made of green paper, folded through the middle of each tree to give a three-dimensional effect. The bears, with markings of chalk and with little pearl buttons as eyes, are felt.

BULLETIN BOARDS DEALING WITH A CATEGORY OF BOOKS. Here are described several bulletin boards that show how posters can be used to interest boys and girls in books of a given type.

1. On a bulletin board entitled "stories about Easter," a large bunny, cut from white construction paper with cotton pasted onto his body, is sitting on the right side of the poster. He is holding in his left arm a small wicker basket containing blown-out egg shells, which have been painted in pastel colors. On the center of the right side of the poster is a tulip plant constructed with a green paper stem and three-dimensional tulips made from pieces of colored egg shell which have been glued together. Pastel colors are used for the tagboard backing and for the lettering.

2. On a bulletin board entitled "Children of Many Lands," a map of the world was portrayed in white with the surrounding water painted blue. Small dolls were dressed to represent a particular country and attached to the map near or on their corresponding countries. The shape of each country for which there is a representative doll was cut from yellow construction paper, pasted over its location on the map, and labeled with its name. The background of the poster can be mounted on white or dark blue construction paper to form a frame around the map.

3. On a bulletin board entitled "Read Science" the background was black tagboard and the lettering was done in red ink on a green strip of paper. The central object was an open book. The front flap was made from red construction paper glued onto the tagboard. Typed on the page were the following headings: "We Read in Science Books," "Science Can Be Fun," "Science Reading Is Different," and "Let's Read a Science Book." The rest of the book consisted of three black tagboard pages. On these pages were pasted magazine pictures from different fields of science. Also included were interesting facts about science. The book was made to stand out by means of triangular-shaped cardboard hinges placed behind the back flap near the binding of the book.

4. On a bulletin board entitled "Read about the City" in the lower right-hand corner were figures of a boy and girl, dressed in clothes cut from material. They were standing at the intersection of four roads. Each road, made from sand glued onto the tagboard backing, lead to a different place in the community — the church, the school, the police station, and the fire station. The buildings were cut from colored construction paper and made to stand away from the backing by pasting them onto a small piece of sponge.

BULLETIN BOARDS TO INTEREST PUPILS IN ANY WORTHWHILE READING. A few bulletin boards to encourage boys and girls in any kind of worthwhile reading are here described.

1. On a bulletin board entitled "Reading Yields a Bountiful Harvest" a three-dimensional cornucopia made from papier-mâché was the central figure. A number of book jackets representing the subject areas found in books were coming out of the cornucopia. The book jackets were made from different colors of construction paper, the lettering was in black ink, and the designs portraying the subject fields were made from cut paper. The background was white tagboard.

2. On a bulletin board entitled "Through Reading Learning Is Exciting" was featured a reader being swept into the clouds on a magic carpet. The figure of the reader was made from construction paper and the carpet was made from colored pipe cleaners that were woven together. On either side of the reader were three real book jackets. A few clouds were represented by cotton. Lettering for the tagboard poster was done with colored pipe cleaners.

3. A bulletin board entitled "Can You Identify These Characters?" was made with a large black question mark cut from felt and pasted to the center of the white tagboard. Surrounding the question mark were illustrations of six characters which the children meet in their classroom reading. Each figure, wearing clothing typical of his character, was painted on the tagboard. The lettering was made of construction paper.

4. A bulletin board was entitled "Meet These Book Friends." The following "characters," painted on

Poster was drawn by Nancy Howard Hickok.

Figure 11.27

Poster was drawn by Jane Schwegler.

Figure 11.28

Poster was drawn by Karen Massie Switzer.

Figure 11.29

Poster was drawn by Janice Sue Woods McPherson.

Figure 11.30

Poster was drawn by Jane Hadley Lewis.

Figure 11.31

Poster was drawn by Barbara Tener.

Figure 11.32

Bulletin Boards about a Category of Books

drawing paper and then mounted on pieces of sponge to give the three-dimensional effect, were connected by yarn to a reproduction of the cover of the book that they represent: the bear from Lynd Ward's *The Biggest Bear;* the steam shovel from Virginia Burton's *Mike Mulligan and His Steam Shovel;* Juan from Leo Politi's *Song of the Swallow;* the kindly policeman from Robert McCloskey's *Make Way for Ducklings;* and the rabbit from Margery Williams' *The Velveteen Rabbit.*

Poster was drawn by Florence Littell.

Figure 11.33 A Bulletin Board to Interest Children in Reading Books of Various Types

Displays

Displays of various types, like those here described, can be exhibited in order to interest boys and girls in reading.

1. In one poster a house was made out of a cardboard box and covered with white paper. The roof was painted green. The words "Come Visit with Us" were cut out of white construction paper and glued to one side of the room. The windows were cut out and a piece of gray construction paper was used as a backing for each of the windows and in front of the gray paper there was a character from a story made of paper and painted with poster paint. Under each window the name of the character was written in black ink. An index card was placed in front of the house listing the various characters and the stories in which they are found. Some characters that were represented were Alice from *Alice in Wonderland,* Huck Finn from *The Adventures of Huckleberry Finn,* and Peter from *Peter Pan.*

2. A folder "Do You Know these Animal Characters?" was made out of poster paper folded in an accordion-like manner. The title was written on the first section of the folder. Pictures of animals from various animal stories had been cut out of white construction paper and colored the appropriate colors with crayon. These figures were pasted on the sections of the folder. The title of the story was written above each picture and the name of the author below it. One side of the folder deals with books for the primary grades and the other side with books for the intermediate grades.

3. A large world map was mounted on poster paper and placed on a table so that it leans against a wall. Ribbons lead from various points on the map to book jackets and to the characters that are displayed. The book jackets were made of colored pieces of construction paper. The title and the name of the author were written on each book jacket. The characters were made of cardboard. Each one also has a piece of cardboard behind it so that the figure stands up. The features were painted on the figures with poster paint. Cotton and wool material were used for the clothing and straw and yarn for the hair.

4. A three-dimensional castle was made out of cardboard. The castle was painted with poster paint and a drawbridge in front was cut out so that it could be dropped as if it were real. Pieces of leather string were used for the chains of the bridge. The window in the castle was cut out and a figure of Repunzel was placed in the window, with her hair hanging out of the window and touching the ground. Various characters from fairy tales were placed around the castle. They were made of cardboard with another piece of cardboard attached to the back of each character to enable it to stand. The figures were painted with poster paint.

5. A large open "book" was made out of poster paper. On one side of the "book" were printed the title *Heidi* and the author's name *Johanna Spyri,* both in ink. On the other side of the "book" was painted a scene from the story. The picture shows a mountain scene with a boy and girl in the foreground dressed in mountain attire playing with a goat. The "book" was propped up by a piece of cardboard and figures of goats of cardboard were placed in front of it. These figures were painted with water colors.

6. A display entitled "Our Animal Friends" was made by placing the branch of a tree in a plastic container into which plaster of Paris was poured. The characters, such as a fish for Golden MacDonald's *The Little Island* (illustrated by Leonard Weisgard), a bear for Lynd Ward's *The Biggest Bear,* and a

Figure 11.34

Display was made by Linda Deuble Lippincott

Figure 11.35

Display was made by Sue Kenworthy and Sandy Bardwell Lee

Figure 11.36

Display was made by Joan Kehl Royer

Figure 11.37

Display was made by Dorothy Wolfe

Figure 11.38

Display was made by Patti Tieken Johnson

Figure 11.39

Displays to Interest Children in Books

swallow for Leo Politi's *Song of the Swallow* were made from construction paper. These figures were suspended from the branch with black thread.

7. To interest children in reading history books dolls can be made out of cardboard and dressed in the costumes of different periods of history such as the Colonial, the Revolutionary, or the medieval period. The clothing can be made of scraps of material. To each character a card can be attached giving the titles of several books about the period represented.

8. A map of the United States can be drawn on tagboard. Characters made of cardboard can stand on the surface to represent a character from a book about a minority group in a given area of the United States. A card can be placed at each character's feet, with the title of the book and the name of the author.

9. The pupils can make dioramas or peep shows to illustrate scenes from a story. The characters can be three-dimensional little figures of clay, plastic or wood or they can be paper-doll representations. The furnishings for a scene can be made of paper, wood, or a variety of other materials. The scenery for the setting can be painted onto the interior sides of the box that houses the peep show.

Display was made by Angela Neasse.

Figure 11.40 A Peep Show as Means of Interesting Children in Books

10. The pupils can make murals to illustrate scenes from books they like. In the primary grades, the boys and girls can draw the characters as well as parts of the scenery on paper and then cut them out and attach them to the appropriate spaces on the mural. Older pupils can draw or paint the parts of the mural directly onto the large paper roll. In some instances the paper may be divided into as many

Display was made by Karen Whipkey.

Figure 11.41 Another Peep Show on a Book

parts vertically as there are scenes to be represented. In other murals one scene may "run" into another without a distinct division of the mural into separate pictures.

11. Book mobiles of various types can "advertise" a single book, or they can illustrate books of a given kind (such as books of biography or animals stories) or they can be representative of a variety of types – possibly favorites of the child who made the mural or a book of each kind that would be good reading for the class.

Other Visual Aids

Reference is made following to a few additional types of visual aids the pupils can make for use in developing interest in good reading.

1. Book jackets. Original jackets for the books, drawn by the boys and girls, can portray for others in the class a reason why the person who drew the picture liked a given book.

2. Paper masks. Boys and girls enjoy transforming paper bags into masks to represent characters from a book they wish to portray.

3. Bookmarks. Pupils can make a variety of bookmarks illustrating favorite books. Sometimes the picture can be drawn by the pupils; at other times pictures portraying scenes or characters from a book can be cut from printed material advertising a book and then pasted onto the rest of the bookmark.

Figure 11.42 Making One's Own Bookmark

4. Scrapbooks. The boys and girls may make notebooks or scrapbooks. In them can be included brief reports of books read by a pupil; pictures — either drawn by the pupil or cut from printed material — representing books that the owner has enjoyed; quotations from books; reports on how to take care of books; lists of books that the owner of the notebook or scrapbook would like to read; poems about books.

5. Puppets. Boys and girls are enthusiastic about making puppets and giving plays to interest others in books. For a somewhat detailed description of puppets, the reader is referred to page 263.

FOR STUDY AND DISCUSSION

1. Devise a questionnaire for help in determining what books to recommend to an individual who is asked, either orally or in writing, the questions you have formulated. Indicate the grade level for which you have planned the instrument.

2. How might you proceed in guiding a child so that he will develop more refined tastes in his reading?

3. On page 230 it is stated that the teacher who in an appropriate manner starts reading to his pupils books of the universal appeal of *Doctor Dolittle* by Hugh Lofting or *The Wind in the Willows* by Kenneth Grahame need not fear that many children able to read such books will not be eager to read them. What are other books in this category that you would recommend for oral reading of the introductory chapter by the teacher?

4. Devise a game that can be used to interest boys and girls in reading worthwhile books.

5. Outline a year's program for any one grade to follow in trying to interest boys and girls in worthwhile reading.

6. Construct one or more visual aids to be used to interest boys and girls in books.

7. Plan a Book Week program for any grade of the elementary school.

8. Consult a professional book on literature for children such as *Children and Books* by May Arbuthnot or *A Teacher's Guide to Children's Books* by Nancy Larrick for suggested readings for boys and girls in any one area of the content subjects. Then read in that area and write brief reviews, possibly on cards, of each book read. Include among other points in your reviews your evaluation of each book. (Some of the titles of books listed under "References" will suggest additional sources for help in choosing worthwhile books. The reader is also referred to Chapter 15 for further listings in the area of literature for children.)

REFERENCES

Adams, Bess Porter, *About Books and Children.* Holt, Rinehart and Winston, 1952. 573 pp.

Arbuthnot, May, *Children and Books.* Third edition. Scott, Foresman and Company, 1964. 688 pp.

Arbuthnot, May; Margaret Clark; and Harriet Long, *Children's Books too Good to Miss.* Western Reserve University Press. Fourth edition. 67 pp.

Association for Childhood Education International, *Literature with Children.* Association for Childhood Education International, 1961. 56 pp.

Hazard, Paul, *Books, Children and Men.* Fourth edition. Horn Book, Inc., 1960. 176 pp.

Larrick, Nancy, *A Teacher's Guide to Children's Books.* Charles E. Merrill Books, 1960. 316 pp.

Walsh, Frances (ed.), *That Eager Zest: First Discoveries in the Magic World of Books.* J. B. Lippincott Company, 1961. 251 pp.

OUTLINE FOR CHAPTER 12

Guiding Growth Through Dramatic Expression

CHAPTER 12

Guiding Growth Through Dramatic Expression

During the past few decades elementary-school teachers have become increasingly cognizant of the role of dramatic expression – which provides communication through speech and through movement – as a vital part of the language-arts curriculum. Trends that seem to be emerging are:

1. A greater number of elementary-school teachers take college courses or attend workshops dealing at least in part with creative dramatics, it would seem.
2. Books and periodicals, dealing exclusively or in part with creative dramatics in the elementary-school classroom, are appearing on the market in greater numbers.
3. More time is devoted in grades 1 through 6 to creative dramatics.
4. Teachers in the classroom are less prone to consider themselves incompetent in guiding growth in creative dramatics.
5. A greater variety of creative dramatics is used in more elementary-school classrooms ranging from the free, unhampered, uninhibited dramatic play of the young child through improvised dramatization to more formal dramatizing, including in addition to dramatic play and the more usual dramatizations, puppetry, pantomime, pageantry, role playing, and verse choirs.
6. The role of the teacher is less directive.
7. Costuming and staging are relied upon less.
8. Greater emphasis is being placed on the variety of values that can be obtained from creative dramatics in the classroom.

VALUES OF DRAMATIC EXPRESSION

Although the values of dramatic expression vary somewhat from one type of dramatics to another, the variance is probably more one of degree than of kind. Here are listed those which more or less pertain to several types of creative dramatics, while on subsequent pages of this chapter attention is drawn, as the types of dramatic expression are discussed, to the contributions each can make.

Provisions for Emotional Expression

One of the chief values of creative dramatics lies in the opportunity it affords for emotional expression. Children, hemmed in by myriads of regulations – many necessary, some not – need the freedom of self-expression that dramatic expression can so well supply. Without such independence the child's world, far from being a happy, carefree one, might be well-nigh intolerable.

It is indeed fortunate that the simplest, freest, most spontaneous means of dramatic expression, namely dramatic play, is almost second nature to the child who, when one minute he plays he is a horse, for all practical effects (that is, for effects on the child's emotional nature) *is* a horse whinnying as he gallops through the dining room, even though the next moment ascending the steps to the second floor, he may be an airplane zooming upward into space. What matter physical restrictions when the spirit is free to abide wheresoever it chooses!

In dramatic play or in more structured dramatization, an observing adult can at times gain insight into the child's emotional life. Care must be taken that neither teacher nor parent assumes diagnostic responsibilities that would baffle an expert psychiatrist, for it is easy to make serious errors in associating dramatic expression with specific underlying and deep-seated psychic deviations. However, persistence in choice of certain roles may well indicate a need. The girl who almost invariably wants to be a princess may have a feeling of deep inferiority. The child who shows cruelty in his dramatic play may be in need of help in freeing himself of asocial impulses.

Development of Personality Traits

Through various types of creative dramatics opportunity for increased self-control, greater poise, more self-confidence is given. The freedom of movement encouraged by liberating dramatic expression fosters gracefulness which in turn affects psychical characteristics. One of the greatest boons of creative dramatics lies in its effects on the imagination. In the young child ample opportunity to engage in creative dramatics gives the imagination of the child free reign. Continued participation in dramatics helps prevent the undesirable inhibitions that typically thwart the imagination of the child as he passes toward adolescence and later into adulthood. Boys and girls receiving the full benefits of creative dramatics at its best may know even when they are grownups how:

> Of the magic things of life, never to tire,
> And how, to renew, when it is low, the lamp of my desire.[1]

Expansion of the Environment

Through dramatics, whether it is the dramatic play of the three-year-old girl who sits on a nest made of mother's shawl as she pretends to breed her chicks or whether it is the twelve-year-old who participates in a Mexican fiesta, there is need, for effective dramatization, of study of the environment, either firsthand through observation or indirectly through pictures, conversation, reading, and the like. The near can become fascinating and the faraway clear and intriguing.

Growth in Sympathetic Understanding

As the child's environment expands through creative dramatics and through related activities, he is provided with the chance to develop in ability to put himself in the place of another, especially when under the guidance of a wise adult. When the bully who is given the role of the bullied, when the boy or girl who once thought of Indians as savages takes the part of an Indian lad or lass as a day on a reservation is dramatized, or when the girl who had been prejudiced against Orientals takes part in a dramatization of "Matsayama's Mirror," the children can hardly avoid developing a feeling of warmth toward the people they portray, for true dramatics is not to *seem* to be but to *be*.

Development of Language Skills

What better reason can there be for boys and girls to develop some of the language-arts skills than that afforded by dramatics? The child who has talked almost inaudibly begins to recognize the value of speech that can readily be heard. Even exercises, if necessary, to get a suitable intonation, to achieve proper pitch, or to speak with convincing tempo make sense to the participant eager to do his best. Drills in the use of exact words to express feeling can become surprisingly important. The script for a dramatization and letters of invitation constitute but a few of the opportunities for written communication provided by creative dramatics.

Development of Work Habits

Important work habits can be formed or reinforced through dramatics. Cooperation, perseverance, critical thinking with need to come to decisions, participation in evaluation, for example, can be practiced in meaningful situations.

Courtesy of the Akron, Ohio, Public Schools

Figure 12.1 Effect of Dramatics on Class Atmosphere

Influence on Class Atmosphere

Repeatedly it has been observed that the whole atmosphere in a classroom can be affected favorably through introduction of dramatics. Boys and girls who previously had lacked interest in school frequently engage happily even in other activities of the school day that formerly had been only boring to them. Pride in the room, joy in teacher and peers, and enthusiasm for school are often the result.

[1] Author unknown

Means of Motivation

Under "Development of Language Skills" reference is made to the power of motivation of dramatics in the area of the language arts. Similarly the social studies, science, art, music, physical education, and health can be vitalized through dramatic expression as the pupils dramatize a folk tale of a foreign country, put on skits showing scenes from the lives of great men and women of science, plan a backdrop for a puppet show, learn songs for use in a pageant, play games of boys and girls in faraway times or places, or make up a good-health play showing the constituents of a balanced diet.

Variation of Procedure

Dramatics can help avoid the sameness in teaching procedure which seems to be one of the reasons why some boys and girls do not like school. Dramatic activities provide not only variety but pleasant variety. To the boys and girls "the play's the thing."

Provision for Enjoyment

Very important among the values of creative dramatics is the fun provided. As "beauty is its own excuse for being," so is pure unadulterated fun that can come from creative expression in dramatics.

DRAMATIC PLAY

Dramatic play, as the term is used here, refers to the spontaneous play that is characteristic of the young child, in which he lives — not merely acts — the part he is portraying. The girl engages in dramatic play when she *is* the mother dressing the baby. The boy takes part in dramatic play when he *is* the engine that pulls the long heavy cars up an almost impossibly steep ascent. For dramatic play no talent is needed beyond that common to childhood. There is no audience to please. The joy of the actor is its reason for being. While props can be used, they are far from essential, and simple props are much to be preferred to the elaborate. The role of a child may change swiftly as after a few minutes of being an airplane — without even a need for transformation, without a fairy wand to make the change — he becomes the milkman or a spider or even a rock. Especially with older children, the same role, as mother, for example, may be continued for week after week.

Values

All of the values listed at the beginning of this chapter probably can be achieved, at least to some extent, in dramatic play. Among those to which dramatic play contributes especially are: (1) provision for emotional expression, (2) development of personality traits, (3) expansion of the environment, and (4) growth in sympathetic understanding. It is through dramatic play that the child can try out the life he observes around him and that which his vivid imagination creates for him. It is through this medium of expression that he can be what he wants to be, ruled by his own spirit not by the physical laws of existence. With utter, joyous abandon he can surmount problems and shortcomings of all types.

Courtesy of the Wichita, Kansas, Public Schools

Figure 12.2 Being, Not Seeming

Role of the Teacher

Maybe the most important function the teacher can fulfill in connection with the dramatic play of the young is not to interfere with it. He should avoid interference by arranging the school program so that ample time is provided, by refraining from any "directing" of the child's play, by making no untoward remarks about his activities, like calling them "dear" or "darling" or "amusing." He can help by setting aside places in the schoolroom where dramatic play can "germinate" and develop. He can provide facilities such as a playhouse unit with its simple household furnishings or a make-believe store. He can help make available to the child large blocks, now common to the kindergarten and first-grade room, from which the children can construct houses, stores, post offices, airplanes, boats, trains, trucks, tractors, whatever fancy dictates. He can make accessible one or more boxes of simple props like an apron for grandmother, a piece of cloth for baby's blanket, high-heeled shoes for mother, long skirts for the ladies, and veiling, hats, pocketbooks for a variety of purposes.

The teacher can also perform an important role by:

1. Conducting discussion that stimulates dramatic play
2. Providing pupils with experiences that lead to dramatic play (such as taking children to a zoo, a farm, or a bakery)
3. Participating, usually only on invitation, in dramatic play (such as tending to the baby when mother needs to cook or having supper in the playhouse or playing the role of a customer in a store)
4. Giving some (but only a few) suggestions as to how dramatic play can be carried on effectively within the limitations of time and space
5. Helping maintain a classroom attitude conducive to freedom without license and with respect for personality
6. Observing the child at his play in order to try to note his needs and his satisfactions.

Examples of Dramatic Play

Interspersed among the preceding pages of this chapter are examples of dramatic play. Following are mentioned additional ones.

1. Being an inanimate object, such as a river, the wind, a seashell, father's rocker, an automobile
2. Being an animal, such as a dog, cat, elephant, duck, goose, robin, eagle, one of the Three Bears, one (or all!) of the Three Little Pigs
3. Playing school, church, Sunday school, a wedding, a funeral, a baptism
4. Baking cookies, fixing baby's bottle, feeding the chickens, sewing a dress, piloting a plane
5. Re-enacting parts of a trip to a farm, a fire station, a bakery, a post office.

DRAMATIZATION

While in dramatic play the accent is on *being*, in dramatization, even the less formal types, there is recognition of the fact that something is being dramatized. The dramatic play of the four-year-old, for example, as he plays house is almost total identification with the role played, with no concern about an audience. In dramatization there is a planned, though often extemporaneously planned, enactment of roles. There is a plot, frequently very simple, with a beginning and a definite ending.

Dramatization can be classified in a variety of ways, these among them: (1) impromptu dramatization, (2) dramatization of a pupil-planned play, and (3) dramatization of an adult-written play. Suggestions for guiding boys and girls in dramatization of each of these three types follow.

Impromptu Dramatization

In the impromptu dramatization, which is sometimes almost entirely extemporaneous, there is relatively little preplanning. After a story has been read during reading class or after the teacher has told or read a story to the class, one child, in a room where pupil expression is encouraged, may ask, "May we play the story?" Even though only a few minutes may be available for following the suggestion, the teacher may assent and help the group to decide quickly what scenes to include, what characters are needed for each scene, and where the setting is to be. After two or three minutes' time, the play may be well on its way. At other times one or more scenes may be enacted even without any preliminary planning other than that of assignment of roles.

With similar lack of emphasis on preplanning the boys and girls can engage in dramatization, with or without words, of activities or scenes about which they have read or which they have seen in life situations. For example, a group of second-grade boys and girls, after having watched workmen build a house, may return to the classroom to decide to put on a pantomime showing the work of builders they have observed. One may be a carpenter, another a plumber, and still another an electrician or a painter. The class can be divided into groups of four (if four workmen are to be presented) with each group assigning one of its members to each of the roles and helping one another re-enact the part of a given workman. Then the groups may pantomime their parts as the audience (the members of the other groups) tell what each person is doing.

Another variation is to have pupils put on impromptu dramatizations of scenes about which they have studied in the content subjects, such as the social studies or the sciences. After having read and heard about life in a Pueblo village, for example, the class may decide on a dramatization of the life of a boy and girl in such a village. After only brief discussion of points that can be brought out in a dramatization, characters can be chosen, the scene dramatized, and a brief discussion held on points of excellence or needs for improvement. Thereupon, again one or more groups of characters may be chosen who in turn will enact scenes. After reading, for example, about Thomas Edison's boyhood and early manhood, the class may determine which scenes would be good for dramatization and then divide into as many groups as there are scenes to be presented. Thereupon each group can plan its dramatization in a different part of the room. Then, for the entire class, the scenes can be presented in appropriate order.

Poetry also can serve as subject matter for impromptu dramatization, as well as for more definitely planned presentation. Many a boy and girl will enjoy responding dramatically to "Paul Revere's Ride" and "Barbara Fritchie," regardless of license in historic accuracy that may have crept into both poems. In "Paul Revere's Ride" some scenes that are brimful of opportunity for dramatization are those that begin with these lines:

> . . . . If the British march
> By land or sea, from the town tonight.
>
> Then he said, "Good night," and with muffled oar
> Silently rode to the Charlestown shore.

What girl in the fifth grade would not enjoy being patriotic Barbara Fritchie when she makes her affirmation,

> Shoot if you must this old gray head,
> But spare your country's flag . . . .

Or what boy in the same grade would not want to be Stonewall Jackson as he says,

> Who touches a hair of yon gray head,
> Dies like a dog. . . .

Points to Observe When Guiding Impromptu Dramatization. In order to help boys and girls receive maximum benefit from impromptu dramatizations, the teacher should keep in mind points such as the following.

1. Presentation to the pupils of many types of subject matter that provide suitable background for dramatic presentation and encouragement in taking part in interesting activities can stimulate the desire to dramatize what they have seen or heard.

2. Because boys and girls become less and less interested in dramatic play (often because of the inhibitions adults have placed upon them) after the early primary-grade years, it is important that the teacher help them preserve the imaginativeness of childhood and develop it as they grow toward adolescence. At first a suggestion to dramatize often must come from the teacher if the boys and girls have been unaccustomed with teachers of previous years to take part in dramatizations.

3. Although there are many values that can be achieved through frequent participation in dramatizations, like most good things they can be overdone. Boys and girls should not be allowed to participate in them so frequently that the excitement, novelty, and joy of participation wear off. To dramatize every story in a reader would probably be almost as detrimental to the child's best growth and development as not to dramatize at all.

4. The slapstick should be avoided in dramatizations. A desire to create a valuable contribution can be encouraged through a discussion beforehand of the mood to be portrayed or the attitude of the character or the style of expression most suitable. Wise use of praise following dramatization can also help set standards for subsequent ones.

5. Criticisms of a child's best effort should be given sparingly lest frustrations and inhibitions result. Emphasis should be placed primarily on points well done.

6. Frequently more than one dramatization of a scene or story could be given, with different pupils taking part.

7. Care should be taken that all boys and girls have opportunities for participation in dramatizations. The temptation to give a part to the child who seems best suited for it can prevent the child who may most need the help afforded by this type of language-arts activity from being able to participate.

8. While it is not important and not possible that every child have the opportunity to take part in every dramatization (often there are not enough parts even if many pupils are intentionally included as characters with minor parts), as a rule no person should be given a part a second time before each child has been assigned one.

Dramatization of Pupil-Planned Plays

As boys and girls progress to the upper primary and intermediate grades, they can increasingly be interested in dramatization that involves more than extemporizing or impromptu presentation with relatively little preplanning. Careful preparation can take place both with stories that the children heard or read or with plays for which they themselves chose a theme and developed the plot.

Dramatization of Stories. In addition to the values of dramatization already listed, dramatization of stories has this important value: boys and girls can gain greater appreciation of literature. If this objective is to be fulfilled, obviously it is important that the teacher guide the boys and girls accordingly.

1. Dramatization as means of increasing pupils' appreciation of literature. One criterion to be observed in order that boys and girls can attain maximum appreciation of good literature through the dramatization of stories is that the stories chosen should be suitable and valuable. First of all, they

should be worthwhile stories, as high on the pupils' level of appreciation as the class can dramatize with success. Dramatization of stories beyond the pupils' power of performance with reasonable success is likely not to instill in them a love of the story. Nor, on the contrary, will stories below the pupils' level of appreciation that they can dramatize reasonably well be likely to foster greater interest in good literature. Some of the requirements for stories for dramatization can be summarized thus.

> The story should be of good literature.
> The story should have vivid characters and swift-moving action intermingled with suspense.
> The story should consist of relatively few incidents.
> The pattern of the story should be distinct, with a forceful beginning, an easily recognizable climax toward which all preceding events lead, and a satisfying ending.
> The story should contain much action on which the theme should rest rather than on beauty of words or philosophy of background.
> The characters should be interesting.
> The story should have emotional appeal for the children.
> Repetition of type of incident or of cause for incidents occurring with almost rhythmic quality in the development of the plot should be one of the points for which to watch in selecting a story for dramatization for the young child.

The reader may have noted that many of the well-known folk tales fulfill the requirements listed. "Rumplestilskin," "The Three Golden Apples," "Hansel and Gretel" all qualify. Modern stories, however, also can be used successfully, as for example *Mary Poppins*, *Mr. Popper's Penguins*, or *Charlotte's Web*.

2. Steps in planning a dramatization of a story. After the story has been selected, what needs to be done next? There is no one series of steps that can be acclaimed as the one and only sequence to follow. The order of procedure here suggested, however, is one that can bring good results.

> Drawing attention to the sequence of events in the story by the manner of reading or telling it to the class, questions by the teacher, or listing of chief events on the chalkboard at the dictation of the boys and girls
> Drawing attention to the characters by asking for the names (to record on the chalkboard) and asking pertinent questions as to the type each is, in terms of motive and actions
> Deciding upon scenes to dramatize and upon the order of these scenes, with emphasis on the action in each
> Determining characters needed for each scene and the role each plays within a given scene
> Discussing general content of what the various characters will need to say in order to portray the plot adequately
> Discussing what would make an effective beginning and a strong ending for the play
> Discussing ways in which the various characters can carry on the story through their words and their nonverbal responses.
> Assigning roles, with care being taken that no pupil need play a part he does not want. (It may be impossible, however, for each pupil to get the part he likes best.)
> Practicing scenes. (At times boys and girls not in a given scene may be engaged in other activities while some of the practicing takes place. At other times the practicing may be done in front of the entire class not in the play for helpful suggestions from them.)

It is often advisable to have more than one pupil work on each of the parts. Opportunity should be provided for each pupil assigned to a given role to be in a dramatization when it is presented to an audience.

Even in carefully preplanned dramatization, the lines frequently are not recorded. The general content of the dialogue should be discussed. There may well be variations each time the story is dramatized. On the other hand there are times when it may seem advisable that the lines be recorded. A variety of procedures can be followed in the writing. For example, a committee under the direction of the teacher may work out dialogue for the first scene. That can then be presented to the class for suggestions, some of which may be incorporated in a rewriting of the parts. Thereupon another committee may proceed with work on the lines for the second scene, to be followed by still another committee or committees whose responsibility it is to write the script for the remaining parts of the play. Even when the script is written, it is not necesary that the lines be memorized. The script can be used merely as guides by the boys and girls.

3. The production. With dramatizations for which there has been careful preplanning, it seems only logical to have an audience for a final performance. Who should be invited should be determined in part by the complexity of the play. The audience may con-

sist of another grade in the same building, the play may be given in an assembly program, or parents may be invited.

Elaborate costuming or stage settings should be avoided. In fact, in some of the best productions from the point of view of the growth and development of the performers, both costuming and stage properties may be lacking. If there is costuming, it is best to keep it so simple that the pupils themselves, not the parents and the teacher, have the experience involved in making the costumes. The same can be said about the stage setting. An apron to suggest that a girl is a grandmother, a hat to show that a boy is a man, long ears made of paper to show that the person is the big bad wolf, often are enough. On the other hand if, for example, a play is worked out on the book *The Door in the Wall* by Marguerite DeAngeli as a culmination for a sixth-grade unit on the Middle Ages, it may be that making costumes by the pupils after adequate research on the dress of that period of history can be a valuable means of integrating the work in the social studies with that in art.

4. Evaluation. After boys and girls have spent considerable time dramatizing a story, they are entitled to the benefit of evaluation. The appraisal should be primarily in terms of self-evaluation, preferably in part, at least, based on criteria that the pupils have helped work out. Points that may be considered in such an evaluation are:

> Did we tell the story well, including important points in a correct sequence?
> Could we be heard easily in every part of the room?
> Did we show by our actions how we felt about what we were saying?
> Did the characters seem true to life?
> Did the play have a strong beginning?
> Did the play have a strong ending?

Probably more permanent values are gained if criticisms by others, including both the teacher and the children, are confined chiefly to favorable points after the final production. As a rule, suggestions for improvement may better be offered before the boys and girls give the play in front of an audience.

Dramatization of Original Plays. Boys and girls in the elementary school often like to plan the plot for plays they present. Sometimes the dramatization may be a series of episodes to illustrate points with a background in the content areas. For example, they may give a dramatization of (1) a Mexican market day, (2) life in Colonial times, (3) life on the Oregon trail, or (4) life during castle days.

Sometimes the dramatization may evolve around a story with a plot which the boys and girls themselves work out. The teacher will frequently need to help them decide on a worthy theme and develop a strong plot around the theme. A decision will need to be made as to what characters are necessary and what scenes to depict in the course of the development of the plot. The boys and girls may want to write the lines for their play or they may prefer putting on the play without use of any recorded lines. Occasionally a boy or girl may want to write a play as an individual creative writing project.

Dramatization of Plays Written by Others

Because of the many values that can be obtained through the very act of working out a play themselves, there has been a tendency among educators to look with disfavor on any dramatization that is not original with the boys and girls. This attitude hardly seems justifiable. There may well be times when boys and girls can achieve some of the objectives of dramatization through dramatizing a play written by others.

Many an adult who has been in a high school or college play or has taken part in community theater will testify that values can accrue from taking part in a play that is published. From and through such activities can result increased cooperation, vicarious experiences with resulting lack of concentration on self, joy in active participation in a joint project, and insight into character development (in case the play is a worthy one).

Especially when plays are based in part on events or conditions in a background of social studies or science or health there is, at times, an advantage in dramatizing a play that has been written by a person who is well acquainted with the background. Unless boys and girls have studied rather extensively – more extensively than time often permits – for example, life in Colonial times they may perpetuate through a pupil-created play ideas about that period of history which can be misleading or outright erroneous. On the other hand, they can receive and give a correct impression if they dramatize a play written by a person well acquainted with customs of Colonial times.

PUPPETRY

Puppetry is becoming more and more popular with boys and girls. It is well that this popularity exists for it can serve as an aid to the elementary-school teacher.

Values of Puppetry

Through puppetry many of the objectives of dramatics listed in the first part of this chapter can be achieved. It can be a means of helping boys and girls in speech training, in reading (including research activities), in writing, and in listening. It can serve as a means of motivation for other areas of learning, giving purpose for some needed activities that otherwise might be monotonous and seem purposeless. It can add interest and understanding to literature as worthwhile stories are being played; it can serve as incentive for living according to laws of good health, when for example, a puppet play shows the importance of the Basic Seven; it can throw light on periods remote in history as children study customs and costumes of the time, for example, when Robin Hood lived, in order to put on a puppet play on *Robin Hood and His Merry Men;* it can give meaning to science as scenes such as the invention of the telephone are dramatized; it can give reason for studying music so that suitable music to accompany the play will be selected; it can give purpose for studying various techniques of artistic production in order to be able to provide a stage setting that is attractive.

Figure 12.3 A Marionette

Figure 12.4 Puppets to Fit Various Needs

One reason why many teachers at times prefer puppetry to other types of dramatization is that everything is in miniature and consequently questions of cost of scenery and costumes present little problem, if any. Another advantage of puppetry is that it is especially helpful for both the shy child and the showoff. The timid child, too self-conscious at first to participate in other dramatization effectively, can, when hidden from his audience by the puppet stage, lose himself in his puppet. Thus he liberates himself for future activity in other types of dramatization and in real life. Similarly the overaggressive child, bent on showing off, soon finds out that in puppetry his antics cannot be seen by the audience. For lack of attention he may decide that acting up is futile. Furthermore, projecting of self into the role of the puppet can serve as balm to the spirit that needs to get beyond itself.

Work in puppetry at school can have a desirable carry-over into the home, especially if the teacher points out some of the possibilities to the pupil and to the parent. Even the only child can work out puppetry plays for presentation at home and at school. Parents can work with their children on puppet plays and in working they can gain a closer relationship with them. They can be instrumental in developing in their children an interest in puppetry that may be of great value to the boys and girls at the time and may lead into a lifetime avocation.

Kinds of Puppets

The difference between a puppet and a marionette should be made clear. The marionette is operated by strings; the puppet is not. Because of the complexity of operating a marionette, it is used relatively little in the elementary school. Consequently discussion in this book is confined to the puppet.

Puppets vary greatly, from the simple ones that even the first-grade child can operate to the elaborate puppets used by professionals. In this chapter puppets are classified as to these three types: (1) stationary puppets, (2) rod puppets, and (3) hand puppets.

STATIONARY PUPPETS. Stationary puppets, also called table puppets, are the simplest of all to operate. In a sense, they need no operator. The puppet is placed on the stage or representation of a stage, maybe even only a table, and there it remains without movement while the puppeteer can concentrate on the thoughts he expresses. This type of puppet is recommended particularly for early puppet dramatization. It also can be used successfully by the teacher who wants a puppet to serve as a mascot or watchman or adviser for the room — one through which he gives some of his directions. He can use it to help maintain a desirable atmosphere in the room.

Figure 12.5 A Puppet Head Made from a Bottle

Figure 12.6 A Puppet Head Made from a Can

Illustrations are here included to show how a bottle and a can are transformed into stationary puppets as they are decorated with water colors or construction paper. Many other media that suit the child's fancy can be used for decoration. Instead of bottles or cans, blocks of wood, balloons, cones made of paper, paper dolls on a stand, cups, water glasses, an interestingly formed branch made to stand up can form the base of the puppet. (It should be noted that when painting on a surface that is likely to repel paint, such as glass, adding a little detergent to the paint often takes care of the difficulty.)

A simple variation of what is usually thought of as the stationary puppet, one very useful in primary grades, is the flannel board puppet. Such puppets are made of flannel or of paper on the back of which are glued strips of flannel or other pieces of material that will make the puppet stick to a flannel board. As the puppeteer tells his story, the puppet to which he is referring is placed on the flannel board. Stories like "The Three Little Pigs" or "The Old Woman and Her Pig," in which the tale is cumulative, are particularly well adapted for use with this type of puppet.

ROD PUPPETS. Rod puppets are operated by means of a rod attached to, in fact often forming part of, the puppet. One of the simplest of these is the paper-mask, in which the mask can be made of construction paper and decorated with paint, crayon, or paper. The rod can be a tongue depressor or a doweling rod or any other piece of wood of appropriate size and shape. For more of a three-dimensional effect a paper-cone rod puppet similar to the one illustrated can be made, or attached to a rod can be any object of paper (created by the children or cut out of magazines) like those in the accompanying illustrations.

With a rod a large variety of puppets can be made. In fact, any flat surface or three-dimensional object to which a rod can be attached can serve as a rod puppet. There is the wood-block rod puppet whose head is a small piece of wood with features painted on or attached. There is the animal puppet in which a three-dimensional duck, dog, rabbit, or any other kind of toy animal is fastened to a controlling rod by masking tape or other adhesive.

A rod puppet can be made by attaching a rod to a head whose basic form consists of a ball of string. A rubber ball, with facial features attached, also can serve as head of a rod puppet. The head of a puppet made of soap can be attached to a rod. (It is recommended that the cake of soap be freshly unwrapped for then it is more malleable.) A puppet can be made by attaching a rod to a stuffed paper bag with features painted or pasted onto it.

A variation of the usual rod puppet is the wooden-spoon puppet in which the handle of the spoon serves as the rod. Another variation is the clothespin puppet. Wire pipe cleaner can serve as arms while features are drawn on and "hair" added.

Figure 12.7 Stationary Puppets

Figure 12.8 Puppets on a Flannel Board

Figure 12.9 A Paper Bag Rod Puppet and a Paper Cone Rod Puppet

Figure 12.10 Rod Puppets made of Paper

Rod puppets made of paper or of a variety of other substances can also be operated from above, to represent a cloud or a bug or a ghost. The "puppet," fastened by thread to the supporting rod, can be dangled onto the scene of action at the appropriate moment.

Hand Puppets. Hand puppets are moved directly by the hand. A typical position of the hand in operating a hand puppet is one in which the forefinger is inserted in the neck of the puppet, the thumb in one arm, and the second finger in the other arm, while the two small fingers are closed. Another position of the hand places the forefinger and the second finger close together into the neck of the puppet, with the thumb controlling one arm and the two smaller fingers, also held close together, forming the control for the other arm. In still another position, with the forefinger in the neck, the thumb can control one arm and the smallest finger operate the other arm while the second- and third-smallest fingers are folded down.

There is possible an almost endless variety of types of hand puppets, a few of which will be briefly discussed. In most cases only the heads are described. For directions for dressing puppets the reader is referred to page 270.

1. The *vegetable or fruit puppet* is made from vegetables or fruits such as the potato, apple, carrot, turnip, onion, orange. A hole can be cut into the vegetable or fruit with an apple corer big enough so that the puppeteer can control his puppet by sticking his forefinger into it. The features of the puppet can be made with ribbon, yarn, tacks, cloves, parts of toothpicks, beads, nuts, or a miscellany of other materials.

2. *Paper bag puppets* can be made in many ways. The whole hand of the puppeteer can be put into a bag that has been decorated to show features. It can be tied around the puppeteer's hand at his wrist. Use of the hand within the bag and motion of the arm give movement to the puppet. A bag also can be used to portray the entire puppet, not just its head. In that case, after the features have been added to the upper part of the bag and a cord tied loosely around that part to form the neckline, holes can be made below the neckline. Through one of these the thumb projects as one arm and through the other another finger, other than the forefinger (which is used for head control) is used as the other arm.

3. *Sock puppets* are especially useful in portraying animals. Of these the stuffed sock-head puppet is perhaps the simplest. For control a four-inch paper tube can be inserted into the neck of the animal puppet. In addition the toe of a nylon stocking can be stuffed to form the head of a puppet, representing a human being. An alligator puppet can be made from an old sock by cutting around the toe end and lining the cut-open part with bright material to represent the

Figure 12.11 More Rod Puppets

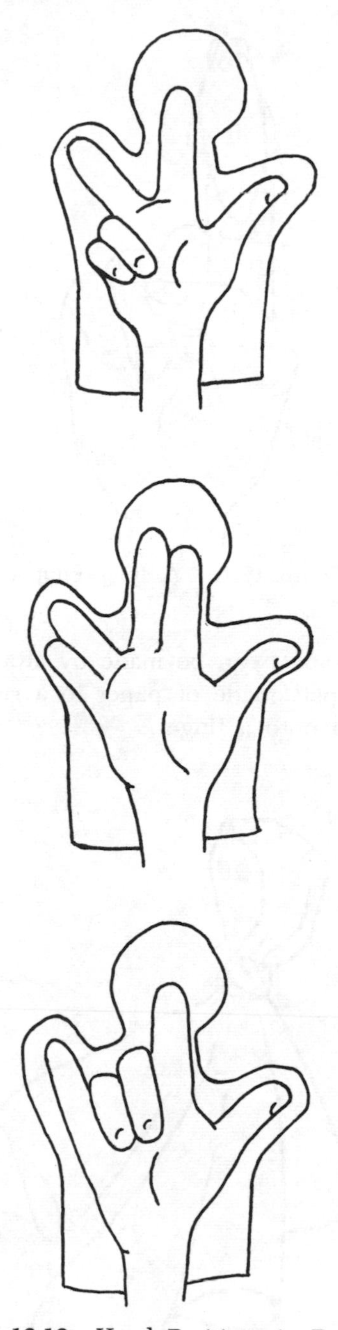

Figure 12.12 Hand Positions in Puppetry

Figure 12.13 A Fruit Puppet

Figure 12.14 A Paper Bag Puppet

Figure 12.15 A Sock Puppet

jaws, to which are attached two pieces of cardboard for stiffening the mouth. Buttons can be used for eyes.

4. *Balloon puppets or ball puppets* can be painted or decorated with construction paper. The forefinger can be securely tied to the end of the balloon. In the case of a rubber ball, a hole big enough for the finger must be cut into it.

5. *A tin-can puppet* can also be made for use as a hand puppet, with features added in the form of paper hair, yarn, rope, pieces of paper, and the like. Care must be taken that the edges of tin cans are not sharp, lest puppeteers cut themselves.

6. A *fist puppet* can be made by painting or by pasting paper cutouts to the hand in fist formation.

Figure 12.16 A Balloon Puppet

Figure 12.17 A Tin-Can Puppet

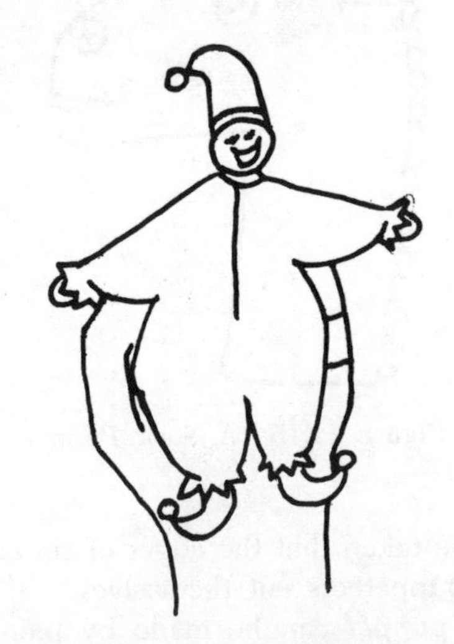

Figure 12.18 A Fist Puppet

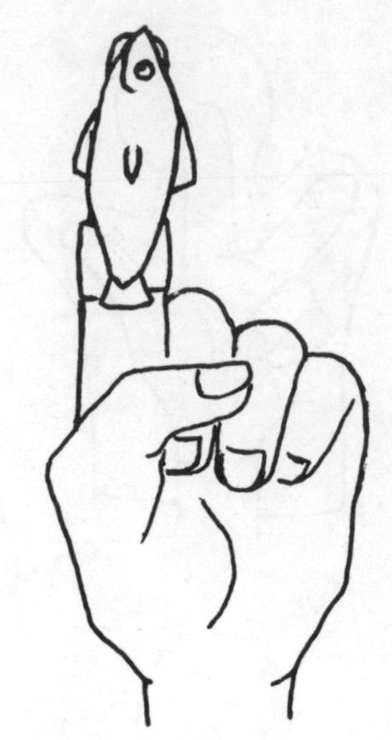

Figure 12.19 A Ring Puppet

7. *Ring puppets* can be made by attaching heads or entire puppets made of paper to a ring made of paper, slipped onto a finger.

Figure 12.20 A Handkerchief Puppet

8. *Handkerchief puppets* can be made by tying a man's white handkerchief around the hand at the wrist, to represent a ghost. (A ghost can also be made by tying a small piece of white cloth around one finger.)

9. *Light-bulb puppets* can be made by painting faces on used light bulbs. Clothes can be glued to or fastened by a rubber band around the neck of the bulbs.

Figure 12.21 A Light-Bulb Puppet

Figure 12.23 A Blockhead Puppet

Figure 12.22 A Rag-Doll Puppet

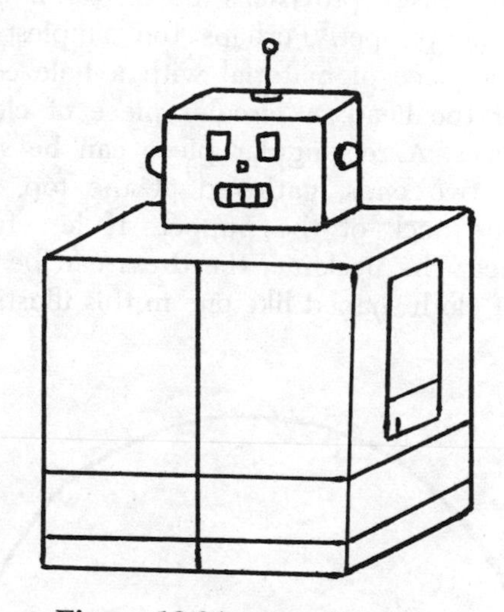

Figure 12.24 Box Puppets

10. The head of a *rag-doll puppet* can be cut from two oval pieces of cloth. The pieces can be sewed together, leaving a hole at one end through which the puppeteer's finger can control the puppet. After the sewing, the cloth should be turned inside out and the head stuffed with cloth, cotton, or crumpled paper, and then (or before) features should be added.

11. *Blockhead puppets,* for which a block is used for the head and nailed to a stick, are another interesting variation of the hand puppet.

12. *Box puppets,* similar to block puppets, can be made with a small box for the head of the character.

Figure 12.25 A Papier-Mâché Puppet Head

13. *The papier-mâché* puppet head can be made simply or elaborately. One of the easiest ways of making it is to crumple paper and then with a string tie it into the general shape desired for the head. Over this basic form thinly-cut strips of paper, dipped in wheat paste, can then be applied. Through an opening left when putting on the strips, at the part that will form the neck of the puppet, the crumpled paper can be removed when the head has dried.

Dressing the Puppet

In some cases the dress of the puppet is made of the same material as the head. For example, in the case of the paper-bag puppet the entire body can be made from a paper bag. In some of the vegetable puppets, too, such as the carrot puppet, the vegetable serves as the whole puppet. In a ghost puppet the handkerchief used for the head also represents the flowing robe.

In many cases provisions need to be made for dressing the puppet. Perhaps the simplest dress is made of a piece of material with a hole cut in the center for the head. A circular piece of cloth for a skirt suffices. A rectangular piece can be sewed together at two ends, gathered at the top, and tied around the neck of the puppet. If less fullness is desired near the neckline, the dress can be cut from a piece of cloth shaped like one in this illustration.

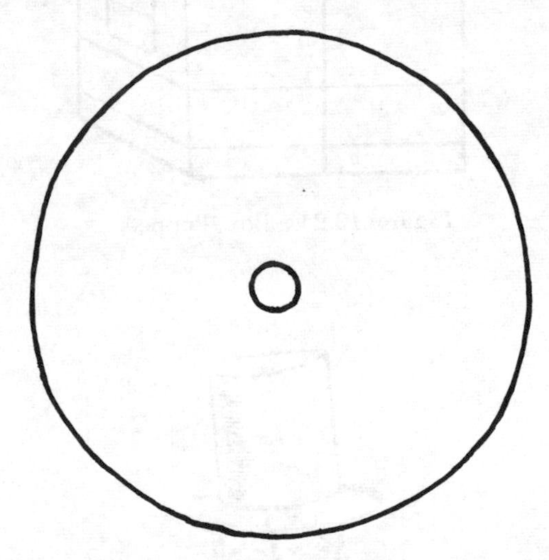

Figure 12.26 Circular Dress Pattern for Puppet

Out of the flowing dress an illusion of the arms can be made by using one or more fingers, as indicated in finger positions illustrated on page 267, or sleeves can be sewed onto the body of the puppet and holes cut at appropriate places in the robe as armholes. Another basic dress pattern is illustrated in the accompanying figure, in which the hands of the puppet are attached to the end of the sleeves.

Figure 12.27 A Basic Dress Pattern for a Puppet

Here are a few pointers to observe when fashioning the dress for puppets.

1. It is good to encourage beginners to test dress patterns by first cutting them out of newspaper.
2. There is danger of making the dress too skimpy. In the case of dresses for puppets representing girls or women, the measurements should be related, in part, to the size of the hand of the puppeteer.
3. A woman's dress may consist of a full skirt that is attached to the waist of the basic dress pattern of the puppet.
4. To sew a dress to the puppet it can be turned inside out over the head of the puppet while being sewed to the head.
5. For the apparel of a woman puppet a straight-lined undergarment can be sewed to the dress before the dress is sewed to the head of the puppet.
6. It is helpful to stuff the trousers of men puppets with crumpled cloth, paper, or cotton.

Puppet Stages

Puppet stages can be classified as temporary and permanent stages.

TEMPORARY STAGES. Stages do not need to be elaborate. In fact, elaborateness of stage can interfere with the effectiveness of the play.

Here are suggestions for a few stages that can be used without bothering to make a permanent stage.

1. The surface of a table, with a cloth draped over it, may be used as the puppeteers stand in plain view.

This type of stage is particularly suited for stationary puppets.

2. A board can be placed across the top of two chairs with backs facing and a blanket draped over the board.

3. A box can be set on a table. The puppeteers present the show using the top of the box as the scene of action. This type also is well adapted for use with stationary puppets but it can serve as stage for both rod and hand puppets if the top of the box is considered the foreground of the scene of action.

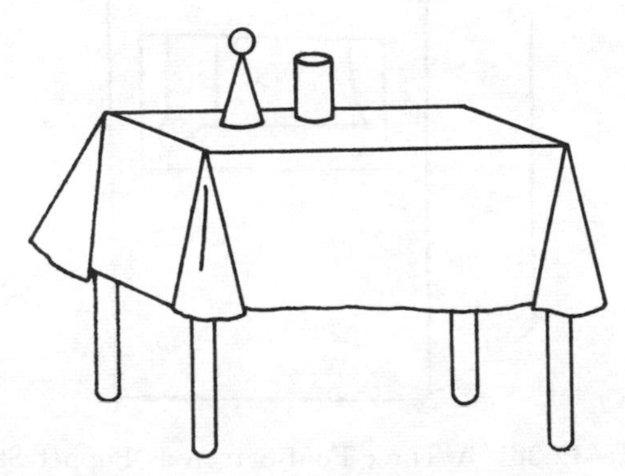

Figure 12.28 A Top of a Table as Temporary Puppet Stage

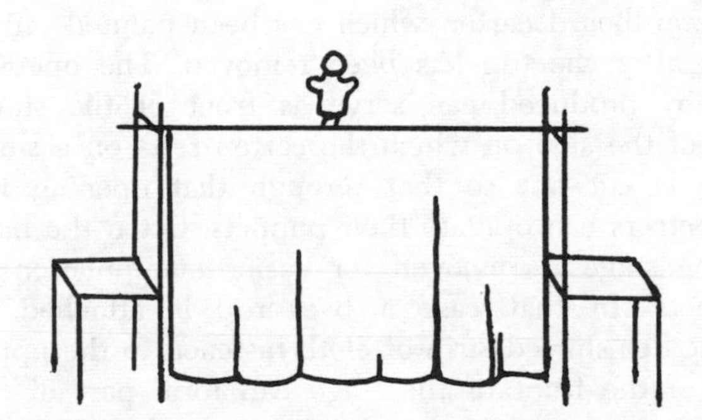

Figure 12.29 Two Straight Chairs Used in a Temporary Puppet Stage

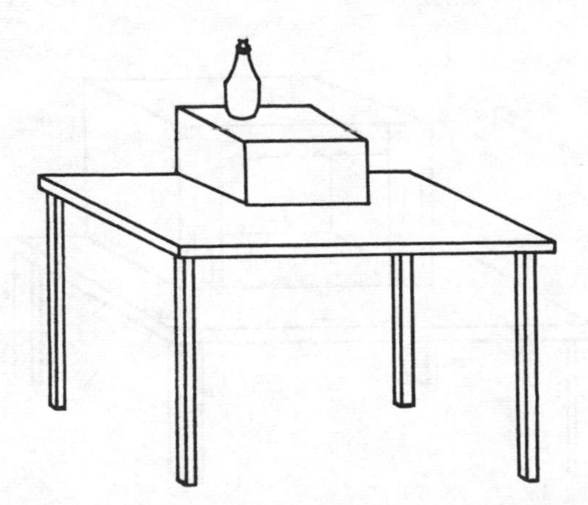

Figure 12.30 A Box on a Table as Puppet Stage

Figure 12.31 A Table on Its Side as Puppet Stage

4. A table can be placed on its side, with the top part facing the audience. A large piece of cloth can be strung as curtains around the sides and front of the stage so that the puppeteers, crouching behind the curtains, can operate the puppets from below.

Figure 12.32 A Doorway as Puppet Stage

5. A curtain can be drawn across the bottom half or so of a doorway by fastening it over a wire stretched across a doorway at whatever height is desired.

6. The window stage, shown in the accompanying illustration, is another simple type of stage.

7. A puppeteer can kneel on the seat of a high overstuffed chair. Kneeling on the seat of the chair he can manipulate his puppets so that they are visible to an audience facing the back of the chair. An empty picture frame can be fastened to the top of the back of such a chair to "frame" the action of the puppets.

8. A low three-part screen behind which the puppeteers are sitting can hide them from view as their puppets are visible over the top of the screen.

Figure 12.33 A Window as Puppet Stage

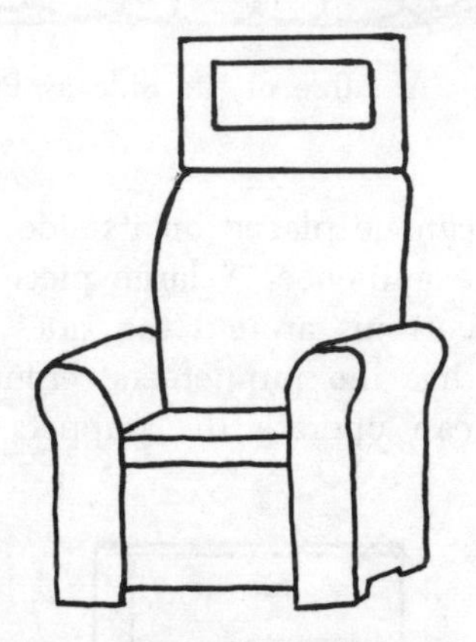

Figure 12.34 An Overstuffed Chair as Base for a Puppet Stage

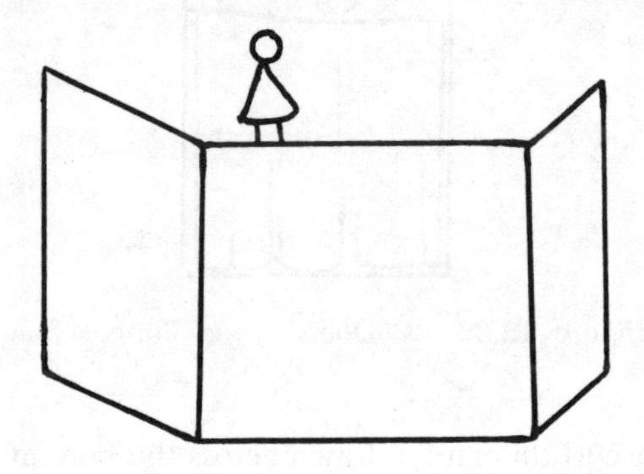

Figure 12.35 A Screen as Puppet Stage

Permanent Stages. As the term *permanent* is here employed it refers to any type of stage that cannot be quickly improvised without committing materials needed to future use as a stage. The degrees of "permanency" vary.

1. An opening to serve as proscenium can be cut into the upper part of the middle section of a three-fold screen. The two side parts of the screen can be arranged so that they are perpendicular to the middle section to hide the puppeteers from view. The puppeteers operate their puppets from a sitting position below the level of the bottom of the opening of the middle of the screen. A curtain can be drawn across the open part of the theater. Across the back of the lower part of the proscenium can be attached a shelf to serve as base of the stage.

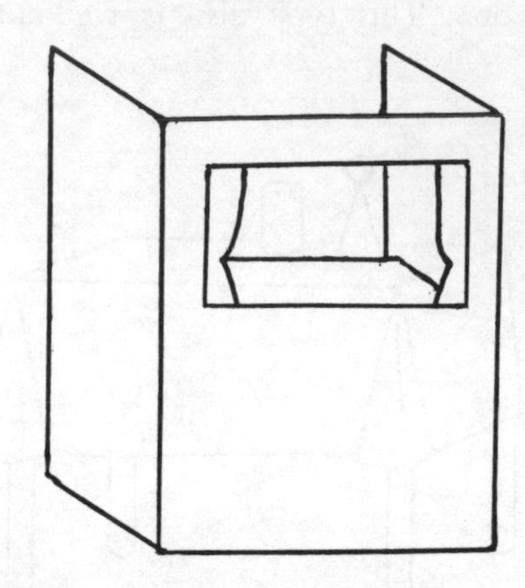

Figure 12.36 A Three-Fold Screen as Puppet Stage

2. A commonly used puppet stage is one made of a cardboard carton which has been painted on all sides after the top has been removed. The opening thereby produced can serve as front of the stage. Part of the side on which the carton rests on a small table is cut out so that through that opening the puppeteers can operate their puppets. Often the back of the stage is removed for easier manipulation of puppets. In that case a backdrop is attached. A pleated or shirred strip of cloth fastened to the upper part of the front of the stage can form part of the curtain. At each side of the front, draw curtains or pull-back curtains made of cloth can be fastened.

3. A stage can be constructed from an orange crate by knocking out the bottom and nailing two

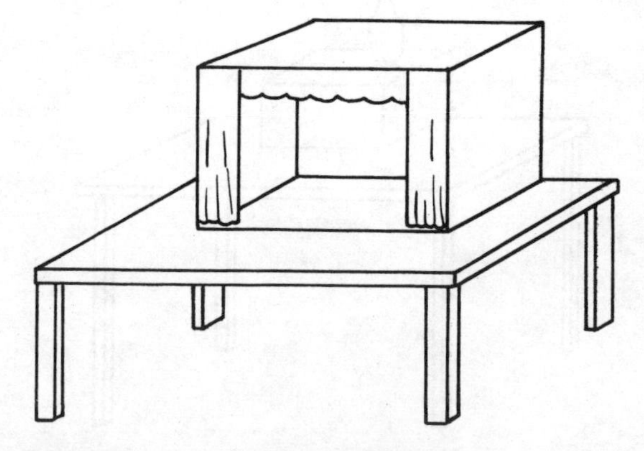

Figure 12.37 A Cardboard Carton as Puppet Stage

sticks to the crate so that they extend as shown in the diagram. To the end of these sticks the backdrop can be fastened.

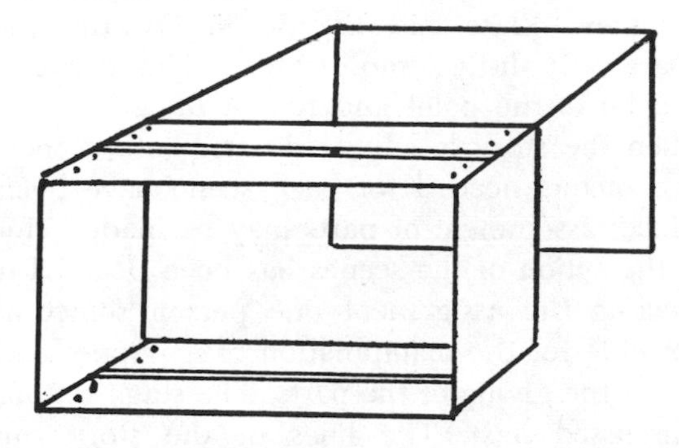

Figure 12.38 An Orange Crate as Puppet Stage

4. Any wooden box of suitable size can be changed into a theater. The accompanying illustration shows the lower side taken out of the box and sawed into about half lengthwise, with one of the two pieces nailed under the box to form a shelf extending a few inches. The effect of a curtain can be secured by attaching a piece of tagboard to the front of the theater.

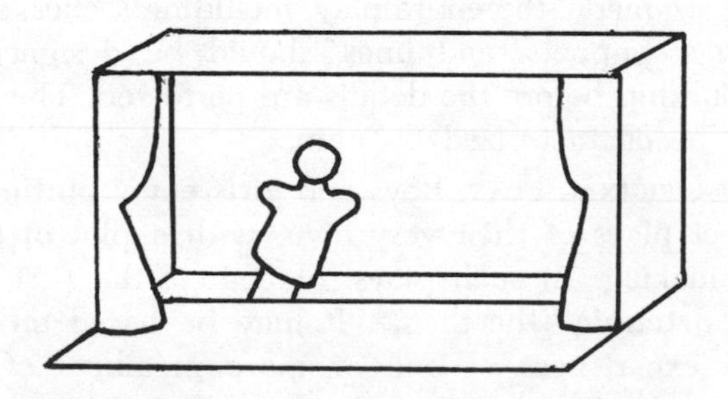

Figure 12.39 A Puppet Stage Made of Wood

5. A variation from the cardboard stage and the stage made from a wooden box is a stage built from wood. It can be made simply or rather elaborately with curtains, floodlights, changes of backdrops (fastened to the theater by a rod). Some teachers like to have one wooden theater in the room for use throughout the year whenever it seems to fit the needs of a production.

6. The puppet tray stage is one of the most interesting stages. It can be made from a cardboard box, into the cover of which two holes are cut. It is through these holes that the puppeteer operates his puppets. The box can be painted, and, fastened with a ribbon to each top corner of the box, it is hung around the neck of the puppeteer.

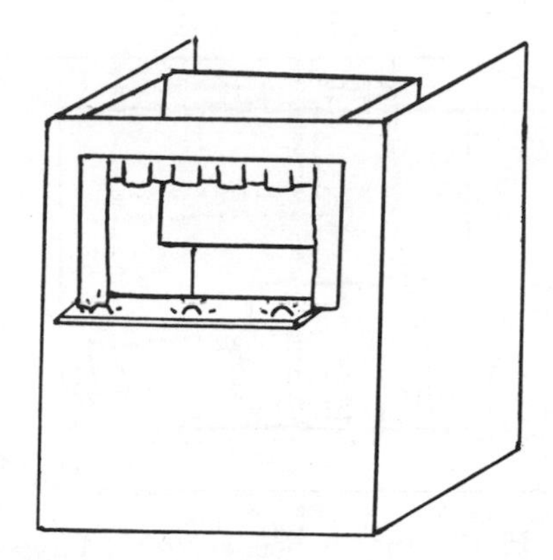

Figure 12.40 Another Puppet Stage Made of Wood

Figure 12.41 A Puppet Tray Stage

Scenery

The scenery, including the backdrop and the side "walls" of the interior as well as the stage setting, should help create the illusion that the little puppets are taking their audience into a fanciful world.

Care must be taken that the background is simple enough so that it truly serves as background and does not "take the show away" from the puppets. The scenery should be suggestive rather than realistic, as a rule. A few paper flowers are enough to indicate that it is spring. The scenery can be painted on a backdrop made of paper. The painted sides also can provide scenery. Usually it is not desirable to paint figures into the background. It is important that the backdrop be larger than the proscenium.

In designing the scenery, the pupils need to give attention to proportionate size. A table in the front of the stage three inches high can hardly serve ade-

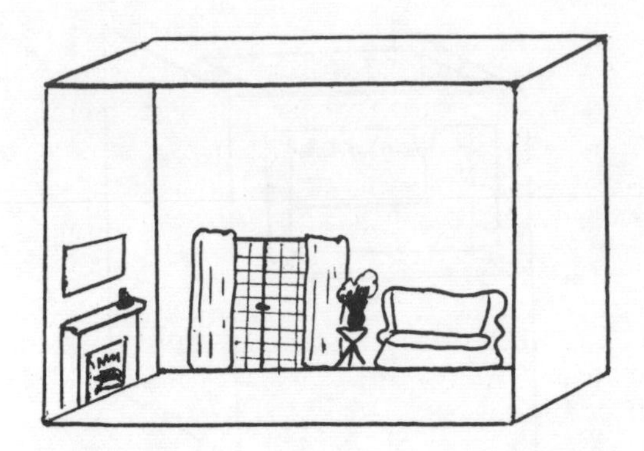

Figure 12.42 Indoor Scenery for a Puppet Play

Figure 12.43 Outdoor Scenery for a Puppet Play

quately as a dining table for puppets twelve inches tall.

If curtains are used, they should help create the atmosphere of fancy. Soft velvet or rich silk, possibly brocaded, helps give the impression of a world that is not commonplace. The draw-type curtain, one on each side of the stage, can be suspended by curtain rings from a rod above the proscenium. With a cord through these rings attached to hooks, the curtains can be pulled open and shut, or simple pull-back curtains can be used.

Steps in Preparing and Presenting a Puppet Play

The steps in presenting a puppet play are similar to those that can be followed in connection with other types of dramatization; however, there is some variation.

A Puppet Play Based on a Story. A story that is well adapted to puppetry should be chosen. The story should be worthwhile, a story that really does something or is likely to do something to the inner nature of the child. It should be dramatic and require but few characters. Those characters should be such that they can be shown in settings easily suggested in puppetry. Most stories need to be simplified before use in a puppet play. Some stories, however, like "Little Red Riding Hood," "The Three Little Pigs," and "Snow White and the Seven Dwarfs" require comparatively little simplification. The conversation should be to the point and full of life.

When the story has been divided into scenes and the characters needed for each scene have been determined, assignment of parts may be made before or after the action of the scenes has been decided upon. In making the assignment one person sometimes is responsible for the manipulation of a puppet and another for the giving of the parts. The stage setting can be discussed next. The lines of the story can be changed into play form by the boys and girls as they "ad lib" or individuals or committees may have the assignment. The pupils can read the parts, memorize them, or say them without memorization. Every performance of the play should be thought of as an opportunity for dramatic experiences, not merely as a time of rehearsal.

Somewhere between the steps indicated, the puppets should be made, the theater selected or constructed, and the scenery, including both "interior walls" and stage furnishings planned, and the plans executed. Regardless of when puppets and stage settings are made, the entire play, including scenes, stage settings, puppets, and lines, should be designed in relationship before the details are perfected. The play must be characterized by unity.

An Original Play. Boys and girls enjoy putting on puppet plays of their very own, with a plot of their own making. In such plays, of course, the first step is to determine the theme. It may be based on personal experiences of one or more members of the group. After a primary-grade class has been on a trip to a farm, they may, for example, decide to enact through puppetry some of their experiences. One puppet could represent all the boys and girls in the room as they meet, in the play, the various animals on the farm. The animals can be drawings on paper attached to dowel rods. The child puppet can be similarly constructed or it can be made more elaborately. Each of the animals can tell the children what it does to help the farmer and other people. A similar theme can be developed after a visit to a zoo. In the play various animals can tell interesting facts about themselves in answer to questions asked by the boys and girls. A health puppet play can be planned, possibly showing what an emaciated-looking, tired, unhappy child learned from various good foods, also in the form of puppets, in order to become the healthy, happy, strong child into which he is being transformed.

In making up an original plot, many boys and girls may need considerable guidance from the teacher. The amount should be determined by the skill of the class. With boys and girls who have had little experience in puppetry, the teacher may need to suggest the general theme while the pupils decide on the details. For example, in the health play to which reference is made in the preceding paragraph, after a study of a unit on the food we eat, the boys and girls may decide which foods the tired child should meet and what each food should teach him.

Following are some other suggestions for topics for puppet plays.

1. A Christmas puppet show in which the pupils work out a series of simple skits showing what boys and girls can do to make others happy at Christmas
2. A Mother's Day play in which a boy and girl find out what different things they can do to make Mother happy not only on Mother's day but the year around
3. A Thanksgiving play in which emphasis is put on reasons for gratitude
4. A puppet show telling important events in the life of an inventor
5. A play emphasizing good manners.

Puppet plays can also be worked out in connection with school subjects such as music, spelling, handwriting, social studies, speech, and foreign languages. For example, one or more puppets can explain the important points of posture to remember when writing.

Availability of Materials

If boys and girls are to be able to make puppetry a creative experience of maximum value, it is advisable to have a large variety of materials available so that they can use their imagination to the utmost. These materials are likely to be of greater value as well as of greater diversity if the boys and girls have a part in collecting them. The smaller materials should be sorted as to type or function and stored in properly labeled drawers or boxes. Pupil responsibility in classification and keeping the collections in usable form is recommended.

The following list suggests a variety of materials, in addition to cartons and boxes of various types, that may be collected: pieces of cloth, including silk, cotton, velvet; pins, needles, and thread; scissors; hammers; coat hangers; glue and paste; paints, including tempera paints; paint brushes; paper, including crepe paper, construction paper of various colors, butcher paper, tagboard, beaver board, cardboard, corrugated paper, contact paper; mailing tubes and tubes from toilet tissue or from paper toweling; paper doilies; buttons; paper clips and brass fasteners; beads; tinfoil from frozen food containers; egg crates; pot cleaners; wood for carving; pipe cleaners; raffia and reed; leather; artificial flowers; pieces of fur; ribbons; braid; small pieces of doll's furniture; plasticine; styrofoam; lace; dowel rods; rulers; nails; plywood; balsa wood; ribbon; twine; crayons; sponges; netting; pictures of people, animals, and inanimate objects; gourds; twigs; wire; rope; old gloves and used socks.

Other Suggestions

Here are a few additional suggestions for use in connection with puppetry.

1. Rod puppets of any kind that make good silhouettes can be used as shadow puppets. A light behind the scene of action throws the shadow on a translucent screen. The puppets can be made of a variety of materials — wood, cardboard, lace doilies, and screening among them.
2. If the eyes of a puppet are close together, the puppet has an older or a shrewder expression than if they are farther apart.
3. For eyebrows of puppets representing children, only a small marking is needed, while strong and/or villainous characters need dark and shaggy eyebrows. Stitches of thread or yarn can produce the desired effects.
4. Pupils often need to be cautioned to hold their puppets erect and at stage level.
5. Puppeteers should speak their lines slowly and distinctly.
6. A puppet who is speaking should face his listeners, at least partially.
7. It is often effective to have a puppet as announcer of a puppet play.

CHORAL SPEAKING

Choral speaking, also referred to as choral reading and verse choirs, has become so common in the elementary schools of this country that no longer is a definition of the term needed in a discussion of this type. Although preparation in directing verse choirs in terms of a college course or workshop on the topic is desirable, it is not essential. The wide-awake teacher can help her pupils gain some of the values of choral speaking without such specialized training. Books and magazine articles and references to the topic in various college courses in the preparation of teachers, especially in courses in literature for children and in methods of teaching the language arts, can furnish valuable background for the teacher or prospective teacher for his work with boys and girls.

Values of Choral Speaking

As the objectives that choral speaking can help fulfill which are named here indicate, a discussion of the topic could appropriately be taken up in various parts of this book – in connection with oral communication or reading, as well as in this chapter on dramatic expression.

1. Through choral speaking the interest of boys and girls in good poetry can be increased. Pupils who have never before felt the joy of reading poetry can be enthusiastic as they look through books on poetry for poems that they can suggest for reading by their verse choir. As they search for suitable poems and discover the treasures of poetry through choral reading some may develop a lasting interest in poetry.
2. Through choral speaking boys and girls can have the satisfaction of giving pleasure to an appreciative audience. When hearing verse spoken with sincerity, the members of the audience frequently show their happiness to the members of the choir by their response to the mood created by the verse choir. The resulting satisfaction to the participants in the choir is one not unlike that which the creative artist feels when he has awakened a responding emotion.
3. Choral speaking can help the participants and the audience to better interpretation of poetry.
4. Participation in choral speaking can be a decided asset in the development of speaking abilities. Pupils see purpose for speaking distinctly, for pronouncing words correctly, for using suitable tone quality, for talking with correct pitch, for good breath control, for correct posture. Furthermore, through choral speaking boys and girls can acquire the self-assurance needed to speak in front of an audience.
5. Taking part in choral speaking can serve as a valuable means of learning to work cooperatively with others – the like and the unlike. In choral speaking "all are needed by each one." The child recognizes the importance of having his voice blend with others. He can appreciate that successful performance is impossible unless each does his part.
6. Through choral speaking the shy, timid child and the overly-aggressive one can be helped. The former, who may be afraid of taking part in a performance in which the spotlight may be on him for a while, can easily lose himself in a group activity such as choral speaking. Furthermore, confidence instilled in him through success in the activity can cause him to be less concerned about himself in the future, regardless of what the activity may be in which he engages. On the other hand, the aggressiveness of the too confident child may be tempered when participating in choral speaking, which could be ruined if he were not willing to submerge himself for the good of the group. The satisfaction he gets from joyous participation in choral speaking even though he is not in the limelight may help him at other times to prefer taking his part with a group rather than showing off.
7. Choral speaking can give release. It seems important that every individual express himself creatively. Some do so through music, others through art, others through writing, others through manual activities. Choral speaking can serve as an outlet for self-expression for every normal child, gifted or not.
8. Choral speaking can be a source of motivation for other worthwhile activities. It is easily conceivable that as a child who has lacked interest in school activities finds pleasure in choral speaking, he may develop a better attitude toward school work.
9. Through participation in choral speaking the child's vocabulary can be enlarged. This improvement can result especially if the teacher makes a point of explaining or has explained some of the words that may be unfamiliar. But choral reading should not become a vocabulary drill. Not every so-called "unknown word" needs to be explained to boys and girls in order that they can understand and interpret a poem.
10. Not least but very important among the values that can be derived from choral speaking are the fun and the joy in the activity itself.

Guidelines

In spite of the many values that can be attained through choral speaking, with some educators it has been in disrepute. A reason for this unpopularity with some seems to be that at times there is failure by teachers to live up to the underlying principles that should govern the use of choral speaking in the schoolroom. Suggestions such as the following should be observed.

1. Care should be taken to avoid overemphasis on words and on rhythm. Important words should be emphasized but overemphasis can lead to loss of meaning or can make the speaking dramatic when simplicity of presentation should be an objective. While the participants should feel the rhythm of the poem and convey it in their interpretation, too much emphasis on rhythm can also cause loss of meaning.

2. Children's voices should be light and expressive. Loud strained voices not only can make the effect displeasing but also can cause permanent injury to vocal cords. A galloping pace, into which some choirs work themselves as they proceed giving a poem, should also be avoided. To meaning and beauty rushing through a poem can be fatal.

3. Overdramatization should be avoided. While with the very young child gesturing is evidence of uninhibited bodily response, frequently with the child in the upper primary or intermediate grades it is put on for effect. When gesturing is not spontaneous, it spells insincerity and thus makes choral speaking lose its charm and much of its value.

4. Costuming and scenery should be kept very simple or not used at all. Costumes of any kind and scenery provided for the stage can easily detract from the boys and girls, the beauty of whose speech and manner should be allowed its full effect upon the audience. While some conductors like to have all the girls dress in white blouses and dark skirts and the boys in white shirts and dark trousers, yet clean and neat cotton dresses, without fuss, and shirts and trousers of any color can make the reading just as effective as similarity of apparel or maybe more effective. A vase or two of flowers is all the decoration any verse choir needs.

5. The teacher who serves as leader of the group must exemplify certain characteristics not only at any program that may be given but throughout the work on choral speaking. He should have a love for poetry and must be able to convey his enthusiasm without in any way trying to exhibit it. True love of poetry must be lived, not forcibly demonstrated. Furthermore, he needs to exemplify in his posture, his voice, his breath control, those characteristics that make for success in verse speaking.

6. It is important that suitable poetry be chosen. For suggestions as to which literature is suitable the reader is referred to page 279.

7. The boys and girls should be encouraged to take part in selecting poems to be read and in planning and organizing choral speaking. They should not, as a rule, be asked to fit into a pattern devised by the teacher or found in a magazine article. Sometimes a pupil well suited to the work may even be chosen as conductor at the time of a performance. However, during practices the pupils usually should have the benefit of the teacher's conducting.

8. In choral speaking a final performance should not be the main objective but the benefits that boys and girls can derive from work on it should constitute the chief aim. In fact, it is questionable whether choral speaking in the primary grades should culminate in a program. When it does seem desirable in the intermediate grades, care should be taken that the chief emphasis is on values gained from practices rather than on production of a polished program.

9. All boys and girls should have an opportunity to take part in choral speaking. If a child's voice comes out in a manner that interferes with the effectiveness of the choir, he may be cautioned, preferably privately, to keep his voice soft. It is questionable whether he should ever be given only a nonspeaking role, like seating visitors or passing out programs. If the true objective of a verse choir is to help the boys and girls gain the values that should be reaped from choral speaking, the teacher will see his responsibility even to the pupils with characteristics that need developing in order for them to be effective participants in verse choirs.

10. Choral speaking should not be made the excuse for forcibly bringing in many voice or speech exercises during a time set aside for choral reading. The help given in these respects should, as a rule, fit right into the ongoing practice.

11. Care should be taken that the overconfident members of a verse choir do not dominate the scene.

12. It is important that all the participants in a choir can hear each other. Consequently a wedge-shaped formation is often to be preferred to the straight-line.

Procedures in Choral Speaking

With these basic principles in mind, let us next turn our attention to the grouping for verse choirs.

Grouping. Even among children in the primary grades there are voices recognizable as higher or lighter than others. In the elementary school the division of a choir is often made into two groups, high and low (or light and heavy.) Not infrequently, a third group — a medium group — is also established. Among elementary-school children some boys and some girls are likely to be found in each of the three groups, for with young children not all boys' voices are low or medium nor are all girls' voices high or medium.

The teacher may be consciously taking note of the quality of the pupils' voices weeks before he starts choral speaking. Some teachers may want to pick out one of the highest and one of the lowest voices beforehand. When they begin the work on choral speaking, they may explain to the boys and girls that speaking voices can be grouped much as singing voices in a choir. The teacher may then point out the importance of having some high voices blend with others that are lower. It is important that he helps the children realize all voices are valuable in a good speaking choir. Next he may tell the class that he has already noticed that [name of pupil] has a rich low voice while [name of a pupil] has a lovely high voice. Thereupon, he may have those two pupils count to ten or give the beginning of the ABC's or say a nursery rhyme such as "Mary had a little lamb." Next each of the other children in the room may be asked to do likewise as the teacher, often with the assistance of the boys and girls, divides the class into two or three choirs. The boys and girls should understand that this grouping may not be perfect and that at times there may be changes made as their voices change or as the teacher, sometimes with the help of the class, for other reasons notes that a voice fits better with a different group.

CASTING A POEM. The term *casting* is used in choral speaking to refer to the division of a given selection (usually a poem, but psalms can also be used very effectively in the elementary school) into parts and assigning these to different groups or individuals. Commonly used methods of organization are here given.

1. *Unison speech.* This method of casting is not to be confused with the nonchoral reading done in concert when all pupils, without being grouped as to voices, speak all lines. When speaking in unison is a method of choral speaking, it means all groups say the same lines but that each group says them according to the voice specification of his division. Although having all choirs saying the lines in unison is the simplest form as far as structure is concerned, it is a very difficult method of choral speaking. In fact, speaking in choruses yet in unison probably constitutes the most difficult type of casting. There are problems in blending and in timing that are not as great in any other type of casting. As a rule unison speech should not be used in the elementary school for entire poems; if used it should usually be reserved for only short parts of selections.

2. *Refrain or chorus.* In poems where there are refrains or choruses the casting is often done by having one group read the choruses while another reads the other parts. The other parts also may be divided among two groups if the total division has been in terms of three groups. Sometimes the arrangement is solo-group. Occasionally the teacher may carry the solo part.

3. *Dialogue and antiphonal casting.* Poems in which considerable dialogue is used lend themselves well to two-part casting. Question-and-answer poems are particularly well suited for this type of casting. One suitable arrangement is to give the question to the high voices and the response to the low. Some question-and-answer poems are cast into three or more groups somewhat equal even if they have no choruses and do not consist of dialogue. Such an arrangement is at times called antiphonal casting.

4. *Line-a-child.* In line-a-child casting three or more children speak separate parts. Each child says at least one line as solo. Some lines may be spoken in unison.

5. *Line-a-choir.* In line-a-choir casting more than two choirs are used for separate parts.

6. *Solo-choir.* A variation from the two-part antiphonal casting is that in which one or more choirs as well as solo parts are used.

7. Other types. Various combinations and deviations from the types of casting described can be made for best interpretation of a poem according to the abilities and needs of a given group of boys and girls.

SUGGESTED METHODS FOR CHORAL SPEAKING. Here are some pointers as to methods of procedure in choral speaking.

1. Before the teacher starts work in choral speaking, with many boys and girls it may be advantageous to interest them in saying poetry by having the group, without any division into choirs, say enjoyable poems in concert.

2. After children's voices have been divided into groups and after a suitable poem has been selected, the teacher needs to present the poem to the class in such a way that the pupils will want to say the poem. This introduction can be made in a variety of ways. On a windy day the teacher may quietly start by saying, with good interpretation but not dramatically, the poem "Who Has Seen the Wind?" There may be a very brief discussion in which some pupils name other signs by which they know that "the wind is passing by." A picture or a series of pictures showing children having fun on a windy day may be used as a point of reference. Then the teacher may say, as he repeats the poem, that some may like to join him in some of the lines. A suggestion from the teacher that the class say the poem by using the choirs into which the group has been divided may bring an enthusiastic response.

3. The problem of memorization can be avoided at the outset of choral speaking if at first the group uses only poems previously committed to memory.

4. Although it is not necessary that every word in a poem not in the pupils' vocabulary should be explained, since the pupils can get the meaning of some words without explanation, nevertheless it is probably

safe to say that as a rule the boys and girls should be helped with words they cannot understand within the context of the poem. The words should not be presented as a formal drill in word study. A somewhat incidental approach is desirable. Sometimes when the teacher knows a few days or longer ahead of time that he will use a given poem in choral reading, he may in his conversation use one or more of the words of the poem that might otherwise cause a problem.

Another technique the teacher may use is setting the mood for a poem and then saying before reading the poem that he would like to introduce the pupils to a few words whose meaning they will want to know in order to understand the poem. He may have these words written on the chalkboard, each in the context of a sentence that helps in their understanding. At times he may refer to a word he has written on the chalkboard as he tells the pupils he thinks he will not need to explain that word since he believes some or all of them may be able to figure out the meaning when they hear it in the poem.

5. The mood for a poem may be created by the teacher's reading it carefully, by discussion preceding the reading, by reading a series of poems before the one to be used for choral speaking is read — all of which are on the same topic such as snow, for example. A series of poems by the same author can be read before the one to be used in choral speaking is presented. Music and art can also serve as means of introduction to some poems.

6. One of the best ways to impress boys and girls with the need of good posture when speaking in a choir is for the teacher to set an example. A discussion of the importance of it may also be beneficial. Drawing attention at times to one or more participants with particularly good posture is another means that can be used effectively. The importance of good posture can also be shown in its relation to another important element of good choral speaking — breath control.

7. The need for good speech can be emphasized in somewhat the same manner as suggested in the preceding paragraph. Again the teacher should serve as a model in his enunciation of words, the clarity of speech, tone quality and pitch, pleasing variation, and lack of overemphasis on words. Help may need to be given with the pronunciation of words for even one mispronunciation can almost ruin a poem. The pupils should be helped to realize that unless the words can at all times be readily comprehended by the audience, unlike singing, the speaking is ineffective. The need for color in the voice, pitch, and tone in choral speaking can well give incentive for practice sessions that may be held at other times of the school day rather than during the period devoted to choral speaking.

8. To help pupils feel the rhythm of poetry, the teacher may read a number of poems in which the rhythm is marked. At times through suitable motions the boys and girls may express the rhythm of a poem that the teacher is reading. They may do whatever the rhythm suggests to them — tapping with pencils or feet, clapping, skipping.

9. With shorter poems as a rule it is not necessary to give pupils a copy, for children usually can memorize such poems with a rather small number of repetitions, especially if they have the intent to learn the poem. When poems are longer it is desirable that each pupil, if he can read, have a copy until he no longer needs one.

10. Just as in singing choirs, in speaking choirs it is important to have a good leader who will mark the time, indicate when different individuals or choirs are to begin, and the like. Like the leader of a singing choir, the conductor of a verse choir may indicate when tones are to be louder and when softer. It is recommended, however, that the leader not use a baton but directly communicate with the participants with his hands or fingers. As boys and girls work on the finer details of reading a poem, the teacher may find it desirable to use fewer and less conspicuous gestures as leader. Furthermore, if a performance is given before an audience, it may be unnecessary to have any guidance from the leader other than for the beginning and at the end of a poem.

11. It is at times necessary that the teacher help the boys and girls comprehend the general meaning of a poem and the relationship of the supporting parts to the general theme. Such help should, as a rule, be given before the pupils are asked to interpret the poem through choral speaking.

12. It is desirable to have the pupils stand when they take part in choral speaking, even during so-called practice periods.

Verse for Choral Speaking

There are various books on the market that contain poems designated as particularly appropriate for choral verse. Some suggest arrangements for casting of poems. A teacher should not be misled by such a listing. Frequently many poems in such a list would be good to use with some boys and girls; however, since different groups respond effectively to different poems, no one list can answer the question for the teacher or for the class, "What poems should we use for choral speaking?" (For a list of books designed for choral speaking the reader is referred to page 321 under "Books on Creative Expression.")

Whether a given poem is listed among these likely to be effective for choral reading or whether it is one that the teacher or a pupil finds in another source, the poem should meet the following criteria. It should:

1. Be a worthwhile poem, one that makes a desirable impression on boys and girls.
2. Be on the level of understanding and appreciation of the pupils.
3. Fit in well, either through conformity or by contrast, with other poems that the pupils have been or will be using for choral speaking.
4. Be a poem which the teacher can present with enthusiasm.
5. Have enough rhythm so that the boys and girls can feel it and interpret it.
6. Have melody.
7. Be relatively short.
8. Not end in tragedy.

FOR STUDY AND DISCUSSION

1. Name examples of dramatic play in which boys and girls in the primary grades can engage that are not listed on page 258 or elsewhere in this chapter.
2. Write a script for a play for elementary-school children on a story or part of a story that fulfills criteria for selection named in this chapter. (See page 259.)
3. With two or more of your fellow students present a short dramatization of a folk tale.
4. Make one of each of several kinds of puppets described in this chapter. Be able to name their uses.
5. A rather extensive listing of puppets is given in this chapter. After reading professional books or magazine articles on puppetry, name, describe, and draw sketches of additional types.
6. Decide on how a flannel board can be used to introduce various scenes of a story progressively to tell to boys and girls in any one grade of the elementary school. Name and describe the flannel board characters and stage settings that you could use in telling the story of your choice.
7. Find a poem suitable for speaking choirs in the primary grades and one appropriate for the intermediate grades. Indicate one desirable way in which each can be cast and be able to give reasons for your choice in casting.

REFERENCES

Arbuthnot, May, *Children and Books*. Third edition. Scott, Foresman and Company, 1964. 688 pp.

Lewis, Shari, *The Puppet Book*. Citadel Press, 1958. 61 pp.

Pratt, Lois H., *The Puppet Do-It-Yourself Book*. Exposition Press, 1957. 75 pp.

Rasmussen, Carrie, *Let's Say Poetry Together*. Burgess Publishing Company, 1962. 114 pp.

Severn, William, *Shadow Magic*. David McKay Company, 1959. 179 pp.

Ward, Winifred, *Playmaking with Children*. Second edition. Appleton-Century-Crofts, 1957. 341 pp.

PART THREE

Specialized Procedures and Resources

OUTLINE FOR CHAPTER 13

Evaluation

CHAPTER 13

Evaluation

Evaluation should be an integral part of the teaching-learning situation, a continuing process in which both teacher and pupils engage. In this book, evaluation is presented in a separate chapter in order to focus special attention on this important aspect of the language-arts program.

BASIC CONSIDERATIONS WHEN MAKING EVALUATIONS

Let us first of all consider these three questions: (1) What are the major purposes of evaluation? (2) What kinds of attainments should be appraised? (3) What are the steps involved in evaluation?

Major Purposes of Evaluation

The possibilities for use of evaluative processes and results for the improvement of instruction are many. Several of the more important functions as they have been identified by Lowry W. Harding[1] are here given. (For various parts of the discussion in this chapter the writer has leaned heavily on the general contributions to the topic of evaluation made by Dr. Harding in *Arithmetic for Child Development.*)

1. Selection and clarification of the goals of instruction, to serve as guides in choosing curricular content
2. Determination of the adequacy of methods and materials of instruction for the needs, interests, and ability of the pupils
3. Identification of rates of pupil growth and progress toward accepted goals
4. Diagnosis of specific difficulties
5. Provision of appropriate practice material for individual pupils
6. Motivation and guidance of learning, especially through self-appraisal by pupils of their own behavior and achievement
7. Establishment of a basis for assignment of achievement marks to pupils
8. Maintenance of efficient planning of work
9. Improvement of curriculum materials of instruction and teaching procedures
10. Provision of a sound basis for public relations, by means of improving reports of pupil progress to parents.

Kinds of Attainment to be Appraised

All too frequently the emphasis on appraisal in schools is directed toward one or two of the desired outcomes of learning experiences – namely on skills acquired or facts learned – often to the almost total neglect of some of the others such as understandings, attitudes, and methods of study. This emphasis persists in many schools in spite of the fact that other desired values are at least as important, if not more so. In written communication, for example, frequently more attention is paid to checking on the mechanical skill that a pupil has developed in terms of sentence and paragraph structure and in capitalization and punctuation than on the attitudes he has acquired toward writing or the growth he has made in expressing thoughts that reveal developing insights.

Steps Involved in Evaluation

The major phases in the evaluation of educational outcomes, as far as the teacher's work is concerned, may be identified in terms of the following seven steps listed by Dr. Harding on pages 333 of the book *Arithmetic for Child Development.*

[1]Lowry W. Harding, *Arithmetic for Child Development.* Dubuque, Iowa: Wm. C. Brown Company, 1964. Page 332.

1. Decide on the objectives and list them.

2. Define objectives in terms of the content involved and the pupil behavior desired. For example, in the objective "ability to give a book report," the desired behavior is *ability* to give a report. Thus the teacher does not want the pupil merely to memorize what points are essential to a good book report, but to be able to give a good report.

3. For each objective, list situations in which the behavior can be shown and sampled. For checking on some of the objectives of the language-arts program, written tests are appropriate; in other situations other means are more suitable.

Here are a few examples of how the pupil can be evaluated in language-arts situations without written tests: (a) In relation to the development of independence of attack in word recognition, the teacher may ask the child to explain the steps through which he goes as he tries to decide on the "names" of given "new" words by means of verbal context clues. (b) If the teacher is trying to find out whether the objective "increasing interest in reading poetry" is achieved, he can make comparisons of the frequency with which a child examines suitable and worthwhile poems placed on a library table, before and after the teacher has through various means tried to help him grow in power to appreciate good poetry. The teacher can also ask others, parents or librarians, to report on the child's "behavior" in this respect. Furthermore, he can ask the pupil directly about his interest in poetry, with emphasis, if the objective is the measurement of growth, on growth.

4. Select specific procedures for getting evidence. The teacher should acquaint himself with the available standardized tests. For the measurement of the results sought in quite a number of the objectives in teaching the language arts, suitable instruments can be found on the market. For evaluating the accomplishment of other objectives, it may be necessary for the teacher to construct tests or check lists of his own.

5. Use the procedures and collect the evidence.

6. Organize and summarize the various types of evidence.

7. Check on conclusions and apply them to improvement of the teaching-learning process.

8. Encourage the pupils to self-evaluation.

EVALUATIVE TECHNIQUES

The following list of evaluative techniques, again to quote Lowry Harding in *Arithmetic for Child Development*, page 337 to 338, shows some of the many means of evaluation that can be used:

Activity records
Adjustment inventories
Anecdotal records
Autobiographies
Case studies

Check lists
Collections and scrapbooks
Cumulative records
Dramatic play
Diaries

Essays, themes, and poems
Flow charts, of play, discussion, etc.
Group discussions
Health and medical histories
Interviews

Intelligence tests
Inventories – of interests, attitudes, etc.
Logs of periods or events
Neighborhood studies
Observation: directed, time-sampling, and informal

Oral reports
Parent conferences
Peer-group studies
Personality inventories
Photographs

Questionnaires
Rating scales
Readiness tests
Recordings and films
Sociograms and other projective techniques

Standardized achievement tests
Teacher-made achievement tests
Teacher-pupil constructed tests
Work samples . . . .

Standardized Achievement Tests

Since with standardized tests there are available scores or norms based on extensive sampling, use of them enables the teacher to compare his pupils with many others. Scores are often expressed in terms of grade levels. For example, if a third-grade pupil at the beginning of October receives a score of 3.1 (representing 3.1 years of school), it means that he has achieved as well as the average third-grade pupil who has completed one-tenth of the third grade; if he receives a score of 4.0, it means that he is .9 of a grade in advance in October of the average third-grade pupil on whom the test was standardized.

To get a quick overview of tests on the market the reader can consult the most recent edition of the *Mental Measurements Yearbook* published by the Gryphon Press, Highland Park, New Jersey. Furthermore, he is referred to page 333 where are given names of test supply companies. For a nominal price, some companies provide specimens of their evaluative instruments. Names of some of the language-arts tests are given in Chapter 15.

Teacher-Made Tests

Standardized tests have several advantages over teacher-constructed tests, in addition to the point emphasized in a preceding paragraph, that they provide a basis of comparison with pupils in other schools. They are, in many instances, constructed by specialists in the field. Usually much more time is spent in construction than that practical for a classroom teacher to use in devising a test.

The advantages, however, are not all on one side. The teacher-made test is often superior to a standardized test in that the former can be constructed in terms of the objectives and learning procedures of a given classroom. The teacher-made test thus may well be more valid for a given group of boys and girls. A safe rule to follow may be to use a standardized test when a suitable one is available and to supplement information gained from it by that obtained from teacher-constructed means of evaluation.

Forms of Paper-and-Pencil Test Questions

Commonly used types of paper-and-pencil test items are essay questions, simple recall questions, completion statements, yes-no (or true-false) statements, multiple choice statements, and matching items. All of these can be used in teacher-made or standardized tests. Seldom, however, are essay questions used in the latter type. Following are one or more examples of test items for each of the foregoing types in the area of the language arts.

1. Essay questions
   (a) Explain what to do when trying to figure out an unknown word in a sentence.
   (b) Why is it important to know how to outline?
2. Simple recall questions
   In which part of a book is the table of contents found?
3. Completion statements
   An adjective modifies a .... or ....
4. Yes-no or true-false items
   (a) Should a comma be used at the end of the greeting of a friendly letter? (Yes, No)
   (b) A comma should be used at the end of the greeting of a friendly letter. (True, False)
5. Multiple choice statements
   The main character of the book is (jovial, pessimistic, unselfish, quarrelsome).
6. Matching items
   Directions: On the line to the left of each item in Column *A* write the letter of the item in Column *B* with which it is associated.

Column A	*Column B*
.... a possessive pronoun	a. children's
.... a proper noun	b. man's
.... a singular possessive noun	c. Washington
.... a plural possessive noun	d. its

EVALUATION IN VARIOUS AREAS OF THE LANGUAGE ARTS

In the preceding paragraphs the description of various means of evaluation is in terms of the type of test items. In this section the classification is according to various phases of the teaching-learning situation in the language arts. For further suggestions for appraising the pupils' achievements in the language arts, the reader is referred to the chapters dealing with the specific areas of the language arts. In the descriptions of methods of procedures given in those chapters, there are also ideas useful in appraisal.

Some points to be observed in setting standards and their use as means of appraisal that apply to all types of activities in the language arts are as follows.

1. The standards should be known not only by the teacher but also by the boys and girls.
2. Frequently the best results are obtained if the standards are made cooperatively by the pupils and the teacher.
3. In the lower grades the wording of the standards will, of necessity, be simple and brief, while in the upper grades the points may be more numerous and more complex in form.

Means of Evaluating Oral Communication

Charts may be made to emphasize points that should be observed during all types of oral communication. One for primary and one for intermediate grades are illustrated.

When We Talk We

1. Speak plainly.
2. Look at our listeners.
3. Express ourselves clearly.
4. Say something worthwhile or interesting.

Points to Watch When We Talk

1. Enunciation
2. Pronunciation
3. Voice
4. Manner
5. Sentence structure
6. English
7. Looking at the listeners

As a variation from the charts given here, a chart illustrated with one or more pictures can be made. Additional standards can be recorded on charts for each type of oral-communication skill such as skill in discussing, taking part in conversation, telling stories.

An individual record should be kept on a 3″ x 5″ card on which are listed the same points for each pupil that are given in a chart publicly displayed. Whenever a pupil gives a talk the teacher, with or without a conference with the child, can put on this card a check in the appropriate column to indicate which points the speaker observed. The date can be recorded at the top and the mark at the bottom of the column.

TAKING PART IN CONVERSATION AND DISCUSSION. The following suggestions indicate how participation in conversation and discussion can be evaluated.

1. With the help of the teacher, boys and girls can draw up a check list for appraisal of the selection of topics for conversation. Points in such a list, depending somewhat upon the age and ability of the boys and girls, may include these among others: (a) The topic should be of interest to most or all of the listeners. (b) The topic should not be one that will be embarrassing to anyone in the group. (c) The topic should not be one that will be likely to induce gossip. (d) The topic should be one that is not likely to encourage unkind comments about other people.

2. A check on the suitability of a pupil's voice can be made through use of a tape recorder. The pupil can then engage in self-evaluation of his voice. In the appraisal questions such as these may be asked: (a) Can I be heard without strain by everyone in my audience? (b) Is my voice too loud? (c) Is my voice pleasant? (d) Do I show variety in my voice? (e) Does my voice express my attitude toward the topic about which I am talking?

3. Pupils can check hypothetical items of conversation in terms of appropriateness for mealtime conversation by indicating which of a list like the following constitutes desirable and undesirable conversation.

.... I wish you would make potato salad the way Aunt Mary makes it. I don't like the way you fix it, Mother.

.... I learned some interesting facts about planets today.

.... I saw a horrible accident on my way home from school today.

.... Good, Mother! I am so glad we have custard tonight!

GIVING TALKS. On page 285 and in the first column of this page are listed points that may be included in check lists on any kind of oral communication. Additional suggestions are given below for check lists and other means of appraisal primarily as they apply to talks or reports the boys and girls give.

This procedure may be followed in working out a check list, possibly at the beginning of the school year, shortly before the boys and girls give their first talks: (a) The teacher tries to interest the boys and girls in the topic or topics about which they will talk. (b) The pupils are helped to realize the need of speaking as well as they can. (c) The pupils name the points that they think they should watch when giving their talks while the teacher lists them, with modifications if necessary, on the chalkboard. (d) The group gives suggestions for observing each of the criteria on the list.

While by no means exhaustive, the following check list can serve as a desirable instrument for the teacher as he helps the boys and girls set standards for the class. It is recommended that not nearly all the items be included in any one list. The wording given here need not necessarily be used.

1. Did I give the topic of my talk (unless it was announced by the chairman)?
2. Is my topic interesting to my listeners?
3. Do I know enough about my topic to make my talk worthwhile for my listeners?
4. Do I have a strong beginning?
5. Do I have a strong ending?
6. Do I keep to the topic?
7. Do I tell points in sequence?
8. Do I stand straight?
9. Do I look at my audience?
10. Am I free of mannerisms that may interfere with my talk?
11. Is my voice pleasant?
12. Can I be heard easily without strain or effort on the part of my listeners?
13. Do I pronounce words correctly?
14. Do I enunciate well?

15. Do I show refinement in what I include in my talk?
16. Do I show refinement in my expressions?
17. Do I use one or more special means of getting and keeping the interest of my listeners (such as giving a demonstration or showing a picture)?
18. Do I give my report without reading it?
19. Do I give my report without using notes?

Since the points for observation drawn up for reports in general also apply to oral book reports, additional specifications may be made for book reports. Points such as these may be listed for evaluation of a book report: (1) title of the book, (2) name of the author, (3) what the book is about, (4) interesting incidents or important information, (5) how I liked the book, (6) where the book can be obtained.

TELLING STORIES. Check lists for storytelling may be drawn up by the class. Such a list can be made after listening to a good storyteller, after reading points about storytelling discussed in a language-arts book, or after thinking of what points one would like to have a storyteller observe.

OBSERVING SOCIAL COURTESIES. Testing techniques similar to the one suggested following for use of the telephone can be worked out for other situations involving courtesies, such as making introductions, acknowledging introductions, being interviewed, receiving callers. In a list like the one given, the pupils can be asked to check those remarks which show courtesy in the use of the telephone.

.... Hello, there! Who's speaking?
.... I know it's past your bedtime, but I wanted to ask you a question before I go to bed.
.... No, Mother is not in. Is there a message for her?

MAKING ANNOUNCEMENTS. The standards for taking part in oral communication of various types listed on page 286, also apply to making announcements. There are some, however, that apply peculiarly to making announcements. Some of particular importance when making announcements are listed here in question form.

1. Have I included all needed information?
2. Did I omit all information that is not needed?
3. Did I tell points in the right order?
4. Did I make my announcement to suit the age level of my audience?
5. Did I talk slowly enough so that everybody could grasp what I was saying?
6. Did I use a visual aid if one would have been helpful?
7. Was I courteous?

Some standards that apply particularly to announcements in the form of invitations are also important for the boys and girls to observe. The following are pertinent when giving announcements to invite a group: (1) The invitation should tell clearly to what the group is invited. (2) The invitation should be definite so that there will be no question in the minds of the audience as to whether or not they are invited. (3) The invitation should tell when and where the event will take place. (4) The invitation should make reference to the fact that the announcer or those for whom he is extending it hope that the members of the audience will be able to accept.

Figure 13.1 A Check on Listening

LISTENING. If standards are drawn up for the evaluation of listening, they should vary with age level. If the points in the evaluation are specific items, they may also vary according to purpose in listening. These are points that may be included in some form in standards set for active listening to a speaker in order to gain information.

1. Looking at the speaker
2. Not playing with anything while someone is speaking
3. Not talking, reading, or doing anything else, as a rule, (other than possibly taking notes) while someone is speaking
4. Noting the speaker's plan of organization
5. Listening with the intent to learn

6. Evaluating what is said, including thinking of points to accept or reject

7. Trying to remember important points made

8. Waiting to make additions or corrections or ask questions until the speaker has finished unless he has specifically indicated that interruptions are all right.

In any evaluation of listening it is important to remember that it defies exact measurement. No instrument has been devised by which the profound changes that can often result from listening can be appraised accurately. Despite this difficulty appraisal that is of value can be made. Through noting the expression on the faces of individuals while they are hearing something, the teacher can get a clue as to how long comprehension continues. The response or lack of it after listening is another index of what has been going on in the mind of the listener. Immediate or delayed questions testing recall can also throw light on the subject. How well children listen to directions or explanations can frequently be ascertained by their ability to follow directions or apply the explanations.

The teacher should not confine his attempts to evaluate to times when the boys and girls are listening to a person speaking to a group. As he talks with a pupil individually and as he observes him in his free conversation with others, during schooltime, before school, or during intermissions, the teacher can obtain information concerning skill in listening. The child who interrupts, who is disinterested unless he himself is speaking or unless the conversation is about him, who leaves the group when someone else is talking, or whose remarks show that he has not been listening — all these give the teacher a clue as to how well he is succeeding in helping boys and girls become better listeners.

Means of Evaluating Written Expression

In schoolrooms where there is much opportunity for written expression, it is not essential that the teacher evaluate every piece of written work. Careful appraisal of everything written, if enough is being done, would take too much of the teacher's time. The boys and girls may at times write a paragraph demonstrating the suggestions they have just discussed and illustrated without even handing their papers in to the teacher. The evaluation in such instances may consist of each pupil checking individually how well he observed the standards for a good paragraph composed by the group. The pupils may practice daily or several times a week writing for a few minutes in a notebook. They may have the understanding that the teacher will not collect the notebooks daily — perhaps not until a pupil has written into his booklet five or six or seven times. Then the teacher will select for detailed analysis one of the reports that the pupil has written since the last time the notebooks were collected. Suggestions to the pupil concerning the one chosen for appraisal should often be in writing so that the next time the child's writings are examined the teacher can check how much the pupil was able to profit from earlier comments by the teacher. When possible, oral conferences with the pupil should implement the written remarks.

Additional suggestions for means of evaluating written communication follow.

1. A check list for skills in written reports can be devised similar in form to the one described on page 286 for oral communication. These points may be listed on a 3″ x 5″ card: (a) neatness, (b) sentence structure, (c) punctuation, (d) capitalization, (e) beginning, (f) interestingness, (g) ending.

2. A neatness scale can be constructed against which points such as these may be checked: (a) placement of writing on paper, (b) freedom from recognizable erasures and from parts crossed out, (c) clean appearance of paper.

3. Pupils can be tested on capitalization and punctuation through exercises like the following.

> *Directions.* Place a question mark, period, or exclamation point at the end of each sentence.
>
> Did you know that we have a pet in our room
>
> Bobby brought a hamster to school
>
> *Directions.* Write these sentences. Use capital letters where they are needed.
>
> We wrote a letter to mr. smith.
>
> he is a farmer.
>
> *Directions.* Write the possessive form of each of the following groups of words:
>
> the books belonging to the boy
> the books belonging to the boys
> the books belonging to the children
> the toys belonging to the babies.

Means of Evaluating Handwriting

Various publishing companies sell handwriting scales. Some of them, such as the Ayres Scale, range from very poor samples of handwriting to a sample representative of superior handwriting. Others have a different scale for each grade from one to six, with the one used for grade six also used to measure handwriting of pupils in the upper grades and high school and of adults.

A few samples of commercial materials that can be used for evaluating handwriting follow; all are available through the Zaner-Bloser Company. Other publishers or distributors of handwriting materials also furnish materials that can be used for evaluative purposes.

1. The worksheets for manuscript and cursive handwriting and for the transition period from manuscript to cursive
2. "Body position charts," illustrating correct position for manuscript and for cursive writing for the right-handed writer and some for the left-handed writer, and "hand charts," showing correct position
3. "Diagnostic rulers" and the "C-thru-Ruler."

Periodically, possibly once a month, the pupils may write a sample of their best handwriting on a uniform size of paper. The writing can be timed, though the major emphasis should be on legibility and form of letters not on speed. After the boys and girls have written for a few minutes and time has been called, they can write in column form, below the sentences that they have written – also in their best handwriting – the following words representing qualities of handwriting: *color, size, slant, beginning strokes, ending strokes, letter spacing, alignment, letter formation,* and *rate.* The teacher can write a characterizing word or group of words to the right of each point listed. For example, opposite the word *slant* he may write either *correct* or *lacking slant* or *too slanting* or *irregular slant.* The rate per minute can then be computed and a quality rating, based on the scale for the grade, can be recorded.

Some teachers may like to use papers of boys and girls in the room to form a scale with ratings comparable to those given on some charts. In some cases the teacher himself may need to furnish one or more samples on the scale for which he did not find comparable samples on the pupils' papers. It is best not to reveal the identity of the writer of any of the samples for fear that the poorer writers may be embarrassed.

Pupils' papers from classes other than handwriting should also be evaluated for handwriting. As a means of appraisal of the neatness of the handwriting in arithmetic papers, for example, a chart can be made without names of pupils, giving samples in which the writing is very neat, average in neatness, and lacking in neatness. If marks are given in handwriting on a report card, in calculating the mark the teacher should count not only the writing in handwriting class but also that done at other times.

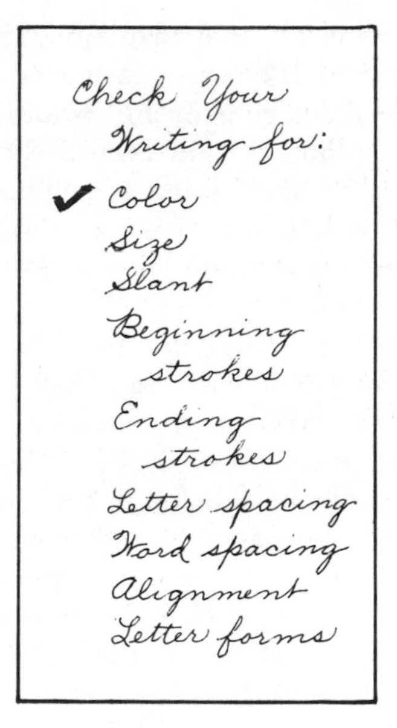

Figure 13.2 A Means of Self-Evaluation of Handwriting

Figure 13.3 Another Means of Self-Evaluation of Handwriting

Means of Evaluating Spelling

In evaluating pupils' spelling papers, these are two questions about which teachers wonder: (1) Should a word be marked wrong if it is poorly written? (2) Should a word be marked wrong if a correction has been made in the writing through erasing, rewriting, crossing out, or writing over one or more letters? Arguments can be given for both sides of these questions. In the opinion of the writer there is more reason for answering the first question negatively than positively if it is clear what letters are intended. Possibly the main argument for counting the word correct if the spelling is right even if the handwriting is poor is that the skill tested is spelling, not handwriting. If there is a question as to what a certain letter is, however, the pupil should not be given the benefit of the doubt.

In regard to the second question, "Should a word be marked wrong if a correction has been made in the writing through erasing, rewriting, crossing out, or writing over one or more letters?" the answer may be "Yes." A person ought to be so certain of the spelling of a word if he has achieved mastery of it that he writes it correctly on first attempt. On the other hand, it may be claimed that the important point is not whether the child writes the word correctly the first time but whether he knows how to write it.

Because pupils seem more likely to spell a word correctly when it is dictated in a list than when it is used in a sentence or paragraph, many teachers have pupils write from dictation a few sentences containing some of the spelling words. Care should be taken that every word in a sentence has been studied or words not studied before are spelled for the pupil, probably on the chalkboard. One recommended practice is that an entire sentence should be marked wrong if only one word in it has been misspelled.

Some teachers check the spelling of boys and girls by having them supply missing letters — frequently those that are assumed to be the letters within a word most likely to be missed such as the *ie* in the word *believe*. It must be kept in mind that unless the teacher pronounces the word in which one or more letters are omitted in writing, the pupil may at times be unable to recognize what word is wanted. Then, it could be argued, if the teacher names the word anyhow, why not have the pupil engage in practice by writing the entire word, not merely supplying the missing letters? The question is justified.

Another means of evaluation is to omit one or more letters in a word which the pupil is to supply when with the incomplete word is given a word or group of words that will help identify the word to be completed. The following is an example of such a listing:

the .... r: belonging to them
bab .... s: more than one baby.

Yet another means, though a questionable one, is that of having pupils detect which words in a list, in a sentence, or in one or more paragraphs are written incorrectly. The danger is that the wrong rather than the right form may be impressed upon the learner's mind.

When dictating words the teacher may like to follow this procedure: (1) Give the number of the word. (2) Immediately after giving the number, say the word distinctly without overpronouncing it. (3) Use the word in a simple sentence that will help the child determine whether he has heard the word correctly and that, in the case of homonyms, will serve as a means of identification of the word. (4) Repeat the word. Thus, if the first word in a list were *walked*, the teacher following these steps may say:

> Number one. *Walked.* The boy walked home. *Walked.*

One means of evaluating the success of a spelling program is by answering questions such as these about the children's spelling and spelling habits: (1) Are they interested in wanting to become good spellers? (2) Are they interested in finding their spelling mistakes in the writing they do throughout the school day and at other times? (3) Are they learning means of finding the correct spelling of words with which they need help? (This question can be asked with profit only after the pupils have learned how to use word lists for that purpose or to look words up in a dictionary even if they do not beforehand know the spelling.)

If spelling is evaluated on report cards or in other ways, not only should the spelling of words studied in spelling class be taken into consideration but also the spelling of words a pupil uses in other written work.

Means of Evaluating Readiness for Reading

A list of tests for evaluating readiness for reading is given on page 333. In using standardized reading readiness tests, the teacher should bear in mind the fact that none of them can be used as a sole evaluative criterion.

Points frequently included in tests of reading readiness are: ability to make visual and auditory discriminations, extent of vocabulary, success in learning new words with a relatively small number of repetitions, ability to follow directions, ability to remember, ability to note relationships. There are other points that are of importance in reading readiness that cannot at present be adequately measured by tests. Examples of such traits are interest in stories and picture books; ability to pay sustained attention; "at-easeness" in group situations; skill in oral communication, voice, vision, hearing, and other matters of physical health and of emotional and social development.

For means of evaluating mental and physical health and determining social development in terms of readiness for reading, the reader is referred to pages 176 to 178. For ways of appraising educational factors, in addition to using standardized reading tests, he is referred to page 178.

A few cautions about evaluation of reading readiness are here in order. (1) It is likely to make a test for some pupils invalid if it is given at a time when they are not "at home" in the school situation. This fact is one argument against giving reading readiness tests to boys and girls the spring preceding entrance to first grade unless they are in kindergarten. It is also argument against giving such tests on the first few days of school in fall. (2) For success in reading it is not necessary that the learner show average or above average ratings in each of the traits that has a bearing on beginning reading. A pupil may even show considerable lack in some and yet be able to learn to read successfully. (3) Evaluation of reading readiness should help determine not only whether a child is ready to begin systematic work in reading but also the type of reading program to which he should be introduced. To be sure, appraisal may sometimes seem to indicate that it is wise to postpone all systematic work in reading. On the other hand, in many cases it is undesirable to postpone it for a long time because of the complex a child may develop who finds himself deprived of the experience that the teacher wisely holds forth to the class as an exciting one – learning to read. In many instances where the pupil is not ready for the type of reading experience from which many in the class can profit, the methods and materials used in introducing him to reading should be so well adapted to his level that he will be successful.

Means of Evaluating Reading Skills

For a long time standardized reading tests examined primarily – some to the exclusion of other traits – rate and comprehension. Furthermore, the aspects of reading rate and comprehension that were tested were limited. In one extensively used test the measure for the rate per minute was based entirely on the speed with which the pupil read during the first minute of testing. Many so-called comprehension tests checked retention chiefly rather than comprehension as the term is used in Chapter 10.

Checking Comprehension. Some of the standardized tests produced within the last few decades check a variety of factors that are components of skill in comprehension. Among these are sentence comprehension, paragraph comprehension, comprehension of longer thought units, ability to grasp the main idea, skill in noting details.

Comprehension can be checked by asking boys and girls questions on what was read of the general type indicated by the questions or directions suggested following.

1. *The ability to comprehend the main idea.* The boys and girls may supply the needed information in following directions like these:

> Put an x on the line to the left of the topic in the list below that best expresses the main idea of the following paragraph.
>
> In your own words write a topic that tells what the following paragraph is about.

2. *The ability to note details.* The pupils can be asked to comply with directions like the following in order to give evidence of the extent of their ability in selecting details.

> Below the following paragraph are listed four statements. Three of them are on details given in the paragraph. Put an x on the line to the left of each of those three.
>
> Below each of the following paragraphs is listed a series of sentences. Some of these sentences contain a detail given in the paragraph. Others give the main idea. Still others give points not mentioned in the paragraph. Put an x on the line to the left of each sentence that states a detail mentioned in that paragraph.
>
> In your own words make a list of the details mentioned in each of the following paragraphs that supports the main idea of the paragraph. (The sentence that contains the main idea of the paragraph is mentioned.)

3. *The ability to comprehend directions.* The boys and girls may indicate by drawing a diagram how to follow directions for getting from one place to another. They may be asked to arrange in proper sequence a series of statements giving directions to proceed from one place to another or statements giving steps for performing an activity such as making applesauce or a papier-mâché figure.

4. *The ability to organize.* To test the pupils' ability to organize what they have read, the boys and girls may do the following:

> Tell which one or more of a series of statements is irrelevant to the other statements in the series.
>
> Arrange a series of points so that they are in suitable sequence.

Fill in the sub-topics in an outline on a given selection for which the main topics (written in outline form) are given. The number of sub-topics to be given under each main topic may be indicated by the number of figures or letters in the parts of an outline. A sample of part of such an outline is given here.

I. Causes of the French and Indian War
 A.
 B.

II. Chief Battles of the War
 A.
 B.
 C.

A variation of the work on outlining suggested is to provide the pupil with the sub-topics for an outline in scrambled order, and ask him to place them where they belong.

5. *The ability to predict outcomes.* Here are ways in which the boys and girls can be tested on ability to predict outcomes.

After the pupils have read part of a selection or after the teacher has read to them, they can be asked to tell which of several recorded statements gives the probable ending.

After pupils have read part of a story or after the teacher has read it to them, they can write a sentence or more summarizing a possible ending.

6. *The ability to evaluate what is read.* The pupils can be tested on their ability to evaluate what they read by:

Telling which of a group of persons whose qualifications are enumerated are best qualified to make a given statement that might be considered controversial or questionable in some other way

Deciding whether given statements are statements of fact or opinion

Rewriting statements of opinion so that they clearly reveal to what extent they are based on fact and to what extent they represent someone's opinion.

CHECKING READING AT APPROPRIATE RATES. Some means of evaluating reading at appropriate rates are by noting the pupils' responses as they engage in activities such as the following:

1. Answer questions as to rates appropriate for reading for various stated purposes

2. Read while being timed for purposes for which different rates are appropriate while at the same time being tested as to level of comprehension through questions suitable for the purpose

3. Take a test on rate of comprehension at the beginning of the time spent on a given selection (perhaps after five minutes of reading) and again later while continuing reading the selection, (in order to check on the "warming-up" period).

CHECKING SKILL IN LOCATING INFORMATION. These are some of the evaluative procedures that can be used to check skill in locating information.

1. The boys and girls can answer questions on various parts of a book such as: (a) In what part of a book is the index found? (b) In what part of a book – the table of contents or the index – are the main entries arranged in alphabetical order?

2. The boys and girls can tell which word of a series would be the most likely one under which, in an index or encyclopedia, information to answer a given question would be found.

3. The pupils can be tested on ability to arrange letters and later words in alphabetical order.

4. The boys and girls can be checked on ability to select the meaning given for a word in a dictionary that fits into the context of a sentence in which the word is used.

CHECKING ORAL READING. Probably the chief value of so-called oral reading tests, such as the "Gray Standardized Oral Reading Check Tests" and the "Durrell Analysis of Reading Difficulty Tests," is that they throw light upon the silent reading abilities of boys and girls. While they do test for word recognition, omission or insertion of letters or words or groups of words, and other skills related to both oral and silent reading, they do not test the reader's skill in interpreting the written word to an audience. A frequently used means of checking oral reading is a check list like the following, sometimes constructed by the class under the guidance of the teacher:

Voice
Enunciation
Pronunciation
Posture
Poise
Interpretation of meaning.

Means of Appraising Independent Reading

The teacher may obtain an estimate of the amount and/or quality of independent reading done by boys and girls by:

READING RATE METER

These rates per minute are figured for every quarter of a minute, beginning with four minutes, for passages of the length indicated.

1400-word passage

350	200	140	108
329	193	137	106
311	187	133	104
295	181	130	102
280	175	127	100
267	170	124	98
255	165	122	97
243	160	119	95
233	156	117	93
224	151	114	
215	147	112	
207	144	110	

1250-word passage

312	179	125	96
294	172	122	94
278	167	119	93
263	161	116	91
250	156	114	89
238	152	111	
227	147	109	
217	143	106	
208	139	104	
200	135	102	
192	132	100	
185	128	98	

1350-word passage

338	193	135	104
318	186	132	102
300	180	129	100
284	174	126	98
270	169	123	96
257	164	120	95
245	159	117	93
235	154	115	92
225	150	112	90
216	146	110	
208	142	108	
200	138	106	

1200-word passage

300	171	120	92
282	166	117	
267	160	114	
253	155	112	
244	150	109	
229	145	107	
218	141	104	
209	137	102	
200	133	100	
192	130	98	
185	126	96	
178	123	94	

1300-word passage

325	186	130	100
306	179	127	98
289	173	124	96
274	168	121	95
260	163	118	93
248	158	116	
236	153	113	
226	149	111	
217	144	108	
208	141	106	
200	137	104	
193	133	102	

1150-word passage

288	164	115
271	159	112
256	153	110
242	148	107
230	144	105
219	139	102
209	135	100
200	131	98
192	128	96
184	124	94
177	121	92
170	118	90

Figure 13.4 A Table for Determining Rates per Minute

READING RATE METER (Concluded)

1100-word passage		
275	157	110
259	152	107
244	147	105
232	142	102
220	138	100
210	133	98
200	129	96
191	126	94
183	122	92
176	119	
169	116	
163	113	

950-word passage		
238	136	95
224	131	
211	127	
200	123	
190	119	
181	115	
173	112	
165	109	
158	106	
152	103	
146	100	
141	97	

800-word passage	
200	114
188	110
178	107
168	103
160	100
152	97
145	94
139	91
133	89
128	
123	
119	

1050-word passage		
262	150	105
247	145	102
233	140	100
221	135	98
210	131	95
200	127	
191	124	
183	120	
175	117	
168	114	
162	111	
156	108	

900-word passage		
225	129	90
212	124	
200	120	
189	116	
180	112	
171	109	
164	106	
157	103	
150	100	
144	97	
138	95	
133	92	

750-word passage	
188	107
176	103
167	100
158	97
150	94
143	
136	
130	
125	
120	
115	
111	

1000-word passage		
250	143	100
235	138	98
222	133	95
211	129	93
200	125	91
190	121	
182	118	
174	114	
167	111	
160	108	
154	105	
148	103	

850-word passage	
212	121
200	117
189	113
179	110
170	106
162	103
155	100
148	97
142	94
136	
131	
126	

700-word passage	
175	100
165	97
156	93
147	90
140	88
133	
127	
122	
117	
112	
108	
104	

Figure 13.5 A Table for Determining Rates per Minute (Concluded)

1. Noting what the pupils are reading when they are at the library table

2. Encouraging the children to bring to school books or magazines that they enjoy particularly, possibly to "share" parts of them with others in the room

3. Noting which books the pupils draw from the room or school library

4. Having the pupils keep a record, under the supervision of the teacher, of books read

5. Asking the pupils to fill out a questionnaire on their reading, as suggested on page 229

6. Discussing significant points of a book with some of the pupils. For example, after a child has read a book on a minority group, the teacher may question him as to his reaction to what he had read. Sometimes the teacher may be able to ascertain whether or not the book has brought about a change in the child's attitude and, if a change was effected, whether it was for the better.

FOR STUDY AND DISCUSSION

1. For somewhat detailed study of criteria on which to evaluate standardized tests, consult books on educational psychology or on measurements in education. Then evaluate one or more tests in the language arts according to those criteria.

2. Make a study of standardized tests, scales, or check lists for evaluation of phases of the language arts. Note which sound objectives of a language-arts program are evaluated by them, at least in part. Also note whether or not there are some important goals of the language-arts program that are not evaluated by the tests you examine.

3. In this chapter are suggested various ways in which phases of the language-arts program can be evaluated. Suggest additional evaluative procedures that can be used.

4. Diagnose a sample of your cursive handwriting as to color, size, slant, beginning strokes, ending strokes, alignment, and letter forms. You may wish to refer to Chapter 7 for ideas useful in making the diagnosis. If you have access to a standardized scale for measuring handwriting, give yourself a general grade for quality according to the scaling of that instrument.

5. Devise an evaluative instrument for use in connection with some important phase of the language arts.

6. Suggest ways in which a teacher can encourage a pupil to self-evaluation in the language arts.

REFERENCES

Ahmann, J. S.; M. D. Glock; and Helen L. Wardeburg, *Evaluating Elementary School Pupils.* Allyn and Bacon, 1960. 435 pp.

Blair, Glenn M.; R. Stewart Jones; and Ray H. Simpson, *Educational Psychology.* Second edition. The Macmillan Company, 1962. 678 pp.

Buros, Oscar K. (ed.), *Mental Measurements Yearbook.* The Gryphon Press, latest edition.

Eson, Morris E., *Psychological Foundations of Education.* Holt, Rinehart and Winston, 1964. 563 pp.

Lindgren, Henry Clay, *Educational Psychology in the Classroom.* Second edition. John Wiley and Sons, 1962. 574 pp.

National Society for the Study of Education (Warren G. Findley, ed.) *The Impact and Improvement of School Testing Programs.* Sixty-Second Yearbook, Part Two, National Society for the Study of Education. University of Chicago Press, 1963. 304 pp.

Thomas, R. M., *Judging Student Progress.* Second edition. Longmans, Green and Company, 1960. 518 pp.

OUTLINE FOR CHAPTER 14

Illustrative Teaching Situations

CHAPTER 14

Illustrative Teaching Situations

Chapter 14 serves as supplementary to the suggestions given in Part Two of this book. It contains listings of (1) steps that can be used in teaching, (2) teaching plans, and (3) descriptions of many other teaching procedures. The organization of the main parts parallels in part that of Chapter 3 through Chapter 10.

ILLUSTRATIVE SITUATIONS FOR DEVELOPING SKILLS IN ORAL AND WRITTEN COMMUNICATION

Since separate divisions of this chapter present suggestions for teaching handwriting, spelling, and reading, in this section none is given on those three phases of written communication other than through incidental reference.

Taking Part in Conversation and Discussion

For background data and additional suggestions to help boys and girls take effective part in conversation and discussion, the reader is referred to page 37.

Developmental Lessons. In planning a developmental lesson in this area, these phases usually should be included as parts of the lesson: (1) motivation, (2) presentation of the new skill, and (3) application of the learning.

1. Motivation. The purpose of the motivation is to interest the boys and girls in learning about the topic, in some cases to help them recognize need for study. Sometimes the motivation may consist merely of a statement by the teacher, in which he explains the lack that he has observed in pupils' conversation. If so, the teacher can tell the class that he will try to help them improve in that respect. At other times the motivation may really be an integral part of the presentation as, for example, when in order to show pupils what to do when two persons start talking at the same time, one skit is presented to illustrate how the problem is handled poorly and another how it is taken care of properly.

2. Presentation. During the presentation the points to be learned during the lesson are emphasized. Often it is preferable to make the presentation through inductive procedures, as, for example, when the pupils are studying the importance of talking only about topics that are not embarrassing to anyone in the group. In such a situation the boys and girls may read two recorded conversations and decide what makes one better than the other. Instead, as already suggested, the points of significance may be brought out through two skits a few pupils have prepared before class with the help of the teacher.

After the new point of the lesson has been developed, it is well for either the teacher or a pupil, preferably the latter, as a rule, to state in a sentence or more what has been learned.

3. Application. During the application phase of the lesson, which should occur during the developmental lesson and usually also at later times, the pupil has an opportunity to use what he has learned. Small conversation groups may be established in which the pupils talk with one another according to the specifications that the teacher may have recorded for them on slips of paper handed to the chairman of each group, or the pupils may judge one sample conversation presented by a small group of boys and girls for the benefit of the rest of the class. In the application of the lesson the pupils should be encouraged to try to apply what they have learned at all times when they engage in conversation.

PANEL DISCUSSIONS. As the teacher plans or helps the pupils plan panel discussions, he will want to keep in mind guidelines such as these: (1) From the continuum of very simple to rather complex procedures that can characterize a panel discussion, choice should be made in harmony with the abilities of the pupils as influenced by age, mentality, grade level, and environmental factors. (2) As a rule, participation in a panel discussion should not be limited over a period of time, to only some of the pupils. (3) Considerable guidance in planning and putting into operation panel discussions should be given, at least occasionally. (4) The audience should frequently be checked on its learnings from panel discussions by means of discussion, oral questions and answers, and written responses.

The following descriptions of possible procedures in a panel discussion indicate, roughly in order of complexity, some of the ways they can be conducted in the elementary school.

1. In a first grade a group of boys and girls, three to five in number, appear in front of their classmates with pictures they have drawn on some one topic such as "My Pet." As each pupil shows his picture, he makes one or more comments about it. When all have shown theirs the teacher, serving as chairman, opens the rest of the period to questions and comments about the pictures or the explanations, first to pupils on the panel and then to the audience. The teacher also may wish to make comments or ask questions. At the close of the discussion there can well be an evaluation of the discussion by the members of the panel, the audience, or the teacher. Questions such as these may be asked in evaluation: (a) Could you hear us? (b) Could you see our pictures? (c) Did we have good posture?

2. After some of the pupils in a third grade have been reading about the food of the Eskimos, they can participate in a panel discussion. A chairman, either the teacher or a pupil, can ask each participant to report on what he learned on the topic, perhaps as each makes several comments. The chairman can then summarize what has been said and ask for additional points or for questions, first from members of the panel and then from the audience. The teacher may wish to contribute also. An evaluation of the discussion can follow.

3. After the pupils in a fifth-grade room have been studying about how to develop skill in conversation, some of the members may take part in a panel discussion on the topic. They can meet beforehand with the teacher to decide what points to discuss in order to be able to help the audience remember what to do to be an effective participant in conversation and to put their knowledge into practice. They may decide upon points such as these: (a) importance of being effective in conversation, (b) helping others take part in conversation, (c) interruptions in conversation, (d) situations in which conversation is out of order.

Next, each participant can be assigned a topic. After each member of the panel has thought for a few minutes about points he plans to stress, he can outline his plans for the panel and ask for suggestions. When suggestions have been made, time can be allowed for the pupils to plan their reports alone. The group may also have a voice in deciding on the pattern of procedure during the time of the panel, which may be as follows: (a) A pupil chairman gives the purpose of the panel and outlines the procedure. (b) All the topics are presented by panel members. (c) Questions and comments are given by the panel members when all reports have been completed. (d) Questions and comments are given by the audience. (e) A summary is given by the chairman. (f) Evaluation of the panel follows by the members of the panel, the audience, and the teacher. After making plans for procedure, the panel is ready to begin its presentation.

SOCIAL USAGES. To supplement the material presented in Chapter 4 on two phases of social usage, namely conversation at mealtime and telephoning, two teaching plans are here given in abbreviated form.

1. *Plan for conversation at mealtime* (adapted from a plan written by two former students, Ethel Klotz Brown and Beverly Lane Koski). This plan may be used in grades three, four, or five if suitable adjustments are made to the personnel of the class.

A. *Pupils' Aim*: To learn how to improve our conversation at mealtime

B. *Materials*:

1. A list of remarks such as the following (written on a piece of paper that the teacher has) to be used to determine which exemplify good and which poor mealtime conversation

   a. Mother, do we have to have vegetable soup every wash day? I can't stand even the smell of it.

   b. Dad, Miss Smith complimented me on what you told me about how the United States got the Statue of Liberty.

c. No, thank you. I don't like spinach. It tastes bitter.
d. Sis, you look nice in that dress!
e. Jim brought a raccoon to school today. He said that the raccoon is so clean that he washes his food before he eats it.
f. Dad, tell Bob to stop teasing me. He has spoiled the whole day for me.

2. A duplicated list of good and poor topics for conversation at the table, preceded by directions such as these: "Below is a list of topics for conversation at the table. Number your paper from *1* to . . . . If a topic on the list below is a good topic for mealtime conversation, write *Good* after the corresponding number. If it is poor, write *Poor*."
   a. A boy at whom you are angry
   b. A bad traffic accident
   c. Something interesting that happened at school
   d. A good story or joke
   e. What you think is wrong with the food
   f. A generous act that you saw.

C. *Outline of Procedure*:
1. Introduction
   a. Discussion of the results of good and poor conversation at mealtime upon the health of the people eating
   b. Statement of aim (See *A*.)
2. Drawing up rules governing good conversation at mealtime, such as the following, as the teacher lists them on the chalkboard: (a) Talk about pleasant topics. (b) Do not criticize the food.
3. Deciding which of a list of remarks are likely to be appropriate at the table (See *B-1*) as this procedure is followed:
   a. The teacher reads a remark.
   b. A pupil tells whether or not the remark is appropriate.
4. Deciding which of a list of topics are good for conversation at the table (See *B-2*.)
   a. The pupils read the directions silently and then tell in their own words what they are to do.
   b. A pupil tells what the answer is for the first item and all pupils record it.
   c. The pupils complete the exercise while the teacher notes study habits.
   d. The pupils correct their papers as the teacher reads the answers while he follows this procedure: (1) giving the number of the item, (b) reading the item orally, and (3) giving the answer.
5. Application
   a. The pupils discuss what changes they can make in their table conversation at home and at school.
   b. The teacher points out the importance of being polite to anyone who disobeys any of the rules as he stresses the desirability of being critical of self and lenient with others as far as adherence to the rules is concerned.

2. *Plan for telephoning.* The following outline of a plan is an adaptation of one prepared for use with a fourth-grade class by two former college students, Betty Baker Trost and Carolyn Dornoff Bilyea.

A. *Teacher's Aims*:
1. To help the boys and girls learn more about good telephone manners
2. To stimulate the boys and girls to try to practice at all times what they know about good telephone manners

B. *Materials*:
1. Skit illustrating good manners

John: This is John Allen calling. May I please speak with Jim?
Jim: Hello, John. This is Jim.
John: Well, Jim, (As John coughs he turns his head away from the phone.) Pardon me. I wonder if we could plan our design for our model airplane this afternoon.
Jim: That would be fine with me. Can we meet in our garage about two o'clock?
John: Oh, that would be fine. I will see you at two. So long!
Jim: So long, John.

2. Skit illustrating poor manners

Joan: Who is speaking?
Carolyn: Carolyn.
Joan: Guess who this is, Carolyn.
Carolyn: Is it Sue?
Joan: No, it is Joan. I have a cold. (She coughs into the telephone.) Can you come to a surprise birthday party for Marj at my home tomorrow afternoon at four o'clock?
Carolyn: (She yells into the telephone.) Oh, I'd love that! I can't wait!

Joan: I'm glad that you can come.
Carolyn: Goodbye, Joan.
Joan: Good-bye.

3. Duplicated copies of conversation illustrating poor manners
Bill (mumbling): I want to speak to Joe.
Joe: This is Joe.
Bill (still mumbling): Joe, this is Bill. I know it's still dark out, but this would be a fine time to dig worms for our fishing trip. I hope you didn't mind getting up at this hour to answer the telephone. You weren't still asleep, were you?
Joe: Yes, I *WAS* asleep. I can't go fishing with you today. You can dig your own worms. Good-bye. (Joe slams the receiver.)

4. Duplicated copies of conversation illustrating good manners
Ellen: This is Ellen Hodgson calling. May I please speak to Louisa?
Louisa: Ellen, this is Louisa. I'm glad to hear from you.
Ellen: What kind of report are we to write for our social studies assignment?
Louisa: First we are to study the questions on the sheet that Miss Grayson gave us. Then we are to write a report that answers those questions.
Ellen: That shouldn't be hard. Thank you very much for helping me. Good-bye, Louisa.
Louisa: Good luck with the report.

C. *Outline of Procedure*:

1. Introduction
   a. Explanation by the teacher that two groups of children are going to dramatize some imaginary telephone conversation that they have prepared beforehand, one group demonstrating good and the other poor manners
   b. Statement by the teacher that the class should note what good and what poor points are demonstrated
   c. Demonstration by the two groups (See *B-1* and *B-2*.)
   d. Naming desirable and undesirable points demonstrated

      If the pupils do not note the following violations, the teacher points them out: (1) coughing into the telephone, (2) yelling into the telephone, (3) asking the other person to guess who is telephoning, (4) asking "Who is speaking?" as opening remark, (5) not waiting to say "Good-bye" until the person who has called shows that he is ready to end the conversation.
2. Formulation of rules for telephoning
   a. Naming rules that have not already been brought out in connection with the two skits (See *B-1* and *B-2*.)
   b. Condensing these rules and dictating them to the teacher, who writes them in a form similar to this:
      (1) Call at times convenient for those you call.
      (2) Tell who you are.
      (3) Speak clearly.
      (4) Make your calls brief.
3. Deciding which rules are obeyed and which disobeyed in telephone conversations recorded on paper (See *C-3* and *C-4*.)
   a. Pupils read silently the conversation under *C-3* to be able to point out which rules are obeyed.
   b. Pupils name rules obeyed in *C-3*.
   c. Pupils read silently the conversation under *C-4*.
   d. Pupils name rules disobeyed in *C-4*.
4. Preparation for dramatization

   The pupils couple up to prepare a telephone conversation after they have decided which rules they want to obey or disobey in their skit, while the teacher helps some of the groups.
5. Dramatization
   a. The teacher explains that not all groups will be called on that day, but that others will have a chance to give their reports at a later time.
   b. The teacher calls on a few groups who give their dramatizations.
   c. Pupils criticize and comment on the manners which are demonstrated.
6. Forward look
   a. The teacher reminds the boys and girls of the importance of the rules they have helped formulate.
   b. A few pupils explain what points they plan to note in particular when next they use the telephone.

Preparing and Presenting Assembly Programs

Following are listed a few ways in which the ideas for assembly programs suggested in Chapter 4 can be put into practice.

1. Boys and girls in the first grade may present a program on the topic "We have Learned to Read." It can consist of: (a) a "movie" (for which the pupils drew the pictures and the teacher wrote the script dictated by the pupils) of a story in their reading textbook; (b) a dramatization of a story; (c) an oral reading of a story in the textbook with the parts of various characters assigned to different children; or (d) a report on a story that the pupils have enjoyed particularly.

2. First-grade pupils can present a program on the topic "Our First-Grade Room." They can display large charts showing drawings of each pupil made by another child. Each drawing can be accompanied by a brief description of the pupil pictured, written by the teacher as dictated to him by the artist (with necessary alterations). A few of the "biographies" may be read as the persons described appear on the stage. A "movie" illustrated by the pupils, with the script written by the teacher, on the occupations of parents of children in the room may be shown. A large map giving the location of the homes of the children can be displayed and explained.

3. Pupils in the primary grades can give an assembly program as a culminating activity for a unit on topics such as "The Farm," "Our Community," "Our Helpers." The program may include oral reading, talks, songs, "movies," and dramatization.

4. A program of Christmas songs, stories, and dramatizations can be presented by elementary-school pupils. One or two lighted Christmas trees on the stage will help create the appropriate mood. At the beginning of the program the audience can join in singing familiar Christmas carols. Then a few short interesting stories can be read or told. A story can be pantomimed or otherwise dramatized.

5. A program on "The Sky Above Us" can follow a unit on that topic by children of the upper intermediate grades. The stage can be transformed into an imaginary observatory with various things on display such as globes, maps, and a planisphere. The program can consist of a combination of some features such as those listed here:

An introductory talk by a guide (a pupil) explaining the value of a study of the heavens and describing the procedure to be followed in the program

An illustrated talk on the importance of the sun to the earth

A demonstration of the rotation of the earth as the cause of day and night

Stories about the moon

A demonstration explaining the phases of the moon

An illustrated talk on one or more of the planets

A demonstration of the relative distance of some of the planets from the sun

A talk on one or more stars or constellations

A demonstration of the revolution of the Big Dipper around the North Star

An explanation of how the Big Dipper serves as the "celestial clock"

A talk contrasting superstitions about comets and meteors with present-day knowledge

A demonstration of Newton's laws of motion as applied to exploration in space

A pupil-made "movie" on the contributions of recent explorers of space

A skit showing an imaginary trip to space fifty years from now.

Following Parliamentary Procedure

The information about parliamentary procedure given here is illustrative of that which boys and girls should follow as members or leaders of clubs.

ORGANIZING A CLUB. It often is wise for the teacher to serve as temporary chairman at an organization meeting. As soon as the temporary chairman has called the meeting to order and has stated the purpose of the meeting, he can ask for nominations for a chairman or president. After the president has been elected, he may take office immediately. Frequently at the organization meeting the other officers are elected also and sometimes other business, such as deciding on frequency of meetings or the date of the next meeting or appointment of committees, is transacted.

ELECTING OFFICERS. When the time comes to elect officers, the chairman frequently asks for nominations. If a member of the group makes a nomination, a second to the nomination is not required. After one or more nominations have been made, a member may move that they be closed. After the group has voted the nominations be closed, the membership votes on the officers, as a rule preferably by ballot. Unless otherwise specified, the person with the largest number of votes may be considered elected. The pupils should realize that it is the responsibility of each member to vote for a well-qualified person.

Duties of Officers. The boys and girls will need to know the duties of the various officers.

Officers	*Duties*
President	To preside at meetings To be in general charge of the organization
Vice-president	To assume the duties of the president in his absence
Secretary	To keep the minutes of a meeting and to read them at the next meeting To take care of the correspondence of the group
Treasurer	To take care of money matters To give a report at each regular meeting on the status of the treasury.

Making and Voting Upon Motions. If a person wishes to have the group vote upon a matter, he can bring it to the attention of the members by beginning, "Mr. (or Madam) President, I move that. . . ." Before there can be any discussion on the topic, someone must second the motion by saying, "I second the motion." Then discussion can follow. When discussion has ceased the chairman may say, "It has been moved and seconded that. . . . All those in favor signify by saying 'Aye,'" Then he adds, "Contrary, 'No.'" The chairman announces whether or not the motion has passed. Voting may, however, be done by ballot.

The boys and girls should not only know the technique for making and voting upon motions but also understand it is important in a democracy that the people vote for motions which are for the good of the group.

Writing the Minutes of a Meeting. During a meeting the secretary should take careful notes on what happens at the meeting and later write the notes more in detail as minutes of the meeting. The minutes should state the time and place of meeting, tell what happened, and indicate that the meeting was adjourned.

Appointing Committees. Usually it is the responsibility of the president to appoint committees. Unless otherwise specified, the person whom the president names first is the chairman of the committee. At times the president may ask the group to elect a committee. At still other times a motion asking a committee be created may specify that it is to be elected, not appointed.

Steps in Conducting a Meeting. The boys and girls should learn the proper sequence of the steps in conducting a meeting. An acceptable order is as follows:

1. Calling the meeting to order
2. Reading and approving (or correcting) the minutes of the previous meeting
3. Presenting reports of committees
4. Taking up unfinished business
5. Taking up new business
6. Giving a program (if there is one to be presented)
7. Adjourning.

Writing a Report

The following teaching plan, an adaptation of one written by two former college students, Sally Atkinson Hudnutt and Elva Pickwick Dunham, indicates one procedure that may be followed as the boys and girls report on a personal experience.

Explanation of Background: We are assuming that third- or fourth-grade boys and girls are writing a series of reports, autobiographical in nature, and then putting them into a booklet for which they will make a table of contents. Some of the topics or titles that may be included in the booklet are "My First Day in School," "A Book I Like," "My Pet," "Something Funny that Happened to Me," "My Family," "My Hobby." In no case will anyone be required to write on a specified topic; he can always choose some other one. Before the children write on a topic, some of the pupils will give talks on it. We are assuming that some pupils have given talks on the topic selected for this plan, "Something Funny that Happened to Me," and that all have prepared oral reports on the topic on which they will write.

A. *Aim*: To write as good reports as possible for inclusion in our booklets

B. *Materials*:
   1. Standards for written reports, given on a chart
   2. Sentences for capitalization on the chalkboard
      a. My first day at school was September 6, 1955.
      b. The first school that I attended was the washington school in winona, minnesota.
      c. My teacher's name was mrs. johnson.

d. On the first friday of school we had a party.
e. after we had had our refreshments, we played ball.

3. Miscellaneous
   a. Pens
   b. Ink (if needed)
   c. Ink paper
   d. Scratch paper

C. *Outline of Procedure*:
1. Introduction
   a. The teacher states that this day the pupils will be given the opportunity to write on the topic of the talks they have prepared.
   b. The teacher encourages the pupils to write as good reports as possible for inclusion in their booklets.
2. Study of points to watch while writing reports
   a. Reading silently the points on the chart (See *B-1.*)
   b. Work on one point on chart (under *B-1*), "Capitalization"
      (1) The teacher explains that the sentences under *B-2* contain errors made in their last papers.
      (2) Pupils name rules for capitalization they have learned. (It is assumed that the pupils have learned to capitalize the following: (a) the first word of a sentence, (b) the name of a person, (c) the name of a place, (d) the names of the days of the week, and (e) the names of the months of the year.)
      (3) The class corrects errors in sentences under *B-2.*
         (a) Pupils read the first sentence silently.
         (b) A pupil indicates the error in capitalization in the first sentence.
         (c) A pupil makes the correction on the chalkboard.
         (d) The same procedure as given under (*a*) through (*c*) is followed for the rest of the sentences.
3. *Writing the report*

   If a pupil needs to find out the spelling of a word, he leaves a space on his paper for it until the teacher, who circulates around the room, comes to his desk, and writes on scratch paper the word(s) he wants spelled.
4. *Forward look*

   The teacher makes arrangement for a time when pupils who have not finished their papers can complete them.

Writing Letters

To help the pupils learn to write letters, exercises such as the following may be used, which supplement those given in Chapter 5.

EXERCISE 1. Write these headings in correct form. Pay attention to spacing, capitalization, and punctuation.

8010 whittier boulevard bethesda maryland 20034
february 28 1966

EXERCISE 2. Write the following address for a business letter, paying attention to spacing, capitalization, and punctuation.

lyons and carnahan 407 east 25th street chicago illinois 60616

EXERCISE 3. Write *Yes* to the left of each of the following items that is a correct salutation or closing for a business letter. If an item is not correct, write *No.*

.... a. Dear Sir,	.... d. Yours,
.... b. Dear Gene:	.... e. Yours truly:
.... c. Yours truly,	.... f. Respectfully yours,

Capitalization and Punctuation

Some suggestions for helping boys and girls in capitalization and punctuation are given in preceding pages of this chapter under "Writing a Report" and "Writing Letters." Some are also given in Chapter 5.

STEPS FOR DEVELOPMENT OF A GENERALIZATION. Following are shown possible steps in developing the generalization that a comma or commas are used to set off the name of a person addressed. The teacher should:

1. Have clearly in mind what generalization he wishes to develop.

2. Determine what background information he needs to review with the class before the boys and girls are ready to note the use of a comma or commas with the name of a person addressed. If necessary, he should, for example, explain the term *the person addressed.*

3. Give the boys and girls reasons for the work about to be undertaken. The teacher may say, for instance, "Today I am going to help you with a use of the comma which you have not been using in your written work because we have not yet studied it."

4. Write five sentences on the chalkboard. Preferably, they should be written on the chalkboard before class. In three of the sentences the teacher may use the name of a person addressed and in two the name of a person not addressed. In sentences with the name of a person addressed, one should have the name at the beginning of the sentence, another at the end, and the third in a medial position, as illustrated in the following:

a. Jane, where are you going?
b. Jane is going home.
c. I talked with Sue.
d. Where are you going, Miss Smith?
e. Where are you going, Herb, after you have finished your work?

5. Ask the pupils to read the first sentence silently. Then the teacher can have someone give the name of the person used in that sentence, tell whether it is the name of a person addressed, and tell whether or not a comma is used with it. The teacher can proceed similarly with the rest of the sentences and, as the pupils respond, record the answers in a table similar to this:

Name of Person Addressed	*Name of Person Not Addressed*
a. Jane (comma)	b. Jane (no comma)
d. Miss Smith (comma)	c. Sue (no comma)
e. Herb (commas)	

6. Ask the pupils what is used to separate the name of the person addressed from the rest of the sentence (to summarize the information in the first column).

7. Restate the summary in terms of the generalization that the name of a person addressed should be separated from the rest of a sentence by a comma or commas.

8. Have the pupils state the generalization.

9. Have the pupils tell why commas are used in some sentences (*a*, *d*, and *e* under *4*) but not in others (*b* and *c* under *4*).

10. In a group of sentences the teacher has written on the chalkboard before class, have some that use the names of persons addressed, without necessary commas, and some that contain the name of a person who is not the one being addressed, and have the pupils supply the required commas.

11. Have the pupils give sentences of their own in which there is the name of a person addressed and ask them to tell where commas are needed.

12. Give the pupils written work in which they can apply the generalization they have learned.

13. Check and correct errors and, if necessary, reteach.

14. From time to time provide opportunities for further application of the generalization learned.

DICTATION. The following description of a procedure indicates how the teacher can use dictation with boys and girls for practice and testing purposes as they learn how to use capital letters and punctuation marks.

1. Write on the chalkboard a list of sentences requiring only the use of capital letters and punctuation marks the pupils have studied. For example, sentences like the following may be used with those pupils: (a) who have studied the need of a capital letter to begin a sentence, the name of a person, the title of a person when used as part of the name, the name of a continent, the word *Indian,* the word *I*, and the names of the week and the months; and (b) who have had work on the use of punctuation marks to end a sentence, with words in a series, with the name of a person addressed, with *Yes* or *No* as part of an answer, and with dates.

a. Will you go with us, Mary?
b. I like books about Indians, animals, and history.
c. No, I cannot go with you on Monday.
d. Columbus discovered America on October 12, 1492.
e. May we have a party, Miss Smith?

2. Ask the boys and girls to follow this procedure as they look at each of the sentences on the chalkboard: (a) Read the sentence silently. (b) Read the sentence orally. (c) Give the reason for each capital letter and each punctuation mark.

3. Give the pupils time to study the list of sentences independently so that later they can write them from dictation. If some words are beyond the pupils' spelling level, the teacher can leave them on the chalkboard during the dictation period.

4. When dictating, follow this procedure:
a. Read the sentence as a whole.
b. Read the sentence in parts.
c. Read the sentence again as a whole.

5. Have the pupils check their papers.

6. Have each pupil write correctly every sentence in which he made an error in capitalization, punctuation, or spelling.

Improving the Vocabulary

Practice exercises similar to the following may help boys and girls in vocabulary development.

EXERCISE 1. As oral and/or written work the boys and girls may substitute one of a list of synonyms for a specified word such as *said,* in sentences like these: (a) Tom *said,* "What a beautiful day!" (b) Evelyn *said,* "It is a beautiful day!"

EXERCISE 2. The boys and girls may match words, given in two columns, that are similar in meaning, such as, for example, those in the following lists:

.... abundant	1. believing
.... trusting	2. quiet
.... silent	3. helpful
.... kind	4. bravery
.... courage	5. wisdom
	6. plentiful.

EXERCISE 3. The boys and girls may substitute "loaded words" for informative words, such as those indicated in these sentences: (a) The speaker told the audience about their *relatives* in that far-off country. (loved ones) (b) They sang songs of their *country.* (native land)

EXERCISE 4. The boys and girls may substitute underlined words in a group of sentences for words that mean about the opposite, as, for example, the word *departed* in place of *arrived* in a sentence like "The train *arrived* on time."

Using Words Correctly

By means of a developmental lesson, using steps like the following the teacher can assist boys and girls with problems of correct use of verb forms: (1) helping the pupils realize the need for the learning, (2) drawing the pupils' attention to specific points (through questioning and comment) in illustrative sentences, (3) stating the generalization, and (4) providing for application of the generalization.

A TEACHING PLAN. The following plan is an adaptation of one written by a former student, Carole Stoffer, that may be suitable for use with a third or fourth, grade, with variations.

> *Background Information.* It is assumed that boys and girls have studied the words *sang, sung, rang, rung,* and *threw, thrown* and that they are familiar with the terms *helping words* and *helper* as used in this plan.

A. *Pupils' Aim*: To learn how to use *saw* and *seen* correctly

B. *Materials*:

1. Board work
   a. Sentences to develop the generalization
      (1) We *saw* four huge fire engines at the station.
      (2) Some of us have *seen* fire engines before.
      (3) The fire chief has *seen* many burning buildings.
      (4) All of us *saw* big ladders.
   b. Sentences for oral practice in which *saw* and *seen* are already included in the sentences
      (1) I have *seen* an elephant at a parade.
      (2) I *saw* an elephant at the circus.
      (3) My mother said she has *seen* my mittens.
      (4) She *saw* them under my coat.
      (5) My sister *saw* the package first.
      (6) We had *seen* many people.
      (7) We *saw* some people whom we knew.
      (8) Our teacher said, "I have *seen* Fred."
   c. Sentences for oral practice for which pupils need to choose correct word forms
      (1) She has (saw, seen) my report card.
      (2) I (saw, seen) her leave the house.
      (3) We have (saw, seen) that movie.
      (4) Tom and I (saw, seen) the team practice.
      (5) We had (saw, seen) the ducks fly south.
      (6) He has (saw, seen) our new neighbors.
      (7) Jane (saw, seen) my ruler.
      (8) I (saw, seen) him on TV.
2. Poster illustrating independence of *saw* and dependence of *seen* on helping words such as *has, have, had*
3. Duplicated copies of sentences for written practice, for which the pupils are to supply the correct form *saw* or *seen*
   a. We .... the new bus today.
   b. Have you .... it?
   c. I .... it last week.
   d. Mary .... it first.
   e. I .... a bigger bus last summer.
   f. Tom had .... a bus like it last year.
   g. We .... the plane land.
   h. She has .... the answer.

i. I .... what I wanted.
j. Suzanne had .... the birthday presents.
k. You .... what happened.
l. They have .... our house.
m. We .... them too late to stop them.
n. Dotty .... a yellow bird in the tree.
o. Mother has .... the bird.

C. *Outline of Procedure*:

1. Introduction
   a. The teacher tells the pupils that boys, girls, and adults often misuse the words *saw* and *seen*.
   b. The teacher tells the class that he has noticed that some of the pupils at times misused *saw* and *seen*.
   c. The teacher tells the class that this day he is going to help them learn the correct use of these words.
2. Development of the generalization
   a. Initial study of the first sentence under *B-1-a*
      (1) A pupil reads the sentence orally.
      (2) A pupil tells what word is underlined in the sentence and tells whether or not the word is used with a helping word such as *has, have,* or *had*.
      (3) The teacher writes the following on the chalkboard as the first entry under the caption "No Helper":
          1. saw.
   b. Initial study of sentences *2, 3,* and *4,* under *B-1-a*
      (1) The teacher asks the pupils to do the following when he calls on them for the remaining sentences under *B-1-a*: (a) Read the sentence orally. (b) Name the underlined word. (c) Tell whether or not a helper is used with the underlined word.
      (2) The teacher writes the responses on the chalkboard according to the reference made under (*1*) so that the following appears on the chalkboard:

Helper	*No Helper*
2. seen	1. saw
3. seen	4. saw.

   c. Giving of summary statement
      The teacher refers to the listing given under *C-2-b-*(*2*) and asks the class which of the words, *saw* or *seen*, is used without a helper and which is used with a helper in those sentences.
   d. Stating of generalization
      (1) By the teacher
         (a) The teacher says that *saw* should never be used with a helping word and that *seen* usually needs a helping word.
         (b) The teacher writes the generalization on the chalkboard.
      (2) By the pupils
         Several pupils state the generalization.
   e. Reference to the poster (See *B-2.*)
      A pupil explains how the poster can help the class remember when to use *saw* and when *seen*.
3. Oral work on sentences on the chalkboard
   a. Work on sentences under *B-1-b*
      Pupils follow this procedure with each of the sentences:
      (1) They read the sentence orally.
      (2) They tell why the word underlined is used, naming the helper if *seen* is used.
   b. Work on sentences under *B-1-c*
      (1) Pupils work on the first sentence.
         (a) The pupils read the sentences silently.
         (b) A pupil tells which word in parentheses should be used.
         (c) A pupil tells why he chose the word he selected.
         (d) A pupil reads the sentence orally.
      (2) Pupils work on sentences *2* through *8*, using the same procedure outlined under (*1*).
4. Written work (See *B-3.*)
   a. The pupils read the directions silently.
   b. The teacher asks the children to refer to the rule on the chalkboard and the poster if necessary.
   c. The teacher states that pupils who finish early should write sentences of their own using *saw* and *seen*.
5. Correcting papers
   The pupils follow this procedure as the teacher gives the number of each succeeding sentence:
   a. A pupil tells what word he chose.
   b. The pupil gives the reason for his choice.

c. The pupil reads the entire sentence orally inserting the correct answer.

6. Forward look
   a. The teacher encourages the pupils to use words correctly at all times.
   b. The teacher asks the pupils to think of words other than *saw* and *seen* which need "helpers" and to name other forms of the same words that should not be used with "helping words."

ILLUSTRATIVE SITUATIONS FOR DEVELOPING SKILL IN HANDWRITING

The following paragraphs show how through a series of lessons the teacher can help boys and girls during the beginning stage of manuscript writing.

1. The teacher writes on the chalkboard something of value to the boys and girls as they watch. On a space ruled with base lines and guide lines, he may write the sentence

Today is Monday.

As he writes it, he may make comments like these: "I am going to write 'Today is Monday.' I start near the left of the line. I make my letters from the top down. I move my chalk from left to right as I write. This is the word *Today.* I am leaving quite a wide space after *Today* because now I am beginning a new word. The word is *is.* Now I leave another wide space for I am beginning another word, the word *Monday.*"

The next day the teacher may say, as he writes while the pupils are watching, "I am going to write 'Today is Tuesday.' I am going to ask someone to show us where I should begin the first word, at this side of the line (as he points near the left side of the space) or at this side of the line (as he points near the right side of the space). Show us where I should start our first word, the word *Today.*" Then the teacher can proceed: "I start the word *Today* up high because the letter is a tall letter. The next letter is not tall. So I start it here (as he points to the correct place on the guide line). The last letter of this word I will start at this line (pointing at the guide line), but I will end it below the line. Now I have finished writing a word. Before I write the next letter I am going to leave a wide space. Why am I going to leave a wide space?" In a similar manner the teacher may continue writing and commenting or asking questions concerning the writing.

Possibly the third day one or more pupils will be ready to copy the first two words of "Today is Wednesday" on the chalkboard directly below the words written by the teacher.

2. The teacher provides a lined space on the chalkboard (permanently lined if the school authorities approve) where the children can write during free time. Every day he may write at the top of the space a word or group of words, which he reads to the class. Some of the boys and girls then can copy it in the space below the teacher's writing. When the teacher has time, he can guide the child who is practicing. At other times a team of two pupils may help each other in evaluation of the writing as first one and then the other of the team writes.

Figure 14.1 Use of a Model in Chalkboard Writing

3. Before handwriting class the teacher may write on five different areas of the chalkboard the letters, words, or groups of words on which there will be practice that day. After he has helped the group during the introduction of the work for the period, five or six pupils can go to the chalkboard for practice in writing a copy of what the teacher has written. As the pupils are writing the teacher may go around to the different pupils and help them as needed. At the same time the other boys and girls can be writing the same material at their seats, from duplicated copies the teacher has given them or from copies in their writing recorders. During handwriting class on succeeding days another group of five or six pupils can also do work on the chalkboard while the others write at their seats, until all have had a chance at chalkboard writing.

4. If pupils have difficulty in knowing where to begin tall letters and where minimum-sized letters, the teacher, using paper ruled with base lines and guide lines, may give a sheet of paper to each child

on which a vertical line double space in height and one a single space in height have been made, each on a separate horizontal line. He can then explain that the first stroke is a stroke that shows the height of a tall letter. Next he can ask the pupils to make a vertical stroke of similar height to the right of it. Then the teacher can proceed similarly with the vertical line indicating the height of a small letter. After the pupils have finished both lines by writing strokes of required height, they can write a line of vertical strokes at the direction of the teacher. Some will be the height of small letters and others the height of tall letters. (Emphasis throughout this exercise should be placed on the fact that the strokes are made from the top down.) A similar exercise can be done with large and small circles. Care should be taken that the circles are the right height and that the direction in making them is correct.

ILLUSTRATIVE SITUATIONS FOR DEVELOPING SKILL IN SPELLING

To illustrate some possible applications of the guidelines for teaching spelling and to supplement other recommendations made in Chapter 8, in this section of this chapter suggestions for a teaching plan are given.

A Teaching Plan

The following plan for teaching spelling in a third-grade class is an adaptation of a weekly plan written by a former student, Jackie Ford Webster. It is intended for use with a consumable spelling book in which the five-day plan is followed, as described in Chapter 8. Naturally many deviations from this plan will be necessary to make it fit the spelling series used if it is not the series on which the plan was based. Changes also will be necessary in terms of the class being taught.

A. *Materials*:

In addition to a copy of the consumable spelling book for each child the following materials will be used.

1. Monday
   a. The list of words (numbered) for the week, written on the chalkboard
   b. A list of words (written on a card for the teacher's use) that may cause difficulties in pronunciation or meaning
   c. A list of words in the story (other than the spelling words) that may cause problems of word recognition (listed on the chalkboard)
2. Tuesday
   Words for special study, written on the chalkboard
3. Wednesday
   Sentences containing words for the week, for use by the teacher when giving the test
4. Thursday
   a. Words missed frequently, written on the chalkboard
   b. Other words needing special attention, written on the chalkboard
5. Friday
   Sentences containing words for the week, for use by the teacher when giving the test

B. *Outline of Procedure*:

1. Monday
   a. The teacher hands back Friday's spelling papers and gives instructions for study of misspelled words.
   b. The pupils look at the picture in the spelling book and talk about it as they get a background for some of the words.
   c. The pupils look at the list of spelling words to see if there are any they cannot pronounce.
   d. If there are questions about pronunciation, the teacher helps the pupils by means of one or more of the following methods: (1) sight, (2) phonetics, (3) structural analysis (syllabication or root words).
   e. If no one asks for the pronunciation of words that the teacher thinks may be difficult for some, he asks the pupils to pronounce those words. (See *A-1-b.*) If they cannot pronounce them, the teacher helps the pupils by means of one or more of the following methods: (1) sight, (2) phonetics, (3) structural analysis (syllabication or root words).
   f. The pupils practice the pronunciation.
      (1) The teacher pronounces each word as he points to it.
      (2) The class say the words after the teacher.
   g. The pupils study the story.
      (1) The teacher indicates the purpose for reading the story.
      (2) The teacher helps the pupils with the pronunciation of the difficult words. (See *A-1-c.*)

(3) The pupils read the story silently.
(4) The pupils answer questions about the story as the teacher checks comprehension.

h. If there are some words of which one or more pupils do not know the meaning, a pupil or the teacher explains and/or uses each one in a sentence.

i. If no one asks for some of the words that the teacher thinks may cause difficulty, the teacher asks for the meaning. (See *A-1-b.*)

j. The teacher points out special spelling difficulties in some of the words.

k. The pupils begin independent study of the spelling words, using this procedure:
(1) They look at the word.
(2) They write the word.
(3) They check their spelling.
(4) If wrong, they repeat the first three steps.

2. Tuesday

a. The pupils note the words which may present special spelling problems.

b. The teacher helps the class with the directions for one or more exercises in the spelling book and makes provisions for those finishing earlier if the work is to be written.

c. The pupils do the exercise(s) in the spelling book (for the second day).

d. The pupils study the words, using this procedure:
(1) They look at the word.
(2) They write the word.
(3) They check their spelling.
(4) If wrong, they repeat the first three steps.

3. Wednesday

a. The pupils study the words independently.

b. The pupils take the trial test, as the teacher follows this procedure:
(1) He gives the number of the word.
(2) He pronounces the word.
(3) He uses the word in a sentence.
(4) He repeats the word.

c. The pupils check their papers as the teacher or a pupil reads the words orally and spells them. (If further check is necessary, the pupils correct their words from a list on the chalkboard or in their books.)

d. The pupils write the correct spelling of words they missed on the trial test.

e. The pupils continue studying the words that they missed on the trial test and on tests of previous weeks, while those who did not miss any words do work provided for them by the teacher.

4. Thursday

a. The class continues oral study of words with special difficulties in spelling.

b. The teacher helps the class with directions for one or more exercises in the spelling book (for the fourth day) and makes provisions for the pupils finishing earlier if the work is written.

c. Pupils do the exercise(s) in the spelling book.

d. The class independently study the spelling words for the week as they pay special attention to words misspelled on the trial test.

5. Friday

a. The pupils take the weekly test as the teacher follows this procedure:
(1) He gives the number of the word.
(2) He pronounces the word.
(3) He uses the word in a sentence.
(4) He repeats the word.

b. The pupils correct their papers as the teacher or a pupil reads the words orally and spells them. (If further check is necessary, the pupils correct their words from a list on the chalkboard or in their books. The teacher rechecks the words later.)

c. The pupils are checked on review words.

Learning the Meaning of Spelling Words

The following steps may be used to help the child acquire the meaning of words in a spelling list if some of them are not in his understanding and speaking vocabulary.

1. The teacher may ask the boys and girls to name any words on the list of which they do not know the meaning.

2. The teacher can help the pupils who do not know the meaning of a word by: (a) explaining a common meaning; (b) asking some one who knows the meaning to explain it; (c) using a sentence or having a pupil use one in which the meaning of the words is "built-in" and, thereupon, (d) asking a pupil who did not know the meaning whether he can tell from the sentence what the word means. In some in-

stances a pupil may demonstrate the word (pantomime it) or draw a diagram to illustrate it.

3. A pupil who had not known the meaning of a word can, after suitable help, be asked to use it in a sentence that shows whether or not he has learned the meaning.

4. If no one asks for the meaning of a word that the teacher thinks some pupils may not know, the teacher can ask a child to use the word in a sentence that indicates its meaning or to explain it. If the child cannot do so, the teacher or another pupil may explain the word, use it in a sentence, demonstrate, or illustrate it. Subsequently the child who had not been able to show that he knew the word can then explain it or use it in a meaningful sentence.

ILLUSTRATIVE SITUATIONS FOR DEVELOPING READINESS FOR READING

This section serves as supplement to Chapter 9, "Guiding Growth toward Readiness for Reading."

The Experience Chart

The points listed following deal with the planning, constructing, and use of an experience chart during the reading readiness period.

PLANNING A CHART. These steps can be followed by the teacher when planning a chart on an experience the boys and girls have had.

1. Provide for the activity about which the chart will tell.
2. Discuss with the children what they did.
3. See to it that the pupils have a reason for making a record of the experience.
4. Help the pupils plan what they wish to include in the chart.
5. Work out with the boys and girls the exact content of the chart. As the teacher records the sentences on the chalkboard, he should watch sentence structure, choice of words, sequence, and unity.
6. Read to the group the tentative list of sentences to find out whether there are to be any changes and then have the necessary alterations made.

When planning a chart on an anticipated experience rather than on one the pupils have already had, the foregoing steps can be followed with but slight alteration in the first three steps enumerated.

CONSTRUCTING AN EXPERIENCE CHART. Frequently the teacher may wish to do the original writing on the chalkboard so changes can be made easily and the first writing can be done with greater dispatch than advisable on a more permanent record. The following are effective procedures for constructing a chart.

1. Use a large sheet of tagboard, newsprint, or lined paper with wide spaces between lines.
2. Decide whether the chart should be illustrated by either a picture drawn by a pupil or a cut-out picture.

Figure 14.2 An Experience Chart

3. Observe the rules for a pleasing balance of items on the chart.
4. Write the sentences in manuscript, making the handwriting almost perfect in form.

USING AN EXPERIENCE CHART AS READING MATERIAL. Even before the teacher has transferred the sentences written on the chalkboard to a large sheet of paper, practice in reading can be provided. After the teacher has read the chart to the boys and girls, it is recommended that they "read" it orally with the teacher as best they can.

During the second reading period, after the teacher has written the chart on a large sheet of paper as suggested under "Constructing an Experience Chart," this procedure may be followed:

1. The teacher reads the chart and then the children join in the oral reading.
2. As the teacher reads sentences in a "mixed-up" order, the pupils find them on the chart.
3. The teacher presents perhaps three or four words which he wants emphasized that he has written on the chalkboard and/or on cards.
4. The pupils find some of the words on the chart.
5. The pupils read the entire chart.
6. The pupils have practice on the words selected for learning as sight words.

Courtesy of the Fargo, North Dakota, Public Schools

Figure 14.3 Practice on Words

Developing Auditory Discrimination

The following list of suggestions as to what boys and girls can do to develop in ability to make auditory discriminations supplements the list on page 181. The pupils can:

1. Try to distinguish, with closed eyes, whether the teacher taps on a table, the chalkboard, a glass, or something else.
2. Dramatize stories in which a variation of soft and loud voices is needed such as "The Three Billy Goats" or "The Three Bears."
3. Draw pictures indicating sounds that the pupils recalled after listening to and discussing with the teacher records in the album "Around the Home" and "Around the Farm," from the record album by Scott Foresman and Company entitled "Sounds Around Us."
4. Name words that begin with the same sound as one given by the teacher.
5. Tell whether two words named by the teacher begin (or end) with the same sound.
6. Draw a circle around each picture in a group, the name of which begins with the same sound as a specified picture in that group.
7. Draw a circle around each picture in a group, the name of which rhymes with the specified word in that group.
8. Orally match words that the teacher gives, with the names of pictures on cards that begin with the same sound.
9. Make up rhymes and then name the rhyming words.
10. Match pictures in one column with pictures in a second column, the names of which rhyme with those in the first column.
11. Tell in which words named by the teacher (such as *cat, race, name, sat*) there is the sound of the short *a*.

Figure 14.4 An Exercise in Rhyming

12. Tell whether a given sound, like *p*, comes at the beginning, middle, or end of words containing the sound that are named by the teacher.
13. Collect or draw pictures, the names of which rhyme.
14. Say the name of a picture and place it in a pocket on which there is a picture that has the same beginning sound.

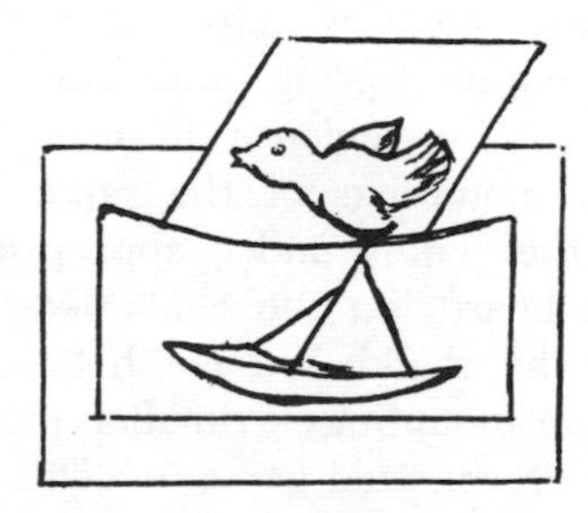

Figure 14.5 Matching Pictures with Same Beginning Sounds

15. Select from a pack of picture cards those that have two pictures the names of whose initial sound is the same.
16. Tell whether the beginning or ending of pairs of words that the teacher names are alike.

Developing Visual Discrimination

The following list of activities are merely suggestive of many others that can be used for developing skill in making visual discriminations. Others are given in Chapter 9. (See page 181.)

1. Matching the cut-off part of each of a series of pictures with the portion of the picture of which it originally formed a part
2. Sorting cards having pairs of like and unlike pictures into two groups, those that are alike and those that are different

Figure 14.6 Matching Cut-Off – Parts of Pictures

3. Showing the relationship between two sets of pictures, with illustrations for words such as the following:

cow	tomato
school	ball
bat	dress
girl	chalkboard
garden	milk

It is suggested that the pictures be mounted on paper of the same size. If the exercise is to be done independently by one person at a time, it is recommended that the child be enabled to check his own arrangement by means of a code on the back of each mounting.

4. Classifying pictures into categories, such as signs of fall, winter, spring, and summer. The pictures, which for convenience in using and storing should be on mountings of the same size, can be arranged by the pupils under appropriate headings on a bulletin board, on the chalk ledge, in a card holder, or on the chalkboard (with tape attached to the back of the mountings). Smaller pictures can be mounted on uniform-sized paper, which one pupil at a time may arrange in proper categories at his seat or at the reading table. So that the exercise can be self-checking, a key can be given on the back of the mountings.

5. Matching geometric forms of various types, possibly also of different colors, such as blue stars, red circles, purple rectangles

6. Matching pieces of paper of various sizes and shapes with symbols of the same size and shape that are given on a chart

7. Arranging in order blocks of similar shapes but of different sizes

8. Answering questions asked by the teacher, calling for discrimination, such as: (a) How are these two puppets different? (b) How are these two chalk marks different?

9. Answering questions such as: (a) What is different in our room today? (b) What is Sue wearing today that she has never before worn to school?

10. Doing jigsaw puzzles

11. Guessing what object is described by the teacher. The description may begin with the words "I am thinking of something."

12. Indicating which of a series of letters or words in each row, such as the following, is different from the first one in that row:

run run ran run run

13. Indicating which of a series of words in a row begin with the same letter (or end with the same letter)

14. Indicating which of a series of pairs of words, such as those listed following, are alike:

form, from; pit, tip; deal, deal; deal, lead.

Some of the pairs may consist of words that may form a problem in reversals for some children. If a pupil makes reversals, such an exercise may be followed with one in which he points out similar letters in a pair of words as he notes that in words such as *was* and *saw* the placement of the letters *w* and *s* is different.

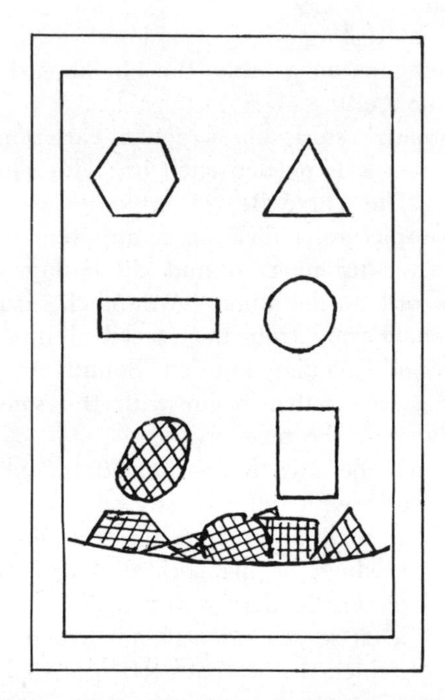

Figure 14.7 Matching Geometric Forms

15. Finding a word card with the same word as a given word on a card holder or on the chalkboard

16. Crossing out in a group of sentences a designated often-repeated word

17. Noting similarities in the beginnings of pupils' names

Figure 14.8 Learning the Initial Teaching Alphabet

Courtesy of the Columbus, Ohio, Public Schools.

18. Looking for words on a chart that begin in the same way as a given word

19. Matching letters or words given in two columns

20. Drawing a circle around words in a row that begin with one letter (or two) used at the beginning of the first word of a line, such as:

*r*ose run fun robin sun
*st*art stone some tore seed

21. Arranging cut-out words on small cards in the order that they are set up in a model that is given the pupil, possibly written on an envelope in which the cut-outs for a given sentence are stored.

ILLUSTRATIVE SITUATIONS FOR DEVELOPING GROWTH IN READING SKILLS

This section contains two teaching plans on reading, one on the first-grade level and the other on the fourth-grade level.

Plan on First-Grade Level

This plan is based on the first story in the revised edition of *On Cherry Street*,[1] first reader of Ginn and Company.

A. *Aims*:

1. To find out what we will be reading about in our new book
2. To find out what Flip did on the first day of school
3. To learn the words we need to know in order to read the story

B. *Materials*:

1. A copy of the textbook *On Cherry Street* for each child
2. Board work
   a. New words (numbered)
      school School
      cannot
      mitten
      Miss Hill
   b. Review words (numbered)
      ready
      something
      Bow-wow, bow-wow
   c. Sentences (numbered)
      Betty and Tom ran to *school.*
      Tom said, "Flip *cannot* go with us."
      Flip saw the red *mitten.*
      Miss Hill said, "I like Flip."
3. Card holder
4. Word cards for new and review words
5. Miscellaneous
   a. Picture of a teacher and of a schoolhouse
   b. A mitten

C. *Outline of Procedure*:

1. Introduction to the new book
   a. The pupils look individually at the pictures in the book to find out what they will read about in their new books.
   b. Some of the pupils refer to pictures they think look particularly interesting.
   c. The pupils find the title of the book *On Cherry Street* on the cover and the title page.
2. Introduction to the first story "We Go to School"
   a. A few pupils tell of experiences that they have had when their dogs have wanted to follow them to school.
   b. The teacher tells the class that in the first story they will find out what Flip did as he followed Tom and Betty to school.
3. Word study
   a. Introduction to word study
      The teacher gives the purpose for the word study. (See *A-3.*)
   b. Presentation of new words (See *B-2-a.*)
      (1) *School*
         The teacher presents the word by:
         (a) Pointing at the new word *school* on the board, pronouncing it, and asking a pupil to say it after him
         (b) Having a pupil match the word card for *school* with the word *school* on the chalkboard as the pupil says the word and then places the card near the picture of the school
         (c) Referring to the word *School* beginning with a capital letter (as written on the board) while he explains that that is how the word is written when it is the first word in a sentence or when it is in the title

---

[1]Odille Ousley and David H. Russell, *On Cherry Street*. Revised edition. Ginn and Company, 1964.

(2) *cannot*
The teacher presents the word by:
(a) Telling the class that the word is made up of two smaller words that they know, as he writes *can* and *not* on the board
(b) Asking a pupil to pronounce the two smaller words and then the entire word
(c) Asking a pupil to match the word card with the word on the board

(3) *mitten*
The teacher presents the word by:
(a) Asking the pupils with what sound the word *mitten* begins
(b) Having the pupils note the beginning sound as the teacher says the word *mitten* while pointing at the word on the board
(c) Asking a pupil to say the word
(d) Having a pupil match the word card for *mitten* with the word on the board and then place it near the mitten

(4) *Miss Hill*
The teacher presents the words by:
(a) Showing the pupils the picture of a teacher and saying that the name of the teacher in the story is Miss Hill
(b) Asking several pupils to say the name
(c) Having a pupil match the word card with the word on the board
(d) Asking a pupil to place the word card near the picture of a teacher.

c. Practice on new words and on review words (See *B-2-a*, *B-2-b*, and *B-2-c*.)
(1) Pupils name new words.
(2) Different pupils name the review words as the teacher points at them on the chalkboard.
(3) A pupil finds the numbered sentence on the board in which the word *mitten* that the teacher names has been underlined and then reads the sentence orally.
(4) In a similar manner the pupils find the other new words in the sentence under *B-2-c* and then read the sentences.
(5) Pupils (a) find the cards with the review and new words as the teacher pronounces them, (b) pronounce the words, and (c) place them in the cardholder.

4. Initial study of the story
a. Name of first group of stories
(1) The pupils find the new word *School* on page 5.
(2) A pupil reads orally the words on page 5.

b. Page 6
(1) The pupils find the title on page 6 as the teacher reads it orally.
(2) A pupil tells what he imagines Mother is saying to Tom and Betty before they leave for school.
(3) The pupils read the page silently to find out what Mother said to Tom and Betty.
(4) A pupil tells what Mother said.
(5) A pupil reads orally the first three lines.

c. Page 7
(1) As the pupils look at the picture on page 7, one pupil tells what he thinks Tom is saying to Flip.
(2) The pupils read silently the page to find out what Flip does after Tom has told him to go home.
(3) Three children read the parts of Betty, Tom, and Flip orally.
(4) The teacher draws attention to the mitten on the sidewalk in the picture.
(5) One or more pupils tell who they think will find the mitten.

d. Page 8
(1) The pupils note who has found the mitten as they look at the picture on page 8.
(2) The pupils point at the word *mitten* on this page.
(3) One or more pupils tell what they think Flip will do with the mitten.
(4) The pupils read the page silently to find out where Flip was running with the mitten.
(5) A pupil tells where Flip was running with the mitten.

e. Page 9
   (1) A pupil, after looking at the picture on page 9, tells what Tom may be saying to Flip.
   (2) The pupils read the page silently to find out what Tom may be saying to Flip.
   (3) A pupil reads orally the lines that tell what Tom said to Flip.

f. Page 10
   (1) The pupils look at the picture on page 10 to see what Flip is doing.
   (2) One or more pupils tell what they think Miss Hill will say when she sees Flip in school.
   (3) The pupils read the page silently to find out what Miss Hill says when she sees Flip.
   (4) One or more pupils tell how they imagine Tom felt when Miss Hill said, "Come in, Flip."
   (5) A pupil reads orally the part that tells what Miss Hill said to Flip.

5. Oral reading of the story
   Five pupils go to the front of the group and each reads a page of the story while the class listen with books closed.

6. Forward look
   a. One or more pupils tell how they think Flip will act at school.
   b. The teacher tells the class that the next day they will find out how Flip acts at school.

Plan on Fourth-Grade Level

This plan is an adaptation of one written by two former students, Nancy Williamson Enochs and Mary Hogan Weaver. The following assumptions are made: (1) The boys and girls have had considerable practice in using the dictionary to look up the meaning of words. (2) This is their first lesson in using the dictionary to find the pronunciation of words. (3) The pupils know the common diacritical markings through the use they have made of glossaries and of material on the chalkboard and on mimeographed sheets.

A. *Aim*: To learn to use the dictionary to find out how words are pronounced

B. *Materials*:

1. Board work
   a. List 1 (numbered)

island	llama
isthmus	guinea pig

   b. List 2 (numbered)

pheasant	electricity	daze
pyramid	hinge	knave
corral	biscuit	cello
caves	giraffe	visor

2. A copy for each child of the *Thorndike-Century Beginning Dictionary*

C. *Outline of Procedure*:

1. Introduction
   The teacher explains the following points: (a) that so far when the pupils have been unable to decipher the pronunciation of words by themselves the teacher has told them the pronunciation or has marked the words for them or they have used glossaries; (b) that this day he will show the pupils how to use the dictionary to find the pronunciation of words.

2. Development of points to keep in mind when looking up the pronunciation of words in a dictionary
   a. Study of the word *island* (See *B-1-a.*)
      (1) The pupils find the word in the dictionary.
      (2) The pupils point at the phonetic respelling.
      (3) The pupils find the markings of *island* at the bottom of the facing pages of the dictionary.
      (4) One or more pupils pronounce the word.
   b. Study of the words *isthmus* and *llama* (See *B-1-a.*) (A similar procedure is followed as for *a.*)
   c. Further study of the key
      (1) The teacher points out the fact that some of the markings in the key at the bottom of the page are different from those they have used (if that is the case).
      (2) The pupils study the words *guinea pig* (listed under *B-1-a*), using this procedure:
         (a) The pupils note the phonetic respelling.
         (b) The pupils find the words in the key that indicate the needed sounds for the word *guinea,* pronounce the word(s) in the key, and give the sound(s).

(3) The pupils discuss why a key to pronunciation is given at the bottom of every other page of the dictionary.

3. Practice
   a. Study of the word *pheasant* (listed under *B-1-b*) as the pupils follow this procedure:
      (1) They find the word in the dictionary.
      (2) They individually decipher the sound of the word.
      (3) One or more pupils pronounce the word.
   b. Study of the other words in the second list (See *B-1-b*.)
      (The same procedure is followed as in *a*.)
4. Forward look
   a. The teacher tells the pupils that they can now use the dictionary to learn the pronunciation of words.
   b. The pupils discuss how knowledge and skill in using the dictionary will help them to be more independent in their reading.
   c. The teacher encourages the pupils to use the dictionary when they need to find out the pronunciation of a word.

FOR STUDY AND DISCUSSION

1. In professional books (including teachers' manuals) or magazine articles locate plans for teaching phases of the language arts. Study them to find additional suggestions for procedure.

2. List procedures for developing auditory discrimination in addition to those given in this chapter and in Chapter 9. Likewise list additional procedures for developing visual discrimination. (You may wish to use the form for recording the procedures that is used on page 311.)

3. Evaluate the teaching plans given in this chapter.

4. Devise a teaching plan in the area of the language arts of each of the following types: (a) a five-day plan for teaching a week's unit in spelling for an intermediate-grade class according to a spelling series of your choice; (b) a developmental lesson presenting work on some phase of critical evaluation in reading; (c) a plan for preparing and using an experience chart as part of the reading-readiness program; (d) a plan for a practice lesson on some phase of handwriting that has previously been presented.

5. In this chapter no illustrative situations are given for developing growth through dramatic expression. Devise a plan for helping boys and girls prepare and present a puppet play. Since such work would need to extend over a number of days, your plan should indicate possible allocation of different phases of the work to the different days to be spent on the work by boys and girls.

REFERENCES

For listings of references for this chapter the reader is referred to those given in the chapters in Part Two and those given in Chapter 15.

OUTLINE FOR CHAPTER 15

Resources for the Language Arts

CHAPTER 15

Resources for the Language Arts

There is at the disposal of the teacher of the language arts a large number of resources, human and material. The ideas the teacher has gleaned through his years of living; materials he has collected; the background of the boys and girls he is teaching; the individuals in any community who can add to the enrichment of the language-arts program; the places, natural and man-made, that can give increased meaning or provide background for the development of greater skill and artistry in the use of the skills of communication; the physical appearance of the classroom, the atmosphere permeating the room – these and many other factors, together with what are commonly referred to as materials of instruction, need to be considered in any comprehensive report on the resources at the command of the teacher of the language arts.

It is not, however, the purpose of this chapter to present an all-inclusive listing of resources. In earlier chapters of this book reference is made to the significance of some of the types of resources listed in the preceding paragraph. In this chapter attention is focused on materials that can be procured commercially.

BOOKS

The first part of this section deals with professional books for teachers, the second with books for parents, and the last three with books for boys and girls – trade books, textbooks, and reference books.

Books for Teachers

The reader may wish to supplement the relatively short listing of professional books given in this chapter by perusal of the catalogs of publishers on the teaching of the language arts.

BOOKS ON THE LANGUAGE ARTS: A GENERAL BIBLIOGRAPHY. In this general bibliography are not included the books listed on subsequent pages in this chapter under the more specific headings such as "Books on Teaching Reading" or "Books on Creative Expression."

Anderson, Paul S., *Resource Materials for Teachers of Spelling*. Burgess Publishing Company, 1959.

——————, *Language Skills in Elementary Education*. The Macmillan Company, 1964.

Anderson, Verna; Paul S. Anderson; Francis Ballantine; and Virgil M. Howes, *Readings in the Language Arts*. The Macmillan Company, 1964.

Burns, Paul C., *Improving Handwriting Instruction in Elementary Schools*. Burgess Publishing Company, 1963.

Dawson, Mildred, and Marian Zollinger, *Guiding Language Learning*. Harcourt, Brace and World Book Company, 1957.

Eckgren, Betty Lois, and Vivian Fishel, *500 Live Ideas for the Grade Teacher*. Harper and Row, 1952.

Eisenson, Jon, and Mardel Ogilvie, *Speech Correction in the Schools*. Second edition. The Macmillan Company, 1963.

Fitzgerald, James A., *The Teaching of Spelling*. The Bruce Publishing Company, 1951.

Greene, Harry, and Walter Petty, *Developing Language Skills in the Elementary Schools*. Allyn and Bacon, 1963.

Herrick, Virgil, and Leland Jacobs, *Children and the Language Arts*. Prentice-Hall, 1955.

Hildreth, Gertrude, *Teaching Spelling*. Holt, Rinehart and Winston, 1955.

MacCampbell, James C., *Readings in the Language Arts in the Elementary School*. D. C. Heath and Company, 1964.

Myers, Emma Harrison, *The Whys and Hows of Teaching Handwriting*. Parker, Zaner-Bloser, 1963.

National Council of Teachers of English (The Commission on the English Curriculum), *Language Arts for Today's Children.* Appleton-Century-Crofts, 1954.

Postman, Neil, *Television and the Teaching of English.* Appleton-Century-Crofts, 1961.

Pronovost, Wilbert, and Louise Kingman, *The Teaching of Speaking and Listening in the Elementary School.* David McKay Company, 1959.

Scott, Louise, and J. J. Thompson, *Talking Time.* Webster Publishing Company, 1951.

Shane, Harold G., et al., *Improving Language Arts Instruction through Research.* Association for Supervision and Curriculum Development, 1963.

Shane, Harold G.; Mary E. Reddin; and Margaret Gillespie, *Beginning Language Arts Instruction with Children.* Charles E. Merrill Books, 1961.

Strickland, Ruth G., *The Language Arts in the Elementary School.* Second edition. D. C. Heath and Company, 1957.

Trauger, Wilma K., *Language Arts in the Elementary Schools.* McGraw-Hill Book Company, 1963.

Wagner, Guy; Max Hosier; and Mildred Blackman, *Listening Games.* Teachers Publishing Corporation, 1962.

Zaner-Bloser Company, The, *Writing on the Board.* The Zaner-Bloser Company, 1958.

BOOKS ON TEACHING READING. In many of the books on the language arts there are chapters dealing with the teaching of reading. Although the following books show the interrelationship among the various facets of the language arts, they place primary emphasis on the teaching of reading.

Austin, Mary C., and Coleman Morrison, *The First R: The Harvard Report on Reading in the Elementary Schools.* The Macmillan Company, 1963.

Betts, Emmett A., *Foundations of Reading Instruction.* American Book Company, 1950.

Bond, Guy L., and Eva Bond Wagner, *Teaching the Child to Read.* Third edition. The Macmillan Company, 1960.

Carter, Homer L. J., and Dorothy J. McGinnis, *Teaching Individuals to Read.* D. C. Heath and Company, 1962.

DeBoer, John J., and Martha Dallmann, *The Teaching of Reading.* Second edition. Holt, Rinehart and Winston, 1964.

Dechant, Emerald V., *Improving the Teaching of Reading.* Prentice-Hall, 1964.

Downing, John, *The Initial Teaching Alphabet.* The Macmillan Company, 1964.

Durrell, Donald D., *Improving Reading Instruction.* Harcourt, Brace and World, 1956.

Fries, Charles C., *Linguistics and Reading.* Holt, Rinehart and Winston, 1963.

Gans, Roma, *Fact and Fiction about Phonics.* The Bobbs-Merrill Company, 1964.

Gray, Lillian, *Teaching Children to Read.* Third edition. The Ronald Press Company, 1963.

Gray, William S., *On Their Own in Reading.* Revised edition. Scott, Foresman and Company, 1960.

Harris, Albert J., *Effective Teaching of Reading.* David McKay Company, 1962.

Harris, Albert J., *Readings on Reading Instruction.* David McKay Company, 1963.

Herr, Selma E., *Learning Activities for Reading.* Wm. C. Brown Company Publishers, 1961.

Herrick, Virgil E., and Marcella Nerbovig, *Using Experience Charts with Children.* Charles E. Merrill Books, 1964.

Hester, Kathleen B., *Teaching Every Child to Read.* Second edition. Harper and Row, 1964.

Hildreth, Gertrude, *Teaching Reading.* Holt, Rinehart and Winston, 1958.

Lee, Dorris M., and R. V. Allen, *Learning to Read through Experience.* Second edition. Appleton-Century-Crofts, 1963.

McKim, Margaret G., and Helen Caskey, *Guiding Growth in Reading in the Modern Elementary School.* Second edition. The Macmillan Company, 1963.

Mazurkiewicz, Albert J., *New Perspectives in Reading Instruction.* Pitman Publishing Corporation, 1964.

Russell, David H., *Children Learn to Read.* Second edition. Ginn and Company, 1961.

Russell, David H., and Etta E. Karp, *Reading Aids through the Grades.* Second edition. Bureau of Publications. Teachers College, Columbia University, 1951.

Smith, Henry P., and Emerald V. Dechant, *Psychology in Teaching Reading.* Prentice-Hall, 1961.

Smith, Nila Blanton, *Reading Instruction for Today's Children.* Prentice-Hall, 1961.

Veatch, Jeannette, *Individualizing Your Reading Program.* G. P. Putnam's Sons, 1959.

BOOKS ON LITERATURE FOR CHILDREN. The following are a few of the many books on poetry and prose. Some are anthologies while others are books devoted primarily to the teaching of literature for children. For additional professional material the reader is referred to books in the preceding listing. Many of those contain chapters on means of interesting children in reading. Additional books of help in guiding boys and girls in the development of lasting, worthwhile interests in reading are listed under "Sources for Book Selection," page 323.

Arbuthnot, May Hill (compiler), *The Arbuthnot Anthology of Children's Literature.* Scott, Foresman and Company, 1953.

Arbuthnot, May Hill, *Children and Books.* Third edition. Scott, Foresman and Company, 1964.

Arbuthnot, May Hill, *Time for Poetry.* Revised edition. Scott. Foresman and Company, 1961.

Ferris, Helen, *Favorite Poems Old and New.* Doubleday and Company, 1957.

Huber, Miriam Blanton (compiler), *Story and Verse for Children.* The Macmillan Company, 1955.

Huck, Charlotte S., and Doris A. Young, *Children's Literature in the Elementary School.* Holt, Rinehart and Winston, 1961.

Huffard, Grace Thompson, and Laura Mae Carlisle, *My Poetry Book.* Holt, Rinehart and Winston, 1956.

Hughes, Rosalind, *Let's Enjoy Poetry.* Houghton Mifflin Company, 1958.

Johnson, Edna; Frances Clarke Sayers; and Evelyn R. Sickels (editors), *Anthology of Children's Literature*. Houghton Mifflin, 1959.

Love, Katherine (compiler), *A Little Laughter*. Thomas Y. Crowell Company, 1957.

Mahoney, Bertha; Louise Latimer; and Beulah Folmsbee (compilers), *Illustrators of Children's Books*. The Horn Book, 1947.

Miller, Bertha Mahoney, et al., *Illustrators of Children's Books: 1946-1956*. The Horn Book, 1958.

Thompson, Jean McKee, *Poems to Grow On*. Beacon Press, 1957.

Untermeyer, Louis (compiler), *The Golden Treasury of Poetry*. Golden Press, 1959.

Untermeyer, Louis, *Stars to Steer By*. Harcourt, Brace and World, 1941.

Werner, Jane (editor), *The Golden Book of Poetry*. Simon and Schuster, 1949.

BOOKS ON CREATIVE EXPRESSION. Many suggestions for creative expression are interspersed among the chapters of the books listed elsewhere in this bibliography. To those the reader is referred as well as to the following which deal primarily with creativity of various types — creativity in writing, creativity in dramatic expression (including puppetry), creativity through choral speaking.

Abney, Louise, and Grace Bowe, *Choral Speaking Arrangements for the Lower Grades*. The Expression Company, 1953.

Anderson, Harold, *The Cultivation of Creativity*. Harper and Row, 1958.

Applegate, Mauree, *Helping Children Write*. Harper and Row, 1954.

Barton, Clifford, *Verse Choir in the Elementary School*. Teachers Publishing Company, 1954.

Batchelder, Marjorie, *The Puppet Theatre Handbook*. Harper and Row, 1947.

Batchelder, Marjorie, and Virginia Lee Comer, *Puppets and Plays — A Creative Approach*. Harper and Row, 1956.

Blackham, Olive, *Puppets into Actors*. The Macmillan Company, 1949.

———, *Shadow Puppets*. Harper and Row, 1960.

Brown, Helen A., and Harry J. Heltman, *Choral Reading for Fun and Recreation*. Westminster Press, 1956.

Burrows, Alvina; Doris Jackson; and Dorothy Saunders, *They All Want to Write*. Third edition. Holt, Rinehart and Winston, 1964.

Durland, Frances C., *Creative Dramatics for Children*. The Antioch Press, 1963.

Ficklen, Alexander, *A Handbook of First Puppets*. J. B. Lippincott Company, 1935.

Fitzgerald, Burdette S., *World Tales for Creative Dramatics and Storytelling*. Prentice-Hall, 1962.

Hoben, Alice M., *Puppets and Marionettes*. Field Enterprises, Inc., 1955.

Howard, Vernon, *Puppet and Pantomime Plays*. Sterling Publishing Company, 1962.

Jagendorf, Moritz, *First Book of Puppets*. Franklin Watts, 1952.

Kerman, Gertrude, *Plays and Creative Ways with Children*. Harvey House, 1961.

Lease, Ruth, and Geraldine Brain Siks, *Creative Dramatics in Home, School, and Community*. Harper and Row, 1952.

Lewis, Shari, *The Puppet Book*. Citadel Press, 1958.

Marksbury, Mary Lee, *Foundation of Creativity*. Harper and Row, 1963.

Mearns, Hughes, *Creative Power*. Revised edition. Dover Publications, 1958.

Pels, Gertrude, *Easy Puppets*. Thomas Y. Crowell Company, 1947.

Pratt, Lois H., *The Puppet Do-It-Yourself Book*. Exposition Press, 1957.

Rasmussen, Carrie, *Let's Say Poetry Together* (Primary Grades). Burgess Publishing Company, 1963.

Richmond, Arthur (editor), *Remo Bufano's Book of Puppetry*. The Macmillan Company, 1950.

Roberts, Bertha, and A. T. Beckman, *Children's Voices*. Silver, Burdett Company, 1939.

Severn, Bill, *Shadow Magic*. David McKay Company, 1959.

Siks, Geraldine Brain, *Creative Dramatics*. Harper and Row, 1958.

Taylor, Loren E., *Pupperty, Marionettes, and Shadow Plays*. Burgess Publishing Company, 1965.

Walter, Nina, *Let Them Write Poetry*. Holt, Rinehart and Winston, 1962.

Ward, Winifred, *Playmaking with Children*. Second edition. Appleton-Century-Crofts, 1957.

BOOKS ON BULLETIN BOARDS. Books that give suggestions on making bulletin boards are listed because much can be done to encourage boys and girls in the development of language-arts skills of all types — skills in listening, speaking, reading, and writing — through effective use of bulletin boards. In addition to the books listed following the reader may find helpful some books on visual aids to lear. ıg such as Edgar Dale's *Audio-Visual Methods in Te. :hing*, published by Holt, Rinehart and Winston (1954); Marjorie East's *Display for Learning: Making and Using Visual Materials*, also published by Holt, Rinehart and Winston (1952); and Walter A. Wittich's and Charles F. Schuller's *Audio-Visual Materials: Their Nature and Use*, published by Harper and Row (1953). Many methods books for elementary-school teachers and several professional magazines also give ideas on bulletin boards valuable in guiding growth in the language arts.

Brantlinger, Fred, *Easy to Make Bulletin Boards*. Hayes School Publishing Company, 1963.

Burgert, Robert, and Elinor S. Meadows, *Eye-Appealing Bulletin Board Ideas*. F. A. Owen Publishing Company, 1963.

———, *Bulletin Board Ideas*. F. A. Owen Publishing Company, 1960.

Cook, Eleanor, *Bulletin Boards Month by Month*. (Grade 1.) Teachers Publishing Company, 1964.

Coplan, Kate, *Poster Ideas and Bulletin Board Techniques for Libraries and Schools.* Oceana Publications, 1962.
Currie, Dorothy H., *Making Dioramas and Displays.* F. A. Owen Publishing Company, 1962.
Dallmann, Martha, *Bulletin Boards.* Teachers Publishing Corporation, 1959.
Dowd, Ann, and Dorothy C. Wass, *Bulletin Boards Month by Month.* (Grade 3.) Teachers Publishing Corporation, 1964.
——, *Bulletin Boards Month by Month.* (Grade 4.) Teachers Publishing Corporation, 1964.
Hamer, Donna, *Bulletin Boards Month by Month.* (Grade 2.) Teachers Publishing Corporation, 1964.
Hein, Robert, *Easy Bulletin Boards.* Easy Bulletin Boards, 1959.
Horn, George, *Bulletin Boards.* Reinholt Publishing Company, 1962.
Kelley, Marjorie, *Classroom-Tested Bulletin Boards.* Fearon Publishers, 1961.
Koskey, Thomas A., *Baited Bulletin Boards.* Fearon Publishers, 1954.
——, *Bulletin Boards for Holidays and Seasons.* Fearon Publishers, 1958.
——, *Bulletin Board Idea Sources.* Fearon Publishers, 1953.
Lee, Carvel, and Lorita Lee, *The First Grade Bulletin Board Guide.* (Also books on bulletin boards available through the publishers for each of grades 2 through 6, as well as other bulletin boards) T. S. Denison and Company, 1963.
Leonard, Mary K., *Let's Create.* (Curriculum Services Series No. 2.) Center for Educational Service, College of Education, Ohio University, 1958.
Liechti, Alice O., and Jack R. Chappell, *Making and Using Charts.* Fearon Publishers, 1960.
Lockridge, Preston, and Ernest F. Tiemann, *Better Bulletin Board Displays.* (Bridges for Ideas Series.) Visual Instruction Bureau, Division of Extension, University of Texas, 1961.
Randall, Reino, and E. C. Haines, *Bulletin Boards and Displays.* Davis Publishers, 1961.
Ruby, Doris, *4-D Bulletin Boards that Teach.* Fearon Publishers, 1960.
Ruby, Doris and Grant, *Bulletin Boards for the Middle Grades.* Fearon Publishers, 1965.
Silcox, Miriam, *Bulletin Boards Month by Month.* (Grade 5.) Teachers Publishing Corporation, 1964.
——, *Bulletin Boards Month by Month.* (Grade 6.) Teachers Publishing Corporation, 1964.
Walker, Shirley, *Fifty Bulletin Board Ideas.* T. S. Denison and Company, 1962.
Warner, Virginia, *Bulletin Boards: Seasonal Ideas.* T. S. Denison and Company, 1962.
——, *Helpful Ideas for Bulletin Boards.* T. S. Denison and Company, 1962.
Weseloh, Anne, *E-Z Bulletin Boards.* Fearon Publishers, 1959.

BOOKS ON CHILD DEVELOPMENT. The following books give helpful background ideas for the teacher who wants to guide the growth of boys and girls in harmony with what can be learned from the field of child growth and development.

Almy, Millie, *Child Development.* Second edition. D. C. Heath and Company, 1959.
Anderson, John E., *The Psychology of Development and Personal Adjustment.* Holt, Rinehart and Winston, 1949.
Baller, Warren R., and Don C. Charles, *The Psychology of Human Growth and Development.* Holt, Rinehart and Winston, 1961.
Blair, Glenn Myers; R. Stewart Jones; and Ray H. Simpson, *Educational Psychology.* Second edition. The Macmillan Company, 1962.
Eson, Morris E., *Psychological Foundations of Education.* Holt, Rinehart and Winston, 1964.
Harding, Lowry W., *Arithmetic for Child Development.* Wm. C. Brown Company, Publishers, 1964.
Havighurst, Robert J., *Developmental Tasks and Education.* Second edition. David McKay Company, 1952.
Jenkins, Gladys; Helen Shacter; and W. W. Bauer, *These Are Your Children.* Scott, Foresman and Company, 1953.
Jersild, Arthur T., *Child Psychology.* Fifth edition. Prentice-Hall, 1960.
Lindgren, Henry Clay, *Educational Psychology in the Classroom.* Second edition. John Wiley and Sons, 1964.
Olson, Willard C., *Child Development.* Second edition. D. C. Heath and Company, 1959.
Pressey, Sidney L.; Francis P. Robinson; and John E. Horrocks, *Psychology in Education.* Harper and Row, 1959.
Smith, Louis M., and Bryce B. Hudgins, *Educational Psychology: An Application of Social and Behavioral Theory.* Alfred A. Knopf, 1964.
Strang, Ruth, *An Introduction to Child Study.* Fourth edition. The Macmillan Company, 1959.

BOOKS ON EVALUATION. Many of the professional books listed in this chapter under "Books on the Language Arts: A General Bibliography," "Books on Teaching Reading," and "Books on Child Development" give information on evaluation. Additional references are:

Ahmann, J. S.; M. D. Glock; and Helen L. Wardeburg, *Evaluating Elementary School Pupils.* Allyn and Bacon, 1960.
Buros, Oscar K. (editor), *Mental Measurements Yearbook.* Latest edition. The Gryphon Press.
Findley, W. G. (editor), *The Impact and Improvement of School Testing Programs.* Sixty-Second Yearbook, Part Two, National Society for the Study of Education. University of Chicago Press, 1963.
Thomas, E. M., *Judging Student Progress.* Second edition. David McKay Company, 1960.
Wood, Dorothy A., *Test Construction: Development and Interpretation of Achievement Tests.* Charles E. Merrill Books, 1960.

Books for Parents

Many parents undoubtedly will find of value some of the professional books listed under various categories in preceding pages of this chapter. Of special interest and help may be some of the books given under "Books on Literature for Children." Of value as a reference book is the publication of The National Council of Teachers of English, by a committee of which Thomas G. Devine was chairman, entitled *Selected Reading List of Books about English Teaching for Parents and the General Public.* From the Children's Book Council can be obtained a bookmark (free with a five-cent postage stamp) designed especially for parents, called *Booklists for Parents,* which names and describes other selected lists for help in guiding children's reading. Additional books giving information of import to parents are:

Ames, Louise Bates, and Frances L. Ilge, *Parents Ask.* Harper and Row, 1962.
Artley, A. Sterl, *Your Child Learns to Read.* Scott, Foresman and Company, 1953. (Of particular value when readers by Scott, Foresman and Company are used.)
Bond, Guy, and Eva Wagner, *Child Growth in Reading.* Lyons and Carnahan, 1955.
Brown, Muriel W., *Partners in Education.* Bulletin 1950, No. 1. Association for Childhood Education, International, 1950.
Frank, Josette, *Your Child's Reading Today.* Doubleday and Company, 1960.
Frank, Lawrence K. and Mary, *How to Help Your Child in School.* Viking Press, 1950.
Gans, Roma, *Reading Is Fun.* Bureau of Publications, Teachers College, Columbia University, 1949.
Gates, Doris, *Helping Children Discover Books.* Science Research Associates, 1956.
Larrick, Nancy, *A Parent's Guide to Children's Reading.* Doubleday and Company, 1958.
Mackintosh, Helen K., *How Children Learn to Read.* Superintendent of Documents, United States Government Printing Office, 1952.
National Education Association, *Janie Learns to Read.* National Education Association, 1954.
Newton, J. Roy, *Reading in Your School.* McGraw-Hill Book Company, 1960.
Strang, Ruth, *Helping Your Gifted Child.* E. P. Dutton and Company, 1960.
Tooze, Ruth, *Your Children Want to Read.* Prentice-Hall, 1937.

Trade Books for Boys and Girls

With the large number of books for boys and girls on the market — some excellent, others ordinary, and still others banal — it is important that both teacher and parent know where to turn for guidance in selection.

SOURCES FOR BOOK SELECTION. Fortunately there are many excellent sources of information to which to turn for help. Three good sources for book lists are: (1) Children's Services Division of the American Library Association, 50 East Huron Street, Chicago, Illinois, 60611; (2) The Children's Book Council, 175 Fifth Avenue, New York, New York 10010; and (3) The Children's Book Center, University of Chicago Library, Chicago, Illinois, 60637. The United States Office of Education also issues bibliographies of books for boys and girls.

The following are some of the much-used and highly-rated publications printed periodically, that evaluate currently written books for children:

The ALA Booklist
Atlantic Monthly
Bulletin of the Center for Children's Books
Chicago Tribune
Childhood Education

Christian Science Monitor
Elementary English
The Horn Book Magazine
Library Journal
New York Times Book Review

Publisher's Weekly
Saturday Review
Wilson Library Bulletin.

The following sources are also recommended. It will, however, be noted that, as the copyright dates indicate, some of them do not include recent books.

American Library Association, *Aids in Selection of Materials for Children and Young People: Books, Films, Records.* The American Library Association, 1957.
——, *Notable Children's Books.* The American Library Association, (annually).
Arbuthnot, May Hill, et al., *Children's Books too Good to Miss.* Second revised edition. The Press of Western Reserve University, 1959.
Association for Childhood Education International, *A Bibliography of Books for Children.* The Association for Childhood Education International, 1962.
——, *Children's Books for $1.25 or Less.* Revised edition. The Association for Childhood Education International, 1961.
Bowker Company, R., R., (edited by Patricia H. Allen), *Best Books for Children.* The R. R. Bowker Company, (revised each March).
——, *Growing Up with Books.* The R. R. Bowker Company, 1965.
——, *Growing Up with Science Books.* The R. R. Bowker Company, 1965.
Child Study Association of America, *Books of the Year for Children.* Child Study Association of America, (published annually).
Dawson, Mildred A., and Louise Pfeiffer, *A Treasury of Books for the Primary Grades.* Chandler Publishing Company, 1959.
Eakin, Mary K., *Good Books for Children.* University of Chicago Press, 1962.
Eaton, Anne Thaxter, *Treasure for the Taking.* Revised edition. The Viking Press, 1957.
Huus, Helen, *Children's Books to Enrich the Social Studies.* National Council for the Social Studies, National Education Association, 1961.

Johnson, Edna; Evelyn R. Sickels; and Frances Clarke Sayers, *Anthology of Children's Literature*. Houghton Mifflin Company, 1959.

Larrick, Nancy, *A Teacher's Guide to Children's Books*. Charles E. Merrill, 1960.

Mathes, Miriam Snow, *A Basic Book Collection for Elementary Grades*. The American Library Association, 1960.

National Council of Teachers of English, *Adventuring with Books*. The National Council of Teachers of English, 1960.

Smith, Dora V., *Fifty Years of Children's Books*. The National Council of Teachers of English, 1963.

Book Awards. The two best-known awards in the field of literature for boys and girls are the Newbery Medal and the Caldecott Medal. The Newbery Medal books date back to 1922 when Frederic C. Melcher made possible the award, given annually for the most distinguished book of the year in the field of literature for children. Himself a publisher, he named the award after the famous publisher of books for children, John Newbery. In 1939, also through the generosity of Mr. Melcher, the first Caldecott Medal was awarded. It is named after Randolph Caldecott, well-known illustrator of books for children during an earlier era. This award is given annually to the book judged to be the most distinguished picture book for children published during the year.

Quite a number of additional awards are now being made. Some of these are:

The Jane Addams Children's Book Award (given by the United States Section of the Women's International League for Peace and Freedom, 2006 Walnut Street, Philadelphia)

Aurianne Award (chosen by the American Library Association)

Child Study Association of American Children's Book Award (awarded by the Children's Book Committee of the Child Study Association of America, 9 East 89th Street, New York)

Thomas Alva Edison Foundation National Mass Media Awards (by the Thomas Alva Edison Foundation National Mass Media Awards, 8 West 40th Street, New York; for three types of books)

Charles W. Follett Award (by the sons of Charles W. Follett; the Follett Publishing Company, 1808 West Washington Boulevard, Chicago)

William Allen White Children's Books Award (by the William Allen White Memorial Library, Kansas State Teachers College, Emporia, Kansas).

For further information on book awards the reader is referred to the fifth edition of *Literary and Library Prizes,* revised and enlarged by Olga S. Weber, The R. R. Bowker Company, (1963) and to the booklet *Children's Books: Awards and Prizes,* published periodically, available through The Children's Book Council.

1. The Newbery Medal Books. For the following books the Newbery Medal has been awarded.

1922 Van Loon, Hendrik. *The Story of Mankind*. Liveright Publishing Corporation
1923 Lofting, Hugh, *The Voyages of Doctor Dolittle*. J. B. Lippincott Company
1924 Hawes, Charles Boardman, *The Dark Frigate*. Little, Brown and Company
1925 Finger, Charles J., *Tales from Silver Lands*. Doubleday and Company
1926 Chrisman, Arthur, *Shen of the Sea*. E. P. Dutton and Company
1927 James, Will, *Smoky*. Charles Sribner's Sons
1928 Mukerji, Dhan Gopal, *Gay-Neck*. E. P. Dutton and Company
1929 Kelly, Eric P., *The Trumpeter of Krakow*. The Macmillan Company
1930 Field, Rachel, *Hitty, Her First Hundred Years*. The Macmillan Company
1931 Coatsworth, Elizabeth, *The Cat Who Went to Heaven*. The Macmillan Company
1932 Armer, Laura Adams, *Waterless Mountain*. David McKay Company
1933 Lewis, Elizabeth Foreman, *Young Fu of the Upper Yangtze*. Holt, Rinehart and Winston
1934 Meigs, Cornelia, *Invincible Louisa*. Little, Brown and Company
1935 Shannon, Monica, *Dobry*. The Viking Press
1936 Brink, Carol Ryrie, *Caddie Woodlawn*. The Macmillan Company
1937 Sawyer, Ruth, *Roller Skates*. The Viking Press
1938 Seredy, Kate, *The White Stag*. The Viking Press
1939 Enright, Elizabeth, *Thimble Summer*. Holt, Rinehart and Winston
1940 Daugherty, James, *Daniel Boone*. The Viking Press
1941 Sperry, Armstrong, *Call It Courage*. The Macmillan Company
1942 Edmonds, Walter, *The Matchlock Gun*. Dodd, Mead and Company
1943 Gray, Elizabeth Janet, *Adam of the Road*. The Viking Press
1944 Forbes, Esther, *Johnny Tremain*. Houghton Mifflin Company
1945 Lawson, Robert, *Rabbit Hill*. The Viking Press
1946 Lenski, Lois, *Strawberry Girl*. J. B. Lippincott Company
1947 Bailey, Carolyn Sherwin, *Miss Hickory*. The Viking Press
1948 DuBois, William Pène, *The Twenty-One Balloons*. The Viking Press
1949 Henry, Marguerite, *King of the Wind*. Rand McNally and Company
1950 De Angeli, Marguerite, *The Door in the Wall*. Doubleday and Company
1951 Yates, Elizabeth, *Amos Fortune, Free Man*. Aladdin Books
1952 Estes, Eleanor, *Ginger Pye*. Harcourt, Brace and World
1953 Clark, Ann Nolan, *Secret of the Andes*. The Viking Press

1954 Krumgold, Joseph, ... *And Now Miguel*. Thomas Y. Crowell Company
1955 DeJong, Meindert, *The Wheel on the School*. Harper and Row
1956 Latham, Jean Lee, *Carry On, Mr. Bowditch*. Houghton Mifflin Company
1957 Sorenson, Virginia, *Miracles on Maple Hill*. Harcourt, Brace and World
1958 Keith, Harold, *Rifles for Watie*. Thomas Y. Crowell Company
1959 Speare, Elizabeth George, *The Witch of Blackbird Pond*. Houghton Mifflin Company
1960 Krumgold, Joseph, *Onion John*. Thomas Y. Crowell Company
1961 O'Dell, Scott, *Island of the Blue Dolphins*. Houghton Mifflin Company
1962 Speare, Elizabeth George, *The Bronze Bow*. Houghton Mifflin Company
1963 L'Engle, Madeline, *Wrinkle in Time*. Farrar, Straus and Company
1964 Neville, Emily Cheney, *It's Like This, Cat*. Harper and Row
1965 Wojciechowska, Maia, *Shadow of a Bull*. Atheneum Publishers

2. The Caldecott Medal books. The Caldecott Medal has been awarded for the following books:

1938 Lathrop, Dorothy, *Animals of the Bible*. J. B. Lippincott
1939 Handforth, Thomas, *Mei Li*. Doubleday and Company
1940 D'Aulaire, Ingri and Edgar, *Abraham Lincoln*. Doubleday and Company
1941 Lawson, Robert, *They Were Strong and Good*. The Viking Press
1942 McCloskey, Robert, *Make Way for Ducklings*. The Viking Press
1943 Burton, Virginia Lee, *The Little House*. Houghton Mifflin Company
1944 Thurber, James (with Louis Slobodkin, illustrator), *Many Moons*. Harcourt, Brace and World
1945 Field, Rachel (with Elizabeth Orton Jones, Illustrator), *Prayer for a Child*. The Macmillan Company
1946 Petersham, Maud and Miska, *The Rooster Crows*. The Macmillan Company
1947 MacDonald, Golden (with Leonard Weisgard, illustrator), *The Little Island*. Doubleday and Company
1948 Tresselt, Alvin (with Roger Duvoisin, illustrator), *White Snow, Bright Snow*. Lothrop, Lee and Shepard Company
1949 Hader, Berta and Elmer, *The Big Snow*. The Macmillan Company
1950 Politi, Leo, *Song of the Swallows*. Charles Scribner's Sons
1951 Milhous, Katherine, *The Egg Tree*. Charles Scribner's Sons
1952 Lipkind, William (with Nicolas Mordvinoff, illustrator), *Finders Keepers*. Harcourt, Brace and World
1953 Ward, Lynd, *The Biggest Bear*. Houghton Mifflin Company
1954 Bemelmans, Ludwig, *Madeline's Rescue*. The Viking Press
1955 Perrault, Charles (with Marcia Brown, illustrator), *Cinderella: or the Little Glass Slipper*. Charles Scribner's Sons
1956 Langstaff, John (with Feodor Rojankovsky, illustrator), *Frog Went a-Courtin'*. Harcourt, Brace and World
1957 Udry, May (with Marc Simont, illustrator), *A Tree Is Nice*. Harper and Row
1958 McCloskey, Robert, *Time of Wonder*. The Viking Press
1959 Cooney, Barbara, *Chanticleer and the Fox*. Thomas Y. Crowell Company
1960 Ets, Marie Hall, *Nine Days to Christmas*. The Viking Press
1961 Robbins, Ruth (with Nicolas Sidjakov, illustrator), *Baboushka and the Three Kings*. Parnassus Press
1962 Brown, Marcia, *Once a Mouse*. Charles Scribner's Sons
1963 Keats, Ezra Jack, *The Snowy Day*. The Viking Press
1964 Sandak, Maurice, *Where the Wild Things Are*. Harper and Row
1965 deRegniers, Beatrice Schenk (with Beni Montresor, illustrator), *May I Bring a Friend?* Atheneum Publishers.

Book Club Selections. Book clubs for children have gained in popularity. They have the advantages and the disadvantages rightly associated with book clubs for adults. A few are named following. For a longer list and for information on each club included, the reader is referred to pages 224 to 226 of the 1964 edition of *Literary Market Place*, published by the R. R. Bowker Company, a copy of which is available in many libraries. Interested persons can write to the sponsors of the clubs for details of membership.

Arrow Book Club (Scholastic Book Services, 33 West 42nd Street, New York, New York 10036)
Best-in-Children's Books (A division of Nelson Doubleday, 501 Franklin Street, Garden City, New York 11531)
The Bookplan (921 Washington Avenue, Brooklyn, New York 11225)
Calling All Girls Book Club (a division of Parents' Magazine Enterprises, 52 Vanderbilt Avenue, New York, New York 10017)
Junior Literary Guild (247 Park Avenue, New York, New York 10017)
Parents' Magazine's Read Aloud Book Club for Little Listeners and Beginning Readers (A division of Parents' Magazine Enterprises, 52 Vanderbilt Avenue, New York, New York 10017)
Teen Age Book Club (Scholastic Magazines Book Services, 33 West 42nd Street, New York, New York 10036)
The Weekly Reader Children's Book Club, Primary and Intermediate (one for each of these two levels; 55 High Street, Middletown, Connecticut 06458)

Young America Book Club (55 High Street, Middletown, Connecticut 06458)
Young Readers of America (a branch of the Book-of-the-Month Club, 345 Hudson Street, New York, New York 10014)

"EASY-TO-READ" BOOKS. Relatively many so-called "easy-to-read" books have recently appeared on the market. These are designed not primarily for the retarded but for the beginning reader. Probably the best known of these books are those by Dr. Seuss, such as *Green Eggs and Ham* (published as one of the Beginner Book series by Random House in 1960) and *The Cat in the Hat Comes Back* (published by Houghton Mifflin Company in 1958). Controlled vocabulary and simplicity of sentence structure characterize the "easy-to-read books," which range in difficulty so that some are suitable for the better reader in the second half of the first grade while others have been rated on a third-grade reading level.

In an article entitled "An Evaluation of Some Easy-to-Read Trade Books for Children,"[1] David Russell, after studying ten such books, states:

> The rise of easy-to-read trade books may be related to the increasing interest in school materials of some trade publishers, to the current emphasis on the individualized reading program, and to a wider concern with do-it-yourself activities in school learning.

Severe criticism has been hurled by some authorities in the field of literature for children against the "easy-to-read books" on the claim that they lack literary value. While recognizing the fact that these books have not contributed to the classic literature of the day, other educators point out that they nevertheless can make a significant contribution to reading if used wisely. An argument advanced by those defending the books is that when children have a severely limited reading vocabulary, they cannot read the books of enduring value for the stories in those books are not couched in a vocabulary that the child recognizes in print. These people will argue that since the "easy-to-read books" help the boys and girls learn to read, unless they are definitely undesirable in content, they can be of value in the achievement of a worthy goal. So that the primary-grade children will not be deprived of enjoyment and learning from the great stories of childhood — written in the more difficult reading vocabulary — some defenders of the "easy-to-read books" favor the teacher's making much use of the classics at this early stage of development by reading and telling the boys and girls those stories that have enduring value, thereby supplementing the reading by the child of books of not-so-good quality.

The following publishers, in addition to Houghton Mifflin Company and Random House, mentioned in connection with Dr. Seuss books, are among those which publish books of the "easy-to-read" type: Beckley-Cardy Company, Follett Publishing Company, Oxford Press, and Harper and Row.

There is an extensive listing of "Recent Easy Books for First-Grade Readers," compiled by Patrick Groff, on pages 521 to 527 of the December, 1960, issue of *Elementary English*. The revised edition (1963) of *Books for Beginning Readers* by Elizabeth Guilfoille, published by the National Council of Teachers of English, is also a valuable reference.

BOOKS FOR THE RETARDED READER. The "easy-to-read books" for the beginning reader are not to be confused with books for the retarded reader. Some of the latter type have been in print a long time although there still is a great lack in this area. To be sure, the retarded reader may enjoy some of the books designed as "easy-to-read" for the normal reader.

The big problem with books for the retarded reader is to be able to provide him with books written in his narrowly limited vocabulary but nevertheless on his interest level, and, in many cases, on his intelligence level. (It must not be forgotten, however, that many intelligent boys and girls are retarded in reading.)

The following listing of books written with the retarded reader in mind is given by Paul S. Anderson:[2]

American Adventure Series. Wheeley Publishing Company
Basic Vocabulary Series. Garrard Press
Cowboy Sam Series. Beckley-Cardy Company
Pleasure Reading Series. Garrard Press
American Heroes. The Bobbs-Merrill Company
I Want to Be Series. Children's Press, Melmont Publishers.

Also of special note for retarded readers are two recent publications by the John Day Company entitled *Stories for Fun and Adventure* and *More Stories for Fun and Adventure*. Another good source of information on books for the retarded reader is the 1964 revision of *Good Books for Poor Readers* by George Spache, published by the Reading Laboratory and Clinic of the University of Florida, Gainesville, Florida.

---

[1]David H. Russell, "An Evaluation of Some Easy-to-Read Trade Books for Children," *Elementary English* XXXVII:475-482, No. 7 (November, 1960.)

[2]Paul S. Anderson, *Language Skills in Elementary Education*. The Macmillan Company, 1964. Page 276.

Textbooks for Boys and Girls

It is with pride that publishers of the outstanding reading series can point to their productions. As both authors and publishers keenly realize, the last word is far from having been said in textbook production in the field of elementary school reading. They are striving for improved instructional materials of all types for boys and girls. Yet the reading series, with supplementary books and with teachers' manuals accompanying them, have improved so much that many criticisms that used to be voiced against them can no longer justifiably be applied.

READING TEXTBOOKS. Reading series differ in various respects — in burden of vocabulary, in nature and quality of the stories and other articles, in format, in underlying educational theory. Each publishing company will point out some of the unique features of its basal readers. Free literature highlighting the points of excellence of each series is available from the publishers.

The publishers of some of the outstanding textbooks in reading are listed following. In parentheses is given the name (or names) of a basal reading series by each publisher.

Allyn and Bacon (Sheldon Basic Reading Series)
American Book Company (Betts Basic Readers)
Bobbs-Merrill Company (Get Ready to Read Series; through third reader)
Ginn and Company (The Ginn Basic Reading Program)
Harper and Row (Alice and Jerry Basic Reading Program)
D. C. Heath and Company (Reading for Interest Series)
Holt, Rinehart and Winston (Easy Growth in Reading Series; also, Winston Basic Readers)
Houghton Mifflin Company (Reading for Meaning Series)
Laidlaw Brothers (Gateway to Reading Treasure Series)
J. B. Lippincott Company (Basic Reading)
Lyons and Carnahan (Developmental Reading Series)
The Macmillan Company (The Macmillan Readers; also The Macmillan Reading Program)
Pitman Publishing Company (i/t/a Early-to-Read Series)
Scott, Foresman and Company (The New Basic Readers)
L. W. Singer Company (Prose and Poetry Series)

Many of the publishers of reading textbooks have more reading books than those that are included in their basal reading stories. Upon request the publishers will willingly supply the teacher or prospective teacher with a list of their publications in the field of elementary-school reading, including, in many instances, supplementary reading series, workbooks, teachers' manuals, and other teaching aids.

OTHER LANGUAGE-ARTS TEXTBOOKS. Although there has been a tendency to integrate the work in "language," spelling, and handwriting, most of the textbooks in these areas continue to deal with a specific phase of the language arts. There are many textbooks or workbooks in spelling, consumable books in handwriting, and both hardback and consumable English books. Notable exceptions are the *We Talk, Spell, and Write* series published by Scott, Foresman and Company and the *Learn to Listen, Speak, and Write* series by the same publishers. *Ginn Elementary English* by Ginn and Company also serves a multiple purpose. There seems to be an increasing amount of attention in textbooks to correlation of the work in one area with that of the other facets of the language arts. For example, in spelling textbooks more emphasis seems to be placed on handwriting in relation to spelling than was formerly evident.

As in the case of reading textbooks, various companies stress different points in their programs in spelling, handwriting, and English. Some series of spellers, for example, make it relatively easy to adapt instruction within a grade to levels of spelling ability. Another differentiating feature lies in the role that phonics plays in the spelling program advocated and incorporated in a spelling series. Handwriting books and English books similarly differ in emphases. For information on the unique features of the various textbooks, the reader may wish to write to some of the publishing companies indicated in the following listings of well-known series of spellers, handwriting materials, and language-arts books.

1. *Spelling series*
   Allyn and Bacon (You Can Spell)
   Follett Publishing Company (Spelling and Writing Patterns)
   Ginn and Company (Spelling)
   Harcourt, Brace and World (Success in Spelling)
   Harper and Row (Basic Spellers)
   Houghton Mifflin Company (Building Spelling Power)
   Lyons and Carnahan (My Word Book)
   McGraw Hill Book Company (Basic Goals in Spelling)
   Charles E. Merrill Company (Spelling for Word Mastery)
   Noble and Noble, Publishers (Better Handwriting for Everyone)
   Silver Burdett Company (Spell Correctly)
   L. W. Singer (Spellingtime)
   Webster Publishing Company (Patterns in Spelling).
2. *Handwriting series*
   Allyn and Bacon (You Can Write)
   Benefic Press (Legible Handwriting)
   The Bobbs-Merrill Company (Bobbs-Merrill Basic Handwriting Series)
   The Macmillan Company (Adventures in Handwriting)
   The McCormick-Mathers Publishing Company (It's Fun to Write)

Noble and Noble (Better Handwriting for Everyone)
The A. N. Palmer Company (Palmer Method)
Parker Zaner-Bloser (Guiding Growth in Handwriting)
Charles Scribner's Sons (Manuscript and Cursive Basic Handwriting)
E. C. Seale and Company (The New I Learn to Write)
Harr Wagner (Our Handwriting Series)

3. *Language series (consumable or hard back)*

Allyn and Bacon (English, Your Language)
American Book Company (Our English Language)
The Economy Company (Keys to Good English)
The Follett Publishing Company (Learning Your Language; a program for slow learners)
Ginn and Company (Ginn Elementary English Series)
Harcourt, Brace and World (Language for Daily Use)
Harper and Row (The New Building Better English; also English Skills and Drills)
D.C. Heath and Company (English Is Our Language)
Holt, Rinehart and Winston (American English)
Houghton Mifflin Company (English for Meaning)
Laidlaw Brothers (Using Good English Series)
Lyons and Carnahan (Mastering Your Language)
The Macmillan Company (The Macmillan English Series)
The McCormick-Mathers Publishing Company (Language Roundup Series)
The L. W. Singer Company (Enjoying English Series).

Reference Books for Boys and Girls

Much emphasis is placed in the modern elementary school on the use of reference books. Publishers are meeting the growing demand for dictionaries and encyclopedias for boys and girls. Selected reference books are named here.

PICTURE DICTIONARIES. Many picture dictionaries can be found on the counters of book stores and of book departments of other stores.

Clemens, Elizabeth, *Pixie Dictionary*. Holt, Rinehart and Winston, 1960.
Courtis, Stuart A., and Garnette Watters, *Illustrated Golden Dictionary*. Simon and Schuster, 1951.
Gatchel, Dorothy, and Margaret Madden, *From A to Z Picture Dictionary*. The Platt and Munk Company, 1960.
Guild, Marion, and Ruth Leder, *My Picture Dictionary*. Maxton Publishers, 1949.
Harper and Row, *Words I Like to Read and Write*. (To accompany the Alice and Jerry Basic Readers) Harper and Row, 1955.
MacBean, Dill W., *Picture Book Dictionary*. Children's Press, 1962.
McIntire, Alta, *The Follett Beginning-to-Read Picture Dictionary*. Follett Publishing Company, 1959.
Monroe, Marion, and W. Cabell Greet, *My Little Pictionary*. Scott, Foresman and Company, 1963.
——, *My Second Pictionary*. Scott, Foresman and Company, 1964.
Moore, Lillian, *The Golden Picture Dictionary*. Simon and Schuster, 1954.
Oftedahl, Laura, and Nina Jacobs, *My First Dictionary*. Grosset and Dunlap, 1948.
Reed, Mary, and Edith Osswald, *My First Golden Dictionary*. Golden Press, 1949.
Reid, Hale C., and Helen W. Crane, *My Picture Dictionary*. Ginn and Company, 1963.
Scott, Alice, and Stella Center, *The Giant Picture Dictionary for Boys and Girls*. Doubleday and Company, 1958.
Watters, Garnette, and Stuart A. Courtis, *The Picture Dictionary for Children*. Grossett and Dunlap, 1958.
Wright, Wendell W., *The Rainbow Dictionary*. The World Publishing Company, 1959.

OTHER DICTIONARIES. Some of the dictionaries used by boys and girls, other than picture dictionaries, are listed below.

Basic Dictionary of American English. Holt, Rinehart and Winston
Funk and Wagnalls Standard Junior School Dictionary. Harper and Row
Thorndike-Barnhart Beginning Dictionary. Scott, Foresman and Company
Thorndike-Barnhart Junior Dictionary. Scott, Foresman and Company
Webster's A Dictionary for Boys and Girls. American Book Company
Webster's Elementary Dictionary. American Book Company
Webster's New World Dictionary. American Book Company
Winston Dictionary for Schools. Holt, Rinehart and Winston
Winston Simplified Dictionary for Schools. Holt, Rinehart and Winston
The Word Wonder Dictionary. Holt, Rinehart and Winston
World Book Encyclopedia Dictionary (Two volumes) Field Enterprises.

ENCYCLOPEDIAS. Encyclopedias for boys and girls include the following:

Book of Knowledge. Grolier Society
Britannica Junior Encyclopedia. Encyclopedia Britannica
Childcraft. Field Enterprises
The Children's Hour. Spencer International Press
Compton's Pictured Encyclopedia. F. E. Compton and Company
The Golden Book Encyclopedia. Golden Press
The Golden Book Encyclopedia of Natural Science. Golden Press
My First Picture Encyclopedia. Grosset and Dunlap
Our Wonderful World. Spencer International Press
Pictorial Encyclopedia of American History. Children's Press
World Book Encyclopedia. Field Enterprises
Young People's Science Encyclopedia. Children's Press.

PERIODICALS FOR BOYS AND GIRLS

According to Lavinia G. Dobler in the Foreword of the index by her name that is listed below, there were in 1960 more than 350 periodicals for elementary-school pupils, with a circulation of 35,000,000. For extensive listings of periodicals for boys and girls, the following are sources.

Association for Childhood Education International, *Guide to Children's Magazines, Newspapers, Reference Books*. Association for Childhood Education International.

Cundiff, Ruby Ethel (compiler), *101 Plus Magazines for Schools*. Grades 1 to 12. Fourth edition. Tennessee Book Company, 1964.

Dobler, Lavinia G., *The Dobler International List of Periodicals for Boys and Girls*. Muriel Fuller (distributor), 1960.

Graves, P. Eileen (ed.), *Ulrich's Periodicals Directory*. R. R. Bowker Company, (published periodically)

Martin, Laura K., *Magazines for School Libraries*. R. R. Bowker Company

Wilson Company, The H. W., *Reader's Guide to Periodical Literature*. The H. W. Wilson Company

A helpful listing of 70 periodicals by Thomas D. Horn, entitled "Periodicals for Children and Youth," is given on pages 342-344 of the May, 1959, issue of *Elementary English*. A list of 41 space magazines, compiled by Willis C. Brown, can be obtained from the Publication Inquiry Unit, United States Office of Education, Washington, D. C.

Periodicals for Class Use

Two publishers put out a series of periodicals that are ordered in large quantities by individual classrooms, with a subscription for each child. One of these companies is American Education Publications, 1250 Fairwood Avenue, Columbus, Ohio 43216; the other is Scholastic Magazines, Inc., 33 West 42nd Street, New York, New York 10036.

PUBLICATIONS BY AMERICAN EDUCATION PUBLICATIONS. Periodicals by American Education Publications include various editions of *My Weekly Reader*.

My Weekly Reader Surprise (for kindergarten)
My Weekly Reader – Picture Reader (for grade 1)
My Weekly Reader – News Reader (for grade 2)
My Weekly Reader – News Story (for grade 3)
My Weekly Reader – News Parade (for grade 4)
My Weekly Reader – World Parade (for grade 5)
My Weekly Reader – News Report (for grade 6)

American Education Publications also publishes *Current Events*, which is designed for grades 6 to 8. It is reputed to have a larger circulation than any other school newspaper. *Read*, published by the same company, is suitable for use in grades 6 to 9.

PUBLICATIONS BY SCHOLASTIC MAGAZINES. Scholastic Magazines publishes the following newspapers that are used extensively in class situations.

News Pilot (for grade 1)
News Ranger (for grade 2)
News Trail (for grade 3)
News Explorer (for grade 4)
Newstime (for grades 5 and 6)

Other Periodicals

The following are among the periodicals of wide circulation, single copies of which are frequently ordered for classrooms or libraries or subscribed for in homes. If the periodical is listed in *The Dobler International List of Periodicals for Boys and Girls*, the age range indicated in the following listing is that given in that index.

American Girl, The. Girl Scouts of the United States, 830 Third Avenue, New York, New York 10022. (Girls, 10-16)

American Junior Red Cross News. American National Red Cross, 17 and D Streets, N.W., Washington, D.C. 20006. (13-18)

Arts and Activities. Jones Publishing Company, 8150 North Central Park Avenue, Skokie, Illinois 60076. (9-16)

Boys' Life. Boy Scouts of America, New Brunswick, New Jersey 08903. (Boys, 8-18)

Calling All Girls. The Parents' Institute of *Parents' Magazine*, 52 Vanderbilt Avenue, New York, New York 10017. (Girls, 7-12)

Child Life Magazine. Child Life, Inc., 36 Federal Street, Boston, Massachusetts 02110. (3-12)

Children's Digest (combined with *Humpty Dumpty's Magazine*). The Parents' Institute of *Parents' Magazine*, 52 Vanderbilt Avenue, New York, New York 10017. (5-12)

Children's Playmate Magazine. Children's Playmate Magazine, Inc., 3025 East 75th Street, Cleveland, Ohio 44104. (6-9)

Highlights for Children. Highlights for Children, 2300 West Fifth Avenue, Columbus, Ohio 43221. (3-12)

Humpty Dumpty's Magazine (combined with *Children's Digest*). The Parents' Institute of *Parents' Magazine*, 52 Vanderbilt Avenue, New York, New York 10017. (3-7)

Jack and Jill. Curtis Publishing Company, Independence Square, Philadelphia, Pennsylvania 19105. (3-10)

Junior Natural History Magazine. American Museum of Natural History, Central Park West at 79th Street, New York, New York 10024 (8-15)

Peck-of-Fun. Clapper Publishing Company, P. O. Box 568, Park Ridge, Illinois 60068, (3-12)

Plays. Plays, Inc. 8 Arlington Street, Boston, Massachusetts 02116. (7-17)

Popular Mechanics. Popular Mechanics, 575 Lexington Avenue, New York, New York 10022. (10–)

Summertime. Scholastic Magazines, Inc., 33 West 42nd Street, New York, New York 10036. (10-12)

OTHER READING MATERIALS

Even a quick glance at the advertising pages of professional magazines for elementary-school teachers indicates the large number of materials in print, other than textbooks, and periodicals, that are claimed to be valuable in teaching reading or the other language arts. An examination of the publicity materials of many publishing companies and distributors of elementary-school supplies also reveals the abundance of such literature. Some of these aids have stood up favorably after scrutiny of research techniques and/or after evaluation in terms of sound educational practice; at the other extreme on the scale of desirability are some that sound dangerously close to quack procedures.

Evaluation

A listing of such reading materials that can be given in limited space can not be comprehensive. An evaluation of them in this chapter would necessarily show many inaccuracies, for the worth of any material is to a large extent a function of the purpose for which it is intended and the methods employed in using it. It is suggested that the reader make his own evaluation as he studies the literature on a given aid, asking himself questions such as these:

1. Is it designed, according to the publicity material on it, to serve a purpose that is important to me? (Care should be exercised so that unsupported claims of publishers or distributors do not mislead the examiner in his appraisal.)
2. Is there evidence to indicate that the claimed purpose is being accomplished through use of the material?
3. Is use of the material in harmony with what we know from the field of child growth and development?
4. Is use of the material in harmony with accepted principles of teaching?
5. Is the time that needs to be spent in the use of the materials reasonable?
6. Can the materials be used without constant supervision by the teacher? (It is not necessarily a score against an aid if constant supervision is needed; however, it is important to note if a teacher is looking for an aid that can be used primarily as a "seatwork activity.")
7. Is the cost of the material in favorable proportion to its usefulness?

When considering possible use of materials dealing with the development of skills in word recognition, the teacher should pay particular attention to the role that phonics plays. He will want to make certain that according to his best insights phonics is neither overemphasized or underemphasized and that methods used in teaching it are in harmony with the teaching principles he accepts.

One further word of caution needs to be expressed. While it is important that a teacher try to justify the use of materials he selects in terms of his best understanding of educational principles and procedures, such consideration should not keep him from refusing to experiment with the new. If all teachers were reluctant to try out materials until their value has been established beyond a doubt, educational progress would be retarded.

Sources of Materials

The teacher in search of materials of instruction of the types to which reference is here made — including reading-readiness materials and those for the development of work-study skills — is advised to write, first of all, for publication lists to the publishing company whose program in reading and in other language arts he is following. An inquiry as to what materials beyond the basal series the company has will likely bring a quick response. If the request is for descriptive literature that will most likely be complied with rapidly also, especially if the teacher indicates that he already is using some of the company's material. Furthermore, the teacher or college student intent upon making a study of available materials may write to any of the publishers of language arts materials listed on preceding pages of this chapter. Some additional publishers and/or distributors of such teaching material in the language arts are listed here.

Beckley-Cardy Company
Benefic Press
Milton Bradley Company
Columbia University, Teachers College, Bureau of Publications

Continental Press
Economy Company
Educational Service
Educational Test Bureau
E. M. Hale and Company

Expression Company
Garrard Press
Globe Book Company
Harlow Publishing Corporation
Hayes School Publishing Company

Iroquois Publishing Company
Judy Company
Kenworthy Educational Service
Learning through Seeing
McCormick-Mathers Publishing Company

Charles E. Merrill Books
Noble and Noble Publishers
O'Connor Remedial Services
F. A. Owen Publishing Company
The Platt and Munk Company

Reader's Digest Services
Remedial Education Center
Science Research Associates
Society for Visual Education

Teachers Publishing Corporation
George Wahr Publishing Company
Webster Publishing Company

Language-Arts Laboratories

Programs in the form of materials for the development of skills have made a considerable impact during recent years on the teaching of the language arts. One such is the *EDL Study Skills Library*, published by the Educational Developmental Laboratories. Science Research Associates has several programs, among them the *SRA Reading for Understanding Laboratory;* the *SRA Reading Laboratory;* the *Basic Composition Series,* of which one part "Writing Skills" is for grades 5 and 6 and the other for grades 7 and 8, published by Science Research Associates; and the *Spelling Word Power Laboratory*. Charles E. Merrill Books has a programed course entitled *Building Reading Power.*

The *EDL Study Skills Library* consists of materials for grades 4 to 9. The *SRA Reading for Understanding Laboratory,* designed for grades 3 through 12, is comprised of 4,000 selections that deal primarily with the development of comprehension skills. The materials are arranged in order of difficulty. The *SRA Reading Laboratory,* for grades 1 through 13, stresses various skills of reading, including rate. On the lower levels considerable emphasis is placed on phonics as a means of achieving growth in word recognition.

Publicity material, available to teachers and prospective teachers for the asking, gives detailed information on the programs incorporated in the language-arts laboratories.

TESTS

To secure a comprehensive listing and evaluation of standardized tests on the markets, the reader is advised to consult the most recent edition of the *Mental Measurements Yearbook,* edited by Oscar K. Buros and published by the Gryphon Press or *Tests in Print,* (latest edition) by the same editor and publisher.

Mental Tests

Mental tests, or intelligence tests, can be classified according to those designed to test one individual at a time and those that are usable in group-testing situations. Much of the individual testing in the elementary school is done by means of one or more of the following tests. (It should be noted that for satisfactory administration of individual tests it is important a person especially trained in that area should give them.)

Arthur Point Scale of Performance Tests by Grace Arthur, for use with language handicaps (Psychological Corporation)
Stanford-Binet Intelligence Scale revised by Lewis M. Terman and Maud A. Merrill (Houghton Mifflin Company)
Wechsler Intelligence Scale for Children by David Wechsler (Psychological Corporation)

A few of the well-known group intelligence tests for elementary-school pupils are:

The California Test of Mental Maturity by Elizabeth T. Sullivan, Willis W. Clark, and Ernest W. Tiegs (California Test Bureau)
The Kuhlman-Anderson Intelligence Tests by F. Kuhlman and Rose G. Anderson (Personnel Press)
The Lorge-Thorndike Intelligence Tests by Irving Lorge and Robert L. Thorndike (Houghton Mifflin Company)
Otis Quick-Scoring Mental Ability Tests by Arthur S. Otis (Harcourt, Brace and World)
The Pintner-Cunningham Primary Test by Rudolph Pintner and Bess Cunningham (Harcourt, Brace and World)
SRA Primary Mental Abilities by L. L. Thurstone and Thelma G. Thurstone (Science Research Associates)

Reading Readiness Tests

Some publishers of basal reading series are producing tests designed specifically to test the readiness of the child for reading the beginning books produced by a given publisher. Since basal readers by various publishers differ in difficulty of material and in types of problems met by the reader, as well as in methods recommended for using the reading materials, the definiteness of purpose of tests of this type gives them a point of superiority over the standardized tests designed with no particular reading series in mind. Another point of advantage of tests planned for a particular series is that some test readiness for reading not only for the initial stage of reading instruction but also for later levels. For example, a test may be included to evaluate a reader's readiness for reading a fourth-grade textbook or to use the dictionary.

Among much-used tests that test readiness for beginning reading not planned to be used primarily with only a given basal reading series are the following:

Gates Reading Readiness Tests by Arthur I. Gates (Bureau of Publications, Teachers College, Columbia University)
The Harrison-Stroud Reading Readiness Profiles by M. Lucile Harrison and James B. Stroud (Houghton Mifflin Company)
Lee-Clark Readiness Test by J. Murray Lee and Willis W. Clark (California Test Bureau)
Metropolitan Readiness Test by Gertrude Hildreth and Nellie L. Griffiths (Harcourt, Brace and World)
Murphy-Durrell Diagnostic Reading Readiness Test by Helen A. Murphy and Donald D. Durrell (Harcourt, Brace and World)
Webster Reading-Readiness Test by Clarence R. Stone and Mary Nila (Webster Publishing Company)

Reading Tests

Some of the following tests of reading ability of boys and girls in the elementary school are primarily survey tests; others are chiefly diagnostic. Some check a variety of reading skills; a few are limited to one phase of reading.

California Reading Tests by Ernest W. Tiegs and Willis W. Clark (California Test Bureau)
Developmental Reading Tests by Guy L. Bond, Theodore Clymer, and Cyril Hoyt (Lyons and Carnahan)
Diagnostic Reading Tests by the Committee on Diagnostic Reading Tests (Committee on Diagnostic Reading Tests)
Dolch Basic Sight Word Test by E. W. Dolch (Garrard Publishing Company)
Durrell Analysis of Reading Difficulty by Donald D. Durrell (Harcourt, Brace and World)
Elementary Reading: Every-Pupil Scholarship Test (Bureau of Educational Measurements, Kansas State Teachers College)
Flash-X Sight Vocabulary Test by George D. Spache and Stanford E. Taylor (Educational Developmental Laboratories)
Gates Advanced Primary Reading Tests (Type AWR, word recognition; Type APR, paragraph reading) by Arthur I. Gates (Bureau of Publications, Teachers College, Columbia University)
Gates Basic Reading Tests (Type GS, reading to appreciate general significance; Type UD, reading to understand precise directions; Type ND, reading to note details; Type RV, reading vocabulary; Type LC, level of comprehension) by Arthur I. Gates (Bureau of Publications, Teachers College, Columbia University)
Gates Primary Reading Tests (Type PWR, word recognition; Type PSR, sentence reading; Type PPR, paragraph reading) by Arthur I. Gates (Bureau of Publications, Teachers College, Columbia University)
Gates Reading Survey by Arthur I. Gates (Bureau of Publications, Teachers College, Columbia University)
Gilmore Oral Reading Test by John V. Gilmore (Harcourt, Brace and World)
Gray Standardized Oral Reading Check Tests by William S. Gray (Public School Publishing Company)
Gray Standardized Oral Reading Paragraph Tests by William S. Gray (Public School Publishing)
Iowa Every-Pupil Tests of Basic Skills: Silent Reading Comprehension by H. F. Spitzer et al. (Houghton Mifflin Company)
Iowa Silent Reading Tests by Harry A. Greene, A. N. Jorgensen, and Victor H. Kelley (Harcourt, Brace and World)
Kelley-Greene Reading Comprehension Test by Victor H. Kelley and Harry A. Greene (Harcourt, Brace and World)
Leavell Analytical Oral Reading Test by Ullin W. Leavell (American Guidance Service)
Lee-Clark Reading Test by J. Murray Lee and Willis W. Clark (California Test Bureau)
Los Angeles Elementary Reading Test by Jessie E. Ingraham (California Test Bureau)
Los Angeles Primary Reading Test by Jessie E. Ingraham (California Test Bureau)
Metropolitan Achievement Tests: Reading by Gertrude Hildreth et al. (Harcourt, Brace and World)
The Nelson Silent Reading Test: Vocabulary and Paragraph: The Clapp-Young Self-Marking Tests by M. J. Nelson (Houghton Mifflin Company)
Peabody Library Information Test by Louis Shores and Joseph E. Moore (Educational Test Bureau)
Primary Reading Profiles by James B. Stroud and Albert N. Hieronymus (Houghton Mifflin Company)
Roswell-Chall Diagnostic Reading Test of Word Analysis Skills by Florence G. Roswell and Jeanne S. Chall (Essay Press)
SRA Achievement Series: Reading by Louis P. Thorpe et al. (Science Research Associates)
SRA Reading Record by Guy T. Buswell (Science Research Associates)
Stanford Achievement Test: Reading by Truman L. Kelley et al. (Harcourt, Brace and World)

Spelling Tests and Scales

Some of the authors and publishers of spelling series have written suggested tests into their books in the form of pretests and final tests for a semester or a year. Some standardized tests dealing with various elementary-school fields of learning include a part on testing of spelling, as, for example, the *Metropolitan Achievement Test* and the *Stanford Achievement Test,* both published by Harcourt, Brace and World, and the *California Achievement Tests* by the California Test Bureau.

Data on some spelling tests are given below.

Ashbaugh, Ernest J., *Iowa Spelling Scales* (Bureau of Educational Research and Service)
Ayer, Fred C., *Ayer Standardized Spelling Scale* (The Steck Company)
Buckingham, B. R., *The Buckingham Extension of the Ayer Spelling Scale* (Public School Publishing Company)
Fitzgerald, James A., *Coordinated Scales of Attainment: Spelling* (Educational Test Bureau)
Greene, Harry A., *The New Iowa Spelling Scale* (Bureau of Educational Research and Service)

Morrison, J. Cayce, and William A. McCall, *Morrison-McCall Spelling Scale* (Harcourt, Brace and World)

Handwriting Scales

Titles of some of the handwriting scales on the market are as follows:

Ayres, Leonard P., *Ayres Measuring Scale for Handwriting* (Cooperative Test Division)
Freeman, Frank N., *Correlated Scales* (The Zaner-Bloser Company)
------, *New Scientific Evaluation Scales* (The Zaner-Bloser Company)
------, *Print to Script (Manuscript) Measuring Scales* (The Zaner-Bloser Company)
Hildreth, Gertrude, *Metropolitan Primary Cursive Handwriting Scale* (Harcourt, Brace and World)
------, *Metropolitan Primary Manuscript Handwriting Scale* (Harcourt, Brace and World)
West, Paul, *American Handwriting Scale* (A. N. Palmer Company).

Other Language-Arts Tests

One source of published tests for the evaluation of language-arts abilities such as capitalization, punctuation, and correct usage is that provided by the publishers of language-arts books produced in consumable form. Some workbooks contain end tests to precede and follow work on the units in the workbooks. Some also include tests to be given at the beginning or end of the year. Other publishers supply separate booklets with their books, which can be used to appraise the success with which the users of the series have mastered the learnings to be acquired through the use of the books. When using any language-arts series the teacher is advised to write to the publisher for information as to the availability of tests to accompany the series.

The following is a listing of some standardized tests that are not planned specifically for the users of a given series of books in the language arts.

The Clapp-Young English Test: The Clapp Young Self-Marking Tests (Houghton Mifflin Company)
Coordinated Scales of Attainment: English (Educational Test Bureau)
Iowa Every-Pupil Test of Basic Skills: Basic Language Skills (Houghton Mifflin Company)
Iowa Language Abilities Test (Harcourt, Brace and World)
Language Essentials Tests (Educational Test Bureau)
Metropolitan Achievement Tests: English Test (Harcourt, Brace and World)
The Pribble-Dallmann Diagnostic Tests in Elementary Language Skills (Lyons and Carnahan)
SRA Achievement Series: Language Arts (Science Research Associates)
Sequential Tests of Educational Progress: Writing (Cooperative Test Bureau)

Publishers and Distributors of Tests

The addresses of the publishers and distributors of tests given following are found in the last part of this chapter under "Addresses of Publishers and Distributors," beginning on page 338. For additional listings of publishers or distributors the reader is referred to the latest edition of *Tests in Print* edited by Oscar K. Buros and published by the Gryphon Press.

Acorn Publishing Company
Allyn and Bacon
American Guidance Service
Bobbs-Merrill Company
Bureau of Educational Measurements

Bureau of Educational Research and Service
Bureau of Publications
California Test Bureau
Committee on Diagnostic Reading Tests
Cooperative Test Division

Educational Developmental Laboratories
Educational Test Bureau
Educational Testing Service
Essay Press
Follett Publishing Company

Garrard Publishing Company
Harcourt, Brace and World
Houghton Mifflin Company
Lyons and Carnahan
Ohio Scholarship Tests

A. N. Palmer Company
Personnel Press
Psychological Corporation
Public School Publishing Company
Science Research Associates

The Steck Company
C. H. Stoelting Company
Webster Publishing Company
The Zaner-Bloser Company

AUDIO-VISUAL AIDS

Although this section deals only with films, filmstrips, and recordings, there are many other audio-visual aids to learning in the area of the language arts which the teacher should use. Provisions should be made, for example, for opportunities for viewing still pictures (including slides), for examining realia, for watching television, for listening to radio broadcasts, and for going on field trips.

For a comprehensive presentation of audio-visual aids to learning, the reader is referred to chapters on the subject in many professional books on teaching methods and to books dealing exclusively with the subject of audio-visual education, such as Edgar

Dale's *Audio-Visual Methods in Teaching,* published by Holt, Rinehart and Winston (1954); *Planning and Producing Audio-Visual Materials* by Jerrold E. Kemp, published by Chandler Publishing Company (1963); and *Fundamentals of Teaching with Audio-visual Technology* by Carlton W. H. Erickson, a 1965 publication by The Macmillan Company.

Films

The films in the language arts may be classified as to (1) films for the teacher and (2) films for boys and girls.

FILMS FOR THE TEACHER. Films for the teacher include (1) those that provide guidance in using films, such as *Choosing a Classroom Film* by McGraw-Hill Book Company and *Film and You* available through Bailey Films and (2) those that give professional information on one or more phases of the language arts such as:

Good Speech for Gary (McGraw-Hill Book Company)
Gregory Learns to Read (produced in the Detroit Public Schools; available through Syracuse University)
How Your Child Learns to Read (produced in the Salt Lake City Schools; available from the Board of Education, Salt Lake City)
Individualizing Reading in the Classroom (Columbia University)
The Lively Art of Picture Books (distributed by Children's Services Division, American Library Association or Weston Woods Studios)
New ETV Handwriting Programs (six films, on the transition from manuscript to cursive writing, to accompany the Guiding Growth in Handwriting texts; The Zaner-Bloser Company)
They All Learn to Read (available through Syracuse University).

FILMS FOR BOYS AND GIRLS. Motion pictures in the area of the language arts that are designed for use by boys and girls may be classified as to (1) films that tell stories, (2) films that provide background for language-arts experiences, and (3) films that give help in development of skills in the language arts.

1. *Films that tell stories.* Films on stories have been produced in series and singly. An example of a series are the films entitled *Picture Book Parade,* available through Weston Woods Studios, Weston, Connecticut. Some of the titles of books in the series are: *In the Forest* by Marie Hall Ets; *Magic Michael* by Louis Slobodkin; and *Pancho* by Berta and Elmer Hader. Examples of films on single stories or books are: *Little Red Riding Hood,* modern puppet version (Encyclopedia Britannica Films); *Night before Christmas* (Encyclopedia Britannica Films); *Heidi* (Teaching Films Custodians); *Perfect Tribute* (Teaching Films Custodians); *Little Red Hen* (Coronet Films); *Three Little Pigs* (Coronet Films); *Andy and the Lion* (Weston Woods Studios); and *Rumpelstiltskin* (Coronet Films).

2. *Films that provide background.* Since the subject matter of language-arts experiences is all of life, the many films suitable for pupils in areas such as the social studies, health, and science – to name only a few – in a sense provide background for development in the area of the language arts. For example, *Animals and Their Homes* (Coronet Films) can be used to enhance the reading of stories about animals, to make more understandable listening experiences the boys and girls may have, or to furnish information for a report they may wish to write. Of similar value are titles as diverse as *Milk* (Encyclopedia Britannica Films), *Minerals and Rocks* (Encyclopedia Britannica Films), *Children of Germany* (Encyclopedia Britannica Films), *How Weather Is Forecast* (Coronet Films), and *Visit with Cowboys* (Encyclopedia Britannica Films). Information to serve as interesting background for Robert McCloskey's books for children is furnished by the film *Robert McCloskey* (Weston Woods Studio).

A rather recent use of films to provide background for reading and to assist in the development of skills is the film reader, the subject matter of which is correlated with selected films. Robert Leestma in the selection "The Film-Reader Program" on page 326 of the book *The Reading Teacher's Reader,* edited by Oscar S. Causey and published by the Ronald Press Company (1958), describes the film readers in which Encyclopedia Britannica sound films are used with correlated reading books published by D. C. Heath and Company and by Harper and Row. Causey states:

> The film reader is an attractive thirty or thirty-six page book closely correlated with the film. On each page of the film reader is an enlarged picture from a significant sequence in the film. Each picture is presented in the order in which it appeared in the film, and hence the sequential nature of the experience is preserved.
>
> At the time of the film showing, the pictorial experience was interpreted verbally in the sound track of the film. The children have been exposed to the spoken words in context by means of the film, and thus an understanding of the relationship between the spoken symbol and the thing it represents is developed.
>
> Accompanying the picture on each page is a series of sentences closely related to the picture. These sentences contain certain of the spoken words and phrases used in the sound track of the film. Thus a relationship between the printed symbols and the spoken symbols is established.

> A key factor in the film-reader technique is the establishment of an easy link between the spoken words in the film and the printed words in the reader. The still picture on each page of the reader provides this link.

It is suggested that the reader who is interested in film readers write to Encyclopedia Britannica, to Harper and Row, or to D. C. Heath and Company, or to consult the article to which reference is made.

3. *Films for the development of skills.* The majority of the films for the development of language-arts skills for elementary-school boys and girls are on the intermediate-grade rather than the primary-grade level. They include a great diversity of topics, as illustrated by the small sampling of Coronet films that follows.

How to Prepare a Class Report
Improve Your Handwriting
Improve Your Pronunciation
Improve Your Reading
Improve Your Spelling
Know Your Library
Verbs: Recognizing and Using Them

Filmstrips

One use of filmstrips that has received considerable attention by educators is that of correlating them with a basic reading series. Such correlation has been made in the case of the *Alice and Jerry Readers,* published by Harper and Row, with filmstrips available through the Society for Visual Education. Another approach to reading through use of filmstrips is that demonstrated by the *Better Reading Series* filmstrips, obtainable through Stillfilms, Inc., Pasadena, California.

Filmstrips for use in connection with language-arts activities include, among many others:

The Comma Series (Society for Visual Education)
Goals in Spelling Series (Popular Science Publishing Company, Audio-Visual Division)
Language (Webster Publishing Company)
American Folk Heroes (Encyclopedia Britannica Films)
Picture Book Parade Filmstrip Series (Frederick Warne)
Filmstrips for Practice in Phonetic Skills (Scott, Foresman and Company)
Basic Primary Phonics (Society for Visual Education)

Many filmstrips not produced as part of a series are available for use in the development of language-arts skills also.

Recordings

One of the excellent series of recordings for boys and girls is that known as Enrichment Records, to accompany Landmark Books by Random House. (Filmstrips are also available for use with these books.)

Another worthwhile series of records is that produced by the National Council of Teachers of English. Titles in this series include, among others: *Children's Arabian Nights,* with selections from "Aladdin and the Wonderful Lamp," "Ali Baba and the Forty Thieves," and others; and *Grimm's Fairy Tales,* featuring "Rumpelstiltskin," "Briar Rose," "The Elves and the Shoemaker," and others. The records by the National Council of Teachers of English also include such titles as *The House at Pooh Corner, Now We Are Six, Rip Van Winkle,* and *Just So Stories.* Two other series are the *Folkways Records,* available from Folkways Records and Service Corporation, and *My First Golden Record Library,* distributed by Golden Records.

Examples of a few other recordings for children are:

Alice in Wonderland (with *Many Moons* and *The Eager Piano* on the reverse side; Columbia Records)
Andersen's Fairy Tales (in three volumes, with "The Nightingale," "The Emperor's New Clothes," "The Steadfast Tin Soldier" in Volume I; Educational Record Sales)
Choral Speaking for Intermediate Grades (Educational Record Sales)
Communities and Community Helpers (Educational Record Sales)
Fun with Speech Sounds (Coronet Films)
Handwriting Demons (National Council of Teachers of English)
Hansel and Gretel (Educational Record Sales)
Importance of Making Notes (Coronet Films)
It's Your Library (Vocational Guidance Films)
Let's Be Firemen (Educational Record Sales)
Let's Pronounce Well (Coronet Films)
Let's Read Poetry (Bailey Films)
Let's Try Choral Reading (Young America Films)
Make Way for Ducklings (by Robert McCloskey; Weston Woods Studios)
Making Sense with Outlines (Coronet Films).

Sound filmstrip sets are on the market in increasing numbers. In these sets records are synchronized with filmstrips. *Crow Boy* by Taro Yashima, *Petunia* by Roger Duvoisin, *Little Tim and the Brave Sea Captain* by Edward Ardizonne, and *The Three Billy Goats Gruff* by Marcia Brown comprise one such set, available from Weston Woods Studios.

Guides to Selection

Many state universities and state departments of education have catalogs of their audio-visual materials. Additional guides to selection of such materials are:

An Annotated List of Recordings for the Language Arts (National Council of Teachers of English)
Audio-Visual Catalog (Materials for Learning, Inc.)
Audio-Visual Materials for Teaching Reading (by Robert Leestma; Slaters Bookstore, Inc.)
Directory of 3660 16mm Film Libraries (by Seerley Reid, Anita Carpenter, and Annie Dougherty; United States Printing Office)
Educational Film (now on cards; in process of publication; American Library Association)
Educational Film Guide (out of print, but still used extensively; by Frederic A. Krahm; H. W. Wilson Company)
Educational Filmstrip Guide (out of print, but still used extensively; by Frederic A. Krahm; H. W. Wilson Company)
Educational Tape Catalog (Magnetic Tape Duplicators)
Educational Television Guidebook (by Phillip Lewis; McGraw-Hill Book Company)
Educational Television Motion Pictures, Descriptive Catalog (National Education Television Film Service, Audio-Visual Center, University of Indiana, Bloomington, Indiana)
Educator's Guide to Free Films (Educators Progress Service)
Educator's Guide to Free Filmstrips (Eduators Progress Service)
Educator's Guide to Free Slidefilms (Educators Progress Service)
Educator's Guide to Free Tapes and Recordings (Educators Progress Service)
Guides to Newer Media (by Margaret L. Rufswold and Carolyn Gauss; American Library Association)
National Tape Recording Catalog (National Tape Library or some state universities, among them National Tape Depository, Audio-Visual Center, University of Colorado, Boulder, Colorado 20004)
New Media Index (McGraw-Hill Book Company)
Sources of Information on Educational Media (by John A. Moldstad; United States Printing Office)
UCLA Children's Film Series (Children's Theater Committee, Theater Arts Department, University of California, Los Angeles)

Producers and Distributors

In addition to the many state universities and the state departments of education that distribute audio-visual aids, some aids are available through book companies and many are distributed as advertising by manufacturing companies, railroads, consuls, and other agencies. A few of the book companies that have one or more types of audio-visual aids for sale are:

American Book Company
Denoyer-Geppert Company
Harcourt, Brace and World
Harper and Row
McGraw-Hill Book Company
Scott, Foresman and Company
Silver Burdett Company

Following are addresses of publishers or distributors of audio-visual aids.

American Library Association, 50 East Huron Street, Chicago, Illinois 60611
American Museum of Natural History, Central Park West at 79th Street, New York, New York 10023
Audio-Visual Research, Department RT-39, 523 South Plymouth Court, Chicago, Illinois 60605
Bailey Films, Inc., 6509 DeLongpre Avenue, Hollywood, California 90028
Children's Record Guild, 27 Thompson Street, New York, New York 10013
Columbia Records, Educational Division, 799 Seventh Avenue, New York, New York 10019
Coronet Films, Coronet Building, 65 East South Water, Chicago, Illinois 60601
Educational Record Sales, 157 Chambers Street, New York, New York 10007
Educators Progress Service, Randolph, Wisconsin 53956
Encyclopedia Britannica Films, 1150 Wilmette Avenue, Wilmette, Illinois 60091
Eye Gate House, 146-01 Archer Avenue, Jamaica, New York 11435
Folkways Records and Service Corporation, 165 West 46th Street, New York, New York 10036
Frith Films, 1816 North Highland Avenue, Hollywood, California 90028
Golden Records, 239 Great Neck Road, Great Neck, New York 11021
The Jam Handy Organization, 2821 East Grand Boulevard, Detroit, Michigan 48211
Keystone View Company, Meadville, Pennsylvania 16335
Language Training Aids, 12101 Valleywood Drive, Silver Spring, Maryland 20902
Magnetic Tape Duplicators, 6766 Sunset Boulevard, Hollywood, California 90028
Materials for Learning, Inc., 1078 St. John's Place, Brooklyn, New York 11123
National Council of Teachers of English, 508 South Sixth Street, Champaign, Illinois 61822
Popular Science Publishing Company, 455 Lexington Avenue, New York, New York 10017
Radio Corporation of America, Audio-Visual Department (RCA Victor Division), Building 15-5, Front and Cooper Streets, Camden, New Jersey 08102
Slaters Bookstore, Inc., 336 South State Street, Ann Arbor, Michigan 48108
Society for Visual Education (Subsidiary of Graflex, Inc.) 1345 Diversey Parkway, Chicago, Illinois 60614
Teaching Films, Inc., 88 Lexington Avenue, New York, New York 10016
Teaching Films Custodians, 25 West 43rd Street, New York, New York 10036
United States Government Printing Office (Superintendent of Documents), Washington, D. C. 20025
University of California (Children's Theater Committee, Theater Arts Department) Los Angeles, California 40524
Vocational Guidance Films, 215 East Third Street, Des Moines, Iowa 50309
Fredrick Warne, 101 Fifth Avenue, New York, New York 10003
Weston Woods Studios, Weston, Connecticut 06883

H. W. Wilson Company, 950 University Avenue, New York, New York 10452
Young America Films (McGraw-Hill Book Company, Text-Film Department), 330 West 42nd Street, New York, New York 10036.

OTHER TEACHING AIDS

Three of the many types of additional aids to the development of skills in the language arts are here considered, namely: (1) educational games, (2) mechanical devices for increasing rate of reading, and (3) free and inexpensive materials.

Educational Games

Criteria for application when choosing games for educational purposes are indicated in Chapter 10. In deciding upon the use of any of the games in publications to which reference is here made the teacher should keep those criteria in mind.

PUBLICATIONS ABOUT GAMES. Brochures by companies publishing textbooks in the language arts, distributed free of charge to teachers using the books of a given company, form an excellent source of ideas for the teacher. Ginn and Company, for example, publishes a booklet entitled "Reading Games and Activities." A publication by Scott, Foresman and Company, "Such Interesting Things to Do! Independent Activities in the Language Arts for the Primary Grades" is another example. Some boards of education in larger cities have also sponsored projects in their school systems in which teachers have prepared for publication lists of games of value in learning the language arts. Some magazines for boys and girls, such as *Highlights* and *Children's Digest,* as well as some professional magazines, such as *Grade Teacher* and *The Instructor,* also furnish many ideas. Reference is here made to a few other publications on the topic.

Abingdon Press, *Games for Boys and Girls.* Abingdon Press.
Dean, John F., *Games Make Spelling Fun.* Fearon Publishers, 1956.
Eckgren, B. L., and V. Gishel, *Five Hundred Live Ideas for the Grade Teacher.* Harper and Row, 1952.
Kingsley, Bernard, *Reading Skills: Simple Games, Aids and Devices to Stimulate Reading Skill in the Classroom.* Fearon Publishers.
Phonovisual Products, Inc., *The Phonovisual Game Book.* Phonovisual Products, 1960.
Russell, David H., and Etta E. Karp, *Reading Aids through the Grades.* Bureau of Publications, Teachers College, Columbia University, 1951.
Starr, John W., *Selected Reading Games and Devices for the Intermediate Grades.* University of Orgeon, Eugene, Oregon, 1958.
———, *Selected Reading Games and Devices for the Primary Grades.* University of Oregon, Eugene, Oregon, 1958.
Teachers Publishing Corporation, *Simple Games for Primary Grades.* Teachers Publishing Corporation.
Wagner, Guy, and Max Hosier, *Reading Games.* Teachers Publishing Corporation, 1958
Wagner, Guy; Max Hosier; and Mildred Blackman, *Language Games.* Teachers Publishing Corporation.
———, *Listening Games.* Teachers Publishing Corporation.

PUBLISHERS AND DISTRIBUTORS OF GAMES. The following are among publishers or distributors of games for use in learning one or more language-arts skills. They are in addition to those to which reference is made in the preceding listing. The addresses are given in the last part of this chapter.

Beckley-Cardy Company
Garrard Press
Ideal School Supply Company
The Judy Company
Kenworthy Educational Service

Parker Brothers
Simon and Schuster
Whitman Publishing Company

Mechanical Devices for Increasing Rate of Reading

For a listing and description of mechanical aids to increase rate of reading, the reader may wish to refer to *Improving the Teaching of Reading* by Emerald V. Dechant, with Prentice-Hall publishing (1964) and *The Reading Improvement Handbook* by John S. Simons and Helen O'Hara Rosenblum, published by Reading Improvement, Box 175, College Station Pullman, Washington (1965).

DISRTIBUTORS. To obtain information on devices for increasing reading rates the reader may write to the distributors for a listing and descriptions of their aids. Distributors include:

American Interstate Corporation, Mundelein, Illinois 60062
Audio-Visual Research, Department RT 39, 523 South Plymouth Court, Chicago, Illinois 60605
Craig Research, Inc., 3410 South LaCienega Boulevard, Los Angeles 90016
Educational Developmental Laboratories, Inc., 75 Prospect, Huntington, New York 11743
Keystone View Company, Meadville, Pennsylvania 16335
Lafayette Instrument Company, North 26th Street and 52 By-Pass, Lafayette, Indiana 47904
Learning through Seeing, Inc., P. O. Box 368, Sunland, California 91040
Perceptual Development Laboratories, 6767 Southwest Avenue, St. Louis 63117

Psychotechnics, Inc., 105 West Adams Street, Chicago, Illinois 60603
The Reading Laboratory, Inc., 500 Fifth Avenue, New York, New York 10036
Science Research Associates, Inc., 259 East Erie Street, Chicago, Illinois 60611
Society for Visual Education, 1345 Diversey Parkway, Chicago, Illinois, 60614

LIST OF DEVICES. Some of the distributors named offer devices not only for increasing rate of reading but also for use in diagnosing reading difficulties as, for example, the EDL Reading Eye (Educational Developmental Laboratories) and for correction of problems of visual perception as, for example, the EDL Reader (Educational Developmental Laboratories). The devices, however, include only those of claimed value in helping boys and girls of elementary-school age in increasing power to read at appropriate rates.

AVR Eye-Span Trainer (used with slides; Audio-Visual Research)
AVR Flash-Tachment (used as tachistoscopic attachment to a slide or filmstrip projector; Audio-Visual Research)
AVR Reading Rateometer (used with nonprojected materials; Audio-Visual Research)
Controlled Reader (used with filmstrips; Educational Developmental Laboratories)
EST 10. Eye-Span Trainer, Model 10 (used with slides; Audio-Visual Research)
Flashmeter (used with slides in an overhead projector; Keystone View Company)
Keystone Reading Pacer (used with nonprojected materials; Keystone View Company)
Phrase-Flasher (used with cards; The Reading Laboratory)
Readamatic Pacer (used with nonprojected materials; Americana Interstate Corporation)
Reading Accelerators (used with nonprojected materials; Science Research Associates)

Sources of Free and Inexpensive Materials

There are many sources of free and inexpensive materials from which can be secured aids of value in the development of skills and abilities in the language arts. Probably the two best-known of the source books are *Free and Inexpensive Learning Materials,* obtainable through the Division of Surveys and Field Services, George Peabody College for Teachers, Nashville, Tennessee, and *Sources of Free and Inexpensive Educational Materials by Field Enterprises,* Educational Division, Merchandise Mart Plaza, Chicago 60654. Both of these publications are revised annually. Others are:

Educators Progress Service, *Elementary Teachers Guide to Free Curriculum Materials.* Educators Progress Service
——, *Guide to Free Teaching Aids.*
Miller, Bruce, *Sources of Free and Inexpensive Teaching Aids.* Riverside, California, (P. O. Box 369)
National Council of Teachers of English, *More Sources of Free and Inexpensive Materials.* National Council of Teachers of English
National Education Association (American Association of School Administrators), *Choosing Free Materials for Use in the Schools.* National Education Association
National Education Association (Association for Supervision and Curriculum Development) *Using Free Materials in the Classroom.* National Education Association
Ohio State University, The, *Inexpensive Bulletins Concerning Teaching Materials.* Bureau of Educational Research, The Ohio State University
Pepe, Thomas J., *Free and Inexpensive Educational Aids.* Dover Publications
Schain, Robert, and Murray Polner, *Where to Get and How to Use Free and Inexpensive Teaching Aids.* Teachers Practical Press.

Various professional magazines (for example, the *NEA Journal, Grade Teacher,* and *The Instructor*) regularly carry a column listing free and inexpensive teaching aids.

ADDRESSES OF PUBLISHERS AND DISTRIBUTORS

In this last part of this chapter are given addresses of publishers and distributors of materials for teaching or learning the language arts, to whose materials reference has been made. Addresses of sponsors of book clubs are given on page 325; publishers of magazines are listed on page 329; and producers and distributors of audio-visual aids are found on page 336.

Because of the many changes constantly being made in addresses of publishers the reader may at times wish to refer to the listing of publishers and distributors of books given in the introductory part of the most recent edition of *Books in Print: Publishers' Trade List Annual,* published by R. R. Bowker Company, which is available in many libraries.

Abelard-Schuman, 6 West 57th Street, New York, New York 10019
Abingdon Press, 201 8th Avenue, South, Nashville, Tennessee 37203
Acorn Publishing Company, Rockville Center, Long Island, New York 11570
Aladdin Books (Discontinued publications; some available through E. P. Dutton and Company or Follett Publishing Company)
Allyn and Bacon, Inc., 150 Tremont Street, Boston, Massachusetts 02111
American Book Company, 55 Fifth Avenue, New York, New York 10003
American Education Publications, 1250 Fairwood Avenue, Columbus, Ohio 43216

American Guidance Service, Inc., 720 Washington Avenue S. E., Minneapolis, Minnesota 55414
American Library Association, 50 East Huron Street, Chicago, Illinois 60611
Antioch Press, The, Yellow Springs, Ohio 45387
Appleton-Century-Crofts, Inc., 440 Park Avenue South, New York, New York 10016
Association for Childhood Education International, 3615 Wisconsin Avenue, N.W., Washington, D. C. 20016
Atheneum Publishers, 162 East 38th Street, New York, New York 10016
Barnes and Noble, Inc., 105 Fifth Avenue, New York, New York 10003
Beacon Press, 25 Beacon Street, Boston, Massachusetts 02108
Beckley-Cardy Company, 1900 North Narragansett, Chicago, Illinois 60639
Benefic Press (A division of Beckley-Cardy Company)
Bobbs-Merrill Company, 4300 West 62nd Street, Indianapolis, Indiana 46206
R. R. Bowker, 1180 Avenue of the Americas, New York, New York 10036
Milton Bradley Company, 74 Park Street, Springfield, Massachusetts 01101
William C. Brown Company, Publishers, 135 South Locust Street, Dubuque, Iowa 52001
Bruce Publishing Company, 400 North Broadway, Milwaukee, Wisconsin 53201
Bureau of Educational Measurements (See Kansas State Teachers College.)
Bureau of Educational Research and Service (See University of Iowa.)
Bureau of Publications (See Columbia University, Teachers College.)
Burgess Publishing Company, 426 South Sixth Street, Minneapolis, Minnesota 55415
California Test Bureau, 5916 Hollywood Boulevard, Los Angeles, California 90028
Cambridge University Press, 32 East 57th Street, New York, New York 10022
Chandler Publishing Company, 604 Mission Street, San Francisco, California 94105
Child Study Association, 9 East 89th Street, New York, New York 10028
Children's Book Center, University of Chicago Library, Chicago, Illinois 60637
Children's Book Council, 175 Fifth Avenue, New York, New York 10010
Children's Press, Inc. (Melmont Publishers), Jackson Boulevard and Racine Avenue, Chicago, Illinois 60607
Children's Reading Service (See Materials for Learning.)
Citadel Press, 222 Park Avenue South, New York, New York 10003
Columbia University, Bureau of Publications, Teachers College, 525 West 120th Street, New York, New York 10027
Combined Book Exhibit, Inc., 950 University Avenue, New York, New York 10052
Committee on Diagnostic Reading Tests, Inc., Mountain Home, North Carolina 28758
Commonwealth Fund (Part of Harvard University Press), Kittridge Hall, 79 Garden Street, Cambridge, Massachusetts 02163
F. E. Compton and Company, 1000 North Dearborn, Chicago, Illinois 60610
Contemporary Press, Box 1524, San Jose, California 95109
Cooperative Test Division, Educational Testing Service, 20 Nassau Street, Princeton, New Jersey 08540
Coward-McCann, Inc., 210 Madison Avenue, New York, New York 10016
Craig Research, Inc., 3410 South LaCienega Boulevard, Los Angeles, California 90016
Criterion Books, Inc., 6 West 57th Street, New York, New York 10019
Crowell-Collier Press (part of Macmillan), 60 Fifth Avenue, New York, New York 10011
Davis Publications, Inc., 44 Portland Street, Worcester, Massachusetts 01608
The John Day Company, 210 Madison Avenue, New York, New York 10016
T. S. Denison and Company, 321 Fifth Avenue South, Minneapolis, Minnesota 55415
Denoyer-Geppert Company, 5235 Ravenswood Avenue, Chicago, Illinois 60640
Developmental Research Institute, Inc., (See also The Reading Laboratory.) 500 Fifth Avenue, New York, New York 10036
Dodd, Mead and Company, 432 Park Avenue South, New York, New York 10016
Doubleday and Company, Inc., 501 Franklin Avenue, Garden City, New York 11531
Dover Publications, Inc., 180 Varick Street, New York, New York 10014
Duell, Sloan and Pearce (part of Meredith), 1716 Locust Street, Des Moines, Iowa 50303
E. P. Dutton and Company, 201 Park Avenue South, New York, New York 10003
Easy Bulletin Boards, P. O. Box 103 Cleveland, Ohio 44121
Economy Company, 24 West Park Place, Oklahoma City, Oklahoma 74103
Educational Developmental Laboratories, Inc., 284 Pulaski Road, Huntington, Long Island, New York 11744
Educational Publishers, Inc., Educational Test Bureau, 720 Washington Avenue S. E., Minneapolis, Minnesota 55414
Educational Services, 1730 Eye Street, N. W. Washington, D. C. 20006
Educational Test Bureau, 720 Washington Avenue S. E., Minneapolis, Minnesota 55414
Educational Testing Service, Princeton, New Jersey 08540
Educators Progress Service, Randolph, Wisconsin 53956
Encyclopedia Britannica, Educational Department, 1150 Wilmette Avenue, Wilmette, Illinois 60091
Enrichment Teaching Materials, 246 Fifth Avenue, New York, New York 10001
Essay Press, Box 5, Planetarium Station, New York, New York 10024
Exposition Press, 386 Park Avenue South, New York, New York 10016
Expression Company, Box 11, Magnolia, Massachusetts 09131
Farrar, Strauss and Company, Inc., 19 Union Square West, New York, New York 10003

Fearon Publishers, 2165 Park Boulevard, Palo Alto, California 94110
The Fideler Company, 31 Ottawa Avenue N. W., Grand Rapids, Michigan 49502
Field Enterprises, Educational Division, 510 Merchandise Mart Plaza, Chicago, Illinois 60654
Follett Publishing Company, 1010 West Washington Boulevard, Chicago, Illinois 60607
Friendship Press, 475 Riverside Drive, New York, New York 10027
Muriel Fuller, P. O. Box 193, Grand Central Station, New York, New York 10017
Garden City Books (See Doubleday and Company.)
Garrard Publishing Company, 1607 North Market Street, Champaign, Illinois 61823
Ginn and Company, Statler Building, Back Bay P. O. 191, Boston, Massachusetts 02117
Globe Book Company, Inc., 175 Fifth Avenue, New York, New York 10010
Golden Press, Inc., Educational Division, 850 Third Avenue, New York, New York 10022
Graflex, Inc., Department AV-111 (See Society for Visual Education.)
Grolier, Inc., (See Spencer International Press.) 47 East 60th Street, New York, New York 10022
Grossett and Dunlap, 107 Broadway, New York, New York 10010
Gryphon Press, 220 Montgomery Street, Highland Park, New Jersey 08904
E. M. Hale and Company, 1201 South Hastings Way, Eau Claire, Wisconsin 54702
C. S. Hammond and Company, 515 Valley Street, Maplewood, New Jersey 07040
Harcourt, Brace and World, 757 Third Avenue, New York, New York 10017
Harlow Publishing Corporation, 532-536 N. W. Second Street, Oklahoma City, Oklahoma 73102
Harper and Row, Publishers, 49 East 33rd Street, New York, New York 10016
Harvey House, Irvington-on-Hudson, New York 10533
Hastings House, Publishers, 151 East 50th Street, New York, New York 10022
Hayes School Publishing Company, 201 Rebecca Avenue, Wilkinsburg, Pennsylvania 15221
D. C. Heath and Company, 285 Columbus Avenue, Boston, Massachusetts 02116
Heritage Press (Part of The George Macy Company), 595 Madison Avenue, New York, New York 10022
Highlights, 2300 West Fifth Avenue, Columbus, Ohio 43216
Holiday House, 8 West 13th Street, New York, New York 10011
Holt, Rinehart and Winston, 313 Madison Avenue, New York, New York 10017
Honor Products Company, 19 Belmont Street, Cambridge, Massachusetts 02138
Horn Book, Inc., 585 Boylston Street, Boston, Massachusetts 02116
Houghton Mifflin Company, 110 Tremont Street, Boston, Massachusetts 02107
Ideal School Supply Company, 8312 South Birkhoff Street, Chicago, Illinois 60620
Initial Teaching Alphabet Publications, Inc. (part of Pitman Publishing Corporation), 20 East 46th Street, New York, New York 10017
International Reading Association, Box 119, Newark, Delaware 19711
Iroquois Publishing Company, Inc., 1300 Alum Creek Drive, Columbus, Ohio 43216
The Judy Company, 310 North Second Street, Minneapolis, Minnesota 55401
Junior Literary Guild Books, 247 Park Avenue, New York, New York 10017 (order to Garden City, New York)
Kansas State Teachers College, Bureau of Educational Measurements, Emporia, Kansas 68802
Kenworthy Educational Service, Inc., 138 Allen Street, Buffalo, New York 14201
Keystone View Company, Meadville, Pennsylvania 16335
Alfred A. Knopf, Inc., 501 Madison Avenue, New York, New York 10022
Laidlaw Brothers, Thatcher and Madison Streets, River Forest, Illinois 60305
Learning Materials, Inc., 100 East Ohio Street, Chicago, Illinois 60611
Learning through Seeing, Inc., P. O. Box 368, Sunland, California 91040
J. B. Lippincott Company, East Washington Square, Philadelphia, Pennsylvania 19105
Little, Brown and Company, 34 Beacon Street, Boston, Massachusetts 02106
Liveright Publishing Corporation, 386 Park Avenue South, New York, New York 10016
Longmans, Green and Company, Inc., (part of the David McKay Company), 750 Third Avenue, New York, New York 10017
Lothrop, Lee and Shepard Company, Inc., 419 Park Avenue South, New York, New York 10016
Lyons and Carnahan, 407 East 25th Street, Chicago, Illinois 60616
McBride Books, 60 Laight Street, New York, New York 10013
McCormick-Mathers Publishing Company, 1440 East English Street, Wichita, Kansas 67201
McGraw-Hill Book Company, 330 West 42nd Street, New York, New York 10036
David McKay Company, Inc., 750 Third Avenue, New York, New York 10017
The Macmillan Company, 60 Fifth Avenue, New York, New York 10011
Macrae Smith Company, 225 South 15th Street, Philadelphia, Pennsylvania 19102
The George Macy Company, 595 Madison Avenue, New York, New York 10022
Mast Development Company, 2212 East Twelfth Street, Davenport, Iowa
Materials for Learning, Inc. (formerly Children's Reading Service), 1078 St. John's Place, Brooklyn, New York 11213
Maxton Publishing Corporation, 1012 West Washington Boulevard. Chicago, Illinois 60607
Melmont Publishers (See also Children's Press.) Jackson Boulevard and Racine Avenue, Chicago, Illinois 60607 (trade orders to Grosset and Dunlap)
Meridian Books, Inc., 12 East 22nd Street, New York, New York 10010 (order from World Publishing Company)
G. C. Merriam Company, 47 Federal Street, Springfield, Massachusetts 01102
Charles E. Merrill Books, Inc., 1300 Alum Drive, Columbus, Ohio 43216

Julian Messner, Inc., 8 West 40th Street, New York, New York 10018
William Morrow and Company, Inc., 425 Park Avenue South, New York, New York 10016
National Council of Teachers of English, 508 South 6th Street, Champaign, Illinois 61822
National Education Association, 1201 16th Street, N. W. Washington, D. C. 20006
Thomas Nelson and Sons, 18 East 47th Street, New York, New York 10017
Noble and Noble, Publishers, Inc., 67 Irving Place, New York, New York 10003
W. W. Norton and Company, Inc., 55 Fifth Avenue, New York, New York 10003
Oceana Publications, 80 Fourth Avenue, New York, New York 10003
O'Connor Reading Clinic Publishing Company, Inc., 1040 East Maple Road, Birmingham, Michigan 48011
Odyssey Press, Inc., 55 Fifth Avenue, New York, New York 10003
Ohio Scholarship Tests (See The Ohio State University Press.)
The Ohio State University Press, 164 West 19th Avenue, Columbus, Ohio 43210
Ohio University, Center for Educational Services, College of Education, Athens, Ohio 45701
Otarion Listener Corporation, Ossining, New York 10562
F. A. Owen Publishing Company, Dansville, New York 14437
Oxford University Press, 417 Fifth Avenue, New York, New York 10016
L. C. Page and Company (Part of Farrar, Strauss and Company), 19 Union Square West, New York, New York 10003
A. N. Palmer Company, 902 South Wabash Avenue, Chicago, Illinois 60605
Pantheon Books, Inc., 22 East 51st Street, New York, New York 10022
Parents' Magazines Publications, Inc., 52 Vanderbilt Avenue, New York, New York 10017
Parker Brothers, Inc., Salem Massachusetts 01608
Parnassus Press, 33 Parnassus Road, Berkeley, California 94708
George Peabody College for Teachers, Division of Surveys and Field Services, Nashville, Tennessee 37205
Perceptual Developmental Laboratories, 6767 Southwest Avenue, St. Louis, Missouri 63117
Personnel Press, Inc., 188 Nassau Street, Princeton, New Jersey 08540
Phonovisual Products, Inc., Box 5625, Washington, D. C. 20016
Pitman Publishing Corporation (See also Initial Teaching Alaphabet Publications, Inc.) 20 East 46th Street, New York, New York 10017
Platt and Munk Company, Inc., 200 Fifth Avenue, New York, New York 10010
Plays, Inc., 9 Arlington Street, Boston, Massachusetts 02116
Prentice-Hall, Inc., Box 903, Englewood Cliffs, New Jersey 07632
Psychological Corporation, 304 East 45th Street, New York, New York 10017
Psychotechnics, Inc., 105 West Adams Street, Chicago, Illinois 60603
Public School Publishing Company, 509-513 North East Street, Bloomington, Illinois 61702
G. P. Putnam's Sons, 200 Madison Avenue, New York, New York 10016
Rand McNally and Company, P. O. Box 7600, Chicago, Illinois 60680
Random House, Inc., 457 Madison Avenue, New York, New York 10022
Reader's Digest Services, Inc., Educational Division, Pleasantville, New York 10570
The Reading Laboratory, Inc. (subsidiary of Developmental Research Institute), 370 Lexington Avenue, New York, New York 10017
Reinhold Publishing Corporation, 430 Park Avenue, New York, New York 10022
Remedial Education Center, 1321 New Hampshire Avenue, Washington, D. C. 20006
Ronald Press Company, 15 East 26th Street, New York, New York 10010
Saalfield Publishing Company, Akron, Ohio
Scholastic Magazines Book Services, 33 West 42nd Street, New York, New York 10036
Science Research Associates, Inc., 259 East Erie Street, Chicago, Illinois 60611
William R. Scott, Inc., 8 West 13th Street, New York, New York 10011
Scott, Foresman and Company, 433 East Erie Street, Chicago, Illinois 60611
Charles Scribner's Sons, 597 Fifth Avenue, New York, New York 10017
E. C. Seale and Company, 1053 East 54th Street, New York, New York 46220
Silver Burdett Company, Park Avenue and Columbia Road, Morristown, New Jersey 07960
Simon and Schuster, 630 Fifth Avenue, New York, New York 10020 (trade order to 1 West 39th Street, New York, New York 10018)
L. W. Singer Company, Inc., (a division of Random House), 249 West Erie Boulevard, Syracuse, New York 13201
William Sloane Associates, Inc. (a division of William Morrow and Company), 425 Park Avenue South, New York, New York 10016
Society for Visual Education, Inc. (a subsidiary of Graflex, Inc.) 1345 Diversey Parkway, Chicago, Illinois 60614
Spencer International Press (a division of Grolier, Inc.), 575 Lexington Avenue, New York, New York 10022
Stanford University Press, Stanford, California 94305
The Steck Company, Austin, Texas 78701
Sterling Publishing Company, Inc., 419 Fourth Avenue, New York, New York 10016
C. H. Stoelting Company, 424 North Homan Avenue, Chicago, Illinois 60624
Frederick A. Stokes Company (See J. B. Lippincott Company.)
Studio Publications, 625 Madison Avenue, New York, New York 10022
Teachers College, Columbia University, Bureau of Publications, 525 West 120th Street, New York, New York 10003
Teachers Practical Press, 47 Frank Street, Valley Stream, New York, (order from Prentice-Hall)
Teachers Publishing Corporation, 23 Leroy Avenue, Darien, Connecticut 06820

Tennessee Book Company, 126 Third Avenue South, Nashville, Tennessee 37202
Time, Inc., Book Division, Time and Life Building, Rockefeller Center, New York, New York 10022
United States Government Printing Office (Superintendent of Documents), Washington, D. C. 20025
University of Chicago Press, 5750 Ellis Avenue, Chicago, Illinois 60637
University of Florida, Reading Laboratory and Clinic, Gainesville, Florida 32601
University of Iowa, Bureau of Educational Research and Service, Iowa City, Iowa 52240
University of Minnesota Press, Minneapolis, Minnesota 55455
University of Texas, Visual Instruction Bureau, Division of Extension, Austin, Texas 78712
Vanguard Press, Inc., 424 Madison Avenue, New York, New York 10017
Van Wagenen Psycho-Educational Research Laboratories, 1729 Irving Avenue South, Minneapolis, Minnesota 55405
The Viking Press, 625 Madison Avenue, New York, New York 10022
Harr Wagner Publishing Company, 609 Mission Street, San Francisco, California 94105
George Wahr Publishing Company, 316 South State Street, Ann Arbor, Michigan 48103
Frederick Warne, 101 Fifth Avenue, New York, New York 10003
Franklin Watts, Inc., 575 Lexington Avenue, New York, New York 10022
Webster Publishing Company (See also McGraw-Hill.) 1154 Reco Avenue, St. Louis, Missouri 63126
Western Reserve University Press, 2029 Adelbert Road, Cleveland, Ohio 44106
The Westminster Press, Witherspoon Building, Philadelphia, Pennsylvania 19107
Wheeler Publishing Company (a subsidiary of Harper and Row) 49 East 33rd Street, New York, New York 10016
Wheeley Publishing Company, 161 East Grand Avenue, Chicago, Illinois 60611
Albert Whitman and Company, 560 West Lake Street, Chicago, Illinois 60606
Whitman Publishing Company, 1220 Mound Avenue, Racine, Wisconsin 53404
Whittlesey House (a subsidiary of McGraw-Hill), 330 West 42nd Street, New York, New York 10036
Wilcox and Follett Publishing Company (See Follett Publishing Company.)
John Wiley and Sons, Inc., 605 Third Avenue, New York, New York 10016
H. W. Wilson Company, 950 University Avenue, New York, New York 10452
The John C. Winston Company (See Holt, Rinehart and Winston.)
Wonder Books, Inc. (See Grosset and Dunlap.)
The World Publishing Company, 2231 West 110th Street, Cleveland, Ohio 44102
The Zaner-Bloser Company, 612 North Park Street, Columbus, Ohio 43215

FOR STUDY AND DISCUSSION

1. Consult the reference librarian in your college as to various volumes, such as *Books in Print,* that give information on books published in the United States.

2. Examine some of the standardized tests listed in this chapter. Make a record of types of questions asked in reading readiness tests, in reading tests, and in other language-arts tests.

3. Become familiar with the classification of tests in *Tests in Print* by Oscar K. Buros, published by the Gryphon Press.

4. Send to a company for a few free or inexpensive materials that should prove helpful in teaching the language arts.

5. If you have access to an audio-visual department, make arrangements to view one or more aids in the field of the language arts. Be able to give your evaluation of the aid(s) that you selected. If you think an aid is worthwhile, be able to explain in detail how it may be used effectively.

6. Start a picture collection that should be of value to you in teaching the language arts in the elementary school.

7. Read parts or all of some of the professional books listed in the first part of this chapter. Be able to tell your classmates of important learnings that you acquired through your reading.